J. E. ATKINSON OF THE STAR

Ross Harkness

J. E. ATKINSON OF THE STAR

UNIVERSITY OF TORONTO PRESS

Foreword

In the summer of 1942 Mr. H. C. Hindmarsh, vice-president and managing editor of *The Star*, assigned Gregory Clark to write the obituary of J. E. Atkinson. As is the practice in newspaper offices, this was to be held in readiness until needed. Clark was told to obtain from Mr. Atkinson, who was then in his seventy-seventh year, information about his early life and his first years with *The Star*, but not to disclose the purpose for which it was intended. For several weeks thereafter an engaging little comedy was played each afternoon in Mr. Atkinson's office, with Clark pretending he was seeking information for record purposes only, his employer pretending he did not know the real design behind the interviews, and each knowing full well he was not fooling the other.

The reminiscences recorded by Clark dealt with major events of Mr. Atkinson's life prior to 1913 and I am indebted to them for much of the material in the early chapters of this book. Mr. Atkinson talked freely of the influences that directed his thinking at an early age along the line of radical social reform, and what he then told Clark provided much of the background for chapter one. He related at some length conversations between himself and such men as Sir Wilfrid Laurier, Timothy Eaton, Sir William Mulock, Senator George Cox, Lyman M. Jones, members of the Massey family, and others with whom he had been closely associated. These were set down by Clark as they were narrated to him, and unless another source is given in the text they are the authorities for the direct quotations from private conversations used in the first seven chapters.

Clark's manuscript was edited by George Maitland, editor-in-chief of *The Star*, who from time to time in the next six years added other anecdotes as Mr. Atkinson told them to him, along with his comments on persons and events. These sometimes casual comments to Mr. Maitland are the source of most of the direct quotations attributed to Mr. Atkinson in later chapters. Much of the Clark-Maitland material was published in *The Star* on May 10, 1948, after Mr. Atkinson's death. Because of his close associations with Mr. Atkinson and *The Star* over a period of forty-eight years as city editor, editorial writer, and finally editor-in-chief and director, Mr. Maitland was an invaluable source of information on Mr. Atkinson's attitude towards public men and affairs, his motives, his partialities, and his prejudices.

Mr. Atkinson was a singularly modest and retiring man, who seems not to have conceived that his personal letters and papers would some day be of interest to historians. He retained only such as were necessary for the lawful and efficient conduct of his business, or were of sentimental value. Fortunately others held his letters in more regard. Thus his correspondence with Sir Wilfrid Laurier, Sir John Willison, R. J. Manion, and Samuel W. Jacobs are to be found among the papers of those gentlemen in the Public Archives at Ottawa. Several persons still living allowed me to examine letters they had received from Mr. Atkinson, or memoranda they had made of conversations with him or Mr. Hindmarsh. No original manuscript of any of his many public addresses survives, but most of them were reported verbatim in *The Star* when they were delivered.

Space does not permit me to name all those employees and former employees of *The Star* who searched their memories, their diaries, and their souvenirs for anything that might add to our knowledge of J. E. Atkinson. But several deserve personal mention and my special thanks. Roy Greenaway generously placed at my disposal the manuscript of his memoirs as a reporter between the two world wars. H. S. Sainthill guided me through the, to me, dubious and frightening mysteries of the business office; his knowledge of Mr. Atkinson's business operations was of inestimable value. Arthur G. Green, payroll accountant, spent an incalculable number of hours combing through the payroll records of the 1930's in a fruitless search for somebody who had been "fired" at Christmas.

My debt must also be acknowledged to that traditional practice of *The Star* of printing interviews with old employees on their retirement or on significant anniversaries of the newspaper. Horatio Hocken, Harry Parr, C. C. Campbell, William Argue, Fred Eatherley, and most of that indomitable band of printers who founded *The Star* in 1892 related at some time or another what they recalled of this newspaper's early struggle for survival. Published interviews with these and other old-timers are the source, except where otherwise noted in the text, of the direct quotations from employees and former employees.

Grateful acknowledgment must be made to those publishers who so generously granted permission to use copyrighted material, in particular to the Ryerson Press for permission to quote extensively from *(CP): The Story of the Canadian Press* by M. E. Nichols, *Down the Stretch* by W. A. Hewitt, and *Ink on My Fingers* by J. H. Cranston; to the Curtis Publishing Company for permission to quote from an article in the *Saturday Evening Post* by David G. Wittels, copyright 1946; and to the publishers of *Time* for permission to quote from its columns.

Finally, I wish to thank Mrs. Ruth Atkinson Hindmarsh and J. S. Atkinson for placing at my disposition letters and documents in their possession, and for never attempting in any way or at any time to influence the manner in which their father was treated in this book. For whatever picture of J. E. Atkinson emerges from its pages I accept total responsibility.

ROSS HARKNESS

Toronto, May 8, 1963

Contents

J. E. ATKINSON OF THE STAR

Chapter 1

A MAN AND HIS BEGINNINGS

"It will never come out of the flesh that's bred in the bone," wrote Ben Jonson. Joseph E. Atkinson used to express the same thought in different words: "Nobody can escape his beginnings, and I despise the man who is untrue to them." Few men were more bound by their beginnings than this self-educated son of a small-town miller who, with his own hands, built one of the world's great newspaper properties and on his death left it to charity. He took neither pride nor shame in his humble birth, neither flaunted nor sought to conceal it. But he never forgot it.

Joseph Atkinson was born in a small house about two miles east of the village of Newcastle, Ontario, on December 23, 1865. He was the youngest child of a family of eight. His parents were John Atkinson and Hannah Story, who came from the Cumberland hills of England, near the Scottish border.

When Joseph was six months old his father was killed while walking home on the railway tracks from an evening in the village. Destitute and with eight little mouths to feed, Hannah Atkinson moved into Newcastle, where she ran a boarding house for workers in Massey's iron foundry, which made plows and other farm implements. Later she rented a bigger house in another part of town, where the boarders were mostly workers in the woollen mill. As her children became old enough to leave school they were sent out to work. Thus Joseph's boyhood was spent in an atmosphere of hard work and poverty. He learned from bitter childhood experience what it meant for a mother to be widowed in a generation in which the only source from which she could expect help was private charity. He learned to count every penny.

Mrs. Atkinson was a deeply religious woman, with the buoyant evangelical Methodist faith that was in such strong possession of a large part of Ontario in the eighteen-seventies. In later years her son recalled that there were only two books in that home, the Bible and a Methodist hymn book, and only one newspaper, a Methodist weekly. At Sunday school he memorized long passages from the Bible, and took a life-long delight in his ability to recall a Biblical quotation to suit any occasion.

When he was old enough to accept some responsibility the Methodist church paid him for odd jobs, such as sweeping the floor and lighting the fire on winter Sundays. The old minute books of the church record that "Mrs. Atkinson's son Joe" was hired to pump the organ; actually her son Tom did most of the pumping, for Joe was not strong enough.

Before his voice changed he had a beautifully clear soprano, which was much admired by the villagers. Sunday mornings he used to sing in the choir of the Roman Catholic church, for which he was paid, then dash around the corner to sing in the choir of the Methodist church, for which he was not paid. His mother believed that if the Lord gave one a beautiful voice one should gladly raise it in praise of the Lord without expectation of recompense in this world, but she thought singing for Catholics was different. In common with most Methodists of that day, she was not sure that hymns sung in a Catholic church reached the ear of the Lord. No matter how far one may stray from conventional religion in later life, the influence of such a home and childhood cannot be wholly erased. Until Atkinson was twenty-seven or twenty-eight years old the strong religious infusion received in childhood and early youth was the dominant and controlling influence of his daily life.

Another impressive influence was the conversation around his mother's table. Most of the boarders were immigrants from English mill towns, and they brought with them the almost ferocious distrust of "the bosses" which characterized early trade unionists. Those were the years when workers were rioting in Britain and the United States, and strikers were being driven back to work by soldiers. Joseph learned of the class struggle from his mother's boarders.

He entered high school at the age of twelve. He must have been a good student, for old newspaper clippings show that at the presentation of prizes at a township festival the next spring he took four awards for scholarship. His mother died at the age of sixty, shortly before Joseph was fourteen, and rightly or wrongly he always believed her death was hastened by hard work and worry. A sister took over management of the household, and he quit school and went to work in the woollen mill.

A few weeks later the mill burned down and he lost his job. Serious as that was for him, it was a calamity for the married workers, for no other jobs were available in Newcastle. Thirty years later, when he was made responsible for outlining a body of social legislation for the Liberal party, at the top of the list he put measures to protect workers and their families from the catastrophic effects of unemployment resulting from sickness or other causes beyond their control.

He returned briefly to school, but when a vacancy occurred at the post office he accepted it, much to the chagrin of his sisters, who wanted him to study for the ministry. A delicate-looking boy with a stammer, he was so small at sixteen that he had to stand on a box at the wicket to serve customers. It was while working at the post office that he began putting an "E" in his signature and signing himself Joseph E. Atkinson. The "E" did not stand for anything, since he had been given only one name at birth, but everybody else had a middle initial. Somehow it sounded important.

When he was eighteen and still earning only nine dollars a month at the post office he decided to look for a better job, and as was the custom in those days he armed himself with a sheaf of recommendations. "I am sorry to part with him, but he merits a higher salary than I can afford to give him," wrote his employer, the postmaster. W. W. Jardine, principal of the high school, wrote that his qualifications and aptitude for learning "render him capable of engaging with success in almost any line of business upon which he may choose to enter . . . I consider him a most desirable young man for any who may require his services . . . His character and habits of life are unimpeachable." The Methodist minister noted that "although the postmaster has been much unwell, yet nothing has gone wrong in the office during that time." He described Joseph as "of respectable family, not rich in this world's goods, but have always borne a good character." "He has secured the approbation and esteem of the whole community," wrote the rector of St. George's Anglican church. "I believe he will fill with satisfaction any position he may be employed in," wrote the manager of the local branch of the Standard Bank. "He is in every way a young man I can confidently recommend," wrote the local druggist. "I cheerfully recommend him for any position his education will permit him filling," testified the grain merchant; and Thomas Miller, general merchant, said, "I have never heard the faintest thing against his character."

He wanted to be a banker, and the local branch manager, W. R. Allen, had recommended him for any opening that might occur for a junior clerk in any branch. But before there was an opening Joseph received a letter from J. D. Trayes, owner and editor of the Port Hope *Times*, asking if he knew of any young fellow with a bicycle who would like a job collecting outstanding accounts in and around Port Hope. One of his tasks at the post office had been to take items of local news from people at the wicket and mail them once a week to the *Times*. He was not a reporter or the local correspondent. He merely took the items, stuffed them in an envelope, and mailed it. In the last budget of news had been a report of a bicycle race in which young men from all the countryside participated.

Joseph did not own a bicycle, but since the job would pay six dollars a week, double what he was earning at the post office, he replied that he would be delighted to do the collecting on foot. "I did not have the faintest intention of becoming a newspaperman when I accepted this job," Mr. Atkinson was wont to recall. "I wanted to be a banker. But six dollars a week was too good to turn down. Thus it was accident, not choice, that set me on my course in life."

A better school in which to learn newspaper work would have been hard to find. The eighteen-seventies and -eighties in Canada was a period of great political activity and considerable intellectual vigour, and newspapers were multiplying like mushrooms all over the country. In this lively little town of Port Hope with a population of six thousand there were no less than three, each furiously waging war on behalf of its own political creed. The *Times* was Conservative, and its publisher spent more time in politics than he did running his paper. Trayes arranged that his new employee receive an identification card from the Canadian Press Association entitling him to reduced fare on the railways. He signed it "J. E. Atkinson, occupation, Reporter." The Canadian Press Association was an organization of newspaper publishers, both daily and weekly, and had no connection with the present news service, the Canadian Press.

Except for the printers, Atkinson was the only employee, and as well as collecting accounts and selling job printing he was expected to be general minder of the office, while his employer frolicked in political pastures with his cronies. To this Atkinson did not object, for it gave him a chance to learn the business end of printing and publishing. Before long he was running the business. Before long, too, he was virtually secretary of the Canadian Press Association. Trayes was the secretary, but he much preferred to let his efficient employee do the work. As a result Joseph acquired a lifelong interest in the association and after he became a publisher himself was for many years its secretary.

When Trayes turned his weekly into a daily, increasing the staff by only one man, Joseph turned his hand to reporting. This earned him a raise in pay to nine dollars a week. Soon he was writing editorials as well, and Conservative editorials at that—which did not bother him in the least. If he held any views on politics at all they were probably those of the foundry workers he had known in his youth—that politicians were all a bunch of rascals who did nothing for the working man.

Meanwhile, Trayes was becoming more and more irresponsible, running off for days at a time to political meetings or the races, leaving Joseph to run the business. From distant points like Montreal, New York, or Toronto would come a flurry of cheques which his youthful employee was expected to persuade the bank to honour. Sometimes it was all Joseph could do to collect enough money to meet them. Of course, no business run in such a fashion can prosper, and about two years after Atkinson went to the *Times* Trayes' creditors closed down on him. A representative of the estate that held the mortgage on the building and machinery approached young Joe, who was not yet twenty-one.

"Atkinson," he said, "We know very well you are running the paper, and we'd like to turn it over to you. Say the word and the paper is yours."

"I couldn't do a thing like that to Mr. Trayes," the young man replied. "He's been very good to me."

So the creditors gave Trayes another chance. Twice again before he was twenty-six Atkinson was to be offered papers if he would assume their mortgage and debts. One was the Stratford *Beacon*, long since merged in the prosperous *Beacon-Herald* partnership, but in 1890 struggling under a load of debt to Toronto paper dealers. The other was the Chatham *Planet*, which vanished in 1923.

If Trayes and his irresponsible ways were a worry to his employee, serious-minded young Atkinson just as thoroughly exasperated his employer. "For God's sake, Joe, why don't you go out and get drunk like any normal man," Trayes exploded one day. Joe mildly retorted that he had seen enough drunkenness among the Newcastle foundry workers to last him a lifetime. His mother's training and his own observation had convinced him the liquor traffic was evil and that no good man would have any part of it. He remained a teetotaller for life. In the hope of bringing him out of his shell Trayes introduced him to the Masonic order, of which the publisher was one of the more exuberant members. Obediently Atkinson joined the Port Hope lodge and regularly attended meetings. But he found them uninteresting and after he left Port Hope he took no further part in Masonic activities.

Trayes found the most vexatious characteristic of his young protegé to be his apparent lack of ambition. He worked hard but seemed to have no goal. Trayes believed he had potentialities if they could be awakened, but his interests were narrow and local and mostly centred around the church. He did not read either for recreation or self-improvement. Trayes was a scholarly man as well as gregarious, and had a large library stocked with books from floor to ceiling. He started inviting the young man to his home, pressing books upon him, trying to open his mind to the great thinkers of the day, and delivering long lectures on his particular hobby, the new social philosophies that were beginning to interest the world in the eighties.

Mr. Atkinson used to recall the complete indifference with which he first encountered the serious literature thus urged upon him. It bored him, but out of deference to his employer he waded through it. Then one evening while reading a book of Canadian biographies by James Dent a paragraph seemed to leap at him with the force of a blow. It told how Leonard Tilley, one of the Fathers of Confederation, had risen from being a clerk in a drugstore to become a great statesman and one of the founders of the nation.

"One can scarcely imagine the curious, thrilling and exciting effect that simple statement had upon me," Mr. Atkinson said. "It had never occurred to me that a clerk could ever rise to such heights. For the first time I realized that life is wider than the bounds of a village or county." Until then he had unquestioningly accepted the humble lot in which God had set him as he thought a devout Christian should. Now he realized that a man is what he makes of himself, and never again could he be content with his lot. But to change his lot he had to know a great deal more than he did.

Feverishly he plunged into Trayes' library like a thirsty traveller into a desert pool, and the days were all too short for the reading he must do.

First he read the biographies of the great for confirmation that a man's beginnings need not hold him back. Then in great gulps he swallowed history, sociology, philosophy, and science. Tolstoy's writings impressed him most—Tolstoy who believed that rich men are wicked and society rotten, but that this rotten society can be regenerated from within. Tolstoy suited his newly awakened mood. Had he not been forced to work as a child of fourteen that rich men might grow richer? Had he not seen his mother worked to death (as he believed) when rich men could have helped her? Had he not seen the workers of Newcastle exploited (as he believed) by rich mill owners? He had never liked rich men, and though he lived to become a very rich man himself he never learned to like them, choosing his friends elsewhere.

At the same time Tolstoy's conception of a society curing itself of its rottenness by regeneration from within along Christian lines appealed to a young man steeped in a theology that taught redemption came only with "conversion." His thoughts turned to how the ills of Canadian society could be cured, and in Trayes' library were books that seemed to him to have the answer—books by such radical and revolutionary writers as Henry George, whose *Progress and Poverty* quickened his interest in social reform; John Stuart Mill, who believed social reform was as important as political reform; and John Ruskin, the moral economist. He read Karl Marx but was unimpressed. As late as 1913 he expressed the opinion that Marx's writings had made few converts and left no permanent impression. His social philosophy took form in his last two years in Port Hope, and the pattern was set to which he was to adhere with unswerving consistency throughout his long life. Like the radicals whose writings most impressed him, and who were then the dominant influence in British trade unionism, he found what he sought in liberalism rather than in socialism.

Morgan Phillips has said of the British Labour party that it derived its beliefs from Methodism rather than from Marxism. So it was with Atkinson. Society must be made good and its injustices corrected. Whether specific wrongs were corrected by socialistic means or otherwise was to him a matter of expediency rather than of principle. And since this was only a matter of expediency, he could support measures that were socialistic without being a socialist, or use the methods of capitalism when they better suited the purposes he sought to further.

After four years on the Port Hope *Times*, at the age of twenty-two, Joseph Atkinson decided he was entitled to a raise, and asked Trayes for ten dollars a week.

"I can't afford it," Trayes replied.

"I know quite well you can," his reporter-salesman-clerk retorted. "I have been in almost complete charge of this business and know what you can and cannot afford."

"I'm nearly broke and going deeper in the hole all the time," the publisher protested.

"I can pull you through if you give me the raise and let me run things," Atkinson told him. But the dollar raise was not forthcoming, Joseph departed to become a reporter on the Toronto *World*, and in due course the Port Hope *Times* was absorbed by a competitor.

Atkinson had met W. F. Maclean, publisher of the *World*, while attending a meeting of the Canadian Press Association, and knew his reputation as a flamboyant and picturesque editor who gave his reporters wide scope to show their initiative and develop their style. Thus when, in October, 1888, he saw an advertisement in the *World* for three reporters he applied for the position, not neglecting to ask how much the pay would be. Back came the reply by wire: "Application accepted. When can you come?" But not a word about money. "Will come for $15 a week," the canny Atkinson wired back. "Salary satisfactory. When can you come?" Maclean replied. Since Maclean seemed to be in such a hurry, Atkinson left for Toronto by the next train. To his dismay the first task given him was to write editorials. The dismay soon passed, for though Maclean was a Conservative, the *World* was the leading exponent in Canada of public ownership, and Atkinson was soon an ardent convert. He remained a public ownership man until his death.

Four months later he was invited by J. S. Willison to join the staff of the *Globe*. That newspaper was being reorganized, with most of the old executives turned out to pasture, and Willison had been hired to shake up the editorial staff. Atkinson declined the invitation. Willison had offered him two dollars a week more than the *World* was paying, but Maclean had promised to send him to Ottawa to cover the next session of Parliament, which he very much wanted to do. Willison had already promised that assignment on the *Globe*'s behalf to Albert R. Carman, who later became editor of the *Montreal Star*. So instead of Atkinson, Willison hired Stewart Lyon, who was then without newspaper experience, but who in the course of time became editor of the *Globe*.

A few months later Willison renewed his offer. This time it was coupled with a promise to let him cover the Legislature, not as important a job as covering Parliament, but still an exceptional opportunity for a young reporter of twenty-three. He accepted.

William A. Hewitt, for sixty years one of Canada's notable sports editors and executives, was then a cub reporter on the *News*. In his autobiography, *Down the Stretch*, he tells of frequently meeting "a smart *Globe* reporter named Joe Atkinson." "Even in my teens I could sense that he was no ordinary news-gatherer," Hewitt relates. "Joe Atkinson was a reserved but friendly rival. He was not a mixer but other reporters respected his ability and integrity."

Mr. Atkinson used to describe his eight years on the *Globe* as "intensely happy and free." He was at liberty to explore at more length the liberal point of view to which his sympathies naturally inclined him, and with every month the liberal idea excited him more. It was not long after he joined the *Globe* that he read Henry George's *Protection or Free Trade*, which had a profound effect upon his rapidly crystallizing point of view. He became a convinced free trader. That led him inevitably into the Liberal party, for in those days the Liberal and Conservative parties in Canada were divided almost solely on the question of high or low tariffs.

At one time his free trade convictions led him to examine the expediency of annexation to the United States, but he decided the prevailing Canadian sentiment made it impracticable. There may have been some truth, however, in charges made later by his newspaper opponents that he would not have objected to annexation on personal grounds. Not long before his death he remarked to one of his close associates, rather regretfully it would seem, that the development of Canada had taken a form that made either annexation or reciprocity impractical.

Aggressive, alert, and superbly edited, the *Globe* at that time was unquestionably one of the great newspapers of this continent, head and shoulders above any other in Canada. For two years Atkinson was a general reporter, covering anything that came along, but he soon distinguished himself as a writer of moving and colourful human interest stories of the kind that later was to make *The Star* famous.

The story that clinched his reputation as a reporter of the first rank was the hanging of J. R. Birchall at Woodstock jail on November 14, 1890. Birchall's arrest and trial was the biggest news event of 1890, and is commemorated in one of Canada's few folksongs. Atkinson's story of that event was not only great reporting; much of it was great writing. But other passages are mawkishly emotional by present-day standards.

Atkinson spent the death watch with the jail guards and the hangman. He was one of two hundred newspapermen and prominent citizens of the community who witnessed the execution the next morning. Not once did he intrude his own personality into his report. He might have been a disembodied spirit dispassionately watching the proceedings. The report he wrote is much too long to be reproduced in full here. It occupied all of page one of the *Globe* of November 15 except the left-hand column, a solid mass of type broken only by an occasional subhead, and turned to an inside page. But from these few excerpts one may judge Joseph Atkinson's skill and style:

The murder of Frederick C. Benwell has been avenged. Reginald Birchall was executed on the scaffold in the yard of Woodstock gaol this morning at about 8:30. He died without confessing, without even alluding in public to his crime. He made no speech or remark of any kind after getting into the gaol yard save a casual one to the executioner. He maintained his nerve throughout, and but for a ghastly pallor gave no evidence of the emotion within his breast. From beginning to end he did not flinch or lose his self-possession. He died bravely, as he said he would die.

The day was bright and beautiful. The yard of death lay in the shadow of the old gaol, and only on one corner of it could the sunlight fall at this early hour. The scaffold was in the shadow, and the whole yard appeared gloomy and frightful contrasted with the brightness that reigned without. Birchall seemed indifferent to the crowd of spectators. His gaze was directed principally towards the dreadful gallows and only occasionally did he meet the eyes of the onlookers, though those of all present were bent with a terrible anxiousness and intentness upon him. When their eyes met he never quailed. He preserved to the last his look of stony determination not to break down, and this was the expression on his face when the hangman drew the black cap down over it and hid it from view. . . .

From here the reporter takes us back to the evening before. After describing the mood of the town he tells how the streets slowly cleared as night fell, and one by one the lights in the homes went out.

Everywhere else the starry mantle of the night wrapt the orderly town in repose and forgetfulness. Everywhere else except in a narrow corridor in the county gaol. A man who had promised to love and cherish a woman through life was bidding her be brave to bear the pain of her near widowhood. A woman who had promised to love, honor and obey a man until death was bidding him bear up under an awful trial and making her last sacrifice on her marriage altar. Only One other knew what they talked about through the fleeting hours until 1 o'clock. . . .

The hangman was J. R. Radclive, an Englishman who worked as a steward at the Sunnyside Boating club of Toronto, and hanged murderers as a sideline. As they sat talking together in the early part of the evening the hangman taught Atkinson how to tie a hangman's noose.

"I don't hang him because I like to do it, but I see no harm in it," said the hangman. ". . . Everyone approves of it except a small, minute minority who have no common sense . . . I shall carry it out as strict and stern as if I was shooting a dog, but I have a good deal of feeling for him just the same . . . I can do it just as steady as I can smoke that cigar . . . As for being a heartless wretch, the public can say as they like, I don't do it for money."

"Do you do it for fame, then?"

The hangman vouchsafed no reply to this, only adding that he hoped Birchall would not confess at the last. If a man insists at the beginning he is innocent he should stick to it. He rolled over on the sofa and in less than a minute was asleep. . . .

Four o'clock came—four hours only of life remained for the man upstairs awaiting death. He was wide awake still. Downstairs, still in a deep sleep, lay the man whose hand was to be the instrument of justice to deprive him of life. . . .

Five o'clock came. The gaol clock hangs in the rotunda, almost immediately under the corridor in which Birchall's cell is situated. Its sharp striking could be heard in the still night in every part of the gaol, and with especial clearness in the condemned cell above it. Birchall hears it, counts the strokes, and knows he has but three hours left of life. . . .

At last morning came, and reporter Atkinson described the ghoulish congregation of two hundred in the jail yard when the doomed man was led towards the place of execution.

Even at this supreme moment Birchall's will sustained him. His face was ghastly pale and, in contrast with his jet black hair, eyes and moustache, looked like marble. Yet he stood there firm and erect, needing no support of any kind, though the sands of his life had run down to the very dregs . . . His gaze was not a stolid one, hardly one of indifference. It was rather one of absolute determination not to show a sign of fear. It was the last venture of a lost man, and it was entirely successful.

Then, in the same dispassionate but expressive language, follows a description of the execution, one of the most dreadful in Canadian annals. The horror of that execution was never erased from Joseph Atkinson's memory. The agony of the condemned man's last hours, the brutishness of the hangman, the whole degrading proceedings, left their indelible imprint on the sensitive mind of the 24-year-old reporter. He could never again condone the death penalty, and his newspapers consistently advocated abolition of capital punishment.

After this Joseph Atkinson was the *Globe*'s ace reporter, though he was all that newspaper reporters were thought not to be. He neither drank nor smoked. He went regularly to the Methodist church and read Henry Drummond's *The Natural Law in the Spiritual World* and his *The Greatest Thing in the World*. He attended Joseph Flavelle's Bible class, forming a lasting friendship with Flavelle, one of Toronto's leading financiers. He joined several other young men in a study group to discuss politics, religion and social problems. He toyed for a while with the idea of becoming a Methodist minister and took private lessons in Latin from city solicitor Chisholm, with the intention of entering Emmanuel College.

"I gave up the idea of the ministry because I couldn't accept the Methodist doctrine of eternal damnation," he related. He was to find as the years passed that this was not the only doctrine of organized religion he could not accept. However, all his life he felt a strange affinity with members of the Christian ministry and no other newspaper in Canada has had as many clergymen on its staff or as contributors as *The Toronto Star*. Or as many former clergymen.

When he was twenty-five a rather remarkable thing happened to Joe Atkinson. He lost his stammer. "I don't know when or how it came about," he related, "but one day I realized somewhat to my surprise that I wasn't stammering any more, and that I hadn't been for some time." But a precise, cautious, almost schoolmasterish enunciation remained as a lifelong reminder of his long struggle to overcome this boyhood affliction.

Atkinson had been on the *Globe* only two years when he won the coveted assignment to the Ottawa press gallery. He covered the six sessions from 1891 to 1896. Here his aloofness was even more noticeable than it had been in Toronto. He became well acquainted with Sir Mackenzie Bowell, the Conservative Prime Minister from 1894 to 1896, but scarcely knew any of the cabinet ministers. His relations with the Liberals, except with their leader Wilfrid Laurier, were almost as formal and distant. "I preferred to stand on the outside looking in," he explained. "Thus my eyes were not blinded by friendship and I was exempt from the temptation to alter or suppress news concerning men with whom I might have been on cordial terms."

His years in Ottawa confirmed his liberal convictions. Things were not going well with Canada. Unemployment was rife and farmers were hard up. Only a Liberal government with genuinely liberal principles could save the nation, he became convinced. He formed a close friendship with Laurier, then the opposition Liberal leader, travelling across Canada with him on his election and speaking tours and helping him write his speeches. He was written up by a magazine in a series it was running on young men who were expected to make their mark in Canada.

When the Liberal party endorsed a policy of unrestricted reciprocity with the United States, the *Globe* sent him on a tour of Ontario to interview manufacturers on the probable effects. It may be, as the government alleged, that he interviewed only manufacturers of known Liberal sympathies, but if so they proved to be uncommonly numerous. Not one interview was repudiated. Among those he interviewed were four men who were to remember him and help him become established in his own newspaper, Lyman Jones, William Christie, Peter Larkin, and Walter Massey.

Between sessions of Parliament he travelled far and wide for the *Globe*, ranging over most of eastern Canada and much of the United States, Canada's first roving reporter. One summer he went to the Maritime provinces, to do a series of articles on business and industry in the East. He was accompanied by C. W. Jefferys, one of Canada's great artists, to sketch personalities and scenes, this being before the day of press cameras and halftone illustrations. It is believed to be the first series of illustrated feature articles to appear in any Canadian newspaper, and the public approval they received convinced Atkinson of the value of pictures. When he had his own paper Jefferys was one of the first men to whom he offered a job.

Perhaps the most quoted of his articles as a reporter is the series he wrote from Iowa and Kansas in the winter of 1893–94. These were prohibition states, and prohibition was a burning issue in Ontario in those days. The *Globe* sent Atkinson, a teetotaller and prohibitionist, and John Ewan, an editorial writer whose leanings were decidedly in the opposite direction, as a team to report how prohibition was working. Each was to write it as he saw it through his somewhat prejudiced eyes. As it developed, Atkinson did most of the writing in an objective, lucid, descriptive style tinged with humour. Here is an excerpt from one of his despatches:

> Perry was the name of the next town we visited. It is a brisk town of somewhere between 2,500 and 3,000 people, situated in Dallas county. Our first aim was to find out, from likely sources, how many places, if any, there are where liquor can be bought. We were told that besides the four drug stores which sell spirits with some caution, there are also two semi-public bars and two semi-private houses where beer could be bought. There was no reason to doubt the accommodating disposition of the druggists and we did not trouble them.
>
> The first saloon we went to was in a small one-storey frame building on a side street. We pushed in the door against the smells, and looking through the super-heated atmosphere, thick from the pot-pourri of cooked orders, saw a rough, unshaven man in his shirt sleeves behind the bar, and a group of just as rough and unshaven men in front of it, engaged in the great American custom of decorative expectoration with the red-hot stove as the object of their designs.
>
> In response to the request for a drink of beer, the keeper of the joint went to fetch a quart bottle, but my colleague, glad of the excuse not to drink in such a hole, excused himself on the score that we wanted only a pint. We discovered

that we could also buy bottled beer at another place. In both places, however, the smallest quantity was a quart, for which a quarter of a dollar is asked; so that drinking under the circumstances is neither economical nor attractive. There was nowhere in the town any sale by the glass, and the hotels do not sell any liquor at all.

Atkinson believed a story should "tell itself." He did not editorialize or dramatize. He wrote what he saw, and left the reader to form his own opinion. This is the kind of reporting he always preferred, and he was suspicious of the reporter who professed to be "an authority." But he could be lenient on a reporter who closed his eyes to troublesome facts if he did so in a good cause.

On one of his first out-of-town assignments he formed an association that was not only lifelong and devoted but also of great moment in Canadian history. While in Berlin, now Kitchener, covering the criminal assizes, he was chatting with John King, one of the defence lawyers, and the talk turned to social problems. "You ought to meet my son Willie," King exclaimed, and invited the reporter to his home that evening. And there he made the acquaintance of William Lyon Mackenzie King, a serious-minded high school student who, like himself, had a passionate interest in sociology. "The life-long bond between us was mutual interest in social problems," King wrote on Atkinson's death in 1948.

While reminiscing with Mackenzie King fifty years later Atkinson recalled the effect on him of his introduction to the King family. King wrote in his diary on April 19, 1943: "(Atkinson) prefaced what he had to say by mentioning that all of his family had had to struggle for their livelihood. None of them had the advantage of special education or association with the learned professions . . . He then said when I came into your home at Woodside, I saw the fire in the library, the books, pictures and all. It was to me as though I had seen for the first time what I had read of in books as the ideal life in country homes in the Old Land. It spoke to me of all that I had most liked and read about."

When King graduated from University of Toronto in 1893 he worked for two weeks on the *News* then went to the *Globe*. He was reading for a law degree in his spare time. For a short time during the 1896 elections King, who was covering the campaign for the afternoon edition, and Atkinson, who was covering it for the morning edition, shared the same desk and occasionally collaborated on election stories.

Two years after Atkinson went to the *Globe* beautiful and talented Elmina Elliott joined the staff, writing a daily column for the women's page under the pen name of Madge Merton. It was the fashion of the day for journalists thus to hide their identities, perhaps in self-defence. She, too, was a liberal and a humanitarian, and they were attracted to each other from the day they met. In 1892 they were married.

A woman of exceptional intellect, great determination, and a somewhat austere cast of character, she has been described as "Joe Atkinson's conscience." J. H. Cranston, former editor of *The Star Weekly,* called her "Atkinson's good angel." She wielded a strong influence over her husband and through him over the policies of his newspapers. Atkinson once approved an article by a *Star* reporter which commented, "Perhaps in the whole history of *The Star* there was not a more important factor than this marriage," and once told George Maitland, "The two greatest influences in my life are the Christian religion and my wife."

Elmina Elliott was a native of Oakville. Her journalistic career began in 1887 when she was twenty with occasional contributions to *Saturday Night,* which Edmund E. Sheppard had founded that year. Sheppard brought her to Toronto to be his society editor. About three years later she went to the *Globe* as editor of the women's page. She was a prolific writer of verse, and in 1915 was awarded the London *Bookman* prize for her poem "Grey Gauntlet." Her columns of 1891 are sprinkled with tender little verses betraying the happiness of a girl in love. Some are gently teasing of her loved one, as the following:

Here a man, stern-browed and weary,
Bends him o'er the printed page;
"There's no time," he said, "for gladness,
Life is naught but care and sadness,
I'll not marry—'tis but madness—
In this age."

On the page, then, Cupid traces—
Wilful, darling little sage—
Maiden's face with brown eyes tender,
And the stern heart makes surrender,
Ah, Love's king, Work but pretender,
In this age.

In a different mood is the little poem entitled "Recollections," which concludes with this verse:

The moonlight slants across the beach;
The shadows nestle 'neath the tree,
But wind and wave and shore and sky
Bring back a time not long gone by,
The night you sang to me.

Mrs. Atkinson became as warm a friend of the King family as her husband, and they were both frequent guests at the King home and even attended King family reunions. In 1947 Mackenzie King wrote Atkinson of a pilgrimage he made to Mrs. Atkinson's grave, to place flowers upon it.

In 1897, after eight years on the *Globe*, Atkinson was offered and accepted the managing editorship of the Montreal *Herald*, then being reorganized and strengthened by its new publisher, Jarvis S. Brierley, formerly of St. Thomas, Ontario. The *Herald* was a Liberal newspaper, and with some associates Brierley had bought it to fight the aggressively Tory *Montreal Star* and the strongly entrenched financial interests that were running the city. Maclean, who had brought youthful Joe Atkinson to Toronto, wrote an editorial in the *World* congratulating him on his new job. "It was seen by all his confreres from the day he entered the newspaper field that he would get to the top," wrote Maclean. Though there was now a daughter, Ruth, Mrs. Atkinson returned to newspaper work to edit the *Herald*'s women's page.

At the *Herald* Atkinson made another lifelong friendship that was, in its way, almost as significant as that with King. It was with J. F. Mackay, who became secretary-treasurer of the *Herald* when Atkinson was appointed managing editor. Mackay later became general manager and in effect publisher of the *Globe*. The two men worked together for years to reform the Liberal party and give it a more social outlook, to strengthen Canadian nationalism, and to establish the Canadian Press on a sound basis.

In a letter to Pierre Berton, of *Maclean's Magazine*, F. W. Sutherland of St. Thomas, a pioneer Ontario newspaperman, recalled an incident when he visited Brierley, his former "chief." The *Herald* at the time

> was engaged in a rapid fire battle against the alleged predatory interests of the city of Montreal . . . The *Herald*'s aggressive attacks included scathing front page editorials from day to day . . . Mr. Atkinson was in his element in this battle, and in his aggressive editorials no holds were barred. He resented the frequent blue pencilling of his copy by Mr. Brierley, and on the day of my visit things were popping. Another of his fighting articles had been severely trimmed by the Chief, and this proved to be the proverbial last straw. Tossing his emasculated copy on the desk, he headed for the office, collected his pay, and without ceremony was gone.

Aggressive blue-pencilling must indeed have been hard to take for a man whose copy had been almost inviolable on the *Globe*. But contrary to Mr. Sutherland's understanding he did *not* quit his job at that time. However, it could not have been many days later that Hugh Graham, later Lord Atholstan, owner and publisher of the *Montreal Star*, offered him a job as managing editor.

The *Montreal Star* had the largest circulation of any English-language newspaper in Canada. It was the rich, powerful organ of capitalist opinion in Canada's richest and biggest city, for the Conservatives what the *Globe* was for the Liberals. That a self-educated, unassuming young man, not yet thirty-four, should be offered the cream of editorial jobs in Canada at a salary no other paper could hope to match was the talk of the Canadian newspaper world. But to the astonishment of all, instead of snapping at the offer, Atkinson asked time to think it over.

For days he wrestled with his conscience while the offer was held open. The temptation was great. But how could he, who firmly believed in a liberalism which at that time was speaking for the trade unions, become the mouthpiece of big business? How could he recant everything he had written about predatory capitalists and become their paid advocate? How could he desert the Liberal party which he had joined from conviction and become a Conservative?

In his indecision he went to Toronto the weekend of November 25, 1899, for a talk with his old friend and mentor of many years, J. S. Willison, editor of the *Globe*. Willison advised him to accept Graham's offer. It was, said Willison, "the second most important newspaper position in Canada." (Evidently he considered his own the most important.) In relating the story, Mr. Atkinson said he retorted angrily that he could not sell himself to the highest bidder or become a renegade to get a better job.

Willison, then, tentatively advanced another suggestion. Would he consider becoming publisher of the *Toronto Evening Star*, though at a salary somewhat less than the *Montreal Star* was offering? Willison explained that at the request of Sir Wilfrid Laurier, who had become Prime Minister in 1896, several wealthy Toronto men, not all identified with the Liberal party, were considering buying the tottering *Evening Star*. Of the six Toronto daily newspapers, only one, the morning *Globe,* supported Laurier. It was felt he should have the support of an evening newspaper as well. Since *The Star* had supported him briefly during the 1896 election, and was for sale, negotiations for its purchase had begun. Senator Robert Jaffray, publisher of the *Globe*, had been asked to recommend a good man to run it.

This information did not come as a surprise to Atkinson, though apparently he did not tell Willison so. Some weeks before Walter E. H. Massey, whom he had known as a fellow member of Joseph Flavelle's Sunday school class, had informed him of what was afoot and indicated the Toronto group would like to meet him. W. A. Hewitt, who had followed Atkinson to the *Herald* to be sports editor, tells of carrying messages, the meaning of which he did not then understand, between Montreal and Toronto. But seemingly Atkinson was not impressed by the prospect and showed only a casual interest.

There was ample reason for an ambitious newspaperman to shun the *Evening Star*, for its uncertain light seemed about to be extinguished. Founded in 1892 by a group of printers with the support of organized labour, it had started brightly enough. But the printers soon ran out of money, organized labour lost interest, and the *Evening Star* had four owners in seven years. With each change of ownership its policies changed, until by 1899 it was unrespected, uninfluential, and almost unread.

Willison arranged a meeting in the office of Senator George Cox, one of the country's leading financial figures and president, among other concerns, of the Canadian Bank of Commerce. To this he took Atkinson. Also attending the meeting was Walter E. H. Massey, president of the Massey-Harris farm implement company, and Lyman M. Jones, managing-director of Massey-Harris, who had been president of the Harris company before it merged with Massey.

They told him the group included Hon. William Mulock, Postmaster General and chief Liberal organizer in Ontario; Timothy Eaton, the department store owner, who had never been identified as a Liberal but greatly admired Sir Wilfrid; William Christie, head of the Christie-Brown biscuit company, who also had not been known as a Liberal, Peter Larkin, founder of the Salada tea company and later Canadian High Commissioner in London; Plunkett Magann, a railway contractor who had made a fortune building the C.P.R. and hoped to make another building the railways Laurier planned; and E. T. Malone, one of the city's leading lawyers and a director of the *Globe*.

Later Joseph Kilgour, president of the Canada Paper Company, M. J. Haney, contractor, lumberman, and founder of the Anglo-Canadian mining exchange, and Henry A. Little, a private banker and financier of Woodstock, each bought stock. But these three came in as investors rather than as contributors to the cause, and were never members of the inner circle. The men named here, or their heirs who were members of their immediate families, were the only persons who at any time have owned common or voting stock in *The Star* from 1899 until its sale in 1958.

Senator Cox outlined the proposition. The backers were pledged to raise $75,000 of which $32,000 would be used to buy the 460 shares of The Star Printing and Publishing Company of Toronto that had been issued. The remaining $43,000 would be available for expansion, promotion, and to meet the losses anticipated in the first few years. The 460 shares would be given an artificial value of $100 each, so that only 320 of them would be distributed to the purchasers, 140 shares being placed in surplus account. Of the 540 unissued shares still in the treasury, 430 would be distributed among the group, to each man in proportion as he met his pledge. This would leave 110 shares in the treasury, after all pledges were met. Cox, Eaton, and Massey had each paid the $10,000 he had promised, and each owned 100 shares, but none of the others had paid his pledge in full. Calls would be made upon them as money was needed. The paper had a reputed circulation of "more than 14,000," Atkinson was told, and was said to have produced $38,000 revenue the preceding year. Would Atkinson come as editor and manager, and if so, at what salary?

Atkinson outlined his terms: a ten-year contract at an initial salary of $5,000 a year, of which $3,000 was to be paid in cash and the rest in stock from the treasury at par value regardless of its actual worth at the time, and an opportunity to acquire fifty-one per cent of the stock in due course.

Cox protested that Atkinson's terms were out of the question. The paper, he said, was being bought for a specific purpose. To assure that purpose would be realized the purchasers had to keep control of it.

"Then, gentlemen, I am afraid you will find my other condition even less acceptable," Atkinson said. "I can come to *The Star* only on condition it is conducted solely in its own interest as a newspaper enterprise. It must be hampered by no other considerations. There has been one *Empire* in Toronto and I have no desire to conduct another." A morning newspaper, the *Empire,* founded some years before to be the official Conservative organ in Toronto, had recently failed and been merged with the *Mail.* It was said to have been the victim of constant interference in its news coverage by the men who had put up the cash.

"But, Mr. Atkinson, you must see that we cannot give you the free hand you ask," Senator Cox protested. "This is something unheard of; an entirely new idea. What assurance have we that you will support the policies towards which we are contributing?"

"Simply this, that I am as warm an admirer of Sir Wilfrid as any of you, and believe as firmly in his policies," Atkinson replied.

In the discussion which followed, Senator Cox came around to Atkinson's view, but not the others, and the meeting dispersed with nothing settled. The following Wednesday Atkinson wrote Sir Wilfrid a long and in places incoherent letter, hastily scrawled in longhand on both sides of four sheets of business letter paper, and bearing every evidence of emotional turmoil. Without any explanation of the disagreement that had arisen, he plunged into an appeal to Sir Wilfrid.

> To me, and I believe to Mr. Cox, it is clear that a paper can be useful politically if it has the confidence of its constituency, and that by having regard to its commercial success, a Liberal paper enables itself to give greater service to its party. . . . I think it would have the effect of strengthening the view which Mr. Cox holds if you were to write him upon this point.
>
> For my part, I am sure I need not say there would [be no] inducements which would take me to an enterprise which, run upon any other basis than its own expansion and success, would be foredoomed to failure, although there might be capital enough behind it to postpone its collapse for years to come . . .

"My Dear Atkinson," Sir Wilfrid replied, "you do not write with your usual lucidity." He asked for an explanation of what the disagreement was about, adding "it seems to be a truism which nobody would dispute that a newspaper can only be useful politically if it has the confidence of its constituency."

In reply Atkinson explained that Mulock, the only politician in the group, wanted *The Star* to be a purely political organ that would have to do whatever was demanded of it by the leaders of the Liberal party, without regard to the long-term welfare of the newspaper. Mulock, he said, wanted it "more ardent and reliable" even than the *Globe* in its partisanship.

"A newspaper is a good ally, but soon becomes useless as the subservient organ of a party," Atkinson warned. Senator Cox, he continued, disagreed with Mulock, and did not want *The Star* branded as a party organ "but on this particular point doesn't want to act at variance with the politicians." If the "mistake" was made of adopting Mulock's view, he said, he would "have to remain in Montreal, and this I would be sorry to do."

The response to this was a telegram from Cox: "Would you please go to Ottawa and see Sir Wilfrid Laurier." In Ottawa he repeated his conviction that no newspaper can be successfully run unless the man at the head of it has final and absolute control over its policy, and that a newspaper must be run in its own best interests rather than that of any party or financial group.

"Who would decide what is in the paper's interest?" asked Sir Wilfrid.

6 O'CLOCK. **THE EVEN[ING] STAR.** A PAPER FOR THE PEOPLE.

THE EVENING STAR, TH[URSDAY], NOVEMBER 3, 1892. ONE CENT.

WORLD OF SPORT.

Helen Nicols Breaks the Record For 2-Year-Olds.

The Filly Goes a Mile On a Slow Track in 1.41 1-2.

Saturday's Football Match—Varsity Defeats Osgoode Hall in the Association Match—Mitchell Explains Why He Assaulted Salvage—Trotting and General News.

TURF NEWS.

ANOTHER PROTEST.

A Resolution Condemning That Lock-out by the Book-binders.

A SERIOUS ILLNESS.

N. G. Bigelow, Q.C., Stricken Down With a Serious Condition.

BIG PURSES FOR THEM.

Where Muscle is More Profitable Than Brains.

The Coney Island Athletic Association Trying to Outbid New Orleans for Fighters.

AN ALLAN LINER ASHORE.

The Sarmatian Goes Out of Her Course in a Snow Storm.

SILVER COINAGE.

The Supply Far Exceeds the Needs of the Public.

Young Men's Liberal Club.

FOR PROHIBITION.

Nova Scotia Legislature to be Asked for It.

A Convention at Amherst Decides to Apply for an Act.

The Leading Lawyers of the Dominion Are of Opinion that the Legislatures Have Power to Act.

DESPOILED THE DEAD.

Ghouls Pounce Upon the Victims in the Roumania Wreck.

But the Robbery Ceased When the Troops Appeared—The Valuables Now in the Hands of the Officers.

THE PROVINCIAL TAX.

Mr. Auge Assails the Obnoxious Measure at Three Rivers.

He Denies That He Has Had Stormy Meetings with Premier DeBoucherville and Says They are a Happy Family.

LOST IN LAKE ERIE.

Changes at the Public Library.

THE AMERICA CUP.

Dunraven Has Decided Not to Sail For It This Year.

SHE SEEKS ALIMONY.

A Deserted Wife Who Was Supported ...

OVER THE OCEAN.

Trans-Atlantic Cables Alive With News.

The London Slander Suit About the Stolen Brooch

Causes Two Gentlewomen to Appear in the Criminal Court—A Publisher Punished For Contempt of Court—Newsy Items of Interest.

THE WINDMILL LINE.

PERSONAL INTELLIGENCE.

NOT AT ALL UNEASY.

O'Neil, the Drummer, Who is Charged With Abduction.

LOCAL HAPPENINGS

What is Going on in the Different Parts of the City.

IAMS' SORE THUMBS.

The Colonel Who Hung Him Up Tells His Story.

A PATHETIC CASE.

How the Railway Wreck at Thirsk was Caused.

WRECKAGE COMES ASHORE.

RIOTS IN MADRID.

The Queen Regent Refuses to Visit the City,

And the Populace Is So Incensed That They Wreck Things.

PERISHED IN THE PACIFIC.

THE CARMAUX STRIKE.

Sparks From the Anvil.

BIRTHS.

The front page of the first issue of *The Star*, November 3, 1892

TOP, left to right: Joseph E. Atkinson at the age of sixteen; at twenty; at twenty-four as a member of the Press Gallery at Ottawa; and at thirty-four when he became editor and manager of *The Toronto Evening Star*

RIGHT: Elmina Elliott at the time of her marriage to Joseph E. Atkinson

BELOW: the house in which Joseph E. Atkinson lived as a youth in Newcastle, Ont. Taken about 1947

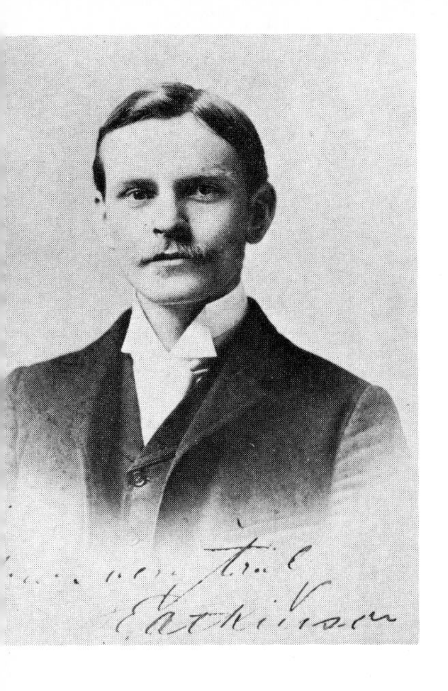

TOP, left to right: Horatio Hocken, foreman of the printers who founded *The Star* and was its first manager; Sir William Gage, owner of *The Star*, August 16, 1893, to December 13, 1895; Frederic Nicholls, owner of *The Star*, 1895 to December 13, 1899

LOWER: four financiers who took a leading part in buying *The Star* and bringing J. E. Atkinson to Toronto in 1899. Left to right: Senator George A. Cox, Sir William Mulock, Timothy Eaton, Peter C. Larkin

Picture of Hocken from oil painting in Toronto city hall; of Nicholls and Cox from photographs in the Public Archives of Canada; Mulock by Frederick William Lyonde and Sons; and Larkin by Bachrach

LEFT: publishers of the two leading newspapers in Toronto in 1900, Senator Robert Jaffray of the *Globe* and John Ross Robertson of the *Telegram*
Photo copyright by Pringle & Booth

BELOW: J. E. Atkinson in 1900 at his first desk at *The Star*

OVER: page one of the first *Star* to appear under Mr. Atkinson's editorship

LAST EDITION

THE EVENING STAR

THE WEATHER

Light, local snowfalls, becoming much colder. Thursday, fine and decidedly cold.

EIGHTH YEAR — TORONTO, WEDNESDAY, DECEMBER 13, 1899.—EIGHT PAGES — ONE CENT

LORD METHUEN MEETS WITH A SERIOUS CHECK.

An All Day Attack Upon the Boers' Position Results in Failure, Though British Hold Their Own.

But as They Are Entrenching It is Feared the Boers May Follow Up Their Advantage—Heavy Loss of the British Who Are in a Very Dangerous Situation.

LONDON, Dec. 13.—Gen. Methuen's report from Modder River shows that he met with a serious check Monday and suffered great losses.

PRETORIA REPORTS HEAVY FIGHTING.

...A, Monday, Dec. 11.--An official report says:

...tle at Modder River began yesterday, with cannon firing, heavy ...g proceeding from 3.30 o'clock in the morning until 2.30 o'clock, with ... Maxims and rifles. A bombardment began at 4.30 o'clock and the ...ill continues. A balloon has just arisen above the British ... where it remained ten minutes, and descended. There were ...ins during the night.

... 9 o'clock this morning a further report was received from Modder ... A despatch rider brought word that all the Boer positions ...een maintained, and that 41 British prisoners had been taken.

...0 o'clock it was reported that the heavy cannon fire had somewhat ...

...he British are constantly using their balloon.

... fighting was still going on at noon.

...mberley is still quiet.

...ORD METHUEN'S REPORT OF THE BATTLE.

...NDON, Dec. 13.—The War Office has received the following despatch ...en. Methuen, dated Tuesday, Dec. 12:

...ur artillery shelled a very strong position held by the enemy in a ...igh kopje, from 4 until dusk, Sunday. It rained hard last night.

... Highland Brigade attacked at daybreak on Monday the south end ...e kopje. The attack was properly timed, but failed. The Guards ... ordered to protect the Highlanders' right and rear.

...The cavalry and mounted infantry, with a howitzer artillery battery, ...ked the enemy on the left, and the Guards on the right, supported by ... artillery. They shelled the position from daybreak, and at 1.15 I ... the Gordons to support the Highland Brigade.

...ne troops held their own in front of the enemy's entrenchments until ... the position extending, including the kopje, for a distance of six ...es towards the Modder River. To-day am holding my position and en...ing myself.

...had to face at least 12,000 men. Our loss was great.

LORD METHUEN IN A DANGEROUS SITUATION.

LONDON, Dec. 13.—Alarm is beginning to be expressed in many quar...as to the situation of General Methuen. The Westminster Gazette ... "If England ever needed a victory it is now, and it is to Buller, ...er, strong, cool-headed and reticent, that the country looks for ... victory."

The other papers are abusing the Government for its "complacent op...mism," and inability to grasp the strength of the opposition it had to ...rcome in South Africa. Considerable significance attaches to General ...ethuen's statement that he is entrenching himself, indicating fear that ... Boers may follow up their advantage, adopt the offensive and attack ...n.

Indeed, the gravity of the situation from the British point of view, can...rdly be over-estimated. General Methuen's long lines of communica...o De Aar are most vulnerable. Should they be cut, General Methuen ... and himself in a very tight place, if only from lack of supplies.

...he news of the British reverse had a bad effect on the Stock ...ge, where there was a general relapse.

...RITISH GENERAL KILLED.

...auchope One of the Victims of the Big Battle.

LONDON, Dec. 13.—The War Of... has received the following des... from Gen. Forestier-Walker : ...e Town, Tuesday, Dec. 12.—Meth... wires that Gen. Wauchope was ... in action yesterday."

...ajor-General Andrew G. Wauchope, ...C.M.G., was a highly distinguish... ...fficer of the British Army. He ... ...ieadier-General commanding ... First Brigade of the ... Expeditionary Force in 1898. ...ntered the army in 1865, was pro...oted Colonel in 1888, served in the ...antee war of 1873, in the Egyptian ...ar of 1882, in the Soudan Expedition ...84, and in the Nile Expedition ...884-85. Gen. Wauchope had been ...nded four times, three times se...erely.

MENELIK MEDDLING?

...w York Paper's Report That Russia and France Are Intriguing.

...W YORK, Dec. 13.—A cable from ...ton to the Journal and Advertis... ...ays that despatches received there ... Cairo and Rome indicate that ...ain European powers are endeav... ...to embarrass England in her ... against the Boers. A Cairo des... ...is quoted as saying: ...peror Menelik of Abyssinia, with ...at force, is moving menacingly ...ard the British possessions on the ...e Nile. His camp is now near ...s Abeba. ...nch and Russian envoys are with ..., endeavoring to rouse him to an ...rgetic campaign against British ..., urging him to assert his ... over the Soudan, which, the ...ys declare, rightfully belongs to ...ain. Menelik's progress is ... The latest advices say he was ...ing over an aggressive move... ...or's court moves with him ... ...baric splendor, and the ...mpanies. ...tch from Rome says that ...ncodicola, the Italian envoy to ...inia, reports the intrigues of ... powers to get Menelik roused ...nst the British in the Soudan. Cic...ola says he fears trouble.

Kaffirs as Laborers.

...YORK, Dec. 13.—A special ...etermaritzburg, Natal, to the ... ...rid yesterday, says that one ... ...ffirs have been sent for... ...o aid the British forces at ... Camp. When they arrived they ...ched into the camp singing war ...gs. It is said they will be em... ...ed with the Army Service Corps ...handling freight and doing fatigue ...

Wounded at Modder River.

...E RIVER, Cape Colony, Dec. ...e hundred and twenty wo... ...have arrive...

LONDON DEDUCTIONS.

An Analysis of Lord Methuen's Report — Not a Bright Prospect.

LONDON, Dec. 13.—Gen. Methuen, as expected, followed up his artillery attack with a general assault on the Boer positions on Monday, and his report shows that the anxiety of the public regarding the result, occasioned by the ominous silence of the War Office, was amply justified. The engagement was evidently of considerable magnitude and the list of killed and wounded will be proportionate, without the compensation which a victory would have brought, if, indeed, the affair does not turn out to be a more serious defeat than General Methuen admits.

The Highlanders, it is believed, must have stormed the Boer position more than once, while the fact that the Guards were ordered to support the Highlanders' rear looks as though the Boers may even have outflanked their attacker.

Another report declares that General Cronje attacked the British. The only compensation the British have been able to discover in the disheartening story is in General Methuen's statement that he maintains his position close to the Boers, thus arousing the hope that he will retrieve the situation.

Apparently the bombardment of Saturday and Sunday did not shake the Boers' grip on their position, and it seems certain they merely withdrew their guns and riflemen under cover, while General Methuen indulged in the usual artillery preliminaries Monday, and that when the British guns were obliged to cease firing owing to the danger of hitting the advancing troops, the Boers speedily re-occupied their trenches and overwhelmed the Highlanders with a terrible fire, probably accompanying this by an attack upon the British right flank and rear.

British Were Surprised.

NORTH OF MODDER RIVER, Monday, Dec. 11.—The Guards and the Highland Brigade early last night moved from the Modder River Camp, marching in a northeasterly direction. The objective of the Highlanders was the eastern spur of the Boer position, the Guards following the bank of the river, while the Yorkshire Light ...fantry moved along the river side. ... before daybreak the Highlanders ... ...b Boer entrenchments at the foot of a hill. Unsuspecting that the Boers were in the vicinity, the British were still marching in quarter column, in close order, when they met a terrible fire from the flanks, and were forced to retire with heavy loss.

Gatacre is moving from Bushman's Hoek to Steikstrom to-day. The magistrate at Steikstrom wires that the situation there has lately improved. Many of the missing have turned up.

French reports that a detachment of cavalry with two guns of the Horse Artillery reconnoitered the enemy's position yesterday at Quiltfontein and Vaalkop, eight miles north of Arundel. They shelled a farm and drove the enemy from Vaalkop. The Boer loss was one killed and several wounded. Our casualties nil.

GRAND TRUNK SCORES A POINT

Lansdowne Avenue Case to Be Re-Opened Before Privy Council Dec. 19th.

THE CITY HAS A CHAMPION

Ontario Government Will Oppose Dominion Interference in Yonge Street.

The Provincial authorities have declared their intention of opposing the Railway Committee's decision to allow the Metropolitan Railway to connect with the Canadian Pacific.

Acting under instructions from the Attorney-General, Mr. Allen Cassels has written the City Solicitor asking for all material and information bearing on the case. Mr. Cassels states that the Legislature will oppose the Railway Committee's decision as being an infringement upon the city's rights.

Lansdowne Case Re-opened.

Corporation Counsel Fullerton this morning received notification from John J. McGee, Clerk of the Privy Council, advising the city that, in accordance with a petition of the Grand Trunk Ry., the Lansdowne avenue matter would be opened up. The case will be dealt with by the Privy Council on Tuesday Dec. 19, at 11 o'clock. The notification is accompanied by a copy of the Grand Trunk's petition, protesting against the action of the Railway Committee in making the company liable for one-third the cost of the subway.

The Solicitors will report the matter to the Board of Works, and recommend what action should be taken.

It will be remembered that this same committee refused to re-open the Metropolitan Ry. case at the city's request.

THEIR FIRST YEAR IN THE NEW HOME.

Methodist Deaconesses Celebrate An Anniversary Pleasantly This Afternoon.

The regular monthly meeting of the Deaconess' Aid Society was held this afternoon in the Deaconess' Home, Jarvis street. The meeting was one of peculiar interest, as it celebrated the first anniversary of the home in its present location. There was a large attendance of members of the society.

Miss Scott, the superintendent of the home, read the report of the last month's work in the home. During the month the deaconesses have paid 1,257 calls, and spent 495 hours in nursing. A distribution of 186 garments was made, and $24.50 of the "emergency money" fund was given out as wages to applicants for relief. There were 24 who were helped in this way last month.

At the conclusion of the business meeting friends of the Deaconess' Home were admitted and a social hour was spent. Dr. Chown gave a short address. Miss Mallough, one of the nurse-deaconesses, who is just home from a course of special training in the United States, spoke on the necessity for having a Deaconess' Hospital in Toronto. Miss Mallough pointed out that six women who had taken the course of training in deaconess' work in Toronto within the past two years, have been obliged to go to the United States in order to secure a course of training as nurse-deaconesses.

The most interesting feature of the meeting was the receiving of contributions and promises of contributions to the Christmas baskets for the poor. It is the custom of the home to provide for each family in whom it is interested a basket of the good things so acceptable at Christmas time. The donations this year were very gratifying to those who have this work at heart, but the fact was strongly dwelt upon, that many more donations would be received with gratitude, as the supply does not yet equal the demand.

Miss May MacWhinney of Portage la Prairie, a student at the College of Music, was present, and sang most acceptably a couple of solos.

CRAZED DURING THE TRIP.

Mary Faust, a middle aged woman who came from Berlin to work as a servant, was sent to jail to-day for medical examination. She went insane during the journey. She has a religious mania, and prayed in the dock.

LIBERALS TO MEET.

The Liberals of the third division of South Toronto will meet in St. George's Hall, Elm street, on Friday evening, December 15th, for organization purposes. The division is bounded by Yonge, Simcoe and College streets, and the bay, but all Liberals are cordially invited to attend.

The Court of Appeal ju... ...ve is...sued an order that, here... ...books must be bound ... ...side h... ...ted ... side ...

GEN. BULLER BEGINS ADVANCE ON COLENSO.

Union Brigade of Fusiliers Advances Within Three Miles and Take Up a Strong Position Without Being Molested.

Gen. Gatacre's Forces Regarded as Safe—In the Stormberg Battle They Simply Rushed at the Nearest Hill Without Orders or Information—Disloyal Cape Ministers.

LONDON, Dec. 13.—A despatch from Frere Camp, dated Tuesday, Dec. 12, says: This morning a union brigade, consisting of English, Scottish, Irish and Welsh Fusiliers, under General Barton, with several naval guns, advanced and took up a strong position three miles from Colenso, meeting with no opposition.

GATACRE ALL RIGHT.

No Anxiety Felt for the Safety of His Troops—Shares Drop.

LONDON, Dec. 13.—Kaffirs and Rand mines dropped 2½ points, and Debeers dropped ¾.

The latest advices from Gen. Gatacre show no anxiety is felt for the safety of his remaining troops, who have been withdrawn to good positions along the railroad south of Molteno.

It is said that Bushman's Hook is impregnable.

The Boers decline to furnish the names of the killed or wounded. They say they buried the dead and are sending the prisoners to Bloemfontein.

BOER LOSS SMALL.

The Boer loss on Sunday is reported to have been four killed and nine wounded. Probably this is correct, as no genuine attack was delivered by General Gatacre's troops, who were completely surprised while in column. The British apparently simply rushed up the nearest hill without orders or knowing where the enemy was.

BULLER'S ADVANCE.

The British were so exhausted from long marches that they were unable to accomplish anything. General Buller's advance in the direction of Colenso seems to have actually commenced.

The military attaches have left Cape Town to join General Buller via Durban.

General White reports under date of Tuesday, Dec. 12, that there are 32 cases of enteric fever at Ladysmith.

DISLOYALTY AT CAPE TOWN.

There are renewed reports of a Cabinet crisis at Cape Town, where it is said that Governor Milner is about to act in consequence of disclosures involving the Ministry's loyalty.

The White Star line steamer Majestic sails from Liverpool to-day for South Africa with 2,000 troops on board.

ANOTHER SHIP CHARTERED.

The White Star steamer Cymric has been chartered for use as a transport.

GOVERNMENT WILL HELP

In the Movement For the Establishment of Better Country Roads.

CONVENTION DOINGS TO-DAY

Hon. E. J. Davis Says "Spend as Much Money, But Spend it More Profitably.

Mr. A. F. Woods, the veteran good roads man of Madoc, presided at this morning's session of the good roads convention. Mr. Kidd of Carlton County was present to-day, as was Hon. E. J. Davis, Commissioner of Crown Lands.

The convention began with the reading of a letter from Judge R. S. Woods of Chatham, suggesting that the Government be urged to take up the work of good road building, the cost to be defrayed one-third by the Government, one-third by the county, and one-third by the municipality. Good roads could be built for $1,500 a mile and maintained for $20.

This report was sent to the Resolution Committee.

THE GOVERNMENT'S RERESENTATIVE.

Hon. E. J. Davis, after dwelling on the old days when he was a county councillor, voiced his belief that York County was the greatest county in the province, and North York the greatest part of the greatest county.

"You are here to discuss a most important question, which has been said by others, and I quite endorse it, to be the greatest public question, the question of good roads. The question of transportation is one of the greatest of the age. The farmer who can get easiest from his barn door to the markets is going to come out best in the great competition of the day.

"It was necessary for the cheese and butter industries that the milk might be got easily to the factories. It would help the new system of postal delivery by wagon, which was said to be cheaper than the old way.

"The question is: How are we to have these good roads? If I were to tell you that, I would spoil the balance of your meeting. That is what you have met to decide. Therefore I will not tell you.

MORE CARE IN EXPENDITURE.

"But there is the question of the expenditure of monies. I don't think the masses of the people will be in love with a scheme which will mean increased taxation. Mr. Campbell's system seems to be a good one—not an increased expenditure, but a more careful mode of spending the money now granted. I think that I need not more than hint, that the minor municipalities jealously guard, and will hold to what they look upon as their right in their road."

Mr. Davis urged very careful consideration before asking legislation, so that when a request is made it may be sufficiently reasonable to be granted.

THE GOVERNMENT'S PROMISE.

"On behalf of the Premier, who asked me to come down here, I want to express to you on behalf of the whole Government, our appreciation of the efforts that you have made in the past, and the efforts you are now making, and to say that anything we may properly do in the interests of the province to aid you in your work, we will do."

ELEVATING THE SU...

Mr. A. W. Cam... ...ced ... municipalities to a national one. Mr. Campbell compared the roads of Hastings, smooth as billiard tables, with the bad roads, ankle deep in mud, of other counties, particularly the "metropolitan bad roads of the County of York."

BIG MONEY WASTED.

"You spend annually $1,100,000 of statute labor on roads, and every farmer will tell you that he believes the statute labor system is the most unjust, extravagant and inefficient system in existence. In the past ten years you have spent $30,500, and the statute labor, equal to $42,000, or its equivalent. Give me that $42,000 and I will undertake to gravel and macadamize every mile of road in the Province of Ontario. Go on in the old way and in ten years there will be little or no improvement, and you will have spent an aggregate of $90,-000,000. You are spending more than the Public Works Department of the Government is spending on its improvements. The statute labor law was made for pioneer days."

The Committee on Resolutions had a session this morning, and discussed resolutions suggesting that the Government take steps to allow suburban railways to enter municipalities, and providing for future meetings of the convention.

MR. CLARKE WILL RUN.

His Committee Arranging to Hold a Ratification Meeting.

It is definitely settled that Mr. E. F. Clarke, M. P., will be a candidate for the Mayoralty for next year.

A meeting of the committee which has had the matter of the requisition in hand was held in the Janes Building last night, at which the decision was arrived at, Mr. Clarke having previously placed himself unreservedly in the hands of his friends, to act as they deemed best in the matter.

The committee estimated that the total names to the requisition is about 7,500, and on the strength of this estimate, and calculating that most of the signatures meant at least two votes, it was decided to put Mr. Clarke in the field.

Arrangements are being made for a ratification meeting.

To-day Mr. Clarke accepted the nomination, and the first organization meeting will be held Saturday evening in Ward One.

RECOUNTS ASKED.

Manitoba Liberals Want Judges to Overhaul Ballots in Four Ridings.

(C.P.R. Despatch).

WINNIPEG, Dec. 31.—Applications have been made on behalf of the Manitoba Liberals for judicial recounts of ballots cast in four constituencies: Rosenfeldt, Saskatchewan, Souris and Brandon City, where the combined majorities on Thursday last were but 43.

CITY SALTED

Must Repay Taxes on Iroquois Hotel and Damages as Well.

Chief Justice Meredith has handed out judgment in the case of Mrs. Mary Horseman, of the Iroquois Hotel, against the city for illegal distress of taxes. The judgment refunds the $987.44 taxes paid under protest and also awards $250 damages.

NEXT BYE-ELECTION

Will Be Held Soon—The Legislature to Meet Early.

Hon. G. W. Ross this morning stated that the bye-elections in East Middlesex would be brought on before the session of the House. The House would meet, he said, in the last of January or first of February.

WS SE... ...E ?

PERSONAL.

PROFESSIONAL.

GENERAL REGRET.

Flags at Half Mast in Memory of the Late Sir George Kirkpatrick.

Sir George Kirkpatrick's death was received with general regret all over the city, and there were expressions of sorrow from citizens of all classes. The flag at the Government House was half masted, and also that at the Parliament buildings. As early as ten o'clock this morning friends began to make calls of condolence, and continued steadily during the day.

The obsequies will take the form of a state funeral. The arrangements are as follows:

The remains will be on view at his late residence, 215 Simcoe street, on Friday afternoon, Dec. 15, from one to three o'clock. The funeral party will leave the house at four o'clock for the Union station where the remains will be placed on a special train of the Canadian Pacific Railway, and will be conveyed over the Canadian Pacific Railway to Kingston, where the interment will take place on Saturday afternoon.

A Kingston Tribute.

Star Special.

KINGSTON, Dec. 13.—The death of Sir G. A. Kirkpatrick in Toronto has caused deep sorrow in his old home, where he was beloved and known by all classes.

In all public matters he was active and generous. He was exceptionally benevolent, and not only money but advice, sympathy and brotherliness, marked his attitude towards the sorrowful and suffering.

His funeral here will be largely attended. His last resting place will be near that of his associates, Sir John A. Macdonald and Sir Alexander Campbell.

C.P.R. DIRECTORS' REGRET.

MONTREAL, Dec. 13.—The news of the death of Sir George Kirkpatrick was received with much regret by the Board of Directors and officials of the Canadian Pacific Railway this morning. Sir George was a director of the great company, and a regular attendant at the meetings of the Board, until laid aside by illness. Several directors have intimated their intention of attending the funeral of their late colleague.

CAR BARN DAMAGED.

Last Night's Little Tornado Ripped Out the Galvanized Iron Wall.

Last night's miniature tornado tore down the south wall of the Street Railway Co.'s new car barn at Dundas street and High Park avenue.

The wall, which is of galvanized iron, is 200 feet long. The wind got a fair sweep in through the open doors and brought the wall down with a crash like a salvo of artillery.

The damage is in the neighborhood of $800.

A number of big board signs in the vicinity were also wrecked.

TO TURN LENNOX OUT

City Authorities Think His Term is Over in the Building.

The Mayor and Controller Burns held a conference with the City Solicitors this morning regarding the taking over of the municipal building by the city. A report has not yet been presented but the Solicitors have expressed themselves as being of the opinion that Mr. Lennox is under no instructions from the courts, and his term of office, as contractor, may be terminated at the will of the Council.

It is understood a report to this effect will be ready in a few days.

CIVIC COMMITTEES.

The petition of the butchers and grocers for early closing will be considered by the Legislation Committee on Tuesday afternoon at 3 o'clock.

The Parks and Exhibitions Committee will meet Monday at 4 o'clock.

"I would have to decide that," Atkinson replied.

"That is the only way a newspaper could be successfully conducted," Sir Wilfrid conceded. He might not have agreed so readily with his young newspaper friend had he been less certain where his loyalties lay.

Atkinson took the night train to Toronto, and the terms of his contract were agreed upon the next day. The Star Printing and Publishing Company of Toronto was formally transferred to the new owners on December 13, 1899. Neither the identities of the new owners nor even the fact that the paper had changed hands were made public. The stock of most of them was held in the name of E. T. Malone, counsel for the group. Malone was elected president, an office he held until November 26, 1910. His brother and law partner, A. L. Malone, was elected a director, while J. H. Mackenzie became secretary-treasurer.

On December 18 a meeting of the shareholders authorized the president to hire Joseph E. Atkinson as manager and editor on conditions set down in the minutes, his employment to be retroactive to December 13. The term of the contract was for five years. Atkinson's name appeared for the first time on the masthead on December 21.

Having agreed that he should be in complete control of policy, there was no longer any point in limiting the amount of stock he might own, and there was no such provision in the contract. On his part, Mr. Atkinson did not insist on having it specifically set out in the contract that he should be able to buy a controlling interest, or in fact any stock whatever other than the twenty shares a year he was to accept in lieu of $2,000 of his $5,000 salary. Atkinson was to claim later that there was a verbal agreement entitling him to first claim on 30 per cent of the stock as it became available, but this was never admitted by the shareholders. It would seem, therefore, that when Atkinson scared away prospective purchasers of *Star* stock with the claim that he alone had the right to buy it, he was bluffing. If so, it was a successful bluff, for he was able to pick up much of the stock on exceedingly reasonable terms—and most of it from the original shareholders.

In fact, few of these gentlemen expected to get their money back. They did not consider *The Star* an investment. They were simply making a donation to the Laurier cause, and mentally they wrote it off. When Atkinson offered them money for their shares, even if it was only fifty cents on the dollar, they snapped at it. And it is certainly true that most of them acted as if they believed Mr. Atkinson was morally entitled to have first offer of their shares, whether or not he had a contractual right to it.

It should be clearly understood that *The Star* was not bought to be a Liberal party paper, in spite of Mulock's wishes. It was bought to support Laurier in putting into effect the platform on which the Liberal party had been elected in 1896 under his leadership. On matters outside this platform, or in provincial politics, it was free to take any position it chose. The Laurier platform was: reciprocity with the United States, Canadian nationalism, opening of the West to settlement, encouragement of immigration, construction of railways, and support for labour unions. The question was to arise later as to whether *The Star* was to support Laurier the man, apart from this platform, or even Laurier's conception of liberalism.

But whatever private and verbal understandings there may have been, a mutually satisfactory agreement was reached and a contract was signed. Joseph E. Atkinson turned down the highest paid job on Canada's biggest and richest newspaper to become editor and manager of Toronto's smallest, poorest, and most discredited newspaper on terms allowing him to give full expression to his essential liberalism, both political and social.

For the next forty-eight years the story of Joseph E. Atkinson is the story of *The Toronto Star*.

Chapter 2

A PAPER FOR THE PEOPLE

The twenty-one printers and four apprentices who founded the Toronto *Evening Star* on November 3, 1892, said they had been locked out in a wage dispute with their employer, the *News*. The proprietors of the *News* retorted that the printers were on strike. In an interview in *The Star* in 1929 Harry Parr, assistant foreman of the printers, said there had been "a mutual agreement that we could not get along together."

The dispute between the *News* and its printers was of a kind not unusual in the last quarter of the nineteenth century when machines were displacing hand labour in so many industries. The *News* had introduced into its composing room a recent invention called the Rogers Typograph which, operated from a keyboard, made it possible for one man to set almost as much type in a day as three compositors of average speed could set by hand. After a flurry of unsuccessful strikes in the United States the Typographical Union had dropped its opposition to these machines provided none but union members were trained to operate them, and a portion of the savings in printing costs was passed on to all union members in the form of wage increases.

Unfortunately no agreement had been reached on a formula for establishing a fair rate of pay, and trouble developed at the *News* over the system of payment. Management offered a piecework rate of fourteen cents a thousand ems instead of the thirty cents paid hand compositors. Theoretically this would enable an operator to earn $14.04 a week if the machine performed as its manufacturers claimed it would. This was considerably more than hand compositors were making. However, the men held out for a straight wage of $14 a week regardless of production. Management retorted that printers had always been paid according to production, and not by the hour, day, or week, and they would not change this traditional system. There the dispute came to a deadlock. The fact was that neither the men nor the owners of the *News* believed the clumsy contrivance would perform according to promise, and both were trying to protect themselves. The wrangle dragged on for weeks while tempers became hotter; having taken a stand neither side would give in.

The climax was reached on the evening of October 24, 1892. The printers met in Shaftesbury Hall over John Scholes' saloon at Queen and James streets and voted to strike if their demands were not met at once. At the same time the proprietors and executives of the *News* met and decided to fire them all. Thus it was that when the printers arrived at the *News* the next morning they found their dismissals nailed to the door before they could deliver their ultimatum. Management had beaten them to the punch.

From the printers' point of view, no worse time for a fight could have been chosen, and they probably had no intention of carrying out their threat to strike. It was said there were two unemployed printers in Toronto for every one that was working. The mechanization of printing plants all over the province was partly to blame, but the main cause was the beginning of one of the worst depressions the country had experienced.

The *News* was able to recruit a full staff of non-union craftsmen and did not miss an issue. To add to the anxieties of the printers, winter was approaching, and the Toronto Typographical Union could promise only seven dollars a week strike pay for married men and five dollars a week for unmarried. It was then they made their momentous decision. They would start a newspaper in opposition to the boss.

It would be no mere strike paper, or even a labour paper, but a serious entry in a field already overcrowded with six fiercely competing dailies. They would put the *News* out of business if they could, but if they could not they stood at least a fair chance of making more than strike pay. It was not quite the preposterous idea one might think, for in those days it cost little more to start a newspaper than to open a grocery store; businessmen with an axe to grind would establish a newspaper as casually as one orders a batch of handbills today.

In years to come their foreman, Horatio C. (Race) Hocken, who lived to be mayor of Toronto and died a senator, claimed credit for the idea. "I started *The Star*," he boasted in an interview in *The Star* when he was appointed to the Senate in 1930. "If I'd known as much then as I do now I'd have kept it." None of the other printers ever disputed his claim, though they agreed credit for putting the plan into effect should be shared with assistant foreman Harry Parr, a labour leader for twenty years and a veteran of the first printers' strike in Toronto, which won a nine-hour day on the *Leader* in 1872.

Some credit should be given also to W. F. (Billie-Bug-Eyes) Maclean, publisher of a morning paper called the *Toronto World*. For some time he had been thinking of publishing an afternoon edition, but he was short of cash. When he learned that Hocken and Parr were looking for a shop in which to print a new newspaper he hastened to them with an offer. His plant was idle during the daylight hours. They could use it. He would even allow them a cubby-hole on the third floor for an office. And it would not cost them a cent: just a 51 per cent interest in the venture.

The printers accepted on condition Maclean be strictly a silent partner, and they were to have a free hand in setting policy and running the business. The remaining 49 per cent of the ownership was to be held equally among themselves. Parr, who was a member of the executive of both the Toronto Typographical Union and the Toronto Trades and Labour Council, persuaded those organizations to back the new venture to the extent of pledging strike pay for six weeks. On their part the printers agreed to draw no wages from the new paper for the same period.

Thus it was that twenty-one printers and four apprentices, with no capital but the craftsmanship of their own hands, were able to found a daily newspaper. Conceived in desperation and cradled in adversity, it could have but little prospect of survival in a city that already had twice too many newspapers; indeed, so remote seemed its chances of success that even its founding fathers abandoned it once the first heady elation of parenthood had passed. But survive it did, to flourish under the direction of Joseph E. Atkinson until it reached its present eminence as one of Canada's greatest newspapers.

The Evening Star its founders called it. It was dedicated to the welfare of the working man. "A paper for the people" was flaunted as a slogan in the upper right corner of page one, while inside was the announcement that *The Star* "is the only exclusively evening newspaper in the city employing union labor." In a manifesto over their names on the editorial page of the first issue the printers defiantly declared: "The owners [of the *News*] seemed eager for a fight and they are having it." After outlining the circumstances leading to the dispute and the difficulty in getting a place in which to print the new paper, the manifesto continued:

> The announcement that the *News* had thrown its men out was heard with astonishment in labor circles. The working men had supported the paper for years, through good report and bad report, and by the influence it wielded through them it became prominent and profitable to its owners.
>
> But through the difference that would have amounted to but $18 a week added to the pay sheet, its faithful employees were turned out of doors. *The Star* has opened up positions for them. Among them are some of the ablest workmen in town, and they are all men who stand well in the city.

There was no explanation of how the figure of $18 was arrived at.

At the end of the manifesto the names of the printers were listed: H. C. Hocken, W. H. Parr, W. Macmillan, Arthur Donaldson, James Melrose, Alf Gautt, Robert Gautt, John Mutton, Harry Stephens, Harry Whittaker, Ed. Reede, W. J. Wilson, Fred Nash, James Farquharson, F. W. Lee, Frank Johnstone, Stanley Jackson, Harry Johnstone, Frank Cormack, Frank Webber, Alf Davis, and the following boys, Charles Gribb, E. Boyd, Frank Brown, and James Simpson.

They must have been a remarkable group of men, for scarcely a one failed to leave his mark in the world of politics, business, journalism, or printing. From them came two mayors of Toronto, a publisher, the manager of a provincial daily, a sales manager, three reporters, and four superintendents of newspaper plants in Toronto, New York, and Detroit.

It was a powerful antagonist they were challenging, for the *News* was a well-established, robust paper, secretly owned by the Riordan Paper Company of St. Catharines, which also owned the *Toronto Daily Mail*. It had stronger financial backing than any other Toronto paper, and a profitable circulation of 20,000 which was only slightly behind John Ross Robertson's *Evening Telegram*. Despite its big business ownership the *News* posed as the champion of the working man, and most of its readers were members of the working class. These were the readers *The Star* intended to woo.

Hocken, as befitted the man with the idea, was business manager. Parr was in charge of the printing. He remained foreman of the composing room on *The Star* until his retirement in 1929 at the age of seventy-seven. Maclean gave them T. A. Gregg, an editorial writer on the *World*, to be editor-in-chief at the splendid salary of $20 a week. Two young men of outstanding abilities who were to play a major part in *The Star*'s rise to pre-eminence accompanied the printers from the *News*. Neither Colin C. Campbell, a reporter, nor Walter Harris, a book-keeper, were personally affected by the dispute, but their sympathies were wholly with the printers. When they learned what the printers had in mind they volunteered their services. Though Gregg was editor-in-chief, Campbell was city editor from the beginning. In the memories of many who served under him in the next thirty years Campbell is enshrined as one of the all-time greats of the North American newspaper field. He came of a family that had been impoverished by the civil war in the United States. As a youth of fifteen he struck out on his own, roaming the continent. He drifted into newspaper work because he liked the excitement, gaining his first experience as a reporter on the Hamilton *Herald*.

Two of the printers were drafted to be the first reporters on *The Star*. Harry Johnstone covered city hall and police courts, and Ed. Reede was commercial reporter. Arthur Donaldson became a reporter later, distinguished himself as publisher of a small city daily, and returned thirteen years later to *The Star* as its expert on type faces and advertising layout. Another printer, Harry Stephens, was the first advertising solicitor. He succeeded so well that the initial issue of *The Star* carried as much advertising as any of its competitors. But he did not like selling, and after trying his hand for a while at reporting left for New York, where he resumed his trade as printer.

Harris helped Hocken run the business office. After Hocken left Harris became business manager, a position he held for forty-two years. He hired *The Star*'s first woman employee, Miss Clara Boake, later Mrs. H. Wrigley. He also hired the first office boy, a red-headed youngster named Lou Marsh who was destined to become the most famous sports editor Canada has known.

Hocken had persuaded a friend, Fred Eatherley, of the circulation department of the *Mail*, to help him get the first issue on the street. He remained with *The Star* until his retirement in 1931, for the last seven years as foreman of the mailing room. Eatherley rounded up a fleet of boys on bicycles to deliver the papers to news-stands while he personally hawked the first copy offered for sale at the corner of King and Yonge streets, then the busiest intersection in the bustling little city of 150,000.

Cautiously they had printed an edition of 8,000 copies, but the demand was so great they ran off a second edition of 2,000 copies.

Everybody in town knew of the dispute between the *News* and its employees, and most of them sympathized with the spunky printers. Notice of their intention to start a new afternoon newspaper in competition with "the boss" had been published in all morning newspapers, and posters had been tacked to poles and fences. But besides that there was not a union man in Toronto who did not know of the venture, for it had been discussed at a mass meeting in Shaftesbury Hall.

Since Maclean had declined to invest any cash in the enterprise the men got their first stock of paper on credit, paying for it out of revenue from street sales. These were astonishingly high. By the third day 12,000 copies of *The Evening Star* were being sold while the news-stands were glutted with unwanted copies of the *News*. Before long reporters, office help, even office boys, were migrating from the *News* to the new sheet.

Six weeks later an alarming report reached the printers. The Riordans had approached Maclean with an offer for his interest, and since Maclean was rarely in his life more than three moves ahead of the bailiff the probability was that he would sell. Once the Riordans had their hands on *The Star* it would be shut down; of that the printers were sure. And even if he did not sell, Wee Willie Maclean was becoming troublesome. He was behaving altogether too much like a majority stockholder for the liking of the printers: he was even talking of the day when *The Star* would be integrated with the *World* as its evening edition, which had been his intention all along.

As a silent partner the printers could tolerate Maclean; as an active partner, never. They had made a deal with him out of desperation, but they had no intention of letting their newspaper fall into his hands. So, hurriedly, they rented an empty building at 114 Yonge Street that had been used as a shoe store, and begged or borrowed enough money from relatives and friends to buy a dress of type. This was a historic building, for it was in a draughting office on the second floor that Sir Sandford Fleming had designed Canada's first postage stamp.

Maclean boggled for a while at selling his interest in the paper—after all, he had not been paid anything for the use of his plant for six weeks—but he finally agreed to transfer it to Hocken in return for a promissory note for $5,000. He also generously sold *The Star* an old Bullock press he was no longer using. Next day the press was seized by the tax collector, with whom Maclean was in a constant state of war when not defending himself against other creditors. The morning *Empire*, which was owned by the Conservative party, printed *The Star* until that misunderstanding was cleared up, though it was a nuisance making up the paper at 114 Yonge Street and lugging the forms two blocks to the *Empire* plant.

Scarcely was the paper in its own quarters than circulation fell alarmingly. It was all very well to be a friend of the working man, but the working man wanted news with his friendship, and that *The Star* was not giving him. It had not the money to hire good reporters or to do the things the other papers were doing. It was poorly printed from hand-set type while the other papers were by then all using clean, new, machine-set type. But saddest blow of all, many of those sturdy unionists on whom *The Star* had counted for support lost their jobs as the depression worsened.

The printers became discouraged. They had agreed to work six weeks without pay while the paper was getting on its feet. The six weeks were now past and there was still nothing left to divide among them after expenses were paid. One by one they began drifting back to the *News*, and the *News* welcomed its penitent sons warmly. *The Star* had cut deeply into the circulation of the *News*, and to the owner of that paper it seemed that the most effective way of eliminating *The Star* as a competitor was to give the printers their jobs back. To make way for them it turned out the non-union printers it had hired. As printers left *The Star* they signed over to those who remained whatever interest they had in a venture most of them had come to consider hopeless.

Even Hocken deserted a vessel he believed to be foundering, transferring his interest to Gregg. He returned to the *News*, became a reporter, then city editor. In 1905 he bought the *Orange Sentinel* and was soon a power in the inner councils of the influential Orange fraternity. In 1913 he was elected mayor of Toronto, in 1917 Conservative member of Parliament for Toronto West, and in 1930 was named to the Senate. Though he remained with it no more than a few months, *The Star* had no reason to be other than proud of the man whose inspiration brought it into being.

Within a few days of Hocken's departure only six of the "originals" were left. Gregg became sole owner when these six gave him their stock that he might pledge it to keep the paper going. "I gave up my share for the sake of the men," Parr said in an interview when he retired in 1929. "Anything to see that the paper was carried on. It wasn't of much value anyway."

Those who stayed with *The Star* were mostly militant trade unionists the *News* did not want back anyway, and the business and editorial staffs, who had more faith in *The Star* than its founders. Campbell, Harris, Parr,

Eatherley, and the apprentice Jimmy Simpson were offered other jobs, but they would not give up. Gregg nursed the paper along for a few months, but there were times when he was able to meet the payroll only because his friend William Bell, an organ manufacturer of Guelph, Ontario, came to his assistance. "We never missed a pay, though sometimes we had to take it in instalments," Campbell recalled in an article written for *The Star* in 1905. "Many a day I had to make the rounds of the paper boys on my bicycle to get enough money to buy paper for the next day's edition," Eatherley related in an interview on his retirement.

Too poor to buy even the equipment he needed, Gregg resorted to scrounging type and furniture from other newspapers. John Ross Robertson of the *Telegram* regarded competition from the anaemic *Star* so lightly he loaned it trucks for the composing room. For years the trials and tribulations of *The Star* were to be a prime source of merriment for Mr. Robertson. They ceased to be some time before his death in 1918.

Eventually the time came when *The Star* could no longer scrounge either paper or equipment and Campbell wrote that one July day in 1893 Gregg dashed excitedly into the composing room. "Stop the press; stop the press, we are finished," he shouted, wildly waving his arms. Then putting on his coat he walked out, leaving word he was going on a voyage for his health. The Great Panic of 1893 had burst upon the United States on June 26 and rapidly spread to Canada, drying up credit, spreading unemployment, and dealing *The Star* what appeared to be a mortal blow. With nobody running the paper it suspended publication.

Three weeks later, on August 19, it was back in business under new ownership. The man who revived it was William (later Sir William) J. Gage, and he did it to fight corruption in politics that had come too close to his own door. The Liberal provincial government of Sir Oliver Mowat had just about put him out of business. Starting with a small stationery store, Gage had become the leading publisher of school textbooks, with a virtual monopoly in Ontario. But unfortunately for him, he was of the wrong political persuasion. When a British publisher sued him for infringement of copyright on a school reader, the Ontario Minister of Education, Hon. G. W. Ross, who later became Premier, seized upon this as an excuse for announcing that hereafter the Department of Education would own the copyright on school texts and would have them printed by the lowest bidder. By a strange coincidence the lowest bidder was the treasurer of the provincial Liberal party.

J. J. Crabbe, former editor of the St. Marys *Argus*, who was running Gage's printing plant for him, persuaded Gage he needed a newspaper with which to fight back. Between them they bought the derelict *Star* for the amount of its debts, and incorporated The Star Printing and Publishing Company of Toronto Limited as owner, with a capitalization of $100,000, divided into 1,000 shares of a par value of $100 each. Gage and Crabbe, contributed $15,000 each; Frederick Roper, an accountant who remained *The Star*'s auditor until 1922, J. H. Cotton, a physician, and Stephen Myers, a St. Marys manufacturer, each contributed $5,000. This was enough to pay the paper's debts and give it a fresh start. Other shareholders came in later for small amounts.

Eight months later Gage transferred his stock to Crabbe, but in return for a chattel mortgage on the company's equipment he agreed to back overdrafts and loans at the bank to a limit of $25,000. Crabbe then became not only president of the company, but editor and manager of *The Star*.

For two years *The Star* was indefatigable in sniffing out scandals in the provincial government. Though it found many, it failed in its objective of defeating Mowat or of driving Ross from office. However, Gage got most of his contracts back and "pork barrel politics" never flourished quite as flagrantly again. Gage was a Conservative, though an independent one, and since the federal government was Conservative too, it enjoyed *The Star*'s support in most things.

Crabbe and Gage were men sincerely devoted to social reform, and one of the more interesting developments of this period was the alliance between *The Star* and Lady Aberdeen, wife of the Governor General, to advance the cause of social welfare. She corresponded with Crabbe, wrote articles under an assumed name for *The Star*, and visited the office whenever she was in town to discuss matters in which she was interested. Her Ladyship's concern for the poor annoyed certain prominent industrialists of Toronto and Montreal, who told her to keep out of business that did not concern her. It was no doubt at her instigation that *The Star* ran a series of articles exposing sweated labour conditions in the Toronto tailoring business, which it ran under the heading " 'Tis a Terrible Tale of Toil." In the depression winter of 1894 it ran the Star Fund for Bread, distributing thousands of loaves to unemployed workers and their families. It vigorously attacked the Grand Trunk Railway for cutting the pay of section hands from $1 a day to 90 cents a day, and won for them a restoration to the former pay scale.

It appealed for help for the missions and havens of Toronto in a series of articles. The first of these was on the Haven and Prison Gate Mission for fallen women. It was a staunch defender of organized labour. It urged free hospitalization for consumptives, and Gage was the founder of sanitaria at Weston and Gravenhurst. The Gage Institute of Toronto is named for him. It waged a vigorous campaign for prohibition and saw Toronto vote by a substantial majority for local option under the Scott Act. It carried to a successful conclusion a campaign against the operation of streetcars on Sunday, a burning issue in Toronto in the 1890's. Gage was a member of the Lord's Day Alliance which was fighting Sunday streetcars everywhere.

It was natural that a paper with such a strong social flavour should attract men of unusual character, and *The Star*'s reporting staff was outstanding. Harvey O'Higgins later won renown in New York as a short-story writer; H. Addington Bruce became a writer of best-selling non-fiction books; Harry Gadsby earned distinction as one of the most witty and brilliant writers in Canadian journalism; Victor Ross became president of Imperial Oil; Tom Banton became financial editor of *The Star* and president of the Toronto Trades and Labor Council, an odd combination.

W. L. Argue came from the *News* as circulation manager and remained in that position until 1939, by which time *The Star* had the largest circulation in Canada, 220,000. Argue's most famous stunt was to buy a horse that had won several races at Woodbine racetrack and use it, hitched to a two-wheeled cart, to beat the *Telegram* delivering papers. Spectators used to line the streets to see *The Star's* fast pacer, usually driven by Eatherley, leave the competition behind.

Almost as thrilling a spectacle was Argue himself as he "scorched" the streets on his bicycle, making the rounds of the dealers, for he was a champion cyclist in a day when bicycle racing was a popular sport. Argue brought out the first noon edition of *The Star* on May 20, 1895, in an effort to beat the *Telegram* to the readers. While the printers had made the *News* their target for personal reasons, Crabbe and Argue realized the *Telegram* was the competitor they had to beat.

"*The Evening Star* in those days was not a 'really,' it was a literary make believe, a newspaper out of a book," reminisced Harvey O'Higgins in an article in *The Star* on August 26, 1905.

> It was a newspaper which employed brilliant young men from the first five chapters of a romantic novel before they accepted positions on the *London Times.*
>
> "Gad" was the hero's name, and whenever Gad spoke he said something so dazzlingly witty that the paper suspended publication while the staff leaned

back and roared. "Jawn" had the second lead. He sat with his hat on the back of his head and smoked a corn-cob and wrote the editorials that were stolen by the country journals. After the paper went to press he put his feet in the top drawer of his desk, lifted his pipe, and ruthlessly defeated the government policies which he had been upholding in his editorials.

The real editor, who was at once managing editor, exchange editor, financial editor, the staff copy reader and the make-up man, was a tyrant called "Bowzer" because his bark was worse than his bite. He did the work of seven men and expected his reporters each to do as much. Whenever Gad paraded up and down Yonge St. for a morning, swinging the tails of his paddock overcoat and smoking his after-breakfast cigar, instead of working on his assignment, the paper was scooped and Bowzer shut himself up in his sanctum and kicked his overshoes around the room. He seemed to think a reporter was paid for gathering news. That was Bowzer's great fault.

Bilk was the low comedian of the office. He wrote an article on the state of the egg market and it was copied in all the papers on the continent and generally credited to Mark Twain, who was so flattered that he did not repudiate it. The others were Davie and Bant and Lou and they were clever enough to make any ordinary paper famous.

Gad had a vocabulary so large that even he himself did not know what all the words meant. And Jawn's editorials were so fearfully potent that he had to write some parts of them in what he called Chinese script so the printers would not be able to set them up. It was generally understood that if the whole of one of Jawn's arguments ever got printed the entire edifice of society would fall in ruins.

The really incredible thing about the paper was the fact that it paid its wages regularly every Friday afternoon and this was so miraculous that the operation always drew a crowd.

The Star must have been quite a paper to work for—and to read—in the days of its rowdy youth.

On the masthead, at the head of the editorial page, Crabbe had nailed this pledge, and it remained there to the end of his editorship:

The Star is a Canadian newspaper. It believes in its country, and gives preference to its news. It is independent in politics, and in federal, provincial and municipal affairs knows no party. It will wantonly attack none for mere partisan reasons, nor will it shield any who are faithless. It aims at the publication of facts, and neither suppresses legitimate news nor distorts.

But although *The Star* was a worthy newspaper, enjoying public confidence and wielding considerable influence while Crabbe was directing its policy, it was not a money-maker. After Gage had accomplished his two objectives of bringing about a clean-up in the department of education and blocking

Sunday streetcars he lost interest in it, and Crabbe could not carry on without his financial backing. The shareholders had sunk more than $60,000 in the paper in a vain attempt to make it pay, but they sold their interest in *The Star* in 1895 for $20,750.

The ostensible purchaser was Edmund E. Sheppard, a former owner of the *News*, founder and publisher of *Saturday Night*, an able editor and a brilliant though injudicious writer, who hated French Canadians, Catholics, Yankees, and the British monarchy. On December 13, 1895, his name appeared on the masthead of *The Star* as "Edmund E. Sheppard, Editor and Proprietor."

"I have returned to daily journalism at a time when a candid and courageous newspaper is needed," he announced in a signed editorial headed "Salutatory." There was no hint anybody else had an interest, though the suspicious reader might have found significance in an editorial on the same page criticizing cabs at the union station as a nuisance to the public and unfair competition to the street railway company, which was giving such splendid service for such a small fare.

Sheppard with his Buffalo Bill hat was one of the more fascinating characters of early Toronto journalism. While proprietor and editor of the *News* he wrote an editorial accusing the 65th French-Canadian Regiment of cowardice in the Riel rebellion, for which he was sued for libel by its officers. Orangemen one and all, Toronto court officers refused to serve the writ on him. However, goaded by charges from Quebec that he was afraid to face a court, he went to Montreal and accepted service. The officers offered to drop the libel action if he would pay the $400 court costs and accept a court order barring him from ever again engaging in daily journalism. He agreed, sold the *News* to the Riordans, and founded *Saturday Night*, which was soon a flourishing weekend newspaper with a large job-printing plant. To this he moved *The Star*'s printing equipment, and for the next nine years *The Star* was printed by *Saturday Night*. For most of that time its editorial and business offices were also in the *Saturday Night* building at 26–28 Adelaide Street West.

In allowing himself to be connected with *The Star* Sheppard flouted the Montreal court order, but nothing was ever done about it. When it was learned he would be running *The Star*, the *World* predicted it would be a mere mouthpiece of the Orange order. Sheppard denied this in a signed editorial, declaring *The Star* would not be "the chore boy of any party, race or creed."

The truth is, Sheppard disagreed with the Orange order on almost everything but religion. He was a nationalist who believed in the separation of

Canada from Britain. He advocated an elected chief executive, or president, instead of a prime minister, an elected senate, abolition of church exemptions from taxation, Canada's right to amend its own constitution, a Canadian flag, election of all provincial and county officials, including sheriffs, prosecuting attorneys, court clerks (but apparently not judges), and school inspectors, and election of the head of the Department of Education by the teachers.

He was a strong supporter of organized labour who never ran anything but a union shop, and in the brief period he edited it *The Star* continued its dedicated support of labour unions. He called himself an independent Conservative, but like hundreds of other prominent Conservatives he supported Laurier in the 1896 federal election, despite his distrust of French Canadians in general. During this campaign *The Star* attained a circulation of 11,553, the highest of its first ten years.

Whenever Sheppard wrote a controversial editorial, particularly one against French Canadians, separate schools, or the British connection, he signed it. "I am not ashamed of my beliefs," he wrote in explanation. "When such an editorial is printed I want people to know I wrote it and that it expresses my personal conviction."

But it turned out Sheppard was only a front man, and a month after the announcement that he had bought *The Star* his designation on the masthead was quietly changed from "proprietor" to "president." The real purchaser was Frederic B. Nicholls, president of Canadian General Electric Company and director of several other firms. Gage was dismayed, for Nicholls stood for everything he was against, and was against everything for which he stood. But apparently Crabbe had known all along that Sheppard was acting on behalf of Nicholls. The final payment was by cheque from Nicholls for $20,000 and it was only then that Gage learned the identity of the real purchaser. Crabbe remained to run the paper, but the identity of its new owner remained a well-kept secret until some years after Nicholls had passed the paper on to new owners.

Nicholls was a Tory of the old school and proud of it. He had founded Canada's first electric company, the Toronto Incandescent Electric Light Company, and was president and director of half a dozen utilities companies and street railway companies. He had been in the vanguard of the fight in favour of Sunday streetcars, because if the fight was won in Toronto the street railway systems he controlled in several smaller cities would probably be given permission to operate on Sunday. He was a former secretary of the Canadian Manufacturers' Association, and founder and publisher of the association's mouthpiece, *Canadian Manufacturer*.

The grievance of Nicholls was against the Toronto newspapers. They were all too "namby-pamby" and "mealy-mouthed." They sentimentalized over the poor instead of realizing the poor got no less than they deserved. But their cardinal crime was in trying to deny street railway companies, electric light companies, and other utilities the right to run their businesses as they pleased. Nicholls bought *The Star* to combat the mischievous tendencies of the other newspapers, and to speak for the only members of the community who in his opinion really mattered—self-made men of wealth and prominence.

Nicholls formally assumed ownership of *The Star* on January 11, 1896, and elected himself president. Sheppard, the minutes of a meeting that day make clear, was no more than a $2,500-a-year employee, though his name appeared on the masthead as president. Crabbe was retained as general manager at $3,000 a year. Sheppard remained little more than a year, for in 1897 Laurier rewarded him for his support in the 1896 election by sending him on a tour of South America to sound out possibilities for Canadian trade, and he did not return to *The Star*.

As long as Sheppard was around he acted as a brake on Nicholls' arrant Toryism, and *The Star* was a reasonably fair paper. But after he left, it became blatantly and unashamedly the organ of predatory financial interests. It called for an immediate stop to the building of schools, and attacked the school board for providing playgrounds in connection with schools. Children, it said, went to school to be educated, not to play. The only reason it did not call for an immediate halt to the construction of the city hall, it explained, was that too much money had already been sunk in the misguided project to stop now. It opposed extension to the waterworks system, but waged a campaign to have drivers of the tank wagons hauling water from the lake provided with louder horns to attract the attention of householders. "The city is poor, and these are hard times," it moaned.

It opposed winter relief for the unemployed, attacking an alderman who had in the past supported the Star Fund for Bread as "leader of the unemployed in a discredited clamor for bread." It opposed a public works program for the relief of unemployment as being too costly, suggesting instead that people who were charitably inclined might give a bag of potatoes to poor families, since potatoes were then selling for twenty cents for a bag of 120 pounds. It even turned against Lady Aberdeen, one of the finest collaborators *The Star* has ever had. When she advanced a plan to provide nurses for pioneer hospitals it spoke of her "overweening ambition completely blinding her judgment."

All the time it was furiously fighting the battle for Sunday streetcars, which Gage thought he had beaten forever, some days running as much as three columns of propaganda on the front page. This gave rise to reports that William (later Sir William) Mackenzie, wealthy contractor and president of the Toronto Street Railway Company, owned *The Star* but actually all the stock was held by Nicholls. However, Nicholls and Mackenzie were men of like mind, close friends and co-directors and co-conspirators in several enterprises. The battle for Sunday streetcars was won in 1897 when the courts ruled they were not contrary to the street railway company's charter.

The years when Nicholls owned it was *The Star*'s darkest period, and the only time in its history when it showed no awareness of a newspaper's public responsibility. Most of its fine staff of reporters left in disgust. After Sheppard's departure it seems to have had no regular editor or editorial writer. Sheppard's assistant had been Joseph T. Clark, assistant editor of *Saturday Night*, but when Sheppard left Clark did too, not to return until new owners acquired *The Star*.

Even by the latter part of 1896 circulation had begun to decline from the election peak, for the paper no longer commanded public respect or confidence. The collapse accelerated after Sheppard's departure until by the end of 1899 circulation was at an all-time low of 7,000.

Nicholls began shopping around for a purchaser on which to unload his unprofitable investment. He found it in that group of wealthy Toronto men who were willing to finance an afternoon newspaper to support the policies of Sir Wilfrid Laurier. He closed the deal on December 13, 1899, for $32,000 cash, making a neat capital gain of 54 per cent in four years. The price was considerably more than the business was worth, but the purchasers did not find out until too late that he had juggled the books to show twice the circulation and considerably more revenue than was actually being earned.

Such was the paper that Joseph E. Atkinson agreed to run in 1899.

Chapter 3

A YEAR OF RECONSTRUCTION

Joseph E. Atkinson plunged with zest into the task of reviving the flagging *Star*. He moved in on December 13, 1899, but spent the first week laying plans for his contemplated assault on a field dominated by such powerfully entrenched rivals as the *Evening Telegram* and the *News*. By December 21 he was ready to run up his name on the masthead: "Joseph E. Atkinson, editor and manager."

It was a new *Star* in appearance and content that he launched that afternoon. Its price was still one cent, but it was bigger, the pages seven columns wide instead of the six to which it had shrunk. The news was differently displayed, and to better advantage. There was more sports news. For the first time in eighteen months the editorial page had something useful to say. There was no advertising on the front page. The women's page had been revamped by Mrs. Atkinson, the able "Madge Merton." The dull columns of household hints and high society doings had been displaced by breezy columns of gossip, advice to the lovelorn and troubled, and light comment on topical subjects.

Another, more subtle, change in *The Star*'s news and editorial policy no doubt passed unnoticed at the time, yet it was the very warp and woof from which *The Star* of the future was woven. *The Star* had become Canada's first "popular newspaper," the first to appeal to the "mass circulation" market. Atkinson "early saw that power was beginning to shift from the rich and important to the little people in the semi-detached houses, and he began to address himself to these alone," wrote B. K. Sandwell in *Saturday Night* on May 15, 1948. Sandwell, a former editor of *Saturday Night*, knew Mr. Atkinson well in the early years of this century. But he was an unfriendly critic who saw in the direction of *The Star*'s news policy only a desire on Mr. Atkinson's part for circulation. "Circulation was the essence of publishing; circulation was all that he cared for," Sandwell wrote. "He went out to get it in every direction, conscious that once he had the biggest circulation in Toronto no advertiser could afford to stay out of his paper no matter how much he disliked it."

But Mr. Atkinson, in an address to students at the University of Toronto in 1901, said a newspaper to be successful must appeal to and serve a certain "constituency," by which he meant a certain element of the community. The wealthy and the intellectual élite were well served by other newspapers. He chose as his "constituency" the industrial workers and the "little people" who had no other spokesman, tailoring the news to their taste and fighting their battles for them in his editorial columns. By winning a massive and loyal circulation among them he knew (and was to prove) that he could be independent not only of advertisers but of political and social pressures as well.

The paper had been purchased with the understanding it had a circulation of 14,000. When Mr. Atkinson asked the young lady in charge of circulation accounts for the exact figure she produced the record book, which showed a circulation slightly in excess of that.

"You understand, though, that everything has been doubled," she said.

"What do you mean, doubled?" her new employer demanded.

"Well, when somebody buys ten papers we enter it as a sale of twenty," she explained. "That way the advertising salesmen can always say the books show a circulation of 14,000 without telling a lie."

"From now on enter the correct figure, and we will be honest with our advertisers," Atkinson instructed.

Knowledge that the records had been deliberately falsified somewhat reduced Mr. Atkinson's distress at having to inform J. J. Crabbe, whom he knew as a fellow Methodist and Sunday school superintendent, that he intended to be his own business manager as well as editor. Crabbe, who had been manager for seven years under two owners, was frankly sceptical.

"Your training has been in writing," he protested. "You don't know anything about the business end of a city newspaper."

"I think I'll manage to pick it up; the paper simply cannot support both of us," Atkinson replied.

Crabbe protested that he had an ironclad contract, entered into with the former owners, and could not be dismissed.

"I'll take this to the courts if necessary," he threatened.

"And you'll tell the court you falsified the books and went around this town claiming 14,000 circulation when you really had only 7,000?" Mr. Atkinson asked. Crabbe decided not to sue.

In extenuation of Crabbe's offence it may be noted that the practice of padding circulation claims was not unusual in the days before audited circulations. When Sir Joseph Flavelle and John S. Willison bought the *News* in 1903 they found the circulation was exactly half what the books showed. When they threatened legal action, the vendors inquired if they thought it a good idea to launch a paper under new ownership with a public admission it had only half the circulation claimed. Unlike J. E. Atkinson, they decided to stand by the inflated figure.

Mr. Atkinson confirmed the other fifty-two employees in their jobs down to the humblest office boy, and most of them remained with *The Star* for the rest of their lives. All were capable men, some were brilliant. Of the originals C. C. Campbell continued as news and city editor though Atkinson was his own managing editor. W. C. R. Harris became Atkinson's right-hand man in the business office. W. L. Argue remained as circulation manager, Harry Parr as foreman of the composing room, and Fred Eatherley as chief of the mailing room. Jimmy Simpson had become a full-fledged journeyman printer, but was anxious to try his hand at reporting, while office boy Lou Marsh was dabbling in sports as a cub reporter. Tom Banton was commercial editor, a title that was later changed to financial editor. Banton had been in charge of the campaign for Sunday streetcars when Nicholls owned *The Star*.

Before long the incomparable "Gad" had returned to the staff—Harry Gadsby, one of the wittiest and cleverest writers Canadian journalism has known—to write feature articles and cover Parliament. He left a year later to become managing editor of the Saint John *Daily Telegraph*, but soon came back to *The Star* as editorial writer. Feelers were put out to Charles W. Jefferys, the noted artist who had so impressed Mr. Atkinson when they toured the Maritimes together for the *Globe*. He did not come at once and Fergus Kyle was engaged as illustrator. Kyle was one of the greatest of a profession that was soon to be replaced by the camera and the halftone engraving.

Under the direction of Campbell, the "Bowzer" referred to by Harvey O'Higgins, whose bark was worse than his bite, *The Star* city news department was soon the most ably staffed and most competently directed in Canada. Campbell was a city editor of a type more often found in Hollywood than in real life. He suffered agonies every time he was scooped by a rival newspaper, and drove his reporters to superhuman efforts to beat the opposition. A writer in the *Canadian Courier,* a monthly magazine, referred to him as "the ablest handler of reporters in Canada," though Mr. Atkinson used to chide him at times for his "Draconian methods." No small measure of credit for *The Star*'s spectacular success in its early years must be given C. C. Campbell, the hard-driving city editor.

The Star became the first newspaper to go to the universities for bright young men, and in the first two years after Mr. Atkinson became publisher the number of reporters and writers was increased from eleven to twenty-three. For several years Mr. Atkinson addressed senior students at the University of Toronto who were interested in journalism as a career. Once, in response to an inquiry from an aspiring reporter, he said the best preparation for a career in journalism was a liberal arts education with emphasis on history, sociology, or political science.

One of the first reporters hired, in February, 1900, was a 22-year-old University of Toronto graduate and lacrosse player named John Ransford Bone. Six months later he was Atkinson's right-hand man in the news department, with the title of assistant managing editor. It was a meaningless title at the time, intended merely to signify that he was responsible to Mr. Atkinson alone, not to Campbell, and was given him after he threatened to quit if he had to take any more "abuse" from Campbell. Bone proved to be an able newspaperman with genuine executive ability. In 1907 he was appointed managing editor and in 1914 a director, positions he held until his sudden death in 1928 at the age of fifty.

Among others hired in the same period were Arthur Roebuck, who became an attorney-general of Ontario and later a senator distinguished for his liberalism, E. J. Archibald, who became editor of the *Montreal Star*, and A. N. Mitchell who became president of Canada Life. Charles E. Fortier, hired a short time later as Atkinson's secretary, was advertising director of the Bell Telephone Company for many years.

Atkinson had long been convinced that the public, and younger people in particular, wanted more sports news. While managing editor of the *Herald* he had lured 24-year-old W. A. (Bill) Hewitt to Montreal from the sports desk of the *News*. Now he lured him back to Toronto with an offer to give him a free hand as sports editor of *The Star*. "Without much coaxing I agreed to come," Hewitt recalls. His experience on the *Herald* had been that "Mr. Atkinson ran a happy newspaper." He was sports editor of *The Star* for thirty-one years. Under his direction the sports pages, which had been humdrum and amateurish, became bright, newsy, and gossipy.

One of his early feats was to scoop all other Toronto papers on the race results from New York and Kentucky tracks in a five o'clock sports edition which he initiated. Race results were not carried by the news services then available, but Hewitt knew a bookmaker in Buffalo who had his own sources of information. Late each afternoon he would telephone this "bookie" for his confidential reports. It was quite some time before the other papers discovered how *The Star* was getting its scoops.

Mrs. Atkinson was responsible for a change that was equally revolutionary in the women's pages. Most newspapers in those days disregarded the woman reader, or if they acknowledged her existence it was to publish "a nice story for the edification of the ladies," as *The Star* had announced its intention of doing in its first issue in 1892. But not long after Madge Merton had moved to the *Globe*, she was demonstrating to its publishers that a well-edited women's page was a powerful circulation builder, just as her famous contemporary, Nellie Bly, was then demonstrating to her employer, the New York *World*, that a woman reporter could hold her own in a profession hitherto restricted to the male sex.

Madge Merton went to the Montreal *Herald* with her husband. She returned with him to Toronto to play a significant part in the meteoric success of *The Star*, not alone as a columnist and head of the women's pages, but also as her husband's trusted confidant and adviser. The first few weeks she devoted to reorganizing the women's department which consisted of only three or four columns, but with the issue of March 31 she began writing an entire page for the Saturday edition on the most amazing variety of subjects. "Madge Merton's Page" it was headed in large type, with a lug at one corner reading "For Women by a Woman" and at the other "Correspondence and Pitter-Patter."

Madge Merton was very much the product of her generation, the late Victorian age. Her writings were popular with the women of that period, whose horizons were still limited by the walls of their homes, but they would scarcely find acceptance with the women of today. Consider, for example, her comforting admonition to a woman of 1900 who sought advice about being overweight. "Some human beings are stout," she replied, "just as some dogs and some horses and cows are of heavy build. You must not find fault with your nature. If your digestion is good and you take sufficient exercise, I wouldn't worry about it, if I were you."

She was a vigorous temperance publicist, a suffragette, a feminist, and a campaigner for the rights of women and children at a time when women were just beginning to realize they had rights. She put *The Star* in the forefront of the campaign for women's suffrage, and served as an inspiration for young women just then breaking into the business world.

Mr. Atkinson personally took charge of reviving the editorial page, which had sunk to a pretty miserable estate after Sheppard's departure. Two of the first three editorials on the day he put his name on the masthead, December 21, show evidence of having been written by the new "Chief" himself, for they dealt with subjects on which he felt keenly. The first, headed "Drop the Racial Cry," was a defence of French Canadians who were being unjustly accused in Toronto of disloyalty because of their lukewarm support of the Boer War.

The campaign of vilification against French Canadians in the Tory press of Toronto had long angered Mr. Atkinson. A personal letter on this subject to J. S. Willison, dated October 25, 1899, is in the Willison papers in the Public Archives at Ottawa.

> There is absolutely no political sentiment in the French-Canadian's attachment to France. French-Canadians have their political aspirations in the future of Canada as a nation, and not as part of the British Empire. In other words, we of English descent have a loyalty to Britain as well as to Canada. French-Canadians have no such dual loyalty, but only one loyalty, and that is to Canada. We have two countries, French-Canadians have one, and surely it would be unjust as it would be useless to demand of a French-Canadian such a feeling for England as we possess.

The other editorial was on "Toronto, a Beautiful City," and could only have been written by one newly returned to a city he loved after an absence of years. It was followed by a flurry of editorials suggesting improvements in Toronto planning. The first of these, on December 24, urged that a street parallel to Yonge Street be opened through from the waterfront to Bloor Street. This was later done, today's Bay Street. At the time, Bay Street ran only from Front Street to the city hall.

A few days later *The Star* urged that negotiations be reopened for the purchase of property for a civic square to set off the new city hall which had been completed the previous September. Some two or three years earlier a group of public-spirited businessmen, headed by Eugene O'Keefe, the brewer, had bought the land now occupied by the west half of Simpson's department store, bounded by Queen, Bay and Richmond streets, and offered it to the city for either $200,000 or a perpetual annual rental of $3,500.

"There is no public demand at this time for a civic square," objected the tax-conscious *Telegram*, branding the project as a scheme of "hungry property owners" to unload their land on the taxpayer, and council turned the project down. *The Star*, while owned by Nicholls, had also opposed the civic square project, but now, under Atkinson, *The Star* sought to revive it. It was again turned down. Once more *The Star* brought it up in 1901, recommending a civic square as a suitable memorial to Queen Victoria. The *Telegram* objected that Toronto already had a memorial to Queen Victoria in Queen's Park, and one was enough, and council again voted it down. Shortly thereafter the property was sold for private use, but *The Star* never lost hope that some day Toronto would have a worthy downtown civic square and repeatedly campaigned for one. Its efforts were crowned with success in 1947, when the ratepayers voted for the present square as part of the new city hall–civic centre project.

These editorials at the outset of his career as a Toronto publisher were indicative of Mr. Atkinson's lifelong devotion to city planning. Throughout most of its subsequent history *The Star* has almost automatically supported any project for the physical improvement of Toronto. It has always, on principle, defended city planners, even when Mr. Atkinson was personally doubtful of the merit of some specific plan. Toronto would be a much more pleasant city to live in had more of its proposals been adopted.

In improving the editorial page Atkinson had the capable assistance of Joseph Clark, the ablest of the editorial writers on *Saturday Night*. For the two years that Sheppard was editor of *The Star* Clark had been his assistant. Since *The Star* was printed by *Saturday Night* and shared offices with that paper, it was natural that Mr. Atkinson should ask Joe Clark to help him out for a few days. And since the association proved to be mutually congenial, it was natural he should ask Joe Clark to stay. With the exception of a brief interruption of two years he remained until his death in 1937, at which time he was editor-in-chief. A gentle, kindly man with a soft pen, Joseph Clark came close to being Mr. Atkinson's conception of the ideal editorial writer.

"I am not much attracted towards the violent type of editorial writing," Mr. Atkinson told a class of aspiring journalists at Toronto University in 1921. "The sane way of appealing to reason pays respect to readers' intelligence. It seems to me that the bludgeoning type does violence to that intelligence. Not that the violent type is not effective, but the violent writer makes an intense appeal to all those whose opinion is reflected in his writing. His articles are futile to persuade those already unpersuaded. Good nature is the finest trait in editorial writing."

Joseph Clark had a very real influence on formulating *Star* editorial policy for many years. Atkinson always listened to him with respect and when their views differed it was very often Clark's that prevailed on the editorial page. His editorials struck the key note for *The Star*. A kindly man himself, he gave people the feeling *The Star* was a kindly newspaper.

Mr. Atkinson had more trouble finding a cartoonist to his liking. He first engaged C. H. Wesler, whose work would stand comparison with the best of today's political cartoons, but Atkinson found his caricatures too waspish and after a few weeks he left. Samuel Hunter, who has been rated by many as one of Canada's all-time greats as a cartoonist, was then persuaded to leave the *World* and draw for *The Star*. He remained only eighteen months. However, Hunter was always Mr. Atkinson's favourite cartoonist because, as he once said, "there is no venom in his work." In cartoons, as with editorials, Atkinson preferred the gentle, humorous touch. But Hunter disliked being tied for long to a steady job, choosing to work when he pleased, selling to whoever would buy. Working this way it was not unusual for him to have as many as seventeen cartoons in the several Toronto papers in one week. His longest association with any paper was with the *World*, though for thirty-seven years he was a welcome occasional contributor to *The Star*. After Hunter left *The Star* in 1901 Kyle drew the cartoon for several months, to be succeeded by Jefferys, who remained for many years. However, *The Star* under Atkinson was not noted for its cartoons and sometimes months would pass without its publishing one.

Three men inherited by Mr. Atkinson from the former regime were to establish *The Star*'s labour policy, and make it the defender of the rights of organized labour at a time when unions were under persistent attack. They were Tom Banton, Fred Bancroft and Jimmy Simpson.

Banton, who was the most able and therefore the most influential of the three, combined what would appear to be the mutually antagonistic occupations of commercial editor and labour organizer. By trade he was a cabinet-maker. Though he did not work at it after coming to *The Star* as a reporter in 1892, it was as a representative of the cabinet makers that he rose through various executive positions to be president of the Toronto Trades and Labour Council for two years and secretary for ten. For years he was accustomed to mount a soap box after leaving his daily work at *The Star* and harangue the homeward-bound crowd. A public-spirited citizen, he was appointed to the public library board in 1896, a position he filled until his retirement at the age of 84. In 1912 he headed a citizens' committee that promoted the annexation of North Toronto to the city.

Bancroft, a reporter, was frequently called upon to arbitrate labour disputes. Once Mr. Atkinson ordered him to give up this outside activity. Bancroft refused and got away with it, for his labour column was one of the paper's most widely read features.

Simpson had completed his apprenticeship and was working in the composing room. Though still in his early twenties, he was already active in labour circles. A deeply religious man, and like his employer a Methodist, he used to say he was a socialist because of his religious beliefs. Atkinson was attracted to Simpson by his active and inquisitive mind, and in the summer of 1900 asked him how he would like to be a reporter, covering municipal politics from the point of view of a working man. For the next eight years Simpson was *The Star*'s reporter at city hall, and for four more years he was municipal editor, writing a column and occasional editorials on municipal affairs. Simpson became one of the country's outstanding labour leaders, and mayor of Toronto in 1935.

Atkinson understood that if *The Star* was to appeal to the little man in the semi-detached house it must have a sympathetic labour policy, but his own experience as a newspaperman had been almost wholly in the political field. His personal inclination was towards political action to right social wrongs, and early editorials indicate a reluctance to condone the direct action of the unions. In 1901, for example, *The Star* referred to the strike as an outmoded method of settling labour disputes. Nevertheless, recognizing his own inexperience, Mr. Atkinson allowed himself to be guided by his three experienced employees.

Thus these three trade unionists were responsible not only for crystallizing *The Star*'s labour policy, but were also largely responsible for Mr. Atkinson's personal attitude towards labour unions. However, the fact that the labour movement in those days was liberal rather than socialistic in its approach, was in fact supporting the Liberal parties in both Canada and Britain, must be counted as predisposing him towards it. Essentially

The Star's labour policy was based upon the liberal principles that workers have the right to organize, the right to join the union of their choice, and the right to peaceful picketing. It has seldom gone beyond that.

The most immediately noticeable change in the news department was the stepped-up coverage of the Boer War, which had been in progress in South Africa for nearly a year. Mr. Atkinson set out to give it the most extensive coverage any war ever had. And it was to be a distinctively Canadian coverage.

Some Canadian troops, mostly volunteers from Toronto, were already in South Africa, and the country was preparing to send another contingent. Excitement in Toronto, the centre of imperialism in Canada, was at fever pitch, and one would think from the editorials in some of the newspapers that the fate of the Empire hung in the balance. Yet those same newspapers were depending for the most part on US news services for their war coverage, and these were uniformly anti-British.

Mr. Atkinson set out to remedy that. He arranged with the *Montreal Herald* to share the salary and expenses of S. C. Simonsky, a correspondent he had sent to South Africa before he left the *Herald*. He sent W. Richmond Smith, a noted writer and artist, overseas with the Canadian contingent then sailing, to prepare illustrated human-interest stories about life in the Canadian army. He acquired the rights to the dispatches of some British correspondents, among them a young fellow named Winston Churchill, who was more fond of reporting his personal exploits than the progress of the war. He engaged a reporter on a London paper to cable any comment, however trivial it might be, on the Canadian war effort.

And he arranged with his friend and one-time fellow reporter Mackenzie King, then studying in Europe on a scholarship, to write special articles. King was to recall after Mr. Atkinson's death that he was the first of a long line of students given financial assistance in this manner by Mr. Atkinson, for the summer or part-time employment of promising young students became a regular *Star* practice. "The payment was a welcome supplement to my slender income," King wrote *The Star* on the death of J. E. Atkinson in 1948.

By January 3, three weeks after Atkinson assumed management, *The Star* was able to boast with complete truth that "*The Star*'s war news is 15 hours ahead of the morning papers, and much of it 24 hours ahead of its evening contemporaries." When the Toronto Company with the Expeditionary Force participated in its first engagement at Dover Farm, *The Star* scored a complete scoop of a day on other Canadian papers, and had human interest interviews and follow-ups for several more days. Soon *The Star* was able to start running a full page of correspondence from Canadian soldiers. As soon as Smith's drawings could be mailed back from England it began a series of front-page feature articles on life aboard a troopship. Every time Canadians took part in an engagement or troop movement, *The Star*'s man in London cabled columns of praise from London editors or leading Britons, while Simonsky reported their activities in the most minute detail.

It is a distressing fact that a war is one of the biggest circulation builders, and *The Star*'s massive coverage of the Boer War in the early months of 1900 attracted many new readers. Nevertheless, Mr. Atkinson was unhappy about it. He was a pacifist and any war to his mind was wrong. This war he regarded as the unprovoked attack of a great imperial power upon a decent and peaceable little republic of farmers, and so more reprehensible than most. He believed that it resulted in large measure from a public opinion whipped to fury by irresponsible British newspapers, and this conviction was to influence the way in which *The Star* handled the news preceding the two world wars. He believed the Canadian government had been stampeded into participating in the war by an inflammatory campaign waged by the *Telegram* and the *World* of Toronto and the *Montreal Star*, and that these three newspapers had been motivated more by a desire to embarrass Sir Wilfrid Laurier than from genuine patriotism.

Thus, though *The Star*'s coverage at first was prodigious in volume for those days, it was remarkably restrained in other respects. It neither reviled the Boers nor extravagantly praised the British. As a newspaperman, Mr. Atkinson had to report the war; as a pacifist, he was determined not to glorify it. Editorially, *The Star* commended the bravery of Canadian soldiers, expressed the hope the "wave of patriotism" would not subside after the war, and commented dispassionately when occasion arose on steps the government was taking, but it never showed any war fever. In a nut shell, it approved Laurier's position that it was too bad Canada had to become involved, but since we were, let us do the best we can.

Once, when there was a lull in the fighting, *The Star* mildly suggested that now would be a good time to negotiate a "peace with honor." The avalanche of vituperation that descended upon his head after this well-meant editorial must have astonished Mr. Atkinson. Peace with honour, the *Telegram* and like-minded newspapers raged, would be equivalent to an admission by Britain that she could not win the war or that the war was an unjust one. None but a traitor to the Queen and Empire would be content with anything short of unconditional surrender by the Boers.

History has justified Mr. Atkinson's judgment on the merits of the Boer War, but it has also disclosed that the pressures pushing Canada into participation were more complex than he suspected. His views on war in general and the Boer War in particular were shared by Mackenzie King, who wrote in his diary after viewing a demonstration in London: "The love of God and War cannot be justified." But King confessed to being thrilled by the pageantry of war and in the end found himself, as Atkinson did, applauding British victories.

After a few weeks the public showed signs of losing interest in the struggle, a circumstance not entirely displeasing to Mr. Atkinson. The war was taking altogether too long to win, and it was becoming quite impossible to maintain interest in a few thousand guerrilla farmers pot-shooting at a few thousand incompetently led redcoats. Besides, *The Star* was running out of money. And so, as abruptly as he had begun his massive coverage, Mr. Atkinson called it off. It was then that there occurred the first of those awesome phenomena which were to become such a familiar idiosyncrasy of *Star* history—the cyclical economy wave.

Harry Parr used to recall with amusement how reporters on assignments had to pay their own street car fares, printers salvaged every shaving of type metal, and Atkinson slipped about turning off unnecessary lights. George Macdonald, an office boy at the time but later a senior member of the advertising department, recalls Atkinson severely admonishing, "George, a fifth of a cent an hour saved" as he turned off a light. Pictures disappeared from the pages, and the paper shrank in size. Yet the public continued to buy it and its circulation continued to increase, for by this time much of the odium that had collected about *The Star* during the Nicholls ownership had been dispelled. It was becoming known as an independent, well-informed, and outspoken newspaper.

It was Senator Cox who recommended this economy wave, but one may be sure it suited Mr. Atkinson's own inclinations, for there was a parsimonious streak in his nature, a hold-over, no doubt, from the poverty of his childhood. It was on Senator Cox's advice also that the practice was adopted of budgeting separately for each department and of not allowing the profits of one department to be applied against the losses of another. "Put each department on such a close budget that it will be next to impossible to keep within it," Senator Cox advised. "That way you keep them on their toes." Mr. Atkinson used to say all he knew of finance he learned from Cox, all he knew of salesmanship he learned from Timothy Eaton, and all he knew of politics he learned from Mulock.

It was not only the Boer War that had eaten heavily into the fund of $43,000 the shareholders had set aside for expansion and improvements. Early in January, 1900, they had authorized a substantial investment in linotype machines, new fonts of type, and a press with a capacity of 24,000 twelve-page papers an hour to replace the old press which could print only 10,000 eight-page papers in the same time. They had also authorized a change in the name of the newspaper from the *Evening Star* to the *Toronto Daily Star*, and this became effective on January 24.

When the new printing equipment arrived it was installed in a building on Yonge Street just south of Adelaide Street. About the same time the business offices were moved to the southeast corner of Yonge and Adelaide Streets, though the editorial offices remained in the *Saturday Night* building until 1905.

Shortly after the new press was delivered Mr. Atkinson called upon Timothy Eaton for whom, among all his financial backers, he probably had the most admiration and respect. He suggested that Eaton's should be the first department store in Canada to publish a full-page advertisement every day. Eaton had stopped advertising in *The Star* when Nicholls ran it into the ground, and though he now owned 10 per cent of the paper he had not resumed advertising in it.

"I don't mix business with my other interests," he told Atkinson. "With the circulation you have it isn't profitable business to advertise in *The Star*."

"But, Mr. Eaton, other merchants are increasing their advertising in *The Star*," Mr. Atkinson protested. "Simpson's is taking a half page or more every day and Adams' nearly as much."

"M-m-m-ff," Mr. Eaton nodded. From a table he took a copy of The Philadelphia *North American*. The back page was entirely occupied by an advertisement of John Wanamaker's store, headed with a big, red streamer "Wanamaker's Daily Store News."

"Can you do that?" Mr. Eaton asked.

"No other paper in North America can or does carry a red line," Mr. Atkinson replied.

"You do it, then come and see me again," Mr. Eaton said. Back Mr. Atkinson hurried to the plant. The pressmen assured him it could not be done, but a telegram to the makers of the press brought a reply that an attachment for colour printing was available.

Eaton had made no firm promise, but Atkinson felt sure he could make the sale once *The Star* could print in colour. But even if he failed to sell Eaton's the space, how splendid it would be for *The Star* to be the first newspaper in Canada with a red line, the first to print illustrations in colour! That would make Toronto sit up and take notice! This eagerness of Mr. Atkinson to adopt new techniques must be counted as one of the factors in *The Star*'s success.

The new attachment arrived just in time for the Easter edition, on Saturday, April 14, and the entire front page was devoted to a three-colour illustration of the resurrection scene by Kyle. The following Saturday the opening of the horse show was heralded with a four-page first section in colour. About three-quarters of page one was occupied by a drawing of horses and riders in hunting costume posed before what appeared to be one of the exhibition buildings. Salada Tea, of which *Star* shareholder Peter Larkin was president, and National Cycle and Automobile Company, of which shareholder Walter Massey was president, shared the back page, the first advertisers in a Canadian newspaper to use colour.

May Day was commemorated on the third Saturday with a front-page colour drawing of maidens in filmy costumes gambolling about a maypole. Featured on an inside page of the colour section was a lengthy article pleading for the abolition of capital punishment, a cause close to Mr. Atkinson's heart ever since he had been revolted by the execution of Birchall.

After this Mr. Atkinson seems to have decided the public was sufficiently impressed, for there were no more Saturday colour sections until the Christmas edition, and that was more restrained than the earlier examples. Truth to tell, these illustrations were not very attractive. As a novelty they called attention to *The Star*, but the colours were watery and the registration poor. Colour printing was still too new an art for it to be a regular newspaper feature.

The first Eaton advertisement appeared on June 6, occupying the entire back page, resplendent with a red line in 48-point square Gothic reading "Eaton's Daily Store News." *The Star* had become the first daily newspaper in Canada and the second in America to use a red line on page one and in an advertisement. Except for the period between June 8, 1921, and September 10, 1923, the back page has been occupied ever since by "Eaton's Daily Store News."

Timothy Eaton took a fatherly interest in the young publisher, often asking the Atkinsons to his home. One Sunday when they were weekend guests at the Eaton summer home a slip of paper was handed the host. Eaton glanced at it, then put it in his pocket.

"Have you any idea what was on that paper, Atkinson?" he asked.

"No, sir."

"That's what the boys took in at the store on Saturday. Do you know what *The Star* took in yesterday?"

"No, I don't," Mr. Atkinson confessed.

"Then you should," the great merchant told him.

Mr. Atkinson often said this advice from Timothy Eaton was the most valuable he ever received. He did not have the staff at the time to prepare the reports, and he used to relate how he would take the day's paper home with him, spread it on the livingroom floor after supper, and he and Mrs. Atkinson would measure the advertisements, comparing them with those in the other papers.

On another occasion when department stores, including Eaton's, were being attacked from some quarters Atkinson asked Eaton what he intended to do about it. "I am going to keep store," Eaton replied. In the years that lay ahead Mr. Atkinson and his newspaper were also to be violently attacked, but except on one occasion when they were particularly vicious he followed Timothy Eaton's precept and "kept store." He used to say the confidence the public was showing in *The Star* was sufficient answer to its critics.

An amusing little anecdote is told of a letter Atkinson once wrote Eaton soliciting his support for some project "as one pillar of the Methodist church to another." Eaton replied that "as one outside pillar" of the Methodist church to another the answer was "No." The close friendship between the two men led to rumours, which were published as fact by other papers, that *The Star* was owned by Eaton's.

Mr. Atkinson enjoyed almost as cordial relations with Senator Cox, despite the fact that early in their relationship he had to rap the distinguished financier over the knuckles for trying to influence the policy of the newspaper—which is not surprising since Cox had a finger in nearly every financial pie baking in Toronto. In 1900 he was behind an offering to the public of shares in the Dominion Coal Company. *The Star* was critical of the methods used to sell the stock, which would not be permitted today. One effect of the frantic and exaggerated publicity campaign was to set off a wave of stock market speculation. In a front-page article *The Star* warned that "a lot of innocent people are likely to have their fingers burned." That night Senator Cox telephoned Mr. Atkinson.

"You have an article on the front page today that contains many mis-statements; do you think it right to print what is untrue?" he angrily demanded.

"Why no," Mr. Atkinson replied. "If you will point out the mis-statements I shall be glad to have them corrected."

Instead of doing so, Senator Cox asked what Mr. Atkinson expected to gain by printing such articles. Without answering directly, Atkinson remarked that he had been informed that William Mackenzie, president of the street railway company, had asked Cox to make *The Star* stop attacking the streetcar system because of its poor service.

"I would appreciate it if you would tell Mr. Mackenzie that *The Star*'s editorial policy is made in *The Star* office and nowhere else," he said.

"Certainly Mr. Atkinson, I would have told him that had I thought of it," the Senator replied. Reading the answer to himself in the retort he had been asked to convey to Mackenzie, Cox did not renew his own complaint. Thereafter he observed the agreement, and did not try to interfere. Not so Sir William Mulock, the only politician in the group. He lived to be 101 and never stopped trying.

Quarrels between Atkinson and Mulock over politics were frequent. George Macdonald tells of one encounter he overheard. "Mulock came roaring into the office one day swearing and cursing (and believe me he knew all the words) over something *The Star* had printed," Macdonald relates. "Mr. Atkinson stared at him a minute. 'When you moderate your language, Mr. Mulock, I will listen to what you have to say,' the Chief said, then turned his back and walked into the composing room."

On one matter, often recalled by Mr. Atkinson, he and Mulock were in agreement. In 1900 a new department of labour was to be established under the general oversight of the postmaster general. Mulock told Atkinson he was having trouble finding the right man to head it and to edit the proposed *Labour Gazette*.

"Why not Mackenzie King?" Atkinson asked.

King was already favourably known to Mulock, having come to his attention as a result of a series of articles he had written for the *Mail and Empire* exposing sweatshop conditions in several Toronto industries. He had also made some private inquiries at Mulock's request into labour conditions in other industries. But at this time he was in Europe, and it was understood he was about to accept a professorship at Harvard. Whether or not it was due to Atkinson's urging, Mulock cabled King in June, 1900, and after some weeks of indecision King turned down the professorship and embarked upon the course that was to make him Prime Minister of Canada.

In midsummer of 1900, Plunkett Magann died and his thirty-eight shares came on the market. He had agreed to take fifty but had not yet been called to pay the balance of $1,200. The lawyer handling the estate encountered sports editor, Bill Hewitt, on the golf course one day and casually suggested he should put in a bid for the stock. Next morning Hewitt told Atkinson of the conversation and asked if he considered *Star* stock a good buy. "Mr. Hewitt, you couldn't buy even one share of it," Mr. Atkinson said sharply. "High or low, no *Star* employee has an access to *Star* stock. My backers have agreed to an arrangement that all stock must be sold to me."

That same morning Mr. Atkinson hastened to the lawyer with a warning that the stock must not be sold to anybody else, then to Senator Cox for a loan. With surprising readiness the Senator arranged for Mr. Atkinson to borrow whatever sum was needed from the Bank of Commerce, of which Cox was president. Mr. Atkinson put in a bid of $2,500 for all fifty shares that had been allotted to Magann. There being no other bidder the stock was knocked down to him at half price.

A few weeks later he bought for $3,000 the fifty shares for which William Christie had paid $5,000, Senator Cox again backing his note at the bank. Thus in the first nine months he had acquired for $5,500 borrowed at the bank 100 shares of a par value of $10,000. Mr. Atkinson repaid these loans at the rate of $1,500 a year out of his salary, keeping only $1,500 a year for living expenses. Mrs. Atkinson was drawing a salary of $17 a week as women's page editor. These purchases gave him an interest in the paper equal to that of each of the three biggest shareholders, Cox, Eaton, and Massey. After the annual meeting of January 26, 1901, had voted him the twenty shares in part payment of his salary, to which he was entitled, he was the largest individual shareholder, owning 13 per cent of the stock issued.

At this meeting he made an unsuccessful attempt to have the shareholders acknowledge that he was in a preferred position in the matter of buying up to 30 per cent of the total paid-up stock of the company. There had been such a verbal agreement, he told the shareholders. He would like it in writing. A motion was passed instructing the president to make inquiries, and if he was satisfied such a promise had been made Atkinson, to write him a letter to that effect. No such letter was ever written.

Mr. Atkinson had been shocked at finding the circulation less than 7,000 when he had expected to be addressing an audience of twice that number. The *Telegram* at the time claimed a circulation of 25,144 and the *Globe*'s circulation was even more. But he wasted no time in idle lamentations. Within a month he was offering pictures of Lord Roberts, the hero of the Boer War, in fifteen colours suitable for framing, for six cents and a coupon from *The Star*. Next it was a picture of Queen Victoria and the Prince of Wales. Then it was a book on the controversy over whether Shakespeare or Bacon really wrote Shakespeare's plays. After that it was an illustrated volume of *Picturesque Canada* for one dollar and a coupon. In the next few years a veritable flood of premiums poured from *The Star*'s circulation department.

Other newspapers wrote sarcastic editorials about *The Star's* premiums and in the fulness of time went to the journalistic graveyard where sanctimonious papers go. Mr. Atkinson "kept store." Premiums he looked upon as merely a means of introducing his product to the public. "This is a promotion scheme," *The Star* frankly confessed on offering a $1,000 accident insurance policy as a premium early in 1901. "*The Star* has no apology to offer. . . . The object is to place the paper in the homes of 30,000 people within the next year." Confident that he was getting out the most interesting paper in Toronto, Mr. Atkinson believed that a considerable proportion of those who were induced to sample his product by the offer of a premium would like *The Star* well enough to keep on taking it.

The first year, however, ended on a note of discouragement. True the paper had added three thousand subscribers, but it was still deeply in the red. The original "kitty" the shareholders had set aside for expansion was nearly all spent, and they were not inclined to put up any more, for none except its youthful editor had much hope it would long survive. Henry A. Little of Woodstock who was not one of the original group was able to buy twenty shares of capital stock from the treasury for $1,000, half the par value. J. E. Atkinson had determined to own *The Star* some day, and was already well started on the way, but that was of small comfort if he could not keep the paper's head above water. "Never mind," encouraged Walter Massey. "I know the other shareholders haven't much interest in the paper any more, but you and I will see it through its troubles."

Mr. Atkinson always looked back on this as a curiously important conversation. Massey was seven years his senior, but they had both grown up in Newcastle, Walter the son of the town's leading citizen, Joe the son of a widow who kept a boarding house. That the head of the family he had been taught as a boy to look up to with respect and admiration should have such confidence in him was all that mattered any more. He never again entertained thought of giving up.

Chapter 4

PUBLIC TASTE THE TEST

It has been said of *The Star* that it broke every rule of orthodox journalism. That may not be literally true, but it broke enough of them that magazine writers were soon commenting in awe on its unconventional behaviour while publishers of more commonplace sheets were whispering at their gatherings that it could not last.

Its most interesting practice was that of turning the entire staff of reporters loose on a big story. A bank robbery would find every reporter in the city room sprinting madly towards the scene of the crime. It may not have originated the practice, but it carried it to an extreme unknown to other newspapers. While *The Star* had its teeth in a big story it did not care on how many little stories it was scooped, for Mr. Atkinson well knew that most of the routine news that fills a newspaper's columns is triviality that will not be missed. While on a recruiting expedition to the University of Toronto in 1905 he assured the graduating class that massive coverage of big stories was one of the secrets of *The Star*'s rapid ascendancy. One of the earliest examples is found in its coverage of the assassination of President William McKinley at Buffalo on September 6, 1901. In its way it is a classic, for it brought into play four *Star* "rules": get the news first; sew it up so the opposition cannot get it; leave not a crumb or a morsel or a tidbit uncollected; play it big.

When the anarchist Czolgosz fired his bullet into the President *The Star*'s man did not wait for more developments. He streaked for the nearest telephone. His breathless bulletin was received as the last edition was being closed. Atkinson ordered the doors closed, lest any hint of what had happened trickle to a rival, then held the edition several minutes past the deadline to allow the printers on the other papers to leave for home before *The Star* broke the story.

The Star hit the streets with the entire assassination story, not just the line, printed in red ink. This was followed by extra after extra until eleven o'clock, giving more details as they were received, still with the entire story printed in red. Opposition papers were caught flat-footed without a staff to print extras. Almost the whole editorial staff was turned loose over night, and the next day the front page was devoted entirely to staff-written stories, mostly interviews with eye-witnesses and Toronto people who had been there, embellished with a large drawing in colour of Liberty in mourning. As McKinley hovered between life and death *The Star* not only printed every morsel available, but put a board in the window with up-to-the-minute details on the president's condition.

When in 1903 R. R. Gamey, member of the legislature for Manitoulin, touched off the greatest scandal until that time by charging provincial cabinet ministers with bribery, *The Star*'s press gallery man did not wait for Gamey to finish his address but telephoned the office while he was still speaking, enabling *The Star* to beat all other papers with an extra. Then, to quote Mr. Atkinson's precise language, "reporters were withdrawn from the other assignments and sent to follow up certain phases of the case." A staff of seven were assigned to report the Royal Commission hearing which resulted, one of the earliest examples of the use of relays of running-copy writers to prepare almost verbatim reports of a court hearing. In the years to come *Star* reporters were to develop running-copy writing into a fine art, carrying to an extreme, some thought, the practice of reporting trials, hearings, and public meetings in direct quotations. It is a high tribute to the accuracy of the reporters that their "quotes" were seldom challenged.

On the occasion of the great Toronto fire of April 19–20, 1904, the whole staff was called out at 8 p.m. and concentrated on the fire. "They remained continuously on duty until the next day's paper was out," Mr.

Atkinson proudly told the college students. Seven pages of the sixteen-page paper contained nothing but fire stories and pictures. The great Ottawa fire and scores of local stories were similarly covered in blanket fashion.

The same rule applied to telegraph stories. The San Francisco earthquake and fire occurred during an "economy wave" but telegraph editor, W. R. Plewman, ignored orders and spent money lavishly to get exclusive rights to the stories of all San Francisco newspapers. Bone grumbled at the cost, but Mr. Atkinson complimented Plewman on a good job.

An article in the issue of August 26, 1905, described how *The Star* editorial staff handled "something stupendous which drops in their midst with a crash." Using the Gamey case as an example, it said "regular assignments were neglected. It took a pretty important event to secure half a column of space as long as the interest in the case was at fever heat, so that the time of reporters on routine work would have been wasted."

Referring to the fire of 1904 it said "very important foreign news was cut to a paragraph. Even the regular departments of financial, sporting, Parliamentary news and social gossip were almost extinguished." Of a big bank robbery in which the watchman was killed it stated: "It is realized at once that this will be the chief thing the people want to read about that day, and the editor tells reporters to hurry through or drop altogether other assignments."

In the case of a bank official who was reported short in his accounts, it said the city editor recognized at once that all concerned would be "secretive" about it. He took every reporter off other assignments, and assigned each to interview one person who might know something about the case. The result was a "scoop" within half an hour. "Each man had but one shaft to shoot," it said. "It was inevitable most would miss. But one hit, ten minutes before deadline."

Speaking generally, the article continued: "Unless it is an especially sensational case, it will have run itself out as a newspaper sensation in two or three days . . . After the first day or two new subjects must serve as the paper's features." This was *The Star*'s method of handling the news for fifty years. It was criticized by some as being sensationalist and unbalanced, but the formula was remarkably successful in building circulation.

In other ways, too, *The Star* was demonstrating its enterprise in a manner that fired public imagination. On August 10, 1903, for example, less than two years after the first wireless message had been sent across the Atlantic, *Star* reporters used this new invention to transmit the results of the Canada Cup races off Hanlan's Point to the office, not only scooping other newspapers but creating in itself a sensational new story that lasted three days. That fall *The Star* sent its reports from the Canadian National Exhibition by wireless, in full view of the public, and anybody could send a wireless message to a friend anywhere in the city for twenty-five cents.

The Star did not consider objectivity necessarily a virtue. The newspaper stood for certain things, for certain principles, and it stood for them in every column from the weather on page one to Eaton's advertisement on the back page. Mr. Atkinson used to say, probably with tongue in cheek, that *The Star* was not a crusading newspaper, yet it was seldom without a crusade. And *Star* reporters always found the evidence and public opinion strongly supporting the cause *The Star* favoured.

Mr. Atkinson had discovered the technique when he toured the country as a reporter for the *Globe* and encountered not one manufacturer opposed to Laurier's low tariff policy. He had not been running the newspaper a month until *The Star* could find nobody in the city opposed to a civic square but dozens willing to go on record in interviews in favour. Near the end of 1901 it showed what a newspaper could really do when it turned the full resources of news and editorial columns loose on the wholly estimable project of saving the Canadian National Exhibition from extinction.

The CNE of 1901 was a financial failure, and just as today, a great clamour arose in the press as to the cause. "The only way to get it back on its feet is to have new buildings," *The Star* declared, but the *Telegram* grumbled that the whole business was a needless expense to the taxpayers and should be shut down. To *The Star*'s alarm, those politicians in the *Telegram*'s pocket seemed ready to carry out its bidding. So *The Star* pulled out all the stops. It devoted the full front page on a Saturday to what should be done to save the CNE, with interviews with everybody of consequence below the rank of governor general. The campaign lasted months, with *The Star* and those it interviewed demanding new buildings, reorganization of management, and shifting of emphasis from the Midway to the exhibits. All three were done, prosperity returned, and the CNE became the world's greatest annual show.

This technique was standard practice on all newspapers sixty years ago; but *The Star* used it more effectively than most. And because it was generally used for ends the public considered desirable rather than for political or class purposes, public confidence in the newspaper was not weakened. As far as news that happened in the ordinary course of events was concerned, *The Star* could be counted upon to cover it more fully and impartially than other Toronto newspapers. Its very impartiality sometimes made enemies, as when it gave labour equal prominence with management in an industrial dispute.

By the end of 1903 *The Star* had surpassed in circulation its three weaker rivals, the *World*, the *News*, and the *Mail and Empire*, and with a circulation of 21,088 was edging close to the second-place *Telegram*. The paper had become so big it was impossible to carry on as it had been doing with editorial, business office, and printing plant in three separate buildings. Accordingly in January, 1904, the shareholders elected J. E. Atkinson a director, and instructed him to secure accommodations adequate for all departments. Thereafter his name appeared on the masthead as managing director, with E. T. Malone as president and his brother and legal partner, A. L. Malone, the third director.

Arrangements were made to buy the office building of the North of Scotland Canadian Mortgage Company at 18 King Street West for $150,000 and to build an addition at the back to house the printing plant. To finance this and to buy new presses and other equipment a $100,000 issue of preferred stock was authorized. This and the initial $100,000 issue of common stock represented the total original investment in *The Star*. Actually only $191,000 in cash was represented, and from this small seed grew the present $25,000,000 enterprise.

Senator Cox again took the lead in the financing and in selecting the persons to be invited to buy preference stock. Atkinson protested that Timothy Eaton's name was not on the list. Cox brusquely retorted that since the paper was not yet paying dividends, though making a profit of about $14,000 a year, he did not think Eaton would be interested. Atkinson appealed to the shareholders, with a request that 40 per cent of the new issue be allotted to him, and this was done. He then called upon Eaton.

"We are having no trouble selling the stock," he said, "but I felt you should be given the opportunity of saying whether or not you want some."

"How much is Cox taking?" Mr. Eaton asked.

"Twenty thousand dollars."

"How much are you taking?"

"I have arranged with the bank to borrow $20,000."

Silently Mr. Eaton made out a cheque and handed it to Mr. Atkinson. It was for $20,000. This stock was held in trust for Eaton by Mr. Atkinson.

By the end of 1904 Atkinson had earned one hundred shares of common stock as salary. But only 110 shares had been left in the treasury when the paper was bought in 1899 and Little had been sold twenty of those. The shareholders decided to pay Atkinson the last ten shares in the treasury and ten shares from the 140 that had been put in the surplus account in 1899. They decided at the same time to divide the other 130 shares in surplus among themselves "in lieu of interest upon subscriptions" the minutes recorded. As purchaser of Magann's and Christie's interests Mr. Atkinson claimed 17 shares. He was given another nine shares on account of the 100 shares he had earned as salary. This brought his total ownership to 226 shares. Cox, Massey, Mulock, and Eaton were each given 17 shares, though Mulock's pledge to invest $10,000 had not been honoured in full. Lesser shareholders were given lesser amounts. A year later *The Star* paid its first dividend; six per cent per annum on both common and preferred stock.

The morning of April 8, 1904, J. E. Atkinson walked briskly into his office, skipped a couple of gay little steps, and explained brightly to his secretary, Charles E. Fortier: "I have a son." Named Joseph Story Atkinson, the son is now president and publisher of *The Star*.

The Star moved its printing plant into its new building described as "the largest and best equipped newspaper plant in Canada" on April 21, 1905. To demonstrate what the new plant and presses were capable of, it published on June 24 the most lavish industrial supplement Toronto had ever seen—forty-eight pages gloriously illuminated with advertisements singing the praises of Toronto, Ontario, and Canada. That one issue earned half the profits for the year.

Business attended to, *The Star* then turned to celebration with another mammoth edition about itself. Employees and former employees reminisced about the tribulations of earlier years, while the readers were instructed in the methods of modern newspapers. A group photograph of the editorial staff shows an amazing collection of youth. At thirty-nine Mr. Atkinson was one of the oldest. Most of them were under thirty. Every editor and executive on the newspaper had been appointed to a senior position while still in his twenties.

Once when Mr. Atkinson was asked how he was able to take a newspaper that was headed for the graveyard and turn it so quickly into a success he responded: "I was young." On other occasions he explained that only a young publisher with a young staff would have had the buoyancy of spirit to withstand the discouragements, the anxieties, and the hard work of building up a newspaper in the face of such strong opposition. To appeal to young people (who are more numerous than old people) a newspaper must be edited by young people, he used to say, and it is doubtful if any newspaper has ever given more rapid promotion to more young men than *The Star*—or demoted them more rapidly when they slowed down.

After moving into its new building the editorial staff was quickly increased in size until *The Star* had more reporters than any other two Toronto papers combined. It had full-time salaried staff correspondents at Ottawa, Montreal, Quebec, Halifax, Winnipeg, and London, England. It had fifty-four correspondents on space rates scattered about Canada and the world. In one typical issue of 1905 it had special stories from its own correspondents in London, Paris, Berlin, Lahore, Glasgow, Rome, and Khartoum, as well as from many centres in Canada.

Among the more notable acquisitions was John Lewis, an able editorial writer. When, to Atkinson's dismay, Clark left in 1906 to become editor of *Saturday Night*, a position he held for two years before returning to the *Star*, Lewis succeeded him as editor. He remained such, in name at least, until he left in 1919 to become editor of the *Globe*, and then head of the Liberal party's information service. A few years later he was appointed to the Senate. Though Laurier and King liked Lewis better than Clark, Atkinson used to complain of what he called "his basswood editorials" which had too little substance. Once he chuckled to George Maitland, who in time also became editor of *The Star*, that "Lewis thinks he is editor but I pay Clark more."

Maitland came to *The Star* in 1906 as a result of an odd "horse-trade" between Atkinson and the publisher of the Stratford *Herald*. He had been city editor of the *Herald* for five years and was looking for wider opportunities, but his employer had nobody to take his place if he left. Atkinson obligingly sent a reporter from *The Star*. Maitland turned out to be one of those useful persons who can do almost anything around a newspaper, and in the next few years he did. He was city editor, news editor, telegraph editor, editorial writer, feature writer, private investigator—in fact, whenever anybody was needed to fill in on a job they "let George do it" in what seemed an endless game of musical chairs. He was city editor at least three times.

There was as yet no Canadian news agency, but *The Star* had contracts with the Associated Press for news from the United States, the Canadian Associated Press (controlled by its competitor, the *Telegram*) for British news, Canadian Pacific Telegraphs, which distributed Canadian news bulletins mostly from the West, the Great Northwestern Telegraph Company's news service, and the privately owned Easson News Service. No other newspaper in Canada and few anywhere could equal its coverage of world events. *The Star* had come a long way in five years.

With a new plant and new equipment Mr. Atkinson determined to publish the best printed newspaper in Canada. With that in mind he invited Arthur Donaldson, one of the founding printers of *The Star*, to return as an expert on type and advertising layouts. Donaldson was twenty when *The Star* was established. He left when the paper temporarily suspended publication the first summer, but instead of returning to his trade he became first a reporter then went into the advertising and business end of journalism. When invited to return to *The Star* in 1906 he was manager of the Galt *Reporter*. He remained with *The Star* until his death in 1941. Atkinson also brought A. C. F. West from the Linotype Corporation to maintain his battery of new machines. He retired as mechanical superintendent in 1946.

About the same time *The Star* had begun using half-tone illustrations on a large scale. In the six years after 1900 the method of illustrating newspapers had undergone a revolution, with the photo-engraved halftone replacing the hand-made woodcut. *The Star* had used halftones as early as 1902, but was slower than some newspapers in adopting the new process because Mr. Atkinson disliked the smudginess of the early engravings. However, with the new presses giving a much cleaner reproduction he became an enthusiastic "picture-man," though his taste was always conservative. Pictures in *The Star* had to be attractive as well as news-worthy. Even as late as 1940 he would not allow *Star* cameramen to use flashlight in taking pictures because he believed it gave too harsh a reproduction.

The big new presses enabled *The Star* to introduce a four-page Saturday comic section on May 5, 1906. The *Sunday World*, founded in 1891, had the rights to the more popular comics such as "Buster Brown" and "Happy Hooligan," but *The Star* was able to secure "Little Nemo in Slumberland," "The Naps of Polly Sleepyhead" and "Uncle Remus" as full-page features, and several smaller ones. The first two daily comic strips, introduced in the latter part of 1906, were entitled "Show Me" and "Isn't it Just Like a Woman." The characters in the latter were ducks.

In the next few weeks *The Star* acquired the rights to just about every comic not appearing in the *Sunday World*. It could not use them all, but comics were just becoming popular and Mr. Atkinson seems to have anticipated how useful they could be. By contracting for them all he not only secured first choice for *The Star* but made it necessary for his competitors to come to him for their comics and be satisfied with the discards.

Shortly after moving into its new building *The Star* surpassed the *Telegram* in circulation, with a daily sale of 37,077 copies. The *Telegram*'s circulation was 31,884. The shareholders were so overjoyed they gave Mr. Atkinson his first raise in pay, to $6,000 a year. For another twenty-seven years, however, the *Telegram* still had the larger circulation within the city of Toronto.

Other publishers were baffled by the friendship between John Ross Robertson of the *Telegram* and Joseph E. Atkinson. By all the rules they should have been at each others throats, yet John Ross took an almost paternal interest in the success of the younger man. Meeting him on the street he would ask, "Well, Atkinson, did you make any money last month?" At first the answer was always "No," to which John Ross would jokingly respond, "Better give it up; I'll give you a job." When at long last the answer was "Yes, we had a little over last month," Robertson tipped his high silk topper in benign congratulations and continued his august ambulation.

M. E. Nichols, in his *(CP): Story of the Canadian Press*, commented in some puzzlement on the "unnatural" alliance of the two men in furthering the interests of Toronto newspapers against what he considered to be those of the rest of Canada, in other words against Nichols' own scheme to make the Toronto papers pay most of the cost of a national news service. "In business affairs of common interest to the Toronto newspaper field Joe could lead John Ross into almost any alley he chose," Nichols wrote.

Gadsby, who wrote a delightful profile of John Ross Robertson for *The Star*, seems to have believed the *Telegram*'s publisher was so serenely confident he was right, and that right would prevail in the end, that he could never take *The Star* seriously. A more likely explanation is that each man respected and admired the other. Each paid the other the compliment of believing he was an honourable man who sincerely held the principles he supported in his newspaper. These principles were poles apart, representing the extremes of conservatism and liberalism, of imperialism and nationalism, but being intelligent men they understood that intelligent men can disagree on matters of fundamental importance.

Perhaps they did not really consider themselves competitors, but neighbours cultivating different fields. A hint of this was given by Mr. Atkinson to the Toronto Advertising Club in 1914 when he said: "No one newspaper can appeal to or speak for the entire community. People by their nature tend to take different views . . . Those who are conservative by temperament line up on the conservative side. On the other side are those who are more sanguine or less cautious by nature." At any rate, *The Star* always treated Robertson with respect, and it was only after lesser minds succeeded Robertson on his death that the *Telegram* began attacking *The Star* and its publisher with such remarkable venom.

From its beginning *The Star* had sponsored funds of various sorts for the relief of sufferers from domestic disaster. Early in 1905 it opened a fund for the relief of sufferers from the great famine in northern Japan, the first of many such funds to aid people in foreign countries. Japan was at the time engaged in a war against Russia, and had the sympathy of most Canadians. In acknowledgment of this aid, the government of Japan presented Mr. Atkinson with three gold *saki* cups and a scroll in Japanese, a translation of which reads: "Count T. Daikiu, president of the Imperial Bureau of Decoration, has the pleasure of presenting to Mr. J. E. Atkinson, representative of the contributors through *The Toronto Daily Star* in the city of Toronto, Canada, one set of gold cups, in appreciation of their contribution of $11,410 to the relief fund for the sufferers of that great famine which took place in 1905 in the north-eastern three prefectures of Japan." And in the following year *The Star* sponsored a fund for the relief of victims from the San Francisco earthquake.

In 1905, *The Star* waged one of its more sensational and successful crusades, a campaign to smash a combine between plumbing contractors and crooked union bosses that had bilked home-builders out of hundreds of thousands of dollars. *Star* reporters had unearthed the combine, and they followed through with a complete exposé. *The Star* was the only newspaper that published a full report of the trials, which resulted in fines of $10,000. The other newspapers knuckled under—when threatened with an advertising boycott by manufacturers.

It was just after this that J. S. Willison, who had recently become publisher of the *News*, had the bad judgment to suggest the Toronto afternoon newspapers should combine to raise advertising rates and the price per copy. "I have given the subject some thought since our conversation but have not been able to decide to enter the arrangement suggested," Mr. Atkinson wrote Willison. "We prefer to hold ourselves free so we can deal without embarrassment with any situation that may arise."

The fact is, *The Star* was doing well playing the lone wolf. The *News* had been dumped by the Riordans and the new owners were attempting to revive it as a high-tariff paper with copious infusions of Flavelle money, while the *World* had begun offering its support (or its silence) to the highest bidder, a practice that contributed in no small measure to its downfall. The *Telegram* had been passed and the *Globe* with a circulation of 50,000, was being overtaken. Why strengthen one's rivals by helping them raise rates?

Until the exposure of the plumbing combine *The Star* had shown no awareness of the pernicious effects of combines. Old-fashioned laissez-faire liberals did not view them with alarm. It seemed to them that if we are to have free enterprise, enterprise must be left free to combine. Thus *The Star* watched with detachment the trust-busting activities of President Theodore Roosevelt of the United States. However, after exposure of the plumbing combine *The Star* began pressing for anti-combines legislation with teeth in it, and by 1909 Atkinson was writing sharp letters on the subject to Prime Minister Laurier. In 1910 Mackenzie King, as Minister of Labour, introduced an anti-combines bill. One result was the first cartoon in *The Star* featuring King. In a letter to Stewart Lyon, editor of the *Globe* on February 21, 1911, King refers to the influence of *The Star*'s campaign in having anti-combines legislation passed.

At the last director's meeting of 1906 Mr. Atkinson again asked for a ruling in writing that he was entitled to an option on 30 per cent of the common stock after he had served seven years. Since there was no unallotted or treasury stock left, what he was actually asking was that the shareholders acknowledge his claim that he had first chance at buying their stock, if and when they chose to sell. The directors decided he should have that option, but the following month the shareholders gave him only until December 31, 1907, to exercise it. Except for this one motion he never succeeded in having the shareholders acknowledge he was in a preferred position with respect to purchase of stock. Actually, the agreement—or lack of agreement—turned out to be of no great importance, for in practice they all gave him first opportunity to buy.

In January, 1907, he heard that Lyman Jones was being pressed by his banker for cash, so he called on the industrialist with a copy of the latest financial statement, which showed *The Star* had made a net profit of $3,735.63 in November.

"What are you showing me this for?" Jones asked.

"I would like to buy your fifty-eight shares of ordinary stock, and I am showing you the financial statement in order that we may arrive at a fair price," Atkinson replied.

"You have only succeeded in convincing me I shouldn't sell," Jones replied. However, his financial position continued to worsen and one day he called the publisher. "Do you still want that stock?" he asked.

"I certainly do," Atkinson replied.

"How much will you pay for it?"

"It's worth between $90 and $100 a share," Atkinson cautiously replied.

"You can have it," said Jones. The company had begun paying dividends but the ordinary shares were still considered somewhat speculative. Jones had paid only $69.50 for his shares in 1899 and had not expected to get his money back. Moreover, he was becoming somewhat disenchanted with Laurier, particularly with his low-tariff policy. Mr. Atkinson was unable to exercise his option to buy within the time limit set by the shareholders, and it was not until 1909, when he was able to secure twenty-seven shares of Joseph Kilgour's common stock (and also the last seventy shares of preference stock in the treasury) that he had acquired the 30 per cent of the common stock he claimed to be his right.

In 1907 John R. Bone was appointed managing editor at the age of twenty-nine. Mr. Atkinson had been gradually delegating more and more authority to him, and he had in fact been managing editor without the title. Atkinson was reluctant to promote Bone over Campbell, his senior in age and experience and in the opinion of many the abler newsman of the two, but Campbell was temperamentally unsuited for executive responsibility; excessive drinking was already becoming a problem with him. J. H. Cranston, who came to *The Star* in 1904 as Mr. Atkinson's secretary and rose to be editor of the *Star Weekly*, commented in his book, *Ink on My Fingers*, on the amount of liquor that flowed, at that time, in *The Star*'s city room.

So Bone was eased gradually into the job. He was sent to various meetings of editors and publishers as Mr. Atkinson's representative, was introduced by the chairman as "the managing editor of *The Star*," and with hardly anybody recognizing quite how it came about, he was soon being deferred to by all, including Campbell, as the man next to "the Chief." It would be hard to find two men differing more in temperament than the phlegmatic Bone and the mercurial Campbell. Put them together and they were a perfect team. "Mr. Bone possesses the mathematical mind which calculates every move to a nicety and weighs every argument with logical exactness," said a writer in *Saturday Night* in 1912. In 1913 a writer in the *Canadian Courier* said of him, "he won his honors by inate ability coupled with tremendous tenacity. If one desired to indicate an outstanding characteristic . . . it would probably be silence. There are no dissipated fireworks along the pathway he has trod."

Bone became recognized as one of the great figures of Canadian journalism, almost unknown to the public, but a power in the inner councils of press associations and publishers' organizations. Some have succumbed to the temptation to denigrate Bone as a mere reflection of Atkinson's prestige, but it is a mistake to do so. Mr. Atkinson chose Bone as his personal representative because he recognized in him a powerful personality, an incisive mind, and a coldly objective brain.

By the time the depression of 1907 struck, the two famous charities supported by *The Star* and its readers, the Fresh Air Fund and the Santa Claus Fund, were soundly based and played an important part in mitigating the hardships of distressed families. *The Star* Fresh Air Fund was actually a revival of a fund that had been established in 1888 with the support of all Toronto newspapers to provide picnics, excursions, and vacations at camps for children of the poor. The man responsible for it was John J. Kelso, a reporter on the *World*, who had founded the Toronto Humane Society in 1887.

When Mr. Atkinson came to the *World* he formed a friendship with Kelso that endured for several years. They went to the *Globe* at about the same time, and when Kelso organized and carried through the 1889 campaign Mr. Atkinson helped him write the publicity. Before long half a dozen rival fresh air funds sprang up, each clamouring for the charitable dollar with tag days and public appeals. The situation became so chaotic the newspapers dropped their fund and ignored the others.

This had been the situation for several years before the summer of 1901 came in with one of the worst heat waves on record. On June 28, 1901, *The Star* announced it was appealing to the public for donations in support of the work of the Toronto Children's Fresh Air Fund, the Fresh Air Fund for the Aged and Infirm, and the Methodist Deaconess' Fresh Air Fund. Daily write-ups on the work these funds were doing were published on page one, with a note at the end of each stating "*The Star* will willingly receive donations." Since the donors rarely indicated to which fund they wanted their donations to go, the writers dropped into the habit of merely asking for contributions to *The Star*'s fresh air work.

The following year no mention was made of the other organizations, readers being advised that if they sent their donations to *The Star* Fresh Air Fund the money would be distributed among several worth-while

The Saturday Night Building where *The Star* was printed from 1895 to 1905

LEFT: Mackenzie King while studying in London and writing for *The Star*

BELOW: crowd in front of *Star* editorial office at Adelaide and Yonge streets celebrating the capture of Pretoria from the Boers on June 5, 1900

RIGHT: the first Star Building, 18–20 King Street West, 1905–1929

THE STAR
THE STAR BUILDING
DAILY STAR
THE TORONTO
DAILY STAR

LOOK - - - in The Star For a House.

THE TORONTO DAILY STAR

READ - - - The Star's Want Pages.

TENTH YEAR. LAST EDITION TORONTO, SATURDAY, SEPTEMBER 7, 1901 WEATHER—SUNDAY—MUCH COOLER ONE CENT

PRESIDENT McKINLEY SHOT

President of the United States Seriously Wounded While Holding a Reception in the Temple of Music at the Pan-American Exhibition---The Would-Be Assassin Was Shaking Hands When He Placed a Revolver Against President's Body and Fired.

PHYSICIANS BELIEVE THAT THE WOUNDED STATESMAN WILL SURVIVE THE ATTACK

Buffalo, Sept. 7.—The President's physicians issued the following bulletin at 6 a.m.:

The President has passed a good night. Temperature 102, pulse 110, respiration 24. (Signed)

F. M. Rixey,
Roswell Park,
George Cortelyou, Secretary to the President.

Buffalo, N.Y., Sept. 7.—The President's physicians issued the following bulletin at 9 a.m.:

The President passed a fairly comfortable night, and no serious symptoms have developed. Pulse, 146; temperature, 102; respiration, 24. (Signed) P. M. Rixey, Matthew D. Mann, Roswell Parke, Herman Mynter, Eugene Wasblin. (Countersigned) George B. Cortelyou, secretary to the President.

Buffalo, Sept. 7.—The stories of the shooting of the President are conflicting. One report says that the Temple of Music was crowded at the time—not more than forty people or so were present. A double rank of marines made an aisle up which the public was to advance to meet the President. Guards and detectives were close by.

The assassin advanced, his hand covered with a handkerchief. Suspicions arose in the minds of several detectives; they moved forward to seize the man and he anticipated them. Shaking hands with the President with one hand, the man shot him with the other. Lightning quick action followed. Guards, marines, and onlookers flung themselves on the wretched man. The negro behind him was one of the first to grasp him, and in a twinkling the scene was like a football match, the assassin below a pile of men. The ever-present dignity of the President abode with him, and in strong contrast with the precipitate rush of his assailant he walked to a bench and sat down. The marines took the situation in hand. They cleared the building. They prepared to get the prisoner away. Without, the crowd, wild with rage, wandered aimlessly and dumbly around, the idea of finding the assassin not yet conceived. A hack stood near a door of the Temple of Music. At a word the marines dashed at the crowd and bore it back, although a moment before it had been throwing the Exposition police about at will. Several men rushed the prisoner into the hack.

TWO SHOTS FIRED.

Another report says that as the man extended his hand to the President, apparently with the intention of shaking hands with him, he fired a shot, which entered the President's right breast, lodging against the breastbone. Another shot was fired immediately, and it entered the President's abdomen.

The assailant was immediately arrested and was thrown to the ground, and quick as a flash twenty men were upon him. When rescued he was covered with blood from a gash in his face. Cries of lynching were heard in every direction, but the police managed to get the prisoner out of the grounds and locked him up in a station house, some distance from the grounds. Later he was removed to police headquarters. Detective Geary was near the prisoner, and the President fell into his arms.

"Am I shot?" asked the President.

The officer opened the President's vest, and seeing blood, replied: "Yes, I am afraid you are, Mr. President."

The President was immediately taken to the Emergency Hospital. The bullet of the first shot caused simply a superficial wound. It was removed within five minutes after the doctors saw the President.

SECOND BULLET NOT FOUND.

The second bullet was not found. An operation was performed at the Emergency Hospital on the Exposition grounds. The President's stomach was opened, but the bullet was not found. Drainage tubes were inserted, the incision was sewed up, and the President was removed to the home of Mr. John G. Milburn. The doctors stated after the operation that they were hopeful, and that the wound was not necessarily fatal.

The prisoner was detained in a side room in the Temple of Music while the President was removed to the hospital. Then, under an escort of police, with a guard of soldiers to fight back the enraged throng in the Esplanade, he was placed in a carriage and driven at a gallop down Delaware avenue, past the home where the invalid wife of the President was waiting for her husband, to police headquarters, where he was locked up.

TRIED TO LYNCH HIM.

Another report says that the thousands who waited about the Temple of Music surged forward when the prisoner appeared, tearing down the barriers of ropes, fighting with the officers and the soldiers, and shouting: "Lynch him, lynch him! Hang him! Kill him!" Some clutched at the horses, others at the wheels of the carriage. The police and soldiers fought back the crowd, and the carriage galloped away. The escape of the would-be assassin from the hands of the infuriated people was in accord with the wishes of the President.

As the President sank back in the arms of Detective Geary and President Milburn, after the shooting, he gasped the name of his secretary, Cortelyou. The secretary bent over him.

"Be careful about my wife," gasped the President. "Do not tell her." Then writhing in the agony of his wounds, the President turned and saw his attempted murderer helpless on the floor, beneath the blows of soldiers and detectives. He raised his right hand, stained with the blood of his wound, and, drawing down the head of his secretary, he whispered, "Let no one hurt him."

Then he sank back, deathly white, but clearly conscious, while they dragged his assailant from his sight.

GREETED THE ANARCHIST.

It was shortly after 4 p.m. when one of the throng which surrounded the Presidential party, a medium-sized man of ordinary appearance, and plainly dressed in black, approached as if to greet the President. Both Secretary Cortelyou and President Milburn noticed that one of the man's hands was swathed in a bandage of handkerchief. He worked his way amid the stream of people up to the edge of the dais until he was within two feet of the President.

President McKinley smiled, bowed, and extended his hand, when suddenly the sharp crack of a revolver rang out, followed by an instant of almost complete silence.

The President stood stock still, a look of hesitancy, almost of bewilderment, on his face. Then he retreated a step, while a pallor began to steal over his features.

Three men at once sprang towards the would-be assassin. Two of them were United States Secret Service men who were on the lookout, and whose duty it was to guard against just such a calamity. The third was a bystander, a negro. The President's assassin was borne to the ground, his weapon was wrested from his grasp, and strong hands pinioned his arms. The crowd that a moment before had stood in bewilderment surged forward, regardless of consequences. Men shouted and fought, women screamed, and children cried. Some of those nearest the doors fled from the edifice in fear of a stampede, while hundreds of others from outside struggled blindly forward in the effort to penetrate the building.

After the first shock of the assassin's shots the President retreated a step, then as the detective leaped upon his assailant he turned, walked steadily to a chair, and seated himself, at the same time removing his hat and bowing his head in his hands.

CRIES FOR "THE ROPE."

As the police were about to emerge from the building with their prisoner, "Lynch him!" cried a hundred voices, and a start was made for one of the entrances of the Temple. Soldiers and police beat back the crowd. Guards and people were wrangling, shouting, and fighting. In this confusion, Nieman, still bleeding, his clothes torn, and scarcely able to walk, was led out by Capt. James F. Vallaly, chief of the Exposition detectives, Commandant Robinson, and a squad of secret service men. Nieman was thrown into a carriage and three detectives jumped in with him. Capt. Vallaly jumped on the driver's seat and lashed the horses into a gallop.

The crowd burst into a roar of rage. "Murderer! Assassin! Lynch, hang him!" they yelled. Men sprang at the horses and clutched at the whirling wheels of the carriage. Nieman huddled back in the corner, concealed between two detectives. "The rope! the rope!" yelled the crowd, and they started forward all in one grand fight, the soldiers to save and the citizens to take a murderer's life.

Soldiers fought a way clear at the heads of the horses, and, pursued by the infuriated thousands, the carriage whirled across the Esplanade, the horses at full gallop, across the Triumphal Causeway, and vanished through the Lincoln Parkway gate, galloping down Delaware avenue until Police Headquarters was reached.

Buffalo, N.Y., Sept. 7.—President McKinley maintains a good measure of his strength, and those who watch at his bedside hold higher hope for his ultimate recovery. The shock from the wounds inflicted upon him by Leon F. Czolgosz seems to be less than was anticipated, and that is regarded as highly favorable to him. It is admitted that the crisis in his condition has not yet come, and that there is the gravest danger until it has been safely passed. Several bulletins came from the chamber of the wounded President during the night and early hours of the morning, and they all indicated a spirit of hopefulness. The President rested well, there were no alarming conditions of temperature or pulse, and the spirits of the sufferer were strong and cheery. The feeling of hope was quite general about the Milburn residence this morning, in sharp contrast to the hopelessness and regret that prevailed last night. Mrs. McKinley bears up bravely in her sorrow, and the physicians in attendance feel but little concern on her account. At the request of the President, whose first thoughts were of her, she was told that he was not seriously wounded, and when she saw him he had rallied from the operation and was suffering but little pain. She was reassured by their meeting, and was content to leave his side during the night and rest herself. The surgeons who operated on the President are in constant attendance with a corps of the most skilled nurses obtainable, and the sufferer is the recipient of every care which their skill and science suggests. They have not publicly discussed the case other than to issue brief bulletins from time to time, but it is understood that they believe the President will recover unless complications not now anticipated come to sap his strength and vitality.

With a common impulse to spare the sufferer the annoyance that noise would inflict, the public avoids the neighborhood where the Milburn residence is located. Early in the night a small crowd gathered near the house eager for news of the President, but the police had no trouble in keeping the people at proper distance.

SOLDIERS ON GUARD.

Early this morning a detachment of the Fourteenth United States Infantry was ordered to the house from Fort Porter. A picket line was established in front of the house, but the sentries found no work to do. Ropes were stretched across Delaware avenue in order to keep teams off that thoroughfare. A party of reporters kept a lonely vigil during the night, but beside them there were not a dozen persons in the neighborhood at 7.30 o'clock this morning. The Milburn residence is a large two and one-half storey brick building, and it stands on the west side of Delaware avenue two doors from the corner of West Ferry street. Graceful ivy climbs over the front of it, and on the large lawn which surrounds it are a number of pretty shade trees. The President lies in the rear room on the second floor. The room was chosen because it insured the greatest quiet. Telegraph wires have been led to the stable in the rear of the Milburn residence and offices opened there. The bulletins telling of the condition of the President are sent there by Dr. Rixey, and at once transmitted to the world.

SEARCH FOR CONSPIRATORS.

Police All Over the United States Trying to Find the Other Plotters.

Buffalo, Sept. 7.—Leon F. Czolgosz, the man who shot the President, slept in comfort after his crime. He was locked up at No. 1 police station, and after he had been interviewed by the officers of the law, a watch of two men was placed on him. He went to his bunk early and was soon asleep. He seemed without regret and undisturbed by the prospect of punishment for his crime. The police machinery of the entire country has been set in motion to expose the plot against the life of the President, if plot there was. The detectives of this city and every other department in the country have joined hands with the great secret system of the Federal Government, and if ingenuity, skill, and energy count, the secrets of the crime will be ferreted out. Czolgosz insists that he alone planned the crime which may rob the United States of its ruler, but that statement is not accepted as true. There is a belief that he was aided by others in a deliberate plot, and that confederates accompanied him to Buffalo and assisted in its execution. The police and secret agents are working privately, and if they have made any progress toward the establishment of the plot theory they have not divulged the nature of it. They do insist that the prisoner locked up at police station No. 1 is not insane, and that his act was not simply the crime of a lunatic with homicidal tendency. Czolgosz is kept in absolute seclusion by the police, and none save the officers have seen him.

BUFFALO QUIET TO-DAY.

The City Filled With Sorrow—Hundreds of Telegrams of Sympathy.

Buffalo, Sept. 7.—The attack upon the President has created a profound sensation, and the people of Buffalo regard it with a feeling of poignant grief. It was at their invitation that the President and his party came to Buffalo, and they have a sense of personal responsibility for his safety. President Milburn and the officers of the Exposition directorate feel the deepest regret. While they had no knowledge or suggestion that there would be an attempt on the life of Mr. McKinley, the subject was one of the matters considered in arranging for the visit. They discussed the matter with the police of Buffalo, and at their request several local officers were detailed to assist in guarding the person of the President. These men were on duty when the attack was made.

Hundreds of telegrams of regret continue to pour in from all over the world. They come from people in all walks of life, and are deeply sympathetic in tenor. All of them express fervent hope for the recovery of the President. The relatives of the President have hurried here, and with them have come a large number of men in public life.

Buffalo is very quiet and there is not the slightest sign of disorder. There was talk of lynching last night, and whenever a crowd assembled there were bitter denunciations of the assailant's work. The police arrested a few men for inciting riot, but let them go soon after.

THE PRISONER.

His Real Name Said to Be Leon Czolgosz—Was an Anarchist.

Buffalo, Sept. 7.—The man who did the shooting when seized by the detectives offered no resistance, and at first refused to give any information about himself. Later he said his name was Fred. Nieman, that he was 28 years old, that he came to Buffalo last Saturday, and had been occupying room No. 8 at 1,026 Broadway. He gave his occupation as a blacksmith, and said he was born in Detroit.

"Why did you shoot him?" he was asked, but he made no answer.

"Are you an Anarchist?" was the next question.

"Yes," he replied.

"Why did you shoot him?" he was asked again.

"I only done my duty," he replied.

Later the police learned that the real name of the would-be assassin is Leon Czolgosz. He was born in Detroit, and came here from Cleveland.

THE OFFICIAL REPORT.

Surgeons Describe the Wounds—One of the Bullets Was Not Found.

Buffalo, Sept. 7.—The following bulletin was given out at the Milburn home at nine o'clock last night: "The President was shot about 4 o'clock. One bullet struck him on the upper portion of the breastbone and did not penetrate. The second bullet penetrated five inches below the left nipple, and one and one-half inches to the left of the median line. The abdomen was penetrated. Through the line of the bullet wound it was found that the bullet had penetrated the stomach. The opening in the front wall of the stomach was carefully closed with sutures, after which a search was made for the hole in the back wall of the stomach. This was found and also closed in the same way. The further course of the bullet could not be discovered, although careful search was made. The abdominal wound was closed without drainage. No injury to the intestines or other abdominal organs was discovered. The patient stood the operation well. Pulse of good quality, rate of 130. His condition at the conclusion of the operation was gratifying. The result cannot be foretold. The condition at present justifies hope of recovery.

"(Signed) P. M. Rixey, M. D. Mann, E. Wasbin, Roswell Park, Herman Mynter; George B. Cortelyou, Secretary to the President."

BUFFALO IN A TURMOIL.

Pan-American Deserted by the Crowds Who Thronged Down Town Streets.

Buffalo, Sept. 7.—The scene of excitement and anxiety displayed on Buffalo's streets last night never had a parallel in the city's history. The Pan-American was abandoned, and the entire population, including the many thousands of visitors, congregated down town blockading the streets while they awaited the frequent reports of the condition of the stricken head of the nation.

The President was first reported dead, but it was soon made known that he still lived, after receiving the two bullets from the revolver of the would-be assassin, and each succeeding announcement was more encouraging, until about 9 o'clock it was given out

(Continued on Page Five.)

THE WEATHER.

TO-DAY—Shifting winds to north-west and north. The breeze will freshen. Local thunderstorms this afternoon and to-night cooler.

SUNDAY—Much cooler.

SEPTEMBER 6TH, 1901.

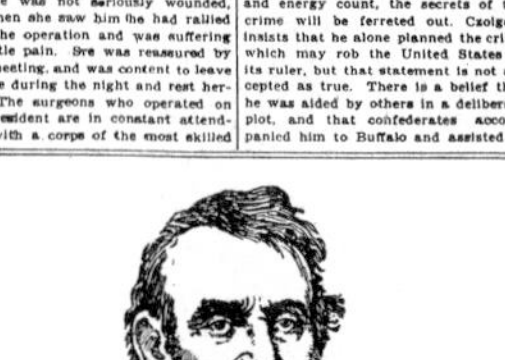
MRS. McKINLEY.

President McKinley at His Desk. The Latest Photograph.

Abraham Lincoln, Shot by Wilkes Booth on April 14, 1865.

A fine-looking page of type, showing the use of line-engravings in those days. The McKinley assassination provided Mr. Atkinson with his first opportunity to give massive coverage to a local story

THE TORONTO DAILY STAR

13TH YEAR — TORONTO, SATURDAY, APRIL 22 1905—TWENTY-FOUR PAGES — Last Edition — ONE CENT

NEW YORK HAS CROWDS AND TORONTO THE GOODS

Member of The Star Staff Finds That Stocks in the Stores in This City are Not Surpassed by Those in the American Metropolis.

VISIT TO A CANADIAN GIRL AND HER FRIENDS

CHARMING ROOMS.

CROWDS ARE FASCINATING.

FIVE WOMEN IN A FLAT.

THE SOCIAL LIFE.

BIG INDUSTRY TO SPEND $750,000

Mr. H. J. Haney Proposes to Locate His Building Supply Shops in Toronto.

HAS LEFT KAMRANH.

Russian Admiral Believes Rojestvensky Has Gone.

WHAT MOVING MEANS

ANOTHER NEW CHURCH IN TORONTO

The Church of the Christian Association in Ontario street, near Carlton, which will be ready for occupation in a few weeks.

BOURASSA MAY BE TROUBLESOME

Will Introduce a Radical Amendment Which Will Bother Quebec Liberals—McCarthy Also Has Amendment.

AN AMENDMENT.

McCARTHY'S COURSE.

WANTS THE GLORY.

CZAR ORDERS FLEET TO LEAVE FRENCH WATERS

Rojestvensky's Squadron Receives Explicit Instructions to Observe Neutrality of France—Japan's Protest at Last Produces Desired Result.

DID ENTER HARBOR.

Useless for Russia to Deny Fleet Used Kamranh Bay.

STOPPED THE DIANA.

KAMIMURA TO CALL.

BUSINESS WINS OVER SENTIMENT

Trollers Will Not Prohibit Saw Mill on Gibson Ave Plain Talk by Mayor.

LORD'S DAY LEGISLATION.

Burke—Ferguson

STREET RAILWAY NOT SO DEFIANT

They Will Try to Find Some Means of Handling Traffic at Ends of Routes.

A FARMER KILLED.

Prominent Man in South Gower Dies From a Fall.

VOTED A BONUS.

WANTED AT INGERSOL.

BURGLARS STOLE $200 AT THEATER

Battered Open the Safe of the Temperance Street Playhouse This Morning.

DIDN'T MARCH OUT.

FIRE IN SPADINA AVENUE.

JAMES BARRY DEAD.

THE LATEST IN EASTER CONCEITS

The face peering over the egg-shell is printed on a postal card, and the idea that of a well-known young lady in this city. The egg and photograph are has made quite a hit in American cities this year.

LYON BEATEN IN GOLF MATCH

Torontonian Did Not Show Up Very Well in a Game With Three Champions.

THE I. K. UNION.

Mrs. Hughes is President—Next Convention to be Held in Milwaukee.

LUMBER LADEN BARGE WAS HEMMED IN BY ICE FIELDS

MIGHT HAVE BEEN MURDER

Rowdies Chased by an Intoxicated Man With a Gun—Where the Police Are Needed.

C. R. HOSMER.

The well-known Montreal financier who has been in England for some time arranging for capital for the company which proposes to build several hundred elevators and two or three flour mills in the North-West.

CASE OF CONSISTENCY.

VESUVIUS IS ANGRY.

THE WEATHER.

Sunday: Fine and mild.

The first front page to be printed in the new building, 1905. An account of the move appears under the head, "What Moving Means"

ABOVE, left to right: Harry Parr, one of the founding printers and foreman of the composing room, 1892–1929; Walter Harris, who joined the printers in founding *The Star* and at the time of his death in 1934 was a director and business manager; Fred Eatherley, who helped distribute the first edition and at his death in 1931 was foreman of the mailing room; William Argue, circulation manager, 1894–1939

LEFT: editorial staff, 1905. Standing, left to right: James Simpson, R. K. Mearns, Charles Fortier, C. W. Jefferys, Charles F. Raymond, John R. Bone, J. Herbert Cranston, Thomas McGillicuddy, Arthur Roebuck. Centre row: W. A. Clark, W. A. Hewitt, Harry Gadsby, Joseph T. Clark, J. E. Atkinson, Colin C. Campbell, W. R. Plewman, H. Dean Carman. Front row: Office boy (name unknown), Lou E. Marsh, Harold Adamson, W. F. Wiggins, office boy

OVER: banners of big events in the early years of *The Star*'s history. The third one refers to the heat-wave that spurred the formation the following year of the Star Fresh Air Fund

THE TORONTO DAILY STAR

ELEVENTH YEAR — TORONTO, THURSDAY, AUGUST 13, 1903—TWELVE PAGES — Last Edition — ONE CENT

CHALLENGER TO-DAY HAS CAPTURED CANADA'S CUP

In the Decisive Race To-day Irondequoit Got the Better of the Start and Held the Lead Throughout.

THE WIND IN FAVOR OF THE AMERICAN BOAT TO-DAY

Though Light at the Start It Freshened Till It Reached 18 Miles an Hour—Another Battle of the Skippers.

	Start	1st Buoy	2nd Buoy	Finish
Irondequoit	11.15.09	12.47.50	1.42.27	2.40.20
Strathcona	11.15.35	12.49.29	1.43.39	2.41.25

Irondequoit Wins by 1 min. 5 seconds.

THE CANADA'S CUP RECORD.

Saturday, August 8—Strathcona won over 21-mile triangular course in 11-mile breeze by 22 seconds.

Monday, August 10—Strathcona won over 9-mile windward and leeward course, in light wind, by 10.05.

Tuesday. Au... 11—Irondequoit won over 2... triangular ...

vis, and the great Canadian skipper is locked up in a struggle with the best man he ever met. Here is a man he can neither bluff or cajole, catch napping, or practice tricks upon. It is an even fight, and the man who makes a mistake, or even hesitates is lost.

When both boats dropped away from the mooring at 9.30 the laziness of breeze was apparent. Both boats fo... first time since the ... opened

a long time fighting every inch of the road. Up aloft the leeches of both club topsails are a-flutter, telling eloquently of how close both skippers are keeping their boats to the wind.

To go back a little in the story, at 11.30 Jarvis made another attempt to get away from Hannan. He swung the Canadian boat about and took the wind over the port rail, but as soon as the Canuck settled away to sail there was Irondequoit perched gaily up in the weather berth.

At 12.20 Irondequoit leads by 145 yards. The buoy is 1 1-2 miles away.

At 12.27 Irondequoit is getting over the water in great shape, but, as in former races, the Canadian boat is pointing up a trifle higher and working out to windward, leaving the American boat to maintain her lead by her fleet heels.

The south-west wind is slowly bringing up a lumpy sea. Strathcona does not like the rough water, and commenced to pound early.

At 11.46 Skipper Jarvis, who had been pinching Strathcona up as high as she would stand, suddenly came about. He beat Irondequoit a few seconds in coming about, and then had clear wind.

At 12.39 Strathcona commenced to leg it along a bit, and was cutting down the lead.

To the uninitiated eye, there has been but little to see on the last stretch on the port tack. Side by side up in front of the following fleet too great white boats sailed in the sparkling sea. There was scarcely a ...ceable change in the position. Their ... shone ... white in the brilli... and from ...

second leg the defender pulled down the advantage held by the Challenger. At 2.25 the question is now is seven miles far enough for defender to cut down that lead of 1 1/2?

She is gaining surely, but oh how slowly. Double the distance and Strathcona will hold that cup.

Two miles and a half down from the second mark the defender had cut the lead down a third and still the challenger was coming back to them.

The wind freshened a trifle as the boats rushed along toward the homeward buoy. Strathcona still continued to gain inch by inch and two miles out Skipper Hannan had a reaching club sail set on Irondequoit. This staved off the Canadian rush.

At 2.35 Irondequoit leads by 300 yards. Finishing buoy one mile away.

Irondequoit finished at 2.40.20 and Strathcona finished at 2.41.25.

THE RACE BY BULLETIN

(By Our Own Reporter.)

Pumping Station at Island, Aug. 13.—9.50—Irondequoit has burst away from her moorings at Island, and goes out into lake at Eastern gap.

9.55—Strathcona now sets out for lake.

10.10—Strathcona beat her opponent at Eastern gap. Both boats sail westward well past starting point. The wind on lake is south-west quarter west and is blowing six ... an hour, there is no seas whatev...

10.45—The re...

The Crowd Reading The Star's Yacht Bulletin

The Daily Star's Yacht Race Reports Are Being Received by Wireless Telegrap[h]

First Use of Wireless in History of Canadian Journalism

T... are busy doings inside a modern ... r office when an event ... popu-

And as the boats go out and near the first buoy the crowd increases in front of the b...

station at the Esplanade, and quick... ...d by special ... messenger, or te...

THE TORONTO DAILY STAR

TWELFTH YEAR — TORONTO, WEDNESDAY, APRIL 20, 1904—TWELVE PAGES — Last Edition — ONE CENT

SWEPT BY FIERCE FLAMES | CONFLAGRATION RACES THROUGH THE WHOLESALE DISTRICT - - LOSS ABOUT $13,000,000

Toronto's Great Mercantile Establishments Wiped Out of Existence in a Fire That Lasted Eight Hours---Thousands of Persons Thrown Out of Work---Help Comes From Buffalo, Hamilton, London---Chief Thompson Injured.

Where the Flames Ate Millions in Property

Starting in Wellington Street West the Fire Raged Through to Waterfront and Along Front Street.

Toronto was scourged last night and this morning as she never was before in her existence. Urged on by a fierce gale from the north-west, a fire which in ordinary course of events would have gutted a couple of important business blocks, swept through the heart of the wholesale and light manufacturing district, and completely gutted it.

There was nothing half way about the conflagration. Almost without exception everything the fierce flames touched withered to complete ruin.

It was a fierce, rapid fire, a reproduction of the great Baltimore conflagration. The rapidity of the fire and the remorseless fierceness of the flames alarmed all who witnessed the march of the fi... fie..t. For several ho... it see...

found that the flames were raging up the elevator shaft. Fanned by the gale, the flames soon burst through the windows and began to reach across the lane to the east toward the big six-storey building of Gillespie & Ansley, also occupied by the Comfort Soap Works. Chief Thompson arrived on the scene about this time and at once set his men to work in an endeavor to save the big building.

WATER SUPPLY WEAK.

The water pressure was not up to the mark, or it failed to overcome the opposition of the gale. Then the Chief took his men and a couple of branches into the top storeys of the building. He had difficulty in getting water, and the fire got away from his control, so the Chief and his men had to retire precipitately. They found the... ...ane from the third storey cut ..., ar... ...agged the hose ... to ...

the west side of Bay street from Wellington street south was intact, but the building at the south-east corner of Bay and Front streets had been attacked by flames, which leaped from the Gutta Percha Rubber Company's warehouse across the street. The firemen turned their attention to this building in an effort to save the block through to Yonge street, but the flames spread too rapidly and they had to retreat. Meanwhile walls were falling in all directions, and hair-breadth escapes were becoming almost too common to notice. Men were taking their lives in their hands at every moment. Suddenly tongues of flame shot across the street from the Gordon, Mackay building to the Goulding building. It burst across Bay street with a roar that seemed almost akin to an explosion, and in one short half hour the whole corner was a roaring furnace. Then commenced the bitter fight down Front street, with the fire in complete possession, almost despite the heroic efforts of the firemen, until at last it was checked at the Customs House and the McMaster building.

ANOTHER BLOCK ON FIRE.

While the fire was thrusting the firemen back along Front street, a back fire had started north from the Goulding building, and soon had the entire block north to Bay and Wellington street in its merciless grip. From there, too, it spread to the Buntin-Reid and F...gour factories, and would have contin... its ... to the north d...pite ... or ...

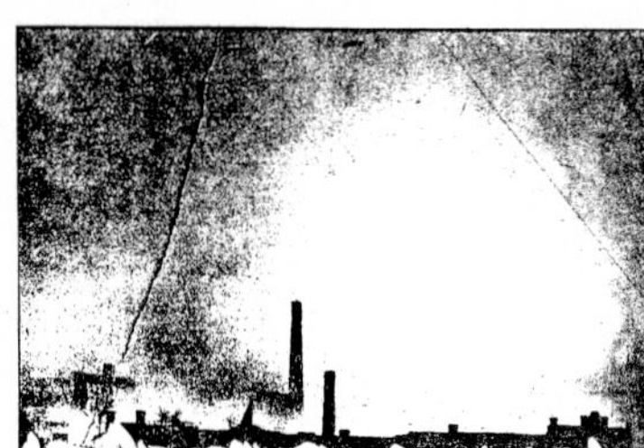

Customs Warehouse Saved, With Costly Goods

Fire Played Havoc in a Big Flour Mill—How the Blaze Raced Through Bay and Front Streets.

The last stand of the fire brigade was made at the examining warehouse of the Customs in the famous Customs issue. It was here that the flames leaped most hungrily for more prey. It was well on to midnight when the flames leaped across Bay street and seized on the big rough stone flour mill of M. McLaughlin & Co., on the corner of the Esplanade, and on their big solid brick mill to the north. In these buildings the fire fiend held high carnival, licking around the insides until not a stick—no, nor a sliver—of wood could be found with a microscope on the naked walls; or, leaping heavenward, as though in exultation. Nor were they content with such harmless exhibitions of their powers, but, leaping on the wings of the north-west gale, they commenced to devour the rear of the buildings on the south side of Front street, and the few structures blocking them in their wild dash for Yonge street.

STEAM ROSE IN CLOUDS.

But they had to reckon with those whose business it ... to fight ... These ... time ...

the brigade operated from the roof of ... engine house.

Mr. Cosgrave, it may be said in passing, has seen the block between Bay and Yonge streets on Front street destroyed by fire on two different occasions, the first time being 37 years ago and the second about three years later. As a result of his faithfulness last night it was possible for the Customs employes to carry out orders from Ottawa to remove the goods from the building, the horses, one of which is in the alleyway referred to, and express wagons being used for the purpose. One consignment of carpets taken out was alone worth $10,000.

It was nearly 3 o'clock when the fire burst out of the buildings opposite the examining warehouse. Firemen inside kept the walls well soaked and firemen outside, played on the walls and roofs, while others on top of the Customs house sprayed the raging furnace that soon took the place of the harmless-looking crockery establishment.

"We're going to save ... " declared a fi... ...r in the alleyway a ... minutes lat... ...h... the words were ... out of his ...

THE TORONTO DAILY STAR

TEN PAGES — TEN PAGES

NINTH YEAR. — LAST EDITION — TORONTO, THURSDAY, JULY 4, 1901 — WEATHER—FRIDAY—UNSETTLED — ONE CENT

AWFUL SUFFERING IN THE HEATED CITIES

Pitiful Scenes Among the Poor in New York—Measures of Relief.

HOSPITAL PHYSICIANS TOIL WITHOUT SLEEPING.

New York, July 4.—A brazen sky that spanned the earth like a fiery furnace; the agony of dumb brutes that dropped dead by the wayside; strong men suddenly stricken down and robbed of vitality and consciousness; the quick rumble of wheels and the clang of the ambulance bell, and over it all the wail of a little child—that is the way I should write the history of yesterday.

Terrible as the heat was for all, it was most terrible for the children. It is always they who suffer most. Rich people gathered up their precious darlings and fled with them to cool forest shades or wind-swept sea sands. The poor could only watch their little ones fade and wither, like blighted flowers, under the pitiless sun, and as I made my way down through the narrow, crowded streets in the tenement district of the East Side I marvelled that romancers should so long have set their most pathetic scenes amidst snow and ice and depicted cold as the climax of human suffering.

Every house, you would think, must have emptied its human hive into the street. The pavements were packed with men and women, half dressed, desperately bringing up the little strips of shade thrown by the buildings, and panting, sweltering, gasping for a breath of the fiery hot air tha... ...e, ... in ... the ...

scene is the presence, in overwhelming number, of the Little Mothers of the East Side. They are not there, as their years entitle them to be, to run with the wind or enjoy the merry romps. They are weighted down with responsibility, care burdened, keeping a watchful eye upon the little brothers and sisters they are sent to mind.

I talked with one Little Mother, nine years old, with her yellow hair in two rigid and uncompromising pig tails behind her ears and an air of worldly wisdom and maternal experience that sat quaintly upon her. In her arms she hushed the most wizened and hideous little creature one could imagine—a tiny bundle of skin and bones with little legs no bigger than a man's finger. Up and down, with that peculiar caressing, soothing, undulating movement that only comes with much experience in handling babies, she moved the little bundle of humanity, while with her foot she kept a rickety perambulator in motion.

"They are twins," she announced exultingly, "and they are six weeks old. I've got five others, all boys, to look after, and it keeps me busy. I'm the oldest."

"What is that you give them to eat?" I inquired, gazing at the peculiar-looking fluid in the bottle one of the twins was imbibing like an old toper.

"It's oatmeal and tea. We've raised all of them on it," she responded.

"Do you like to come down to the pier every day?" I asked.

"It doesn't make any difference whether I do or not," she answered, with the fatalism of the poor; "I've got to get these twins through this summer."

"W... ...'t you like some sc... ...nd cand... ...ggest... and fr...

Temporary Lull To-day, But No Sign of Permanent Cessation of Warm Wave.

COOLER NIGHT FOLLOWED BY RISING TEMPERATURE.

	Deaths.	Prostrations.
New York	200	250
Chicago	2	7
Philadelphia	19	125
Pittsburg and suburbs	97	[illegible]
Cleveland	7	22
Washington	5	15
Wilmington, Del.	3	15
Boston	[illegible]	7
Baltimore	4	32
Detroit	2	0
Milwaukee	[illegible]	12
Indianapolis	2	12
St. Louis	2	7
Cincinnati	1	17
Toledo, Ohio	3	[illegible]

New York, July 4.—It was much cooler in this city to-day than it has been for a week, and in consequence there was a much decreased death list. At 11.30 a street thermometer registered 82 degrees. At the same time yesterday this thermometer showed a temperature of 96.

Washington, July 4.—While the slight showers and wind of last evening gave the people of Washington a comfortable night's rest, the temperature was again high this morning, the thermometer recording 82 degrees at 8 o'clock, and 86 degrees at 10.30.

Philadelphia, July 4.—There has be... a drop in the tem... ...re this ... the ...

VISIT TO A FRESH AIR HOME.

Twenty-six boys to care for; twenty-six boys who are new to the country, and to whom the country is new; twenty-six boys perpetually surprised; twenty-six boys who take a toad for a frog; twenty-six boys all anxious to go fishing, to dig in the sand, and to go swimming in the lake. If you want to see lively boyhood, bursting with energy, playing all day tirelessly, and sleeping the sleep of the weary at night, go down to the Fresh Air Home at Whitby.

They came down from Toronto on Tuesday, and were just in the full tide of exuberant surprise on Wednesday afternoon when a Star representative visited at the home. The party includes 18 from the Fred Victor Mission and eight sent by the Toronto Fresh Air Fund, and none of them has ever been in the country before.

They are not being pampered, but they are being made comfortable. The house in which they live is none too large, and the ingenuity of the workers is taxed to make four rooms, with two beds in each and two others made up in the hall, accommodate 26. There is no space lost. Two boys sleep in every bed, and in some of the extra large ones three are tucked away.

But let none think they are crowded and lack air. The breezes from the lake come fresh to lungs that have only breathed the close cooked airs of the city streets and lanes. Every room has a window, and there is one at each end of the hall, through which the breezes play freely. The boys find it too cool, and last night the windows had to be closed to keep them fro... catchi... colds. Nor ... Tuesday a co... night, ... hose whe...

find new strength in the ozone of the country, which may add years and happiness to their lives.

The amount of money required to send a child to one of these homes for a fortnight is small. Three dollars will ...over the cost of board and care at ... of them ... some cases there is an ...ional c... of 25 cents ... for ...

POLICE REPLY TO CHARGES BY A.J.H.

Chief Grasett Declares There is No Favoritism for Coroner Greig.

FIGURES SUPPORT THE DEPARTMENT'S POSITION.

The charge that the police show favoritism in the matter is denied vigorously by the officials.

"If there was any motive in such a procedure then there might be something in such a charge," said Chief Grasett to-day. "The story that the police are coerced into favoring Dr. Greig is nonsense, for Dr. Greig could not revenge himself upon a policeman who did not favor him in the matter of inquests, for he has absolutely no opportunity. His position as one of the junior police surgeons brings him in contact with the officers in the eastern portion of the city, but he could not get a man placed on the sick leave list or give him any other privilege worth anything. All sick leaves have to be passed by Dr. Sprague after personal investigation of the case.

"Another thing, Dr. Greig has not had a majority of the inquests, but even if he had the explanation would have been simple. When the police come in contact with a case which looks a little suspicious, they immediately notify the nearest coroner. Now Dr. Greig is right in the heart of the most populous districts of the city. He is right on the borders of the two largest divisions in the city, the divisions where the most violent deaths occur. There isn't anything more natural than that he should be summoned to a majority of the investigations, for he is always the handiest man.

"If there is any favoritism shown it is among the doctors themselves. Nine cases out of ten the police know nothing of the death until the warrant is filed. The doctors who are called notify the coroners if they consider the matter worth investigating. If one coroner has more friends in the fraternity than another, it is surely no fault of the police officials.

"I have investigated the matter thoroughly, and find that there is not the slightest foundation for the allegations of favoritism among the police."

A statement of the number of warrants filed by the different coroners since January, 1900, is as follows:

Coroner Johnson, 43; Coroner Greig, 39; Coroner Duncan, 25; Coroner Young, 24; Coroner Cotton, 12; Coroner Powell, 8; Coroner Aikins, 6; Coroner Spencer, 4; Coroner Lynd, 4; Coroner McConnell, 3; Coroner Wilson, 2; Coroner Orr, 1.

"I think that the centralization of coroners' warrants would be a good thing," said the Chief. "If we had fewer coroners the inquests would be better conducted. Those who conduct them would have more experience.

"This talk of favoritism to coroners is all bosh," is the emphatic way in which Inspector Hall of Court Street Station deals with the matter.

ALL CITY CORPS TO COME TO TORONTO

Big Military Display When the Duke of Cornwall Arrives in the Queen City.

ARRANGEMENTS MADE BY THE DEPARTMENT.

Special to The Toronto Star.

Ottawa, July 4.—The Militia Department is making elaborate arrangements for the military celebration at Toronto on the occasion of the visit of the Duke of Cornwall and York. It has been practically settled that every city corps in Ontario will be mobilized for the occasion.

NO SIGN OF COOL WEATHER.

Toronto and Halifax Had the Highest Temperatures in Canada Yesterday.

The Observatory to-day reported: The temperature has moderated a little in Ontario and Quebec, but at present there is no indication of cool weather. The highest temperatures reported yesterday were 84 at Toronto and Halifax. Showers and thunderstorms are prevalent in the North-west Territories and Upper Lake region.

AMERICANS WON A SECOND HEAT

They and the Leanders Will Row for the Big

agencies. It was made clear *The Star* was acting only as a collecting agency, but would make certain the money was usefully spent. In 1902 only a little more than $1,000 was raised, but in 1906, when the beginning of a depression left many men out of work, donations took a sudden spurt to more than $1,700. In 1907 collections were slightly higher. Then they declined for a while, but gradually increased as the city and *The Star*'s circulation grew, to reach a new peak of $5,328 in the 1913 depression year.

At first the emphasis was on picnics and excursions, usually a day-long boat trip on the lake or a picnic in the country to which mothers and children were transported free by the old Belt Line railway. It was not until the 1930's that the emphasis shifted to camps in the country to which children could be taken for two or three weeks. Recently the emphasis has begun to shift back to picnics and day camps in city parks. Mrs. Atkinson has often been credited with suggesting to her husband that the old newspaper fresh air fund be revived, but if so one may be sure he needed slight persuading, for he was a man of generous private charity.

The Star Santa Claus Fund was established in 1906. The need was great, for the beginnings of the depression were already severely pinching many families. Early in December, Rev. Peter Bryce, a young minister working among British immigrants in York township, and later a Moderator of the United Church of Canada, appealed to Mr. Atkinson for help. Thirty families in his district were utterly destitute, and a hundred children faced a Christmas without Santa Claus. Atkinson at once assigned George Maitland to investigate the need, and when he confirmed Mr. Bryce's report *The Star* Santa Claus Fund was launched.

An experience of Mr. Atkinson's own childhood assured that needy children at Christmas should have his sympathetic attention. He had been sitting one day on a log by a pond watching other children skate when a woman whose name he never knew but whom he recalled as young, beautiful, and kind asked why he was not joining in the fun.

"I have no skates," he replied.

"Would you like skates?" she asked.

"Oh, very much," he told her.

On Christmas morning a pair of skates was left at his home. He was to remember this as the happiest Christmas of his childhood. The purpose of *The Star* Santa Claus Fund was to make sure that no child twelve years of age or under in greater Toronto was overlooked by Santa.

These two funds were dear not only to Mr. Atkinson but to all members of his family. *The Star* has always paid the full costs of administration. For many years Mr. Atkinson personally ran both funds, and the early accounts, even the reports on specific cases, are in his handwriting. When his daughter, Ruth, was old enough she helped pack Santa Claus parcels, and after her marriage she and her husband, H. C. Hindmarsh, took over the keeping of accounts, often personally investigating cases and checking final lists. If in any year not enough money was raised to meet the need of every child, *The Star* made up the difference. These funds were never used to promote *The Star* or to increase its circulation, and on several occasions other newspapers invited their readers to contribute to *The Star*'s funds. It has been said that the surest way for a young reporter to attract the Chief's attention was to write Fresh Air Fund or Santa Claus Fund appeals. Certainly almost every man who got anywhere on *The Star* during Mr. Atkinson's lifetime had to do it at one time or another.

The Star was assiduous in promoting projects for the betterment of the city. It backed the Ontario Association of Architects when they asked for the widening of Yonge Street and the extension of James Street south of Queen. "If these improvements are not made now they will never be done," it warned. The *Telegram* opposed them all. *The Star* sponsored the acquisition of the water lots along the lake frontage which today form the city's beautiful entrance from the west. "In advance of Toronto's need," the *Telegram* grumbled, and when its obstructive tactics failed it complained that "organized interests always conquer abstract righteousness when the two forces come into conflict." *The Star* led the drive in 1907 to prevent the railways from locating their eastern entrances to the city along the waterfront, and in 1909 began the campaign to have the city's water supply chlorinated and filtered. The *Telegram* opposed chlorination, but when a typhoid fever epidemic broke out in 1910 it flagellated council for not chlorinating the water.

In those days, however, *The Star* had slight influence in municipal politics, for almost half its circulation was outside the city. It tried to establish a reputation for independence by devoting its attention to principles rather than personalities. It had not yet adopted the modern Toronto newspaper practice of endorsing a slate for all elective offices, but it always supported for mayor a man in favour of public ownership of utilities. If he was a Methodist and a teetotaller so much the better, though it was not essential. Neither was it essential that he be a Liberal, but it was a decided disadvantage to be either an Orangeman or active in Conservative party affairs.

In 1909, just under ten years after Mr. Atkinson had assumed direction of the feeble little newspaper, *The Star* moved into first place among Toronto dailies, with a circulation of 56,733. Now it was surpassed in all Canada only by two Montreal newspapers, the *Star* and *La Presse*. With the French language field almost to itself, *La Presse* had a circulation of about 105,000. In a cheerful little letter to Sir Wilfrid Laurier, Mr. Atkinson made the strange comment, which may have been an admission, that "if *The Star*'s influence would keep pace with the increase in the number of its readers, there would be nothing left for us to wish for."

To anticipate the future, the *News* tottered along until 1919, when its name was changed to the *Times* for a few brief weeks before it gave up the ghost. The *World* stopped reporting its circulation in 1911, though it survived until 1921, to be merged at last with the cannibalistic *Mail and Empire*. In 1923 *The Star* passed the *Montreal Star* in circulation, and in 1930 it topped *La Presse*. Since then its circulation leadership among Canadian dailies has never been seriously challenged.

Comparison of circulation growth does not present a picture that is quite fair to the *Telegram*, for the readership of the two newspapers was quite different. *The Star* aimed for a wide appeal and a large part of its circulation was outside the city of Toronto. The *Telegram* deliberately chose to appeal to a specialized audience and it reigned in the hearts of Tory Toronto until 1932.

Nor did *The Star*'s circulation represent readers taken away from other newspapers. The population of Toronto and Ontario was increasing rapidly, and in those years when "foreigners" were pouring into the city *The Star* spoke for them, and sought their support. The other newspapers spoke with the voice of Old Canadians and for British immigrants. But though *The Star* did not actually take readers away from the other newspapers, its aggressive news and circulation policies prevented them from expanding as they might otherwise have done, and thus weakened their competitive positions. As *The Star* had observed editorially in 1906, though all Toronto dailies were growing in circulation and appeared to be prospering, there was neither room nor need in Toronto for six newspapers. Sooner or later the weaker ones had to go.

The remarkable success of *The Daily Star* led Mr. Atkinson to consider the possibilities in a weekend newspaper, but from the start most of his associates tried to dissuade him. However, he insisted, and on April 9, 1910, the first issue of *The Star Weekly* rolled off the presses. It was slow in catching on and lost money for several years but eventually became Canada's most popular national periodical. The story of *The Weekly* is told in more detail in Chapter 11.

At the annual meeting of November 26, 1910, E. T. Malone informed the shareholders that he wished to be relieved of the duties of president. J. E. Atkinson was the unanimous choice to succeed him, but Malone and his brother remained as the other two directors. Malone still voted the biggest block of stock, most of which he held in trust for other shareholders, though Atkinson was the biggest individual shareholder.

Various explanations have been advanced for the remarkable success of Atkinson and for the meteoric rise of *The Star* in ten years to first place among Toronto newspapers. Some have been put forth in malice. Others have arisen from the painfully widespread inability of members of the human race to believe in the honesty of their fellows. A good many of them, one must suppose, have no other origin than the myth-making instinct whose pervasiveness is perhaps not fully appreciated by any except newspapermen. The least credible is the one expounded by M. E. Nichols, former president of the Canadian Press, in his history of that news distributing agency. It is that John Ross Robertson and his successors as publishers of the *Telegram* did not really care, and that *The Star* owes much of its success to the "passive policies" of its principal competitor.

Comforting as this idea may be to those who cannot conceive the idea that a newspaper can honestly believe in liberal principles or the public be honestly attracted to them, it does an injustice to the *Telegram*. That newspaper may have been obdurate but it never was passive. It, too, triumphed over rich and powerfully entrenched rivals. Having chosen its constituency—the Conservative, Protestant, Empire-minded element of the community—it fought for it vigorously and sometimes passionately. Nor does Nichols' supposition explain the rapidity with which *The Star* knocked out the *News* and the *World* as serious competitors and overhauled the influential and respected *Globe*.

Nichols came closer to the truth when he stated that "as a merchandiser of news Atkinson was not surpassed by any publisher in America," though he sourly added that "not so much can be said for his merchandise." But even this reluctant tribute is not a wholly satisfactory explanation. How did Mr. Atkinson explain it?

"The building up of goodwill is one of the most difficult of sciences as evidenced by the multitude of failures that have taken place and are continuing to take place annually among aspiring publications," wrote Mr. Atkinson in *The Star*'s special edition of 1905. "But sometimes after a hundred have failed another will come and build upon their ruins a great newspaper property. The latter apparently had no better opportunity than those who went before. To those outside his success looks like a mere accident. In reality he had the genius of appealing to the public. He had a clear perception of public taste. In other words, he was closest to the people, and therein is probably the greatest requisite for successful journalists."

And therein is the real secret of *The Star*'s success. It was closest to the people. It reflected the hopes, the yearnings, and the aspirations of the common man. It reported the events that affected his life in language he understood. Joseph Atkinson came from the common people, and with the instinct of generations he was in tune with them.

Nevertheless, to say as Mr. Atkinson himself did on occasions without amplification that *The Star* was guided by "popular taste" is to risk being misunderstood by the readers of today, when popular taste is equated with rock-'n-roll, westerns, and sex. *The Star* was certainly flamboyant, clamorous, and "razzle-dazzle," but it was neither yellow nor sexy. It carried more foreign news than any other Toronto newspaper and less crime news than most. As a measure of its accuracy it had not a libel suit in seventeen years. Mr. Atkinson was attacked by opposition newspapers for saying, as he did in the same exact words in at least three public addresses, that "what is a matter of individual taste need not necessarily be bad principle, and the newspaper's business is to serve and suit public tastes." He was accused of suggesting a newspaper should serve "the lowest common denominator." His retort was that the lowest common denominator no more represents public taste than the most prissy highbrow.

Thus, though *The Star* might on occasion gild the lily, sugar-coat the pill, and interpret the budget in terms of its effect on the pocket-books of the working man rather than on gross national product, it did not cater to the lower appetites. Most of the accusations of bad taste that were hurled against it were for uncovering social abscesses some people preferred to keep hidden, or for reporting when police clubbed strikers back to work, or for not disguising its opinion that the commander-in-chief of British forces in Canada was a silly ass.

Mr. Atkinson had an almost mystic conception of the function of the press, and of its responsibilities. "Civilization itself rests upon the mind and conscience of the whole people, and for this mind and conscience the press is the best vehicle of expression the world has yet evolved," he told a group of Presbyterian divines in 1901. "It is closer to the people than courts or Parliament and closer too, if you will let me say so, than the Church itself . . . What man will say, then, that the press should conform to his particular tastes and ideas? The editor who publishes his newspaper strictly according to his personal taste and liking would make of it a failure."

The public taste of the times in which he spoke can only be understood when viewed in the context of the tremendous events that were shaking Canada to its foundations in the first decade of this century. Canada had entered the twentieth century a colony, its people poor, its resources underdeveloped, only a third of its arable land settled, and so under Britain's thumb it was not allowed to negotiate even the simplest agreement with its next-door neighbour. For the next fourteen years immigrants by the hundreds of thousands poured into the West, factories sprang up in the East, mines undreamed of were discovered in the North, railways extended their tentacles, and Toronto grew more in ten years than it had in the preceding fifty. It was a period of expansion unequalled again until the booming 'fifties.

Small wonder, then, that most Canadians believed with Sir Wilfrid Laurier that the twentieth century belonged to Canada. The result was the development of a vigorous nationalism of which *The Star* was the leading exponent in English Canada. Among Toronto newspapers only *The Star* and to a lesser extent the *Globe* recognized that a new and rebellious mood was stirring the country—or if the others noticed they did not approve.

For the first time Canadians had a pride of country distinct from pride of Empire and *The Star* fed that pride. Its reporters roamed the Dominion, sending home stories of its greatness. They rode on immigrant trains to the West, camped with prospectors among the rocks of New Ontario, and ate with railway construction crews. In the light of hindsight some of their predictions appear ludicrous, as that Canada would have a population of fifty million by 1950, and Toronto a population of six million; that Canada's centre of population would move north of Lake Superior and cities greater than Toronto would arise in northern Ontario; that Canada would soon outstrip Britain as a manufacturing nation. But they believed them and most Canadians wanted to.

The "public taste" of the early 1900's was not for sex or crime but for nationalism. When *The Star* blustered in 1902 that Canada should "kick the Yankee poachers out of Hudson's Bay" and not be deterred by "fear of Uncle Sam" from sending Captain J. E. Bernier to the North Pole it was expressing popular sentiment.

To most Canadians, as to *The Star*, it was clear Canada would never realize her destiny while she remained colonial in spirit, and subject to imperial restraints. But to many estimable people whose spokesman was the *Telegram*, the British Empire as it then stood was as eternal and immutable as the heavens, and the right of Englishmen to rule no more to be questioned than the divine inspiration of Holy Writ. To harbour other thoughts was, in their eyes, dangerous treason to the King, the Flag, and the Empire.

The Star probably has the distinction of having been more misrepresented than any other newspaper in Canada. To a vociferous minority, some of whom sat in high places, it was the destroyer of old ways, old traditions, old loyalties, and they hated it. But others in larger numbers saw it as the champion of reform and the enemy of privilege, and they loved it. As a consequence *The Star* also had the distinction of having the most devoted following in Canada. It was no accident that in the inflamed atmosphere of the early 1900's it was *The Star* and the *Telegram*, the newspapers that spoke most vigorously for the extremes, that emerged on top.

Nor should we discount the importance of the fact *The Star* was the only Liberal afternoon newspaper in Toronto at a time of Liberal ascendance, whereas Conservative readership was divided among two afternoon and two morning newspapers. There is an advantage in being on the popular side. It was the only champion of labour at a time when industrial workers were swelling the population of Toronto from 150,000 to 450,000. Its news policy pleased the public, while the liberalism of its editorial policy appealed to the intellectual minority.

Chapter 5

THE SHAPING OF POLICY

The period between 1900 and 1911 was one of great importance in the development of *Star* policies, for not only the news pattern but the editorial pattern as well was set for half a century. *The Star* under the direction of J. E. Atkinson did not burst upon the world with a program in full bloom. In the beginning it could be summed up in five words, "Laurier and the little guy." At first they seemed synonymous.

George Maitland, who worked as closely with Mr. Atkinson as any man for more than forty years, summarizes *The Star*'s policies as they eventually took form as (*a*) a sturdy and self-reliant Canadianism, (*b*) public ownership of public utilities, (*c*) equal rights and full civil liberties for minorities, (*d*) the right of labour to organize and strike, (*e*) town planning, and (*f*) freedom of the individual from fear, want, and injustice. Mr. Atkinson's inclination was to support any party that furthered these ends, oppose any party that did not.

In the beginning it was the first two of these that were pursued most diligently and that had the greatest influence upon *The Star*'s fortunes.

In latter years it was the sixth. All were enunciated before 1911, though the social welfare program did not take concrete form until Laurier had passed from the scene. Until the defeat of Laurier in 1911 *The Star* acquiesced right down the line with the Liberal government at Ottawa. Mr. Atkinson felt he could be as independent as he liked in provincial and municipal affairs, and he did not hesitate to defy his financial backers when he disagreed with them, but he was morally obliged to support Laurier's policies. He was not always happy about the direction some of these were taking. Laurier remained to the end of his days a Gladstonian Liberal and a firm believer in the economic doctrine of laissez-faire. On the other hand, Atkinson from his youth had been attracted by the "radical" or "reform" liberalism then dominating the British Liberal party. Reform liberalism had developed in Britain in response to the inequalities of wealth and privilege that had resulted from the unrestrained free enterprise of the classical Liberals.

H. H. Asquith, leader of the British Liberal party, was declaring the state must deal in an organized manner with unemployment, old age, and infirmity, while his deputy, Lloyd George, urged that "the state should step in to the utmost limit of its resources" to mitigate the hardships of individual poverty due to personally unavoidable circumstances. Here was not yet the complete program of the welfare state, but the germ is discernible. In some minds, including Laurier's, this sort of liberalism was confused with socialism, and this confusion was compounded by the fact that occasionally the reform Liberals and the socialists made common cause against social evils, as in the first British elections of this century. But in Atkinson's mind there existed no such confusion. Liberalism stands for maximum freedom of the individual. The individual cannot be free if he lives in fear of poverty, unemployment, illness, and exploitation. It seemed clear to him that Liberals had to remove those fears.

In time the gap between Laurier Liberalism and Atkinson liberalism became so wide the latter was to lament that "there is no liberal party left in Canada." Because Laurier and Atkinson had a fundamentally different conception of what Liberalism stood for, there were times when *The Star* had to reverse policies it was advocating to conform with announcements of government policy from Ottawa. This it usually managed to do with remarkable agility though with much inner resentment.

No such problem existed so far as the Liberal government in Ontario was concerned. *The Star* went through the motions of supporting the Ross government, but without enthusiasm and largely, it would seem, because of pressure from Cox and Mulock. But it was with some relief that Mr. Atkinson saw the Liberals defeated in 1905, for the government was both corrupt and incompetent. *The Star* gave the new Premier, Conservative J. P. Whitney, a warm welcome and supported him throughout most of his ministry.

Atkinson's disenchantment with Laurier took place gradually. In the 1904 election *The Star* wholeheartedly advocated his re-election. The Laurier government had removed the restrictions on picketing and union organization. It had passed the Conciliation Act of 1900, founded the Department of Labour in 1900, and passed the Railway Labour Disputes Act in 1903. It had initiated an aggressive immigration policy, it was pledged to an aggressive railway building program, it had brought about the removal of the last British garrisons from Canada, had asserted for Canada the right to negotiate its own treaties, had withdrawn the Canadian militia from British army command, and was rapidly turning Canada from colony into nation. These were all policies *The Star* and its publisher could support with a whole heart.

But by the time the 1908 election was held, to quote the *Canadian Annual Review* of that year, the old Canadian Liberal party, "with its policy of United States reciprocity, stringent economy, antagonism to protection, and intense democracy had passed away. In its place was a government led by a Chief of marked personality and dominant power, surrounded by a phalanx of devoted followers, supported by an organization of great and far-reaching strength. . . . The Liberal party went to the voters on the practical claim that Canada had prospered under Liberal rule."

The Star supported Laurier almost entirely on the grounds of "Liberal prosperity" and tried to ignore charges of corruption in the constituencies at the grass roots level. But it was deeply disturbed by them, the more so that their truth could not be denied. Laurier won, and the next day *The Star* warned the government that "it would be a great mistake to interpret the Liberal victory as a declaration that the rank and file of the Liberal party are not sensitive about the charges of graft that have been made in the past year. What the Liberal electors have said is that they believe Sir Wilfrid Laurier and his colleagues to be honest and public spirited men . . . who will make reforms wherever they are necessary." A few days later *The Star* proposed that "in order to maintain the independence of Parliament, Parliament ought to enact a law compelling the publication of contributions to campaign funds." It has been saying this ever since.

In the 1911 election *The Star* supported Laurier and reciprocity so vigorously and so extravagantly as to provoke derision. Maitland, who was writing editorials at the time, says Mr. Atkinson believed passionately in reciprocity, though his original belief in free trade with the whole world, a classical Liberal doctrine, had been somewhat tempered by the failure of the rest of the world to co-operate. Laurier's success in negotiating a reciprocity agreement with the United States wiped the slate clean, so far as he was concerned, of all past sins of omission.

But for all that, Laurier's rejection by the electors was not the bitter blow it would have been a few years earlier. Perhaps the fact that it ended *The Star*'s obligation to support the federal Liberal party did much to reconcile Atkinson to the defeat of a cause he had supported with such conviction. It relieved *The Star* of an obligation to defend measures many prudent people believed would end in disaster, as indeed some of them did. He must have felt most keenly, for example, the restraint on his freedom to criticize Laurier's railway policy.

The first campaign Mr. Atkinson launched after becoming publisher of *The Star* was for public ownership of public utilities, including railways, a cause many Liberals, including Laurier, believed to be quite un-Liberal. It resulted in more disputes with his financial backers than anything else he ever did. It brought *The Star* into conflict with Laurier's railway policy, and it was *The Star* that had to back down at the risk of appearing inconsistent. It resulted in Atkinson being accused at first of being a Conservative, later of being a socialist.

The campaign began with an attack on the street railway company in January, 1900, less than a month after Atkinson took over *The Star*. It demanded that the city expropriate the company or, failing that, compel it to give the public better service. Before long *The Star* was advocating public ownership of power plants, gas plants, railways, telephones, telegraphs, and even coal mines. It supported public-ownership men for public office.

The Star was always embarrassed by Laurier's coolness to public ownership at a time when the Conservatives were enthusiastic about it. R. L. Borden, chosen leader of the Conservative party in 1901 and a man Mr. Atkinson much admired, said "everybody in Canada supports it." The Conservative government of Ontario introduced a bill to expropriate power companies that charged too much. A Conservative manufacturer, Adam Beck, led the movement for public ownership of hydroelectric power resources in Ontario. *The Star*'s Conservative competitors, the *World*, the *News*, and the *Telegram*, supported Beck and backed the Conservative party in advocating construction of the proposed transcontinental railway by the government rather than by private capital, as the Laurier government contemplated.

Mr. Atkinson was well aware of the inconsistency between classical Liberalism and public ownership. "Some Liberals might shy at public ownership because they think it is against the old liberal doctrine of free individual action and competition," *The Star* said editorially in 1907. "That is a splendid doctrine when it is applicable, but it does not apply to conditions where competition is impossible. Competition is impossible when an individual or a corporation or a combination of these gets control of the coal lands, or the oil lands, or the water powers in a country. Then the question is not between individualism and public control, but between public control and monopoly." In this respect *The Star*'s policy was remarkably like that enunciated by Pope Leo XIII in the encyclical *Rerum novarum* of May 15, 1891, a document with which Mr. Atkinson must have been familiar.

However, under the compulsion of supporting Laurier, *The Star*'s railway policy progressed from one of outright public ownership to one that was close to outright private ownership. This was an era of tremendous national expansion, with hundreds of thousands of immigrants pouring into the West. Every Canadian was convinced new railways had to be built, none more so than the publisher of *The Star*. The only question was: who was to build them?

In 1901 *The Star* was declaring public ownership of railways an "impregnable position (to which) we must advance." By 1902 it was finding the "project so large . . . the public is not prepared for this step . . . The effects of education in the nationalization principle must be waited for." In 1903 it considered "government ownership of railways a sound principle" when the public approves but not otherwise. When Hon. A. G. Blair, Minister of Railways, resigned in July, 1903, as a protest against Laurier's decision to let private capital build all but the unprofitable section of the transcontinental railways *The Star* said "the country is not willing that its money should be spent in a government railway to the Pacific."

On May 26, 1904, Borden unequivocally placed the Conservative party solidly behind public ownership of the proposed railways. "If the government doesn't run the railways the railways will run the government," he said in language reminiscent of *The Star*'s own words three years before. The *Star* omitted relevant portions from its report of his address, and did not comment on his statement for two days. Then it weakly remarked that the only real difference between the railway policies of Laurier and Borden was that "the government intends to carry out its pledges and the opposition doesn't."

Before the end of 1904 it had given unqualified approval to Laurier's disastrous partnership between the government and the Grand Trunk Railway, whereby the government was to build the uneconomic link across northern Ontario between Winnipeg and Quebec City. Before long it was even supporting its old enemies Sir William Mackenzie and his partners D. D. Mann and Senator Nicholls in their equally disastrous Canadian Northern Railways project. Thus at the very time it was attacking Mackenzie for greedy mismanagement of the Toronto street railway and the Toronto Electric Company, it was also lauding his noble vision as a great builder of transcontinental railways.

The inference is clear. *The Star*'s railway policy was not set in *The Star* office but by Sir Wilfrid Laurier. In provincial affairs it was free to support the plans of the Ontario Conservative government to build as a public project the proposed railway to James Bay, the present Ontario Northland Railway, but in federal railway matters it had to toe the Laurier line. And one may be sure that Mr. Atkinson was reminded of his duty. Senator Cox was deeply involved in the railway business, both as a director of the proposed Grand Trunk Pacific Railway and as head of the financial institutions that were raising the money. Other *Star* shareholders had lucrative construction contracts, and Mulock had emerged as Laurier's hatchet man.

Almost every newspaper in the country except those tied to the Liberal party and those with big business connections, such as the *Montreal Star*, opposed Laurier's railway policy. Senator Cox was pictured in the minds of the public as the evil genius behind the financial machinations, but, oddly enough, he was supposed to have conspired in some way with Senator Jaffray, owner of the *Globe*. His relationship to *The Star* was still a well kept secret. The *Telegram* had once tried to sniff out such a link, but it was so well hidden the *Telegram* apparently decided the only one was that they were both scoundrelly Grits.

But *The Star* never gave up its insistence that, however they might be built, the railways and the rates they charged must be under strict government supervision. On this point, too, it was criticized by doctrinaire Liberals at Ottawa who believed any form of government supervision was un-Liberal. "It is not true liberalism to say the railways must be allowed to manage their own business," *The Star* lectured them. "They are managing the people's business and partly governing the people under borrowed powers . . . To preserve our liberties either the government must operate the railways or it must insist on . . . strict regulation of the railways."

Several of Mr. Atkinson's financial backers were engaged in various operations with public utilities from which they hoped to garner a bountiful harvest, and their newspaper's espousal of public ownership did not sit well with them. Senator Cox and Hon. William Mulock both tried to get *The Star* to drop its support of a city plan to buy the Toronto Electric Company for $40 a share in 1901. "Disgraceful bullying," Senator Cox called it, while Mulock, who became Sir William a year later, blustered it was "pure confiscation." He had paid $71 a share for stock in September, he told Mr. Atkinson.

"But Mr. Mulock, this proposal to buy out the company for $40 a share was being discussed in the press all summer," Mr. Atkinson reminded him. "Surely you had enough warning not to pay $71 for it."

"I didn't know what was going on in the press," Mulock replied.

But he evidently knew what was going on in the minds of the Ross government, for a short time later it rewarded its political friends by giving their electric company, which Senator Cox headed, a franchise to develop electricity at Niagara Falls. It followed this a few months later by giving a second company a similar franchise.

Toronto will not get cheap electricity "if we allow the intervention of private capitalists," *The Star* raged impotently, and urged that the city also apply for a franchise and develop its own power. However, when Sir Adam Beck produced his proposal for a provincial hydro-electric power commission to generate all power, selling it to the municipalities, *The Star* endorsed it as the better plan. Since Laurier was in no way involved in the power controversy, *The Star* was free to advocate whatever course it chose.

When the Ontario Hydro Commission and the city bought out the Toronto Electric Company in 1908, Sir William and the other shareholders were reported to have received $160 for their shares. In return Hydro got only a franchise that should never have been awarded, and a generating plant that had to be scrapped. Largely because of Whitney's favourable stand on public ownership and Hydro, *The Star* supported Conservative governments in Ontario until 1919.

In those years *The Star* advocated public ownership of gas companies, coal mines, and oil wells for the same reason it supported public ownership of Hydro—they were basic sources of energy. Mulock and Mr. Atkinson quarrelled again when *The Star* supported a proposal before the ratepayers that the city buy the Consumers' Gas Company, of which Sir William was a large shareholder. The purchase was approved by the electors, but because of political obstruction it was never completed.

Sir William gave Mr. Atkinson more trouble than any other shareholder, always telling him how to run the paper and even what candidates to support in civic elections. Mrs. Atkinson once told friends her husband would come home trembling with rage after an encounter with Sir William at a shareholders' meeting, while Maitland relates how he tried to take advantage of Mr. Atkinson's absence in Europe in 1909 to change *Star* policy on some matter by claiming to be "in charge" while Atkinson was away.

"You never do anything I ask you," Sir William peevishly complained on one occasion.

"It must be that my judgment is not as good as yours," Atkinson smiled.

"No, it is usually better," Sir William handsomely conceded. "It must be something else."

Nevertheless, though Sir William opposed public ownership in principle, when Mackenzie King, then Deputy Minister of Labour, reported sweat-shop conditions among women employees of Toronto and Montreal telephone exchanges, he veered towards support of government-owned telegraph and telephone systems, to be run by the post office. *The Star* at the time was backing a move by city council to expropriate the telephone company, but when that fell through it urged federal ownership. Neither Mulock nor *The Star* pressed the issue when Laurier disapproved. Some years later *The Star* opposed a proposal that the Bell Telephone Company be nationalized. It did not advocate public ownership for its own sake, it explained, but only where public ownership would better serve the public interest. It believed the private company was serving the public well.

While public ownership was the cause of most of Mr. Atkinson's disagreements with Cox and Mulock, Lyman Jones quarrelled with him over tariffs. Jones had supported Laurier's low tariff policy when it seemed to mean increasing the farmers' prosperity, and thus the sale of farm machinery, but he turned against it when he found "Made in U.S.A." implements competing with those manufactured by the company he headed. "That fellow Atkinson, I helped put him where he is today and now he is trying to ruin me," Jones complained to a fellow businessman.

That may explain why Jones was so ready to sell his *Star* stock in 1907, for he was not so hard up that he had to sell it for less than it was worth.

But as for the other shareholders, they might grumble, and might regret the power they had given their managing director, but being businessmen they were not disposed to quarrel with success. The astonishing prosperity of *The Star* did much to reconcile them to policies that must have seemed pernicious to most of them.

Laurier's most notable contribution to Canadian development was along constitutional lines. He was a pronounced nationalist, and Canada achieved actual national status under his guidance. He thus laid the groundwork for transforming the old British Empire into the present Commonwealth of free and equal nations. In his nationalism he had the unremitting support of *The Star,* for nationalism has been *The Star*'s most consistently proclaimed policy.

The twentieth century opened with most Canadians quite content with their colonial status and serenely certain of the eternity of the Empire and its everlasting goodness. There is slight indication Atkinson gave any more thought to imperial affairs than the majority of his fellow citizens until compelled to do so by the exigencies of his new status as a publisher. At first he approached them hesistantly and with some uncertainty, and except for an occasional editorial on the Boer War and its aftermath *The Star* had little to say on imperial relations throughout 1900 and most of 1901.

However, on September 3, 1901, it devoted its entire editorial page to a discussion of Canada's relations with the Empire and the United States. This was inspired, it would seem, by the activities of certain persons in the United States who hoped to detach Canada from Britain and annex it. At the same time, in England Joseph Chamberlain and his Radical-Unionists were advocating that Canada virtually merge its existence with that of Britain, while others were insisting with the kind of obtuseness that led to the American Revolution that Canada should contribute taxes towards the maintenance of the Royal Navy.

"In geography alone we have the guarantee of independence in our union with Great Britain no matter how close that union may grow to be," said *The Star*. "Absorbed in the United States we would take pot-luck with the rest of the continent and find our most intimate affairs managed for us by representative bodies in which our delegates would have only a trifling influence. . . . Patriotism may some day quarrel with Imperialism and provide justification for independence, but not while independence is feared to be a prelude to annexation."

It envisioned for the future an equal partnership between Britain, Can-

Joseph E. Atkinson at 43, when *The Star* moved into first place among Toronto newspapers in circulation

RIGHT: Joseph T. Clark, editor-in-chief, 1900–1906, 1908–1937

BELOW: Lou E. Marsh, first office boy, 1893; sports editor, 1931–36; Tom Banton, labour reporter, 1894–1924; commercial editor, 1924–1934

LEFT: John R. Bone, managing editor, 1907–1928

BELOW: C. W. Jefferys, artist, 1900–1913; W. R. Plewman, 1903–1954, war news analyst and editorial writer

General Section **THE TORONTO STAR WEEKLY** General Section

FIRST YEAR. THE TORONTO STAR WEEKLY. 5c PER COPY.

Points

IT is all very well to say that a man should learn to sacrifice money when necessary, but how is he to learn when it is necessary?

WHY do the newspapers always say, when a man allows his name to be mentioned for such a post as Medical Health Officer, that he is "after it"? The term seems to suggest a person pursuing a job that is too good for him.

NO doubt Capt. Midford is all right as an engineer, but when he says that on one occasion he was introduced to Dean Galbraith as "the most resourceful engineer I have ever met," he should remember that the point is, not to whom he was so introduced, but by whom.

THIS is the way the London Chronicle refers to a speech by Winston Churchill: "Mr. Churchill's masculine mind and vigorous intelligence presented a striking contrast to the wriggling nihilism of Mr. Balfour."

DR. SCHWENINGER of Nice, by whom the King of Sweden is being treated, was Bismarck's doctor. When they first met Bismarck objected to answering so many questions. "Very well, then," said Schweninger, "you had better call in a veterinary surgeon. He won't ask any questions."

WE must confess to a distinct shock on seeing in an English journal a reference to "Hon. Joe" as "Mr. Jas. Martin, M.P." But his name will become familiar right soon.

AN English journal is carrying on a discussion as to whether it is lawful to lie in politics. It may be unlawful, but we see very few punished for it.

REFERRING to the error by which this journal credited a photograph showing a great delivery of agricultural implements at New Liskeard as a scene at Haileybury, the New Liskeard Speaker says: "Of course, this was an unfortunate mistake for The Star to make, because, while Haileybury is a mining town, New Liskeard is the greatest agricultural town north of Orillia."

DUMMY directors directors who say nothing at board meetings sometimes find their voices in court.

AGAIN a Frenchman has flown off with a big prize in sky-racing. Bleriot and Paulhan have won places in history.

MR. C. C. JAMES must have been misreported about those alleged wild pigeons' eggs when he said that "plenty of robins stray away from the general migrations and nest earlier than others." Those eggs were white, and no robin would stray so far away from the habits of its family as to lay white eggs.

CANADA [illegible] ancing. Time was [illegible] a purse of $120.- [illegible]

ENVY IN CANADA

Rather Too Much of It—As If the Change From Grape Juice to Lemon Juice had Affected the National Character

THERE is scarcely any quality in the human character less admirable than envy of success. Am I unduly pessimistic in thinking that this unamiable trait is beginning to cut too large a figure in Canadian life? For long years this country produced few outstanding personalities, except the politicians. We know how they fared. George Brown, a type of vigor, courage, and public spirit, was pursued as if he had been a modern Attila. Sir John Macdonald was vilified with a sort of melodramatic ferocity that smacked of the dime novel. Alexander Mackenzie's honesty and devotion to principle were greeted with sneers and gibes. Not being rich, having no literature to speak of, possessing no quality that drew the world's attention, Canada produced few men of real distinction in letters, art, science, or commerce, and, consequently, we jogged on from year to year in a tolerably good imitation of Christian charity, at peace with ourselves and our neighbors. Now, we have suddenly stepped into the automobile of progress, and are whirling down the world's highway without any speed limit. To be a Canadian is to be known. Germany begs us not to be too hard on her with our cruel tariff. President Taft ogles us into a friendly business arrangement. Our London representative is one of the half-dozen conspicuous figures in English life. Our banks are said to be the greatest ever. We have arrived—and so, on a large scale, have envy, malice, hatred, and all uncharitableness.

THE intoxicating atmosphere of success generates a tribe of petty gossips, who whisper their detractions into the too-ready ears of the laggard, the incompetent, and the jealous-minded. A Canadian, by pluck and ability, gets his head a little above the crowd, and is at once assailed by the shafts of ridicule and censure. The press gets the credit, in popular opinion, of leading the hosts of malicious critics. In point of fact, the newspapers are innocent lambs in this line of activity. It is in social life that you hear the unkindest comments. Here are hatched the most malignant satires. Over the dinner table, at the club, in the stock exchange, on the way home from the theatres, the successful man, the handsome woman, or the clever artist is put into the frying pan, and disposed of. We are a very temperate people in the use of drink, and lemonade is producing a decidedly acid disposition. Spite and envy pose as virtues. Let us, they declare, avoid the American habit of boastfulness and self-praise. Let us be candid and cultivate the critical faculty. This is merely the mask of envy. It hates success, and desires to make success as difficult of achievement as possible.

YOU and I know a Canadian, who, for many years, has been foremost in philanthropy. Instead of devoting his surplus time to horse-racing or the game of bridge, he is warm-[illegible], unselfish, a[illegible] full of plans to help the [illegible] unfort[illegible] he [illegible] the

ciated at their true value. No one seems eager to print them, and one editor, who shook his ponderous head with a peculiarly exasperating smile at a fine ode to Niagara Falls, is known to be utterly lacking in taste. He has been seen to steal quietly away to the baseball game, leaving priceless manuscripts on his desk to be fingered by the vulgar. Such a man is not envious, because he is incapable of any strong passion. In the haphazard incongruity that disfigures our social machinery, he is simply out of place. He should be shining shoes, but, unhappily, chance has made him—but temporarily, thank Heaven!—an arbiter over the disposal of literary masterpieces. A century hence my manuscript poems will be found in Mr. Fraser's archives, and given to a delighted generation. The author will chuckle in the spirit world over the editor's discomfiture. There is no envy in this feeling. Mine is merely honest indignation.

THE Canadian has much to learn of his own land, the achievments of its pioneers, the books of its writers, the pictures of its artists. He bestows far too much time on Mr. Teddy Roosevelt, the House of Lords, and the eruptions of Mount Vesuvius. There is work to do at home. There are useful periods in our history unstudied and economic problems not yet elucidated. This is not due so much to slothful indifference as to an envious timidity lest some Canadian shall be discovered worthy of fame and to be even now doing original work. There is lack of generous effort to uncover national merit. In the middle of a campaign of much party bitterness Mr. Lloyd George and Mr. Balfour met at a public luncheon in London. Did you observe the enthusiasm of the Liberal for the fine talents of the Conservative? There was no touch of envy, of grudging admiration. Big men in a big sphere are not petty. One cannot imagine Socrates jealous of Plato. Cromwell certainly admired the dashing tactics of Rupert. There is something suggestive of greatness in the meeting between Lee and Grant at Appomattox. The quality of envy, however, is peculiarly the characteristic of the small-minded. It is ever active to see who makes progress and to put, if possible, an obstacle in the path of a rising man. Instead of industriously pursuing his own way through the world, the envious person loses time watching the ascent of others. What pangs he suffers, what transports of disappointment seize him! It would be far wiser of him to greet a winning Canadian as a national possession, to congratulate him heartily, and to reap encouragement from the example.

THE under-rating of the individual goes hand in hand, as one would naturally expect, with an enhanced national self-importance. To a reasonable extent, optimism and patriotic fervor are go[od] things. Until recent times, Canada lacked self [illegible]. But that [illegible] is over. No fo[illegible] can now [illegible]

THE COMBINE BILL
Hon. Mackenzie King (meditatively). "Otherwise, I suppose, possibly, the Bill's all right!"

The Name of "York"

THE name Toronto, generally held to be the Indian word signifying "place of meeting," is one of the most euphonious ever bestowed upon a city. Its origin, as anyone who knows his Scadding will tell you, dates very far back. In 1686, as a letter in the French archives shows, it was spoken of by the Marquis de Denonville as the portage of Toronto. For a time the Humber was called the Toronto River, and what we now call Humber Bay was once Toronto Bay. The Indians used to bring their furs down Toronto River from far distant Michilimackinac, and a great trade was done. The French fortified trading post, officially styled Fort Rouille, was established here, but it was most frequently named Fort Toronto. The interior region, as far back as Lake Simcoe, was known as the Toronto region, and that lake itself was Toronto Lake before it was named after Upper Canada's first Governor.

Why, then, was Toronto called York for such a long time? There is an interesting anecdote about this. When Capt. John Denison, the first of that family to settle here, came to Canada in 1792, he stayed with his fr[illegible] Gov[illegible] at Newark [illegible]

The Onlooker

A CANADIAN Associated Press despatch from London tells us that "several recent meetings in London of the Empire Pioneers have been broken up with much disorder, and the Imperial orators have been unable to obtain a hearing." Many who saw this despatch in the daily newspapers must have wondered what it meant. Who are the Empire Pioneers? If they are Imperial orators, how did their oratory become Imperial?

In Battersea and other districts of London where work people reside, meetings are being addressed by three speakers, who are called the "Imperial Pioneers." They are: Mr. Frank Fox, of Australia; Mr. P. J. Hamon, of South Africa, and Mr. L. W. R. Mulloy, of Canada. They are talking as spokesmen from the Dominions over sea, an[d] urging the Briti[sh] [illegible] to abandon fre[e] [illegible] and adopt tariff reform with co[illegible]

Observations

THE DAILY STAR may think that the popular songs of to-day are superior to the popular songs of twenty years ago, but I don't. From a musical point of view this generation hasn't anything on the generation that have come and gone in my time. "Annie Rooney" and "After the Ball," "Ta-ra-ra-boom-de-ay," and "Comrades," had very little to commend them, except the catchy air, but what makes me despair now is the vogue of Harry Lauder, a pompous, piffling and conceited buffoon, whose songs have a swing and a verve that "catch," but are marred by a vulgarity that convict the maker of a vulgarity. A Scotchman himself, he must assume the responsibility for the stage Scotchman that now caricatures the race in vaudeville, as the stage Irishman burlesqued a whole race beyond the limit of a patience that had a sense of humor back of it and a knowledge that no caricature could mar the original. You see the stage Scotchman now in every imitator of Lauder. He knows he has to be vulgar, if he would be like Lauder, and he is foolish enough to essay the role.

IF there could be such a thing as copyright on a joke, the joker would be justified in calling it a jest protector.

TALKING about the mutations that time produces, I think the greatest has to do with the business of banking. My first knowledge of a bank manager had to do with a magnate who sat in his office while the man who sought to do his business with him, approached through the styled door to the inner chamber, which was a sweat-box if there ever was one. He made you feel at once that you were suspected of attempting to defraud the bank and, if you cleared yourself of that unspoken charge, you put yourself under obligation to him for a favor, which made you pay eight or ten per cent. interest, and placed you under obligation to one of two friends, whose name, or names, graced the reverse side of a small, but important, piece of paper.

That was my first experience. My last was a more pleasing one. I cannot describe the enjoyment I felt when canvassed for business by several bank managers. It did my heart good to see the aristocrats of the commercial world out hustling for business like the rest of us.

DO you recall the country funeral of 38 or 40 years ago? The long procession of wagons well-laden with men and women, boys and girls, paying the last tribute of respect or affection to the "dear departed." There was little sham about it in those days. I don't think any one joked about it. To-day what do you find? Those who attend—many of them—but the less said of this the better. It makes me sad to think what they will say when they are attending our ow[n] funerals. I recall the slow, measur[ed] [illegible]

ABOVE: a cartoon of Mackenzie King appears in the first issue of the *Star Weekly*

BELOW: an example of the intensive campaign *The Star* waged for Reciprocity in the 1911 election

THE TORONTO DAILY STAR

19TH YEAR. TORONTO, THURSDAY, SEPTEMBER 14, 1911.—TWENTY-TWO PAGES. Last Edition. ONE CENT

Prices in Buffalo and Toronto Compared

FOOD EXHIBIT IN STAR WINDOW A GRAPHIC DEMONSTRATION ON COST OF LIVING

Actual Purchases Made in the Two Cities

PURCHASES MADE BY THE STAR SHOW THAT FOOD SUPPLIES IN TORONTO ARE MATERIALLY HIGHER THAN IN U.S.

While the Price Farmer Gets in Canada Is Lower Than Across the Line.

PRICES OF LONG LIST OF ARTICLES COMPARED

Pork Products, Cooked Meats, Salt, Milk, Canned Goods Included in Exhibit.

SOME STRIKING CONTRASTS

Details of How Purchases Were Made—Prices and Times Normal in Buffalo.

To-day The Star windows at 18 King street west attracted more than usual interest. Indeed some people were inclined to affirm that they created a sensation.

The reason was a food exhibit. Reporters on this paper have for the past few days been making purchases of various staple articles of food in the cities of Buffalo and Toronto, with a view to presenting a comparison of actual conditions in the cost of living. The list includes a great variety of smoked and cooked meats, pork products of all sorts, condensed milk, salt, and a large assortment of canned goods. The display does not include the more perishable commodities, such as fresh meats, because as yet The Star's store-keeping facilities in the way of ice boxes, refrigerators, and general accommodation are somewhat limited. In passing, it may be said, however, that from the prices quoted to The Star a striking contrast in the prices of fresh meats in Toronto and in Buffalo is to be found.

Quality Corresponds.

Every precaution was taken to make the price comparisons accurate. In the matter of quality in foodstuffs, it is quite impossible to be dogmatic, and [illegible], so that what one thinks is the best brand may not suit another at all, but an earnest effort has been made to get prices in the two cities for the corresponding brands of the various articles. For example in bacon, there are many brands and varieties. In Buffalo The Star purchased what we were assured was the best bacon to be had anywhere in the United States. To compare with this we purchased a piece of what we were assured was the best bacon in Toronto. In the type of stores also, as far as possible, the standard of quality and the street locality were taken into consideration. There is in Buffalo a string of meat stores known as the Kamman stores, 13 in number, scattered all over the city, in the same fashion that the Wm. Davies Company stores are scattered over Toronto. Several purchases were made from the Davies firm in Toronto and the Kamman firm in Buffalo, respectively. It may be recalled that some years ago the Wm. Davies Co. started up in business [in] Buffalo and [illegible]

BUFFALO AND TORONTO PRICES

Table Showing Cost of Articles Purchased for Food Exhibit Now in The Star Window

PORK PRODUCTS.	Toronto	Buffalo
Best smoked bacon	24c	20c
Same sliced	27c	21c
Best smoked ham	20c	17c
Same sliced	25c	21c
Best boiled ham	35c	24c
Pure lard	15c	11c
SLICED COOKED AND SMOKED MEATS.		
Sliced cold tongue	40c	22c
Sliced roast pork	38c	32c
Sliced spiced beef	30c	25c
Jellied tenderloin	35c	30c
Jellied veal	30c	23c
Ham bologna	17c	10c
Beef bologna	12c	10c
Wiener sausages	12½c	10c
CANNED GOODS.		
Tomatoes	12½c	10c
Wax beans	10c	8c
String beans	10c	8c
Best red salmon	22c	18c
Corn beef	20c	18c
Peas	11c	10c
Cherries	15c	12c
Canned pears	15c and 18c	10c
Canned Pumpkin	10c	8c
MISCELLANEOUS.		
Salt (3-lb. bag)	5c	3c
Evaporated milk (Buffalo can is 1 inch taller, price the same)	10c	10c

An early morning crowd in front of The Star Building looking at the exhibits of foods bought in Toronto and in Buffalo, with the prices, which show that the cost of food in this city is much the higher. All day long people have been stopping in front of the windows, looking at the meats and canned goods, and exchanging comments on the difference in prices. At the noon hour the crowd was so large it flowed out on the roadway.

DEARER HOGS, CHEAPER BACON

While the Cost of Hog Products to Buffalo Workingman Is Less Than in Toronto, the Canadian Farmer Gets Less for His Live Hogs.

While The Star's exhibit shows that pork, bacon, ham, and other products of the hog can be bought cheaper in Buffalo than Toronto, the fact remains that live hogs fetch a higher price on the Buffalo market than in Toronto. Not satisfied with paying as little as possible to the farmer, the Canadian packers squeeze as many cents per pound as possible out of the consumer. In order that there may be no doubt as to the prices paid for live hogs in the Buffalo and New York market, The Star herewith reproduces the schedule of average prices since 1906, as it appears in the official return which was printed by order of the Canadian Parliament.

	Light Hogs. Buffalo.	Heavy Hogs. Buffalo.	Medium Hogs. New York.	Choice Selects Toronto.
1906	$7.05	$6.65	$6.83	$6.81
1907	6.73	6.66	7.02	6.43
1908	6.05	6.13	6.57	5.95
1909	x7.47	7.69	7.98	7.29
1910	9.43	9.32	9.76	8.68
x1911	7.38	7.11	7.54	6.80

xFirst six mo[nths] [illegible]

[illegible] total for [illegible] high cost of living are fro[m] all quar[ters] [illegible]

BORDEN-BOURASSA ALLIANCE SADDENS CONSERVATIVE CLERGYMAN; "LAURIER IS NOT PLIABLE ENOUGH"; SITUATION PATHETIC

"Spectator," in Canadian Churchman, Discusses Situation in Quebec—Borden Will Have to Make Concession to Roman Catholic Church and to Bourassa's Anti-Imperial Campaign—The Understanding Between Nationalists and Conservatives.

Who is Henri Bourassa? The Toronto News says he is a patriot; the World and London Free Press are committed to his praises. Mr. Borden's candidates in Quebec are pledged to his policy of "no naval contribution." Mr. Borden's own naval policy has been modified so as to meet with his approval. Mr. Borden's French-C[onservative] daily [in Q]uebec is [illegible] ed. He is the man who has attempted to scare the mothers of Quebec with fairy stories of the likelihood of conscription, and who has pictured the sons and fathers torn from their families to take arms against some far-off foe.

A Conservative Opinion.

But who is Bourassa? He is Sir Wilfrid Laurier's most bitter enemy, as well as the Bordenites' [mo]st secret frie[nd] [illegible]

[At] the same time Mr. Bourassa repudiates Mr. Borden as a leader. At a great Nationalist meeting in Montreal last week at which "Spectator" was present the name of Borden received but the coldest acknowledgment, while the Nationalist leader was tremendously cheered. We say that the situation in Quebec is a pathetic one from every point of view, from the point of view of the leaders' place in public esteem [illegible]

ON THE MORNING AFTER

Probable Article by Mr. Maclean in the World of September 22nd

It is the invariable habit of Mr. W. F. Maclean to come out with a scathing article on the front page of the World on the morning after an election in which his party has been defeated, giving some plain talk to his party leaders and the party followers. As Mr. Maclean is very busy just now, and may not get time to give that article of his the time and attention it deserves, we venture to prepare it for him in advance and publish it now for his future approval. This, then, is, in part, about what Mr. Maclean may be expected to say in the World on the morning of the 22nd:

Well, here we are again, just about where the World expected the Conservative party would be this morning. One trouble with the party made great by John A. Macdonald is that it smokes too much. If it didn't hit the pipe and have fine dreams about winning victories which it stands no earthly chance of winning, perhaps it would get down to real business and listen to practical advice from such a man as the Conservative candidate in South York yesterday, or such a man as Mr. W. F. Maclean, or such a newspaper as the World. But we must confess that we do not expect to see much of a change for the better until Father Time, who slays fools with reluctance, can shirk his duty no longer, in regard to a bunch of Conservatives who lived in the last century, who exist in this, but who really belonged to the seventeenth, or an earlier period, and who, no doubt, would have been on earth then except for some blunder in the eternal bookkeeping. We have always thought, and awaited an opportunity of saying, that Mr. Foster should have debated theology with John Knox. But they did not meet—the appointment was not kept—and this morning we see in the election returns one of the consequences.

The men who sat around Sir John Macdonald in office should have been satisfied to get out of Parliament after the defeat of 1896 and make room for new men. The time had come for new men. But the only way the country could get them was by electing Laurier in 1896 and by keeping him there. Laurier saw the point. He kept shifting his men, renewing his colleagues, until now there is scarcely a man in his Cabinet who was there at first. But across the aisle in Parliament the Conservative party kept in the front seats—always ready to frown upon new men and new ideas—the indestructible, immortal, and too-familiar countenances of a group of men whose only claim to rank as statesmen was their occupation of the seats they sat in. They had talked one generation off the boards, and were ready for another. Many a time when the member for South York has uttered a modern opinion in Parliament he has expected to see everybody in the front row of the Opposition, from the Speaker's throne to the chair of the sergeant-at-arms, swoon and lurch forward on their desks as if hit by a horizontal shaft of lightning. It is a frightful handicap when the progressive men of a party have to modify their opinions to suit the embalmed intelligence of contemporaries of Pharoah.

In this election we were out-generalled by Laurier. In fact we were not generalled at all on our side. The men who framed up the fight against reciprocity were not politicians seeking the welfare of the Conservative party, but a group of millionaires as yet in the cocoon stage of development. A fat lot they cared about the Conservative party. A big ado was made about eighteen Liberals who joined us. Well, some of them represented interests which would have made it advisable to whisper the news of their joining us, instead of yelling about it. Mr. Sifton joined us. That was all right. But it was not all right to take this discard from Laurier's hand and let everybody see that it was the best card in our pack. He had been abused by us so long that we couldn't turn around and praise him. It was a fool thing to do. If the party had possessed any sense it would, when it saw the kind of people who were coming to it, have locked the door. But it didn't, and Bourassa got in. Having got in, the whole house was made his. Mr. Borden acted exactly like one of those easy-going citizens, who, at Exhibition time, will give up his bed to any comer and sleep on the floor. We woke up one morning with the French tricolor over the door. One result was that half our election printing was rendered useless, unless the Albany Club will pay for it, and use it as fuel during the coming winter.

Those people who think they know how to run the Conservative party only know how to ruin it. They represent the corporations, and are entirely out of touch with the people. They cannot see beyond their noses. Would Sir John have left Fred Haultain unseen and unreasoned with until he had blurted out his real opinions in the Saskatchewan Legislature? Would Sir John have let Dick McBride accept a banquet at Ottawa without getting his promise to contest a seat in British Columbia? Would he have let Bob Rogers, after all his brag and bluff, shirk a personal run in Manitoba? Would he have sold out a half-interest in all the principles and fixtures of the Conservative party to Bourassa without requiring Bourassa to come into [illegible] his own [illegible] would not have made [illegible] ada, Australia, and South Africa "which will mean that the United States, instead of being bounded on the north by a colony of a European power ripening to the harvest, will be bounded by an Empire no less firmly set as an American power than it is as a power in Europe." There is no suggestion here of a chafing at colonialism, and if any resentment is discernible it is against American annexationists rather than against British imperialists. Yet little more than a year later *The Star* was in almost open revolt.

The cause was the Alaska boundary dispute. The United States had bought Alaska from the Russians in 1867 but the boundary between British Columbia and the "panhandle" had not as yet been settled. When President Theodore Roosevelt laid claim to a much wider strip than Canadians believed the United States was entitled to, and threatened to land troops to back up the claim, Britain declined to support Canada. Canadians were shocked, and shock soon turned to anger. When Canadians found they were not even to be allowed to "dicker for ourselves," as *The Star* suggested, they were outraged. Britain had asked Canada to go to war against the Boers; it should be ready to go to war for Canada, *The Star* fumed.

When the British member of the tribunal voted with the three US members against the two Canadians, thus agreeing on a boundary that cut off most of Canada's northwest territories from access to the sea, *The Star* reviled it for "politics, not Imperial, but English and insular." It is clear, it said, "that Britain has an Empire she will protect only against weak aggressors."

A short time later the Toronto branch of the British Empire League declared that "Canada needs the protection of the British navy" and should contribute to its financial support. *The Star* lashed back: "Canadians are unable to perceive wherein the backing of Britain and her navy have benefitted Canada a cent's worth in the Alaska boundary dispute. All that a foreign nation claimed from us has been taken from us . . . just as surely as if the Dominion were a young orphan at the mercy of the world . . . The Canadian navy, which does not exist, was just as much use to us as the British navy, which does exist."

Violent as these expressions were, they truly represented the nationalistic mood of Canadians, and must be counted a significant factor in *The Star*'s rocketing rise. In five years while the controversy over Canadian relations with the Motherland was raging *The Star* added 30,000 circulation, the Empire-minded *Telegram* 6,700.

Yet *The Star* never advocated separation from Britain. "In a hundred ways the British connection is of immense value to us," it commented. In the main it endorsed Laurier's conception of the Empire as a group of autonomous nations with a common king, "bound together by a treaty" and mutual self-interest rather than by sentiment, and with each nation "pledged" to defend the others.

In 1909 Mr. Atkinson made his first trip to England as one of the fourteen delegates from Canada to the Imperial Press Conference. George Maitland, who was city editor at the time, said he returned with an anti-British prejudice that remained with him for life. He still believed Canada should remain within the Empire because it was of practical value to this country, but he was more than ever convinced Canada should assert its complete equality with Britain, and have nothing to do with a proposed imperial defence force.

But at the same time he was made aware of the fact that news of significance to Canadians was not confined to Canada and the United States. So, later that same year he sent Gadsby to Ireland to cover the Irish insurrection, Maitland to London to get the British side of the Irish question, and J. T. Clark to England to cover the elections. This marked the beginning of *The Star*'s practice of sending reporters anywhere in the world to cover important events. But world events were treated like domestic stories, to be cleaned up as quickly as possible by a reporter or reporters sent out from home. *The Star* did not favour permanent bureaux, fearing that a man left for long in one post would get too friendly with the natives. Roving reporters were preferred, and even when a London bureau was opened it was looked upon more as a convenient base of operations from which to cover Europe.

Mr. Atkinson had always had a sort of romantic conception of life in "the old country," but on his visit in 1909 he was shocked and appalled by the extreme poverty of the workers in contrast with the extreme luxury in which the aristocracy lived. He was incensed by the arrogant attitude of British officials and politicians towards delegates from the "colonies" to the Imperial Press Conference, and their disrespect for Canadian public opinion. And he was angered at the unconcealed efforts of the British government to bludgeon the colonial publishers into supporting the British policy of one navy to be paid for by all, but which would be run by Britain.

After the second day *The Star* moved reports of the conference from page one to an inside page and cut them to a couple of paragraphs. Mr. Atkinson declined to serve on any committees, refused to give interviews to the British press, and abandoned his intention of addressing the conference.

J. S. Brierley, of the *Montreal Herald,* and J. A. MacDonald, editor of the *Globe*, were quite as angered as Mr. Atkinson and, according to a London newspaper, "stated Canada's position with a vigour that astounded the conference." MacDonald further vented his ire in a dispatch to the *Globe* which raked British morals, manners, and mores from Limehouse to the House of Lords. *The Star* reprinted it.

On the other hand Hugh Graham, publisher of the *Montreal Star*, told the conference that Canadians were done with "sponging on the Empire" and were prepared to contribute through their taxes to the support of the British fleet, while M. E. Nichols, then editor of the Winnipeg *Telegram*, assured the British press in an interview that such men as Atkinson, MacDonald, and Brierley did not represent any significant number of Canadians and had no influence in Canada. Nevertheless, it was papers like Nichols' that the public deserted, not those that preached nationalism.

One of the themes British speakers kept reiterating during the conference was that Germany was out to conquer the world, and that only a united Empire could stop her. Conceding that Germany and Russia were both bent on conquest, and that it would be a sad day if Germany should win a war, *The Star* nevertheless commented that "it would be an equally sad day for the world if all units of the British Empire were subordinated to London."

There is in England, said a later editorial, "a party that is out for glory and conquest, for great military and naval careers, for expansion, for centralization and for aggression. There is another party that believes the great need of England is social and domestic reform and betterment of the conditions of the people. It is upon the side of the latter party that the people of Canada would naturally be arrayed."

These two parties came to grips in the British election of 1910. Canadians believed this election to be of vital concern to them, for the Liberals and Conservatives went to the country with totally different concepts of how the Empire should be organized. The Liberal program of a Commonwealth of equal nations came close to that advocated by *The Star*, but Mr. Atkinson was even more attracted by the Liberal promise of social and constitutional reform.

The Star sent J. T. Clark to cover the campaign. The *Telegram* sent its editor, J. R. ("Black Jack") Robinson, described by the British press as "a radical Imperialist." Stewart Lyon represented the *Globe* and J. S. Willison the *News*. Clark arrived in England on December 13, 1909, and immediately began sending to *The Star* dispatches described by the *Cana-*

dian Annual Review as expressing "a strongly radical view of English conditions." His articles were syndicated throughout Canada and the United States. "Here is a country where sooner or later the cards must be put back in the pack and a new deal called for," he wrote in one of his first stories. "Here the past oppresses the present and the people are preserving the scenery at the expense of the race."

As the campaign drew to a close the Conservatives tried to make imperial preference rather than social reform the issue. In an editorial commenting on this on January 15, 1910, *The Star* made a statement that was to be quoted as the perfect condensation of its Empire policy: "The British Empire will not be saved by restrictions nor lost by freedom. It is worth preserving, not as a trading concern, but as a league of free nations."

The Liberals won the election and their victory marks the end of what might be called the militant phase of *The Star*'s nationalism. Apparently *The Star* believed that with a party pledged to transform the Empire into a league of free and equal nations in power in the old country the struggle was won. Thereafter it concerned itself mostly with urging removal of such vestigial remains of colonialism as appeals to the Privy Council, a British governor general, and lack of a national flag.

The Imperial Conference of 1911 was the first at which the dominions met as equals with the motherland, but Britain and Australia came with proposals for a centralized imperial parliament or council that would have made the Empire virtually a federal union. Sir Wilfrid Laurier led a successful fight for the present loose association. On the Prime Minister's return from London in June, 1911, Mr. Atkinson wrote Sir Wilfrid: "Canadians owe you a debt for the way you have steered the ship through very difficult waters towards a sane, safe and enduring Imperialism. Your supporters and friends never trusted you or admired you more than they do today." Atkinson used the word Imperialism as it was used in 1911, meaning the relationship of the Dominions and colonies in general towards Britain, and not in the narrow sense in which it is used today. "The misfortune for us is that in such a country as this such principles cannot be asserted without at once being the butt of old prejudices which even when dormant are sure to re-appear," Laurier replied.

The Star was as slow as other Canadians in understanding that there were a great many people within the Empire who did not want to be there, but after it did it was persistently critical of the refusal of Britain to give freedom to people who wanted it. It supported home rule for Ireland and independence for India. "Everybody in Canada believes in it," it said. The real danger to the Empire, it commented, lay not in extending freedom to such countries as Canada and Australia, but in withholding it from others like India. "If ever the Empire is wrecked it will be by such countries as India, that do not have self-government," it warned.

Just as Mr. Atkinson's social and economic convictions were derived more from Methodism than from Marxism, so were his moral and ethical convictions derived more from Methodism than from liberalism. He believed in censorship of books, periodicals, motion pictures, and plays, and during his life *The Star* reflected his views when it spoke on the subject at all. To those who said: "I have a right to read what I like," his retort would be: "Yes, but nobody has a right to publish what he likes, if what he publishes corrupts." "The motion picture is a great educational medium, but education should not be in the use of guns," it said in 1914. It once succeeded in having the Victoria Theatre closed for presenting a play that was considered immoral, and it urged the duty of librarians to use discretion in the selection of books.

The Star might be sensational at times, and not all it published was edifying, but Mr. Atkinson was always most careful that nothing it published would corrupt or tend to lower public or private morals. At the same time he drew a sharp distinction between religion and morality. An example is his attitude towards Sunday observance, which he considered purely a matter of religion, and properly exempt from government regulation. When Laurier introduced the Lord's Day Act *The Star* mildly observed that the birds continued to sing, the winds to blow, and the sun to shine without respect to it.

Mr. Atkinson's early training and his emotional reaction to the evils he saw in the liquor traffic made him a prohibitionist. He wanted desperately to believe that drunkenness, alcoholism, even poverty, could be wiped out by act of law; yet reason told him they could not. He first faced this conflict in 1902 when a prohibition referendum was held in Ontario. In his irresolution *The Star* took no stand until two days before voting, when reason prevailed over emotion.

"Prohibition would be a disastrous failure," *The Star* warned then, in a remarkably prophetic editorial. "Business would be dislocated, many evils would be brought upon society, law and order would be brought into contempt, education and work along temperance lines would be suspended, and all for the sake of an unenforced statute which could be repealed or become a dead letter because it is in advance of public opinion." Perhaps in this editorial we find the hand of Joe Clark rather than that of Joe Atkinson. In another editorial the same day it said the bigotry of many prohibitionists "tends to drive thousands to refuse to identify themselves with a cause in which they will be associated with people entirely unguided by reason and ready to malign people of the noblest qualities who happen to disagree with them." This editorial resulted from an attack by prohibitionists upon a respected Anglican clergyman who had expressed his personal opposition to prohibition.

By 1904 *The Star* was tentatively suggesting a system of strict government control which would discourage the use of alcohol while making it available to those who insisted upon using it. This eventually became *The Star*'s policy, though how weakly it was held at first was demonstrated in 1916 when *The Star* called for total prohibition as a wartime measure without either a plebiscite or referendum. It campaigned vigorously on behalf of prohibition in the 1919 referendum.

For several months after Mr. Atkinson became publisher *The Star* ran an occasional advertisement for a Toronto brewery. But he soon decided that to publish liquor advertising was inconsistent with his temperance convictions. However, while his conscience would not allow him to accept liquor advertising in his own paper, he told the Toronto Advertising Club he did not condemn newspapers that did.

The Star vigorously supported Laurier's policy of admitting Europeans of any nationality and creed in as large numbers as they could be induced to come, provided they were of good character and health. It conceded a possibility there might be trouble in the future with Doukhobors and Mennonites, and was not too sure about some of the "undesirables from Britain," but on the whole it was pleased.

In an entertaining little story in 1906 on the changes taking place in Toronto it noted that in five years Jewish newsboys had almost totally displaced Anglo-Saxons. "They are a better class and easier to handle than newsboys used to be. They are also more trustworthy . . . The street sales of *The Star* fall off 1,500 to 2,000 on Jewish holidays," it also noted.

At the same time it agreed with Laurier on a "white Canada" policy. "To hold up the ideal of a white Canada is not to foster race prejudice or to condone injustice to men and nations of other races," it asserted on September 23, 1907. "A nation has a right to determine the quality of its citizenship . . . Canada must consult her own interests."

For a time *The Star* toyed with the idea of Canada "expanding towards the equator" to counterbalance our frozen north, but when a movement for annexation of the West Indies developed in 1905 it was hostile on the grounds it would result in immigration of Negroes. At the same time it defended the rights of members of coloured races already in this country. "They are Canadians," it reminded, and should be treated in every respect the same as white Canadians.

Mr. Atkinson was at first a firm believer in the Lemieux Act of 1907 which provided for compulsory investigation and either arbitration or conciliation before a strike in any public service utility. However, an unfortunate experience in 1910 caused him to doubt whether either was practical. In that year Mackenzie King, by then Minister of Labour, appointed him chairman of a conciliation board of three to arrange a settlement of a railway wage dispute. The board recommended substantial increases, amounting in some cases to 18 per cent, but short of what the unions wanted. CPR trainmen accepted the award and the CPR said it would be made immediately effective. Neither the Grand Trunk Railway nor its employees accepted the decision, and a strike was called which lasted two weeks.

Mr. Atkinson was the only newspaper friend the unions had in Canada at the time, but the strikers attacked him as being "pro-boss." For years this rankled and he would never again serve officially as a labour conciliator. But he blamed the railway as much as the unions, and firmly believed unions were necessary if the working man was to escape exploitation. He was often consulted unofficially, and frequently found a basis for settlement agreeable to both parties. As the Laurier regime drew to a close *The Star* was to deplore on many occasions the failure of the Canadian Liberal party to follow the example of the British Liberals in labour and welfare legislation.

Atkinson believed in free trade, but he was also a pragmatist. Not long after becoming publisher of *The Star* he began to question whether Canada could remove its tariffs while the rest of the world taxed imports from Canada. In an editorial in 1900 *The Star* conceded free trade might be "impracticable" on that account. Moreover, as his nationalism strengthened he found that free trade and nationalism were mutually incompatible. In the struggle in his own mind it was the desire to industrialize Canada that won. But the question that always bothered him was: how far should a government go in taxing wage-earners and farmers to promote industry? In the end he came to believe that reciprocity with the United States offered the solution.

In 1903 *The Star* supported a British preferential tariff which Laurier was negotiating, but at the same time it conceded the possibility that public support of imperial preference was "more a re-action of hostility to the United States" over the Alaska boundary dispute than of regard for Britain. *The Star*'s enthusiasm for imperial preference dimmed when it became apparent the extreme imperialists in Britain (and some in Canada) regarded it as the first step towards an empire federation. The Liberals made much of the benefits of empire preference in the 1904 election, but *The Star* said it had nothing to do with their victory. During the 1906 British election it said it did not object so much to imperial preference as to the people who advocated it. Meanwhile it indicated it was prepared to accept a moderate "tariff for revenue," which was the term being used by Ottawa Liberals to rationalize their support of tariff increases, and in the 1908 federal election it cut loose entirely from its former free trade convictions. "We believe," it said editorially, "that no reasonable advocate of a low tariff would . . . propose that Canada should confine itself to farming, lumbering, fishing and extracting mineral wealth from the soil . . . It is not necessary to argue the relative merits of free trade or protection . . . The only controversies that arise are controversies upon the amount of duty to be levied."

When the Laurier government began its reciprocity talks with the United States in 1911 *The Star* welcomed them. "Canada," it said on January 16, "has such natural facilities for industry as would induce many manufacturers to locate here instead of in the United States" if the tariff barrier were removed. To suggest, as the anti-reciprocity campaigners were doing, that Canadians could not compete with Americans, is "an insult to Canada and an insult to Canadians."

The 1911 federal election was possibly the most bitterly fought in Canadian history, with *The Star* supporting Laurier and reciprocity with a vigour and extravagance that was not seen again in any election for forty years. Men who had played a prominent part in *The Star*'s affairs turned against both it and their party. John C. Eaton (later Sir John) who had inherited his father's shares in the newspaper, and Z. A. Lash, *The Star*'s lawyer, were among eighteen prominent Toronto Liberals who signed a manifesto against reciprocity. Lyman Jones "stumped the country" organizing a rebel movement among Liberals. Among all that group of 1899 financiers who were left, only Cox, Mulock, and Larkin remained true to Laurier.

The Conservatives succeeded in making the issue one of loyalty or treason. "The Conservative party stands for reciprocity with Britain," boomed Borden. "The issue is not reciprocity but revolution," clarioned the *World,* while the *Telegram,* which had condemned Laurier for his Canadianism, now accused him of "hauling down the flag of Canadianism." *The Star* vainly insisted the issue was between "the privileged few and the unprivileged mass." It filled its window with a display of food bought in Buffalo and in Toronto, with prices attached. "The food monopolists who have been able to play both ends against the middle for the benefit of themselves will have their exorbitant profits cut down to the advantage of both classes of their victims," the consumers and the farmers, it said.

But the very wind of nationalism *The Star* had helped fan defeated Laurier, as *The Star* was among the first to acknowledge. Many voters, it said the day after the election, "believed they were making a declaration of national independence." For this "spirit of Canadian nationality . . . there can be nothing but the deepest respect." It ran an amusing front page cartoon showing "Diogenes Laurier" seeking a Liberal in Ontario.

"A man clean through is Sir Wilfrid's successor," it said in a front-page editorial. "R. L. Borden, the new Premier, is a gentleman in the full sense of the word." He has "distinct executive ability" and he has "character." To make sure there was no mistaking its admiration for Borden a second laudatory editorial was published on the editorial page. They were sincere tributes. Atkinson had always admired Borden. When he became leader of the Conservative party in 1901 *The Star* was most complimentary, and at no time did it ever attack him personally. As a matter of fact, Borden was closer than Laurier to *The Star*'s position on public ownership and social legislation.

Mr. Atkinson deeply regretted Mackenzie King's defeat in his home riding of Berlin. During the campaign he had written King offering his "personal assistance," an extraordinary offer in view of Atkinson's aversion to the political limelight. King had been lifted from the civil service only a short time before the election and appointed Minister of Labour. His defeat left him without a job. Mr. Atkinson offered him a position as editorial writer at $3,000 a year, and when he declined that, he asked him—also in vain—for articles on the political situation from time to time.

The Star accepted the vote of 1911 as settling the reciprocity issue for all time, and did not again allude to it. Indeed Mr. Atkinson seems to have decided protection was here to stay, for in identical letters to King and Laurier in 1916 he suggested the Liberal party should cease its attacks on the principle of protection. Laurier disagreed. One might expect that *The Star*'s support of a cause which, in the light of the vote, must have been unpopular, and the defeat of the party it had so staunchly supported, would adversely affect its fortunes, but such was not the case. Its circulation continued to increase at the same steady rate. Obviously in other ways it was pleasing its readers.

Laurier's defeat was one of the momentous milestones in *The Star*'s history. It ended for all practical purposes the pact of 1899. Laurier was out of office and would never return. All planks in his platform of 1896 had been implemented but this one, reciprocity, and it was rejected by the electors. There was no longer a Laurier platform to support. Hereafter *The Star* could go its free and independent way with no curb on its publisher but his own will.

The final seal on its independence was set when Mr. Atkinson became the majority stockholder in 1913, though Mulock and Larkin, militant Liberals both, remained minor stockholders for many more years, importunate but impotent.

After 1913 nobody was ever in a position to control, affect, or materially influence the policies of the newspaper except J. E. Atkinson. Even before 1913 he had been remarkably successful in maintaining his independence against pressure from shareholders. He could not challenge them collectively, but he could challenge them one by one, for there was nothing to hold them together but the slender thread of Laurier policies and even that wore thin.

Why should *The Star* ever again submit to outside influence? It was a large and prosperous institution, free of debt by 1913, and never again under obligation to any man, combination of men, or party. Quite aside from moral considerations and the reluctance which many men feel to selling their souls, it provided J. E. Atkinson and the members of his family with all the income required to live in the unostentatious manner they preferred.

Hereafter it was a liberal paper solely because J. E. Atkinson was a liberal. It opposed the Conservative party because Mr. Atkinson believed Conservatism would be harmful to the well-being of Canada and its people. At times it supported Progressives and Socialists because, to quote Maitland, "they were giving bigger licks to the Conservatives than the Liberals were." Except for a few short periods it supported the Liberal party for it, in the main, was furthering liberal principles and a platform Atkinson had helped to draft.

Chapter 6

THE BREAK WITH LAURIER

The years after 1911 were critical ones for *The Star*, as they were also for Canada. The golden age of Laurier prosperity and national expansion, which had lasted fifteen years, was drawing to a close, soon to be followed by a depression, then by war. The Liberal party was in eclipse, riven by factions that were almost to destroy it, and *The Star* felt compelled to support those who broke away from the leadership of the old leader. Nationalism, a keystone of *Star* policy, was sunk in the effort to win the war and was soon to be discredited in English Canada by the excesses of the Quebec Nationalists led by Henri Bourassa.

The defeat of Laurier freed *The Star*, indeed compelled it, to review some of the policies it had supported, but it had to do so without appearing to desert outworn causes or old loyalties. This it did by keeping mum. Between 1911 and 1916 *The Star* rarely expressed strong convictions in national affairs, contenting itself with the reasonably safe position of a fair and moderate opposition newspaper in both federal and provincial affairs. It had resumed its support of the provincial Liberal party after Newton W.

Rowell was chosen leader in 1911. "He is a noble fellow, worthwhile fighting alongside of," Atkinson wrote Mackenzie King.

For a while Mr. Atkinson busied himself getting the recently organized Canadian Press Limited soundly established in Ontario and Quebec as a co-operative news-gathering association. Until 1910 most eastern Canadian newspapers had received their wire news from Canadian Pacific Telegraph Company, and their cable news from Canadian Associated Press. But in that year the telegraph company announced it was giving up the news-distributing business, and was prepared to surrender the rights to Associated Press, which it held for Canada, to whatever news-gathering organization the publishers set up.

Eastern publishers quickly incorporated Canadian Press Limited to be a holding company for Canadian rights to AP. As president and secretary-treasurer respectively, J. F. Mackay of the *Globe* and J. E. Atkinson signed the first contract with AP. The following year negotiations were begun with Western Associated Press, a co-operative that had been serving newspapers west of the Lakehead since 1907; the object—to form a national news service.

Head of Western Associated Press was M. E. Nichols of the *Winnipeg Telegram*, and he and Atkinson clashed immediately on the way costs of bridging the long, unpopulated gap between East and West should be shared. The westerners wanted the cost apportioned among individual newspapers in proportion to their circulations. The easterners argued that the two associations should retain their separate identities within the proposed national organization, and that each association should be charged an equal share of the cost.

The main flow of news was from East to West, and the western newspapers would benefit a great deal more from bridging the gap than newspapers in the East. Under the western cost-sharing plan, said the easterners, the much more numerous eastern dailies would, in effect, be subsidizing the western papers. Aside from the cost of bridging the gap, there was the cost of servicing western newspapers strung along two thousand miles of territory. Eastern newspapers were in a compact group that could be economically served, and they objected to subsidizing uneconomic operations in the West.

During negotiations "the West had in Eddie Macklin (manager of the Winnipeg *Free Press*) a master poker player, seasoned in experience," Nichols wrote in his *(CP): Story of the Canadian Press*. "The East had its protagonists in Joe Atkinson, whose inexperience in the noble game found ample compensation in his intuitive understanding of it."

Due, said Nichols, to "Atkinson's finesse" the six Toronto newspapers and two English-language newspapers of Montreal presented a united front the West could not crack. He blamed chiefly the *Globe*, the *Telegram*, and *The Star* of Toronto, "and Atkinson shaped the policy of the trinity." P. D. Ross, of the *Ottawa Journal*, who believed eastern publishers should make some sacrifices in the cause of national unity, also blamed the Toronto newspapers for "relying on their geographical position, which gives them an advantage."

The westerners pictured the "big eastern publishers" as opposed to co-operative news-gathering. This may have been true in the case of E. F. Slack, of the Montreal *Gazette*, who spoke for the Montreal newspapers, and of Mackay of the *Globe*. As heads of morning newspapers with many correspondents and a wide circulation outside their own cities they regarded the small city daily newspapers as competitors. But neither Mr. Atkinson nor John Ross Robertson held any such narrow view. Atkinson was, in fact, actively promoting co-operative news-gathering by Ontario newspapers. Canadian Press Limited had been incorporated only to serve as a holding company for AP rights, but Mr. Atkinson was mainly responsible for having it turned into a news agency serving all Ontario newspapers.

Having lost their fight to have the eastern newspapers subsidize their uneconomic operations, the western publishers began to pressure the government for a subsidy, and they found many allies in the East. Mr. Atkinson believed a government subsidy could endanger freedom of the press in Canada, and he opposed it, ably seconded by Robertson. After war broke out in 1914 the newspapers succeeded in persuading the government that the wartime need for national unity made a subsidy essential, but to make clear he would have no part of it Mr. Atkinson resigned as secretary-treasurer of Canadian Press.

"J. E. Atkinson cheerfully accepted office as secretary-treasurer of Canadian Press Limited in the hope, I think, that when tempers subsided he could be of assistance in making it a living thing," Nichols wrote. "When four years passed without evidence of progress he resigned, which was unfortunate . . . He declined to accept policies which were acceptable to most of his colleagues."

Nichols does Atkinson an injustice. Though still far from national, Canadian Press was very much "a living thing" in Ontario and Quebec, due largely to Mr. Atkinson's efforts. There had been real progress. And what Nichols dismisses as "policies," Atkinson held to be vital principles, essential to preservation of freedom of the press. The fact that "most of his colleagues" accepted these "policies" did not make them right in Atkinson's eyes.

By 1913 Mr. Atkinson had acquired a majority interest in *The Star*, and he chose to announce this to the other shareholders in a manner that tickled his sense of humour as well as his love of the dramatic. The annual meeting of December 8 was attended by shareholders Sir William Mulock, P. C. Larkin, E. T. Malone, and A. L. Malone. A heated discussion arose over some matter of policy, with Sir William laying down the law as usual and Larkin agreeing with him. Mr. Atkinson listened courteously for a while, then interrupted to state he intended to follow a course quite different from the one suggested.

"And on this occasion I can present my views with authority, because I am now the owner of a majority of the stock of *The Star*," he smiled. He used to look back with considerable delight on the shock this announcement gave Sir William.

The company records do not show whose shares he acquired to give him his majority, for the stock of the major shareholders was held in trust by E. T. Malone. The records merely indicate a transfer from E. T Malone to Mr. Atkinson of 201 ordinary shares and 335 preferred shares, and from Henry A. Little to Mr. Atkinson of twenty-two ordinary shares. But at any rate, as of record on April 15, 1914, J. E. Atkinson was owner of 534 shares of ordinary stock. Five other shareholders owned the remaining 466 shares. Cox was the only shareholder who had acknowledged in writing the right of J. E. Atkinson to have first chance to buy his shares, and most of the stock transferred in Malone's name undoubtedly came from him. The senator, then seventy-four, had been ill for five months and died only a month later. The inventory of his estate, as published by his executors, of which Malone was one, did not show that he owned any *Star* stock at the time of his death. Mr. Atkinson may also have acquired Malone's personal holdings, the extent of which were never disclosed for a notation the following June indicates he had divested himself of all *Star* stock he owned. Timothy Eaton had died in 1907 and his son John (later Sir John) Eaton owned his shares. Massey's shares had passed to Chester Massey, then to the Massey Manufacturing Company, and shortly after this date to Vincent and Raymond Massey. At this same meeting in 1913 Sir William Mulock's shares were transferred to William Mulock, Jr., who was to prove almost as bothersome a thorn in Mr. Atkinson's flesh as his father had been.

On April 20 A. L. Malone resigned as a director and was succeeded by Mr. Atkinson's personal physician and friend, Dr. Wilbur Harris. E. T. Malone did not attend any more directors' meetings and on June 29 he too resigned. He was succeeded by Walter C. R. Harris, the bookkeeper who had left the *News* with the strikers to found *The Star* and was now business manager. A few months later J. R. Bone succeeded Dr. Harris as a director. Bone and W. C. R. Harris had each acquired thirty shares of preferred stock from Malone in 1914, much to Atkinson's chagrin. They were the only employees who ever succeeded in buying stock in *The Star* during Mr. Atkinson's lifetime, apart from the one share needed to qualify as a director, but even they could not acquire common stock. Mr. Atkinson purchased their stock after they died.

Before his death in 1948, Mr. Atkinson had acquired all the stock except the Mulock interest. He paid $50 a share for his first purchase, $5,000 a share for his last. He tried repeatedly to buy out William Mulock, Jr. Once, shortly before Mulock died in 1928, H. S. Sainthill, *The Star*'s chief accountant, encountered him on the stairway.

"The old boy tried to buy me out again," Mulock chuckled, jerking a thumb towards Mr. Atkinson's office. "He offered me - - - - -," naming a figure.

"That's a pretty good price," he was told.

"Ha!" Mulock snorted. "If he offers me that much you may be sure it's worth more."

Mr. Atkinson had no sooner acquired the majority interest than he had the delight of seeing *The Star* emerge as a power in municipal politics. Not only did *The Star*'s candidate for mayor, H. C. Hocken, wipe the floor with McBrien, the *Telegram*'s candidate, in the voting on January 1, 1914, but James Simpson was elected to board of control with the biggest majority ever given anybody for that office to that date.

The contest had been widely regarded as a test of strength between *The Star* and the *Telegram*. Each paper had picked a complete slate of candidates for mayor, board of control, and city council. All but five on *The Star*'s slate were elected. Of several questions put to the electors, all those supported by *The Star* carried while the only one supported by the *Telegram* was lost. The day after the election *The Star* printed a cartoon on page one of a voter holding his nose with one hand and dropping a dead cat he was holding by the tail, labelled "the *Telegram*," into a garbage pail.

Victory was all the sweeter because in the preceding election *The Star* had taken quite a beating. Simpson had been snowed under and a modified single-tax plan advocated by *The Star* had been defeated. Ever since he had read Henry George as a young man Mr. Atkinson had been attracted to the idea of a high tax on land, a low tax on buildings and improvements. Several times *The Star* had tentatively suggested Toronto might experiment along those lines, and had published an occasional article on Henry George's tax theories.

After the electors turned down the proposal in 1913 *The Star* dropped the single-tax idea and thereafter advocated that the city buy enough additional land when a public project was undertaken to assure that the taxpayers rather than speculators benefit from any increase in property values resulting from the expenditure of public monies.

Early in 1913 Bion J. Arnold, the man who had electrified New York's suburban railways, advised city council to buy the street railway system, as *The Star* had long advocated. Mr. Atkinson personally took an active part in the ensuing campaign for purchase of the streetcar system, addressing public meetings and clubs, and there can be little doubt that his campaign on behalf of public ownership and city planning was an important factor in the election in 1914 of Hocken as mayor and Simpson as controller. Both advocated purchase of the streetcar lines.

Simpson had left *The Star* in 1912 to become a full-time labour organizer, but Mr. Atkinson still considered him a *Star* protegé. He had been elected to board of education in 1905, and had run unsuccessfully for mayor and three times as a Socialist candidate for the legislature. *The Star* gave a banquet to celebrate his election to board of control, to which all employees were invited. Mr. Atkinson was master of ceremonies and his delight was unconcealed. In fact, he so far succumbed to the spirit of *bonhomie* as to light up a cigarette with the guest of honour, though after a few tentative and distasteful puffs he put it aside. He did not become a smoker until after his wife's death in 1931. Simpson was presented with an illuminated address on behalf of his former editorial associates.

Atkinson had become alarmed in 1909 at the arms race between Britain and Germany, fearing it would rule out possibility of a peaceable settlement of problems vexing the two countries. He was horrified when the Conservatives at Ottawa used their large majority in 1913 to ram through Parliament a bill to donate a dreadnought to the British navy, but *The Star* based its opposition on constitutional grounds.

"Is it to be self-government or centralization?" it demanded. "Is the process of evolution which has brought Canada up to its present proud position to be continued, or to cease? Are we to take the new path . . . which tends to place Canada in a position analogous to that of one of its provinces?"

Laurier used the large Liberal majority in the Senate to veto the gift. When Conservatives threatened to abolish the Senate for thus thwarting the will of the Commons, *The Star* said it hoped they would—it should have been abolished long ago, and one useful deed did not compensate for forty-six years of inactivity.

When a Serbian terrorist assassinated the Crown Prince of Austria at Sarajevo on June 28, 1914, *The Star* carried the story on the front page. But as soon as it appeared this might be the spark to set off a general conflagration all stories dealing with the crisis in Europe were moved to inside pages, where they remained until the declaration of war by Germany on Russia on August 1, 1914.

Mindful of the part he believed British and Canadian papers had played in fomenting the Boer War, Mr. Atkinson was determined *The Star* would not be guilty of any part in increasing the war fever. So far as anybody reading the news pages of *The Star* might know to the contrary all was sweetness and light in Europe. Editorially it conceded the danger of war, and as relations worsened took issue with those in Britain who said the way to prevent war was to be so powerful Germany would not start anything.

"There is another way, but it has been suggested it may be too pusillanimous," it said, continuing:

> That would be to recognize the fact that the time has come when the defence of a nation ought to be taken out of the hands of the armed man and put into the keeping of the statesman, the banker, and the merchant. Now that war cannot be confined to the land and the surface of the sea, but rises into the clouds and follows the depth of the sea, is it not reason to hope that mankind will see the cost and peril will far exceed any use that remains in it to nations that subsist on industry and trade and must perish of famine without them? It is getting pretty near time for the Parliament of Man to hold a session.

Germany declared war on Russia on a Sunday. Monday, August 2, was civic holiday, and for the first time *The Star* published on a holiday to give the public the latest news on the impending crisis. W. R. Plewman, a scholarly student of history and foreign affairs, who had been telegraph editor and foreign news analyst for nine years, wrote the first of the daily "The War Reviewed" columns that were to win him international commendation for their insight and objectivity.

The day Britain declared war he wrote a remarkably lucid and restrained exposition of the conflicting historical forces that had helped bring about the struggle. "The most curious and humanly interesting fact of all," he wrote, "is that in Germany and Austria, in Russia and France, in Britain and Belgium, wherever people are sharpening their swords or loading their muskets, pious persons are addressing prayers in their various languages to the same throne of heaven asking for aid in their warfare and for success of their arms in the struggle that has been unjustly forced upon them by their enemies."

Once the nations of the world were irrevocably committed to war no newspaper supported the Canadian war effort more vigorously than *The Star*. "*The Toronto Star* was influential in (Liberal) party councils because of its ability, and it took the clear line of liberty and loyalty," stated the *Canadian Annual Review*. "Tested and tried by the fiery ordeal of war, British unity seems to be strong, while each part of the Empire enjoys liberty to go its own way and is developed along its own lines," *The Star* said editorially. "Experience has been the best vindication of freedom. Surely the lesson is that freedom ought to be extended not contracted."

At the same time it warned against the suggestion, which originated in Britain but with which Borden seemed to be toying, that Empire armed forces should be pooled under British command, and that conduct of the war should be entrusted to an Empire Parliament or council. "By all means let there be consultation and co-operation for common ends," it said, but consultation was as far as it thought Canada should go.

Gradually it enunciated the principles that (*a*) there should be no election until the war was won, (*b*) the war should be prosecuted by a non-partisan or union government, and (*c*) there should be conscription of both wealth and men. By conscription of wealth, it explained later, it meant a graduated income tax, which Canada did not have at the time, and an excess profits tax. It did not favour a coalition government, which would mean a balancing of Liberals and Conservatives, but rather a national government of "the best men" regardless of party, with the prime minister going outside Parliament if necessary for cabinet material.

J. Castell Hopkins, distinguished writer and editor, and a Conservative, wrote in the *Canadian Annual Review* that while *The Star*'s proposals were realistic and sensible, its motives were suspect by the Conservative press. Although *The Star* was almost daily advocating National government with a non-partisan cabinet, he observed that it was unceasing in its harsh criticism of the Borden government's war effort, and particularly of its financial policy. Was it advocating National government as a means of ousting the Tories? Some suspected so. Conservatives were alarmed also at its advocacy of "conscription of wealth."

The fact is that the Canadian war effort was being ineptly handled and there had been some bad examples of incompetence and of profiteering on war contracts. Moreover, Borden was hampered by the fact he was dependent upon the support of some twenty Quebec Nationalists who were absolutely opposed to Canadian participation in the war. *The Star* urged Borden in 1915 and early 1916 to cut these Nationalists off from the Conservative party and accept Laurier as the only authentic voice of French Canada. The conscription issue had not as yet arisen and Laurier was co-operating closely with Borden.

While Atkinson had been out of sympathy with Laurier for several years, the actual break when it came was over Laurier's war policies. The first major dispute followed the introduction of the Borden government's budget in February, 1916, providing for an excess profits tax. Both *The Star* and the *Globe* approved of this feature, and they did not immediately find fault with the budget. Sir Wilfrid promptly fired off letters to Mr. Atkinson and to Stewart Lyon of the *Globe* expressing his displeasure.

Mr. Atkinson replied with an eight-page letter containing a detailed analysis of the budget, which he suggested might be helpful to the Liberal financial critic. *The Star*, he said, had merely held its fire until it could study the budget at greater length. The one thing, he said, which he could not find fault with was the excess profits tax.

Sir Wilfrid retorted that such a tax was inexcusable, and he gave his reasons in detail for finding it wholly unacceptable, chief of which was that it would lower incentive to produce. Mr. Atkinson wrote Sir Wilfrid by return mail:

> Please do not think I am writing in this way because I set my opinions against those which you in Ottawa have arrived at, but it can do no harm that you should have put before you the view that the wisest course, if I may say so without presumption, is to leave the government the responsibility for adopting this means of raising its war revenues, on the condition that the bill shall contain provisions for its application with a minimum of inequity and handicap to those businesses which are being conducted in accordance with sound financial principles, and without offering immunity to those other businesses which have been in the field of stock jobber and inflator.

Dealing with the incentive motive editorially, *The Star* said it could not believe Canadian industrialists would help their country win the war only if assured of exorbitant profits.

"I am sorry to say that we are at the very antipodes on this question," Sir Wilfrid replied to Mr. Atkinson's letter. "The whole scheme seems to me wrong from the start. No amount of amendment can eradicate this fatal defect. I do not think it would be advisable further to carry on this discussion beween us. I hope, however, that your last word has not been said upon it." Here was the Gladstonian Liberal pleading that free enterprise is entitled to its profits.

A month later *The Star* was calling for what must have appeared to Laurier like a reversal of his railway policy. The Grand Trunk Pacific and Canadian Northern Railways had got into financial difficulties and were asking for some form of financial relief. "A conviction grows that the only permanent solution will be found in nationalization," *The Star* said. "The longer it is delayed the more difficult it will be, and the greater the burden the country will have to assume . . . The country must not be frightened by the magnitude of the undertaking, or the responsibilities that will have to be assumed."

When Conservative newspapers reported that Sir Wilfrid was opposed to nationalizing the railways *The Star* hotly retorted: "A campaign of persistent and malignant lying has been carried on against Sir Wilfrid Laurier." It said nationalization of the railways would have the support of the Liberal party. *The Star* was mistaken in this, as it should have anticipated because of Laurier's conception of Liberal principles.

A year later a royal commission appointed by Borden to investigate the railway problem recommended nationalization and reported: "The shareholders of the company have no equity either on the ground of cash put in or on the ground of the saleable value of the property as a going concern." *The Star* heartily endorsed the report, particularly the suggestion the country should take the railways without compensation. The people, it argued, "should not assume a ruinous obligation." The CPR could join the national system or not as it liked, but *The Star* saw no objection to a government-owned and a privately owned railway competing with each other. Later in 1917 it modified its position, urging nationalization of the CNR and GTR "on equitable terms" after an independent appraisal.

Meanwhile, Ontario and western Liberals had been growing restive under Laurier's passive leadership. This was particularly true in the case of Rowell, the Ontario leader, who had virtually made a truce with the provincial Conservatives and was devoting most of his time to patriotic work. *The Star* was still outwardly devoted to Laurier, though once it made a significant reference to him as the greatest statesman "not in office," and Mr. Atkinson tried to conciliate the two factions. On May 17 he invited Laurier to Toronto to meet a few friends. "I sincerely hope some way out of the present situation may be found in which the convictions of neither group of friends need be compromised," he wrote. Laurier replied that he had contemplated coming to Toronto anyway to meet Atkinson, Rowell, and others "with a view to making a last attempt to come to a solution of a situation which has become intolerable, so far at least as I am concerned." The conference achieved little.

At the same time *The Star* was becoming increasingly critical of the Borden government and its "sham taxing of excess profits." There should be "a real appropriation of them by the state," it declared. "The war destroys the force of the argument that profit is necessary to stimulate business." The year ended with its hinting at the need for conscription and declaring "there should not be a party in office at a time like this . . . The country should have a non-partisan war administration."

On May 28, 1917, Borden asked Laurier for a conference. He informed him that compulsory military service was, in his opinion, necessary and explained the provisions of the conscription bill he proposed to introduce. He invited Sir Wilfrid to join him in forming a coalition government. Laurier declined, and said conscription should not be enforced without a referendum of the people.

That same evening Mackenzie King wrote Mr. Atkinson asking him if *The Star* would support Laurier in a call for a national referendum on conscription. "Once the measure is carried by this way, by referendum, there would no longer be questions as to the attitude which all parts of the Dominion should show towards it," he wrote. He described Laurier as "genuinely distressed" over the possibility a situation may be created "which is going to be extremely difficult to deal with . . . if Canada is to be spared grave misfortune." Atkinson's reply is not on record, but it was evidently unfavourable, for a few days later Laurier asked him to come to Ottawa for a conference. Mr. Atkinson replied:

My Dear Sir Wilfrid, I shall gladly come down to Ottawa . . . I should deeply regret it if we should not be able to respect each other's opinions when, as the case is, they are sincerely held. I have believed and expressed in connection with this situation that there is no alternative to your leadership. It is the bridge to future re-union of the party and country, but in the immediate future the differences which exist between those who support and those who oppose conscription ought to be frankly and tolerantly recognized.

This appears to be the last correspondence ever exchanged between Mr. Atkinson and Sir Wilfrid Laurier. They had, in fact, never corresponded regularly, and this flurry of letters in 1916 and 1917 was unusual. For sixteen years Atkinson's contacts with the higher echelon of the Liberal party had been almost entirely through Sir William Mulock. Hereafter it was to be almost entirely through Mackenzie King.

"The Liberal party is split, and it is hard to see how during the war it can come together again," *The Star* commented. It said conscription was of such "absolute necessity" that as long as Liberals are divided on that, no other issue or combination of issues can conceivably reunite them.

The break with Laurier became complete on July 25, 1917. "Sir Wilfrid Laurier has been a great figure in this country," *The Star* commented. "But in this crisis he has chosen Quebec as his kingdom and Canada can no longer choose him as the man to govern." If an election were held before the new year, as Borden had intimated, the Liberals remaining true to Laurier would go into the election "on old and obsolete issues as dead as Julius Caesar."

The following day representatives of twenty Ontario Liberal daily and weekly newspapers met in Toronto. *The Star* was represented by J. R. Bone and J. T. Clark, who played a prominent part in drafting a resolution "to stand squarely for compulsory military service" and in the impending election to support no candidates except those who stood for that policy. At the same time they declared "Sir Robert Borden and his government have proved themselves unequal to the task."

Commenting on this *The Star* said the country wanted neither Laurier nor Borden. It wants something more than "a patched up Borden ministry." It is "sick and tired of Sir Robert Borden, [Hon. Robert] Rogers [Minister of Public Works who had been the principal target of Liberal attack], and the rest." It called the moderate income tax introduced in the preceding budget "a fraud on the electors" intended to cover the government's abject surrender to profiteers, and demanded a still higher excess profits tax.

On July 25 and later *The Star* ran whole pages of telegraphed answers to the question of whether or not the time had arrived for "the prime minister to bring into his cabinet representatives of all parties and the ablest businessmen available, thus organizing a truly national Canadian government." Those questioned were all the reeves, mayors, and presidents of Canadian clubs and boards of trade in the country, with no attempt to pick and choose or select answers. On various days the replies ranged from 70 per cent to 80 per cent favouring a national government.

All Liberal and most independent newspapers followed the lead of *The Star* in calling for the resignation of Borden and his replacement by a non-political figure as prime minister, but Conservative papers professed to find a political motive behind the movement. Perhaps there was, for unquestionably the accession of some of the leading Liberals to Borden's union government greatly strengthened the Conservative party and weakened the Liberals.

Meantime Mr. Atkinson was speaking at various centres in the province on behalf of conscription and his proposed National government. Typical was an address he delivered at his old home town of Newcastle in August, when he presented the town with a flag pole and flag in commemoration of the third anniversary of the outbreak of war and of the Newcastle volunteers who were fighting for their country.

"Canada has done well!" the local paper quoted him as saying. "Yes, but some have done badly. Those who do nothing have no share in the honor coming to Canada. We need conscription, not only of bodies but of wealth, to strike the blow at war-lordism. The new democracy is coming, paid for in blood, when men shall come more directly into their own."

The paper reports that "Master Joe Atkinson Jr." was given the honour of raising the flag, marching from the bandstand with the Newcastle cadet corps providing him with a guard of honour. The letter of thanks from Newcastle council for the flag pole was signed by Reeve J. Coulson, who had been a classmate of Atkinson's in public school.

Though *The Star* had attacked Borden for incompetence and for not suppressing profiteering, it supported the Union government after it was formed in October, 1917. "It is as representative of both political parties throughout Canada as could be expected," it said. It was preferable to a coalition government which could not have succeeded in view of Laurier's adamant stand against conscription, but it fell short of the ideal national government of the best brains, which *The Star* had advocated.

Laurier Liberals were highly incensed at what they regarded as an act of treason by *The Star*. To mollify them Atkinson sent Maitland to Montreal to meet the leading Quebec Liberals. His instructions were not to argue, not to apologize, not to try to explain *The Star*'s reasons, but to listen patiently while they blew off steam, and to assure them that once the period of post-war reconstruction was over *The Star* would again support the Liberal party.

In the election of December 17, 1917, *The Star* was solidly behind the Union government and the pro-conscription Liberals who supported it. It contributed $1,000 to the Liberal-Unionist election fund. The Conservative press, led by the *Telegram*, violently attacked Quebec as treasonable and anti-Canadian, but *The Star* was more tolerant. "We in Ontario and the West regard the war as a Canadian question, and Quebec does not," it remarked. Mackenzie King ran in North York but took little part in the campaign outside his own riding. He was the only official Liberal candidate in Toronto and the Yorks *The Star* did not oppose, but shareholder P. C. Larkin financed King's campaign. King was defeated.

The electors returned Borden's Union government, thus endorsing conscription. The day after the election Mr. Atkinson received the following personal note from Borden: "You are the first man I thank after our victory, for you are one of the few who never asked anything of me." But to the man who had never asked anything of him Borden offered a baronetcy, which was promptly turned down. Borden believed in titles and was more lavish in their distribution than any previous Prime Minister. He had elevated Hugh Graham, publisher of the *Montreal Star*, to the peerage as Lord Atholstan, knighted Willison of the Toronto *News* for changing his politics, and on the slightest excuse was making a "Sir" of any millionaire "for distinguished service towards winning the war."

In a lengthy letter Mr. Atkinson told Borden he had supported Union government entirely from motives of patriotism and without any hope or expectation of reward other than the satisfaction which comes from the knowledge one has done right. "There is nothing within the gift of the government that I want or will accept," the letter concluded.

Presumably Mr. Atkinson was to have been given a title in the King's birthday honours list of June 3, 1918, but to make his position clear, in March *The Star* ran five strong editorials against the institution. "There will never be any complaint in Canada that titles are too few," it said in the first, on March 8. "Titles are bought and sold over the counter" for political support, it charged the next day. "During the war the sowing and harvesting of titles goes on as never before," it commented in the third editorial. In the fourth it suggested that Parliament give no more titles for the duration of the war and the year following, and in the fifth it said it "has heard no indignant protest at the suggestion they be abolished."

The Star was not alone in its protest. In Toronto four of the five newspapers, including the *Telegram*, were against titles, as was every western paper. In consequence only five persons were given titles in the King's birthday honours list, and the following year titles were abolished.

Since 1916 *The Star*'s circulation had been declining. During the 1917 election campaign it fell by 6 per cent while the *Telegram* pulled ahead of it again. In 1918 circulation declined another 10 per cent and *The Star* dropped into third position in Toronto. It barely held its own in 1919, then began to recover. But it did not regain its 1915 circulation of 105,000 until 1922, when it again drew abreast of the *Telegram*.

It may be that in a period of wartime emotionalism the *Telegram*'s strident imperialism and "hate Quebec" campaign was more fitted to the mood of Toronto than *The Star*'s moderation. Perhaps, as a Liberal paper, *The Star* suffered because of the general decline of Liberal popularity, despite its support of conscription and its break with Laurier. Perhaps, as some have suggested, the break with Laurier was the more important cause, and it was true-blue Laurier Liberals who stopped reading it. Perhaps it was a combination of all three.

Mr. Atkinson believed it was because of the decline of the Liberal party. The Liberal party had nothing to fight for except issues "as dead as Julius Caesar." It was riven by bitter hatreds, and there were in sight no leader, or platform, or issues to heal the breach once the war was over and conscription need no longer divide.

Joseph Atkinson was ready to provide it with all three, and thus restore not only the fortunes of the Liberal party, but those of *The Star* as well.

Chapter 7

A NEW PROGRAM FOR LIBERALS

Joseph E. Atkinson began the task of drafting a new platform for the Liberal party early in January, 1916. He was then fifty years of age. He had been appointed chairman of an advisory subcommittee of the National Liberal Association to study and report upon a program of social reform and health legislation.

The appointment came as no surprise to him; he had been angling for it for months. Ever since Laurier's defeat in 1911 he had been urging upon party leaders the necessity of framing a wholly new program on advanced liberal lines to replace the old Laurier platform which had been largely implemented while what little remained was outmoded. For several years he had been writing and making public speeches on the need for social reform.

He had watched with sympathetic interest the efforts of the British Liberal party to improve the conditions of the depressed classes, but at first he did not believe that Canada needed such a sweeping welfare program. Canada, *The Star* said editorially, is a vigorous young country with opportunities for all and no oppressive aristocracy.

However, in discussing old age pensions in 1907 *The Star* said "it is impossible to deny the logical force of Ruskin's contention that the old soldiers of the ploughshare are as much entitled to recognition as the old soldiers of the sword." The public should not too hastily conclude "that the debt cannot be paid." About the same time it began discussing compensation for injured workmen.

The depression of 1913 swept away what complacency Mr. Atkinson had about Canada's fortunate position. He was appalled as the roll of unemployed mounted during the winter of 1913–14 and indignant that city, province, and Dominion alike disclaimed any responsibility for feeding the hungry. *The Star* ran a fund throughout the winter for the relief of the unemployed, but that thousands must thus subsist on private charity angered him.

"Canada must have some form of unemployment insurance," he told the Toronto Moose Club on February 19, 1914. "The large and apparently inevitable degree to which the province is affected [by the depression] urgently demands some such provision being made by legislation, as is already in operation in the Motherland." Thereafter he did a great deal of speaking on social problems before various organizations, apparently with no political objective in mind. His purpose seems to have been only to stir up public interest in such matters. Mr. Atkinson was more outspoken in his public addresses than *The Star* was editorially.

"Before the war materialism was the keynote of all the nations, Canada included," he declared before the Canadian Club of Toronto on November 30, 1915. "In Canada we have had for the past 25 years a government which in its outlook was conservative, no matter what its name. Material prosperity has long occupied the attention of the people and the government of Canada. After the war things will not be the same as they were before. Many pet prejudices will have to go by the board, and more attention and sympathy will have to be devoted to the everyday life of the people." He looked forward, he said, to seeing old age pensions and sick benefits for workers adopted in Canada. Even tariffs should have built-in protection for the workers and consumers, he said on a later occasion. "The human element in the manufacturing industry, the quality and standards of living of the workers and workmen, is more important than the product," he declared. A tariff act should contain provisions forbidding manufacturers to form combines and providing some method of establishing fair wages and a fair price for a protected article.

The question naturally arises as to why Atkinson took a stronger line in his personal addresses than he did in his newspaper. The explanation may be that *The Star* was still ostensibly the spokesman for Laurier and the Liberal party and they were for free trade and against "government interference" in economic affairs. He may also have felt that since his speeches were widely reported, even in newspapers competing with *The Star*, he was reaching a wider audience than could be reached by editorials.

The first man to whom Mr. Atkinson wrote after his appointment as chairman of the Liberal health and welfare subcommittee was Mackenzie King, then working for the Rockefeller Foundation in the United States but still attached to Liberal headquarters. In a somewhat lengthy letter he explained the subcommittee's purpose as being "to study and report upon a comprehensive program which shall include such measures as (1) old age pensions (2) national insurance for sickness and invalidity and (3) insurance against unemployment in certain occupation and industries." He invited King to join the subcommittee and forward any ideas he might have.

Two days later on January 15, he wrote King that he was going to Ottawa to meet other members of the subcommittee, which included Hon. W. S. Fielding, former minister of finance, Alphonse Verville, Labour member of Parliament for Maisonneuve, J. J. Hughes, M.P. for Kings, P.E.I., Samuel W. Jacobs of Montreal, president of the National Liberal Association, and P. C. Larkin.

Within two months the Atkinson subcommittee was able to report progress, and since King was in the United States and nearly all the other members were occupied in Ottawa with the session of Parliament, one may suppose the progress was mainly due to the chairman's activity. At any rate, on March 16, 1916, Mr. Atkinson wrote identical letters to Sir Wilfrid Laurier, Samuel Jacobs, and Mackenzie King, far too long to be more than summarized here.

"Old age pensions would naturally be the first plank in a program," he wrote. He had studied and made a digest of the old age pensions legislation of Denmark, New Zealand, three states of Australia, and Britain, and suggested following the example of Denmark. "I have also endeavoured to estimate the outlay which would be involved in Canada by the adoption of the Australian rate of pensions applied to the pensionable age which Great Britain has adopted, namely 70 years and over. I have no thought of doing more than approximating what an old age pension act would mean to Canada, but even that involves considerable study," he continued.

Next most important, he declared, is widows' pensions, "which really are pensions for the children of widows . . . These two features make a strong appeal to popular opinion and do not involve a very burdensome obligation." Then, he added, there must be maternity allowances, and pensions for people "who become totally incapacitated at an earlier age than the pensionable one."

"The principle underlying unemployment insurance is thoroughly sound and should form part of a Liberal program," he declared. "The report to the unemployment commission in Ontario is an ample justification for the adoption of a scheme in which the employer, the state, and the employee cooperate. The commission had not the courage to recommend such insurance although it showed not only the necessity but the equity of it."

Another plank should be a Dominion workmen's compensation act covering disability accidents to workmen. He referred to the Ontario law as "a very good measure that might well form a model for federal legislation." Shortly after this date the Borden government passed such an act. It was hailed by Mr. Atkinson in a public address as "the most liberal act ever passed by a Canadian government, Liberal or Conservative."

He advocated a minimum wage and maximum hours act for women and children. Such legislation had been advocated before, but the Canadian Manufacturers' Association had prevented its adoption. He suggested the Industrial Disputes Investigation Act should be supplemented by legislation providing for the establishment by simple machinery of local wage boards similar to those which for several years had been in operation in Australia. "They would be useful in connection with the equitable operation of the tariffs insofar as seeing fair play to wage earners is concerned," he suggested. Dealing with tariffs he said:

> Perhaps you will allow me to express here my opinion that the proper fiscal policy for the Liberal party in the light of present conditions is a cessation of attacks upon the principles of protection in our tariff and the plain and emphatic acceptance of the obligation which must rest upon any government which extends tariff advantages to certain industries:—
>
> (a) to see that the protective duties will not remain higher than the lowest point at which an industry (which deserves to be preserved in Canada) can make for its proprietors reasonable profits on the capital employed
>
> (b) to see that there shall be protection to the consumer against unfairly high prices, and
>
> (c) to provide machinery also which will protect workmen against unfairly low wages.
>
> Make it an all around protection, or as they use the phrase now in Australian politics, "new protection." This can be done by a tariff commission with ample powers. . . . The matters I have been referring to are all parts of one program;

they are like the fingers of a hand. If we are going to acknowledge our obligation to introduce social reform legislation, let us extend to the wage earner not one finger or two fingers, but our whole hand in fellowship with him.

Jacobs replied to the letter with a simple acknowledgment of receipt. Sir Wilfrid Laurier thought the subjects mentioned would require a great deal of study and investigation, and should not be adopted without ample consideration. King replied enthusiastically by return mail. The only changes he would make in Atkinson's welfare program would be to add the establishment of government labour exchanges which would provide the necessary machinery for the registration of individuals entitled to unemployment insurance and pensions. He was doubtful about amending the Industrial Disputes Investigation Act, and thought the tariff should be kept distinct from welfare. "Let us not confuse the issue," he said, "by rousing prejudices in a discussion on tariffs."

Apparently Fielding was as unenthusiastic as Laurier, but after several conferences with him Atkinson was able to write King that they were "pretty close together." The subcommittee met in Laurier's office on July 18. A press release was prepared on the new "social reform program" though Laurier was still doubtful about it. He felt he was being rushed into something by King and Atkinson, as indeed he was. This was not a case of Atkinson leading King or King leading Atkinson, but of two men in complete agreement on what needed to be done leading the party.

The press release was in the papers of July 21, though Laurier had not approved it. This was Atkinson's doing. He hoped that by giving the program wide publicity he would make it impossible for Laurier to disown it. The following day Atkinson sent King clippings of editorials from the *Telegram* and the *News* indicating "the confusion it has caused in Conservative ranks," and "the conflict of treatment they will probably show until they have settled upon a policy regarding it." He observed that by way of ridicule the *Telegram* said "the only thing not insured against is the necessity of making one's own living." He thought the Conservatives would be compelled by public opinion to adopt a favourable attitude towards old age pensions and mothers' allowances. King replied that "the Tory party will probably favor old age pensions and mothers' pensions, and where they do not openly combat, say very little about the rest."

Though his name had not been mentioned in connection with them, before long it was generally known that Mr. Atkinson had framed this Liberal welfare program. "He is the most dangerous force in Canadian journalism today," wrote Britton B. Cooke, in the *Canadian Courier*.

> I say dangerous having regard only to the feelings of certain classes in the community . . . So far he has loved democracy and shown a steady faith in the right instincts of the common people of this country. Too long-headed to be a mere Hearst, too sincere . . . to be a Northcliffe, unless he is deflected from his course he promises to do effective execution one of these days. It will be the more effective because almost noiseless in approach. . . . He is the big force not merely in Canadian journalism but in Canadian politics of the future . . . master of a paper built, not by dead men but by his own hands. He is a near-genius, much more to be reckoned with than a real genius.

But the *Telegram* dubbed him "Whispering Joe," in sly derision of his preference for operating behind the scenes, and began to hint he could be bought off with a title and probably would be, an innuendo that was meant to be an insult, for *The Star* had been campaigning for the abolition of titles since 1900.

Sir Wilfrid Laurier made his first public reference to the welfare program in a speech at Montreal in September. It was a rather grudging reference, for the old leader devoted more attention to the tariff, fiscal problems, and the Liberal good roads policy. Nevertheless Mr. Atkinson effusively congratulated him. "The allusions to the problems of the working classes must gratify all who are at the same time your friends and the friends of labor," he wrote Laurier. "Your inclusion in a specific way of the welfare of the working population as the object of special thought and solicitude broadened the basis of your appeal by reducing it to terms of human beings." Sir Wilfrid's acknowledgment was a brief thank you. Thereafter he virtually ignored the welfare program.

But Mr. Atkinson continued his speaking campaign, and *The Star* began crusading for welfare legislation. The Brantford *Expositor* referred to an address by Atkinson before the South Brant Reform Association in Brantford on January 8, 1917, as "tinged with emotion and complete with statistics." "Of all the causes of poverty the greatest is low wages," he said on that occasion. "The greatest single social reform would be to raise the wages of the worst paid workers. This cannot be done by legislation only. That will be opposed by the workers themselves, who oppose legislation fixing wages. Sickness and unemployment insurance, however, work indirectly to ameliorate conditions." The state, he said, must assure workers that they receive a greater share of the product of their labour.

Shortly after this Mr. Atkinson eased off on his campaign for social legislation, turning his energies within the Liberal organization towards bringing about Union government. After the 1917 election, with the Liberal remnant in Parliament consisting mostly of members from Quebec hostile to social legislation, campaigning along this line almost ended, and the effort was directed towards winning the war. However, he kept in close touch with Mackenzie King, giving his addresses and writings wide publicity, boosting the man rather than the party or program.

When King's book, *Industry and Humanity*, was published in December, 1918, *The Star* printed a long review of it. "There are many sections which are positively exciting, dealing with the world's great ferment," the reviewer said. It was, in fact, a very dull book that only the most dedicated humanitarian ever finished reading. The main point it made is that modern industry involves four partners, capital, management, workers, and the community. The old industrial aristocracy of capital and management must be replaced by a system in which workers will be consulted. The part of the community, through its elected representatives, is to investigate, inform, and provide an elaborate system of social services. Socialism was rejected as merely substituting, a state monopoly for the old monopoly of private ownership.

Laurier died on February 17, 1919, and when King came to Toronto in March *The Star* welcomed him almost as effusively as it had welcomed Laurier in the past. It published his speech before the Empire Club on March 18 in full, picking highlights from it to set in large type in a two-column box, as though it were an important public pronouncement. In a way it was, for it reopened the campaign for social security legislation. King stayed at the Atkinson home while in Toronto, and the strategy leading up to his bid for leadership at the convention to be held at Ottawa in August was discussed.

At the time *The Star* was in an awkward position politically for circumstances compelled it to straddle the fence. It had advocated formation of a national or union government not only for the duration of the war, but for the period of reconstruction after. Therefore, it had to stay with the Borden government for the time being. Officially it supported the Liberal-Unionists, and was thus looked upon with suspicion by the stalwarts who had stayed with Laurier. It had not yet regained the right to suggest to the Liberals whom they should choose as leader, and its endorsement of any candidate might be the kiss of death for him. The best it could do for King, therefore, was to keep boosting him as a great man with a great mission and act very surprised when he was mentioned as a possible Liberal leader.

Moreover, Mr. Atkinson had two strings to his bow. There was talk of the Liberal-Unionists and the Conservatives coalescing to form a permanent new party that might be more liberal than a Liberal party restrained by

Quebec. The former Ontario Liberal leader, N. W. Rowell, had been one of the strong men of the Union government and a member of the imperial war cabinet. There was a distinct possibility he might emerge as the leader of the new party. A liberal in the truest sense, a man of high principles and fine intelligence, Rowell had enjoyed Atkinson's confidence for years. "Rowell is the one man in politics whose leadership I could unquestionably follow," Mr. Atkinson told a colleague.

The Liberals under King or the Unionists under Rowell—Atkinson was prepared to support either. And until he saw what the Liberal convention did he was keeping the way open for a move in either direction. However, *The Star* went so far as to call upon the Liberals to adopt a platform "at once sane and radical." "The old stuff of party conventions will not do," it warned, "nor will the people be satisfied with perfunctory, vote-seeking declarations." The world was in a ferment, with the common people almost in a state of revolution against age-old inequalities and injustices, and even Canada and the United States could not count on escaping. "Bolshevism seems to have the power of making converts as Mohammedanism did, and suppression alone will not prevent its spread," it declared. "The only way to allay the unrest is to guarantee the people justice and security."

"We are opening a new chapter in Canadian history," it said in another editorial, warning the Liberals not to succumb to the desire "to play safe" which besets political parties. "It is earnestly to be hoped," it added, "that the Liberal convention will satisfy those who are Liberals not only in name but in love of reform, of liberty, of liberality, of broad and liberal views upon public questions."

The convention adopted the kind of liberal platform *The Star* had urged, and it chose as leader King, the dark horse, largely on the strength of what was called at the time his "labour speech." This was almost exactly the program presented by Mr. Atkinson in 1916, reinforced by reasoning from King's book, *Industry and Humanity*.

"It was a particular pleasure to me in drafting the labour part of our policy to go over the work of the committee of which you were chairman and to embody in the platform the program of social reform which you sought so eagerly to have adopted," King wrote Atkinson. "I look forward with intense eagerness to continuing our efforts together to give expression in legislation to the principles and beliefs we have so much at heart."

"I am sure none of your friends feel greater pleasure about your election than those who live on the hill here," Atkinson wrote King the day after his nomination.

We, Mrs. A. and I, could not sit down to dinner until the final result was telephoned up from the telegraph office. There was rejoicing when it came. I am certain it was the very wisest course the convention could have taken.

Looking back at the perplexities of the years since 1911, one sees something very like destiny in the decisions which were so repeatedly reached to remain in public life, in spite of attractions which held out their hand from the other side of the line, and discouragements in the political field at home. "Seek ye first the Kingdom of God and His righteousness and all else will be added unto you." The older one grows the oftener one sees the truth exemplified. I look forward to a talk with you about it all.

One of your early, if not earliest concerns will naturally be the completion of the reconciliation of the elements of Liberalism in Canada which are still looking a little askance at each other. I wonder if I may suggest if North York gives you the banquet which I see mentioned, it will be well, as your first public appearance as leader, if representative unionist Liberals were urged to attend. They will hesitate to break the ice but if, at the banquet, their rapprochement is not evident it will be a pity.

King replied that the first telegram of congratulation he had received was from Atkinson. It was sent over the open wire *The Star* had into the convention hall. The letter continued:

I am in most hearty accord with your suggestion that every effort should be made to emphasize the rapprochement which has already been effected in such large measure between unionist and other Liberals. In this matter there can be but one attitude from now on . . . I shall continue to look to you for counsel, advice and guidance in all matters of public policy, and I shall be grateful if in matters of public interest you will permit me to share at all times the same intimacy which I have been privileged to enjoy in matters of private and personal concern.

In its editorial comments on the platform adopted by the convention *The Star* ignored all but its labour and welfare planks, and as a matter of fact King paid but slight attention to the others either. "A progressive labor platform associated with an unsympathetic leadership might mean very little; such a platform with Mr. King as leader means a great deal," *The Star* said. Thereafter it stressed the theme of Liberal unity with "peptalk" editorials of the "Let's all get together, boys, for the grand old cause" variety. Atkinson was indefatigable in organizing dinners and luncheons and banquets at which those he referred to as "the separated brethren" might get together in a friendly atmosphere. They were not without their embarrassments, as when the president of the Toronto Women's Liberal Club (true-blue Laurier) led her clucking brood from a banquet hall at which King was to speak because she had glimpsed Atkinson and other former Unionists in the audience, and she would not break bread with them.

"I wonder how long it will be before those of us who supported the Union government will feel at home at Liberal party gatherings?" Atkinson wrote King. ". . . What with those Liberals who will have nothing to do with Unionist Liberals, and those other Liberals who want no alliance with the Progressives, we seem to need a peacemaker in this province."

"I can assure you, you do not feel half as indignant as I do myself at the kind of behaviour to which your letter refers," King replied. "Did I not have before me the representations of your letter I should not have believed possible anything so stupid and short-sighted as the incident to which it refers."

While Atkinson was working behind the scenes to reunite the Liberal party, *The Star* was supporting the Borden government's post-war reconstruction program, true to its promise of 1917. Though praising King and the new Liberal platform, it did not try to obstruct the Borden government or indicate dissatisfaction with it. Rowell left the Borden cabinet in 1920 and retired from politics in 1921, to become in due course one of the more distinguished members of the judiciary, but some other Liberals remained, and these were gently treated. With Rowell's departure from politics Atkinson lost whatever hope he might have had of a liberally inclined Unionist government, and thereafter he pinned his hopes on King.

Borden resigned in July, 1920, because of ill health, to be succeeded as Prime Minister by Arthur Meighen. "The new Premier of Canada is a man of character, resource, industry, ability and courage," *The Star* commented. "Mr. Meighen has won his way fairly to the top. He is the logical leader of the Conservative party." There was a touch of sly humour in this last statement, for privately Mr. Atkinson referred to Meighen as "the high priest of high finance." In Atkinson's opinion, that made him a proper Conservative leader.

The Star continued to give moderate support to the Meighen Government even after most of the Liberal-Unionists had departed, either to become Liberals again or to join the new Progressive party, which was the arm in federal politics of the farmers' organizations. It approved Meighen's conduct at the Imperial Conference of 1921 at which he virtually forced the British government to abandon the Anglo-Japanese alliance. Both Meighen and *The Star* believed the United States would be a more trustworthy ally than Japan, and the Anglo-Japanese alliance was much disliked in the United States.

An indication of *The Star*'s attitude towards King is conveyed in a letter from Atkinson, dated April 1, 1921, apologizing for an article from its Ottawa correspondent, J. A. Stevenson, which had been published the previous Saturday. The article contained statements, Atkinson wrote, "which must have appeared to you as less than friendly. They pained me greatly. I want you to believe that I am extremely sorry about them. Nothing of an unsympathetic character about you should appear in *The Star* as though it represents the paper's viewpoint, or the opinion of its special representatives."

Stevenson was a close friend of Hon. T. A. Crerar, a former Liberal who had served in the Union government but left it to become leader of the Progressive party. King was always suspicious of Stevenson, and on at least one occasion tried to have Atkinson dismiss him. However, he remained with *The Star* for another two years. Atkinson considered him a valuable contact with the Progressive party, one of the few Ottawa correspondents the Progressives trusted. He would be an invaluable man should the Progressives win the next election, which Atkinson thought quite possible.

The election was held December 6, 1921, and *The Star*'s position can only be described as anti-Conservative. As between the Liberals and Progressives it held the scales evenly. It expressed the opinion Mackenzie King would be the next prime minister, but it was more vigorous in defending Crerar from Conservative attacks. Its one recurrent theme was "defeat the Tories," and that, it said, could be done by voting either Liberal or Progressive. "Do not worry what the Liberal party or the Progressive party or both will do the country's welfare; they will do it good," it assured a couple of days before polling.

Such a position angered Meighen and he wrote a bitter letter to Atkinson. He could have understood and forgiven *The Star* had it supported either the Liberals or the Progressives, but that it should be neutral between them while making "get rid of Meighen" the sole issue was infuriating. If *The Star* was to be independent, it should treat all three parties equally, he protested.

But *The Star*'s position was simply that the Progressives were "separated brethren" who should be wooed back into the Liberal fold rather than be antagonized. Most of them had been Liberals and their program was liberal, differing only in the particular planks they emphasized from that of the Liberal party. *The Star* looked confidently to them being reunited under Mackenzie King. King had adopted the same position, but some of the older Liberals wanted to fight the Progressives as hard as they were fighting the Conservatives. King was opposed to running Liberal candidates in ridings it seemed likely a Progressive or Farmer candidate could win if the vote were not split, though sometimes he was over-ruled by local Liberal associations. After a Farmer-Labour coalition won the Ontario election of October 20, 1919, he wrote in his diary: "The Farmers' movement is a people's movement and as such the truest kind of Liberalism. The same is true of Labor."

Atkinson and King seem to have arrived independently at the conclusion that the federal Liberals should conciliate the Progressives and Farmers rather than fight them. This is not surprising, for both were conciliators by temperament, believing a soft voice was more effective than a big stick. But having decided independently as to the most effective tactics, they seem to have consulted frequently on their application. There is slight record of correspondence between them, but there are too many examples of statements by King following closely upon the heels of speculative stories or editorials in *The Star* for them to have been accidental. Moreover, their visible harmony on almost every matter that arose indicated prior consultation.

This may have been by telephone, for Atkinson preferred to telephone rather than write. We know, also, that King was a frequent visitor at the Atkinson home. Mr. Atkinson's daughter, Ruth, recalls King stomping out of the bathroom in the morning, face covered with lather, and demanding what had happened to his favourite razor strop.

The Liberals won 117 seats in the 1921 election, the Progressives 64, the Conservatives 50, and other parties four, thus the Liberals had one member less than the combined opposition. When King was called to form a government, *The Star* advised him to choose his cabinet impartially from Liberals and Progressives. This proved to be impossible, for the Progressive members decided to remain a separate group.

The Star's comment on Meighen's defeat was: "The financial group in Montreal betrayed Mr. Meighen, but overplayed its hand." It did not amplify this somewhat cryptic statement. Privately Mr. Atkinson remarked: "Meighen is too honest to be a good politician; he is well out of it." Though Atkinson had no confidence in Meighen's policies, he had a high personal regard for him.

After King's victory, Atkinson restricted his personal participation in politics to acting as peacemaker between the Progressives and the Liberals, and his public speeches became fewer. One reason may have been that

The Star was demanding more of his attention. It was still trailing the *Telegram* and the *Globe* in circulation, while the *Star Weekly*, founded in 1910, was losing money. It was important to him that he get his papers back into first position, and on a sound financial basis.

At the same time he was somewhat impatient with the Liberals. He had confidence in King, but because of the influence of older, more conservative men like Fielding and Sir Lomer Gouin, the leader of the Quebec bloc, the party was dragging its feet in implementing the reform platform approved by the 1919 convention. On the other hand the Progressives were acting as he thought Liberals should act. In editorials in *The Star* and in personal letters he advised King to take the risk of antagonizing the right-wing Liberals, adopt a position left of centre, and make the fiscal changes the Progressives were demanding. This King did in his budget of April 10, 1924. He cut the sales tax, which *The Star* had always argued was a tax on the poor, gave relief to farmers by reducing the duty on agricultural implements, provided free entry for raw materials and semi-manufactured materials essential to industry, and increased the income tax exemption for dependent children.

"I am glad again to have a Liberal cause to fight for," Atkinson wrote King. "Don't be afraid of protectionists either in Parliament or out, for the protected interests are most to be feared when tariff changes are a matter of prophecy rather than experience." Thereafter *The Star* was unswerving in its support of Mackenzie King.

King's move to the left of centre proved to be a wise one politically. The Progressives supported the Liberals and eventually were absorbed into a stronger, more vigorous Liberal party. At the same time the reactionary Quebec wing remained loyal to the party though its influence was reduced.

Chapter 8

THE CHIEF PICKS A SON-IN-LAW

Harry Comfort Hindmarsh did not become managing editor of *The Star* until June, 1928, but some people have dated the beginning of the Hindmarsh era in the news department from one o'clock the afternoon of November 7, 1918, when a flash from New York was received in the wire rooms of Toronto newspapers: "Armistice signed. War over." It was four days premature but everybody had been expecting such an announcement. So the newspapers got out their extras and the sessions of the High Court at Osgoode Hall were adjourned for the day.

Owen McGillicuddy, who was covering courts for *The Star*, had the brilliant idea of persuading John Philip Sousa, who was in Toronto with his famous band, to stage a victory parade along King Street to *The Star* office. Sousa's publicity man thought it a grand stunt to advertise the concert to be held in Massey Hall that night, and the white-coated bandsmen went swinging along to *The Star*, where they played to a huge crowd until the news agency responsible for the error sent out a correction.

But mistake or not, city editor Hindmarsh was so delighted with Mc-

Gillicuddy's inspiration that he gave him a two-week vacation in New York with his wife. "The finest bit of public relations work around here in years," Hindmarsh declared.

Few realized at the time that this event was prophetic or that the Hindmarsh era was about to begin, when money was no object provided a scoop resulted, and reporters were encouraged to be original, imaginative, and just a little bit mad. In a few years *The Star* was known as the "wackiest" newspaper in the world, and one of the most successful.

The Hindmarsh era lasted about forty years. It did not begin all at once, of course. The cautious and tight-fisted Bone was still at the head of the news department, and was to remain there for another ten years. But as Atkinson gradually loosened the purse strings it seemed to many that he was pleasurably surprised by the exciting results. Bone was left firmly clutching the brake, which was a good thing, but Hindmarsh wrested the steering wheel from his hands. It was not until Bone's restraining influence was removed by death that *The Star* began to have the staff troubles which worried Hindmarsh yet were an inevitable part of his *modus operandi.*

This man whose influence on *The Star* was to be second only to that of J. E. Atkinson was hired, almost by accident, on November 30, 1911. The reporter assigned to cover a civic ball in honour of the new Governor General, the Duke of Connaught, had been so overcome by the festive spirits of the occasion that he was not only quite incapable of writing the story but he was unable to find his way back to the office for three days. Scanning the guest list for someone who, at 7 a.m. after an all-night ball, might be able to give a substitute reporter a run-down on what happened, city editor Colin Campbell recognized the name of teetotal Harry C. Hindmarsh, former editor of the student newspaper, the *Varsity*, briefly a reporter on the *Globe*, and then editing a little financial sheet for the brokerage firm of Erickson, Perkins, and Company. He got him out of bed. Would he come down to the *Star* office and help them out of a hole? Hindmarsh would be delighted to.

His story, written in haste from memory and without notes, so impressed Campbell he offered the young man a job at $22 a week, starting at once. Hindmarsh accepted the offer on the spot, for it could not have been made at a more opportune time. He was thoroughly fed up with writing financial stories and bored to tears by the brokerage business. *The Star* was his kind of a paper, liberal, rebellious, brash, and a little bit crazy. Moreover, he had printer's ink in his veins from both sides of the family, and it was boiling to get out. His maternal grandfather, Hiram Comfort, was one of the founders of the St. Thomas *Times*, and his father's brother George was a reporter on the Brooklyn *Eagle*.

His parents moved from St. Thomas to Bismarck, Missouri, where Harry was born on January 13, 1887. Despite a markedly German appearance and bearing, he was descended on his father's side from a long line of English sea-captains, one of whom is commemorated by a monument in Australia for his service to the Empire. On his mother's side he was of United Empire Loyalist descent. His father, a railway employee, died when he was an infant, and his mother returned to her parents in St. Thomas.

Young Hindmarsh wrote his first newspaper story at the age of fourteen when, on a visit to Scotland with his mother, he sent back reports of what he saw to the St. Thomas *Times*. On leaving high school he joined the land rush to the West, where he filed on a homestead near Carbon, Alberta. A year later he decided farming was not the life for him and returned East, to enrol in the Arts course at the University of Toronto, majoring in modern history. His first summer vacation he worked half-heartedly on his homestead, but the next, between his second and third years, he stopped off in Detroit on the way West and got no further. Walking along the street he saw an advertisement in the window of the *Detroit News* for a reporter, and decided to give big-city newspaper work a try. He was so enthralled by the life of a reporter that instead of staying only for the summer vacation, as intended, he remained out of university a year.

"Every day (in the life of a reporter) is filled with surprises," he wrote later in the *Varsity*. "Every day is an education. The newspaperman must ever be on the alert, ever on his mettle; and it is this war of intellects, mind striving against mind, which keeps men young. . . . Be he a veritable pygmy he (the reporter) may quiz the grandest minion of the law (I mean cop) with impunity. Mention the magic word 'reporter' and this dweller on Olympus becomes as other men are and holds speech with you. . . . Let the university men of the continent take hold of its great newspapers."

In his final year, 1909, he was appointed editor of the *Varsity*. He promptly turned it from the literary journal it had formerly been into a newspaper of student activities, jazzed it up with pictures and bigger and meatier headlines, and tried to make it a daily. He failed in the latter attempt, and settled for tri-weekly publication.

Big, slow-moving, calm of demeanour, and quiet of speech, Harry Hindmarsh was the last man one would suspect of being a rebel, yet his appearance was deceptive. As an undergraduate he was almost at once identified with the "angry young men" at the University. In his sophomore year he and his close friend, the present Senator Norman Lambert, were suspended two weeks for leading a student insurrection against the hazing practices then in vogue which sometimes caused damage to university property and a number of cracked skulls.

In his third year he organized a Democratic League to have college fraternities banned as undemocratic, snobbish, discriminatory, and contrary to Canadian conceptions of equality. His league succeeded in defeating every fraternity man who ran for office in the student elections, and the newly elected anti-fraternity student council passed a resolution asking that fraternities be banned from the campus. They failed in this objective, but Hindmarsh continued to fight what he considered the pernicious influence of fraternities throughout his university career. However, he joined the University Masonic Lodge on the grounds that the Masonic order was a true fellowship, open to men of all social strata regardless of race, religion, or colour. He became the master of the University Lodge, and went on to become a 32nd degree Scottish Rite Mason.

The next time he attracted attention was when he moved before the University debating club "that Canada should declare her independence at once," and spoke so eloquently in support of the motion that the judges had to give him the decision. Then the judges, all faculty members of sound imperial convictions and correct political complexion, called him before them.

"Did you believe what you were arguing?" he was asked. "I believe Canada should remain within the Empire," he replied, thus skilfully bypassing the matter of the exact relationship between Canada and Britain.

"We're glad to hear that," one of the judges told him. "If you had said otherwise we would have had to expel you from the University."

A short time later a similar proposition was placed before the Historical Club. This time Hindmarsh spoke just as eloquently against the motion, and it was defeated.

After graduation he was elected president of the University College Literary Society as leader of the Social-Democrat group, defeating the official candidates of the Liberal and Conservative clubs. The first man he invited to address the Society was Sir Wilfrid Laurier. The second was President William H. Taft. Both accepted. Hindmarsh was elected to a second term as president by acclamation, the first to be thus honored in sixty years. This time he presented himself as a Liberal with Socialist support.

Hindmarsh's rebellion against injustices and social ills was in no sense motivated by an experience of youthful poverty, as was that of Atkinson. He had been raised in circumstances of better than average comfort, and he confessed to Pierre Berton, who interviewed him for an article for a national magazine, that he had been spoiled by an overly generous and indulgent mother. Nor was it influenced to any extent by books or studies.

His approach to liberalism was almost wholly emotional. There was something wrong with society or there would not be the poverty and inequalities one saw on every hand. Exactly where the trouble lay or how it could be cured he had not yet decided, for by temperament he was more inclined to come out swinging wildly at things he did not like than to analyse them. Moreover, in those days at University, liberalism afforded greater scope than conservatism for exercise of his instinct for leadership.

J. E. Atkinson, on the other hand, was not a rebel. With the impersonal detachment of a physician he had diagnosed society's ailment and prescribed liberalism as the remedy. Once Hindmarsh was brought into contact with *The Star*'s liberalism he embraced it with an enthusiasm not surpassed by Atkinson. But even so, his liberalism always tended to be emotional and partisan rather than intellectual. In the end it became confused with paternalism.

His first job after leaving University was as cable editor of the *Globe*, and by a strange coincidence the story that got him off the cable desk and onto the reporting staff was a report of a hanging. At the same age, twenty-three, J. E. Atkinson had written his memorable story of the hanging of J. R. Birchall.

Ivan Stefoff, a Bulgarian immigrant with a string of murders to his discredit in the Balkans and the United States, was to be hanged on December 23, 1909, for the hatchet killing of a Toronto man. The *Globe*'s police reporter refused to witness the hanging, as reporters were supposed to do in those days, and Hindmarsh volunteered to take his place. Relating the incident to Berton thirty-five years later, he recalled how he had peered into the open trap to watch the final contortions of the dying wretch, then raced downstairs to see the body cut down. His story was a bald recital of facts, utterly devoid of the human interest and passion that had made Atkinson's story so moving. There was no evidence of Atkinson's revulsion at the brutality of hanging, but rather an impression that Hindmarsh thought the victim got what he deserved. "There was no miscarriage of justice," he stated in the lead. His story was on an inside page near the back of the paper, but this, and the complete suppression of the human interest angle, may have been due to a change in *Globe* policy rather than a reflection on the competence of the writer. By 1909 the *Globe* was already evidencing the stodgy respectability that was to result in its decline from first place to fourth among Toronto papers.

A few months after the hanging Hindmarsh left the *Globe* for the brokerage office, but soon found the sheet he had been hired to edit was far from being the respectable financial paper he had expected. It was, in fact, a tipster sheet, its purpose to push the occasionally none-too-reputable stocks the firm was handling. He had already made up his mind to leave before receiving Campbell's welcome offer.

On his second day as a reporter for *The Star* Hindmarsh was assigned to the city hall staff, where he learned to write "running copy" in *The Star* manner. He soon distinguished himself as a meticulous and thorough reporter, though his writing was always heavy.

Many years later a young reporter, Miss Betty Thornley, complaining to Mr. Atkinson about the changes Hindmarsh, then city editor, was making in her copy, said "I wouldn't mind if he just cut out what he doesn't like, but when he writes something in he spoils it. Mr. Hindmarsh writes like an elephant while I write like a bunny rabbit." After leaving *The Star* Miss Thornley gained some prominence as a writer for *Vogue*.

Hindmarsh's big break came when the Titanic struck an iceberg and sank on April 14, 1912. A *Star* crew of several reporters and photographers under Lou Marsh was sent to Montreal and New York to interview survivors. The papers were full of stories that panicking male passengers had pushed women and children out of the way to clamber into lifeboats and save themselves. After interviewing many passengers Hindmarsh wrote a dispatch stating these stories were untrue. The male passengers had been ordered into the lifeboats by the ship's officers to provide oarsmen, otherwise the boats would have been swamped and everybody drowned, he wrote. He quoted Major Arthur Peuchen of Toronto as saying: "Every woman who cared to go was taken off," and that lifeboats with a capacity of sixty were lowered with only twenty-three in them while men stood by.

Hindmarsh was called into Mr. Atkinson's office on his return. "I hope you can substantiate your story," the Chief warned. "I can," Hindmarsh replied, and from his pocket he took written statements he had secured from ships officers to the effect they had ordered men into the boats. The statements contained the names of men so ordered, some of whom had been accused of cowardice. He also had copies of the written orders some of the male passengers had insisted upon being given.

From that time on Mr. Atkinson had his eye on Hindmarsh. In 1913 he was put on the "rim," editing copy. For ever after he was convinced no reporter was worth his salt until "seasoned," as he called it, on the rim. In a few more weeks he was assistant city editor.

Meanwhile, the news editor, J. S. Crate, had resigned, and George Maitland, who had been writing editorials, was made news editor. A few weeks later Maitland was called back to the editorial page, with no successor named to the news desk. Campbell promptly promoted himself to be news editor, and Hindmarsh just as promptly promoted himself to be city editor, calling on a reporter to assist him as needed, which was seldom, for Hindmarsh was quite happy doing the work of two men.

Such queer self-promotions were not unusual on *The Star*, for Mr. Atkinson had an aversion to pinning anyone down to a specific job or handing out titles, apparently on the principle that if he shuffled everybody around until all were thoroughly confused the best man would emerge on top. Only four years earlier J. H. Cranston had appointed himself news editor by simply walking in one morning, saying he was it, and nobody contradicted him.

But this double Campbell-Hindmarsh shift seemed to puzzle even Mr. Atkinson. "Didn't I tell you when I called you back to write editorials that you were still news editor?" he asked Maitland. "No, Mr. Atkinson, I understood I was taken off the news desk for good," Maitland responded. "Odd," said Atkinson. "I thought you were still news editor."

Hindmarsh's next move was to do exactly what Bone had done ten years before—he told Atkinson he would not work another day under Campbell. And Atkinson did exactly as he had done ten years earlier—he made Hindmarsh assistant managing editor, and confirmed him as city editor. Hindmarsh's rebellion was not a mere display of prima donna temperament. Cranston wrote that when he was Campbell's assistant "I was limp with exhaustion by early afternoon. He had a picturesque, expressive and explosive vocabulary." Only a meek man could work long with Campbell, and Hindmarsh was anything but meek.

On the news desk Campbell grew increasingly irascible and unpredictable. The man who had been described as the greatest handler of reporters in Canada now wanted only to be the "master-mind" and leave the handling of reporters to others. At the same time he insisted on reading every line of copy written by reporters and flew into a ferocious tantrum when a story was not handled to his satisfaction, which was several times a day. Only the imperturbable Hindmarsh kept the news department on an even keel.

Mr. Atkinson was reluctant to hurt Campbell, for he recognized that his genius as a newsman had contributed in no small measure to *The Star*'s success. Yet something had to be done. So it happened that mysterious troubles began unaccountably to develop with make-up, troubles that it seemed only Campbell could iron out. Before long Campbell was spending more time on make-up than he was on editing. Hindmarsh eased into his chair and Maitland seemed to be spending a lot of time at the city editor's desk for one who was supposed to be writing editorials. Without anybody quite knowing when the changes took place, Atkinson began referring to Campbell as "make-up editor." The office of news editor disappeared for several years, for Hindmarsh was officially "assistant managing editor and city editor."

About this time Mrs. Campbell, who was a Christian Scientist, persuaded her husband to consult a Christian Science practitioner for his alcoholism. He swore off the bottle and never touched another drink. He retired in 1929 and died in 1946 at the age of 85.

"There was no sweet reasonableness about C.C. on the warpath," wrote E. J. Archibald, editor of the *Montreal Star*, on Campbell's death. Archibald began as a reporter under Campbell. "His reporters held him in deep and abiding affection, but would gladly have strangled him a dozen times a day. They had to be on the scene before any others, and each *Toronto Star* reporter was expected to be better than any three from any other newspaper. The amazing thing is that he got his reporters to believe they were."

In those days the Atkinsons were accustomed to entertain senior members of the staff at their home, a practice for which Mrs. Atkinson was mainly responsible. She used to return their visits with "afternoon calls" on their wives, as was the custom of the time. So no one thought it particularly significant that Mr. Atkinson should invite Hindmarsh to his home for an evening or a Sunday dinner. But when the invitations increased in frequency there were knowing winks, for Ruth Atkinson was a remarkably attractive girl and the apple of her father's eye. As a matter of fact, Ruth's popularity had been causing her parents some worry, for not all the swains then paying her court were regarded as eligible for their only daughter's hand. It was this circumstance that had led to the first invitation to Hindmarsh.

"I'm going to introduce you to a real man, my girl," Mr. Atkinson told his daughter one day, and next evening brought home Harry Hindmarsh. Ruth was impressed—with his bulk—but to demonstrate her independence she went out for the evening with her girl friend, leaving her parents to entertain the suitor they had chosen. However, Hindmarsh was a personable young man, and persistent, her coolness soon thawed, and in the fulness of time Mr. Atkinson was able smilingly to inform his editorial writers that he was delighted his daughter had "settled her affections" on such a reliable young man as Harry Hindmarsh. The same day Mrs. Atkinson told one of the wives she had hoped Ruth would not marry a newspaperman because they lived such a turbulent existence.

No sooner were they engaged than Mr. Atkinson fired his prospective son-in-law. "I decided long ago that my son-in-law should not work at *The Star* but would have to make his own way," he explained. Hindmarsh said he would leave at once for Detroit, where a job was awaiting him on the *News*. Atkinson demurred; he wanted to keep his daughter nearer home. So Hindmarsh applied to Atkinson's old boss, Sir John Willison, publisher of the Toronto *News*, for a job. Although Willison was friendly, he explained that since *The Star* and the *News* were rivals he preferred not to have a son-in-law of Atkinson serving as a pipeline into his office. When Hindmarsh relayed his conversation, Mr. Atkinson realized at once that a pipeline might work both ways. "I can see," he said, "that it is not practical for two closely related men to hold key positions on rival newspapers. You'd better stay with *The Star*."

Harry Hindmarsh and Ruth Atkinson were married on November 27, 1915. The groom had the satisfaction of having proven his merit before marrying the boss' daughter.

Chapter 9

A MOVE TO THE LEFT

The end of the First World War marked the beginning of a new era for *The Star* as clearly as the defeat of reciprocity in 1911 had marked the end of an old one. The ten years immediately following the war were years of extraordinary activity on the part of Mr. Atkinson, and of expansion on the part of his newspapers.

The war had broken out only seven months after Mr. Atkinson had gained control of *The Star* and whatever ambitious plans he may have had in mind had to be shelved until it was won. But now the war was over. He was in the middle of his vigorous fifties with five lost years to be regained. As owner of one of the most profitable newspapers in Canada, and with a substantial reserve from profits he had been unable to spend because of wartime restrictions, he was free to play almost any part he willed in the journalistic, political, or business life of the community.

We have already observed his activities in the political field. In the journalistic his first task was to restore *The Star* to first place among Toronto newspapers. With a dynamic news policy for which his son-in-law,

H. C. Hindmarsh, was largely responsible, and with an editorial policy so radical that many considered it Bolshevistic, it regained first position by 1922, where it has remained ever since—the most controversial newspaper in Canada.

The *Star Weekly* was changed into a different kind of publication, and by 1925 its circulation had zoomed to first place among Canada's national publications. The London *Advertiser* was bought in what appears to have been an experimental step into chain journalism. The pioneer radio station in Toronto and one of the first in Canada, CFCA, was established and operated for twelve years. A syndicate was founded, headed by Andrew Miller, to distribute the reports of *The Star*'s staff writers and correspondents, and the British and US services for which *The Star* held Canadian rights.

And to house all this a twenty-three-story building was raised in the heart of down-town Toronto near the end of the decade, as a symbol of *The Star*'s success.

The most momentous development was a radical shift to the left in *The Star*'s editorial policy. Until 1919 *The Star* had been traditionally Liberal, like half the other newspapers of Canada. If it differed from the general run of Liberal newspapers it was only in being more nationalistic than most of them. When it was attacked it was because of its nationalism which most Conservatives and some Liberals regarded as anti-British and disloyal. After the war it was to be attacked because of its advanced liberalism in social matters.

The war had ended with the world in a ferment, and this ferment had spread to Canada. The One Big Union and the Industrial Workers of the World were organizing unskilled labourers, mostly foreign-born immigrants from eastern Europe who had been exploited as cheap labour by mine, forest, and construction industries. Soviets on the Russian model had been established in Toronto, Ottawa, Winnipeg, Brandon, Saskatoon, Calgary, and Vancouver, but conventional labour unions were also busily organizing, for only 249,000 of Canada's 1,800,000 workers were unionists. The objectives of the unions seem moderate today—an eight-hour day, the right of workers to bargain collectively through organizations of their choice, a minimum wage law, and open hearings of deportation proceedings.

As strikes spread throughout the country in 1919 *The Star* placed the blame squarely on those industrialists who refused to bargain with "moderate labor unions." By their refusal, said *The Star*, they were driving reasonably-minded workers into extremist organizations. "Labor unions," it declared, "are opposed by all those extremists who prefer industrial war to industrial peace. The labor unions constitute the conservative force, the force which makes for conciliation and cooperation. The employer who recognizes this is working on the side of industrial peace. The employer who refuses such recognition is, consciously or unconsciously, promoting strife and unrest. . . . Capital is always organized. The mere possession of capital represents organized power." To negotiate on equal terms labour must also be organized.

When the Winnipeg strike occurred in May, 1919, and normal activities were at a standstill for two weeks, *The Star* sent three of its top men to cover it, W. R. Plewman, Main Johnson, and J. J. Conklin. Nearly every other newspaper in the country blamed "the Bolshevists," but *The Star* said the strike resulted from the stubborn refusal of certain employers to negotiate with moderate unions, thus playing into the hands of extremists.

When the strike collapsed and the leaders, including J. S. Woodsworth, were arrested *The Star* expressed fears lest "a great state trial" be held, which would be bound to antagonize organized labour. It warned against allowing inflamed tempers and fears to deny a fair trial and justice to the accused. "Government and the social fabric cannot remain stationary," it said. It is no crime, it observed, to advocate another economic or social system. The crime is in advocating or attempting to bring about changes by force. Liberty is equally endangered by the timid and the reactionary who would deny people the right to advocate changes, as by those who exhort to violence.

On another occasion it said: "Two movements characterize the ceaseless efforts of national groups to react to environment—first the conscious, subversive elements such as Socialists, Communists and what not, and secondly the evolutionary tide of human energy . . . working for the gradual transformation of society." It was this evolutionary tide *The Star* supported, a tide it believed was furthered by welfare legislation, labour unions, and liberalism. At the same time it believed it was foolhardy to ignore the other forces, or to pretend they did not exist.

The Star did not defend communism or Russia, or excuse their excesses. But from them it drew the lesson, expressed in an editorial on April 14, 1919, that "the fanaticism of Bolshevism is serving the useful purpose of making men examine the workings of Democracy." Like every other newspaper in Canada it had welcomed the Russian revolution as the overthrow of one of the last remaining despotic governments in Europe and the worst of the lot. It deplored the usurpation of power by the Bolshevist Lenin from the liberal Kerensky, and for the next ten years had little good to say of Russia. It published a series of articles on the difference between communism, which was bad, and socialism, which contained some good.

But whereas a sizable number of Canadians in troubled 1919 were demanding that local communists be thrown in jail and labour be prevented from organizing, *The Star* took the position that such methods would only strengthen communism. Out of this year of unrest emerged *The Star*'s unswerving support of democratic labour unions as a stabilizing element in the social structure, and the surest defence against communism.

At the same time *The Star* was looking with a sympathetic eye on the nationalistic aspirations of other countries, warning that intervention on behalf of conservative elements is more likely to promote revolution than pacification. As an example, when the US Senate held its "Mexican policy debate" in 1919, *The Star* mildly suggested it might consider a policy of "Mexico for the Mexicans." Mexico was then behaving much as Cuba did in the first four years of Castro's regime.

The Mexicans, *The Star* said, "are entitled to get their land back, and their oil back from the oil barons, and their railways back from unscrupulous foreign investors." Such statements were not calculated to endear it to industrial and financial leaders, some of whom were beginning to regard *The Star* as dangerous.

One of these, it would seem, was *The Star*'s third biggest shareholder, Sir John Eaton, who had inherited from his father 11.7 per cent of *The Star*'s stock. While Mr. Atkinson had been a warm friend and admirer of Timothy Eaton, he and Sir John were uncongenial personalities. Sir John was a Liberal and vice-president of the Reform Club of Toronto, but he believed the Atkinson-King program of the Liberals went too far to the left. Several times he protested against "the Bolshevistic trend" he thought he saw in *The Star*. "I don't tell you how to run your store," Mr. Atkinson is quoted as protesting after one encounter, but Eaton claimed the right as a shareholder to make his opinions known.

Atkinson had been trying to buy Eaton's shares since 1912, and in May, 1920, Sir John agreed to sell, possibly because of his dissatisfaction with *The Star*'s policy. A year later, on June 8, 1921, the T. Eaton Company, *The Star*'s largest and most valued advertiser for twenty years, withdrew its advertising. It did not return until June 28, 1922. The ostensible reason for its action was an increase in advertising rates from ten cents to thirteen cents a line by *The Star* at a time when the *Telegram* did not increase its rates.

When Eaton's withdrew, the Robert Simpson Company immediately increased its advertising from the half page it had been taking to two full pages a day, while several other large downtown stores increased their advertising. Simpson's wanted the back page Eaton's had occupied, but this Mr. Atkinson would not give them. However, he began printing *The Star* in two sections, placing Simpson's on the back page of the first section, a position they still occupy. Pending the expected return of Eaton's he directed that the back page be kept free of advertising, and it was made a page of pictures. This Picture Page was a popular feature for the next thirty-five years, though it was moved inside after two years.

Atkinson knew circulation might be adversely affected by the loss of Eaton's advertisement, and in the long run that could be more harmful than the loss of advertising revenue. Surveys have consistently shown that next to the front page Eaton's advertisement is the page most read by women. He therefore added several new features, and considerably enlarged the reporting and writing staff. The result was beyond expectations, for the year ended with *The Star* showing a larger increase in circulation than it had ever had in any previous twelve months, while that of the *Telegram* declined. Both parties to the dispute adopted a posture of unconditional surrender. Mr. Atkinson forbade Arthur Donaldson, advertising representative, to have any contacts whatever with Eaton's, or to solicit them to return. Sir John ordered his advertising manager, Ivor Lewis, to break off his friendship with Donaldson and never to enter *Star* premises. The two men, however, continued to meet in secret, frequently lunching together in obscure restaurants.

"Once a newspaper allows an advertiser to think he can influence its editorial policy it loses its independence," Mr. Atkinson told Donaldson. On another occasion he said: "I'll say what I like in the *Daily Star* and make my money if necessary out of the *Star Weekly*." The *Star Weekly* had just begun to show a profit.

Relations were still frozen when Sir John died on March 30, 1922, but the thaw set in shortly after. Eaton's began advertising in the news section of the *Star Weekly* in May. On June 28, after an absence of thirteen months, it returned to the daily with a two-page advertisement, but not in the old position on the back page. It was another eighteen months before the picture page was moved inside and Eaton's was back where it began.

This episode is significant in the light of an address Mr. Atkinson gave early in 1924 before his favourite forum, the senior class in Arts at the University of Toronto. "When people say newspapers are too dependent upon advertising they have the shoe upon the wrong foot," he said. "A newspaper is dependent upon advertising as a whole, but the individual advertiser is more dependent upon the newspaper than the newspaper is upon the individual advertiser."

The Star occasionally adopted what some advertisers regarded as a cavalier attitude towards them, but Mr. Atkinson regarded *The Star* as first and foremost a newspaper, and moreover, a newspaper with a mission. Advertising was a necessary evil and when advertising, such as liquor advertising, conflicted with the mission of the paper, it was sacrificed. When it threatened to restrict *The Star*'s freedom to cover the news, then also it was sacrificed.

Moreover, Mr. Atkinson took a singularly personal view of his newspapers, regarding them almost as an extension of his own personality. On one occasion he called the advertising manager to his office and asked if his solicitors were calling on a certain manufacturer. Told they were, he instructed: "Don't have them call on him any more." Some months later he explained the reason for his action. He had attended a meeting of prominent citizens at which the manufacturer had expressed opinions Mr. Atkinson found repugnant. Watching this man across the table later the thought crossed Mr. Atkinson's mind: "How I would hate to have to ask that man for anything." This was followed by the thought: "How I would hate for *The Star* to have to ask that man for anything." And then the thought: "Perhaps *The Star* is asking him for something, advertising." Until Mr. Atkinson's death advertising from that firm, one of the largest in its field, was accepted when offered, but it was never solicited.

One of the more serious disputes with an advertiser occurred in 1928, when Henry Ford introduced his new Model "A" car. Lack of liaison between advertising and news departments was in part to blame. For twenty years Ford had made the Model "T" "with constant improvements but no new yearly models." By 1928 it was apparent drastic changes would have to be made to maintain sales. It is hard today to imagine the excitement with which the introduction of the new Ford was awaited. Every major newspaper on the continent had reporters in Detroit trying to find out what the new model was like, while Ford was trying just as hard to keep it a secret until the official unveiling.

One day a man contacted Harry H. Johnson, assistant to Hindmarsh on the city desk, offering to sell him photographs which he said were pictures of the new model. Hindmarsh spread them on his desk before automotive editor Warren Hastings. "Are these Ford's new car?" he asked. "They are, I'll bet anything they are," Hastings exclaimed excitedly. So the pictures were printed.

Next morning two representatives from Ford were waiting for Mr. Atkinson when he arrived for work. They demanded the name of the individual who had given the pictures to *The Star*. If the name was not given, Ford would stop advertising. Mr. Atkinson telephoned Bone.

"Did we get those pictures in a legitimate manner?" he asked the managing editor.

"We did," Bone replied.

"Gentlemen, I cannot give you the names of any of the persons concerned," Mr. Atkinson said firmly. Ford stopped advertising in *The Star* for several weeks, resuming only after one of the biggest automobile agencies in Toronto threatened to cease handling Ford cars unless they were advertised in *The Star*.

What angered Ford was that shortly before the pictures were published it had delivered photographs of the new model to *The Star*'s advertising department on condition they would not be published until the advertising campaign. The news department had not been advised of this arrangement. Mistakenly, Ford believed *The Star*'s advertising men had broken faith until their own investigation disclosed the source of the pictures.

In imperial affairs, *The Star* continued to affirm that Canada must assert its sovereignty, and since the Empire had progressed to the critical point at which it was about to be transmuted into the Commonwealth, tempers were more inflamed than they had been at any time in the past. Looking back this distance of years it is hard to understand why anybody should have opposed the Commonwealth conception or the autonomy of Canada, yet prominent citizens and leading statesmen of both parties did. It is implicit in *The Star*'s editorials at the time that it regarded the post-war conferences as fortuitous occasions for manoeuvring other countries into recognizing Canada's autonomy, after which it could not be denied either by Britain or by imperialists in this country. Thanks largely to Borden, the manoeuvre was successful.

Chief exponent of the imperial and Conservative viewpoint was the *Telegram*, and in its fury at *The Star* for what it considered "disloyalty" and "Bolshevism" it descended to a level of personal invective unknown before or since in Canadian journalism. Day after day Mr. Atkinson was pictured to readers of the *Telegram* as an evil old man, hunched in his office spinning Machiavellian plots for the destruction of the Empire, Protestantism, and Western civilization. Since the *Telegram* still had a circulation within the city greater than that of the next two papers combined, most residents of Toronto knew Atkinson only from the distorted picture presented to them by his enemies. The *Telegram* had never attacked Mr. Atkinson personally while John Ross Robertson was living, but Robertson had died in 1918 and the paper he had founded was under the direction of men unable to distinguish between personalities and principles. It was edited by a man who regarded personal abuse as the most effective form of argument.

Under these men the *Telegram* denied Mr. Atkinson credit for sincerely holding the liberal principles for which he contended. It professed to find a plot for his personal aggrandizement in everything *The Star* did. Thus when *The Star* advocated widening Bloor Street the *Telegram* ran a picture of his home in Forest Hill. He wanted, the *Telegram* accused, a nice, wide thoroughfare "to speed along en route from his home in Forest Hill to his office in Toronto." Actually Bloor Street crosses the route he travelled at right angles. When *The Star* advocated a larger and better paid police force for Toronto, the *Telegram* sneered that since Atkinson lived in Forest Hill he would not be taxed to pay for it. *The Star*, in fact, was one of the larger taxpayers on downtown property.

This sort of harassment continued for years, though the *Telegram*'s most fatuous effort was probably in 1924 after the defeat of the British Labour party. It ran, side-by-side, pictures of Atkinson and William Randolph Hearst, the US publisher notorious for his anti-British attitude, under the caption, "Routed by the Electors of Britain."

This attempt to identify Atkinson with Hearst, with whom he had little in common, continued for years and was carried to ridiculous extremes. For example, the *Telegram* cited as "proof" that Atkinson and Hearst were two of a kind the fact *The Star* carried the comic strip, "Bringing Up Father," which originated with a Hearst newspaper and was Hearst's favourite. When George McManus, creator of the comic strip with its famous character Jiggs, came to Toronto to address the Canadian Club in 1923 the *Telegram* urged that he be boycotted because he drew pictures Hearst and Atkinson liked. When Mr. Atkinson was asked, after delivering an address at Sigma Delta Chi fraternity in 1924, why an irresponsible publisher like Hearst had the influence he did the *Telegram* ran a report of the address under the heading, "Fired Query About Hearst at Local Sponsor of Jiggs." Mr. Atkinson's reply to the question was that Hearst's newspapers apparently "suited the taste" of a considerable segment of the American public.

An example of the kind of language used by the *Telegram* in attacking Mr. Atkinson is to be found in that newspaper in 1926 after the *Star Weekly* ran an article on the marriage of Sir Henry Thornton, president of the CNR, to an American girl. Said the *Telegram*: "The publisher of the whistle on the peanut roaster of partisan slanders against Lord Byng and patron of a glorification of Sir Henry Thornton has made Canada ridiculous in the U.S. section of the civilized world." It devoted an entire page, with great type and headings, to this one topic, in the course of which it reprinted most of the *Star Weekly* article with its own comments interpolated.

The reference to "the partisan slanders against Lord Byng" was, of course, an allusion to the federal election campaign of that year in which the issue was the propriety of the Governor General's action in calling upon Arthur Meighen to form a ministry after rejecting Mackenzie King's request for a dissolution of Parliament. As a matter of fact *The Star* had paid but slight attention to the constitutional issue during the campaign, in the belief the question was too academic to have much influence on the vote. It did not attack Byng, though it had expressed the opinion when he refused dissolution to King that he erred in judgment. Instead it concentrated its attacks upon Meighen and the personalities in his cabinet. In an editorial the day after the election it said, however, that maybe the Conservatives would now admit there had been a constitutional issue.

Vigorous as was *The Star*'s campaign, it had slight influence in its own circulation area. Central Ontario sent an almost solid phalanx of Conservatives to Ottawa. The *Telegram* ran a cartoon that was widely reprinted in Conservative papers showing no Liberals elected "within 65 miles of *The Star* office" and "none as far south as Washington." But Senator Buchanan's Lethbridge *Herald* said that *The Star*'s vigorous campaign was responsible for the Liberals' "splendid gains made in Ontario."

It was not only opposition newspapers that attacked *The Star*. Extremists of all shades and complexions took offence at its tolerant liberalism. Communists and fascists, socialists and Conservatives, Orangemen and Roman Catholics all condemned it for giving the other extreme a hearing. It seemed that Atkinson could do nothing right except publish a newspaper most people in Toronto appeared to like.

When *The Star* commented favourably on the Farmer-Labour government of Premier E. C. Drury of Ontario, the *Telegram* accused it of socialism. When it criticized Drury the *Farmers' Sun*, organ of the United Farmers of Ontario, called it "a partisan paper which resents seeing the Liberal party out of power." When the *Star Weekly* printed a full-page article by Bishop O'Brien of Peterborough presenting the case of Roman Catholic schools for a larger share of taxes, the *Telegram* called Atkinson "Pope Joseph I" and *The Star* "his Vatican organ." When a week after Bishop O'Brien's article the *Star Weekly* printed an article by H. C. Hocken, local head of the Orange order and one of the founders of *The Star*, presenting the other side, the *Catholic Register* attacked Atkinson for "Methodist bigotry."

The *Telegram* had discovered the entry in the old minute books of Newcastle Methodist church hiring "Mrs. Atkinson's son Joe" to pump the organ, and over a period of years it delighted in reprinting this note with the comment that Joe was still "pumping an organ" for the Liberals, the Catholics, the Communists, or anybody else the *Telegram* did not like.

The disputes between the *Telegram* and *The Star* were not the mere acrimonious wrangling between business competitors that one might be tempted to judge them—and as, indeed, many people did dismiss them. The two newspapers were poles apart in their approach to social, economic, and political problems. Mr. Atkinson could understand the *Telegram*, for it spoke with the voice of sane, respectable, property-owning, Conservative Anglo-Saxons of the Victorian age. But the *Telegram* could never understand Atkinson, whose voice was the radical voice of the rising new labour unions and the industrial class they represented. And because it could not understand him, it could not believe in his honesty.

One of their most violent disagreements was in 1922, over what *The Star* called "the waterfront grab." This was a monstrous proposal by Sir Adam Beck that the city transfer to Hydro for one dollar a strip of the waterfront parks 105 feet wide and eight miles long along the lakeshore. On this he planned to lay six tracks of an electric railway to Niagara Falls, which would completely cut off access by the public to the waterfront. He proposed to bring electric cars downtown along city streets.

The fight over public-owned "radials," as these were called, was one of the most bitterly contested issues there has ever been in Ontario politics, for not only was the immense prestige of Beck, the father of Hydro, behind it, but also the provincial Conservative party, then in opposition, and the financial resources of railway contractors and manufacturers of electrical equipment. It was opposed by the Farmer-Labour coalition government of Premier E. C. Drury. *The Star* devoted six pages, including most of the front page on December 30, 1922, to beating the "grab," and the property-owners of Toronto voted on January 1 to turn it down. To announce its victory *The Star* published an extra on New Year's Day. The "grab" was supported by the *Telegram* and the *Globe*, but the *Mail and Empire* joined *The Star* in opposing it. In most of the years between the wars that is the way the Toronto newspapers divided on civic matters.

Mr. Atkinson was to say later that defeating this "grab" was the greatest single act of public service *The Star* ever rendered Toronto. "The city has been saved from an abyss," *The Star* commented the next day. The water-front had been preserved for the enjoyment of the public. The taxpayers had been protected from the expenditure of a vast sum for a type of inter-urban transportation that buses and trucks were already making obsolete. And the Canadian National Railways, also owned by the public, were protected from the competition of another publicly owned railway that was not needed. Nearly every one of the radials Beck wanted to build would have duplicated an existing CNR line.

Five years later the *Telegram* got its revenge when, after one of the most infamous and prolonged of all its attacks on the publisher of *The Star*, it brought about the defeat of one of the boldest and most imaginative plans for the redevelopment of downtown Toronto that had ever been produced. The "crooked lane," the *Telegram* called it, a masterpiece of sly innuendo hinting at secret dishonesty and at the same time belittling the project. The "crooked lane" was only one of several proposed new streets in the down-town area; it was to be a hundred feet wide, and it would have passed along the west side of the skyscraper *The Star* was then building on King Street West, presumably enhancing its value.

It had first been proposed by E. W. Beatty, president of the CPR, in an interview in the *Telegram* early in 1927. The Union Station had just been opened, and the Royal York Hotel across the street from it was under con-struction. Beatty proposed that instead of extending University Avenue south from Queen Street, where it then ended, a diagonal street a hundred feet wide should be cut through run-down old buildings from the intersec-tion of University Avenue and Queen Street to a square in front of the Union station. On behalf of the railway he offered to give the city some property the CPR owned for part of the right-of-way.

City council asked Basil Campbell, a consulting engineer, and Eustace G. Bird, an architect, for a report. They approved of it. Council then ap-pointed an advisory planning committee headed by H. H. Williams, a prominent realtor, financier, and philanthropist. This committee prepared a master plan for downtown redevelopment, the main feature of which was a sort of Piccadilly Circus at University Avenue and Queen Street from which eight streets 100 feet wide would radiate. It estimated the cost at $10 million. If the entire plan was not accepted, it recommended that at least the diagonal street suggested by Beatty be opened, though with a bend in it to provide better intersections with cross streets.

"The committee is recommending a University Ave. corkscrew extension . . . for the benefit of two newspapers," the *Telegram* declared. It had learned that the *Mail and Empire* had also bought property on King Street for a new building. It doctored maps distributed by the planning committee to make it look as if the street beside *The Star* building was the main feature of the plan. Before long it was running its own distorted maps showing it as the only feature. It charged *The Star* with having had advance notice of the recommendation, though actually *The Star* had bought its property a month before Beatty made his suggestion and nearly a year before the committee was appointed. It even ran a fanciful story of plans being stolen from the city hall, presumably by agents of *The Star*. It claimed the only reason *The Star* supported the redevelopment plan was because Mr. Atkinson owned some lots he hoped to sell to the city for an exorbitant profit. It ignored his offer to resell them for what he had paid.

This plan was submitted to the electors in December, 1929, but by that time the "crooked lane" had been straightened into a broad thoroughfare that would run midway between Bay and York streets from the union station to a proposed civic square on Queen Street. By that time, too, a hostile city council had tagged a number of unrelated street widenings and straightenings to the master plan for downtown redevelopment, raising the estimated cost to $19,000,000.

Nevertheless, the *Telegram* continued to call it the "crooked lane" plan, and when a number of prominent citizens, including Sir Joseph Flavelle, Sir James Wood, Canon Cody, and former Premier Sir William Hearst organized a "citizens' committee for a Greater Toronto" to support it, the *Telegram* refused their advertising on the grounds it was "calculated to deceive."

When the *Telegram* could not find any potential candidate for mayor opposed to this far-sighted plan, it ran its city editor, Bert S. Wemp, against Samuel McBride in the December, 1929, election. But the *Telegram* virtually ignored McBride and campaigned against "Holy Joe" and his "crooked lane." Wemp was elected, and the redevelopment plan was defeated by 2,200 of 55,300 votes cast. "A catastrophe," declared the citizens' committee, as most persons familiar with downtown Toronto today will agree. Until death relieved them of their duties in 1948 the then publishers of the *Telegram* delighted to refer to *The Star* as "the newspaper on crooked lane."

While *The Star* and *Telegram* were engaged in bitter rivalry and differed on almost everything under the sun, on one point they were united. That was on the preservation of the freedom of the press. Joseph E. Atkinson and John Ross Robertson had been opposed to Canadian Press Limited accepting a subsidy to defray the cost of bridging the news gap between eastern and western Canada, believing that the press of a nation could not be free as long as it was dependent upon government grants for any portion of its news. When it looked as though they were to be overruled by a majority of their fellow publishers, Mr. Atkinson resigned as secretary-treasurer rather than have any part in it.

According to Nichols, "Atkinson stood aloof from proceedings when the subsidy was granted" by the Borden government in 1917, thus making Canadian Press a national service, but no sooner was the war ended than he began the fight to have it removed. The amount was $48,398 a year. He had accepted a seat on the directorate of the new co-operative Canadian Press in 1917, but resigned after a year, to be succeeded by John R. Bone as *The Star*'s representative. To clear the decks for action Bone resigned in 1919.

Most Canadian publishers justified, or rationalized, acceptance of a government subsidy by Canadian Press on the grounds it was needed to "bind the nation together." Similarly they extenuated a subsidy by the British and Canadian governments on trans-Atlantic cable news on the grounds it was needed "to bind the Empire together." Mr. Atkinson's argument was simply that politicians, being as they are, would soon start meddling in the affairs of a subsidized news agency.

The question of government-subsidized news came up at the annual meeting of Canadian Press on May 19, 1920, with all members represented. A motion was presented authorizing Canadian Press to enter into an agreement with the Canadian and British governments for a subsidy of $20,000 a year to help defray the cost of cable tolls on British news transmitted to Canada. *The Star*, the *Telegram*, the *Globe*, and the *Montreal Star* immediately protested. They objected not only to subsidies in general, but in particular to the British government providing the Canadian Press with hand-picked and slanted British news at reduced cost. They lost the battle before Canadian Press, but won the fight at Ottawa when Premier

Meighen declined to pay the Canadian share of the subsidy though his predecessor Premier Borden had agreed to it. Meighen was accused in some papers of "taking fright" at the campaign of *The Star* and *Telegram* against "subsidy hunters."

Claims that the subsidy was "essential" were quickly disproven. Canadian Press increased the levy on its member newspapers, made an arrangement with the independent British news services for their news, and within a few weeks was providing its members with an improved cable service free of any suspicion of slanting by British or Canadian governments.

Shortly thereafter *The Star* and *Telegram* renewed their campaign to have the government subsidy to bridge the East-West gap dropped, and for the adoption of the Associated Press' system of apportioning the cost among newspapers. Mr. Atkinson was represented on CP by his managing editor, the impassive, subtle Bone. John Ross Robertson had died in 1918 and the *Telegram* was represented by his erratic son, Irving.

Their first move was to call for a special general meeting of CP members to examine, among other things, "the present inequitable system of overhead costs for the safeguarding of eastern interests." J. F. B. Livesay, general manager of CP, proposed costs should be apportioned among newspapers according to their ability to pay. *The Star*, *Telegram*, and some of Ontario's small city dailies argued for the AP system of regional subdivisions, with each subdivision paying its own costs. Their contention was that under a regional system the newspapers of Ontario and Quebec could support an independent and unsubsidized news service. Whether or not the western newspapers chose to accept government money would then be a matter for them alone to decide, but the East at least would have a press free from the threat of government interference. They were defeated 72 to 10, and the subsidy was continued.

The publishers soon had cause to regret their decision, for beginning in 1922 members of Parliament of all parties began sniping at the CP, claiming the right to interfere in its affairs by reason of the subsidy. The attacks of private members were bad enough. Much more serious was the intervention by the Minister of Labour, Hon. James Murdock. Displeased by CP reports of a strike in Cape Breton, he wrote CP general manager Livesay a letter criticizing them. "Having in mind that your organization receives from the Dominion government a very substantial grant in aid of its undertakings, you will, I am sure, realize my right to lay the matter before you," he wrote. This was exactly the kind of interference Mr. Atkinson had feared. The matter was brought to a head when Canadian Press refused a franchise to W. F. Herman of Windsor, publisher of the *Border Cities*

Star, for a newspaper in Ottawa. There was no Liberal newspaper in the capital and Herman's application was sponsored by no less a personage than the recently elected Prime Minister, Mackenzie King. It was rejected on the grounds there were already two newspapers in Ottawa.

Conservative and Liberal Parliamentarians alike insisted that as long as Canadian Press received a government subsidy it must grant a franchise to all applicants. Prime Minister King told Parliament he disagreed with this view, for which the *Telegram* accused him of "talking sheer, shallow nonsense." When it looked as if members of all parties would combine to strike the subsidy from the estimates, King intervened with a promise that if it was approved in 1923 it would not be in the 1924 estimates.

Once more it was proven a government subsidy was unnecessary. Thrown on its own resources, Canadian Press pulled up its socks, the publishers dug deeper into their pockets, while *The Star* and the *Telegram*, having won their fight for a news service free from the threat of political interference, agreed to contribute more generously to the costs of the service.

Canada has a free and independent news service today because Joseph E. Atkinson and his opposite numbers on the *Telegram* were able to bury personal animosities for the time being and fight shoulder to shoulder for a principle in which they profoundly believed.

Many people found *The Star*'s attitude towards religion baffling and at times contradictory. Its general tone was puritanical, a true reflection of Mr. Atkinson's austere disposition. It had one or two pious articles a week on its editorial page. It covered religious news extensively. But at the same time it based its social program on intellectual humanism rather than on religion, and it gave sensational treatment to congregational wranglings and the transgressions of clergymen.

One cause, however, had its unswerving support. That was the movement for a union of Protestant churches. From the time Mr. Atkinson took over *The Star*, the negotiations leading to a union of Methodist, Presbyterian, and Congregational denominations were fully and sympathetically reported. As a prominent Methodist on terms of close personal friendship with the leading personalities of that denomination, his advice and guidance were frequently sought. When at last it became evident that a considerable element within the Presbyterian church was unwilling to unite with Methodists on the basis that had earlier been agreed upon, he could scarcely be restrained by editor Clark from hurling *The Star* into the fight on behalf of Church union. One morning he burst into Clark's office. "Mr. Clark," he declared, "we've got to have an editorial tomorrow on church union."

Patiently Clark repeated what he had said so many times before—that a dispute over doctrinal matters was not something a secular newspaper should deal with; that no good end would be served by an editorial along the lines Atkinson wanted; that it would only inflame still further tempers already too hot; and that much of the anger would be turned upon *The Star*.

"But, Mr. Clark, Church Union is so important we can't keep silent any longer," the Chief protested.

"Mr. Atkinson, in spite of you I shall prevent *The Star* from doing something that can only harm it," Clark said with determination. "I will not write such an editorial myself, nor will I instruct any of my staff to write it." Mr. Atkinson glared at his editor for a moment, then turned on his heel and left. The editorial was not written.

Mackenzie King was a Presbyterian unfriendly to church union, and when a bill giving legal sanction to the union of the three denominations into the United Church of Canada was introduced in Parliament in 1924, he had attached to it an amendment suspending church union subject to a decision of the courts on certain technical points. Mr. Atkinson immediately sent a lengthy telegram to King. This amendment, he said, "would undo the work of eighteen years." He said he could not hold with the technicality on which it was proposed to delay the union, because the idea of "the immutability for all time of church doctrine has been outgrown in the country in which it was raised," namely England, where a number of Presbyterian sects had been united. "It is distressing to think that a movement in which the great majority of three Canadian churches have been engaged during so many years should be wrecked," he protested. He referred to the proposed union as "a matter in which my heart and mind are so deeply engaged . . . I appeal to you."

In response to vigorous protests from supporters of Church Union, King withdrew the proposed amendment. The bill was passed substantially as the uniting churches requested, and the United Church of Canada came into being on June 10, 1925. That same day *The Star* had its first editorial on the subject, a pleasant, non-committal one that might have appeared with equal propriety in any church paper. However, for the week preceding, when the uniting denominations were holding their final conclaves, *The Star* had devoted dozens of columns to their deliberations, with great headlines on page one, making it clear to the public that this was the greatest event in Canada since Confederation.

Some years after church union Atkinson expressed disappointment in its results. "The zeal of the Methodists has been dampened by the coldness of the Calvinists," he complained. On another occasion he said the United Church had become "too sacerdotal."

His personal religion was a strange mixture of intellectual liberalism and old-time Methodism. He seemed to feel the church's theology was questionable but its ethical teachings were sound. Thus *The Star* could always be counted upon to support the churches in good works, but at the same time to publicize doctrinal disputes or the rebellion of a clergyman against the discipline of his superiors or congregation. This ambivalence with respect to organized religion sometimes brought accusations of hypocrisy upon Atkinson, one of the accusers being his son-in-law, who was often impatient when treated to scriptural quotations. However, Mr. Atkinson sincerely felt that the ventilation of sectarian disputes revealed how petty most of them were, and in the long run promoted religious tolerance.

It has been said that though Mr. Atkinson kept his extensive personal charities a secret he blazoned the charities of *The Star* to the world. Nothing could be further from the truth. Certain charities, such as *The Star* Fresh Air Fund and the Santa Claus Fund depended upon public support and had to be highly publicized. Certain other works were undertaken as "promotion" for *The Star*, and they too were publicized. But commencing around 1918 or 1919 it was a rare year in which unpublicized donations by *The Star* failed to reach $25,000 to $30,000. The YMCA received $1,000 to $5,000 a year. Bolton Fresh Air Camp, the Federation of Community Services, and Toronto Western Hospital in some years each received as much as $2,500. Banting Institute got $5,000, the Art Gallery of Toronto $2,500, and shaky little Brandon Baptist College out in Manitoba was more than once saved from sinking by *The Star*.

In 1918 all employees were paid a "war bonus" of six per cent on their salaries. This had been negotiated by the mechanical trades, but was voluntarily extended to non-union employees as well. The following year the bonus was doubled to twelve per cent, without having been negotiated. In December, 1919, *The Star* began the practice of giving one week's salary to every employee as a Christmas bonus, it was said at the suggestion of Mrs. Atkinson. This practice has been continued ever since. Mrs. Atkinson was always urging her husband to pay higher salaries, and it was not

The present Star Building, completed in 1929

LARGEST CIRCULATION IN CANADA

THE TORONTO DAILY STAR

READ NIGHT EDITION of The Daily Star at 4.30 o'clock every evening

36TH YEAR (MARCH CIRCULATION, 173,877 COPIES DAILY) TORONTO, MONDAY, APRIL 16, 1928—40 PAGES 5 O'CLOCK EDITION TWO CENTS

STAR PLANE PICKS UP IRISH FLIER

Labrador Coast in Grip of a Violent Gale With the Heaviest Fall of Snow

TWO GERMAN FLIERS STAY ON GREENLY IS. TO REPAIR THE PLANE

Only Determination and Strong Will to Succeed Got Bremen to Greenly

GAS DIMINISHING

Crashed Through Ice in Landing on Small Lake—Airmen Escape Injury

Second Attempt To Reach Island Gets Under Way

WIND PACKS ICE MONTCALM HELD FROM CONTINUING

Steady Southeast Wind Rafts Ice on North Shore

120 MILES AWAY

Need North Wind Before They Can Go to Help of Bremen

Star Representatives Reach Bremen Fliers

THIS IS MOST RECENT PICTURE OF CONQUERORS OF ATLANTIC

SCHILLER AEROPLANE AT GREENLY ISLAND BEARING STAR AGENT

Flight of Noted Aviator From Murray Bay Is Successful

MONTCALM IS STUCK

Two Other Aeroplanes Winging Way Toward Scene of Flight

Brown Lauds Achievement of Bremen Crew

PARENTS GLAD SCHILLER REACHED GREENLY ISLAND

They Knew Son Would Do Because "He Ayways Finished What He Starts"

AWAIT HIS LETTER

Flier's Brother Composes March Honoring Exploit

MONTREAL IS CHOICE FOR NEXT SWIM DERBY

Toronto Has No Chance If Water Is Available—Many Entries

OFFER IS ACCEPTED FOR STORE CHAIN

The Canadian Department Store Bondholders Approve Sale—Price Around $4,000,000

BALKED ELEMENTS RENEW ONSLAUGHT ON BREMEN PLANE

Work of Repairs Going On in Face of Violent Gale

MACHINE STILL SAFE

German-Irish Fliers Still Confident of Continuing the Journey by Air

Moving Picture Camera Operator Off to Greenly

FABULOUS PRICES OFFERED FOR SEAT IN RELIEF PLANES

Movie Men and Reporters Overrun Sleepy Quebec Town

WEATHER IS BAD

Frantic Bidding Marks Efforts to Reach Ocean Fliers

CANNOT ENTER CLASS WEARING SMELLY BAG

Must Wear It to Save Self From Disease, Mother Says

COL. RALSTON DELIGHTED AT STAR PLANE'S SUCCESS

CURRIE LIBEL ACTION STARTS BEFORE A JURY OF YEOMEN

No Returned Soldiers on Panel for Trial of Celebrated Case

ARMY OF PRESS MEN

Hanna Smiles As He Returns to 'Legitimate' Job

THE WEATHER

ABOVE: the story of the rescue of the German fliers ranks as one of the great newspaper scoops of this continent. The spelling of the island was later standardized as *Greenely*.

RIGHT: the front page of the first issue of *The Star* printed in its present building, February 4, 1929

LARGEST CIRCULATION IN CANADA

THE TORONTO DAILY STAR

READ NIGHT EDITION of The Daily Star at 6 o'clock every evening

TH YEAR (DECEMBER CIRCULATION 174,186 COPIES DAILY) TORONTO, MONDAY, FEBRUARY 4, 1929—36 PAGES 5 O'CLOCK EDITION TWO CENTS

DISASTERS ON LAND AND SEA TAKE 44 LIVES

HENOMENAL FRIGIDITY AND GALES TAKE TOLL FORTY-FOUR ARE DEAD

orms of Unprecedented Sever-y Bring Hardships to Many European Centres

ERMAN CREW LOST

nstantinople Shut Off From World by Blizzard—Wolves Attack on Roadway

London, Feb. 4 (AP).—At least 44 sons met death in Europe over a ek-end of unprecedented storm and d conditions, the Balkan states and rkey being particularly heavy ferers.

hipping everywhere was deranged, pecially in the Black Sea, where merous minor wrecks were reported. The most serious disaster was off coast of Portugal, where the Ger-n freight Deister foundered yester-y after being driven on the rocks ring a violent gale. The crew of assembled on the topmost deck, but huge wave hurled 20 of them into . The remaining six went down h their vessel.

he second largest disaster was on Russian Turkestan town of Alma where a landslide on Saturday pt 11 persons to their deaths. It in this town that Leon Trotsky, mer leader of the Red Army, was exile for many months.

hour workmen sent to clear the ks of the Simplon Express in arian Turkey were frozen to th and the work of digging out the train, which has been blocked by snow for three days, was called off.

Three persons were frozen to death in Budapest and many others were suffering from exposure. It was the coldest day in 50 years, the temperature dropping to 20 below zero centigrade in some places of Hungary.

Heavy Fog in London

While London groped through a choking fog, which was the worst one

(Continued on Page 2)

STARTS MAIL SERVICE

Col. Charles Lindbergh "Lucky Lindy," flying a United States mail plane took off from Miami, Fla., to-day on the first leg of a 2,327 mile trip to Cristobal, canal zone. To-day's flight starts an air mail service which will put any point in South America just a week distant from the canal.

PERFECT START BY LINDBERGH ON LONG FLIGHT

Inaugurates New Air Mail Service to South American Points

REACHES HAVANA

His Next Stop Will Be Belize British Honduras, on Mainland

Miami, Fla., Feb. 4 (UP).—Col. Charles A. Lindbergh is celebrating his 27th birthday to-day by flying a United States mail plane. He hopped off from here to?day at 6.08 a.m. on the first leg of a 2,327-mile flight to Cristobal, Canal Zone.

The take-off of the Sikorsky plane was perfect in the dim, gray dawn. With the familiar Lindbergh flourish it shot from its resting place, motors roaring, to leap into the air as the old mail flier was wont to do.

With Lindbergh in the plane was Jet Trippe, president of the Pan-American Airways, sponsors of the new air route; John Hambleton, vice-president of the same concern, and Harry Buckey, mechanic and radio operator. Their objective was Havana, first stop of the flight.

The flight starts an air mail service to South America.

Reported Nearing Havana

Havana, Feb. 4 (UP).—Radio reports received here at 7 a.m. said Col. Charles A. Lindbergh, en route from Miami, was flying low at 100 miles an hour, headed west-southwest. Light head winds prevailed. Lindbergh was expected here in an hour.

A later report from Havana states: Col. Charles A. Lindbergh landed here at 8.20 a.m. to-day, completing the first stretch of the new Pan American airways route from Miami, Fla., to Cristobal, Panama canal zone.

He will remain in Havana for about half an hour and then leave for his next stop, an overnight one, at Belize, British Honduras, on the central American mainland.

May Get High Post

Miami Beach, Fla., Feb. 4 (UP).—President-elect Hoover is drafting a comprehensive scheme for development of aviation, one of the major objectives of his administration, in which Col. Charles A. Lindbergh, youthful master of the skies, may have a prominent role.

Takes Off Again

Havana, Feb. 4 (UP).—Col. Charles A. Lindbergh left here to-day at 9.21 for Belize, British Honduras, on the second section of his flight from Miami, Fla., to Cristobal, Panama Canal Zone.

To Try Long Distance Flight

BRITAIN'S "SILVER TORPEDO"

Latest addition to English aviation, "Silver Torpedo," the largest cantilever aeroplane constructed in England, will seek the non-stop long-distance record held by Italy, with its Rome to South America flight. It was put through successful tests recently in preparation for the flight from Capetown, South Africa, to northern Scotland. It is a Fairy-Napier monoplane. (1) The "Silver Torpedo"; (2) Flight Lieut. Eric Victor Major, navigator, and (3) Squadron Leader Arthur Gordon Jones-Williams, chief pilot.

Life Begins to Throb In The Star's New Home

"Boys of the Old Brigade" Clear Their Throats When They Leave the Former Abode—Work of "Producing and Expressing" Starts Anew

By R. E. KNOWLES

hey do say that the fitting of The ly Star was the greatest "fly-by-ht" achievement since the children Israel set out on their great hegira. for here we are, this bright and y Monday morning, all settled n at 80 King St. W.—and the en is purring on the hearth! st Saturday afternoon marked, to (as to The Daily Star) a waterfall he stream of time.

was right touching, in all earnest-s, to see some members of The r staff, especially "the boys of the brigade," trying to say good-bye 8 King W., that bring the exact at which The Daily Star passed steady and inexorable pace, from aping to a great tree, among whose nches some 600 workers carry on, beneath whose umbrageous shade dry hundreds of thousands take r ease and their journalistic pabu-

happily fell to my lot, by accident, e in the sanctum sanctorum, where Chief's" invisible hand so long has the throttle-valve. It was early rnoon—and suddenly there appear- the substantial form of one of "the old guard." His first name, not inferentially employed, is "Bill." He did not sit down, nor otherwise linger. He just was about to pull out for 80 King St. W. So was the Chief.

But this modern Harvey (Harvey "invented" Circulation — but of the blood) walked straight up to his Chief, held out his hand, smiled deliberately and heroically, and said: "Well, I just came in to say good-bye to you—we've been here together quite a while, haven't we?" and then he cleared his throat.

And the Chief stood up, and took the offered hand, and said: "Yes, about 29 years we've been together anyhow—it's quite a while—good-bye," with which he too cleared his throat. Then the circulationist walked out of the door, and so did I, also indulging in a little dredging of the thorax. And I suppose these two colleagues met, very shortly after the farewells, at 80 King St. W.

But, nevertheless, I thought it one of the most appropriate and significant valedictory scenes I had ever witnessed.

An hour later something of the same kind transpired in the (big—or display) advertising room on the ground floor. The chief figure was one of

(Continued on Page 3)

Flowers Express Mayor's Good Wish

Beautiful Building Demonstrates Toronto's Growth, He Tells President of The Star

The mayor added to his presence at the new Star building to-day a beautiful bouquet of flowers addressed to the president with wishes for success and happiness to The Star.

"Nothing could demonstrate the growth of Toronto," said Mr. McBride, "better than this beautiful building and its really amazing equipment."

At the ceremony of the turning on of the presses, Thomas Peck superintendent of the presses, and several members of his staff were introduced to the mayor.

MAYOR DEMANDS FURTHER INQUIRY INTO BY-ELECTION

Aims at Having Contest Comply Strictly With the Law

BENSON WILL RUN

With respect to the contention that the holding of a by-election to fill the vacancy on the board of control in compliance with the order of the master-in-chambers would be illegal Mayor McBride told The Star to-day that everything would be done to comply strictly with the law.

"I don't want anything to happen such as happened in connection with the last election," said Mayor McBride to The Star. "We don't want to hold this election and then run the chance of somebody protesting it. Therefore, I have asked for a further opinion on the question from both the city solicitor and the corporation counsel to make it absolutely sure that we have a right to go on with this by-election."

City Clerk Somers stated that he regarded the order of the master-in-chambers as an order of the supreme court and he was continuing his preparations for the by-election to fill the vacancy in the office of controller.

Demanding action on the question of their qualification, Alderman J. W. Benson (Ward Five) has announced that he will resign and run for controller, making the disposition of three city aldermen whose taxes were unpaid at the time of election the chief plank in his platform. He will further bring up the question of preventing the future nomination of unqualified persons.

The council turned down Alderman Benson's motion for an investigation of the recent election and also his motion to have all members file affidavits that their taxes were paid when they were nominated. Mr. Benson's

(Continued on Page 2)

Arrest Provides First City Copy In New Building

Walking into a restaurant on Church St. early this morning, Plainclothesmen McKay and Mann of west Dundas St. station arrested William Dunn, who gave his residence as Bond St., on a charge of registering and recording bets.

A large quantity of alleged betting slips and racing material was seized by the officers.

The accompanying story, telling of the arrest in the city of a man on a betting charge, was the first local news item to pass through the copy desk of this newspaper in the new Star building to-day. It was shortly after 6 a.m. when the reporter on the night police beat handed in the copy.

EXPECT PRICE ON NEWSPRINT TO BE SET TO-DAY

Settlement of Rate for 1929 at $55.50 a Ton Anticipated in Montreal

WILL BE INCREASED

Special to The Star by Staff Reporter

Montreal, Feb. 4.—Settlement of the newsprint price for 1929 at $55.50 a ton is expected at Montreal to-day or to-morrow. The announcement will be made by Col. P. B. Wilson, director of the Canadian Newsprint Institute.

"Ninety per cent. bunk," was the comment of a prominent newsprint manufacturer of this city on the dispatch from New York quoting an interview with a Canadian manufacturer obtained by Editor and Publisher before the conference left New York for Montreal, that the International Paper Co. is playing a "heads I win, tails you lose" game with the other manufacturers in the newsprint price situation.

"I've been at a good many of the conferences," he said, "and I never heard anything to suggest that the International Paper Co. 'had us licked before we started, and is simply shaking the Canadian manufacturers by the throat while they are down.'

"The Canadian manufacturers, as a matter of fact," said this manufactur-

(Continued on Page 2)

WANT TO SET OWN LIMIT

Hon. George S. Henry, minister of highways, to-day promised to consider a request of a deputation from East York township to give municipalities adjacent to Toronto permission to set their own speed limit for automobiles. It is claimed that the present limit of 35 miles per hour is too high for some municipalities.

CALLED WITHIN BAR

Mr. Justice Jeffrey called Thomas F. Battle, K.C., within the bar at weekly court at Osgoode Hall to-day, when he presented his patent to the court. His lordship paid a tribute to his long acquaintance with Mr. Battle and expressed personal pleasure at the opportunity afforded him.

HULME DESCRIBES HIS TRIP BY SKI FROM FAR NORTH

Writes of Twenty-Day Undertaking Made for a Wager of $250

MAKING PROGRESS

The following story of his trip and adventures on the route is being written exclusively for The Star by Kennelm Hulme, who has undertaken to ski from Timmins to Toronto in 20 days on a wager of $250.

By KENNELM HULME

Special to The Star. Copyright

New Liskeard, Feb. 3.—I have been on the trail six days and am a little over a quarter of the way to my destination. It was just ten to five when Jack Forbes and I pulled into New Liskeard to-day, so I decided to call it a day and put up for the night, having covered 31 miles. We left Timmins on Tuesday, Jan. 29, at 8.10 a.m.

There was a big snowstorm driving in our faces all day long and both highway and track were unbroken after we passed Golden City. However, we pushed on to Connaught, arriving there just about dusk.

Wednesday morning when we got ready to start out on the trail again I found it was necessary to wax my

(Continued on Page 2)

TROTSKY REPORTED SAFE IN RUSSIA

Moscow Reports Deny That He Was Drowned in Black Sea

Berlin, Feb. 4 (AP).—Despatches received here to-day from Moscow state that Leon Trotzky was still in Russia and reports that he had been drowned while crossing the Black Sea to Constantinople were without foundation.

Ship Was Delayed

Constantinople, Feb. 4 (UP).—The Soviet steamship agency said to-day that the steamer Krasnyflott was safe. The ship was merely delayed by bad weather and probably would arrive Wednesday, the agency said.

MAN IS ASSAULTED

Michael Stiss, 24, 97 Sydenham St., received severe scalp wounds in a brawl at 362 King St. E. last night, resulting in the arrest of Rode Diminoff, living at the King St. address, on a charge of aggravated assault. Stiss was taken to St. Michael's hospital for treatment, where several stitches were required to close the wounds. Police say the injured man was felled by a stick wielded by Diminoff.

THE FOX

The mocking bird of the mammals is the fox, which has been heard to bleat like a lamb, and on occasions, to mew like a kitten.

BIG THREE HOLD COURT SPINNING HUMAN FATE IN WEB OF RUM-RACKET

Detroit's Underworld Organized to Last Detail on Basis of Booze

20,000 SPEAKEASIES

Star Reporter Conducted on Survey of America's Blind-Pig Capital

Special to The Star by Staff Reporter

Detroit, Feb. 4.—There's a bar down East Jefferson Ave. in Detroit where three men preside over the destinies of America's greatest "racket." Three three men—two Italians and one American—control the underworld of the rum capital of America.

That's the difference between the speakeasies of Buffalo and Detroit. The speakeasies of Detroit are more organized. The blind pig operator in Detroit is more often the professional gunman. In fact, there is no comparison between the number of speakeasies in the two cities. In Buffalo there are 1,500. In Detroit there are 20,000. Commissioner of Police Wm. P. Rutledge set the figure two years ago at 15,000.

Our first visit to the blind pigs of Detroit made us aware of "the grapevine around Detroit and Windsor," as our guide described the organized underworld. If we did not get into the presence of the Big Three in the East Jefferson saloon, we got close enough before self-preservation whispered the old adage that discretion is the better part of valor.

There was no doubt about our guide. A few weeks ago he figured on the

(Continued on Page 2)

LEAVES FOR TURKEY

Leon Trotsky, Russian war-time revolutionary leader, exiled from Soviet Russia, predicts that a Napoleon will rise in Russia and overthrow the revolutionists. The steamship Krasin, on which he is believed to be travelling, is missing in a terrific hurricane raging over the Black Sea. Grave fears are entertained for the safety of the vessel.

HOWLING LUPUS OF THE BUSH MET DEATH ATTACKING BOYS

At Least That's How Story Goes and Battered Pelt Is Offered as Proof

PAWS WERE INJURED

Special to The Star

Chapleau, Feb. 4.—Has a timber wolf at last come out into the open and attacked a human being?

Marshall King and William Hall, pupils at the Indian school here, say that it has. For proof of their statement they offer the body of a full grown timber wolf which they have turned in for government bounty to Carl Fadden, game warden at Chapleau.

They claim they clubbed the wolf to death in a twenty minutes battle, precipitated when the wolf launched his attack.

Driving a team of horses, drawing a sleigh load of wood, the kids say they encountered the animal about a mile from the school. Dashing from the cover of the dense brush at this point, they claim it made several attempts to jump into the sleigh. At first believing it was nothing more formidable than a vicious husky, the lads belabored it with slabs of wood, but when it returned again and again to the attack, they discovered they were faced by a wolf.

Halting their team, the lads seized the sleigh skates from the side of the vehicle and, leaping to the ground, battered the animal about the head and body. Handicapped as it was by two mangled front paws, injuries no doubt occasioned by having been caught in a steel trap, the wolf put up a magnificent fight as the courageous lads attacked from the front and the rear. Finally a well directed blow delivered on the head by King knocked the animal unconscious, and a few moments later the boys realized they had won when the wolf stiffened and died.

They placed their trophy on the sleigh and brought it to Carl Fadden, Chapleau, game warden, and entered a claim for the government bounty. Although many stories have been circulated in the Chapleau district dealing with wolves attacking humans, this is the first instance where yarns have been partially substantiated by the battered and mutilated presence of the pelt.

Please Give Us Time to Arrange Things for You

The Star is in its new home to-day and, after a week or two devoted to getting settled, will welcome visitors who may desire to see the new building and the new plant.

For the present, however, we are in the position of those who have just moved into a new house. We are experiencing a period of inevitable unsettlement, with many things that will require arranging and tidying up.

During this interval The Star asks the indulgence of its friends and requests them to defer their social visit until a later date. Arrangements for showing visitors through the building will be announced publicly in due course.

This note does not apply, of course, to those having direct business which they wish to transact with The Star; all facilities for such business transactions are already in operation.

THE WEATHER

MONDAY-TUESDAY, FEBRUARY 4-5

The local forecast is: Lower Lake Region and Georgian Bay—Moderate winds, shifting to easterly; mostly cloudy with local snowfalls or flurries to-day and Tuesday; stationary or a little higher temperature.

The observations at noon to-day showed: Highest temperature yesterday, 23; lowest this morning, 13.

Yesterday's mean temperature was 13, or 9 degrees below the average. The mean temperature for the corresponding day last year was 23, or 3 degrees above the average.

Time	Temp	Wind	Weath	Hum
8 a.m.	19	N.W. 5	Cloudy	84
Noon	21	W. 2	Cloudy	75

Handy Reference Calendar

Sun	Mon	Tues	Wed	Thur	Fri	Sat
3	4	5	6	7	8	9

The meteorological office estimates that the lowest the temperature will drop during the night is 14 degrees above zero, while its highest mark to-morrow is estimated at 26 degrees above.

To-day's Calendar

Sun rises .... 7.32 a.m.
Sun sets .... 5.33 p.m.

Synopsis of Weather Conditions:

Pressure is high over the eastern part of the continent and over the far northwest, while a shallow trough of low pressure extends from Manitoba to the southwest states. Except for light local snow in Southwestern Ontario and in Manitoba the weather has been fair in all provinces. It has been cold in Eastern Canada and decidedly cold in Saskatchewan and Alberta.

STEAMSHIP ARRIVALS

Steamer	At	From
Cameronia	Halifax	Glasgow
Westphalia	Halifax	Hamburg
Polonia	Halifax	Copenhagen
Gripsholm	Halifax	Gothenburg
Can. Volunteer	Halifax	W. Indies
Elerinno	Halifax	Cepitia
Doric	Halifax	Liverpool
Milverton	Saint John	Hull
Can. Inventor	Saint John	Antwerp
Maid of Andros	Saint John	Oran
Metagama	Saint John	Liverpool
Marta	Trapani	St. John
Hada County	Rotterdam	St. John

EKS TO STRIKE OUT CLAIM OF J. DENISON

Jdgment Reserved on Defendant's Motion in Denison Estate Case

D. Porter, counsel for several defdants, by counter-claim in the ac- to claim title and repossession of Denison estate, moved before the ster at Osgoode Hall to-day to strike the amended counter-claim filed John Denison pursuant to the ster's order of November 14. Judg-nt was reserved.

Mr. Porter moved on the ground t the amended counter-claim does comply with the order in that does not set forth the title which Denisons assert, or the grounds on which they claim possession of lands and premises in question.

The lands in question are valued at lions of dollars and lie on the west of Dufferin St. between Bloor College Sts., and include Dufferin track and a number of industrial premises.

The original action was brought by . and Effie Watson and Robert therston, for a renewal of the r of the lands. Watson was the ginal assignee but he had assigned leases to others. This action was ontinued, and John Denison, rles Fisher Denison and Margaret nison Featherstonhaugh continued r counter-claim for repossession of lands.

he Orpen, Cruden and Adams, kenson Dye Works and the or-al plaintiffs were made defend-s to the counter-claim.

The only facts they set forth as porting to set forth their title," Mr. Porter, "is that George Tay-Denison in his lifetime, was seized the lands. Then they quote a sage from G. T. Denison's will in ch he gives to his son, Charles lie Denison, a life interest in the ds with power of appointment to children.

Then they say that John Denison the sole surviving executor of rles Leslie Denison, and as such cutor, he is now owner of the ds to which he claims possession.

They don't show how John Denison has any interest in the lands at all. A life estate, and an executor he would not have any right to turn the lands over.

"The facts should set up and show a chain title from George Taylor Denison to John Denison. There is a big skip there."

Mr. Porter also pointed out that only John Denison had filed the amended counter-claim. Either the other two must join or the claim must be stricken out.

SPRING FLOWERS GREET THE STAR'S PRESIDENT

When the president of The Star reached his office in the new building this morning he found his desk almost buried under beautiful flowers.

One huge basket filled with spring blooms was accompanied by a card, "with best wishes from the staff, February 4, 1929."

Other lovely flowers came from Mayor McBride, Mr. J. H. Gundy, Mr. J. A. C. Kemp, of the Toronto branch of the Canadian Bank of Commerce and Mr. W. A. Lydiatt, president of "Marketing."

Canadian Papers Join in Greeting The Daily Star

The president of The Star received this morning the following telegram from Henri Gagnon of Le Soleil, Quebec, president of the Canadian Daily Newspapers Association:

"I very much appreciate the privilege accorded me to-day as president of the Canadian Daily Newspapers Association to offer you sincere congratulations on the occasion of the inauguration of your new building and your new presses. Not only the fellow-members of our association but the whole population of the Dominion should be proud of your great achievement in placing the press of Canada on a standing equal to that of the best newspapers of any country. Accept also the best personal wishes of the managing director of Le Soleil."

PROPERTIES CHANGE HANDS

Total of $69,000 Reached in Three Sales To-day

Three property sales totalling $69,000 were recorded at the city registry office to-day. John Alva Carveth has purchased the property at 28-30 Grenville St. for $31,000. The site, located between Bay and Yonge Sts., has a frontage of 50 feet on the north side of Grenville St., with a depth of 150 feet. Vendors were the executors of the estate of the late Randal English.

Title to a property formerly owned by the McLaughlin Building Construction Co. has been acquired by Benjamin Swartz, 336 Dundas St. W. This has a frontage of 30 feet on the south side of Gerrard St. E., with a depth of 100 feet. The purchase price was $20,000.

Frank A. Deering has purchased a property having a 25-foot frontage on the west side of Main St., with a depth of 150 feet. The vendor was Charles F. Kennedy, the purchase price being $18,000.

GENERAL BOOTH LEAVES HIS SOUTHWOLD RESIDENCE

Army Heads Speculate as to Significance of Return to His Home Near London, Although His Secretary Explains That It Is for the Purpose of Treatment

London, Feb. 4 (AP).—Salvation Army circles wondered to-day just what significance to attack to General Bramwell Booth's journey yesterday from his sickbed at Southwold to his home at Hadley Wood, Barnet.

General Booth's secretary was quoted as saying the move had been undertaken at his doctors' request to facilitate application of the specialized treatment.

But others say the general himself decided to return to be near the scene of action in the conflict which is looming between himself and members of the high council, which is seeking to depose him as commander-in-chief of the army.

At Hadley Wood, it is stated, he might easily, given physical fitness, help his daughter, Catherine, to conduct matters in his behalf. Attention is called to Hadley Wood being just 12 miles from London, whereas Southwold was four or five hours' away at best.

Friends say the aged general enjoyed yesterday's motor trip very much. It was a clear cold day and the 126 miles were travelled in something more than four hours.

A new resolution was drawn up by the council Friday and forwarded to the general, asking him to appear before it and defend himself against the charge of his physical incapacity.

WATERLOO VICTORY COSTS BELGIUM $20,000 A YEAR

London—More than a century has passed since the Duke of Wellington, aided by German, Belgian and Dutch troops, defeated Napoleon at Waterloo. For this feat of arms the Belgians must pay a perpetual annuity to the duke's heir amounting to approximately $20,000.

After Waterloo the Duke of Wellington received the Belgian title of Prince of Waterloo together with revenue from the property situated in the famous battlefield. The present beneficiary is Arthur Charles Wellesley, fourth Prince of Waterloo.

Honduras Chief Escaped Bullet When in Parade

Tegucigalpa, Honduras, Feb. 4 (AP).—There had been no arrests or explanations to-day because of a shot fired yesterday at President Vincente Mejia Colindres in the parade preceding his inaugural.

The shot was fired while the inaugural party was proceeding from the cathedral to the presidential palace, but it missed the president and buried itself in the wall of the Casino Hondureno near one of the newspaper correspondents.

President Colindres was elected Oct. 27, 1928, on a coalition ticket to succeed former President Paz Baraona.

REVOLT IN SPAIN LESSENS AFTER 61 ARRESTS ARE MADE

Captain General of Valencia Is Awakened From Sleep and Taken to Prison—Former Premier Surrenders and Assumes All Responsibility for Outbreak

Valencia, Spain, Feb. 4 (UP).—The arrest of 61 alleged revolutionists, including Castro Girona, Captain-general of Valencia, appeared to-day to have improved the situation here where an outbreak against the government threatened yesterday.

Girona was awakened from his sleep last night immediately after the arrival of Gen. San Jurjo by automobile from Denia, and sent under a heavy guard to Madrid where he was imprisoned.

Girona was alleged to have been one of those involved in the revolution which was planned to break simultaneously in all parts of Spain last Tuesday and for which former Premier Jose Sanchez Guerra has surrendered, assuming all responsibility.

REPORT THREE BURGLARIES

Two Houses and a Store Entered by Thieves Over Week-end

Using a key on a side door thieves entered 167 Cambridge Ave., some time between 8 o'clock and 12 o'clock Saturday night and stole a silver brooch and some beads.

The home of O. M. Walter, 119 Constance St., was ransacked last night by thieves and a suit of clothes, a watch and ring stolen. Entrance was gained by an unfastened side kitchen window.

McDonald's grocery store at 223 Sorauren Ave., was broken into through a rear door and $45 stolen from the cash register.

Peeress 'Flunked' In Aviation Test Would Try Again

New York, Feb. 4 (AP).—Lady Heath, British aviatrix, who has flown 1,300 hours, flunked a non-technical examination for an American transport's license and wants to take the examination all over again and at once.

Her flying ability met with all the requirements and her physical condition was found perfect but she was unable to rate 70 per cent. on navigation and department of commerce regulations.

Protesting she was a stranger in this country and that her livelihood had been taken from her on account of a technical interpretation Lady Heath has wired to the department of commerce asking full particulars and permission to repeat the examination immediately.

The city desk in the first Star Building, about 1914. Left to right, R. K. Mearns; William Wallace, later advertising manager (1936–1947) and a director;

W. F. Wiggins, 1902–1954; H. C. Hindmarsh, then city editor, president 1948–1956

J. E. Atkinson and son Joseph S. in a moment of relaxation at Bigwin

Mr. Atkinson's favourite pastime was driving a fast motorboat

In 1927 Mr. and Mrs. Atkinson, speaking from Mr. Atkinson's office in Toronto, made the first commercial trans-Atlantic telephone call

Mrs. Joseph E. Atkinson

unusual at a *Star* picnic or one of the staff get-togethers which were held fairly frequently in those days for her to call an employee over and say: "Joe, I don't think you are paying Mr. X enough." And what could Mr. Atkinson do but give the man a raise?

After Mrs. Atkinson's death in 1931 of a long and painful illness, raises were less frequent and the pay gap widened between the small group of stars and the "workhorses" who formed the majority of editorial office employees. Since the mechanical trades were represented by a strong union which negotiated wages and working conditions, the working conditions of printers improved while those of reporters deteriorated. In 1900 a reporter was paid 50 per cent more than a printer. The time was to come when a linotype operator was paid twice as much as a reporter with a university degree.

Mr. Atkinson did not often presume on his friendship with King to recommend appointments, but on December 2, 1927, he suggested Sam Clarke of Cobourg for the Senate. King replied that he already had in mind a man for the vacancy. Who that man was, he informed Atkinson in a letter dated December 23. It was J. E. Atkinson.

"In the course of my public life you have been at all times a very true and loyal friend," he wrote, "and I feel I owe very much to your helpful co-operation. *The Star*'s advocacy of Liberal principles and policies and its support of myself and my colleagues have been of the utmost service to the party and to the government, as was also the case with the [London] *Advertiser* under your direction. But quite apart from all this, your own high character, your deep personal interest in and knowledge of social and political problems as well as the years of public service you have given to our country, have more than merited this recognition on the part of the administration. The years of public usefulness which I pray may still be before you would make your presence in the Senate a valuable addition to the Parliament of Canada."

There is no record of Mr. Atkinson's reply to this offer, but obviously he turned it down. He probably did so by telephone, for unless there was some particular reason for writing he preferred to telephone, and it was not unusual for him to conduct quite important transactions in that manner, leaving no record of them. He wrote much of his correspondence in long-hand, keeping no copy, or tapping it out on a typewriter himself.

Two years later the *Telegram* reported that Mr. Atkinson was offered a seat in the Senate "for the fourth time." If this was true, only one offer was made in writing. Mr. Atkinson could not conscientiously have accepted. Not only was *The Star* advocating abolition of the Senate, but nearly ten years earlier it had expressed opposition to newspapermen in the Upper House. "The practice is not one to be encouraged," it said in 1918, "because the associations of a senator are apt to conflict with the duties of an editor."

The failure of the Home Bank in 1923 enabled Mr. Atkinson to acquire the 53 shares of *Star* stock owned by M. J. Haney for $24,723.98. Haney was a former president of the Home Bank. In order to protect depositors from loss when it failed, a levy was made on officers and shareholders. Haney had to raise a very considerable sum in a hurry. In disclosing the transaction, the *Telegram* asserted that the stock had a true value of about $159,000 based on the price at which newspapers of comparable size to *The Star* were changing hands in the United States. But because after he got control of *The Star* Mr. Atkinson had reduced the dividend rate to 6 per cent on the par value of the original issue of $100,000 common stock, Haney was realizing a total dividend of only $318 a year on his shares. "A minority shareholder may find that his stock is of very little value when one man has control of the company," commented the *Telegram.*

Most of the disputes between Mr. Atkinson and three generations of Mulocks were due to their efforts to have a larger share of the profits distributed to the shareholders. But Mr. Atkinson had plans for expansion, and wanted to plow the profits back into the business.

For some years Vincent and Raymond Massey each owned eighty-three shares which had come to them from their uncle, Walter Massey, by way of the Massey Manufacturing Company. Mr. Atkinson acquired these shares and fifty shares owned by Miss Aileen Larkin in 1929. Thereafter William Pate Mulock, whose father, William Mulock, Jr., had died in 1928, was the only owner of *Star* stock outside the family.

By the mid-twenties *The Star* had outgrown the building it had occupied since 1905 and Atkinson began looking about for a new location. Early in 1927 he learned the Baldwin estate which owned the property on which buildings number 72 to 102 King Street West inclusive were situated, and the Jones estate, on which 70 King Street West was situated were in a mood to sell. However, they owned only the land, the buildings being the property of ten different owners who occupied the land on lease.

Quietly he engaged the real estate firm of Robins Limited to negotiate for the properties, and on June 29, 1927, he was able to inform the shareholders they were successful. The buildings, land and leaseholds with a frontage of 288 feet on King Street and extending back to Pearl Street could be bought for $715,700, *The Star* getting possession November 1. The firm of Chapman and Oxley, architects, estimated a twenty-three-storey building of the type he contemplated could be built for $1,500,000 while he figured at least $700,000 worth of new equipment and presses would have to be bought. As is not unusual in such cases, the estimate was about $1 million too low, and the total cost proved to be close to $4 million. Much of the additional cost was extras not contemplated by the architect in the original estimate, for Atkinson wanted this to be the most beautiful skyscraper in Toronto, as well as the most functional, a symbol of *The Star*'s success. Large sums were spent on decorative work that would not be considered by any builder today.

On the weekend of February 2–3, 1929, *The Star* moved into its new building, which it had numbered 80 King Street West. It is still the largest and finest newspaper plant in Canada. It was built on a frontage of 170 feet, the westerly 105 feet of property being kept for future expansion, while 13 feet on the east was cleared for a lane.

The move to the new building began at 2 o'clock on the afternoon of Saturday, February 2. It was described in an article in *The Star* at the time as "the most stupendous moving job in Canada." In order to avoid the necessity of dismantling machines with consequent loss of time, holes were knocked in the brick walls and through these the machines were hoisted in three steel cages that had been specially fabricated for the occasion. The biggest firm of household movers in Toronto had a force of seventy men engaged for forty hours in the transfer, while sixty of *The Star*'s own staff installed the machines in their new locations and readied the offices for Monday morning. The transfer was completed in time for the first edition to roll off the presses Monday, not a moment late.

Chapter 10

FROM SCOOPS TO NUTS

When the war ended *The Star* had fourteen reporters, two girls writing society news, and W. R. Plewman doing special features. This was the largest reporting staff it had ever had. But within five years the number of reporters was increased to twenty-four and in the next year to thirty-two.

Among those hired in this relatively short period were James A. Cowan, who was to become one of Canada's top public relations men; Gordon Hogarth, later a director of publicity for the Ontario government; Frederick Griffin and Robert C. Reade, who with Gregory Clark were to become the "big three" of the *Star Weekly* feature writing staff; Wilfred G. Palmer, now personnel manager and secretary of the board of directors of *The Star*; Main Johnson, who had worked some years before for *The Star* as a student and had been principal private secretary to N. W. Rowell; Henry Somerville, a scholarly Englishman who became *The Star*'s resident correspondent in London and later editor of the *Catholic Register*; Charles B. Lanphier, who became famous as Toronto's "radio priest"; Kenneth A. McMillan, later a financial editor and now circulation manager of *The*

Star; Charles Vining, who was war-time head of the Canadian government's information services; Foster Hewitt, Morley Callaghan, and Ernest Hemingway.

Some of these men were hired by Bone but most of them by H. C. Hindmarsh. In 1924 alone Hindmarsh hired such able newsmen as Gordon Sinclair, Thomas J. Wheeler, who rose to be managing editor and who now heads his own public relations service, H. R. (Barney) Armstrong, who headed *The Star*'s Ottawa bureau for eight years and at his death was assistant editor, Keith Munro, who became publicity agent for the Dionne quintuplets, David B. Rogers, now editor of the Regina *Leader-Post*, Harvey Hickey, former city editor of the *Globe and Mail* and for many years that newspaper's highly respected chief of its Ottawa staff, and Clifford S. Wallace. In the same period the *Star Weekly* was busily building up a staff of free lance reporters.

Several years ago a national magazine published an article headed: "Everybody Has Worked at *The Star*." To old-time newspapermen almost everybody who counts has. At a dinner tendered H. C. Hindmarsh by alumni of *The Star* in 1955 among the two hundred who attended were nine publishers and editors, six well-known authors, three professors, two artists, directors of five corporations, a priest, and a few score others who have made their fame in radio, public relations, or other occupations.

In unpublished reminiscences he set down several years ago, Roy Greenaway, a University of Toronto honours graduate who abandoned his intention of being a high school history teacher to come to *The Star* as a $15-a-week reporter in November, 1918, describes Hindmarsh's method of training a reporter. "For days I handed him my masterpieces," Greenaway wrote. "Silently he glanced at them and dropped them into the wastepaper basket at his knee. Not a word of criticism was forthcoming and, puzzled, I would stand around doing nothing for the rest of the day . . . Somehow I must have learned my lesson for one morning HCH mumbled: 'I guess you'll be a newspaperman now,' and threw my copy over to the deskman for editing." Greenaway had been hired by Bone, but he noted everybody recognized that Hindmarsh was in the process of taking over. The hours were incredibly long, the discipline firm, even harsh, and the pressure tremendous. "Testing a man's endurance was probably often deliberate," Greenaway continued.

> The cold fact was always plain, if you couldn't take it you could leave. Most did, and only one man in scores hired stayed very long . . . Those who remained did so because they felt they were with a winner. It was a period of 'scoops'

and, sparked by HCH, *Star* men went out to get them or be forgotten with the rest.

Star practice, contrary to that of the *Telegram*, was not to keep a man for long on a specialized beat. *Star* men started in the courts, writing running copy or dictating stories on the telephone. Then they were quickly pushed through the whole reporting business and were soon far afield on important out-of-town assignments to demonstrate their ability and self-discipline. If a reporter wanted to hold his job he had to show he had a wide general knowledge, the ability to write clear, forceful narrative, the talents of a good detective, and above all, better than average physical and mental endurance.

For its noble reporting staff *The Star* had no rewrite men, and never had until recently. Mr. Atkinson did not believe in rewriting, for he wanted preserved the freshness of style of the individual reporter. "I don't like a newspaper that seems to have been all run out of one mould," he used to say. If a reporter showed anything distinctive in his style he was certain of quick advancement, and the desk always had the names of several writers whose copy was never to be changed—which used to irritate some sub-editors no end.

Hindmarsh did not like a rewritten story either, seeming to feel that a hastily written story or one dictated by a reporter over the telephone and taken down verbatim implied to the reader a sense of urgency. A rewritten story is a work of art; Hindmarsh wanted his news stories to be slices of raw life. Fine as this may sound in theory, not all reporters have a popular style and not all are good writers. Thus a certain amount of rewriting was always necessary. Much of this was done by the city editor himself or by copy readers on the "rim." But generally speaking, stories were printed very much as the reporter wrote them.

Star city editors were the hardest working in the business, and it was a rare man who stood the pace for more than three or four years. Greenaway relates how, a few weeks after he started work in 1918, a man he refers to as the "city editor," but who must have been Hindmarsh's assistant, returned to the office one afternoon after an unsuccessful attempt to find comfort in a bootlegger's merchandise and began hurling typewriters at reporters to whom he had taken a dislike. Before he was brought under control nearly every typewriter in the city room was a wreck. To this episode Greenaway attributes the rule, followed for forty years, that reporters had to make do with cast-off typewriters from the business office.

In succeeding years everything from scissors to chairs were hurled at Hindmarsh. If they seemed about to hit him he would move out of the way, but otherwise gave no sign of perturbation. He was a man of personal courage, tremendous vitality, and extraordinary imagination who drove himself as hard as he drove his staff. He never understood why weaker men could not stand the pace he set for himself.

Mr. Atkinson had been in the habit of making a personal trip to the University every spring to look over the new crop, but after 1924 he left the hiring to his son-in-law. Hindmarsh took on as many as ten students at a time in the summer holidays, in the hope of finding one or two newspapermen among them, and many a student worked his way through college as a *Star* reporter prior to 1930. Hindmarsh always had a kindly feeling for these student reporters, remembering that he got the taste of printer's ink while working at a summer job with the *Detroit News.*

Some of these students were incredibly green, but their very greenness paid off, as in the case of Vining. Fresh out of the University of Toronto, he was sent to Quebec with a photographer to report the arrival of the new Governor General, Viscount Byng of Vimy, a routine assignment good for no more than a half column. As he left the office Hindmarsh casually remarked he might try for an interview. Hindmarsh knew governors general were not supposed to give interviews, but Vining did not know—and neither did Byng. So Vining got his interview. An hour later he received a frantic telephone call from Byng's senior ADC telling him it could not be printed. Vining was abashed for only a moment. "Sir," said he, "no rule has been broken. Lord Byng will not be Governor General until he is sworn in at noon tomorrow."

It was lucky for Vining he was such a quick thinker, for all the king's men could not have prevented Hindmarsh from printing the interview which was by that time in his hands. In telling the story Vining always remarked that of course Hindmarsh was only joking, and no doubt he was. But those who were familiar with Hindmarsh's propensity for such jokes understood that back of them always lurked a hope.

One of the "scholars" Hindmarsh hired was Major Claude Pascoe, a former teacher at Ridley College. Pascoe had been an officer with the ill-advised international expeditionary force sent against the Bolsheviks after the war, for which there was a price on his head in Russia, and he had served in Ireland with the notorious Black and Tans, for which there was a price on his head in Ireland.

He was hired to write a series on his adventures, but after the first two or three articles Mr. Atkinson decided they were too rich for the blood of a newspaper which believed in home rule for Ireland and recognition of Russia. Nevertheless Pascoe remained twenty years with *The Star*, most of the time as real estate editor, a useful contact with people who believed as he did that employees who join a labour union are disloyal, and anybody who makes a lot of money is the finest type of citizen. He left on retirement allowance after suffering a disabling heart attack.

Until 1920 *The Star* had its cuts made by a commercial photo engraver, but in that year it established its own photo-engraving department with a staff of four men. There was a boom in pictures, in which Hindmarsh was every bit as interested as his father-in-law. In 1923 he set out to strengthen the picture department. *The Star*'s first photographer had been Fred Foster, uncle of Foster Hewitt, but he had left. Hindmarsh hired Fred Davis, who had learned picture-taking on the *World* but was at the time staff photographer on the *Mail and Empire*. Characteristically, he hired Davis because he liked a pretty scenic shot he took, for Hindmarsh, like Atkinson, wanted his pictures to be attractive as well as newsworthy.

The invention of the wire-photo was seized upon by *The Star* as a means of getting pictured news as quickly into the office as written news. On July 27, 1928, it joined a number of United States newspapers to transmit pictures of the Tunney-Heeney prize-fight, the first commercial use of wire-photo in the world. There was no wire-photo network as there is today, and the pictures were developed in two hospital ambulances parked outside the Yankee stadium in New York. From there they were transmitted by wire to several distribution points, from which they were sent by conventional means to newspapers in the area. Cleveland was the closest distribution point to Toronto, and *The Star* had an automobile there to rush them to its newsroom. The cost was $105 per picture. Before long *The Star* was bringing pictures by wire into its own office, though it was not until 1939 that it joined the AP wire-photo network.

Though *The Star* used a prodigous number of pictures and kept a half dozen or more photographers busy on assignments, Fred Davis was one of the few photographers on staff during the Hindmarsh regime. For several years he was the only one. The others were paid only for pictures used and were officially free lances. This provided a useful cushion when Hindmarsh exceeded his budget, which was often. He would simply stop buying pictures and illustrate the paper with old photographs from the library. Thus when the Prince of Wales visited the Riviera one might find half a page of pictures of girls in bathing suits with some such caption as "H.R.H. will see beauties like these on the Riviera." While most of the photographers earned only a bare living, some earned more than if they were on staff and

Hindmarsh was shocked to find that one year photographer Tom Wilson, who also had the darkroom concession, made more than he did.

Mr. Atkinson had originated the practice of sending almost the whole reporting staff out on a story. Hindmarsh, with a staff of thirty or more to work with, was to carry it to an extreme undreamed of by its originator. He founded *The Star*'s famous flying squad, equipped with staff cars, who were on call twenty-four hours a day, seven days a week, ready to go on a moment's notice anywhere in Ontario or adjacent parts of the United States. Keith Munro was its first member, and the number was soon increased to four.

On a big story the entire flying squad might go into action, transporting other reporters and photographers in their cars. On arrival at its destination the squad would fan out, dropping individual reporters here and there to scout for information. Invariably one task force would be assigned to pick up every available picture before the opposition arrived. Members of the flying squad sometimes accomplished amazing feats, as when Alf Tate tracked down a murderer in the wilds of Haliburton, shared a dinner of canned beans with him, got his exclusive story, and persuaded him to surrender to police without a fight.

While he was city editor Hindmarsh personally directed every activity of his large force, organized every foray, and more often than not presented it with a complete plan of campaign. Helen McMillan, who came to *The Star* from the *London Advertiser* as women's editor in 1926, recalls her first sight of Hindmarsh dashing madly down four flights of stairs two steps at a time because the elevator was too slow, in order to give last minute instructions to the flying squad embarking on some campaign.

Hindmarsh put great value on speed and on a "scoop," and as was inevitable accuracy suffered. Whereas *The Star* had gone fifteen years without a libel suit against it and twenty-five years without having to contest one in court, now libel suits began to come thick and fast. In 1926 alone *The Star* was sued by Mayor Foster, Premier Ferguson, Hon. H. H. Stevens, chief Conservative whip W. A. Boys, and ex-mayor T. L. Church, not to mention half a dozen lesser persons.

Hindmarsh loved to see the city room in a turmoil. There were never enough desks, enough typewriters, enough telephones. "This crowding gives a sense of urgency," he once remarked. Years later Churchill was to say the same about the House of Commons when plans for enlarging it were under discussion.

Yet for all this contrived sense of urgency, a reporter who had nothing to do never felt he had to take his feet off the desk when Hindmarsh walked by, for Hindmarsh knew that five minutes earlier this same reporter might have been working at break-neck speed, and might be again in the next five minutes. Occasionally, however, Mr. Atkinson would poke his head in the door and a few minutes later the city editor would be ordered to tidy up the place, get those papers off the desks, pick the rubbish off the floor.

Occasionally Hindmarsh would bemoan that his reporters were growing soft because the *Telegram* was giving them so little competition. During one such period he decided to provide them with competition from inside, and detached three good reporters from the city staff, assigning them to dig up good stories on their own. Soon dubbed "the nuts department" because of the kind of stories they favoured, they were such a howling success that before long all had become editors.

During this period of extraordinarily rapid expansion the managing editor was John R. Bone, but Hindmarsh virtually ignored him. As city editor he had never paid much attention to Bone, for which he was only mildly rebuked by Mr. Atkinson. As time went on he began, as "assistant managing editor"—a title that had been given him originally for prestige purposes only—to invade areas that were not strictly within the purview of a city editor.

Bone used to feel that Hindmarsh was trading on his relationship with Mr. Atkinson in these invasions, and it is true there were times when subordinates, faced with conflicting orders from Bone and Hindmarsh, decided it was safest to obey the boss' son-in-law. But Hindmarsh was by nature a man impatient of authority, and even had there been no family relationship he would have clashed with one anyway.

In view of his character, the passivity with which he accepted direction from his father-in-law seems surprising. Even when arbitrarily overruled his reaction was usually a quiet, "It's his paper." In possible explanation, men who worked with him for years say he was interested only in news, knowing or caring little about business or politics. When told by his father-in-law that certain things should or should not be done for business or political reasons, he accepted his judgment without question.

One gnawing grievance of HCH was Bone's little sideline of corresponding for British and U.S. papers, an activity forbidden other employees. When Bone got a query from an out-of-town newspaper he would assign a reporter to do the story for him, for which Bone was paid while the reporter got nothing though he may have had to work overtime. If the story carried a byline it was that of J. R. Bone. Hindmarsh considered this unfair to the reporters and he used to try to intercept these queries and assign reporters himself, in which case he always made sure the reporter rather than Bone was paid. Once he handed Roy Greenaway a request from Sir John Willison for a feature article on some subject for *The Times* of London. "Don't accept less than $20 for this, and don't split with Bone or Willison," he directed. Several days later he asked Roy if he had got $20 for the article. Roy said he had. "Did you give Bone anything?" HCH demanded. Roy said he had not. "Good," Hindmarsh exclaimed. "If you did I'd have fired you."

There were other sources of friction. Bone was so excessively parsimonious as to be almost miserly, whereas Hindmarsh was a lavish spender who never failed to be amazed when told his budget had been exceeded. Bone was so secretive he kept his office door locked even while working inside, and he would cover papers on his desk or clutch them to his chest so visitors could not see them. Hindmarsh was a frank and open personality who did not care who knew what he was doing.

Sooner or later there would have been a show-down between these two had it not been averted by Bone's untimely death of a heart attack suffered while at work in his office on June 7, 1928. He was in his fiftieth year and had been managing editor of *The Star* for twenty-one years.

"I never knew a man in whom I had more implicit confidence," was the tribute of Irving Robertson of the *Telegram*, with whom Bone had worked to free the Canadian Press of government domination. Few men of his ability would have been content to submerge their personalities so completely in that of *The Star*. He was succeeded as managing editor and director by Hindmarsh, who was shortly thereafter appointed vice-president.

While son-in-law Hindmarsh was building up his staff of city reporters, Mr. Atkinson was also engaging special writers whose work he liked and occasionally fighting for their right to report the news as they saw it. Some of the sternest battles were with Mackenzie King who was slow in learning that though Atkinson was his friend and supported his policies, *The Star* was neither a King nor a Liberal organ. Several times in the first few years of his leadership he tried to have *The Star* assign a reporter of his choice to the Ottawa bureau. His recommendations were invariably ignored.

He protested against *The Star* engaging J. A. Stevenson, whom he described as "Mr. Crerar's most intimate personal friend," and tried to have him dismissed. "Among the opponents of the government no one has been more unfair and bitter than Mr. Stevenson," he wrote Atkinson in 1922. Mr. Atkinson tartly replied: "I think no bias against the government is present in his dispatches." In August, 1923, King asked Mr. Atkinson to send "a special correspondent" to the Imperial Conference in London "who will be sure to present in a sympathetic light the attitude to be taken by my colleagues and myself." Atkinson replied merely that Stevenson would not be covering the conference since he was leaving *The Star*'s employ within a few weeks. The reason for his going was one that caused many another reporter to sever his connection with *The Star*—he had written articles of which Atkinson disapproved for other publications. In this instance they were two articles critical of King. Not unreasonably Mr. Atkinson told Stevenson he must not write articles unfriendly to King while he was *The Star*'s Ottawa bureau chief, since they might tend to discredit the paper's support of the Liberals. Stevenson retorted that what he wrote on his own time for other publications was none of *The Star*'s business. He was given two months' notice, and left to become Ottawa correspondent for *The Times* of London, a position he filled with distinction until his recent retirement.

They parted friends, for Stevenson was always well regarded by Mr. Atkinson, and had been an occasional weekend guest at the Atkinson home. He recalls that on one of these visits, while they were discussing politics, Mr. Atkinson remarked: "I'm a bit of a socialist, you know." His impression is that Mr. Atkinson had no real liking for King but supported him as the only political leader pledged to introduce the social welfare program on which his heart was set. This could well be so, for though their relationship was to be close for many years it had many of the aspects of an alliance rather than a friendship. Mr. Atkinson was always reluctant to be put in a position where one could make demands upon him, even demands of friendship, and as J. W. Pickersgill has observed in his excellent book, *The Mackenzie King Record*, King shunned close friendships for a similar reason.

The Star did not send anyone to the Imperial Conference and it was covered by the London bureau chief, Henry Somerville. King need not have worried about the kind of coverage the conference would be given. The Home Bank failed, wiping out the life savings of thousands of depositors, and some of its officers were arrested, the Prince of Wales was touring Canada, and Lloyd George was on a triumphal visit to this country and the United States. With such sensational competition at home slight attention was paid to the talks in London.

Lloyd George's visit led to one of those piquant incidents which, with the passing of the years, became enshrined in *Star* folklore—the departure from the staff of Ernest Hemingway. Hemingway had submitted his first article as a free lance writer to the *Star Weekly* in February, 1920. Before that he had been knocking about the United States and Canada for several months, never holding a job for long. On a visit to Toronto he met Gregory Clark and Jimmy Frise because, as Clark relates, "we were the easiest to meet around the place." Clark introduced him to J. H. Cranston, editor of the *Star Weekly*.

Cranston was not particularly impressed with the tall, black-haired, lanky youngster not yet twenty-one, but Hemingway assured him he could write. He had worked for a few months on the Kansas City *Star* before joining an ambulance unit when the States entered the war. He had just come from Chicago, he said, where he had applied for a job on the *Herald-Examiner*. They turned him down because he did not know any policemen.

Cranston accepted a short article about a group of young matrons who had organized a circulating library of paintings by modern artists. Published as a filler in the news section on February 14, it was no better than one would expect of any cub reporter. He was paid five dollars for about seven hundred words. His second article, submitted three weeks later, written in terse, short paragraphs and laced with humour, was an utterly delightful piece relating his experience in getting a free shave at a barber college where students learned their trade by practising on courageous or penniless volunteers. It was printed under his by-line, perhaps the first time the by-line of Ernest Hemingway appeared in any publication. This was followed the next week by a hilarious pen picture of Toronto's sporting mayor, Tommy Church, at a boxing match during which His Worship never allowed events in the ring to distract his attention from the serious business of wooing the voters.

Greg Clark recalls that after this article was published Bone called Hemingway into his office and offered him a job. Hemingway came dashing out of the office waving his arms and shouting: "I've got a job; I've got a job." But after a short time on general assignments he asked to be taken off the payroll. He was working on a book, and was determined that such frivolous considerations as earning a living should not be allowed to interfere with it. But Bone gave orders that as much feature work as he would do should be given him.

He remained in Toronto for two years, living off his earnings as a free-lance contributor to the *Star Weekly* and *The Daily Star*. These would have averaged about $45 a week, which was somewhat higher than reporters were earning on most American newspapers at that time. But he only took the time to write for pay when he needed money.

Few of his friends in Toronto were among working newspapermen. He preferred the company of other intense young devotees of Sherwood Anderson, Ford Madox Ford, Ezra Pound, and James Joyce. Occasionally he would bring an article he wrote to show fellow reporters. If they said they liked it, he would throw it away. If they said they didn't like it he would send it to Paris for criticism by one of his heroes.

In December, 1921, he went to Europe as roving correspondent for *The Daily Star*. Though he drew regular cheques from *The Star* and was bylined "Star Staff Correspondent," he was not on the payroll.

In the autumn of 1923 Bone persuaded him to return to Toronto. He went on the payroll on September 10 at a salary of $75 a week. Only one reporter was paid more. He came with considerable reluctance, for he was beginning to suspect that newspaper work was not his true vocation. "This godammed [*sic*] newspaper stuff is gradually ruining me," he wrote his friend Sherwood Anderson. Besides, he had formed a profitable association with Hearst's International News Service which he would have to surrender. However, *The Star* was insistent and Bone outbid Hearst for his services.

The first major assignment given him after his return was to meet Lloyd George in New York and accompany him on his tour. And Hemingway was scooped. He duly reported Lloyd George's arrival and in the first two days he wrote eight news despatches and interviews totalling more than 5,000 words. But he failed to report the surly welcoming speech of deputy mayor Hulbert of New York. With an eye to the Irish vote, Hulbert had greeted Lloyd George with a lecture on Britain's sins, Europe's shortcomings, and an admonition to Europeans to model themselves on the blameless and wise inhabitants of the land of the free. "An insulting speech," the New York *Herald* called it, and *The Star* hadn't a line.

Mr. Atkinson learned of it when reading the New York papers at home the next night. He telephoned the night editor to "take that man Hemingway" off the Lloyd George tour at once. Next morning Hemingway came storming into the office. He had got more scoops for *The Star* than any other reporter, and anyway this was a silly speech that didn't deserve reporting, he raged. He had a row with Bone, and another with Hindmarsh. Hindmarsh proceeded to give him "the prima donna treatment" he reserved for reporters who, in his opinion, had got too big for their breeches.

It consisted of either ignoring the reporter or giving him unpleasant assignments. Hemingway's by-line disappeared from *The Daily Star* after October 6, while he covered fires, labour meetings, and conventions.

But in the three-month period when city editor Hindmarsh was giving him only piffling assignments, Hemingway was doing some of his best work for *Star Weekly* editor Cranston. In thirteen weeks he contributed seventeen full-length magazine articles. When he wrote two articles for the one issue he used the by-line John Hadley on one of them.

One day in late December Hemingway was assigned to cover an address by Count Apponyi of Hungary before a luncheon club. He had breakfast with the count and borrowed some important documents relating to Hungarian aspirations which he planned to use as background material for a story. He sent the papers by messenger to Hindmarsh with a note explaining they were to be kept carefully. When he got back to the office the papers could not be found.

Hemingway blew up, accusing Hindmarsh of deliberately destroying them. He sat down at his typewriter and wrote a letter of resignation of more than two thousand words in which he dealt at length with the alleged deficiencies of Hindmarsh as a city editor. Then he pasted the sheets on which it was written into a ribbon sixteen feet long, and fastened it to the bulletin board for all to read. There it remained three days. Hindmarsh walked past it a dozen times a day, but neither glanced at it nor ordered it taken down. The writer was completely ignored, his beautiful letter a dud. The third day Hemingway removed it.

"I want to show it to my wife," he explained lamely to fellow reporter Roy Greenaway. On December 31, 1923, Ernest Hemingway went off *The Star*'s payroll. He left almost at once for Europe as correspondent for INS.

In the four years he had been associated with *The Star* as free lance writer, roving foreign correspondent, and staff reporter, he had sixty-seven feature articles of three thousand words or more published in the *Star Weekly* and many more than that number of shorter feature articles published in *The Daily Star*. An account of the first bullfight he had ever seen was published in the *Star Weekly* issue of October 20, 1923.

Thirty years later, while in an expansive mood during negotiations with the newspaper guild, Hindmarsh told the committee Hemingway was temperamentally unable to conform to the routine of newspaper work or accept direction. On one occasion, he said, Hemingway had to be called off a labour story because instead of reporting objectively he made himself the advocate of the workers. "However," Hindmarsh added, "I should have made some effort to persuade him to stay. I made a mistake in the way I dealt with him." The truth is, with a man of Hemingway's genius the parting could only have been delayed, not prevented. He told colleagues on *The Star* that he did not like newspaper work "for always the questions are who, where, when, how, but never why, which is the most important question of all."

Hemingway was not the first and by no means the last to be given Hindmarsh's prima donna treatment. Mr. Atkinson did not share his son-in-law's aversion to reporters who did not conform, though he had slight use for a reporter who thought he knew better than the editor how *The Star* should use his high-priced talents. Once when irascible news editor John Drylie summarily fired a reporter, the latter appealed directly to the Chief. As the reporter later related the incident, Mr. Atkinson telephoned Drylie in his presence.

"Has this young man's work been unsatisfactory?" he asked.

"His work is fairly good but he is insolent; in the interest of discipline I had to dismiss him," Drylie replied.

"Mr. Drylie, insolence and insubordination are fairly common in newspaper offices," Mr. Atkinson remarked. "That is one of the crosses editors have to bear." The reporter was reinstated.

Mr. Atkinson told a group at the University of Toronto that reporters and writers should be given their head to develop their own style and demonstrate where their interests lay. A good writer and reporter, he implied, was a rare and erratic bird, and occasional lapses should be expected and condoned. *The Star* in its time has employed some rare birds.

Among the more exotic fauna were certain gentlemen of the cloth who, for one reason or another, found it expedient to earn their livings in a profession more tolerant of personal eccentricities. The most famous of these was the Reverend R. E. Knowles, who for seventeen years had been pastor of the second largest Presbyterian congregation in Canada, Knox Church at Galt, Ontario. As a preacher he was nationally famous for his eloquence, his learning, and the power of his Gospel message. He had also made something of a name for himself as a novelist, and had been the subject of one of the first personality sketches in the *Star Weekly* after it was founded in 1910.

Then, at the age of fifty-one and at the height of his career, he suffered a shattering experience. He was severely injured in a train accident and the man in the seat beside him was killed. After months in hospital he tried to resume his church work, but collapsed completely. That was in 1915. He spent much of the next five years in a psychiatric hospital in Toronto. He left the hospital a changed man in some respects, but with his power of oratory and his writing ability unimpaired.

Knowles began writing for *The Star* on a free-lance basis in 1920 and for the next twenty-six years his ripe and purple prose was one of its most distinctive features, the object at once of ridicule and admiration. His first articles were undistinguished, for he was still a sick man, shrinking from contact with unfamiliar people. But he seems to have regained his confidence on a trip to Europe in 1921 from which he sent back a series of articles in the style for which he was to become renowned.

In an article he cabled *The Star* on October 2, 1921, he described his first airplane flight, from Paris to London, in these words: "It was wonderful! Simply wonderful! Next to falling in love for the first time flying is the greatest experience in life. A parable on wings—an allegory in the sky—the combination of a thousand thrills, of wonder, terror, rapture, triumph." Characteristically, he told of admonishing a woman who was worried about the safety of some Venetian glass in her luggage: "Madam, it ill becomes you, or any of us, to be concerned at such an hour as this with these petty baubles, for we are pilgrims of the skies—and it would better become us to think of our latter end." After this he was a regular contributor to *The Star*.

Knowles' real forte was interviews, and in the course of his career he interviewed almost every celebrity and notable in the world, including every prime minister of Canada and of Britain in his time. Movie stars, sportsmen, fashion experts; the famous, the notorious and occasionally even the obscure were grist for his voracious mill. To be interviewed by Knowles was an experience unlikely to be forgotten, for he had the manner and mien of an ancient Shakespearian actor spouting Job instead of Hamlet. "What is this that thou has done unto me? How could'st thou beguile me so?" he quoted despairingly in an interview with Sir Alfred Mond when he left the British Liberal party. Interviewing Nellie McClung he described her "serenity" as "like the repose of Mussolini, at which one could not but marvel."

When in the full flood of eloquence Knowles was grandly disdainful of geography, historical fact, the accuracy of literary quotations, and the exact meaning of words. While covering the first general council of the United Church of Canada for *The Star* he somehow got thinking of China, with this result: "There is always something of portent, half of hope and half of fear, when China looms before us. 'Yonder sleeps a giant,' said Napoleon from his vessel's deck as he pointed to the Chinese shore: 'Let him sleep—for when he wakes he will shake the world.' " Jokingly the *Telegram* remarked that these words were really spoken by Napoleon as he crossed the Alps in an open boat

Knowles wrote about everything from sports to politics. He was once sent to Britain to cover an election, *The Star* using the reports of news agencies to inform the readers what was really happening while Knowles awed them with a sumptuous display of gorgeous verbiage. This is how he reported the election of Ramsay MacDonald and the British Labour party in an article cabled to *The Star* on July 4, 1929:

> There is a stern restraint of fear—fear of the great people of England—that will forbid the presumptuous scorn and factious destructive vigilance (as though some dangerous things were to be hunted down) which in 1923–24 lay in wait for the "Socialists" whose name was once that of outlaws, later that of importunate upstarts, now that of an inherently sacramental significance which needs restraint, requires vigilance, stands in need of chastening—but which at the heart of it has the throb of human right and is the blood relation of the Sermon on the Mount and the Carpenter who proclaimed it. . . . I know that I was present at the deliverance (though with instruments) of a Man-child whose life all the outraged Herods of class and heredity and privilege, and the worshippers of Things As They Have Always Been, can not destroy.

What did it mean? Only R. E. Knowles and perhaps J. E. Atkinson knew, but there were another thousand words in similar vein. The readers of *The Star* seemed to love such writing marvelling at Knowles' rich command of language and his ability to clothe inanities in pomp and solemnity. But the *Telegram* endlessly ridiculed him, dubbing him "the interviewer who interviews himself." This was a not unmerited description, for his interviews were copiously larded with poetic quotations, narrations of his own emotions, and statements designed to show he knew as much, or more, about the subject as the person interviewed. "The first essential of an interviewer is to have a fine opinion of himself," Knowles confided to the Toronto Women's Press Club. "There is no such joy to the interviewee as to find a man of magnitude interviewing him."

"I often think, Mr. Knowles, that you are the intellectual superior of anyone you interview," Mr. Atkinson once remarked, though one may suspect with tongue in cheek. But the fact is, Mr. Atkinson admired Knowles' style. He wrote some pretty exotic prose himself on occasion. Though Knowles was one of *The Star*'s most notable writers for many years with a front page interview almost daily, he was on staff for only a part of the time. He preferred to work on space at an unusually generous rate. "That's why I pad my interviews with quotations," he joked once with a reporter. "I enjoy getting paid for something Shakespeare wrote."

Most controversial of the reverend writers for *The Star* was probably Salem Goldsworth Bland, who wrote a column on the editorial page under the heading "The Observer" for twenty-five years. At a time when the *Telegram* and others were trying to persuade the public that *The Star* was "a Communist paper" Dr. Bland was singled out for attack, not because of anything he wrote for *The Star* but because of his record before he came to this newspaper.

After seventeen years as professor of church history at Winnipeg Wesley (Methodist) College, Dr. Bland was dismissed in 1919 because certain of the larger financial contributors objected to his attitude on social questions. In 1918, for example, he wrote: "There is nothing in the history of the world to equal the injustice of the distribution of wealth." In 1919 he warned in a letter to the editor of *The Star*: "Canada is not going to escape the wild storm that has already broken over other lands." It was only a few weeks later that the notorious Winnipeg general strike occurred.

After dismissal from his professorship he became pastor of Broadway Methodist Tabernacle, Toronto, but by July a majority of the congregation voted to ask him to leave because "his preaching conduced to lawlessness." The Methodist conference supported him, however, and he remained until 1923, though often in hot water. He was accused of disloyalty by not offering prayers for the King and of not allowing the choir to sing the National Anthem as part of the service. In 1921 he campaigned for the Progressive party. He was a favourite target of "fundamentalists" in both the Baptist and Methodist churches, and of the "wets," for he was also a prohibitionist.

He began writing for the *Star Weekly* in 1924 on social and religious matters, and before long had a regular column in the daily. In 1931 the *Telegram* accused him of being a communist and of aiding in fomenting the Winnipeg strike, charges he was easily able to disprove. Though a socialist, he declared: "It is inconceivable to me that Russia's way could be our way." His articles on *The Star* editorial page seem mild and innocuous today, but in the 1930's when fear of communism kept many otherwise sensible people a-tremble in their beds at night they were considered by some as dangerously inflammable. He remained a regular contributor until his death in 1950 at the age of ninety.

Little less controversial was the Reverend Charles H. Huestis of Edmonton, a Methodist (later United church) minister, a Socialist and a pacifist, who also wrote two or three times a week for the editorial page. Dr. Huestis was dropped for a while after the outbreak of the Second World War because of his extreme pacifism, but was taken on again and wrote until his death in 1951. Though his personal life was less stormy than that of Dr. Bland, his articles were even more outspoken.

In an article he wrote after Mr. Atkinson's death, Huestis said Atkinson agreed with the pacifistic sentiments he expressed, and to some extent with his socialism. The fact that the capitalistic system enabled an individual to make great wealth is not necessarily proof that he condoned the system, Dr. Huestis wrote, and he said he believed Mr. Atkinson felt there was something wrong with a system that allowed him to make so much money, while others lived in poverty.

The Star's library, the finest newspaper library in Canada, was organized on its present basis in 1923 by another clergyman, the Reverend Adam Fordyce (Biddy) Barr. An extraordinary man, able, learned and of noble character, Barr had been a star member of the Varsity football and lacrosse teams in his student days, and was for many years honorary football coach at the University of Toronto. He was ordained an Anglican priest in 1901 after teaching a year at Ridley College. In 1913 he gave up his parish after a disagreement with his bishop on theological matters, and came to *The Star* as a reporter, but he remained for most of his life assistant minister at one of the larger Toronto Anglican churches. During the First World War he left to help organize the production of munitions, returning to *The Star* as a reporter after the war.

The nucleus of the library goes back possibly to 1909, when Cranston, who was doing a number of odd jobs as a sort of assistant to Bone, started a daily questions and answers column. He was provided with a good collection of reference books, but soon began clipping items of interest from various newspapers and filing them away. As a sideline he organized a better system of filing used cuts and photographs.

Before long everybody from Mr. Atkinson down was being pestered by letters from an accountant in an office supply firm named John J. (Jerry) Elder, pointing out errors in the answers. An omnivorous reader with a pack-rat mind, Elder's hobby was accumulating and cataloging general information whether useful or not. After a blizzard of letters he was invited to become Questions and Answers editor, an offer he accepted with alacrity. Given a small room off the newsroom, he was soon practically living in it, surrounded by clippings, paste pots, reference books, newspapers, and periodicals. It became almost impossible to shoo him home from his clippings at night, while his wife complained of the way he was overworked. The night of his daughter's "coming out" party he was so intent on hunting down elusive facts he forgot the party entirely. Since he and his wife were temporarily not on speaking terms and it was his habit to crawl in the back window rather than use the front door, he did not recollect it until a clipping with an account of the event was posted on the bulletin board the following day.

Elder had an interesting hobby—searching out the almost unbelievable blunders and contortions of the *Telegram*'s editorial policy from the earliest days. These he printed and filed in the library under the mystifying heading of "Aerobatics." It is too bad nobody has kept his collection up to date.

After two or three years Elder had amassed so many clippings that an assistant was required and Frederick Griffin, a young immigrant from Northern Ireland, was hired. A few months later Hindmarsh transferred Griffin to the reporting staff, where he was to win fame as one of Canada's great reporters. In late 1918 Hindmarsh assigned his most junior reporter Hugh Halliday to help Elder. Halliday had asked for a raise. "There is no use putting one through for you because Bone will turn it down," Hindmarsh told him, "but if I put a raise through in connection with a transfer he might pass it." So Halliday, now a popular nature writer for the *Star Weekly* and author of several nature books, became assistant librarian to qualify for a five-dollar raise.

Meantime Elder's health began to fail. When Hindmarsh entered the library one day to find him doubled over in a paroxysm of coughing he sent him home, called a doctor, and ordered him to take a rest on full pay. Barr was assigned to run the library and when Elder returned in 1921 he was relieved of all work except the Questions & Answers column. In 1923 Barr introduced the scrapbook system of keeping clippings, still in use, and greatly expanded the library's services. Under his able direction it attained its present high degree of efficiency.

In the twenty-seven years Barr was with *The Star* he was regarded almost as staff chaplain, playing his part as priest at christenings, marriages, and funerals of members of the staff and their families. A noble and dignified figure, with a fine leonine head, he was paid a tribute of love and respect by his fellow workers such as few men merit. On his death in 1940 he was succeeded by Miss Marion Thompson, a trained librarian, who had been his assistant.

As well as being a haven for off-beat clergymen, *The Star* also welcomed disillusioned theology students who decided midway in their course they were not cut out for the ministry. At the same time it helped several theology students complete their courses by providing part-time employment. It was said by cynics that the surest path to advancement on *The Star* was to be very religious, very irreligious, or an alcoholic. Total abstainers were given no particular credit, since it was assumed any decent man abstained from drinking, just as he abstained from beating his wife.

The Star had always been a great newspaper for promotions and stunts, as witness the first use of wireless telegraphy in 1903. Around 1921 Mr. Atkinson appointed Main Johnson promotion manager, the first of several men whose task was to keep *The Star* forever before the public eye. Promotions ran the gamut from who could make the ugliest face to symphony concerts. Zebras were given to the zoo and Shetland ponies to children. There were oratory concerts with first prize a trip to Europe, essay conests, freckles contests, baby contests, beauty contests, and cooking contests.

The Star sponsored the first public demonstration of radio in Canada at the CNE, as it had earlier sponsored the first demonstration of wireless telegraphy and was later to sponsor the first demonstration of television. In 1926 when an eclipse of the sun was obscured by clouds it sent an aeroplane aloft to take photographs, and describe the sight by radio.

In 1927 Mr. Atkinson made the first trans-Atlantic business telephone call, speaking with London correspondent Henry Somerville. The toll charge was $150. A few weeks later a *Star* reporter made the first telephone call from Canada to Mexico City, and on January 2, 1932, Matthew Halton made the first telephone call to South Africa, interviewing the governor general, who had once farmed in Ontario. To maintain the record of telephone firsts, *The Star* put through the first commercial telephone call to England when the trans-Atlantic telephone cable was inaugurated on September 25, 1956.

Just as it was first in telephone, wireless and radio, *The Star* tried to be the first in the air. It was the first newspaper in Canada to use an aeroplane to transport reporters to the scene of a story and to fly back pictures. On August 28, 1929, it entered a plane in the Toronto Flying club's Toronto to Cleveland race, and a month later sponsored a plane in a race from Toronto to St. Catharines. Lindbergh's famous flight two years before had started a rage for aeroplane races. In order to be the first newspaper in

Canada to distribute newspapers by plane it sent a shipment of one edition to St. Catharines by air on September 14, 1928. Later it pulled the spectacular stunt of flying newspapers to Kitchener with a report of the first horse race, and having them on sale at the track before the second race began.

It made frequent use of planes on "errands of mercy," searching for lost hunters, of whom it found several, combing Lake Ontario for missing pleasure craft, or Lake Erie for fishermen adrift on a floe. Usually there was sound reason for this prolific use of aeroplanes, for it resulted in *The Star* getting many an exclusive story. But often some of the stunts verged on the ridiculous, as is evidenced by the authentic story of the reporter bearing milk and bread who landed in a ski-equipped plane on the field of a snow-bound farmer, only to find cans overflowing with milk the farmer had been unable to get to market and his wife taking a batch of freshly baked bread out of the oven.

Dumping his gifts on the table the reporter hastened away across fields to the next starving, snow-bound farm family, for when Hindmarsh sent reporters on errands of mercy "neither snow, nor rain, nor heat, nor gloom of night stopped these couriers from the swift completion of their appointed rounds" in time to telephone their stories for the night edition.

One of Johnson's more lasting promotions was *The Star* Free Concerts in various churches and institutions, beginning in January, 1922. The first of their kind anywhere, and enormously successful, they were widely copied in other cities. As many as 45,000 persons attended in a season, and more than 2,000 musicians participated in the first five years. These concerts were dropped in 1938, but resumed by Hindmarsh in 1949. Out of these concerts developed the first radio concert broadcast in Canada by live musicians, on March 28, 1922, and from this it was a natural step for *The Star* to put in operation the pioneer radio station in Toronto, with promotions manager Johnson running it.

Chapter 11

THE STAR WEEKLY

The *Toronto Star Weekly* had been founded by J. E. Atkinson in 1910, but it was not until 1919 that anybody in the organization but Mr. Atkinson took it seriously. Mr. Maitland has said it was started because Mr. Atkinson did not like to see Linotype machines idle between daily editions and he wanted to give the operators something to do. J. H. Cranston said it was because Atkinson was convinced a weekend newspaper "would add prestige to the *Daily Star* and would eventually become a profitable venture." Nobody else expected it to pay.

Atkinson was more attracted to the English type of Sunday newspaper than to those published in the United States. He wanted it to be a newspaper, rather than a medium of entertainment. He chose to call it *The Toronto Star Weekly* rather than the *Sunday Star* as some of his executives wanted it named. He felt that to call it the *Sunday Star* would be misleading, because since 1906 the federal Lord's Day Act has forbidden the publication of a newspaper on Sunday, and it would have to be published Saturday afternoon. Moreover, the idea of a newspaper capitalizing on Sunday was repugnant to both him and Mrs. Atkinson.

J. T. Clark was appointed editor, Lewis still being editor of *The Daily Star*. Clark's idea was to turn out an unpretentious friendly journal which would not aim at a large circulation. Being modestly printed on newsprint, and without an illustrated section or comics, he believed it would pay its way from the start. He brought Harry Jakeway from *Saturday Night* to be assistant editor in charge of theatre and book reviews, music, and other cultural features.

The first issue, on April 9, 1910, contained a short story by Robert W. Service, an article by a staff reporter of *The Daily Star* on the boom in Haileybury, and another staff-written article entitled "How Will Toronto Deal with the Skyscraper Problem." This latter article was undoubtedly inspired by Mr. Atkinson's interest in city planning. There was a four-page sports section, but the editorial page was very philosophical and the rest of the paper very intellectual. It was a flop. News-stands returned most of the copies.

The second week a four-page picture section was added, printed from fine-grain halftones on machine-finished stock, and Cranston was appointed picture editor. The paper was a bit more newsy, less bookish.

By the end of the year the *Star Weekly* had a circulation of 16,000 but it was no longer the kind of paper Joe Clark had envisioned. He was unhappy about the trend to make it more competitive with the popular *Sunday World,* and asked to be relieved of the editorship. He was succeeded by Cranston, who wrote in his book, *Ink on My Fingers*, that Mr. Atkinson instructed him "to produce a weekly paper which would be welcomed in any home, and which would provide a medium for young Canadian writers, in addition to publishing material from those who have already made a name for themselves."

Herb Cranston, who was to be editor for the next twenty-one years, was then thirty. A sober, religious-minded young graduate of McMaster University, he had come to *The Star* in 1905. In 1906 he was Mr. Atkinson's private secretary "to see the paper from the inside and get a view of the business end of things." He covered the 1907 session of Parliament. After a stint on the sports page he became a sort of handyman to Bone for two or three years, during which he wrote appeals for the Fresh Air and Santa Claus Funds, ran the Questions and Answers column, occasionally wrote a feature story, and for a brief time basked in the title of News Editor.

On his appointment as editor of the *Star Weekly,* Cranston was authorized to draw upon the *Daily* for staff-written articles, and one-seventh of the *Daily* editorial payroll was charged against the *Weekly*. In spite of this, for some time circulation manager William Argue complained that he could not sell the *Weekly* against *Sunday World* competition "because there is nothing in it but the street cries of London and Greg Clark's baby."

Gregory Clark, son of J. T. Clark, had left the University of Toronto after his freshman year to become a reporter, and had been contributing a whimsical column to the *Weekly* in which his offspring found frequent mention. Jimmy Frise, a youngster of twenty, who was then retouching photographs for *The Daily Star*, used to illustrate them, the beginning of a partnership that was to last thirty-eight years. Frise became the most famous artist and cartoonist *The Star* ever had, and possibly the most widely known in Canada, but he never had a formal art lesson in his life. A boy from the farm, his first job in the city was marking areas for settlement on maps. One day, tickled by a letter from a farm-hand challenging the editor of *The Star* to a milking contest, he mailed a cartoon to the editor showing him milking a cow from the wrong side. The cartoon was printed, but since he had neglected to give his address they did not know where to mail his cheque. However, the next day he came to the office with the clipping in his hand, and was hired immediately.

In spite of one or two good features the *Star Weekly* remained a hodgepodge of articles written by run-of-the-mill reporters or bought cheaply from syndicates. A typical issue contained a couple of pages of sport, a couple of pages of financial news, a couple of pages of women's news and fashions, a page of old country news clipped from British papers, a sermon, a Sunday school lesson, a page on plays and theatre, a heavy book review section, almost a page about music on which was printed the words and music of a popular song, a serial story, and an editorial page that was neutral and non-controversial, since the *Star Weekly* was supposed to be independent.

It was not until July 5, 1913, that the *Star Weekly* carried its first comics in a modest four-page section, though the Saturday edition of the daily had been printing comics for several years. It would be pleasant to be able to report that these were memorable and historic features, but the truth is that few addicts would recognize their names today. Who has heard of "The Dream of Rarebit Fiend," " 'Brick' Bodkins' Pa," "The Terrors of the Tiny Tads," "Uncle Mun," or "Mr. Twee Deedle"? They were decidedly second-rate, for the *Sunday World* still had the best ones under contract, while the better of those available to *The Star* were kept for the daily's Saturday comics section. Nevertheless after the introduction of comics circulation increased by 4,000 to 26,000.

Cranston reported that comics would have been introduced sooner but for Mrs. Atkinson's dislike of them. If so it may be that she was responsible for the fact that three of the first five comics were in the nature of artistically illustrated fairy tales. He told of a visit to the Atkinson home during which Mrs. Atkinson expressed her disapproval of comics quite vigorously.

"My dear," he quoted Mr. Atkinson as saying, "I am not running a Sunday school paper."

"I rather wish you were," she replied. She feared the introduction of comics would open the way to turning the *Star Weekly* into the kind of yellow journalism represented by most American Sunday papers, and which she abhorred.

Seven years after it was founded the *Star Weekly* was still losing money and still badly trailing the *Sunday World* in circulation. Advertisers had no confidence in it, while the advertising department complained that every advertisement they managed to sell for the *Weekly* represented so much space lost to the *Daily*.

But Mr. Atkinson remained convinced the *Star Weekly* could be made to pay once it hit upon the proper formula. He refused to listen to suggestions it be merged with the Saturday edition of *The Daily Star*, but neither would he spend the money needed to get it out of the rut. The entire editorial staff consisted of Cranston and Jakeway. During the First World War circulation had increased slightly, for readers were eager for war features, and it broke even on more issues than it lost money. But the war ended with it still in a precarious condition.

Then, early in 1919, Mr. Atkinson made the momentous decision to do with the *Star Weekly* what he had done with the *Daily*—make it a newspaper for the little fellow who lived in a semi-detached house in the suburbs and wanted entertainment more than education in his weekend newspaper. Hereafter emphasis was to be placed on lighter material, humour, and fiction with a more popular tone.

Cranston remained as editor with Jakeway as his assistant, but his budget was increased. He was instructed to engage the finest staff of feature writers he could get, and authorized to pay up to $100 for a good feature from free-lance contributors, at that time about as high as any Canadian publication paid.

The childish comics of earlier years were discarded for such popular (and high-priced) ones at "Mutt and Jeff," "Bringing up Father," "The Captain and the Kids," "That Son-in-Law of Pa's," and "Mr. & Mrs." by Briggs. Before long they were joined by "Happy Hooligan," Jimmy Swinnerton's immortal "Jimmy," and Outcault's dog "Tige," which had made its appearance in the first comic strip of all, "The Yellow Kid." Among these were the most famous, the most popular and the most indestructible comics of all time. "Roughneck comics," Cranston called them, heretofore considered too coarse to be introduced into *Star Weekly* homes.

To print them the first four-colour presses were bought in 1920. They remained in use until 1934, though other units were added to the original four as circulation increased or more colour pages were needed. At the same time the first rotogravure press in Canada was installed, a two-unit monotone job, to print the eight-page picture section.

The post-war automobile boom had begun and a motoring section was introduced, edited by Warren Hastings, who later was general manager of the Ontario Motor League. After he left it was edited by W. Frank Prendergast, who recently retired as assistant to the president of Imperial Oil. One of the more popular of the earlier features, "A Page About People," was kept but brightened by changing the nature of the articles from biographical to anecdotal and keeping them short. Less space was given to the doings of Toronto's high society, more to fashions and household hints for women of moderate means. The "news" section was separated from the "magazine" section, which consisted of articles and fiction.

The changes were put under way in the early half of 1919, though naturally it took many months to build up a staff and a pool of contributors. Nevertheless, the effect was immediate and beyond even the most optimistic dreams. In the twelve months beginning July, 1919, circulation increased from 79,000 to more than 122,000, exceeding that of *The Daily Star*. Atkinson was so confident the *Weekly* had struck upon the right formula to win public approval that on August 14, 1920, he raised the price from five cents to ten cents a copy. The price had to be increased if the *Weekly* was to continue paying salaries and rates high enough to attract the best writers.

The immediate effect of this price increase was a drop in circulation of 20,000 and thus the average shown for the year is 110,000 rather than the peak it had reached. But gradually it crept back. Readers who had deserted the *Star Weekly* for the *Sunday World*, which was still selling for five cents, decided it was worth the extra nickle and returned.

W. F. Maclean, publisher of the *World* newspapers, had been teetering on the brink of insolvency for twenty years, and in 1921 he sold out to the Douglas brothers, owners of the *Mail and Empire*. The morning *World* was merged with that paper, giving it just enough additional circulation to put it ahead of the *Globe* for the first time, but it was decided to continue the *Sunday World* as the weekend edition of the *Mail and Empire*.

With stronger financial backing and new editors, the rejuvenated *Sunday*

World presented a stronger challenge to the *Star Weekly*. The *Star Weekly* met this challenge by "beefing up" the features at considerable expense and adding eight new comics printed on four extra pages. These included "Barney Google," "Clarence," "Tillie the Toiler," "Polly," "Toots and Casper," and "Reg'lar Fellers." Cranston attributed the slaughter of the *Sunday World* that followed to these additional comics more than to anything else. "It was disconcerting to the editor and writers that the formula for getting more circulation was the addition of more comics," he wrote in the Midland *Free Press-Herald* in 1940.

Be that as it may, in a matter of months the *Sunday World* dropped 20,000 circulation and soon had only a third as many readers as the *Star Weekly*. Mr. Atkinson offered its publishers $80,000 for the name and subscription list. They accepted, and on November 15, 1924, the *Sunday World* was quietly chloroformed. By this time the *Star Weekly*'s circulation of 153,000 was the largest of any Canadian publication.

Meantime Cranston had been busily building up a staff of writers. Once the general policy had been laid down he seems to have been given a remarkably free hand in putting it into effect, and the selection of articles and the writers to be engaged were left pretty much to his discretion. Usually he was called to account only when he made a mistake. There were, however, certain general rules to be observed, chief of which was that since the *Star Weekly* was read by all members of the family it should contain nothing distasteful to anyone. Ladies in pictures had to be fully clothed, fiction dealt only with love at its purest, and articles dealt only with nice people and nice things.

As the *Star Weekly* demonstrated, nice people, pure love, and fully clothed ladies are quite as interesting as the other kinds, and few even in this sophisticated age would find the *Star Weekly* of the 1920's noticeably prudish or moralistic. The only people who seemed to complain were the ones who complain most loudly today—writers who have an off-colour story rejected.

Cranston recalled as one of the incidents that remained in his memory being called on the carpet for running a picture of a girl in a bathing suit of immodest proportions by the standards of those days. He attributed this to Mrs. Atkinson, but Mr. Atkinson was quite as insistent as his wife that nothing in the *Star Weekly* should give offence. This policy with respect to pictures was continued in both *The Daily Star* and the *Star Weekly* long after Mrs. Atkinson's death, and the story is still told of the day Mr. Atkinson "came dashing up the steps two at a time" commanding that a picture of a girl in a bathing suit be removed from page one of the *Daily*.

Over a period of five or six years there was built up on the *Star Weekly* a galaxy of writers the like of which no Canadian publication had ever seen before or is likely to see again. On the staff at one time were Gregory Clark, Frederick Griffin, Robert C. Reade, Charles Vining, John Herries McCulloch, Roy Greenaway, and William McGeary.

The first staff men transferred from the *Daily* to the *Star Weekly* were Clark and Frise, fresh from the war. Both had done work for the *Star Weekly* before going overseas and they were reassigned to their old jobs. Clark had matured considerably while overseas, and instead of writing the frothy column he had formerly done, he did some really sound reporting. But his knack was for stunt stories, such as frying an egg on the city hall steps on the hottest day in summer, or trying to buy a necktie with a $1,000 bill.

At first Frise drew a half-page panel called "Life's Little Comedies" modelled on a popular syndicated US feature, but it dealt with city people and city situations and Jimmy was a farm boy. He never liked it himself and it did not catch on with the readers. In 1920 he began a half-page cartoon based on village life, the famous and popular "Birdseye Centre." By 1923 "Birdseye Centre" and its characters were known all over the country, and in 1926 readers of the *Star Weekly* voted it their best-liked comic. "Birdseye Centre" was based on Jimmy's native Port Perry, but it typified hundreds of provincial hamlets. An attempt was made at one time to syndicate it in the United States and the spelling was Americanized to "Center" but it did not go over. Perhaps it was too Canadian in its humour. Or perhaps Jimmy's kindly treatment of a "hick town" and "hick people" did not appeal to the sophisticated readers of American Sunday papers.

At the same time the feature he was to do for many years with Clark was taking form. Greg had begun writing humorous articles on the strange characters he met on city streets, which Frise illustrated. Before long these developed into weird or humorous adventures that were pure fiction. In addition Greg was occasionally called upon to do special articles and interviews for both *Weekly* and *Daily*.

Frederick Griffin was the second man to be added to the writing staff. He had joined *The Star* as assistant to librarian Jerry Elder. Transferred to the *Daily* as a reporter he broke his leg on his first assignment, chasing a fire truck on Yonge Street. Back at work after recovering, he began submitting stories to the *Weekly*, though at that time *Star* employees were not paid for *Weekly* articles. Two years later he was on the *Weekly*'s full-time staff.

Griffin has sometimes been referred to as "the greatest reporter in Canada." Though Irish, he was lacking in humour, but he had the Irishman's emotionalism and sentiment. He had a gift for pathos, and his wide and rich vocabulary and fine feeling for words made him a master of the telling phrase. Truth was a passion with him, and he was never satisfied until he got to the bottom of a story. He prided himself on reporting facts without taking sides, but being emotional and warm-hearted he sometimes took sides in spite of himself. By nature he was temperamental, for which Cranston made allowances. But Hindmarsh, who succeeded Cranston, did not understand temperamental "prima donnas." As a result Griffin's last years on *The Star* were bitter and unhappy. He died of a heart attack in 1946.

Robert C. Reade, one of the first Rhodes Scholars from the University of Toronto, was perhaps the most brilliant of the group, a sparkling writer and intelligent reporter. On his return from Oxford in 1922 he joined the staff of *The Daily Star* but was soon transferred to the *Weekly*. Before long he was known for his well-written features and his pungent paragraphs on the editorial page. Unfortunately, at the height of his career his health collapsed and he had to give up writing. After a long period in hospital he returned to *The Star* to spend the latter part of his life in a relatively minor and undemanding editorial position.

Charles Vining and Merrill Denison, the latter now an internationally known author and playwright, collaborated on stunt stories with Clark before becoming popular in their own right. After only a year on the *Daily* Vining was sent to London as managing editor of the ill-fated *Advertiser*, a Liberal paper *The Star* had bought to be the first in a proposed chain. After the *Advertiser* was sold in 1926 he joined the *Star Weekly* as associate editor but became better known for his feature articles. He left *The Star* to become president of the Canadian Newsprint Association.

None of these men were hired in the first place by Cranston, but he had the authority of Mr. Atkinson to pick the top writers off the reporting staff of the *Daily,* Hindmarsh did not like having his best reporters snatched from him in this manner, but there was not much he could do about it at the time. In addition to men transferred from the *Daily* to the *Weekly* staff, Cranston was occasionally allowed to draft such writers as R. E. Knowles, Gordon Sinclair, sports columnist Lou Marsh, and others for special articles.

Equally important to the success of the *Star Weekly* were the brilliant young free-lance writers who wrote more or less regularly on assignment.

Unknown then, most of them became nationally, some internationally, famous in the next few years. Morley Callaghan wrote his first article for the *Star Weekly* at the age of eighteen, while he was still in high school. It was about a meeting of a street corner evangelist at the corner of Yonge and Albert streets. Callaghan earned pocket money while attending university by writing at space rates for both the *Daily* and *Weekly* papers, and on graduation joined the staff of the *Daily*. But he remained only a short time, for he found newspaper work uncongenial. "You present the whole problem of the university man," Hindmarsh told him on parting. "You have never been broken to harness."

B. K. Sandwell was a regular contributor while he was earning his living as a free-lance writer between his departure in 1925 from Queen's University, where he had been a professor of English, and his appointment as editor of *Saturday Night* in 1932. Laura Goodman Salverson also drew regular cheques from the *Star Weekly* while writing her now-famous Icelandic-Canadian novels. Louis Arthur Cunningham, the author from the Maritimes, was an occasional contributor.

Claire Wallace, whose two brothers were on *The Star* and whose father had been assistant city editor for a short time, was sent to Cranston by Hindmarsh to whom she had applied for a job. Her brothers tried to dissuade her from newspaper work, but she soon distinguished herself as a writer of imagination and initiative. Some time later she was transferred to the *Daily*, which she left to go into radio work, becoming an outstanding success.

Arthur D. (Cowboy) Kean thrilled the *Weekly*'s readers for years with his stories about horses, but he never was a cowboy and detested the name. He came to Mr. Atkinson with a letter of introduction from Sir Edward Beatty, president of the CPR. He had some two hundred and fifty animal yarns, real and fictional, published in the *Star Weekly*.

Other regular contributors were Ernest Hemingway, Mary Lowrey, Chief Buffalo Child Long Lance, the Alberta Indian writer who became highly popular in England, Nina Moore Jamieson whose humorous stories delighted readers for years, Bruce Hutchison and Grattan O'Leary. And among established writers who wrote regularly for the *Star Weekly* were Stephen Leacock, Nellie McClung, Ring Lardner, and H. G. Wells.

The *Star Weekly* was always alert to get articles by famous Canadian personages, sometimes ghost-written but usually written by themselves. One of these was by W. E. Raney, Attorney General of Ontario, and as a result of a statement he made the *Star Weekly* contested its first libel suit

Joseph E. Atkinson's favourite photograph of himself — by Violet Keene

Four things an Executive Should Know

MEMORANDUM

Mr.

(1) What ought to be done

(2) How should it be done

(3) Who should do it

(4) Has it been done.

May 1st, 1940

Executives were given these rules in Mr. Atkinson's handwriting on promotion

Frederick Griffin, feature writer and war correspondent, 1919–1946

Gregory Clark, *Star Weekly* feature writer and war correspondent, 1913–1946

Matthew Halton, foreign correspondent, 1932–1945
Ashley & Crippen

Jimmie Frise, *Star Weekly* cartoonist, 1913–1947

Ernest Hemingway, staff writer and foreign correspondent, 1920–1923

Roy Greenaway, staff writer, 1918–19—

R. E. Knowles, feature writer and interviewer, 1920–1946

Robert C. Reade, *Star Weekly* writer, 1922–1956

Gordon Sinclair, staff writer and globe-trotter, shown here with Dr. Allan Roy Dafoe, was one of Canada's earliest radio interviewers

Canada's first portable radio unit toured Ontario fall fairs in 1922–23, to popularize *The Star*'s station, CFCA

in fifteen years. There had been other cases in which libel was charged, but they never reached court. The *Star Weekly* won its case, but on appeal a retrial was ordered on a technicality. Evidently *The Star*'s lawyer considered the technicality was sound, for an out-of-court settlement was reached. *The Star* paid the plaintiff a considerable sum, but did not admit it had committed libel.

Among artists who earned their "bread and butter" illustrating for the *Star Weekly* while earning a name for themselves as creative artists were Franz Johnston, Manly MacDonald, Arthur Lismer, E. J. Dinsmore, Fred H. Varley, J. E. H. MacDonald, Franklin Arbuckle, Tom Mitchell, L. A. C. Panton, H. W. McCrea, Estelle M. Kerr, Grant H. MacDonald, Lydia Fraser, and Charles Comfort. Some of C. W. Jefferys' finest historical paintings were introduced to the public by the *Star Weekly*.

Friction was developing between Cranston and Hindmarsh. Technically they were equals under managing editor Bone, each running his separate show, but they were both ambitious men. Cranston had a well-developed sense of his own importance, while Hindmarsh, an aggressive, dominating personality, would let nothing stand in his way when it came to getting news. Men who worked with them say Cranston felt that by marrying Atkinson's daughter Hindmarsh had cut him off from advancement, and Hindmarsh once expressed the view that Cranston's resentment on this point had made it impossible for them to work together.

The first clashes arose when Hindmarsh began to ask for the services of *Star Weekly* staff writers to cover major news stories for the *Daily*. Usually these centred around Frederick Griffin. Cranston accused Hindmarsh of "drafting" his staff, but actually Bone's approval had to be obtained first, and he would not assign Griffin to a *Daily* story unless he considered it of more importance than the *Weekly* feature on which he was working. The so-called "drafting" was not entirely one-sided, for Cranston did not hesitate to call upon space writers like Hemingway, R. E. Knowles, and others upon whom Hindmarsh was counting for *Daily* features, while occasionally top *Daily* writers like Gordon Sinclair were assigned to him. Cranston had also drawn most of his staff from *The Daily Star*.

On Bone's death in 1928 Hindmarsh became managing editor of both the *Daily* and *Weekly*, responsible only to J. E. Atkinson. For a couple of years he devoted his attention almost entirely to the *Daily*, but around 1930 he began taking a more personal interest in the conduct of the *Weekly*. The *Weekly* was still gaining in circulation, but the rate of increase was slowing, and it was still pretty much a Toronto paper. Hindmarsh believed it had got into a rut, and indeed it had changed little in the previous ten years.

Twenty years later Cranston wrote in his book that Hindmarsh thought the *Star Weekly* needed "more zip and boom and hurrah, and should follow more closely the highly successful pattern of Hearst's *American Weekly* . . . I did not know to what extent The Chief was in accord with those ideas, having no direct word from him, but I naturally struggled to maintain the Canadian characteristics which up to that time had had Atkinson's approval and backing." An examination of the *Star Weekly* files of those years discloses that few of Hindmarsh's innovations even remotely resembled Hearst's *American Weekly,* unless one accepts timeliness and interest as exclusively Hearst characteristics. In fact, Hindmarsh's effort was to make the *Star Weekly* like no other paper anywhere. Nevertheless, the changes he made were drastic, and to one of Cranston's religious nature and conservative temperament they may have appeared Hearstian.

Out went the sugary fiction that had become a characteristic of the *Star Weekly* with such titles as "Flowers of the Soul" and "Her Great Moment," to be replaced by westerns, mysteries, sports stories, humour, and romances with a less tepid love interest. More space was devoted to articles of international importance. Staff writers were sent out on articles with real meat in them instead of writing on bee-keeping in Fergus or the southerly migration of birds. Greg Clark's whimsical little features that had so appealed to Cranston disappeared, and Greg was assigned to doing good, punchy interviews. It was with the encouragement of Hindmarsh that the Greg-and-Jim series flowered and eventually became the most popular feature in the paper, with Clark writing a half page of copy and Frise drawing a half-page illustration.

Religious articles had been gradually increasing in number, reflecting Cranston's interest, until there were sometimes two or three in one issue. These were drastically reduced in number. Dr. Salem Bland, who had been writing what were little more than sermons, was encouraged to turn the powerful searchlight of his pen on social problems, and became one of the most notable and controversial writers the *Star Weekly* ever had.

Historical features, which also had been running sometimes two to an issue, were discarded entirely to be replaced by such things as a signed article by Mussolini, an interview with Gandhi, an article by Griffin on Chicago's gangsters, or a story on the Toronto branch of the Ku Klux Klan joining US Klansmen in raiding Negro homes, all of which appeared in one issue. Topicality was of the essence.

To the regular contributors were added Matthew Halton as staff correspondent in London, and Pierre van Paassen as a roving correspondent in Europe. Van Paassen, a former *Globe* reporter, had been for some time with the Paris bureau of the New York *World*.

Halton had come to *The Star* in 1931 after studying a year in England on an IODE scholarship. He was an undistinguished cub reporter until sent with the usual *Star* multitude to cover the imperial economic conference in Ottawa in 1932. As the junior member of the team he had nothing much to do, so he occupied his time writing whimsical "Alice in Wonderland" stories about the conference. News editor Drylie tossed them in the waste basket as they were received.

One day Drylie was sick. His substitute did not know Halton's stories were not supposed to be any good, and put one on the front page. Within minutes after the first edition was delivered to Mr. Atkinson the news editor's telephone rang. The delightful articles of that young man Halton were to be featured every day on page one. Furthermore he was to be given a shockingly large increase in pay. A few weeks later he was sent to London as correspondent for both the *Star Weekly* and *The Daily Star*. His reports were among the most popular features of both papers.

Soon staff writers were being sent to Russia to report what the communists were doing, to Italy to report what the fascists were doing, and to Germany to report what the Nazis were doing. Others were sent on assignments all over Canada, to the United States, and to Latin America. "World news is Canadian news," Hindmarsh said. On another occasion he said he wanted the *Star Weekly* to be "Canada's window on the world." Whether this new emphasis on foreign news was Atkinson's idea or Hindmarsh's is unclear. At any rate it had Mr. Atkinson's approval for on occasion he gave instructions himself to foreign correspondents.

The *Star Weekly* continued to depend primarily upon Canadian writers, artists and photographers, but there was no striving for a "Canadian angle" to an international story. The objective was to view the world through Canadian eyes and to report world events that interested Canadians. At the same time it gave some opportunity to staff writers on British and American periodicals to express themselves on foreign affairs with a frankness that would not be tolerated by the editors for whom they worked. On moving into the new building in 1929 Mr. Atkinson had colour rotogravure presses added to the original monotone press. Colour has been used in every issue of the rotogravure section since, greatly adding to its attractiveness.

The changes made by Hindmarsh were all for the better and increased the popularity of the paper. Whereas circulation growth had slowed to under 5,000 a year by 1930, it increased by more than 9,000 the year Hindmarsh took over, and by more than 18,000 the next year. But Cranston saw in the changes a reflection on his editorship and resented them—and even openly resisted them.

He was proud of what he had accomplished with the *Star Weekly*, as he had every right to be. His error lay in failing to realize it could not stand still, and that public interests change. Had he worked as enthusiastically in 1930 as he did in 1919 to put the revamped *Star Weekly* across he might have spent many more useful years as its editor.

Nevertheless, Cranston was given nearly three years to put Hindmarsh's ideas into effect, for it was not until the first week in June, 1932, that Hindmarsh "moved in" and made it clear he was the unmistakeable "boss." He ordered Cranston to let him see all the manuscripts that had been accepted for publication. There were more than forty and some had been around for quite some time. Three days later Hindmarsh ordered them all returned, paying about $800 to authors to soothe aggrieved feelings.

On December 8 that year, Main Johnson was appointed editor. Johnson had left *The Star* four years earlier to be promotions manager for the Robert Simpson Co. after having been successively promotions manager of *The Star* and manager of radio station CFCA which *The Star* owned. But he had found his venture into the world of merchandising less pleasant than he had anticipated. Cranston remained another eight weeks as associate editor before resigning.

Cranston's own version of the events of 1932 indicate that Hindmarsh had the full support of Mr. Atkinson in the changes he had made and was probably encouraged by him, for The Chief must have known the *Star Weekly* could not long survive the dullness that had crept into its columns. Moreover, Atkinson was already turning over in his mind the feasibility of making the *Star Weekly* a national publication. As yet two-thirds of its circulation was in Toronto and its suburbs, while the other third was restricted for the most part to central Ontario. The response of readers to the broader appeal Hindmarsh had given it encouraged him to believe its bounds could be extended.

However, 1933 turned out to be one of the worst years for the publishing industry. The depression was at its severest, and the circulation of almost every publication in Canada fell off. The *Star Weekly* experienced its first decline since 1917. Even *The Daily Star* gained only 794 while all other Toronto dailies lost. The *Globe* never recovered. Mr. Atkinson intended to expand into the West where there would be no competition, but with the price of wheat at an all-time low and much of the West in the grip of a drought he decided to wait for a more propitious time.

That came in 1934 when the West had begun to recover. Early in the year Mr. Atkinson called his circulation and advertising managers into conference and asked them respectively if they could sell the paper in the West and if they could sell advertising on the basis of western circulation. Both replied they could. Circulation manager Ralph Cowan was accordingly given a budget of $80,000 for sales promotion. This was increased the next year to $110,000.

The response exceeded expectations, for the *Star Weekly* caught on with western readers at once. In 1934 it added more than 40,000 circulation west of the Great Lakes. By 1939 it had increased by a total of 131,000. On January 22, 1938, its name was changed from the *Toronto Star Weekly* to simply the *Star Weekly*, which better suited a national publication. On April 9 of the same year it began printing its rotogravure picture section in tabloid form. A special bulldog edition of the news section was printed for western readers: thus it still presented the appearance of a weekend newspaper. A bulldog edition of the news section had been printed for Ontario readers outside Toronto since 1931. The paper did not go on sale in Toronto until Saturday, and the Toronto news section carried up-to-date news printed the same day. It was not until 1942, when newsprint became scarce, that the news section was dropped and the practice began of putting it on sale earlier in the week.

The magazine section, illustrated in colour, consisted almost exclusively of fiction and articles which had become increasingly serious with the passing years. It always had one and frequently two articles on foreign affairs by such writers as Matthew Halton, who reported the British viewpoint, Maurice Hindus, the expert on Russia, and Pierre van Paassen, the student of fascism, and Nazism, and foreign intrigue. It had an article, sometimes two, on a Canadian subject by a staff writer. It had a light and frothy, or occasionally humorous, article by a Canadian writer. It had an article of the escapist type which might be an adventure story from a foreign land by Gordon Sinclair, or an article on elephant-hunting or bronco-busting.

Its fiction followed just as strict a formula—a love story, an adventure story, a funny story, and a western. Occasionally it had two love stories, one a tale of gay young love, the other of mature devotion, or of a husband and wife brought together after an estrangement. The adventure story might be of crime or detection or even sport. It was a successful formula for it provided both fiction and non-fiction for every member of the family and to suit every taste. It did not change for years. Even the comics section, one of the biggest in America, had at least one feature for each age group.

Main Johnson was editor of the *Star Weekly* until 1938, when he became financial editor of the *Daily*. He was succeeded by T. J. Wheeler, a young man who had had a somewhat meteoric rise on the *Daily*, and now found himself managing editor of both publications. Wheeler remained two years, resigning in December, 1939, to establish his own authors' agency and syndicate service. He was succeeded by George Rogers, who first had the title of executive editor but became articles editor when it was decided to divide responsibility for fiction and magazine features. Rogers remained for eighteen years.

But no matter who was the ostensible editor, the real editor of the *Star Weekly* from 1939 until his death on December 20, 1956, was H. C. Hindmarsh.

Chapter 12

TORONTO'S PIONEER RADIO

Joseph Story Atkinson was one of the early "ham" wireless operators in America, building his first set while a student in his early teens at the University of Toronto Schools. In those years immediately after the First World War transmission was still in dots and dashes, and young Joe used to sit up half the night with his half-kilowatt rotary spark transmitter and crystal receiver talking with other "hams" in Toronto and nearby cities.

After legislation was passed in 1922 requiring amateurs to be licensed, the call letters 3EC were assigned him by the Department of Marine and Fisheries. J. E. Atkinson was therefore aware of the tremendous advances that had been made in radio transmission in the immediate post-war years.

Mr. Atkinson followed with a lively interest the introduction of voice transmission by wireless in early 1921, though his son remained a dot-and-dash enthusiast. *The Star* reported the appearance of the first commercial stations in the United States using voice in November of that same year, and Mr. Atkinson was quite familiar with this new marvel when his promotions department suggested *The Star* might duplicate its feat of being the first newspaper to use wireless by being the first to transmit voice and music by radio. He learned that the Independent Telephone Company, which distributed the components used by most Toronto amateurs in making their sets, had established an experimental broadcasting station at the Canadian General Electric factory on Wallace Avenue, and was having some success broadcasting records.

Mr. Atkinson was impressed by the promotional value of *The Star* being the first newspaper in Canada to broadcast a live concert; this could be made the occasion for a great public exhibition. Accordingly he authorized promotions manager Main Johnson to arrange a demonstration of "wireless telephony" in the form of a Star Free Concert, with the public hearing the entertainment by means of a wireless loud speaker. With the utmost secrecy arrangements were made with the Independent Telephone Company to broadcast the concert over its station 9AH, musicians were hired and sworn to silence, and the Masonic Temple was engaged for the main concert. A second loud speaker was set up at Christie Street Military Hospital.

The concert was broadcast on the evening of March 28, 1922, just six weeks after Marconi's experimental station broadcast its first "entertainment" in Britain. The publicity bomb had been exploded the preceding day with an eight-column line in 72 point on page one. "This is an experimental undertaking," the accompanying story stated. "*The Star* cannot and does not guarantee a perfect demonstration but it has secured careful preliminary tests which give reasonable assurance the experiment will be highly interesting and successful. The wireless telephone has not attained perfection. There are certain crudities and defects in it yet." Amateurs were asked to stay off the air between 8.15 and 10.15 p.m. so that they would not interfere, and a similar request was made to Buffalo "hams." The power was 100 watts, the wavelength was 415 metres, but that did not mean much, for those primitive broadcasting stations wandered all over the dial, and it was often impossible to tune out a station that was stronger or closer.

Bone, the managing editor, was chairman at the Masonic Temple. "It is quite within the realm of possibility, indeed I should say probability, that this occasion is the forerunner of a development which will alter our customs and habits to as great an extent as that occasioned by the invention of the original telephone, or of the phonograph, or even of the motor car," he told the 1,100 people who jammed the auditorium.

Perhaps it was with intention that he did not make *The Star*'s intentions too clear, for nobody knew how successful the demonstration would be. Thus at one point he said *The Star* had put on the demonstration as "the most practicable way of dealing with wireless from a news point of view," implying that this was just another big story, while later he referred to "the services which *The Star* will send out hereafter." As a matter of fact, *The Star* had already been granted a licence for a broadcasting station.

Bone introduced W. A. Fowler, of the Independent Telephone Company, as the man "who is doing the delicate tuning necessary, fussing with condensers, moving vernier adjustments to hair breadth accuracy" on the clumsy receiving set which occupied a table in the centre of the stage. Dr. Charles A. Culver, chief radio engineer for the same firm, announced the program from the studio two miles away.

The artists on the program were Mrs. R. J. Dilworth, soprano; Evelyn Chelew Kemp, pianist; Victor Edmunds, tenor; Romanelli's Orchestra; Boris Hambourg, cellist; Alberto Guerrero, pianist; and Henri Czaplinski, violinist. The program was a tremendous success, not only with the public which jammed the Masonic Temple but also with the estimated thousand owners of private radio receiving sets in the Toronto area. It was the first live radio program of entertainment broadcast in Canada, and it was not until three months later that Europe heard its first live music broadcast from a garden fete at Hampstead, England. *The Star*'s report of its experiment was ecstatic.

"Twenty-five hundred years ago Belchazzar and his thousand roistering lords were stricken with fear of a mystic hand that wrote a flaming message on the walls behind," wrote the anonymous reporter. "To these people in the Masonic Temple last evening came an even stranger manifestation, yet they do not fear. Only a great wondering that such things could be." But *The Star*'s music critic, Augustus Bridle, opined that "the soprano voice will never be transmitted with true fidelity by wireless," a straight crib from Edison's famous comment on the soprano voice and the phonograph.

At once *The Star* put into effect its plans for a regular broadcasting service without waiting to build its own station, renting time on 9AH. *The Star* has been careful not to claim it had the "first" radio station in Toronto, though it had the first to broadcast regular programs. Instead it has claimed it had the "pioneer" radio station. It had hoped to be the first newspaper to go on the air, but the Vancouver *Province* nosed it out by a few days. However *The Star*'s claim to the distinction of initiating the first regular broadcasting service in Canada and the first programming of live entertainment is sustained by the *Canadian Annual Review* of 1922. *The Star* "took up the subject [of radio broadcasting] with ability and energy," that publication stated.

The Star broadcast a second concert on April 4, and a third, picked up in a public auditorium in Peterborough, on April 6. It began broadcasting the first daily radio service in Canada on April 10. This consisted of an evening program, beginning 7 p.m. with a children's story by Miss Ruth Strong of the Toronto public library, followed by news read by one of *The Star*'s editors, a summary of closing market reports by financial editor, Kenneth McMillan, and a summary of the results of big league baseball games. Interspersed with these throughout the evening were selections of popular music on records. Twice a week it broadcast a live concert.

The same day it began its daily radio programming *The Star* started a daily radio column edited by a very junior reporter named Foster Hewitt. Most of the articles were tips on how to build a set since most people in those days had to make their own. Only four stations were listed in the program, WGR, WWJ, WJL and WBZ. Later KDKA was added. There was no network and no other stations, Canadian or American, within reach of the Toronto listener.

The Star's own station went into operation on June 22, 1922, with the call letters CFCA and a wavelength of 400 metres. At the same time the Canadian Independent Telephone Company's station 9AH was assigned the new call letters CKCE. However CKCE did not broadcast regularly and for twenty-five months *The Star*'s station CFCA had the Toronto field virtually to itself. In August both the *Telegram* and the *Globe* were awarded licences, but neither ever operated a broadcasting station.

When *The Star*'s station went on the air there were only four commercial stations regularly broadcasting in the United States, of which one, WEAF, was experimenting with sponsored programs. There were some fifty stations similar to the Independent Telephone Company's station operated in conjunction with radio supply stores. It was not until August, 1922, that Britain's first radio station, 2LO, went on the air with regular programs, while the BBC was organized in November as the sole agency broadcasting programs in Britain.

Main Johnson was the first manager of *The Star* station, a position he held for seven years. The studio occupied a couple of small rooms in *The Star* building at 18–20 King Street West until it was moved to Yonge Street and St. Clair Avenue in 1924. Shortly after it began broadcasting, CFCA organized the first studio orchestra in Canada under the direction of Reginald Stewart, musical director of Hart House. Stewart conducted the first fifty-piece orchestra ever to broadcast a live program; Foster Hewitt was the announcer.

While still using CKCE *The Star* radio was the first in Canada to broadcast a church service, the Easter morning service of Rev. W. A. Cameron of Yorkminster Baptist church. After it had its own station Cameron became Canada's first radio preacher. For almost ten years he was on the air nearly every Sunday, drawing mail which at times assumed mountainous proportions. The combination of his weekly column in *The Star* and his Sunday radio sermons made him Canada's best-known pastor.

In 1922 *The Star* sponsored the first public exhibition of radio broadcasting and receiving at the Canadian National Exhibition. During the summers of 1922 and 1923 it sent a van fitted with radio receiving equipment to fall fairs throughout Ontario. This van, which was in charge of Foster Hewitt, and the publicity given radio in *The Star* are credited with initiating the tremendous boom in radio listening in the province in those two years.

CFCA was the first radio station anywhere to broadcast a hockey game. Foster Hewitt recalls how one night in March, 1923, as he was preparing to leave the office, he was assigned to try a new experiment—a play-by-play broadcast of a hockey game from the Mutual Street Arena.

"It wasn't a request, it wasn't even an invitation, it was one of those 'into the jaws of death' commands," he related in an interview in *The Star*. "At Mutual Arena I sat, or rather hunched, on a stool with sawed-off legs in a glass box four feet high and three feet square. At that time a crowd noise was something to be avoided at all costs, so the box was air tight. As the game progressed vapor clouded the glass and created the impression that players were skating in a thick fog." Thus was Foster Hewitt launched on the career that was to bring him fame as one of Canada's great sports announcers. Before long he was devoting full time to radio, being succeeded as radio editor of *The Star* by Frank Chamberlain, now a public relations man. At first the announcing, including reading of news bulletins, was done by Edward J. Bowers, the radio engineer. He was succeeded in both jobs by Gordon McClain in 1927.

In February 1924, CFCA became the first radio station in the world to broadcast a news service to newspapers. One of the worst storms to hit this province had virtually destroyed telephone and telegraphic communications. At the request of Canadian Press, which found most of its wires down, CFCA broadcast a condensation of the regular CP service to provincial newspapers. That summer Foster Hewitt began broadcasting baseball and football. In May 1925 he broadcast from Toronto's Woodbine track the first commentary on a horse race to go on the air waves anywhere.

The Star's station joined US stations in the first experiments with network programs, participating in the first hook-up of several stations. In 1925 it experimented with remote control broadcasting, bringing the Champlain tercentenary celebration from Orillia by long-distance telephone. By 1926 it was leading all Canadian stations in remote control programming. It was the first station in North America to pick up a European program by short wave and rebroadcast it. On February 9, 1928, it rebroadcast a program from 2LO, London, beating NBC by several months. Two weeks later it rebroadcast a program from Australia, and three weeks later a speech the Prince of Wales was delivering in London. It was commended for its enterprise by a Washington radio editor.

In those days both receiving and broadcasting equipment were so elementary it was impossible to avoid interference, thus the federal government would allow only one station at a time to broadcast in any one city. However it issued licences to more than one station, leaving them to work out among themselves how the time would be apportioned. Thus within three years CFCA found itself with two competitors, but it was able to reserve the choice early evening for itself.

Interference was so bad between nearby stations that when *The Star* broadcast the Dominion election results in December, 1926, station WKBW in Buffalo courteously went off the air. As an experiment CFCA and CKNC tried broadcasting at the same time at 357 and 500 on the dial on New Year's eve, 1927, but they interfered so badly CFCA went off the air.

Only once did CFCA get into trouble about anything it broadcast and that was in 1926 when it cut off the evening sermon from St. Michael's Cathedral. Arrangements had been made for a series from the Cathedral called "Catholic Truth." After the first two or three sermons CFCA asked Reverend G. J. Kirby to alter their tone, which it felt were attacks on Protestantism rather than expositions of Catholicism. This Father Kirby declined to do. On March 21, 1926, CFCA cut off Reverend Father Greely, SJ, of New York in the midst of a Lenten sermon in which he was contrasting Catholic "tolerance" with Protestant "bigotry." The following day it informed Father Kirby it would no longer broadcast from St. Michael's Cathedral. This resulted in the first of many attacks on *The Star* by the *Catholic Register*, now the *Canadian Register*—attacks which were to continue for another twelve years. The *Register* accused *The Star* of "imperiously setting itself up as a Methodist censor of Catholic doctrine." It referred to Toronto as a city "whose intellect is chloroformed by the old Protestant tradition," and accused all Toronto newspapers of "maliciously distorting" what Father Greely had said.

For several years radio stations in Canada and the United States had been broadcasting copyrighted musical works without compensation to the composers as a result of which, in December, 1926, the Canadian Performing Right Society Limited obtained an injunction against most stations forbidding them from "performing in public any musical work or works or any part or parts thereof, the sole right to perform which in public is owned by the plaintiff." The Society controlled the performing rights in Canada of Canadian and British authors, composers, publishers, and other owners of copyrighted music. The injunction was served on CFCA on December 29, 1926.

A suit by the composers against Famous Players Canadian Corporation for compensation for music performed in their theatres was made the test case, and in the next two years it progressed through the Canadian courts to the Privy Council. In anticipation of an adverse verdict, the radio stations appointed Mr. Atkinson and P. R. du Tremblay, director of *La Presse*, Montreal, which had operated a radio station since the fall of 1922, to bring pressure upon the Canadian government to amend the Copyright Act to "protect" the interests of the broadcasters.

They met Prime Minister King, who did not offer much encouragement to the heads of the two most powerful Liberal newspapers in the country, referring them instead to Hon. Fernand Rinfret, Secretary of State. Mr. Atkinson followed up these interviews by sending Rinfret a draft copyright bill prepared by his solicitors, which he suggested should be adopted. When no action resulted from this he wrote King in April, 1928, expressing his "regret" at the government's failure to introduce copyright legislation at the current session of Parliament.

At the same time he wrote Rinfret that unless the copyright legislation he suggested was passed, "music performing organizations throughout Canada would be subject to whatever toll might be levied upon them by the very aggressive gentlemen who have discovered this means of filling their pockets." It was in the public interest, he said, that "organizations interested in the public performance of music" should not be "at the mercy of the Performing Right Society."

In news reports in *The Star* at the time there was no hint that the interests of composers and writers were concerned. It was pictured as solely a dispute between sheet music publishers on the one hand, and theatre and radio owners on the other. Actually the Performing Right Society was defending the right of composers to be paid when their works were publicly performed by commercial organizations. Composers had derived their income in the past from royalties on the sales of sheet music, but radio was putting the sheet music publishers out of business. Radio, which had become the chief beneficiary of his talent, should therefore pay the composer, said the Performing Right Society.

In opposing this logical argument, Mr. Atkinson revealed a facet of his creed that puzzled many. *The Star* was always at hand to defend the defenceless, to fight the fight of those who were suffering injustice through no fault of their own, to proclaim the right of the weak to organize. But Mr. Atkinson felt it was under no obligation to fight the battle of the strong. Composers and song writers were organized in the powerful Performing Right Society. The antagonists were evenly matched. Both sides were justified, therefore, in using any lawful means of getting the better of the other, he reasoned.

He applied this same reasoning to labour unions. Workers had the legal right to organize and were protected against intimidation by employers. He was prepared to fight to the limit in defence of these rights. But if certain of his employees did not exercise their rights, they were at fault, not him, if he took advantage of their submissiveness. By the same token, if they were organized, he felt justified in using every lawful means of besting them.

This was sound liberal doctrine in the generation in which Mr. Atkinson grew up, but it has been often attacked even within Liberal parties. Doctrinaire liberals held that, if the employer was free to exploit his workers if he could and the workers were free to organize as they saw fit to resist exploitation, a compromise would be reached. Those opposed to this doctrine, particularly in England, France, and Sweden, insist that more often it results in both sides taking such an adamant position that compromise is impossible.

The Copyright Act was not amended until June 11, 1931, and it did not embody the changes Mr. Atkinson sought. It may have been because of this dispute that *The Star*'s radio station leaned so heavily for the musical part of its programs on classical and semi-classical works on which the copyright had expired, and broadcast very little popular music. CFCA was a decidedly high-brow station, musically speaking. It also tended strongly towards public service and news broadcasting, covering such events as conventions, political meetings, and events at the city hall.

It was banned from the city hall throughout 1930 when Bert Wemp, the *Telegram*'s city editor, was mayor unless another radio station was represented at the same event. Since other radio stations were not interested in such public service broadcasts, CFCA was effectively barred.

For some time CFCA had shared its wavelength with two other stations, each operating a third of the day, since by international agreement only one wavelength was allotted to Toronto. But when Toronto was awarded three wavelengths in 1928, CFCA was given a clear channel while four other stations shared two channels. At once charges were made, in Parliament and in opposition newspapers, that *The Star* was the object of political favouritism. *The Star* was vulnerable to such attacks, for its power was still only 100 watts, the weakest in Toronto, and its equipment was undeniably obsolete, whereas the other stations were more modern and more powerful and gave a superior signal.

"Making all reverential allowance for antiquity, it does not seem right that a covered wagon should be given right-of-way over an up-to-date locomotive," the *Telegram* observed, while the *Globe* demanded that CFCA either modernize its equipment or give up its licence. But speaking in the House of Commons, Hon. P. J. A. Cardin, Minister of Marine and Fisheries, said licences were given to newspapers in preference to other applicants. He cited as evidence that political favouritism was not involved the fact licences had been awarded Conservative newspapers in London and Halifax. Moreover, he said, he did not believe it in the public interest to give the only clear channel in Toronto to a distillery, Gooderham and Worts, which owned CKGW, even though it was the newest and most powerful station.

The *Telegram* had been broadcasting over CKGW as a "phantom station," using the call letters assigned to it in 1922. A "phantom station" was a licensee who had no broadcasting equipment of his own but rented that of another station. Some twenty "phantom" licences had been granted in Toronto, but by 1928 the system of "phantom stations" was being replaced by the present system of sponsorship of programs.

By 1929 the radio situation in Canada was in a muddle with all sorts of people scrambling for the few channels the United States in its generosity had allowed Canada to have unencumbered. Early that year the federal government appointed a commission headed by Sir John Aird, president of the Canadian Bank of Commerce, to hold hearings in Canada and other countries and recommend a radio policy.

The commission reported on September 11, 1929. Briefly it recommended complete government ownership of all broadcasting, cancellation of all licences to private broadcasters, and the establishment of a trans-Canada chain of seven 50,000 watt stations which it believed would blanket all populated parts of the Dominion. The recommendations were approved by most newspapers. The *Telegram* violently dissented on the grounds (*a*) that Mackenzie King would turn a government system into a political organ and (*b*) that somehow "Holy Joe" would manage to wangle exorbitant compensation from the government for the loss of his station.

The Star was perhaps the only newspaper in Canada to pass no judgment on the report, a circumstance soon remarked upon by the *Telegram* and the *Globe*. As *The Star* continued to remain silent these two newspapers began to "needle" it. Was this "public ownership" newspaper which was the private owner of a radio station for or against a publicly owned radio system, they demanded.

The Star gave its answer on March 7, 1930. It was unequivocally for a 100 per cent government-owned radio broadcasting service, as recommended by the Aird commission. "Radio stations constitute a monopoly service by reason of the limitation on their number, which is unavoidable," it declared. "Where a public service in its nature is a monopoly, public ownership of it becomes necessary sooner or later." This was followed by editorials declaring that only public ownership could prevent the air of Canada "from passing into the control of a private U.S. monopoly," and that the issue was not between private or public ownership "but between Canadian control or U.S. control."

"*The Star*," it declared on April 1, "would favor private ownership in its own interest did it not feel that in the public interest radio broadcasting is a natural monopoly that should be under the public ownership of the nation." In another editorial it declared, "private ownership is not going to stand up to its job on Canada's behalf in the radio field." However, it added, "if radio remains in private hands [*The Star*] will have a powerful new plant."

The province of Quebec and certain private radio interests with which *The Star* had no connection challenged the right of the federal government to regulate radio, and the controversy subsided for a year while the Privy Council considered the constitutional question of whether the federal government or the provinces had control. Its decision, given in 1932, was in favour of the federal government.

At once *The Star* renewed its campaign for a government radio system, while the *Telegram* renewed its cry that *The Star* was only interested in dumping its "pile of junk" on the taxpayers. *The Star* retorted with a promise that if the government ever expropriated CFCA "the money paid for it will be paid over by *The Star* to one of the city hospitals." At the same time it predicted the government would buy only one station, the new and powerful CKGW. In fact the government did take over this station, but it only leased it.

The Star's station was broadcasting programs of local origin almost exclusively, with a heavy content of news and public service features, while the *Telegram* was sponsoring NBC network shows over CKGW. Thus, while the *Telegram* was abusing *The Star* for its alleged "poor programs and poor equipment," *The Star* was pointing to the *Telegram*'s US imported programs as an example of what would happen to Canadian radio under private ownership.

Meanwhile R. B. Bennett and his Conservative government had succeeded the Liberals at Ottawa. Bennett acted quickly after the way was cleared to bring in radio legislation, but the Liberals in opposition criticized every move the government made in that direction. At last, on May 12, 1932, after the Liberals had been particularly obstructionist, Mr. Atkinson fired off a sharp telegram to King.

"The report of the radio committee and the support Parliament is giving to nationalized broadcasting is highly gratifying to *The Toronto Star* and, if I may say so, to me personally," he said. "The delay which has already occurred in putting into effect this great service to the people of Canada makes it important that legislation be not postponed but be passed by Parliament this session. It is natural to suppose that those who are opposed to nationalization will endeavour to get legislation put over for another year, but the people of Canada would be deeply disappointed." King replied that "there is no disposition on the part of the opposition to seek postponement of legislation."

The Broadcasting Act was passed on May 18. The debate on the measure had consisted mainly of attacks by Conservative cabinet ministers and Conservative members from Toronto upon *The Star* and station CFCA. Their criticism was not wholly unjustified. CFCA still had a power of only 100 watts while CFRB was broadcasting 10,000 watts, and CKGW had applied for an increase from 5,000 to 10,000 watts. CKCL and CKNC, the other two Toronto stations, each had 500 watt transmitters. Moreover, until *The Star* installed new equipment in early 1933 its waveband was so broad it interfered with neighbouring stations.

But Mr. Atkinson was on the horns of a dilemma. When he tentatively applied for an increase in power, Conservative members of Parliament and private ownership people roared that this proved his support of public ownership was insincere. Since it looked as if his application for increased power for CFCA might be used to defeat public ownership, he hastily withdrew it. All he could do, therefore, was promise in *The Star*, as he did again and again, that if the government decided upon a system of private ownership *The Star* would immediately provide CFCA with the most modern and most powerful broadcasting equipment in Canada. The *Telegram* retorted that this promise was of no value, since the Bennett government would not give *The Star* authority to increase the power of its station.

The Broadcasting Act, which came into effect in late 1932 provided that, as the Aird report recommended, the commission would operate a system consisting of a sufficient number of 50,000-watt stations to blanket the southern portion of Canada, but that private owners would be allowed to operate stations of not more than 100-watt power. As had been predicted by *The Star*, the radio commission leased CKGW for ten years, assumed its contract with NBC, and changed the name of the call letters to CRCT. The other Toronto stations were ordered to cut their power to 100 watts.

CFCA ceased to operate on September 1, 1933. Mr. Atkinson was convinced that radio was now firmly established as a government monopoly, and that there would be slight place for private radio stations. It would cost $100,000 to bring the equipment of CFCA up to date even with a power of only 100 watts, and he decided the scope of a privately owned radio station would be so restricted it was not worth while. His judgment was no doubt influenced by the fact CFCA had been started as a promotional gimmick for *The Star*, and he was unaccustomed to thinking of it in any other light.

"As our readers know," *The Star* said in a front-page statement, "we have been advocates of nationalized broadcasting and have always supposed the ultimate result would be elimination of privately operated stations. It seemed to us that with the revenues available to the radio commission, programs would be produced with which private stations could not compete, and could not therefore long continue to hold the interest of the public. This view is proving to be the correct one."

The Star said it had thoroughly surveyed the field open to a 100-watt station and concluded "there is not a worthwhile future for such a station in Toronto in competition with the government's local station of a power of 50,000 watts and with the treasury of the Dominion behind it." Despite this, it declared, "our share in bringing into being the Radio Commission we, of course, do not regret."

If it is true that misery loves company, Mr. Atkinson may have derived some satisfaction in later years from the knowledge that owners of ten other radio stations in Canada thought as he did and closed down. However, seventy remained in operation. Before long they were allowed to increase their power and improve their programs. Not only did the public demand a wider selection of programs than the government system was providing, but improvements in both broadcasting and receiving equipment eliminated most of the interference between stations.

The very week *The Star* closed its radio station it was giving the Canadian public the first demonstration of live television at the Canadian National Exhibition, in co-operation with RCA-Victor. The show was opened by Jessica Dragonette, who was in Toronto to give a concert for *The Star* Fresh Air Fund. Gordon Sinclair interviewed her and other prominent visitors at the exhibition from a specially constructed studio, and thus he qualified as the first television interviewer in Canada. Miss Kathleen M. Taylor, a school teacher, interviewed visitors to the exhibit. They could watch themselves on nearby monitors. "The transmission was sent from a medium-sized but over-heated room, dark as the inside of a grave except for a flood of yellowish light," Sinclair wrote the next day, describing his interview with Miss Dragonette just before her concert.

The hostility between the Bennett government and *The Star* was not reflected in the new radio commission, and a few days after closing its own station *The Star* began broadcasting for two fifteen-minute periods a day from CRCT as a "sustaining program," that is, paying nothing for the time it was given. This arrangement, which was made verbally, was confirmed in an exchange of letters between F. L. Tate, business manager of *The Star*, and Lieut.-Col. W. A. Steel of the Canadian Radio Commission. The Commission, said Colonel Steel, conceded *The Star* had "a moral right" to free time for news broadcasting by reason of its priority in the broadcasting field in Toronto, and because it had abandoned its own station without compensation. Fred Hotson, former CFCA newscaster, began the newscasts over CRCT but he was soon succeeded by Walter Bowles, who remained *The Star*'s newscaster for another ten years.

After a few years the Canadian Radio Commission was succeeded by the Canadian Broadcasting Corporation, and in 1937 it also acknowledged *The Star*'s right to free time. "I have felt that your zealous work and your pioneering have deserved special treatment, nevertheless it has to be kept in mind that sooner or later the situation will have to be regularized in terms of the press as a whole," wrote Gladstone Murray, president of the CBC, to Tom Wheeler, assistant managing editor of *The Star*. Conservative members of Parliament were beginning to complain that *The Star* was being given preferential treatment in the matter of free time.

In 1939 Canadian Press began negotiations with the CBC with a view to the withdrawal of all newspapers from the field of news broadcasting, and asked for legislation banning commercial sponsorship of news. This was opposed by both *The Star* and the *Telegram*, the latter newspaper having a popular newscast over CFRB. Eventually a contract was signed with Canadian Press, but *The Star*'s arrangement was continued as a moral obligation recognized by the CBC.

It was cancelled as a result of an attack in Parliament in August, 1946, led by John Diefenbaker, on the alleged favouritism shown *The Star*. A committee of Parliament held a hearing at which it was disclosed the CBC paid Canadian Press $70,000 a year for its news service and British United Press $25,000 a year. Diefenbaker maintained that with such an outlay there was no demand for additional news services such as that provided by *The Star*, though Dr. Augustin Frigon, general manager of the CBC, told the committee *The Star* performed a public service by providing local news outside the field covered by Canadian Press.

Chapter 13

THE DEAD HORSE

"In no part of Atkinson's great achievement is there to be seen evidence of a major error bearing on the fortunes of his property. He may have lost a quarter of a million or so in his attempt to storm the London, Ont., newspaper field, but his general operations were unaffected. He had the wisdom to refrain from flogging a dead horse." Thus wrote M. E. Nichols in (*CP*): *The Story of the Canadian Press.*

The loss was considerably more than a quarter of a million, for when Mr. Atkinson bought the London *Advertiser* in December, 1922, he made one of the few serious mistakes in his business career. For some time he had been mulling over the idea of establishing a chain of newspapers. *The Star* and the *Star Weekly* were both profitable. Why should not their success be duplicated elsewhere?

It was still only a vague but appealing idea in the back of his mind when H. B. Muir, managing director of the *Advertiser*, paid him a hurried visit one day late in 1922. The *Advertiser* was about to be sold to W. F. Herman, who also dreamed of owning a chain of newspapers, and Muir was in a pickle. He had given up a well-paid job as advertising manager of the London *Free Press* only a few weeks before to accept an offer from T. H. Purdom, the London lawyer and utilities man who headed the interests that owned the *Advertiser*. Muir had a contract, but Herman balked at signing the final papers unless Muir would tear it up for a quite inadequate settlement. No doubt the contract could be enforced, but it would be a messy job all around.

On the spur of the moment Mr. Atkinson decided to buy the *Advertiser* and keep 32-year-old Muir as managing director. In a matter of days the deal was completed, *The Star* taking over in December. The price was $95,000 for the entire stock of the London Advertiser Company of a par value of $300,000. In addition *The Star* paid off debentures of the company amounting to $75,000 and back interest amounting to close to $10,000, for a total purchase price of approximately $180,000. A few months later *The Star* guaranteed a loan to the *Advertiser* of $50,000 for the purchase of new equipment, including a $32,000 press.

The *Advertiser* was regarded as the Liberal organ in south-western Ontario, and was the only Liberal newspaper of consequence in Ontario that had remained true to Laurier on the conscription issue. As a result thousands of Laurier Liberals had transferred their subscriptions to the *Advertiser* from other Liberal newspapers, notably from the *Globe*, boosting its circulation from 29,000 in 1916 to a high point of 41,000 in 1920, exceeding that of the Conservative *Free Press*.

But it was a dangerous kind of circulation, for in attracting Laurier Liberals from points as distant as Toronto and Windsor, it had alienated Unionist Liberals in its own circulation area. Once the breach was healed under the soothing influence of Mackenzie King its new and distant readers returned to the *Globe* or local newspapers, but those it had angered in its own community were slower to forgive. As a result its circulation plummetted in two years to 26,500, less than it had been in 1916. The *Advertiser* was not yet losing money, but Purdom had lost heavily on other investments, bleeding the *Advertiser* to cover his losses. Thus when its circulation began to fall off the paper had no reserves, and neither Purdom nor the *Advertiser* had the resources needed if the decline was to be stemmed.

This, then, was the newspaper *The Star* bought, a once-great and still respected journal but already on the skids which, in the preceding eight years, had carried thirty-eight Canadian dailies to oblivion. This was the period of greatest newspaper mortality Canada has known, but Mr. Atkinson was confident that with *The Star*'s resources he could make the *Advertiser* the metropolitan newspaper of the rich southwestern Ontario region.

He had originally intended to put Hindmarsh in charge of it, but while the Hindmarshes were packing to move he suddenly changed his mind and decided to send Bone instead. Probably he had in mind clearing the way to promoting his son-in-law to managing editor of *The Star*. However, Bone declined to go on a permanent basis, though at the outset he went for a few days or a week at a time. Maitland also declined to go on a permanent basis, though offered an increase in salary. "Neither Bone nor I had much confidence in the future of the *Advertiser*, and did not want to be identified with what looked to us like a sure loser," he commented later.

In the end Charles Vining, only a year out of university, was sent as managing editor. But the *Advertiser* continued to lose readers, while local merchants showed a decided preference for the locally owned *Free Press* as the medium in which to display their bargains. Circulation campaigns with premiums and hoop-la that had gone over big in Toronto fell flat in London. Just over three years later, in February, 1926, with circulation down to 23,000, Mr. Atkinson had had enough. He asked his close friend of thirty years, J. F. Mackay, who had left the *Globe* and was running a financial agency specializing in the buying and selling of newspapers, to find a buyer for the *Advertiser*.

The only interest shown was by the *Free Press* and it was finally sold to them for $112,500, this price to include the new press and other equipment *The Star* had provided. The *Free Press* kept the *Advertiser* going for another ten years. Vining was recalled to Toronto to be associate editor of the *Star Weekly*.

In the little more than three years Mr. Atkinson had owned it the *Advertiser* lost $292,214.82 on operations and another $189,839.09 on surplus account, for a total book loss of $482,053.91. But if one counts the great deal of free services *The Star* gave the *Adveriser*, such as news from its correspondents at home and abroad, special writers for special occasions, the free use of circulation and advertising experts, and the like, whose salaries were paid by *The Star*, the loss was considerably more than that. Some of the loss on operations could be charged to *The Star*'s profit and loss account to reduce its taxes, but this did not amount to a great deal. Taking everything into consideration, therefore, estimates made at the time that Mr. Atkinson dropped a half-million in this ill-fated venture were not far from the mark.

Many inquests were held by newspapermen over the *Advertiser*, the general verdict being that it just goes to show a successful big city publisher does not necessarily know how to please the readers of a small city newspaper. That was Mr. Atkinson's verdict. "I can't understand it," he remarked frankly to H. S. Sainthill, his chief accountant at the time and later internal auditor. "Everything I do in Toronto is right, yet when I did the same thing in London it was wrong."

Charles Carruthers, the city editor of the *Free Press*, said at the time, "We licked the *Advertiser* by concentrating on local news, particularly anything connected with the tax rate or the cost of living, and by thoroughly covering the news in the small towns of Western Ontario that did not have a daily newspaper, whereas the *Advertiser* was loaded with dispatches from *The Star*'s hot-shot correspondents in Europe." A similar opinion has been expressed by Arthur Ford, editor of the *Free Press*, who added "we were ahead to start with and they couldn't catch us." On the other hand the Ottawa *Journal* placed the blame almost entirely on the economics of the business. "The cost of producing a newspaper has become so high, requiring huge revenues, that all over the country amalgamations, and eliminations have been found necessary," it observed.

Costly as this experience with the *Advertiser* was, it may have been a good thing in the long run for *The Star* and Canadian journalism. Though Mr. Atkinson never admitted an ambition to be a press lord with a string of newspapers, his son believes he had some such idea in mind. If he ever had such a design he dropped it after 1926, concentrating his talents, his attention and his financial resources on building up his Toronto properties.

Chapter 14

YOUNG JOE LEARNS THE BUSINESS

Mr. Atkinson wanted his son, Joseph Story Atkinson, to go into the editorial department when he graduated from the University of Toronto with a B.A. degree in 1926, but Mrs. Atkinson vetoed that. The news department was Harry's domain, and perceptively she foresaw a clash of personalities if son were placed under son-in-law's command.

Since both were able and ambitious men and potential heirs to the Atkinson empire, friction was inevitable, but she sought to minimize it. Thus "Young Joe," as he was to be known until after his father's death, was assigned to learn the business and production sides of publishing. He learned them from the bottom up. His first job while still a student at the university was working in the accounting office during summer vacations for $15 a week.

After graduation he spent a short time in accounting, then went to the composing room where he held copy for the proofreaders. For a while he worked under Walter Harris on the display advertising control desk. He tried selling advertising for a while but did not like it and returned to the office. He worked for a few weeks as secretary for his father, and was recalled several times when the regular secretary Wilfred Palmer was away. The elder Atkinson was a perfectionist and it was from him that "Young Joe" learned to pay the meticulous attention to detail that is one of his outstanding characteristics today.

Mr. Atkinson was a strict but wise counsellor, though there were some who thought he drove his son a little too hard and did not make enough allowance for inexperience. If this is true the explanation may be found in the advice he gave his son when he started work.

"Joe," he said, "because you are the boss' son you will be facing problems that other young men do not have when they start in business. Your fellow employees will be looking for you to presume on your relationship, and your position may be embarrassing." Then he gave this advice: "When you want somebody to do something for you, no matter how humble their position, ask them to do it, don't tell them."

J. S. Atkinson says today that he regards this as the most important advice his father ever gave him. By following it he found the way made easier in his difficult early years in the organization. Even today, when he is president and publisher of *The Star*, he is reluctant to give an order if a courteous request serves the purpose.

His mother was also an important influence in his life. In the top drawer of his desk in the office once occupied by his father is a little leather case about four inches long, the first thing he sees when he begins work each day. In it is a slender rule which unfolds to a foot in length. It is made of solid gold, and was a present from his mother on his twenty-third birthday, April 8, 1927. "I am giving you this," she told him, "in the hope you will always live by the golden rule. Keep it close by you as a constant reminder." It has never been far from him since.

A third influence in his life was Mackenzie King, for whom he had considerable admiration. For many years King was a frequent visitor at the Atkinson home, and despite their differences in age a warm friendship developed between the young man and the Liberal leader. Thus, not only his personal bent but also his admiration for an older man of distinguished station inclined him towards King's social philosophy.

In December 1926, the year he joined the staff, he attended his first meeting as a shareholder. By this time the only owners of common shares outside the Atkinson family were William Mulock, Jr., Miss Aileen Larkin, and Vincent and Raymond Massey. The Masseys and Miss Larkin never attended a meeting but were occasionally represented by their solicitors.

Mrs. H. C. Hindmarsh had been a shareholder since 1917, when the one share held by Dr. Wilbur Harris was put in her name on his resignation as a director, but she did not attend meetings and it was not until after he became a director in 1928 that Hindmarsh held any stock or attended any meetings. He never owned more than one share.

On July 24, 1928, JS was named a signing agent for the firm with his father and Walter Harris, the business manager. His natural inclination led him to the production department, for since school days when he had built and operated one of Canada's first amateur radio stations his interest had been in things technical and mechanical. In 1929 he was appointed production manager, an office he held until he became president in 1957. "I thought it considerate and clever of Dad that when he wanted to give me a promotion and title he appointed me to a job nobody else had ever had round here," JS comments. "Thus nobody had to be displaced and nobody had any reason to feel I was promoted over his head."

That same year, 1929, he had his first experience in labour relations, participating with his father in negotiating the contract with the Toronto Mailers' Union Local 5, which he signed on behalf of *The Star*.

One day JEA threw an arm across his son's shoulders. "I'm so proud of you," he exclaimed, "you are carrying so much more weight around the office than you used to." Young Joe's chest was nearly bursting with pride at this unexpected tribute from his father, but he was soon deflated. "Yes, sir," said his father, standing back and eyeing him judiciously. "I'd say about twenty pounds more." He had estimated accurately. JS had put on about twenty pounds since starting work.

When JS became production manager his father scribbled for him on an ordinary office memo pad, in longhand, his "Four Things an Executive Should Know." These are:

1. What ought to be done.
2. How should it be done.
3. Who should do it.
4. Has it been done.

The original memo has not been preserved, but one in JEA's handwriting given an executive of another company, and by him to JS, hangs framed in a prominent position on the wall of J. S. Atkinson's office. Another piece of advice given to his son by J. E. Atkinson is that he should never hesitate to make a decision for fear he may be wrong.

As production manager J. S. Atkinson was in charge of the garage which, at the time he assumed its management, was on Dalhousie St. It was overcrowded and inconvenient, and in 1930 he persuaded his father to allow him to buy property on Albany Street on which the present commodious garage was built, opening in January, 1932. At the same time he began modernization of *The Star*'s large fleet of trucks.

In December, 1933, the original company, The Star Printing and Publishing Company of Toronto Limited, surrendered its charter, transferring the *Daily Star* and the *Star Weekly* to a new company, The Toronto Star Limited, of which J. E. Atkinson was president. The real estate holdings of the original company were transferred to a new subsidiary, Toronto Star Realty Limited, of which J. S. Atkinson was president. Thereafter JS was in charge of administering the real estate as well as of production and distribution.

On April 17, 1931, *The Star* printed the largest newspaper that had ever been printed in Canada up to that time, sixty-four pages. It was said the press run of 195,000 copies represented a strip of paper the width of a page extending from Montreal to Vancouver. At the request of the library J. S. Atkinson estimated that 160 cords of pulpwood would have been required to make the newsprint. The same year *The Star* led all other Toronto newspapers for the first time in the number of birth and marriage announcements printed. Heretofore the *Telegram* had led. In another ten years *The Star* was to wrest from the *Telegram* its cherished slogan of "The Newspaper with the Want Ads."

By 1934 *The Star* was carrying more display advertising than any newspaper in America except the *Washington Star*. It has not always maintained that position, but for many years it has been among the top four or five in the amount of advertising carried. Simpson's advertisement of January 31, 1934, consisting of eighteen pages, was the largest until that time ever published in any newspaper. Both the circulation and the size of the newspaper had increased so much that seven new press units had to be added to the original twenty-eight units installed when *The Star* moved into its present building in 1929.

In the meantime J. S. Atkinson had been gradually assuming more responsibilities in the business office because of the ill health of Walter Harris, who had been business manager almost since the founding of *The Star*. Harris was also secretary-treasurer of the firm, and when he became critically ill in December, 1933, JS was appointed assistant secretary, though with the full responsibilities of the office. On Harris's death on February 24, 1934, he succeeded him as secretary-treasurer, and was appointed assistant to F. L. Tate, the new business manager. He became vice-president in charge of production and administration in 1940.

Despite his increasing administrative duties after 1933, J. S. Atkinson retained his interest in things mechanical, and established *The Star*'s research department with laboratories in the new garage. Head of this was R. Edgar Wallace, a man considerably older than JS and who had been connected with radio since its inception; before coming to *The Star* he was with the Columbia Broadcasting system. When scarcely out of his teens he had invented a radiant electric heater which had considerable popularity, and he was always working on some invention or other.

J. S. Atkinson and Wallace together invented the Wallastar bundler which is now used by many of the larger newspapers of America for tying bundles of newspapers with wire. How they came to devise it is an interesting story. A representative of a US manufacturer of bundling machines had tried to persuade JS that *The Star* should rent machines from them. The rental would be moderate, but *The Star* would have to contract to buy all the wire used from this firm. Like the manufacturers of safety razors, who make their profit from the sale of blades, it expected to make its profit from the sale of wire. Mr. Atkinson objected to such an arrangement, since wire probably could be bought cheaper elsewhere, but the manufacturer refused to sell the machines outright. The discussion ended with JS suggesting *The Star* might build its own machine, and the manufacturer's agent telling him, with a laugh, to go ahead and try if he thought they could.

JS consulted Wallace and they decided to build a bundler. Wallace proposed that instead of twisting the ends of the wire together, they be welded electrically. To demonstrate it could be done without setting fire to the newspapers Wallace poured a pile of gunpowder on a bundle of newspapers, set two wires on it, and welded them without igniting the powder.

The first model of the Wallastar bundler, so named by combining Wallace and Star, has been described as "a real Rube Goldberg contraption," but it was soon perfected under experimental use in *The Star*'s mailing room. Thomas Sykes, who became head of the research department after Wallace's death in 1945, redesigned it to be completely automatic, the first of its kind, and added other improvements.

The Star manufactured thirty-eight machines which were sold in several countries, but some directors did not believe a newspaper should be in the manufacturing business. Accordingly, to assure that the machine would continue to be manufactured, about ten years ago J. S. Atkinson agreed to a decision of the board of directors giving Cline Electric Company the right to make it in the United States. Cline subsequently went bankrupt and patent rights were transferred to the Goss Company of Chicago. The British United Supply and Machinery Company manufactures it in England for the British and certain foreign markets.

Subsequently *The Star* research department developed a complete line of mailing room equipment with the exception of a stacker. These grew out of a works simplification study in the mailing room about ten years ago, the purpose of which was to reduce the amount of hand labour. These automatic machines were patented under the trade name of *Torstar*, and *The Star* experimented with the feasibility of manufacturing them in its own shops, and contracting with other newspapers to convert their mailing rooms to automatic operation. One of its first contracts, and the largest, was the mailing room in the new plant of *La Presse* in Montreal.

However, a decision was reached to place the manufacture and distribution of Torstar equipment in the hands of the Goss Company also, retaining only the right to manufacture machines for its own use. Torstar equipment has proven remarkably successful, and is used by newspapers throughout the world. Among the larger plants now using these machines are the London *Daily Mirror* and the New York *Times*.

The research department is still an important unit of *The Star* organization, still working on improvements to the equipment used in newspaper plants.

One day in 1937 a man named John E. T. Musgrave called on J. S. Atkinson. He had recently lost his job with a British manufacturer of printing inks, he said, but he knew all the formulas and given the equipment he could make just as good ink as any in the business. He proposed *The Star* should make its own inks. JS thought it a good idea but his father had his doubts. They would have to prove to him they could make as good ink as any commercial manufacturer, and make it as cheaply, before he would invest any substantial sum in their project. JS accepted the challenge and accompanied by Musgrave and Wallace he began hunting for second-hand machines that could be adapted to grinding the pigments and mixing the inks.

They found some in a junk yard, three old chocolate-grinding mills that had been discarded. Bought for $100 each, with only slight modifications these proved to be exactly what was required. They supplied the *Daily* with its first black ink on November 22, 1937. By the end of February, 1938, they were making coloured ink for the *Star Weekly*. In an interview in the *Star Weekly*, Musgrave was quoted as saying they experimented with ninety blacks, twenty reds, twenty blues, and twenty-five yellows before they got the right combination of pigments.

The first ink plant was over the garage on Dupont Street, but it is now adjacent to the new *Star Weekly* building on the waterfront. *The Star* manufactures for its own use only, but its consumption is so large, approximately three million pounds a year, that the saving in manufacturing its own supply has amounted to hundreds of thousands of dollars.

Other useful inventions perfected by Wallace while with *The Star* were a carbondioxide fire prevention system and a device for checking printing registers on rotogravure presses. Wallace died in 1945 at the age of fifty-two.

J. S. Atkinson was bothered by the fact *The Star*'s large fleet of delivery trucks engaged in runs outside Toronto was not being put to the most efficient use, since trucks returned to the city empty. Before the introduction of the Public Commercial Vehicles Act in September, 1928, *Star* trucks had picked up an occasional load of merchandise at the end of their run to bring back to Toronto, but the new act made such traffic illegal without a licence.

An application by *The Star* for such a licence was refused on the grounds it should restrict its business activities to publishing. It was suspected Premier G. Howard Ferguson had personally intervened against *The Star*'s application. This may not have been literally true, but *The Star* had been fighting Ferguson ever since he entered public life, and during the Ferguson regime it was not unknown for government officials to discriminate against *The Star*, knowing it would please the Premier. Nevertheless, some months later *The Star* was granted a class "C" licence which permitted it to transport goods of only one shipper in any one cargo, and only between Toronto and points specified in the licence. This was too restrictive to be of much value, and most of its freight consisted of cordwood hauled from Orillia.

In 1931, Ferguson having been succeeded by George Henry, *The Star* applied for and received a broader license. It held it for only a few months. In a public address on November 26, 1931, before the Automotive Transport Association of Ontario, Premier Henry announced he had personally ordered *The Star*'s licence cancelled because it was offering to haul wood from Orillia for fifty cents a cord less than the railways were charging and this, said Henry, was "unfair competition."

In 1935 Henry was defeated by M. F. Hepburn and *The Star* tried again.

It purchased the business of Lakeshore Transport Company and with it the unrestricted class "C" licence held in the name of Alex Anderson, for which it paid $1,100. This would allow it to operate its trucks on any road in the province and between any two points, but it could haul the freight of not more than ten customers with whom it must have contracts.

Early the next year a subsidiary company called Starways Limited was incorporated with J. S. Atkinson as president, and the Anderson licence and some trucks were transferred to it on March 10, 1936. However, before it could begin operations a new set of regulations under the PCV Act was introduced, abolishing the unrestricted class "C" category. This made it necessary for Starways to apply for the new class "D" licence, which was substantially the same as the former unrestricted class "C."

Anticipating no trouble in getting this licence, Starways Ltd. went after business with determination, and by the end of summer it had contracts with ten industries to haul freight from their plants in provincial cities to Toronto. Three of these contracts were approved by the Department of Highways before the licence was granted and Starways began hauling shirts from Kitchener and flowers from Brampton. Its operations were under the general direction of C. P. Roberts.

However, Starway's application was opposed by the Automotive Transport Association of Ontario, the CNR, and the CPR. Hearings were held before Eric Cross, chairman of the Ontario Railway and Municipal Board on January 18 and 25, 1937, as a result of which Cross denied the application. Starways, he held, was "offering no special service not already available by common carriers." It continued to operate under its old, more restrictive licence, but most of its contracts had to be cancelled.

A year later a commission under Mr. Justice Chevrier held hearings to determine what government policy should be with respect to the transportation industry. J. S. Atkinson presented a brief on behalf of *The Star* and Starways Ltd., on which he was questioned in a somewhat hostile manner by counsel for competing industries. In reply to questioning he emphasized that *The Star* has always argued that the public interest is best served when competition is free of artificial restraints designed to protect the less efficient members of an industry. Asked if he believed a new company should be allowed to put an old established firm out of business, he indicated he was prepared to go that far if the new company was giving better or more economical service.

Evidence had been given at both this hearing and the one a year earlier that some industries had contracted with Starways because its trucks ran on a strict timetable due to the necessity of delivering newspapers without delay. Atkinson testified that where its routes competed with a railway, Starways charged the same rates as the railway, but that when its competition was only with other trucking firms it charged lower rates.

However, as a result apparently of recommendations made by Mr. Justice Chevrier, the Ontario minister of highways notified Starways that its licence would be cancelled as of March 19, 1938. Since then Starways has been dormant, and *The Star* has not renewed its efforts to engage in hauling general freight and express.

The Star did considerable experimenting with various types of trucks and bodies, and one designed to be safer and more convenient for the "hoppers" who throw off the papers at city delivery points was widely adopted. Successive improvements have now made it obsolete, but *The Star* still uses only trucks built to its standard.

Somewhat less practical, though they served their purpose for the time being, were multiple-engine trucks to deliver papers to Kingston. Four tons of *Star*s were being trucked to Kingston compared with one ton of *Telegrams*. No manufacturer at the time was making a fast four-ton delivery truck, and the *Telegram* was regularly beating *The Star* on this route. To get enough power to give *The Star*'s heavier load the speed of the *Telegram*'s lighter trucks, JS had two engines mounted on one chassis. Performance was good, but not all that was required, so a truck with three engines was built. It was a bit complicated to handle, but it had a terrific pick-up and passenger car performance on the road, substantially reducing the running time to Kingston. However, before long manufacturers were bringing out standard trucks with similar performance, and the three-engine model was discarded.

While J. E. Atkinson's interest was entirely in publishing, and he thought of expansion in terms of larger circulation or more publications, his son would have preferred diversification, particularly into fields related to the printing and publishing industries. He had regretted the decision to scrap *The Star*'s radio station in 1933, and later persuaded his father to join with him in an unsuccessful attempt to acquire control of CFRB. He would have liked *The Star* to acquire some interest in the mills that supplied it with paper, but his father declined.

One is tempted to label any man who leaves a fortune of $25 million a financial genuis. He is certainly a man of more than ordinary business acumen. But in the eyes of J. E. Atkinson, the immense fortune that came to him was but a by-product, the reward of being a good newspaperman.

He did not value wealth for its own sake, and did not deliberately set out to become wealthy. When he had more money than he needed he spent it lavishly on his newspapers instead of in ways that would make him more money. When he economized it was for the sake of his newspapers, not to save money for some other purpose. By plowing his money back into *The Star* Mr. Atkinson made it the liveliest and newsiest newspaper in Canada, and despite the maledictions of the politician and the Pharisee, the public responded with as devoted a show of confidence and affection as has ever honoured any newspaper.

In spite of this, one must concede *The Star* would rest on a more solid foundation today had J. E. Atkinson adopted more of his son's ideas. Subsequent events demonstrated they were sound and would have been profitable. And *The Star* would not have suffered as a newspaper, for in some years money was spent more lavishly than was necessary.

In his later years J. E. Atkinson seems to have become converted to his son's conception of vertical integration, for at the time of his death they were planning a newsprint mill on the waterfront site now occupied by the Richard L. Hearn generating station of the Ontario Hydro commission. When efforts to buy control of CFRB failed consideration was given to establishing an FM radio station. The idea was dropped as being premature, which it was at the time.

Chapter 15

FROM RUM TO CIO

The return of the Liberals to power in Ottawa in 1921 brought *The Star* once more into the Liberal ranks so far as federal politics were concerned. Not so in Ontario.

After 1905 *The Star* had supported the Conservative government of Sir James Whitney, a public-ownership man who gave the province Hydro and the Ontario Northland railway. It swung back to the Liberals briefly when N. W. Rowell was appointed their leader in 1911, contributing $2,000 to the Liberal campaign fund. When Rowell called a wartime truce with the new Conservative leader, W. H. Hearst, *The Star* did the same, and when Rowell left provincial politics in 1917 to join the Union government it supported the Hearst government rather than the Liberals in the legislature.

Hearst was a man very much to Mr. Atkinson's liking—honest, puritanical, a prohibitionist, and a friend of public ownership. The prohibition issue arose in 1916 as a war measure, and whatever doubts Mr. Atkinson may have entertained as to its practicality in 1902 appear to have been calmed by 1916. "Pass a war measure at once, without any referendum or device for delay," *The Star* urged. "After the war have a referendum or plebiscite."

The Hearst government did so, and thereafter *The Star* was as staunchly Conservative in provincial politics as any newspaper. This was the easier for it after Rowell left, as the provincial Liberals were ineptly led, badly divided, and devoid of any program.

The Liberals held a provincial convention in 1919 to choose a new leader and their choice fell on Hartley H. Dewart, an anti-prohibition, anti-conscription, anti-public-ownership man who had devoted most of his time in the preceding two years to attacking Rowell as a turncoat. His political record alone was reason enough why *The Star* could not support him, but there was a much more personal reason as well. Hartley Dewart had got the better of *The Star* in a libel suit.

In February, 1915, a domestic servant named Carrie Davis had been charged with the murder of her employer, Charles Albert Massey. She pleaded self-defence and was acquitted. Several women had recently been acquitted in Ontario on murder charges, and the *Star Weekly* ran an article summarizing them all. The article was innocent enough, but the heading was "Ontario Is Easy On Murderesses." Of course, if they were acquitted they were not murderesses, and Miss Davis sued for libel.

Hartley Dewart had been her lawyer in the murder case, and because the woman was poor he had received no fee. Mr. Atkinson believed Dewart persuaded her to sue *The Star* that he might collect his fee from the settlement. The case was settled out of court for a substantial sum, and Dewart got his money. However, this bit of cleverness may have cost him the premiership of Ontario, for orders were given that his name was never to be mentioned again in *The Star*, and publicity is the breath of life to a politician. His name could not be omitted when he was chosen leader, but to show its displeasure the *Star* ran the report of the Liberal convention on page five and made no editorial reference to it.

In the election of October 20, 1919, *The Star* supported Hearst as "the prohibitionist leader of a party opposed in the past to prohibition." A referendum was taken on the same day, giving the electors a choice between prohibition and varying degrees of government control. *The Star* called for "a sweeping verdict for prohibition," declaring that "a province that has experienced the blessings of prohibition is not going to welcome back the liquor traffic." Before the election it sent reporters into counties that had prohibited liquor for many years under the local option provisions of the federal Scott Act. They described how crime was less, health better, poverty reduced, and even industrial disputes less acrimonious in counties where liquor was forbidden.

The referendum resulted in a resounding verdict for prohibition, but also a resounding defeat for the Hearst government which had made prohibition its main plank. Both Hearst and Dewart were personally defeated. The winners were a farmer-labour-veterans coalition without a leader and with a variety of platforms that promised anything to anybody, including prohibition. A few days later E. C. Drury was sworn in as Premier.

The Star had not been caught napping, and was on the Drury bandwagon before one could say "John Wesley." In his behind-the-scenes manoeuvring to heal the breach in federal Liberal ranks Mr. Atkinson had become aware of the strength of the agrarian movement in Ontario, and the possibility a Progressive party might appear on the provincial scene. Moreover, the year after the war had been one of great labour unrest and of political activity on the part of labour. As soon as the war ended he had assigned W. R. Plewman, whose "The War Reviewed" column had been a popular daily feature, to keep him informed on the progress of the farmer-labour political movement. There were only three farmer members of the Legislature, but Plewman cultivated them assiduously, through them won the confidence of leaders of the movement, and soon was able to report to his employer that it was stronger than most people suspected, though even Plewman did not suspect its real strength.

Plewman was a strange man to be sent to ingratiate *The Star* with a left-wing movement. He was the only Tory Orangeman on the writing staff, and how he got on it is an interesting story. In 1903 he gave up the study of law because he wanted to marry his childhood sweetheart, the daughter of H. C. Hocken. On his way to the *News* to begin work as a reporter, a job Hocken had got him, he had to pass *The Star*, and on impulse went in to see Mr. Atkinson. "We need a man of your convictions here," Atkinson told him at the end of an interview. "Every reporter and writer we have is a Liberal. You can keep us from being too one-sided." Plewman remained with *The Star* more than fifty years, half that time as an editorial writer, proudly proclaiming that he was still a Tory Orangeman and that he had never been asked to write anything contrary to his political or religious convictions.

Thanks to Plewman, when the Drury government took office *The Star* had a man close to its leaders and sufficiently in their confidence to exert some influence upon them. In fact, his influence was so widely recognized that a *Telegram* cartoon pictured him as the puppeteer pulling the strings to which Drury danced.

Mr. Atkinson had known and admired Drury ever since the new Premier, as the first president of the United Farmers of Ontario, had backed his demand for conscription of wealth as a wartime measure, and was, therefore, predisposed to support him. Drury chose W. E. Raney, a prominent Toronto lawyer, a Methodist, a leader in the temperance movement, and a personal friend of J. E. Atkinson, to be Attorney General.

In office Drury proved to be a man of liberal temperament. He set up a minimum wage board, broadened the Mothers' Allowance Act, initiated a program of forestry conservation, abolished party patronage, improved the calibre of magistrates and coroners, began an extensive good roads program, and made a determined attempt to enforce prohibition. At the same time he opposed Sir Adam Beck's grandiose scheme for a network of electric railways operated by Hydro, which *The Star* was fighting. As a result he enjoyed the enthusiastic support of *The Star* in nearly everything he did in the four years he was in office.

"Any man who is truly a liberal must desire to see progressive and liberal policies introduced and furthered, even though his own party may not be in office," *The Star* declared. "A newspaper that advocates reforms must be prepared to accept and approve of them and to consider the province fortunate if any fortuitous combination of circumstances makes it possible to see the interest of progress and reform advanced at a pace which would ordinarily not be looked for." King wrote in his diary that the farmers' movement was liberal, but Arthur Meighen called the Drury government "Bolshevists" and by association imputed like character to newspapers and others who supported it, including *The Star*.

Shortly after the Drury government took office, the same split that was plaguing the federal Liberals manifested itself in the Ontario Liberal party. On one hand were those die-hards represented by Dewart who wanted no truck nor trade with the Progressives or the UFO, which was really the Progressive party in Ontario. On the other hand were men like Wellington Hay, house leader of the Ontario Liberals, who believed as *The Star* and King did that the UFO, the Progressives, the Labour party, and all the rest were really liberals who should be wooed back into the Liberal party. At a convention on March 1, 1922, to choose a leader to succeed Dewart, Hay was elected on the first ballot.

"It is evident that Mr. Hay, by adopting sunny ways in the legislature with the farmer government, has followed a policy that has met with the general approval of the party," *The Star* commented the following day. "This may not have found favor with some who prefer to see fighting whether there is anything to fight about or not."

Meantime G. Howard Ferguson had emerged as leader of the Ontario Conservatives. A shrewd politician of vindictive temperament, Ferguson had been involved in a scandal in the forestry department of which he was minister in the Hearst government. When *The Star* sought to have the scandal investigated in 1922, he sued it for libel, but dropped the action before it came to court.

The Star was evidently prepared to pursue the policy in the 1923 election that had proven so successful against Meighen in the federal field, that is, concentrate on attacking the Conservatives while plugging for the Liberals and the UFO-Progressives to get together. But unfortunately for this plan, no sooner was the campaign under way than Drury slammed the door on any deal with the Liberals, and Hay was no Mackenzie King to bring about a reconciliation. The "grass-roots" on the back concessions had seized control of the farmers' political organization in Ontario with results that were to be disastrous to it.

The UFO had been split almost from the beginning between those who wanted a party established on a democratic base broad enough to appeal to all liberal-minded people, and those who wanted an aggressively agrarian party with members of the legislature no more than mouthpieces for farmers' organizations. For nearly four years Drury, the liberal, had successfully held out against the increasingly aggressive attacks of J. J. Morrison, secretary of the UFO and leader of the grass-roots wing, but a month before election day he surrendered. In a public statement he agreed the UFO should be a party for farmers only, even if the result might be to reduce it to an opposition bloc.

The Star reasoned that it could not support a "class party" despite the fact that "in no similar period has so much progressive legislation been put through in Ontario." It did not repudiate Drury, but neither did it endorse him. As for Hay, his campaign was so colourless and the Liberal party's program so uninspired there did not seem much point in supporting them.

Nevertheless, *The Star* attacked Ferguson with extraordinary bitterness, mainly on his record as minister of lands and forests. "Is this the man to be made Premier of Ontario?" it headed a series of front page editorials dealing with his personal career and his alleged leniency towards capitalists who were attempting to get control of Ontario's forests. It barely stopped short of accusing Ferguson of being personally corrupt.

Canadians have shown repeatedly that they do not like a "class party" whether it be farmer, labour, or big business, and the UFO was almost wiped out in the election. The Liberal representation was reduced in number. The Conservative victory, *The Star* commented, was the result of two parties of common aims being unable to come together, combined with the last-minute proclamation of the UFO that it was a party for one class only, the farmers. The farmers, it was to comment later, would have accomplished more for themselves had they recognized the legitimate aspirations of other elements of the community and supported Drury in his policy of democratic reform. Most of the members re-elected by the UFO eventually drifted into the Liberal party. One of them, H. C. Nixon, became Premier of Ontario. Another, Farquhar Oliver, was for years leader of the Ontario Liberal party. Both enjoyed the support of *The Star*.

The Star had suggested as early as November, 1920, that the Drury government might not be re-elected because of its class alignment. Nevertheless, it was shocked by the crushing extent of its defeat, for until the last it had hoped enough UFO and Liberal members would be elected to make a coalition government possible. The elevation to the premiership of G. Howard Ferguson it regarded as a calamity. The only consoling feature it could find was that Ontario had returned to the two-party system. What worried it most were hints from Ferguson that he might liberalize the Ontario Temperance Act. "The Ontario Temperance Act is the best law on the statute books," *The Star* warned the new Premier.

Since 1916 *The Star* had been militantly prohibitionist, and as pressure for the repeal of the OTA increased after 1920, so did *The Star*'s militancy on its behalf. Editorials were infrequent, but the paper was loaded with "news" stories and feature articles purporting to show the great benefits that had resulted from prohibition. *The Star* admitted that prohibition as it was being enforced was ineffective, but even so it believed it better than either open sale or government sale, and that it could be enforced if the government was determined to do so. When enforcement agencies pleaded the difficulty of getting evidence, *The Star* sent its own reporters to visit bootleggers and "blind pigs," and published the evidence they found.

Gordon Sinclair has said that many of the stories were deliberately faked by eager-beaver reporters who knew what would please the Chief. One can readily believe this after reading a series by an anonymous writer purporting to disclose the crime and debauchery allegedly rampant in British

Columbia, where liquor was sold under government control. According to these articles, prominently displayed on page one, the jails were filled, insane asylums were overflowing, opium dens flourishing, white slavery rampant, crimes of violence out of control, half the homes of the province shattered, and wife-beating a normal practice.

It may be that Mr. Atkinson did not find such stories unbelievable for his hatred of the liquor traffic knew no bounds. He believed that because of the enormous revenue to be derived from liquor, greedy politicians would inevitably turn government "control" into government "sale," and all the evils that had existed during private sale would reappear. On the other hand J. T. Clark did not believe prohibition could ever be made to work and tried to dissuade Mr. Atkinson from supporting it. This may account for the fact it was the news department rather than the editorial page that carried on the fight.

Sinclair was referring mainly to reporters sent to probe conditions in Toronto. His comment can not be applied to the series of articles written over a ten-year period by Roy Greenaway, one of the more conscientious and resourceful reporters *The Star* has had. They brought to *The Star* an international fame and to Greenaway a citation and an honorary membership in the Michigan State Police, which he still holds. He became recognized as Canada's leading reporter on the activities of gangsters, rumrunners, and other criminals, and was one of the few to interview Al Capone.

Greenaway's famous series began in 1920 when he was sent to Windsor to investigate the charges of Reverend J. O. L. Spracklin, a young Methodist minister and former motor mechanic, that the Canadian side of the Detroit river was lined with "dens" catering to Detroit residents, and that drunkenness, debauchery, and gambling "were unparalleled since the wide-open mining camps of the West." He reported that Spracklin had not exaggerated.

On July 27 Spracklin was appointed by the provincial government to head a special enforcement squad to clean up the border. For five months Greenaway lived with this special force, accompanying them on their raids. More than once he narrowly escaped death as gangsters fired from ambush on law-enforcement cars or boats in which he was riding. His assignment came to an end when Spracklin, during a raid, shot and killed Beverley Trumble, operator of the most notorious of the roadhouses, and the special force was disbanded. *The Star*'s only editorial comment on the affair was to criticize the government for not giving Spracklin enough men, squad cars, and armed boats to do the job properly. Raney admitted Spracklin had too few men and announced the regular law-enforcement agencies would be augmented. "The government has intimated it will employ a regiment of soldiers if necessary. That is the right spirit," *The Star* approved.

By 1923 Greenaway was established as an international authority on rum-running and his articles in the *Star Weekly* were being widely reprinted in US publications. In February 1923 he secured pictures of a rum-running detachment of some seventy-five men hauling sleds loaded with whisky across the frozen Detroit river. The following November, accompanied by an RCMP corporal, he drove a high-powered speed-boat into the midst of a rum-running fleet of twelve fast launches out in the Detroit river, and with the policeman operating the boat he took a number of pictures. That same day he was sworn in as a special RCMP constable which permitted him to carry a gun legally and accompany RCMP patrols. His articles and pictures led to a strengthening of US law-enforcement units at Ecorse, Mich.

It has been argued with considerable justification that Greenaway's articles had an effect exactly the opposite to that intended by Mr. Atkinson. Meant to prod the government into stricter enforcement of the law, instead they convinced the public of the ineffectiveness of prohibition, and thus contributed to the defeat of the Drury government.

Nevertheless, *The Star* set out to prove to the new government of Premier Ferguson that all that was wrong with the Ontario Temperance Act was lack of enforcement. In January, 1924, it began publishing a series of articles by Greenaway on bootlegging in Toronto, which it described as "reading like a 17th century adventure story." In February it sent him back to Windsor, where he engaged a boat, loaded it with Canadian whisky, and, accompanied by a Detroit photographer, joined the rum-running fleet. On some of his trips he was accompanied by an RCMP constable in plain clothes.

Two years later, in August, 1926, Greenaway was sent again to Windsor, this time on behalf of the Federal Liberals. The Mackenzie King government had been defeated in the House in June and Arthur Meighen was Prime Minister again. Meighen in his turn was quickly defeated in Parliament and called an election for September 14. This was the election in which King made the issue the constitutional impropriety of Governor General Byng calling Meighen to form a government. The Conservatives tried to make the issue a scandal in the customs department while King was Prime Minister. *The Star* set out to demonstrate that conditions were even more scandalous under the Conservatives. This was to be done by getting evidence that rum-runners, with the connivance of customs officers, were clearing loads of liquor for export which they then "short-circuited" to roadhouses and bootleggers on the Canadian side.

Accompanied by Charles H. Gundy, a reporter who was a competent short-hand writer, Greenaway hired a boat from a known rum-runner, cleared it for export, and openly made deliveries to roadhouses along the Canadian waterfront. He described the roadhouses well enough for them to be identified, but did not name them. He made a similar investigation of rum-running out of Port Colborne to Buffalo.

Premier Ferguson immediately ordered the owners of the Windsor roadhouses arrested, and had summonses issued for the appearance of Greenaway and Gundy as Crown witnesses. The trial was set down for three days before the election. Ferguson's intention was plain. If Greenaway and Gundy observed the practice of most reporters and refused to testify against sources of information the bootleggers would be acquitted, with doubt thrown on the accuracy of *The Star*'s charges against the customs department in time to affect the election. If Greenaway testified he would be branded as a "government spotter" and his usefulness as a crime reporter ended. Ferguson thought he stood to win either way.

An employee in the attorney general's department tipped *The Star* to Ferguson's intentions in time for it to hide its two reporters before the subpoenas were served. In announcing what it had done, *The Star* said it had acted to prevent the use of its reporters as "government spotters." They were kept in seclusion until after the election, which resulted in Meighen's defeat and the return of King.

The *Border Cities Star* described the trial, which was held September 18, as "the most amazing episode in the administration of justice in the province of Ontario." The prosecution made no pretence that it had prepared a case against the bootleggers or intended to convict them. The intention had been solely to embarrass *The Star*. Since Greenaway and Gundy declined to testify, the charges were dismissed in ten minutes. That night the owners of eight roadhouses and of the dock used by the rum-runners treated Greenaway and Gundy to a banquet in their honour at the Chappell House, where Spracklin had killed Trumble six years before.

Possibly this episode did more than anything else to establish Greenaway in the minds of both the police and the underworld as a reporter who could be trusted, and make it possible for him to develop some extraordinary "scoops" both in Canada and the United States. Some of his exploits rivalled those of the fictional "private eye," but his quiet, unassuming personality did not lend itself to exploitation, and he was never as colourful a writer as some of his colleagues.

After the era of gangsterism ended he became *The Star*'s reporter at Queen's Park, the provincial legislature, respected by members of all parties. His hobby is painting and one of his pictures was bought by the provincial government. It hangs in the office of the premier. Another is owned by former Premier Leslie Frost.

Mr. Atkinson was always convinced prohibition could be made to work if "the liquor interests" had not bribed and corrupted the politicians, and he was forever hoping to uncover the corruption he believed existed. This led to a mysterious incident that has never been adequately explained.

From a source he had reason to believe was trustworthy he received information regarding payments allegedly made to a member of Premier Ferguson's cabinet by a bootleg ring, supposedly to buy "protection." While still having this investigated he received threats on his life, which he took sufficiently seriously to notify the RCMP. And the RCMP was sufficiently impressed to give Mr. Atkinson a gun and a bodyguard. Close-mouthed reporter Claude Pascoe, a former major in the "Black and Tans," was made a sort of decoy, shadowed wherever he went by the RCMP in the hope his apparent activities would lure the supposed gangsters into the open.

After two weeks of this Mr. Atkinson received word from Ottawa that his life was not in danger. Were the threats a hoax? Or did the RCMP arrest somebody? It was never disclosed. Mr. Atkinson had given orders that no member of his family or of *The Star* organization except Pascoe was to be told of the threats, and all Pascoe was told was that he was no longer needed as a decoy. Years later members of the family were mystified at finding a revolver among their father's possessions. As for the exposé Mr. Atkinson hoped for, it was never published, but it was not revealed whether he discovered it was a frame-up or merely dropped it for lack of sufficient evidence.

The Ferguson government went to the electors in December, 1926, with a pledge to introduce government control if elected. *The Star* attacked Ferguson almost entirely on his liquor policy. Nobody knows the extent of Mr. Atkinson's personal contributions towards the cause of defeating Ferguson though they were considerable, but *The Star* gave the Ontario Progressive party $5,000 and the Ontario Temperance Federation a like amount. There is no record of any contribution from the newspaper to the Liberal campaign fund, though this does not rule out a personal contribution from Mr. Atkinson.

While the campaign was in progress *The Star* ran a series of revelations of the day-by-day life of Mussolini. In connection with these Gregory Clark wrote an article in the *Star Weekly* comparing Mussolini's daily life with that of "the two Canadian Mussolinis," Howard Ferguson and Mayor Foster of Toronto.

The Conservatives were re-elected and on June 1, 1927, the Ontario Temperance Act was superseded by the Liquor Control Act. "It's a mistake," Mr. Atkinson told Maitland, but after the heat of battle had died down he conceded the possibility that a policy of strict government control which made it possible but not easy for determined drinkers to buy a bottle might also serve the cause of temperance. However, he held that people who did not drink should not be encouraged to do so by advertising. *The Star* has not advocated prohibition since 1927, but has persistently opposed any relaxation of liquor laws.

While the introduction of government control ended *The Star*'s militant prohibition policy, it by no means ended its fight with Premier Ferguson. This reached its climax in September, 1930, when Ferguson ordered all Ontario government offices throughout the province closed to *Star* employees and correspondents.

The Star had been carrying speculative stories for several weeks predicting a reorganization of the Ferguson cabinet. There had been scandals and rumours of impending scandals in several departments, and *The Star* was trying to smoke them into the open. It had five reporters at Queen's Park in addition to the regular correspondent, each assigned to keep constant watch on a particular cabinet minister. Some ministers were under virtual 24-hour surveillance.

High on the list of those likely to be removed stood the name of Dr. Forbes Godfrey, Minister of Health, who among his other sins had been so indiscreet as to add this postscript to a letter written a constituent: "I trust you will vote Conservative next time." On September 16 Dr. Godfrey was summoned to the Premier's office. While waiting in the anteroom the reporter assigned to trail Dr. Godfrey heard him shout loudly and angrily, "I won't resign, Ferguson." He telephoned what he had overheard to the office, and a story was published to the effect that Ferguson had demanded Dr. Godfrey's resignation, but that the minister had refused, defying the Premier to force him out. Godfrey's words were quoted.

In an interview in the *Mail and Empire* the following morning Ferguson called *The Star*'s story "a falsehood from beginning to end with not the slightest vestige of truth in it." Later that day he wrote a long letter to Mr. Atkinson, copies of which he gave the other newspapers, demanding that *The Star* retract its report. "I am prepared to issue instructions to every department head, cabinet minister and every official of the Buildings to refuse *The Star* news and not let their representatives in any office," he warned. "Further I will fire anyone who disobeys the instructions and does give them news. In doing this and demanding a retraction I am determined to show the people of the province that what they read in *The Star* regarding Queen's Park is neither authentic nor official." The letter was printed in *The Star*.

"It is quite unnecessary for Mr. Ferguson to 'show' the province that *The Star*'s news reports about Queen's Park are not official," *The Star* retorted. Ferguson therefore issued his order on September 18. At the same time he sent a lengthy letter to *The Star*, which concluded with the statement: "This attitude is not to be construed in any sense as a reflection upon the reporter who has been representing you at the Parliament Buildings."

"The press is an institution like the Legislature that goes on and on while men come and go," *The Star* chided. "Man is like the grass which groweth up in the morning and in the evening it is cut down and withereth. Even Premiers tarry but a little while. Mr. Ferguson is the seventh Premier of Ontario *The Star* has seen in office and it will see many more of them, some of whom will bluster and threaten even when the skids are under them and they are on their way out . . . No doubt *The Star* vexes Mr. Ferguson from time to time . . . Mr. Ferguson frequently vexes *The Star* . . . We don't get along." The Biblical language stamps the authorship. It was written by Mr. Atkinson himself, according to Joe Clark the first editorial he had personally written in twenty-one years.

The Star refusing to retract the story, the ban at Queen's Park went into effect and the following day was extended to include provincial police, magistrates, and all other government employees and officials throughout the province. Without expressing an opinion as to the accuracy of *The Star*'s report, the *Telegram, Globe* and *Mail and Empire* instructed their reporters at the Parliament Buildings to furnish *The Star* with carbon copies of everything they wrote.

"There is a distinction between personal courtesies and those official facilities which a newspaper requires in order to secure routine news for its readers," observed the *Telegram*, adding that Ferguson had a right to break off personal courtesies extended *The Star*, but that was as far as he should have gone. On the other hand the *Globe*, which had been assailing *The Star* for alleged pro-communism, accused it of colouring the news from Queen's Park, while *Saturday Night* observed that *The Star* "has wilfully misrepresented him [Ferguson] and his colleagues on many occasions."

It is true *The Star*'s attacks on Ferguson throughout his administration were exceedingly bitter, but whether he was "misrepresented" is another matter. Twice Ferguson issued writs for libel against *The Star* but failed to pursue them, and he persistently refused to permit public inquiries at which accusations made by *The Star* could have been disproven had they been false.

In general the provincial press chided Ferguson for his ban, but was not as forceful in supporting *The Star* as Mr. Atkinson could have wished. Indeed he felt somewhat hurt at the indifference it showed. In fighting the Ferguson administration Mr. Atkinson believed he was fighting for honesty and integrity in government. He believed Ferguson's ban on *The Star* was not only unlawful, but also an unjustifiable restriction on the freedom of the press to get news, and he had expected the other newspapers to take the same position.

It may have been that other newspapers were unconvinced of the accuracy of *The Star*'s report. Two days after its editorial reproving Ferguson, the *Telegram* reported it had interviewed the reporter who wrote the story and he said he had been dismissed. Ferguson also issued a statement that the reporter had been "fired" for deliberately writing an untrue story. This was an unusual statement from Ferguson. Usually he charged that stories he claimed were untrue were "fabricated in *The Star*'s office."

It is a fact the reporter went off payroll the day after the article appeared, but so did eleven others at the same time for reasons of economy. His name reappears on the payroll a week later, which suggests he may have been suspended a week without pay. It is impossible to ascertain the facts now. *The Star* said it had printed the report in the belief it was true. Thus, though never insisting on the story's truth, it did not retract it, for which it was criticized by the *Financial Post*.

W. H. Price, who was Ferguson's Attorney General, told the present writer in 1961 that Ferguson and Dr. Godfrey had explained to the other cabinet ministers at the time that all that had been asked was Godfrey's resignation as medical health officer at the Ontario Hospital, a mental institution at Mimico, near Toronto. Price said that because of attacks by *The Star* Ferguson had ordered his ministers to resign from any other offices they might be holding. Dr. Godfrey had been MOH at this hospital for twenty years, regarded it as his hobby, and refused to give it up. The reporter had heard the words correctly, but jumped to the wrong conclusion. That, at least, was Ferguson's explanation.

On the other hand the reporter always insisted, both to his editors and to other reporters, that he had spoken to Dr. Godfrey immediately after the meeting, and that Dr. Godfrey had confirmed that he had been asked to leave the cabinet. Ferguson, he maintained, had seen an opportunity to deliver a wicked kick at *The Star* and had seized it.

Two days after imposing his ban Ferguson left on a trip to Europe. He never resumed active responsibilities as premier, for the newly elected Prime Minister, R. B. Bennett, appointed him High Commissioner to London. On October 7, 1930, Leopold Macaulay, provincial secretary, informed his department heads in writing that "*The Star* is entitled to any public information that it wants," and his example was quickly followed by other ministers. The ban had lasted three weeks. It had not prevented *The Star* from getting what information it wanted, though it added to the difficulty.

Shortly before the federal election of 1930, Mr. Atkinson had written King: "Hope has come to me out of your leadership. You personalize the social and economic liberalism which has in our generation succeeded to the older political liberalism whose principles are now universally accepted." But King was defeated and Bennett, a man for whom Atkinson had but slight regard, was in his place.

When the *Mail and Empire* referred to *The Star*'s "dislike" for Ferguson and Bennett, *The Star* responded with a gentle editorial that was Joe Clark at his best.

> *The Star* entertains no dislike, neither hearty nor otherwise, for either Mr. Bennett or Mr. Ferguson. With the policies of these public men we disagree. With the courses they take, the speeches they make, it happens we very often find fault. They belong to a school of political medicine which we distrust, and they dose the body politic with nostrums in which we have no faith. But as for these men personally, we entertain no dislike whatever, and can readily understand how it is that they enjoy a great popularity with their own political following.

When Ferguson's resignation as Premier of Ontario was announced in

December *The Star* reprinted Mr. Atkinson's editorial about premiers withering like the grass, with a short "We told you so" introduction and a concluding sentence hoping Mr. Ferguson was ashamed of himself. When asked if this wasn't "rubbing it in a bit" Joe Clark tilted his cigar at a rakish angle, winked, and replied, "That's what The Chief intended."

Before Ferguson sailed for England, without consulting his party he named as his successor "Honest George" H. Henry, a man Mr. Atkinson and most of the Ontario cabinet ministers considered unfit for the office. He demonstrated the justice of their judgment by never winning an election, though *The Star* can claim slight credit for that. He was defeated by a Liberal leader it had accepted reluctantly and with misgivings.

The sad state of the Ontario Liberal party had long caused Mr. Atkinson considerable concern and as early as March, 1926, he had written King on the necessity of strengthening the leadership. Since their defeat under Wellington Hay in 1924 the Liberals had been led in the legislature by W. E. N. Sinclair, but the office had gone to him by default and he was not the choice of a convention. If there is to be a change, Mr. Atkinson told King, "it is necessary to know in advance upon whom the mantle is to fall."

There was not a prospect anywhere in sight, and it was not until 1930 that the Ontario Liberals decided in desperation to call a convention. The date was set for December 18. As the day approached it became apparent the mantle was likely to fall upon either Mitchell F. Hepburn, MP for Elgin West, or Elmore Philpott, associate editor of the *Globe* but inexperienced in politics. *The Star* did not think much of either of them, and for that matter neither did Mackenzie King.

The day the convention opened, it hopefully reported a rumour Hepburn had decided to remain in federal politics, and advanced the names of several "dark horses" as possible candidates. But when a "draft Hepburn" movement developed it gave it extensive publicity with a friendly biographical sketch. After the convention had elected Hepburn, it continued to ignore him on the editorial page, while commenting with approval on the platform the convention had adopted. It contributed generously to the Liberal war chest in 1932 and 1933, and to individual Liberal candidates in the 1934 election, including Philpott. But it was not until Hepburn won the election that it became reconciled to his leadership, and then with reservations.

"I think Hepburn is strengthening the Liberal cause in Ontario," Mr. Atkinson wrote King. "This is so at present, whatever may be the result ultimately. My opinion of him has become more favorable since the elections. I can see nothing but a sweeping victory in this province when the federal elections come off."

Atkinson's first judgment of Hepburn was to prove the more accurate. Ultimately, Hepburn wrecked the Ontario Liberal party and did his best to wreck the party federally. On the other hand, the forecast of a Liberal sweep in the federal elections proved correct, and King was returned to office in 1935. Scarcely had the ballots been counted than Hepburn was off to Ottawa to tell King whom he should appoint to his cabinet. As the boy wonder who had saved Ontario from the Tories in 1934, he claimed most of the credit for the Liberal sweep of his province in the federal election and demanded the homage he felt his due. When it was withheld he turned against King with venom.

King believed Hepburn was a demagogue, a fascist at heart, and a threat to democracy, and by 1937 Atkinson was ready to agree with him. Hepburn opposed the welfare state, so cherished by Mr. Atkinson, as contrary to "true Liberalism," but at first *The Star* preferred to remain silent where it could not agree with him. But the time was soon coming when it could remain silent no longer. That time came in April, 1937, when Hepburn formed an alliance with George McCullagh, the new publisher of the *Globe and Mail*. The two simultaneously declared war on the CIO (the Committee for Industrial Organization), "foreign troublemakers," "international labor agitators," and Prime Minister Mackenzie King. McCullagh had proclaimed his newspaper the voice of "true Liberalism," by which he meant laissez-faire liberalism as opposed to King's concept.

The CIO had been formed in the United States in 1935 to organize the workers in such industries as mining and automobile manufacturing in which the craft unions, by the limitations of their trades, performed only a minor role. Employers resisted labour organization on an industry-wide basis, and there were many strikes with some violence. When the CIO began to organize workers at the General Motors of Canada plant at Oshawa into the United Automobile Workers, Premier Hepburn vowed he would "keep the CIO out of Canada." *The Star* admonished him that industrial unions were "the next step in the inevitable progress of trade unions."

"We do not profess to know," it said a few weeks later, "but it seems to us that about every 50 years trade unionism needs to revise its technique in an industrial world which, over the heads of labor, is changing itself in a most revolutionary manner . . . Employers, and indeed all who want the capitalistic system to continue, must reconcile themselves to industrial negotiations in which labor will be on a more even footing with capital."

When the workers went on strike at Oshawa on April 8, 1937, and Hepburn vowed he would smash their organization, *The Star* took no sides upon the merits of the dispute as regards wages and working conditions, but it took a very emphatic stand upon the impropriety of the government seeking to deny workers the right to belong to a union of their choice. "Employees have the right to organize, the right to select whatever union or form of unionism or affiliation they may desire, the right to choose their representatives, and the right to bargain collectively . . . ," it declared. "No government is warranted in forcibly interfering with labor so long as labor is doing only those things which the law sanctions." When the CIO was attacked because it was controlled in the United States, *The Star* said: "For 60 years the effective trade unions of Canada have been international unions. They will necessarily be international in the future."

When Hepburn mobilized a force of three hundred provincial police and swore in two hundred university students as special police to suppress the Communist uprising he professed to fear at Oshawa, *The Star* warned of the dangerous course he was taking. "The fear of Communism by which Mr. Hepburn is trying to excite the people of this province is the pretext that Fascism is using in all countries as it pushes its advances in its efforts to overthrow Democracy," *The Star* declared on April 14, 1937. It added that regrettable as was the violence that accompanied some strikes, it was not because of this that industry opposed the CIO but because "industrial organization gives workers their maximum strength."

Mr. Atkinson was deeply disturbed by Hepburn's attitude. He believed it to be a denial of basic democratic rights that could only end in catastrophe for the provincial Liberal party. On April 9, the day after the strike began, he called upon the Premier in his office at the Parliament buildings to plead with him to reconsider the course upon which he was embarking. The meeting took place in the presence of Provincial Secretary Harry Nixon, and Attorney General Arthur Roebuck. It began on a conciliatory note, with Mr. Atkinson hoping to persuade Hepburn of the error of his ways, but it ended in a violent quarrel.

While testifying a year later at a meeting of a special committee of the Legislature investigating Hydro, Hepburn related his version of what had happened. "Mr. Atkinson said if I continued to disagree with him on the CIO question he would persecute me, and attack me personally, and would not let up until he had driven me from public life," he said. "Mr. Atkinson shouted so loud he could be heard in the outer office. He was in a terrible frame of mind and argued and raved to almost inconceivable length over the action the government had taken to prevent the CIO invasion of the peaceful Oshawa scene. I was amazed at the effect and that he could be in so violent a temper."

"As was his way, Mitch over-dramatized what happened," Nixon told this writer. "The men disagreed, but I don't recall Mr. Atkinson making any threats."

"Absurdly untrue," said Roebuck in an open letter to the press the day after Hepburn gave his version of the meeting. "I was present at that interview from beginning to end . . . and I am definite in saying there is not one word of truth in all that paragraph. There was no threat of any kind; there was no loud talk; Mr. Atkinson was not in a terrible frame of mind, and he showed neither violence nor temper."

The "terrible frame of mind" seems to have been all on Hepburn's part, for it was at this meeting, in the presence of Atkinson and Nixon, that he turned on Roebuck and angrily dismissed him from the cabinet for questioning his CIO policy. Later that day he called reporters to his office, including Keith Munro of *The Star*, and in their presence dictated a letter to Roebuck formally notifying him of his dismissal. Roebuck testified at the Hydro hearing that George McCullagh, publisher of the *Globe and Mail*, was present with the reporters. He said Hepburn had told him earlier that McCullagh had said he would drive him, Roebuck, out of public life unless he was dismissed. David Croll, Minister of Labour and Welfare, resigned April 14 over Hepburn's CIO policy. Both were later elected to the House of Commons and subsequently appointed to the Senate.

After this abortive interview Mr. Atkinson assumed personal direction of the campaign on behalf of the Oshawa automobile workers. There were no pretentions *The Star* was neutral or that it was covering this as "just another news story." It was fighting for the right of workers to join the union of their choice, and its position was that those who opposed that right had no case worthy of presentation. H. C. Hindmarsh, who was by this time vice-president as well as managing editor, was absent on vacation and thus had no responsibility for subsequent events.

Frederick Griffin and Roy Greenaway were sent to Oshawa to cover news developments, Atkinson instructing them to report directly to him rather than to the city editor. It was not unusual for him to telephone them three and four times a day with instructions, and he personally edited their copy. H. R. Armstrong and T. J. Wheeler were assigned to write front-page editorials on aspects Mr. Atkinson suggested. Some days the editorial page was almost entirely devoted to the strike.

At the same time Mr. Atkinson was in almost daily communication with the union leaders, and it was on his suggestion that Hugh Thompson, international organizer for the CIO, withdrew from negotiations, leaving C. H. Millard, chairman of the Oshawa local of the United Automobile Workers, as chief negotiator. Thompson was a Canadian, but as head of the CIO representation he had been attacked as a "foreign trouble-maker," and Hepburn had refused to allow negotiations to proceed as long as he had anything to do with them. His withdrawal permitted Hepburn to resume discussions with both parties without losing face.

The strike was settled April 23 on terms suggested by Mr. Atkinson. As he related the story three years later, early on the morning of April 20 there came a knocking at his door. It was a deputation from the Oshawa local of the UAW. They told him both parties were eager for a settlement, but both had made such extravagant statements that neither could back down without losing face. Could he suggest a formula that would make it appear neither side was surrendering to the other?

He suggested that the contract should be between the company and "its employees who are members of the UAW," without any mention of the CIO. Even the UAW as an organization need not be a party to the contract. Both sides accepted this formula. The company signed a collective agreement with employees who were members of a CIO union, and all who signed on behalf of the union were CIO officials. But so far as the company was concerned, it was signing with its own employees, not with the CIO, and it had not "recognized" the CIO.

The *Telegram* and the *Globe and Mail*, who did not know of the part Mr. Atkinson had played in bringing about a settlement, proclaimed that the strike had been lost and the CIO kept out of Ontario—a claim that was quickly disproven. Thompson, the CIO organizer, protested at first that the local UAW leaders had no authority to act without prior approval of international headquarters, then was silent.

Though *The Star* placed the blame for the strike squarely upon Hepburn's shoulders, saying that the company and the union would have settled their dispute peaceably had they been left alone, General Motors had warned Atkinson that if *The Star* continued to support the strikers it would withdraw its advertising. Since Mr. Atkinson would never submit to dictation by advertisers, this threat was ineffective. As a result General Motors and about thirty other firms connected with the automotive industry, including manufacturers of tires, batteries, and other components, stopped advertising in *The Star*.

One of the complaints of the company was the activities of Griffin, which it believed exceeded the bounds proper to a reporter. Though his news reports were factual, he had become emotionally involved on behalf of the strikers, and had been indiscreet enough on one occasion to address a strike meeting. On his return to work Hindmarsh, who was never as extreme in his labour views as his father-in-law, was quite upset at the way the strike news had been handled. Griffin, whose salary was reduced, always believed he was unfairly penalized for his part in it, for he had been working directly under Mr. Atkinson's instructions.

General Motors withheld its advertising for several weeks. Friendly relations were restored when its general manager, H. J. Carmichael, called upon Mr. Atkinson and they had a chat in which Atkinson explained that *The Star* had never disputed the right of an employer to use any legal means to get the better of a union in a labour dispute. Its quarrel had been with the intervention of the provincial government on the side of one party, and the attempt to deny employees a right of choice permitted employers. "We believe that in great industries great unions are necessary," the *Star* commented. "Believing so, our course was plain . . . The result shows that we were right."

With the rights of labour established, *The Star* hastened to make clear that it held no anger against Hepburn, only sorrow. "*The Star* has been a supporter of Premier Hepburn and we hated to go back on him," it said in an editorial May 1. "But we, as a liberal newspaper, hated to see him suddenly become a more Tory Premier than this province has ever had in office. He acted upon his large fund of inexperience in connection with trade unionism, which was greatly augmented by his intimacy with the new publisher of the *Globe and Mail*, who knows nothing of trade unionism, but who is deeply concerned with gold mining . . . The objection we took to the action of Mr. Hepburn was the futility of it."

The *Ottawa Journal* had reported during the strike that not only did George McCullagh attend upon Hepburn both before and after strike conferences, "but he is reported to have been with Mr. Hepburn during actual strike negotiations." The *Windsor Star,* which supported Hepburn, quoted him as telling its correspondent "the strike there [at Oshawa] is merely a pawn in a much larger game." The "larger game," he explained, was the drive of the CIO to organize the gold-miners. Roger Irwin, former secretary to David Croll, wrote in the *Nation* that the campaign against the CIO was dictated by gold-mining interests who had persuaded Hepburn to make Oshawa the battleground. Irwin later joined the staff of *The Star* and played a prominent part in the first attempt of editorial workers to get a contract. It was recalled that William H. Wright, the gold-mining man who financed McCullagh's purchase of the *Globe*, said he did so to give mining a voice. "Anything that is of advantage to mining is of advantage to the country as a whole," Wright said in an interview.

In a remarkable series of conciliatory editorials beginning early in May *The Star* reviewed Hepburn's record which it found on the whole to be good and, except in labour affairs, generally liberal. Clearly it was prepared to let by-gones be by-gones if he would drop his feud with the CIO. Imagine its horror, therefore, when Hepburn tried to negotiate a coalition with the Conservative opposition to set up a one-party government in Ontario the better to fight communism, socialism, labour unions, and Mackenzie King. Fortunately Earl Rowe, who was then leading the Conservatives in Ontario, would have none of this.

Even then it did not slam the door, and in the provincial election campaign of October, 1937, it was cautiously pro-Liberal. This was after the quarrel in Hepburn's office, but before Hepburn had accused Atkinson of threatening to hound him from office. When Hepburn made his accusations, Atkinson commented that the fact *The Star* had supported Hepburn in an election was "sufficient refutation" of his "wild charge" that he had threatened to drive him from office. *The Star*'s final editorial before the voting was a notably impartial and somewhat lengthy summing up of the issues and personalities, but it concluded with this statement: "We think there is more to be hoped for from a Liberal than from a Conservative administration in Ontario during the next four years."

A year later it would have willingly eaten even this mild endorsement. Hepburn formed what C. D. Howe, speaking in Port Arthur on December 10, 1938, called "an unnatural political alliance" with Premier Duplessis of Quebec to force the resignation of King and establish a one-party National government at Ottawa "which would be largely controlled by the provincial governments at Toronto and Quebec." The following day King made a similar reference to this "alliance." *The Star* likened this Hepburn-Duplessis axis, as it was called, to Mussolini's march on Rome which overthrew a democratically elected government and established a fascist dictatorship. Hepburn, it declared, is no longer leading a Liberal party but "some sort of third or fourth party . . . that substitutes uncouth rudeness for courtesy in public life, promotes Canadian disunion instead of unity, and is allied with a non-Liberal party in Quebec which is led by Mr. Duplessis." Hepburn by this time was opposing the St. Lawrence seaway, which *The Star* and the federal Liberals supported, and insisting Ontario be allowed to export power, which *The Star* and the federal Liberals opposed. The time is coming, said *The Star*, when Ontario will not have enough waterpower for its own needs. That time came sooner than even *The Star* expected.

In December, 1938, it was running almost hysterical editorials on the front page, two columns wide and the full depth of the page, calling on all Liberals to stand firmly behind Mackenzie King and democracy and against Hepburn's destructive ambitions.

When George Drew was chosen leader of the Ontario Conservative party on December 8, 1938, it came close to welcoming him as the saviour of Ontario. It gave the convention that selected him bigger coverage than it had ever before given any political convention, not even excepting the one that chose King. It chose to forget that Drew was the leader of a faction within the Conservative party that had wanted to join Hepburn in a one-party government, for by this time it believed the most important issue in Ontario politics was getting rid of Hepburn. It even forgave Drew for magazine articles he had written that were critical of King and his minister of defence.

It did not exactly say it would support Drew, but it began laying the groundwork for doing so if Drew proved amenable to reason. Its first comment, the day after the convention, was one of satisfaction that the schemes of the *Telegram* and the Toronto Tory organization had been foiled, for neither wanted Drew. This it regarded as a major point in his favour. A week later in a friendly editorial it observed that he began as provincial Conservative leader "with a clean slate," and could make what he wished of his political career. Though Mr. Atkinson personally distrusted some of Drew's friends, *The Star* said his victory "is a victory over the old guard." He was a young man, it said. It had great hopes for him and it wished him well.

A year later it was attacking Drew as fiercely as it had ever attacked Hepburn, for instead of being the white hope who would unseat the renegade provincial Liberal leader, he had formed an alliance with him and McCullagh to unseat King. The "Toronto clique," the *Telegram* named this association, for it distrusted it as much as *The Star* did. For the next ten years it was to be one of the most unsettling influences in Canadian politics.

Chapter 16

RAZZLE-DAZZLE AND ROYALTY

Ad Astra

To Hindmarsh and Knowles Mr. Atkinson spoke:
If we don't sell more papers *The Star* will go broke:
I've three super-salesmen who say they can sell
They're Jesus and Dickens and Edith Cavell.

CHORUS:

Come fill up our columns with sob stuff and sex
Shed tears by the gallons and slush by the pecks.
Let the presses revolve like the mill-tails of hell
For Jesus and Dickens and Edith Cavell.

As a lover this Dickens is really the bunk
His letters are long and his technique is punk
But he looks kind of sexy, his whiskers are swell
And besides we've got Jesus and Edith Cavell.

Edith Cavell is the best of the lot
It's always hot news when a woman is shot.
Get plenty of pictures for those who can't spell
Of Jesus and Dickens and Edith Cavell.

CHORUS:

Then hey for the paper that strives for the best
(If Jesus makes good we'll put over Mae West)
With the cuties and comics and corpses and smell,
And Jesus and Dickens and Edith Cavell.

This derisive bit of doggerel written in 1934, it is alleged by two anonymous members of the Toronto Writer's Club, ridicules one of the distinctive practices of *The Star* which reached its apex in the 1930's—that of reprinting popular literary works that lend themselves to exploitation. While most newspapers ran serial stories that were really a form of "soap opera" in print (one such serial ran nearly twenty years) Mr. Atkinson was always on the alert for good non-fiction. Among his early ventures along that line were excerpts from the biographies of Queen Victoria and General Lord Roberts in 1902. In 1923 *The Star* had run Winston Churchill's history of the First World War.

In 1934 it exceeded anything it had previously done. The year before had been the worst of the depression and, as already noted, almost every newspaper in the country except *The Star* lost circulation and even *The Star* gained only 794. Within the city of Toronto *The Star* lost 1,200, but since the *Telegram* lost 6,000 the year-end found *The Star* leading its rival in the city by about 4,000, the first time its city circulation had ever exceeded that of the *Telegram*. With a total circulation of 210,788 it was outselling the *Telegram* three to one in the suburbs and ten to one in the province outside the suburbs. Undoubtedly the *Telegram*'s support of the unpopular Bennett government lost it readers, while the social welfare legislation advocated by *The Star* could not but be popular in a time of depression.

Once city circulation was ahead of the *Telegram*, Mr. Atkinson determined to keep it there. There was a proverbs contest, not very successful for the first prize was only $200. On January 25 *The Star* began running two to four pages a day of official Canadian and British army photographs from the First World War, including some of the most gruesome pictures ever published. This accounts for the reference to "corpses and smell" in the last verse of the poem. On March 5, 1934, it began serializing *The*

Life of Our Lord by Charles Dickens, overlapping the war pictures. This was followed, beginning March 21, by a serialization of *The Crime That Shook the World*, the biography of Edith Cavell, the British nurse who was executed by the Germans.

The "three super-salesmen" did an excellent job, for in March and April, when these three features were running, *The Star*'s circulation reached a peak for the year that was unusually high. Circulation declined, as it always does, with the approach of summer, but the average of 225,000 for 1934 was the highest of any year to that date. Thereafter *The Star*'s circulation forged rapidly ahead while that of the *Telegram* remained relatively unchanged until about 1945.

But was the job of the "three super-salesmen" solely, or even primarily, to sell newspapers? Many, including the authors of the poem of 1934, thought it was. Others, like *Time* magazine, sensed a more profound purpose behind the publication of these pictures and articles.

"Leading the anti-war campaign is Canada's largest newspaper, the rich, radical Toronto *Star*," said *Time* in an article in 1935 on the spread of pacifism. Pacifism at the time was strong everywhere but in Germany and Japan, and student pacifist leagues were being organized in Canada, the United States, and Britain. As a pacifist, Mr. Atkinson was sympathetic towards these movements, but he chose to support them by publishing graphic proof of the horror of war rather than by editorials lauding the pleasures of peace. The Edith Cavell biography and the 1934 series of war pictures were not overtly pacifistic, but their lesson was clear. When, in 1935, *The Star* ran a second series of war pictures it chose to point the lesson more emphatically. Here are some of the headlines that appeared over full-page spreads in 1935: "Modern War Seeks in Vain to Appear Heroic," "How Can Heroism be Applied to Peace?" "Who Will Dream for Us a Fairer Vision than War for the Use of Man's Divine Gifts." This series showed soldiers dying horribly of poison gas, soldiers of several nations fighting and drilling with the same make of machine gun, and preparations in Paris, Berlin, and Tokyo to protect civilians against gas attacks. In two years, *The Star* ran more than 8,000 war pictures. At the same time *The Star*'s two correspondents in Europe were hammering daily at the threat of Hitler, Mussolini, and the rise of fascism to peace, while the pacifistically inclined articles of Dr. Salem Bland and Rev. Charles H. Huestis were being published regularly on the editorial page.

Whether Mr. Atkinson's hope was that these pictures would fire a determination to stop the dictators or whether they were intended to encourage neutralist sentiment in Canada is not clear. Perhaps he had no very definite intention. They showed how terrible war was, and he may have thought that justification enough.

"Three super-salesmen" whose real purpose was perceived by so few at the time! They sold newspapers because they appealed to the deep longing for peace in the hearts of men and women, but they also strengthened that longing. Quite often Atkinson did things the real purpose of which was not perceived until much later.

The Star never tried to "put over Mae West" as the anonymous poets hinted, but in 1936 it "put over" another movie star, Mary Pickford, serializing a novel published under her name.

The 1930's were years of great expansion for *The Star*. Depression years though they were, economic and political conditions favoured it. The Conservative party and conservative principles, for which the *Telegram* stood, were at their lowest in public esteem and were soon to be rejected by the voters in every province. Even Tory Toronto was to give the Conservatives only 38 per cent of the popular vote in the 1935 election.

But even allowing all reasonable credit to favourable circumstances, these alone could not have given *The Star* such commanding leadership in almost every field. The major credit must be given *The Star*'s aggressive news policy, its imaginative promotion, and its progressive editorial policy. The welfare state was taking form in Canada and the United States, and people liked it. They had had enough of the depression's hardships and worries. They wanted security, and the newspaper that fought for security for the little man was given his support.

"Fun poking aside, 'sob stuff and sex . . . comics and corpses' are by no means the major product of *The Toronto Star*," commented *Time* in printing the verses at the head of this chapter. "It is a thoroughly highly organized newspaper. No venture is too great or too small for its attention. . . . Spectacled, meticulous, kindly, Publisher Atkinson is called 'ruthless' by his competitors, 'determined' by his friends. He wields great political influence."

One day a senior executive of *The Star* in Montreal on business was invited to the home of Lord Atholstan, the former Hugh Graham, publisher of the *Montreal Star*, shortly before the latter's death in 1938 and they chewed over *The Star*'s phenomenal success in a period when so many other papers were folding. "It's too bad Atkinson didn't take that job with me when I offered it to him," Atholstan said. "There's no telling where the two of us couldn't have gone together."

"Gone together!" Mr. Atkinson hooted with laughter when told of this conversation. "Nobody ever 'went together' anywhere with Hugh Graham. He keeps his executives on too short a halter." Atkinson's faithful retainer restrained himself until he was out in the corridor, then he, too, hooted with laughter. Look who was talking about a short halter!

The 1930's have been called "the razzle-dazzle period" of *The Star*. There had always been a bit of razzle-dazzle about the newspaper. Mr. Atkinson liked it, his son-in-law even more. Until about 1927 its activities were limited by financial considerations. But the time came when the newspaper owed nobody a cent, when it was making more money than its owner could use for his own needs. If he chose to spend money lavishly to get wildly fantastic scoops, there was no reason why he should not. And that was his choice. Some have said he did it because he loved the excitement. Others that he realized it was good business to expand while his competitors were cutting their budgets. Perhaps both considerations played their part.

"The razzle-dazzle period" of tremendous scoops really began in September, 1927, when Hindmarsh got Mr. Atkinson out of bed one night to overrule Bone. There was a terrible storm on the upper lakes and great freighters had gone down or were missing. The *Agawa* was a wreck with some of her crew members who had been saved in serious condition in hospital at Mindemoya. The *Lambton* was on a reef, the *Martian* was aground, the *Kamloops* was missing, and the *H. W. Oglebay* was on fire. Every available reporter was sped to the scenes of the wrecks.

Greenaway and Griffin arrived in North Bay to find no way of getting to Manitoulin Island except by train the next afternoon. Hindmarsh wired them to hire a special train, and when Bone refused to OK the expense of $562 Hindmarsh got Mr. Atkinson out of bed to authorize it. Thereafter Bone was little more than a figure-head in the news department. As yet without the title, Hindmarsh was already in fact the managing editor.

Griffin worked thirty-eight hours without going to bed and filed 12,000 words on this story. To get it all in, with pictures, the size of the paper was increased by four pages. Ken MacTaggart, then a reporter, relates that a few days later Hindmarsh stomped into the office with a sheaf of papers in his hand.

"Who authorized Mr. Lawson [Lawrence B. Lawson, a reporter] to hire a taxi and drive all around Manitoulin Island at a fare that must have been only slightly less than the value of his cab," he demanded.

"Not I," the city editor hastily disclaimed.

"I'm afraid I'm to blame," confessed his young assistant meekly. "I'm sorry that without special thought I let *The Star* in for such an expense."

"I only wanted to know who to commend," Hindmarsh rumbled. "Thanks to you, Mr. Lawson and Mr. Greenaway (whom he met in Little Current) were the only reporters in America to get any pictures."

How they got the pictures is an amazing story of ingenuity. This was in the days before electric flash bulbs, the time was night, and the only cameraman available was an amateur with a No. 3 folding Kodak and no flash powder. "What is the composition of flash powder? Isn't magnesium its main constituent?" asked the doctor at the hospital in Mindemoya. He routed out the high school chemistry teacher, who confirmed his opinion, and got some magnesium from the school laboratory. They just about set fire to the hospital with their home-made flash, but they got a good picture which they were able to rush to Toronto in time for the next day's paper.

Jimmy Nicol tells a story which illustrates Hindmarsh's recklessness with money when a news scoop was concerned. Nicol was night editor in the first days of the war when a submarine was reported in the St. Lawrence. He hired two planes to take reporters and photographers to Montreal, and a couple of other planes to stand by in Montreal in case they were needed. A few hours later the submarine was identified as a floating barrel and an expenditure of close to $1,000 had gone for nothing. Trembling in his boots, Nicol awaited Hindmarsh's arrival next morning.

"I guess I pulled a boner," Jimmy said tentatively.

"I guess you did," Hindmarsh replied severely.

"I guess I'm in trouble?" Jimmy hazarded.

"I guess you are," Hindmarsh retorted, "but," rolling his cigar in his mouth, "in not nearly as much trouble as you would have been in if there had been a submarine and you hadn't sent those planes." And that was the end of the matter.

The most spectacular scoop *The Star* ever made was in April, 1928. It still remains one of the great scoops of newspaper history, for *The Star* beat all news services and some of the greatest newspapers in America.

The story began when word was received that the German aeroplane, *Bremen*, attempting to make the first east-to-west non-stop flight of the Atlantic, had been forced down on Greenely Island, off the Gulf of St. Lawrence near the border between Quebec and Labrador. Their goal had been New York. Only the year before Lindbergh had made his famous flight in the much easier west-to-east direction. The crew of the *Bremen* consisted of Baron Guenther von Huenefeld, who had contracted in advance to sell his story to the Hearst newspapers, Major James Fitzmaurice, of Ireland, who had contracted to sell his story to the New York *Times*, and Capt. Herman Koehl, who as a simple crewman was being left out of the big money. *The Star* had arranged with Hearst for von Huenefeld's story.

The crash made it anybody's story who could get there first, and no sooner was the "flash" on the crash landing received in newspaper offices than the New York newspapers, news agencies, syndicates, and newsreel companies began the most exciting race for a story this continent has seen. It cost the life of one aviator, the famous American flier Floyd Bennett. Pitted against the great newspapers and news services of the United States, *The Star* in two exciting weeks got and printed an unparalleled spread of exclusive news stories and pictures, including the first published photographs of the wrecked *Bremen* and its crew.

When *The Star* learned that "Duke" Schiller, the veteran bush pilot, accompanied by Dr. Louis Cuisinier, was going to try to rescue the fliers from the island seven hundred miles from the nearest settlement, it arranged to pay him $7,000 for his exclusive story, any pictures he could take, and anything he could get from the fliers. It contracted with the North American Newspaper Alliance to syndicate these in the United States. Then it ordered Frederick Griffin and photographer Tom Wilson to Murray Bay, the end of steel on the north shore below Quebec city. When they found more than sixty reporters and photographers waiting at Quebec for the one train a day, they shared the cost of chartering a special train with the Fox Newsreel people. They had to call on the train crew to help throw off other newsmen who tried to clamber aboard, but they beat the pack to Murray Bay.

Schiller was unable to land within fifteen miles of Greenely Island and had to complete his rescue mission by dog sled. On his first trip out he brought Major Fitzmaurice and the only pictures of the three fliers taken at the wreckage, flying them to Lake St. Agnes, the Murray Bay airport on which planes landed on skis in winter, pontoons in summer.

By this time competition was so hot one US agency tried to buy Lake St. Agnes to keep all but its own planes from landing on it; another syndicate bought all the gasoline at Quebec airports in the hope of grounding competition. A New York newspaper offered $20,000 for a single picture, while another offered $3,500 for a roll of film taken on an amateur camera. A newsreel photographer paid $20,000 for a seat on a small plane two reporters had chartered. Bad weather prevented it from getting through. With the bidding so fierce, Schiller's pictures found their way into the pocket of a New York newsman. Griffin, a big man, beat him up and took the pictures away from him.

There were only three telegraph lines from Murray Bay. The New York *Times* leased one of them and Griffin tied up another by giving the operator a copy of the *New Republic* to file to *The Star*. This left only one telegraph line for forty reporters, and *The Star* and the New York *Times* were the only newspapers to get out complete stories that day. The *Times* threatened to sue Fitzmaurice for breach of contract because of an interview he gave Griffin, and which ran under his by-line in *The Star* several hours before the first of his by-lined stories could be published in the New York morning newspaper.

Meantime Griffin had dispatched two planes to Montreal, the first conveying Tom Wilson's pictures of the arrival of Fitzmaurice at Lake St. Agnes, the second the pictures taken by Schiller of the *Bremen* crash which Griffin had secured too late to send on the first plane because of the aforementioned difficulties. The first plane reached Montreal where it was met by Roy Greenaway, who put Wilson's pictures on the night train to Toronto. But the second plane, with the much more important pictures, was forced down at Quebec by bad weather. *The Star* chartered a special train to bring them from Quebec to Montreal, where Greenaway had a set printed for North American Newspaper Alliance. He had written authority in his pocket to charter a special train from Montreal to Toronto, but decided to bring them in by taxi, driving all night in bad weather. He pulled up at *The Star* office in the morning to find J. E. Atkinson standing on the sidewalk to welcome him. At noon and without rest Greenaway was ordered to Murray Bay to replace Griffin, who was being sent to New York to cover the arrival of the fliers in that city. Greenaway arrived at Lake St. Agnes to find that von Huenefeld and Koehl has not yet arrived from Greenely Island. They were to be flown out in a New York *World* plane piloted by Bernt Balchen.

By being the courteous gentleman he is by nature, Greenaway persuaded the airport manager to allow him the use of the lookout tower in which was the only telephone to town. While less mannerly reporters fought and jostled to interview and photograph the fliers, Greenaway sat comfortably in his big window, telephone in hand, seeing and hearing everything that was done and said on the ground below, and dictating his story to W. O. Trapp, New York *World* reporter, who was sitting at a typewriter in the Murray Bay telegraph office.

Greenaway and Trapp had earlier made an agreement. Greenaway was to be the legman, getting the story, while Trapp, a fast man at a typewriter, was to write it for both newspapers. To keep two telegraph lines open they had filed to both *The Star* and the *World* the same copy of the *New Repub-*

lic Griffin had used. After their stories had been sent they closed the wires to competing newspapers by the same means.

At 5 o'clock Hindmarsh in Toronto received a pleading telephone call from United Press in New York. "Every paper in the United States is waiting for news of the rescue of the fliers, and we learn your man has the wires tied up," he was told. Hindmarsh made a deal on the spot to sell *The Star*'s exclusive to United Press.

This was the last time in Canada a reporter was permitted to hold a telegraph wire open to his paper by filing a magazine or book. The howls of rage against Griffin and Greenaway for the trick, which newspapers had practised for years, was so great that Canadian telegraph companies adopted a regulation that wires could be reserved only if legitimate news was being transmitted.

Griffin's scoop on the *Bremen* rescue was included in a book *Behind the Headlines*, published in 1932, as one of the fourteen greatest stories by North American newspapermen. He was the only Canadian mentioned.

To do justice to the razzle-dazzle exploits of *The Star* and its indomitable band of reporters in the next twelve years would require a book much larger than this one. Merely to mention them all would fill pages. They had the opposition dizzy, while editors from afar viewed with amazement. When *The Star* set out to get a story no expense was spared and reporters on out-of-town assignments had the expense accounts of minor Oriental potentates.

"I really don't know whether these scoops pay or not," Mr. Atkinson remarked to W. G. Wittels, of the *Saturday Evening Post*, who had asked him if all this expenditure of money and energy was worth while. "I have never sat down and figured just what effect they have on circulation. But," and his eyes twinkled, "they are a lot of fun." Reporters found them a lot of fun, too.

No doubt Mr. Atkinson was being facetious, for every day his circulation manager laid on his desk a report of the number of *Star*s the public had bought the previous day. He knew to the last nickel how much every big scoop brought in. As early as 1921, when *The Star*'s total circulation was still under 100,000, an exclusive interview with escaped murderer Norman Garfield resulted in a one-day increase in sales of 32,000. The next day the Chief gave the reporter who got it a big increase in pay; he knew the value of a scoop, all right! And with the kind of raises he gave, reporters knew it, too.

In 1929 *The Star* sent Gordon Sinclair on the first of his famous tours of the world in the course of which he visited more than eigthy countries in ten years. Though he had been a good general reporter for several years, he first attracted public attention when he joined a party of hoboes in the spring of that year and "bummed" his way to New York. This was in boom times, just before the depression broke, when "tramps," as they were called then, were a novelty.

Sinclair's articles from faraway places were sheer escapism, a valuable and popular safety valve in such times of tension as the depression. He did not concern himself with politics, or wars, or rumours of wars, leaving that to men like Griffin, Clark, Halton, van Paassen, and others. He wrote about the romantic places everybody wanted to visit, and things everybody wanted to see, and old and young alike thrilled to his adventures in India, Africa, and the South Sea Islands. On his departure for a trip in 1933, he was given such an enthusiastic send-off Massey Hall could not hold all who wanted to wish him "bon voyage."

What he wrote was not great literature or enduring literature, and his observations when he ventured into making any were superficial, but he became the most popular of *The Star*'s corps of writing stars. In the intervals between his trips overseas Sinclair served in a variety of strange occupations. One year he was a sports columnist, another year women's editor. But usually he was a general reporter, and an exceptionally able one, for he was a newspaperman of initiative as well as a pungent writer.

In the 1930's other *Star* staffers covered two wars and trouble spots on every continent but Australia. Hindmarsh had said "World news is Canadian news," and he was accused by his critics of regarding world news in the same light as domestic news—just another story to be cleaned up in a hurry by a staffer sent from the office. This does both Hindmarsh and *The Star* an injustice. *Star* reporters did some of the most vigorous and well-informed writing to come out of Europe in those years. The misfortune is they were too often lonely voices.

In 1932 the newspaper profession was given dramatic and tragic demonstration of the circulation-building power of a story that tore at the heart. On March 1, 1932, the 19-months-old son of Charles and Anne Lindbergh was kidnapped from the family home. On May 12 the body was found; the child had been murdered. In the two-and-a-half months between the kidnapping and the discovery of the body public interest was at fever pitch. A graph kept by *Star* librarian "Biddy" Barr shows circulation rising to an unprecedented peak while the search for the kidnapper was at its height, then dropping sharply with the solution to the crime. That was one of the few years in which *The Star* did not use an artificial circulation booster in March, but the average circulation gain for the year was more than 19,000, the largest in any single year to that date. The experience of newspapers in the United States was similar. No other news story had a like effect on the circulations of Toronto newspapers until Hurricane Hazel struck the city in 1954.

The Star was in the throes of one of its drastic economy waves when, on May 28, 1934, a one paragraph "flash" from its North Bay correspondent reached telegraph editor Gerald Brown. A woman named Dionne had given birth to quintuplets at an obscure crossroads hamlet called Corbeil. The story was already hours late, for Dr. Alan R. Dafoe had puttered around most of the forenoon in a daze after his shattering experience of delivering the five before he thought of telephoning the news to the North Bay *Nugget*. Brown barely had time to rush the "flash" into the Home and Sport edition, closing time 1:30 p.m., under a two-column heading.

Then he began gnawing his finger nails. All photographers but Tom Wilson had been laid off, and Tom was also running the darkroom. Reporters could not be sent out of town except on the most earth-shattering stories. Long-distance telephone calls had to be cleared in advance with the news editor, Drylie. Brown decided to follow the rules in an economy wave. He wired the correspondent to send a 300-word interview with the father. It arrived in time for the next edition. "I'm the kind of a man who should be put in jail," said Dionne under a two-column heading.

For three days *The Star*, like every other newspaper in the country, used Canadian Press stories originating with the *Nugget* and photographs by Richard Railton, a North Bay photographer. Dr. Dafoe said two of the babies were going to die anyway; if they did, it was not a story anymore. Then R. E. Knowles, returning from a visit to his home town of Galt, got into conversation with the man in the seat beside him on the train, who introduced himself as Charlie Blake of the Chicago *American*. He was on the way, he told Knowles, to North Bay with an incubator for the quintuplets and a shipment of frozen mothers' milk. The two weaker quintuplets had fooled everybody by living for three days. The Chicago *American* was going to try to keep them alive.

Knowles' report threw *The Star*'s top brass into a state of consternation. Economy wave or not, *The Star* could not allow any other newspaper to get ahead of it in exploiting a story in territory it regarded as its own. Hastily a nurse was hired, a large incubator procured, and five complete layettes bought. These, with Gordon Sinclair and Fred Davis, were piled into the powerful Graham-Paige automobile kept for *The Star*'s flying squad, and with Keith Munro at the wheel they set off for Corbeil and the quintuplets.

Blake, travelling by train, beat them there but the incubator he brought was only big enough to take one infant, the smallest and weakest one. The other four were put in *The Star*'s incubator, while the trained nurse took over from the two practical nurses who had been looking after the babies. *The Star* sent three more incubators the next day. Meantime, the quints got the jaundice, Mrs. Dionne got the 'flu, and it was several days before Davis was able to take any pictures.

And unfortunately, in sending Sinclair *The Star* had forgotten that so far as its readers knew to the contrary he was still looking for adventure in Grand Bassam on the Ivory Coast. Sinclair had returned only a few days before from a trip to far-away places, and as often happens in such cases *The Star* still had a half-dozen of his unpublished stories on hand. It would be confusing to have him filing stories simultaneously from Corbeil, where a woman had five babies, and Grand Bassam, where a man had five wives. It was decided to leave him, figuratively, on the Ivory Coast until his series had been published. He therefore had to stand by while Munro wrote how *The Star* was saving the quints from perishing in much more restrained style than Sinclair would have used.

Meanwhile the big US syndicates and news services had become aware that something of a miracle was happening in Corbeil, and began bidding with the four guardians the Ontario government had appointed for exclusive rights to stories and pictures of the quintuplets. *The Star* bid too, but was soon eliminated, for no single newspaper could compete against the money these big groups were offering. World rights were sold to Newspaper Enterprises Association, on terms which realized about $117,000 for the quintuplets, and from them *The Star Newspaper Service* acquired exclusive rights in Canada. Fred Davis was hired as official photographer, a position he occupied for five-and-a-half years until the exclusive rights expired. In 1937 the Ontario government appointed Munro business manager for the quintuplets.

The Star had been winning commendation for its newspaper excellence for many years. "One of the liveliest and most progressive (newspapers) on this continent . . . rated among America's finest," was the praise of Frank Parker Stockbridge, editor of the *American Press*, after one of its successful news beats. Not all its awards were for editorial excellence. In one year, for example, it won two awards from *Editor & Publisher*, one for imaginative circulation promotion, the other for the promotion of its great news scoops, that is, for letting people know when it gained a scoop. This was largely the responsibility of circulation manager Kenneth McMillan, who had begun as a reporter, and the various promotion managers who were associated with him from time to time, but everybody in the organization played some part in them.

Sometimes it was hard to draw the line between promotion and legitimate news, or even between promotion and charity. One of these borderline cases occurred in November, 1935, and though nothing *The Star* ever did brought it more favourable and widespread publicity, newspapers throughout Canada and the United States paid it the compliment of ascribing its act to genuine humanitarianism without ulterior motive.

In November, 1935, Harry O'Donnell was arrested for the brutal sex killing of Ruth Taylor in a Toronto ravine. Mrs. O'Donnell was in hospital very ill after giving birth to a baby. She had heard of the discovery of the girl's body just before leaving for the hospital and expressed violent loathing for the murderer. Hospital authorities had kept from her the papers reporting her husband's arrest, but she kept calling for a daily newspaper and asking whether the criminal had been found.

City editor John R. Heron remembered the old story of how a newspaper had eased the dying hours of a British statesman by printing for him a one-copy edition omitting reference to his incurable disease. The day of O'Donnell's arrest he had the forms for two pages broken after the edition had been run off the press, cut out O'Donnell's name wherever it appeared, and inserted new leads and new headlines. A single copy was sent Mrs. O'Donnell at the hospital, while police had the arrested man send his wife a note saying he had influenza and wasn't allowed to see her. For eight days Mrs. O'Donnell got her special edition of *The Star* before the doctor decided she was strong enough to be told what had happened.

Newspapers all over the continent reported what *The Star* had done and many wrote editorials commending it. The *Christian Science Monitor* spoke of *The Star*'s "delicacy of feeling." *Time* wrote: "City editor John R. Heron is a man with a good heart, prime news sense, and a taste for old anecdotes. Last week he combined all three with dramatic results."

In the municipal elections of December, 1935, *The Star* astonished everybody, not the least the candidates, by opposing the re-election of James Simpson as mayor. After his defeat in 1914 because of his socialism, Simpson was out of politics until 1930, when he was elected to board of control with the support of *The Star*. He was elected mayor for 1935, again with *Star* support.

Simpson made the mistake of trying to be mayor and continue his activities as labour leader at the same time, and these latter took him away from the city for considerable periods at a time. Most of the load was carried in his absence by Samuel McBride, a former mayor who had returned to municipal politics and was president of the council. In mid-term Mr. Atkinson sent Maitland with a warning to Simpson. Either he give up his labour work and attend to business as mayor, or *The Star* would not support him for re-election.

"Nonsense!" Simpson retorted. "J. E. Atkinson will support me in any election I run in," and he paid no heed to the warning. When McBride announced he would oppose Simpson, *The Star* supported him, giving as its reason Simpson's lack of leadership. The *Telegram* ran a cartoon of a dagger dripping blood, captioned, "*The Star*'s Christmas present to Mayor Simpson." McBride was elected.

In this election Mr. Atkinson had to choose between two men he liked. In a long political career, including two years as mayor, McBride had stood for the progressive legislation supported by *The Star*, including downtown redevelopment. They had fought side by side for a more humane approach towards the distribution of relief which had been carried out in a manner seemingly deliberately designed to humiliate.

As a controller from 1932 to 1936 McBride had campaigned to have relief paid in cash instead of in clothing and food. When McBride first suggested cash relief *The Star* ran a strong editorial opposing it, saying it would lead to abuses. The next day it reversed its stand, saying McBride was right and *The Star* had been wrong. Women, it said editorially, should not have to go dressed in a uniform just because they were poor, and that would be the result if the relief department distributed clothing bought in mass quantities. It conceded some cash relief might be misspent, but it maintained it was an affront to human dignity to deny relief recipients the right to spend their money as they chose. Eventually relief was distributed in cash.

On October 31, 1933, H. C. Hindmarsh was appointed vice-president. At the same time Vernon Knowles, the Knowles referred to in the ditty at the head of this chapter, was named managing editor. Knowles, like Mr. Atkinson, had once contemplated entering the ministry but gave it up to become a reporter. After a distinguished career in the United States and Western Canada he was brought East by *The Star* to be news editor. He remained only a short time before moving to the *Mail and Empire*, but quarrelled with the publishers of that newspaper when they introduced sweeping pay cuts.

Readers of *The Star* must have found the announcement of his appointment and Hindmarsh's promotion somewhat confusing. Pictures of the two men were run side by side in three columns, with separate cutlines under each picture. "Mr. Hindmarsh has been managing editor of *The Star* and now, without relinquishment of his past responsibilities in connection with the news department, has been made vice-president of the company," said one set of cutlines. "Vernon Knowles has resigned his position as executive editor and director of the *Mail and Empire* to assume direction of the news department of *The Star* as managing editor," said the other set of cutlines.

That is, Hindmarsh was not "relinquishing" his responsibilities but Knowles was "assuming" them. Before long Knowles was complaining that he was only a figurehead, and was beginning to suspect that the only reason he had been hired was to prevent him from going to the *Telegram*. He left *The Star* on December 31, 1936, to become public relations adviser to the Canadian Bankers' Association. Hindmarsh continued for several months as his own managing editor, but in mid-1937 appointed T. J. Wheeler, a young man who had been associate editor of the *Weekly* since 1935.

There were other important staff changes in those years. W. A. Hewitt, who had come to *The Star* from Montreal with Mr. Atkinson, resigned as sports editor in October, 1931, to become manager of the new Maple Leaf Gardens, taking his son Foster with him as manager of the Gardens' radio department. Hewitt was succeeded as sports editor by his assistant Lou Marsh, the first office boy hired by *The Star* after it was founded. He became the most famous sports editor in Canada.

Hewitt had set the pace in 1900, putting *The Star* in the lead as a sports paper, and it was never overtaken. There was scarcely a sport in which he was not interested, and at one time he was said to be on the executive of twelve sports associations. But his greatest contribution was to the development of hockey, John Ross Robertson of the *Telegram*, who was also an ardent hockey fan, referring to him as "the miracle man of hockey." It was the newspapers of Toronto that put the game on the map, and nobody did more than Bill Hewitt. Possibly his zeal exceeded his prudence in boosting hockey, for a month after his departure the two afternoon papers imposed a ban on advance stories on any professional game. Amateur sports were exempt. The publishers said in explanation that professional sports is a business, and should be treated like any other business, but Mr. Atkinson's chief concern was to prevent professional sports from corrupting the integrity of his writers.

Marsh was a cub reporter on general assignments when Mr. Atkinson came to *The Star*, but had already distinguished himself in several fields of sport. He was known for the sometimes incredible distances he ran, carrying his copy to the office so no other newspaper could beat *The Star*. At Hewitt's request he was transferred to the sports department, and his column, "With Pick & Shovel" became one of the most widely read features in any newspaper.

In 1925 Alexandrine Gibb, Canada's leading woman athlete and Olympic star, began covering women's sports for *The Star*, and her column, "No Man's Land of Sports," also attracted wide readership. When Marsh was appointed sports editor she became assistant editor. Her column was discontinued during the war.

Marsh died March 5, 1936, at the age of fifty-eight after having worked forty-three years for *The Star*. "Surely the most fascinating personality in the sports world," Gregory Clark wrote in his obituary. Marsh founded the sportsmen's fund for the Star Santa Claus Fund and each year raised a large sum for that charity from the sporting fraternity. In 1908 he took Tom Longboat, the Indian runner, to the Olympics and fame; once on a bet he swam from Niagara Falls to the bellbuoy and back, a distance of fourteen miles; a man of great courage he is known to have saved at least fourteen lives.

Marsh was more than just a sports writer; he was a notable athlete in his own right. He played almost every game, and at the time of his death was said to have refereed more hockey matches, professional and amateur, than any other man. He refereed thousands of boxing bouts. The *Mail and Empire* said his "opinions influenced policies and actions of sports officials throughout Canada," while the *Globe* referred to him as "one of the all-time greats of hockey refereeing."

His funeral was the biggest Toronto has ever seen, and *The Star* devoted more columns to his passing than to that of any other man until the death of J. E. Atkinson. For this it was criticized by the *Telegram*, which remarked that *The Star* gave 1,700 inches to the death and funeral of Marsh compared with 1,250 inches to the death and funeral of King George V. "There is no comparison between the death of a king and the death of a sports editor," the *Hamilton Spectator* chided the *Telegram*. "No attempt should be made to make one. No death among the world's great touches quite the same spot in the heart as the passing of a friend. And many thousands of individuals thought of Lou Marsh as a friend."

In Marsh's memory Charles E. Ring, sportsman and investment broker, donated the Lou Marsh Trophy to be awarded each year to Canada's outstanding athlete. Miss Gibb was named secretary of the awards committee.

The office of sports editor was left vacant for almost a year. Among others called upon to try their hand at it was Gordon Sinclair. However *The Star* announced on April 1, 1937, that Fred Jackson, who had begun as a "printers' devil", would be the new sports editor. Two years later he was succeeded by Andy Lytle, who had come to *The Star* in 1934 from the *Vancouver Sun*.

Death and retirements took their toll of other old-timers. Harry Parr, one of the founders of *The Star* and foreman of its composing room for thirty-seven years, died in harness in 1929. Fred Eatherley, who helped get out the first *Stars* in 1892, retired as foreman in the mailing room in 1931. Tom Banton, one of the first reporters, retired in 1932. C. C. Campbell, *The Star*'s first city editor, retired in 1929 but lived on to the age of eighty-five. Walter Harris, who came to *The Star* when it was founded and was for many years a director and business manager, died in 1934 at the age of sixty-seven. W. L. Argue, who started as a door-to-door canvasser for subscriptions in 1894, died in 1939. When he became circulation manager *The Star* had a circulation of 6,000. On his death its circulation was 220,000. Frederick B. Housser, financial editor, died January 15, 1937. Housser's financial ideas were called "heretical" by businessmen, for he wrote incessantly against the paradox of poverty existing in the midst of plenty. Most of Atkinson's financial editors were chosen more for their social ideals than for economic orthodoxy.

The man whose passing was most poignantly felt by those who knew him was Joseph T. Clark, *The Star*'s editor-in-chief, who died July 23, 1937, of a heart attack. He was in his seventy-first year. "He was as incapable of malice in his writings as in his personal relations," wrote Hector Charlesworth, the famous editor of *Saturday Night*. "His style was clear and flexible, and his resources of ironic banter large. Yet beneath the surface he was of very firm convictions, democratic not merely in his surface relations with everybody, but by intense personal conviction. . . . He did a great service to *The Star* by maintaining a dignified and humorous tone in all matters of controversy. The fiercest diatribes were parried by penetrating thrusts, always smilingly delivered. . . . The public loses a man who gave genuine savor to the life of the community."

The *Telegram* saw in his death the closing of an era that had been marked by great Canadian editors who set the standards by which their newspapers were judged. Other newspapers remarked on the number of "partnerships" between great publishers and great editors there had been in Canadian journalism, and saw in this the ending of one of the few remaining.

Joe Clark had been editorial writer or editor for fifty years, an amazing record for any man. His most famous expression, "the twentieth century belongs to Canada," was first used in an editorial written for *Saturday Night* shortly before he came to *The Star*. The *Canadian Annual Review* of 1907 incorrectly stated that Clark used this expression first in an editorial in *The Star*, though it is true he used it in *The Star* before Laurier adopted it as the Liberal campaign slogan in 1900.

Clark was one of the few writers whose editorials were rarely changed by the Chief. Mr. Atkinson did not believe in editorial conferences, and writers were usually free to write on whatever subjects attracted their fancy. They edited their own copy and sent it to the composing room. Mr. Atkinson first saw the editorials in proof the next morning. No attempt was made to "keep on top of the news" and sometimes several days would pass without an editorial on some topical subject, for Mr. Atkinson distrusted snap judgments.

Clark was succeeded as editor-in-chief by George Maitland, who had been his assistant for several years, but the gentle urbanity he had given *The Star*'s editorial page was never recaptured. In his memory the Joseph T. Clark Memorial Cup is given each year to the best newspaper in centres of 1,500 or less population. Maitland remained editor-in-chief until December 31, 1954.

Although *The Star* was attacked in the 1930's mainly on the grounds of its alleged sympathy for communism, there was still in the minds of some people the misconception that it was in some manner hostile to the British connection. *The Star* was, in fact, less hostile to the Commonwealth ideal and the institution of royalty than some British newspapers of the same time. It was commended in the British press for its moderation in handling the crisis which led to the abdication on December 11, 1936, of King Edward VIII. While other newspapers were carrying sensational stories of the King's romance, *The Star* played it down until the British government admitted a crisis existed, a few days before the abdication. Then it treated it as the great world news story it was.

It never lost its sense of proportion, observing that "the event is more interesting than important." After it was over it commented with satisfaction that the Commonwealth rests on a more substantial foundation than the personality of a king. "The view taken by us," it explained, "was that we saw no reason for discussing the issue until the issue took such form that we could be sure what it was. Was it all about a woman, or was it about several things?"

When George VI was crowned the following year *The Star* went the limit in covering the event, hiring Dick Merrill and Jack Lamb to fly the pictures across the Atlantic in order that it might be the first newspaper on this continent to publish them. The race to be first was so intense, and the likelihood a rival newspaper might try to hi-jack the pictures so probable, that Merrill was instructed to deliver them to nobody without the password: "Times are wasted." Merrill won the race, and *The Star* was the first with the pictures.

Two years later the need to fly pictures across the Atlantic no longer existed. An April 5, 1939, the first pictures were sent across the Atlantic by cable, a vast improvement over the radio transmission that had come into use five years earlier. *The Star* had participated with the Associated Press in preparations for the first trans-Atlantic cable-picture service, and for a considerable time was the only Canadian newspaper represented on the AP wire-photo network.

About the same time *The Star* equipped its flying squad with a portable wire-photo unit, under the direction of reporter Alf Tate. Using Bell telephone wires, it was possible to lay down pictures in the office twenty minutes after they were taken anywhere in America. Tate was killed in 1955 when, seeking a feature story, he flew into the eye of a hurricane in the Caribbean.

This portable unit was given its most severe test during the Royal Tour of 1939 when King George VI and Queen Elizabeth visited Canada. In May Gerald Richardson, one of the top free-lance photographers serving *The Star*, had visited Buckingham Palace with Matthew Halton and taken an extraordinary collection of photographs of the royal family, which were subsequently printed in *The Star* and the *Star Weekly* and were widely syndicated.

Gregory Clark, Jessie MacTaggart, Frederick Griffin, and Andy Lytle travelled on the royal train throughout the Canadian tour, with Richardson as official photographer. Gordon Sinclair had a roving assignment, unattached to the royal party and writing what he wished. Other reporters and photographers were assigned to cover the party by automobile, particularly while they were in Ontario. Tom Wilson was loaned to the government and took the official photographs available to all.

On May 22, 1939, the *Star Weekly* published a Royal edition, crammed with pictures and stories about the royal couple. The demand for it was so great news-stands were soon sold out and a second run was necessary. That week the *Star Weekly* sold 75,000 more copies than on any previous week in its history. On June 17 when *The Daily Star* published sixteen pages of royal pictures it sold 300,000 copies or 70,000 more than the normal run.

One of the more famous of the thousands of photographs taken on that tour was the work of Tom Wilson. It shows Their Majesties at Banff with Prime Minister King, and has been reprinted thousands of times in booklets and magazines. The one that caused the most comment among the newspaper fraternity, however, shows the King and Queen gazing up at an enormous picture of themselves and children, taken by Richardson, centring the decorations on the front of *The Star* building in Toronto as they rode past in their open car.

The idea of this picture originated with Hindmarsh, and it was Major Claude Pascoe who "set it up." The driver of the royal car was a fellow member with Pascoe of the Black Watch Club, and a personal friend. Pascoe arranged to have him point suddenly to the picture as they drove by, knowing Their Majesties would instinctively turn their heads in the direction. Several photographers were spotted at strategic positions, so that if one missed another would get the picture. The ruse worked, and *The Star* got a picture that was not only good promotion, but that showed Their Majesties exhibiting a very human interest in an attractive display.

Hindmarsh personally directed the Royal Tour coverage, coming to work as early as 5 a.m. to select pictures and read the overnight stories. More than forty reporters and photographers participated at one time or another in covering the tour, and the cost to *The Star* exceeded $100,000.

Politically *The Star* remained unswervingly Liberal throughout the 1930's. In 1930 the federal Liberals were defeated and R. B. Bennett became Prime Minister. "No defeat of a government was ever more undeserved," Mr. Atkinson wired King, and in a following letter assured him he would be back in office if "the future policy of the party . . . contains some advanced proposals" and "progressive Liberalism." For Bennett he had slight regard. "A platform politician," and "a political lawyer" he had called him when he was mentioned for a cabinet position in the union government of 1917.

The Star's attitude towards Bennett was usually one of studied contempt, and it began a campaign against him as early as 1926. In that year the *Star Weekly* published an article disclosing how he had acquired his large fortune by inheritance rather than by merit. When he was chosen leader of the Conservative party its editorial the next day was devoted almost entirely to his eloquence, with his platform mannerisms described in detail. His oratory, it said, "is more after the manner of New York than of old York." It called him "instinctively a Tory." Over its story of the first session of Parliament after Bennett was elected it put the heading, "Pooh Bah is on the Job at Capital." Once it sarcastically commended him for his temerity in "walking up to the very verge of doing something."

On the other hand, when some western newspapers reported that he had brought about the court martial of a US army officer who had "affronted" him on a visit to Ottawa, *The Star* promptly declared the report could not be true, because Bennett was not the kind of a man who would do such a thing. "*The Star* disagrees with him on a great many subjects, but it has no low estimate of his personal character," it said.

Almost from the beginning of the widely publicized dispute between Bennett and H. H. Stevens, his Minister of Trade and Commerce, over government regulation of business, *The Star* suggested the whole affair was "too carefully staged and manipulated to be genuine." The controversy began with a series of addresses in Toronto, Kitchener, and Galt in which Stevens advocated "legislation to force those who fail to recognize (business) ethics to conform." He condemned businessmen for cutting wages and exploiting workers.

"Hon. H. H. Stevens has ideas," said *The Star* editorially on March 19, 1934. "He always did have them. Some of them have not been as good as some others. Just now he has nearly all the ideas that the Liberal party and CCF possess . . . Mr. Stevens would not kid the public, surely, by staying in the Bennett government while out-talking the radicalism of Elmore Philpott and Agnes Macphail, M.P."

In an editorial a few days later it wondered if it was proposed that both Bennett and Stevens should remain in the same cabinet, "playing both ends against the middle." On several occasions it saw significance in the fact that often Stevens' most sensational speeches were delivered to audiences Bennett was originally to have addressed and that, though Bennett was continually reprimanding his minister, he also continued to send him on speaking tours. When Bennett went to Europe while five by-elections were being held, leaving Stevens to conduct the campaigns, *The Star* said it was convinced now the whole dispute between the two men was a "put-up job," and that Bennett was using Stevens to test public response to a Conservative party in the guise of defender of the common man. The Conservatives lost four of the five by-elections.

Even when it was being widely believed that Stevens was leading a palace revolt within the Conservative cabinet, *The Star* expressed skepticism. It said that when Bennett reprimanded him "his shifts, evasions, denials, explanations . . . show very clearly that Mr. Stevens is not built of the stuff out of which insurgent leaders are made." It said his responses to Bennett "range from the petulant to the pathetic."

The Star welcomed the establishment of the Royal Commission on Price Spreads, but after Stevens made a speaking tour during a recess of the commission it called for his resignation as chairman. He had, it said, demonstrated that "he lacks the judicial temperament" and "cannot perceive the difference between allegations and established evidence." It was particularly harsh in its condemnation of a speech he made in Toronto attacking the alleged methods of chain stores before any evidence concerning chain stores had been placed before the inquiry. The Stevens inquiry, it said, was producing too much hearsay and allegations and too little proof. When Stevens resigned from the cabinet shortly before the 1935 election *The Star* commented that Bennett had evidently decided the Conservatives could not win an election on a reform program that merely duplicated those of the Liberals and CCF.

Atkinson could not believe that Bennett was sincere when he proposed more liberal social legislation in 1935. "If he is penitent on account of his past, and if he now sees the light, he should, at the present session of Parliament, undo some of the sins perpetrated by him in the last three or four sessions of Parliament while he was a Prime Minister living in the dismal dark of his former state, before he had read a certain book and had conversations with a man from Moscow which, he says, influenced him," *The Star* commented in an editorial on February 18, 1935. It accused him of talking "of new remedies" without repudiating the "old cure of high tariffs" with which he "dosed the country." After Bennett's defeat in October, 1935, *The Star* observed with considerable satisfaction that he left the Conservative party in ruins.

Why *The Star* should have taken such an uncompromisingly hostile attitude towards Bennett is not clear. It may have been a personal matter on Mr. Atkinson's part. He had been known to take what Maitland called "a scunner" against people. He seems to have believed that Bennett was all oratory and no action. Bennett was also a very rich man who stood, until the very end of his parliamentary career, against almost everything Mr. Atkinson supported. Atkinson may also have regarded him as the greatest threat to Mackenzie King the Conservatives had produced, and been a bit afraid of his influence.

At a convention on July 8, 1938, the Conservative party chose R. J. Manion as its new leader—a choice welcomed by *The Star* with an enthusiasm it usually reserved for Liberals. On three successive days it had editorials on what a splendid choice had been made, and there is little doubt they were sincerely meant. Dr. Manion had been originally a Liberal who had been elected in 1917 as a supporter of the Union government and remained with the Conservatives. His election and the adoption of a platform he favoured by the convention represented, *The Star* believed, a break with the imperialism and Toryism that had heretofore been dominant in the Conservative party.

Dr. Manion lived up to expectations, for immediately after the convention he embarked on a country-wide speaking tour that must have caused many members of his party to shake in their shoes. In September he delivered an address in which he warned that reform of the existing social order is the only alternative to "wreck, anarchy and revolution." In the same address he declared "well-timed reform alone averts revolution." For these opinions he was violently assailed by a section of the Conservative press and by certain big businessmen. The *Telegram* called it "political tripe," while the Montreal *Gazette* said "a turn to the left is not progress ahead." Dr. Manion wrote Mr. Atkinson asking for a kindly word of encouragement from *The Star*. Atkinson replied:

I have long been one of your well-wishers and admirers, and now your speeches are justifying the good opinion I have long held. I hope the endorsation by *The Star* of the progressive character of the speeches will not add to the resentment of your reactionaries against them. I am encouraged, however, on that point by your letter. It happens that we had an article waiting in proof which is in today's paper. Perhaps it may be too much to hope that we will see eye to eye on all political questions, but at least we are on agreement that there must be changes if our capitalist economy is to continue.

The article Mr. Atkinson referred to was used as the lead editorial in *The Star* of September 12. It commended everything Manion had said, praised him for his courage, and told the Liberal party at Ottawa it "could learn a lesson from Dr. Manion." The expression "your reactionaries" in Atkinson's letter was a reference to Bennett's farewell address at the convention in which he castigated "reactionaries" within the Conservative party for preventing him from being the reformer he said he wanted to be, and thus contributing to the defeat of the Conservatives in 1935.

After this "unveiling," as *The Star* called it, of the inner conflicts within the Conservative party *The Star* became more lenient on Bennett than it had been—indeed it went out of its way to exculpate him of much of the blame for the reactionary policies of his Government. The reactionary Tory elements within the Conservative party were too much for any one man to combat, it conceded. At times after this it was almost kindly in its treatment of Bennett. It could not forgive him for giving up his Canadian citizenship to accept a title in England, instead of staying here to fight for what he claimed to believe in, but even on that point it was not harsh.

It was Mr. Atkinson's belief that every page of *The Star* should reflect its social philosophy, and sometimes this was reflected in ways little suspected by the readers. In the depression years of the 1930's the emphasis of *The Star* Fresh Air Fund and *The Star* Santa Claus Fund underwent a subtle change that was scarcely noticeable for all its significance. Heretofore they had been wholly charitable in purpose, but with the advent of the depression Mr. Atkinson appears to have recognized their value as a means of publicizing the need for social reform. People would not have allowed his reporters into their homes if they came only to hold them up as examples of poverty and poor housing, but when they came in the name of charity they were welcomed.

Thus for several years such able reporters as Gregory Clark, R. E. Knowles, Archibald Lampman, Jessie MacTaggart, Alexandrine Gibb, and others were allowed to enter freely the poorer homes of the city,

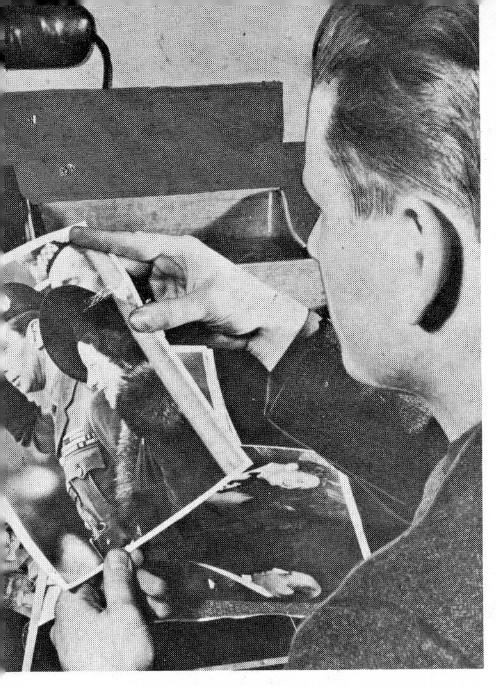

The Star was a pioneer in the transmission of pictures by wire, installing its first receiver during the royal tour of 1939

King George VI and Queen Elizabeth looking at a picture of themselves and their family on the Star Building during their tour of 1939

INDEX
Amusements—30 Serial—38-39
Births, Deaths—31 Sports—14-17
Comics—37-39 Suburban—10
Markets—18-19 Want Ads—31-36
Radio—24 Women's—26-29

THE TORONTO DAILY STAR

THE WEATHER
Moderate to fresh, north winds, partly cloudy and Thursday, moderate winds; with slightly higher tempera

44TH YEAR ★ TORONTO, WEDNESDAY, APRIL 22, 1936—42 PAGES MARCH CIRCULATION 256,785 COPIES PER DA

RESCUED

Both in Good Shape

DARING MINERS BREAK WAY INTO 10-DAY PRISON OF TORONTO MINE MEN

Doctor and Stretchers Rush Down Shaft to Administer First Aid and Bring Men Up to Surface—Big Crowd Gathers

SENDING UP OF MINE GEAR FIRST NOTICE OF RESCUE

Dr. Robertson Appeals for Hypodermic to Ease Pain of Himself and Scadding—Minister of Health Takes It

Moose River, N.S., April 22. — Rescue workers broke through early this afternoon to a clear shaft leading to two Toronto men entombed in the Moose River gold mine since April 12. Stretchers were taken down from the surface.

The entombed men were reached at 12.36 noon, Toronto time.

A huge crowd seething with excitement was being held back from the Reynolds pit mouth by Royal Canadian Mounted Police.

Spectators cheered or burst into hysterical sobbing.

A hacksaw and extra blades were sent down into the mine after word had reached the surface rescuers had broken through.

Long after first word reached the surface word was flashed up that there still was work to do—clearing away shale and stone and 'enlargement of the hole so that the entombed men might be removed.

It was believed they could not be brought out for at least an hour, possibly longer.

Dr. D. E. Robertson and Alfred Scadding were expected to be carried to the surface as soon as they were treated by Hon. F. R. Davis, minister of health, who volunteered to go down with rescue leaders and administer hypodermics because the men had reported they were in great pain.

The stretchers were carried down the shaft only a few minutes after an excited digger had rushed to the surface and shouted 'We've got through to Dr. Robertson and Scadding."

It was expected the men would be carried to the surface with the body of their companion, Herman Magill, who died early Monday, after they had been given hypodermic injections to relieve the agony of hunger, cold and inertia.

The men, however, were not brought immediately to the surface.

Appeal for the hypodermics came from Dr. Robertson over a miniature microphone with which he has kept contact with rescuers. Dr. F. R. Davis, volunteered to climb down the treacherous passage to the 141-foot level as soon as the appeal was received.

Medical supplies, blankets and hot water bottles followed Dr. Davis and his hypodermic into the shaft.

The men were to be revived with stimulants before the difficult task of taking them to the surface was begun.

Miners Line Shaft Sides

Dr. Davis hastily donned miner's togs and dungarees before entering the life-saving tunnel. On both sides of the rescue shaft, from the subterranean chamber to the surface, grimy mine workers lined up in human chains to aid the passage of Robertson and Scadding.

The approach was made through dangerous "live earth", along channels that had been closed by the cave-in. Daring draegermen from Stellarton and unmarried volunteers "with guts" had burrowed their way through this channel which threatened to collapse on top of them at any moment. Every foot of the way had to be propped.

The cave-in which trapped the men had affected a wider area than was at first thought and hindered rescue attempts from the beginning.

On the surface, an area 150 feet long, 75 feet wide was sunken 15 feet.

The way was along a twisting, narrow, low channel and stretchers with rope supports had been devised to carry them out. Miners feared to jar sides of the tunnel for fear of collapse. It was not known how long it would take to get Scadding and Robertson and the body of Magill to the surface, but it was believed it would be perhaps an hour or more.

Fragmentary reports brought to the surface indicated the rescuers had made only a small opening at first and that it might take some time to enlarge the passage sufficiently to take the men out of their prison 141 feet below the surface.

The fighting draegermen were triumphant and great grins spread over the faces of those on the off-shift. Jim Simpson, their leader, George Morrell, a draegerman, and H. Hirschfield of Goldenville, had

HOME AND SPORT EDITION

RESCUED BY HEROIC DRAEGERMEN

Entombed in the Moose River mine for ten days, Dr. D. E. Robertson and Alfred Scadding have been rescued by the heroic efforts of miners and draegermen who broke through the last barrier of rock to reach the trapped men after days of frantic digging in the dangerous Reynolds shaft, where their lives were continually threatened with the possibility of new cave-ins. (1) Alfred Scadding dressed in mining clothes at the Moose River mine. (2) Dr. D. E. Robertson. Copyright, The Toronto Star.

PROVINCIAL HEALTH MINISTER DESCENDS TO AID CAPTIVES

By FREDERICK GRIFFIN

Moose River, N.S., April 22.—At last rescue crews are through to Dr. D. E. Robertson and Alfred Scadding. They got through before 12.30 Toronto time. Dr. F. R. Davis, provincial minister of health went down on a life-saving mission.

Stretchers stand ready at the mouth of the tunnel.

worked steadily and frantically since 9 a.m. in the last big push.

It was those three who first opened the Reyonlds shaft, through which the approach was begun, and it was they who tore out the last rock from the rescue tunnel.

They were the "face workers" who tore material blocking their progress from its place with bare hands or picks. In an unpropped tunnel going through an area that has already collapsed. That is one of the most dangerous jobs an man could take on.

Hard-bitten coal miners from Stellarton who carried forward the brunt of the work, were laboring toward the last on the flat of their stomachs, so low was the passage. They had to enlarge this and then cut through decayed timbers.

The ambulance waited with its motor running to carry the men across a mudd field to an improised hospital as soon as they could be brought out. Other physicians also waited there. Several spectators burst into hysterical sobbing.

At the top of the narrow hole which was drilled into the underground chamber four days ago, H. F. Hannigan was talking to the two men below. It was impossible to learn what Robertson and Scadding said to Hannigan, or wha he told them.

Wives of the three men entombed Easter Sunday were waiting anxiously in the mine office seve hundred yards away from the Reyonlds shaft for rescue to be effected. Mrs. Magill had returned h from Halifax, where she went after learning of husband's death Monday morning.

Mrs. Scadding arrived here last night with F Scadding, younger brother of Alfred Scadding.

Mrs. Robertson has been on the scene since week ago Tuesday when she arrivd with Mrs. Ma and Charles Ivey of London, Ont., her brother. Ivey and Fred Scadding were waiting at the Reyno shaft-head for the men to be brought to the surface

As the rescue crew cleared away more of debris in the shaft it was established that they w able to talk to the two men. It was said at 1.30 p that only a few small rocks and broken imbers blocked the way.

In the hospital, nearly a mile away, beds w warmed with hot water bottles and preparatic completed for emergency treatment of the men w were subjected to more than nine days of hung camp, cold, and darkness.

Surgical instruments were made ready for possible operation on Scadding, whose feet becar swollen and infected from wading in cold water. oxygen tent also was set up for treatment of pn monia, which it was feared Dr. Robertson might ha contracted.

At 2.04 p.m. (E.S.T.) rescue squads had not started out with the entombed men, but talked the prisoners and learned that they were in "goo shape," although they were known to be ill from co and exposure and were suffering from inertia.

At 1.30 p.m. (Atlantic time) a miner rushed from rescue shaft and was reported to have told Hon. Michael Dwy minister of mines, that the rescue crew "Thinks they' through".

The minister put on oilskins and went into the pit wi the miner. Stretcher bearers, accompanied by Dr. H. MacDonald, also went into the rescue shaft.

It was pointed out that Joe Simpson's crew of "mucke

(Continued on Page 2, Col. 1)

WAVE OF REJOICING SWEEPS CONTINENT AT NEWS OF RESCU

Heart-Rending Concern Relieved When News of Rescue Is Flashed

SORROW WITH JOY

Herman Magill, Companion of Robertson and Scadding, Died Monday

10-DAY ORDEAL ENDS

Hope Had Almost Been Abandoned Until Men's Voices Heard Sunday

MINERS DEFY DEATH

STAR GAVE NEWS OF RESCUE FIRS

The Toronto Star beat all Ca with the story of the rescue of Toronto men entombed in Scotia to-day, both on the air on the street.

At 12.47 The Star radio annou gave out the good news, eight utes ahead of the next broad and at 12.53 the first Star reached King and Bay, nine mi ahead of the other evening pap

A few minutes later a call made upon The Star to hook u a continent-wide broadcast thr NBC, and organization of new The Star office, supplied by Fr ick Griffin, Gregory Clark other staff writers at the scene. the press service, enabled The to provide a complete story of thrilling last minutes in the re shaft.

An epic chapter of collective heroism was written posterity to-day on Canada's scroll of honor as weary resc brought to a glorious end their dramatic struggle to libe two Toronto men, imprisoned for ten days in the dange depths of Moose River mine.

Seldom before, when tragedy or disaster cast its sha over a community, have Canadians followed with such he rending concern a fight against perilous odds to save hu life. A wave of rejoicing swept across the country when dramatic news was flashed that Dr. D. E. Robertson Arthur Scadding had been released from their prison of hor It relieved pent-up tension which was almost world-wide.

The joy, however, was tempered with deep sorrow fo the three so suddenly trapped Easter Sunday, one failed survive the ordeal. Herman Magill, who was unwell wher entered the shaft, died from the effects of the terrif experience.

Through the years there has never been such concer

(Continued on Page 2, Col. 5)

How *The Star* played one of the most dramatic news stories of the thirties.

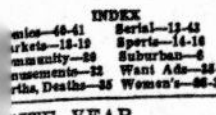

TORONTO DAILY STAR

THE WEATHER
City and Lower Lakes—Mostly fair and warm today and Friday; scattered thunder showers tonight. Low tonight, 58; high Friday, 75.

47TH YEAR — TORONTO, THURSDAY, AUGUST 24, 1939—44 PAGES — 3c PER COPY, 18c PER WEEK

TORONTO MAN NEW SALVATION ARMY HEAD

Duce 'Strongly Advises' Hitler to Avoid War

HOME AND SPORT EDITION

F.D.R. Pleads With King Of Italy to Save Peace

'GOD KNOWS I HAVE DONE ALL POSSIBLE,' SAYS CHAMBERLAIN 'BUT WAR PERIL IS IMMINENT'

British Government Is Given Authority to Mobilize and Ration Supplies—Start Removal of Britons From Germany —Nazi Troops Stand Ready for Orders

AMERICAN TOURISTS GIVEN WARNING TO LEAVE BRITAIN, GERMANY AT ONCE

(United, Canadian and Associated Press Despatches)

An Exchange Telegraph dispatch from Warsaw to London today reported a German patrol had crossed the East Prussian frontier and penetrated almost a mile into Poland. The dispatch said the Germans occupied the Bagno estate, in the Ilawa district. Berlin denied the report.

President Roosevelt today appealed to King Victor Emmanuel of Italy to exert all possible influence to preserve peace. A personal message from the president was delivered to Victor Emmanuel by the U.S. ambassador at the king's summer residence.

Great Britain began mobilizing a fleet of liners and cruise ships for use if necessary to transport an expeditionary force to France.

The liners Alaunia, Montcalm and Montclare, which had planned cruises from London to Madeira on Saturday, were held at London. Previously the government had taken over the Voltaire and other vessels.

Travellers arriving from Scandinavia reported that their ships were convoyed through the North Sea by British destroyers, presumably on the lookout for submarines.

The mobilization of vessels extended throughout the Empire. Ships were ordered to cancel previously scheduled cruises. The North Sea fishing fleet was recalled. All trawlers, which can be used against submarines, were instructed to remain in port.

The King held a privy council at Buckingham Palace today and signed orders-in-council under the great seal authorizing the government to mobilize the navy, naval reserve and the territorial army when necessary.

The King gave Edward Leslie Burgin, minister of supply, full powers to conserve supplies, issue ration cards and commandeer all transport.

Reserves in all the armed and civilian British services were warned to be ready for call; more were summoned for active duty; the civilian populace was mobilized for defensive action.

Police circulated an order throughout London providing for a permanent "blackout." All lights must be blacked out or extinguished every night as soon as darkness falls.

Anti-aircraft guns pointed skyward, the air force was tuned and manned for instant action, and the great home and reserve fleets were in the North Sea.

Some British warships were reported in the Skagerrak, between the Danish and Norwegian coasts, where they can recall vividly to German imagination the "hunger blockade" imposed by the navy during the world war.

The British Museum was closed to the public today to permit necessary measures to preserve its valuable collection from damage in the event of an air raid.

START MOVING BRITONS FROM GERMANY

British consular authorities in Berlin were instructed to start removing British residents from Germany.

Joseph P. Kennedy, U.S. ambassador to Britain, advised American tourists to leave the British Isles.

The United States embassies in France and Germany also advised Americans to leave those countries.

France mobilized a fifth class of reservists, adding approximately another 150,000 troops to the men already under arms. Previous

(Continued on Page 3, Col. 1)

Asks Wide Emergency Powers "In Face of Grave Situation"

"GERMANY FULLY READY FOR WAR"

Hitler Spurns All Warnings, Demands "Free Hand" in Eastern Europe

London, Aug. 24.—Prime Minister Chamberlain told parliament today that Great Britain "finds herself with an imminent peril of war."

Germany is now "in a condition of complete readiness for war," the prime minister stated. He asked parliament to give the government wide powers to deal with the international situation.

Adolf Hitler has told Britain that Germany wants a free hand in eastern Europe and that if Britain or any other country intervenes there, they must accept blame for the ensuing conflict, Chamberlain told the House of Commons.

"If war comes, we shall be fighting to prevent destruction of those principles which hold all possibility of peace and security for the peoples of the world," Chamberlain said. "We have a united country behind us. As we think, so shall we act unitedly." The House rose to its feet and cheered.

"God knows I have done all that is possible in efforts for peace," said the prime minister after he had declared Britain's obligations to Poland "remain unaffected" by what he termed an imminent peril of war.

Chamberlain spoke to a virtually unanimous House. Arthur Greenwood, acting leader of the Labor opposition, described the prime minister's statement as one of "gravity" and approved the government's policy of firmness.

"Let no man abroad," he said, "think Labor will be a willing party ever to acquiesce in any further acts of aggression."

Sir Archibald Sinclair, Liberal leader, also approved the government's policy. "Now that we are in a crisis, criticism must be put aside," he said.

The prime minister, grave-faced, was cheered as he entered Commons. Mrs. Chamberlain accompanied him from No. 10 Downing St. and crowds greeted them with applause along the short route to parliament.

Text of Speech

The text of the prime minister's speech follows:

"In the last debate we had upon foreign affairs, which took place July 31, I observed that the Danzig situation required very careful watching. I expressed my anxiety about the pace at which the accumulation of war weapons was proceeding throughout Europe. I referred to the poisoning of public opinion by propaganda which was going on, and I declared that if that could be stopped, and if some action could be taken to restore confidence, I did not believe that there was any question which could not be solved by peaceful discussion.

"I am sorry to say that there have been no signs since of any such action, but on the contrary the international position has steadily deteriorated until today we find ourselves confronted with the imminent perils of war.

"At the beginning of August a dispute arose between the Polish government and the Danzig senate as to the position and functions of certain Polish customs officials. It was not a question of major importance. Many more acute difficulties have been easily settled in the past in less tense conditions and even in this case discussions had actually begun between the parties last week.

"While these discussions were in progress the German press opened a violent campaign against the Polish government. They declared that Danzig could not be the subject of any conference or any compromise, but that it must come back to the Reich at once unconditionally.

Resembled Last Year's Charges

"They went further, and linked up the question with the question of the Corridor and attacked the whole policy and attitude of the Polish government and published circumstantial accounts of alleged ill-

(Continued on Page 12, Col. 1)

SALVATION ARMY ELECTS NEW GENERAL

Commissioner George Carpenter, now territorial commander for Canada, has been elected commander of the Salvation Army by the grand council meeting in secret session in London, England. He will succeed General Evangeline Booth, who retires this October. General Carpenter was born in Australia, but has been many years in Canada.

GEO. CARPENTER ASSUMES OFFICE HELD BY BOOTHS

Has Been Territorial Commander for Canada Since May, 1937

BORN IN AUSTRALIA

Wife, Now in City, Author of Many Denominational Biographies

London, Aug. 24—(CP and UP)—Commissioner George L. Carpenter of Canada today was elected commander of the Salvation Army.

He succeeds General Evangeline Booth, who is retiring because of the age limit.

Commissioner Carpenter was appointed territorial commander for Canada in May, 1937. Before that he was stationed in South America. He was born in Australia, where he began his army career 45 years ago.

Commissioner Carpenter's wife is known as author of army biographies. She also is an Australian.

Carpenter joined the Salvation Army when he was 19. He was literary secretary to Bramwell Booth for 12 years.

The final vote of the 51 members of the army high council on the five candidates nominated yesterday was as follows:

Commissioner Carpenter, 35; Commissioner Catherine Bramwell Booth, of England, 8; Lieut.-Commissioner Albert Osborne, of Scotland and Ireland, 6. There were two blank ballots.

Lieut. Commissioner William Dalziel, of eastern Australia and Commissioner Benjamin Orames of the western United States were the other candidates.

Lives on Belsize Drive

Since he became territorial commander for Canada in 1937, Mr. Carpenter has made his headquarters in Toronto residing in a modest dwelling on Belsize Drive. He left Toronto the first of August to attend the high council meeting, at which he was elected. They have two children, a son in England and a daughter here.

Mrs. Carpenter was today attending a conference of Salvation

(Continued on Page 12, Col. 4)

'THRILLING AND TENDER ROYAL TOUR COLOR FILM IS REALLY MARVELLOUS'

How Wonderful If All History Could Have Been Preserved Like This

FRESH AND VITAL

Star's Movie at Exhibition Shows Again the Queen's Beautiful Clothes

By FREDERICK GRIFFIN

What a marvellous thing if we could thus have had preserved for our eyes to see the action and color of say the Field of Cloth of Gold!

Or the meeting of King John and the barons at Runnymede. Or Columbus setting sail on his western voyage. Or the crusaders. Or Napoleon in a succession of moments. Or Queen Victoria when she was a young mother. Or a thousand and one other historical episodes that come easily to mind.

That is the thought I had on seeing a preview of the color film of the royal tour of Canada and the United States which The Toronto Star has collected, selected and prepared for public presentation at the Canadian National Exhibition. How wonderful, I thought, if all history could have been preserved for us like this! It was actually possible to imagine oneself for a precious half-hour or more living again those great crowded weeks of their majesties' visit.

The Star, anxious not merely to meet the public hunger for a reseeing of the King and Queen, but to do this in a worthwhile way, spent months collecting color film from many sources, to find and make available the best.

It was found that the Canadian Corps association had secured a wealth of fine footage, particularly in Ottawa and Toronto. So had the Toronto Amateur Movie club. Both co-operated. The Cunard White-Star Line made available beautiful official film taken in Quebec and Montreal.

The Star advertised and inquired and all over Canada from Halifax to Vancouver contacted photographers who had made color movies of their majesties' visit.

Finally the Eastman Kodak Company made available the exclusive color film of the United States visit which they were making specially to present to their majesties. Selections from this are incorporated in The Star feature.

The search took many shapes, met many snags, overcame them. It became a race against time to collect and select. Toronto Star representatives made many visits here and there to see and negotiate. The

(Continued on Page 17, Col. 1)

BUSINESS ON MEND U.S. BUILDERS SAY

Construction Boom Some Places, Survey Shows

New York, Aug. 24—(AP)—A survey of 2,000 small firms engaged in the construction industry shows an improvement in business, the F. W. Dodge Corporation, building statisticians, reported today.

"In an investigation of conditions throughout the 37 states east of the Rockies," said the company, "a majority of small firms contacted by the Daily Construction news service said their business was in an upswing which varied from five per cent. to boom proportions."

The survey showed 59 per cent. of the firms describing business as better, 18 per cent. unchanged, and 23 per cent. worse.

THIS WAY TO THE BIG SHOW COME AND SEE STAR EXHIBIT

Big Parade of Scientific and Pictorial Marvels Opens Tomorrow

STARTS AT 10 A.M.

Hamburgers do a cakewalk, hot dogs wriggle, onions weep in rehearsal—for tomorrow is the zero hour.

Along the midway, barkers gargle to put an edge on their voice. They yodel to give them tone. Everyone else is a-hurrying and a-scurrying. In the buildings is a last minute rush of banging and clanging. In the grounds the grass is spring-green and the flower beds are sheer loveliness. Everywhere is the smell of fresh paint. Not an orange peel, not a banana skin, not a scrap of lunch paper anywhere—yet. No lost children.

That's the Exhibition on the eve. Tomorrow not only does the world's greatest annual fair begin but The Toronto Star's big parade at the big fair begins too.

This way, ladies and gentlemen —come one, come all . . . and see The Star's great galaxy of attrac-

(Continued on Page 7, Col. 2)

MANY STAR READERS LOOKING FOR HOMES

There's no doubt about it, a lot of people are in the market for homes to buy and to rent. One advertiser told The Star that he has sold four out of five houses he has recently advertised. Another said he had at least 30 enquiries about the 6-roomed bungalow he quickly sold through Star Want Ads. And it's the same story with rental ads—plenty of prospects and good tenants obtained in quick order. But when you stop to consider that over 210,000 people buy The Star every day, it is not surprising that there are plenty of prospects for buying and renting homes among this great number of Star readers. To advertise, call Waverley 3636.

ROOSEVELT ASKS MEDIATION OF KING OF ITALY IN CRISIS

Urges Him Directly "To Formulate Proposals for Pacific Solution"

Washington, Aug. 24 — (AP) — President Roosevelt renewed today his efforts to avert a European war.

He appealed to King Victor Emmanuel of Italy "to formulate proposals for a pacific solution of the present crisis."

Ambassador William Phillips, on arrangements made by Mussolini and Foreign Minister Count Ciano, had an audience with King Victor Emmanuel and presented the president's message orally.

Following is the text of the president's message:

"Again a crisis in world affairs makes clear the responsibility of heads of nations for the fate of their own people and indeed of humanity itself.

"It is because of traditional accord between Italy and the United States and the ties of consanguinity between millions of our citizens that I feel that I can address your majesty in behalf of maintenance of world peace.

Predicts Devastation

"It is my belief and that of the American people that your majesty and your majesty's government can greatly influence the averting of an outbreak of war. Any general war would cause to suffer all nations, whether belligerent or neutral, whether victors or vanquished, and would clearly bring devastation to the peoples and perhaps to the

(Continued on Page 3, Col. 3)

HOLLAND STARTS MOBILIZING ARMY

The Hague, Netherlands, Aug. 24—(UP)—The government ordered preliminary mobilization of its armed forces today.

KING CABINET MEETS DEFENCES ARE READY

50,000 Militiamen Are Said Ready for Call—Veterans as Guards

Ottawa, Aug. 24.—(CP)—Prime Minister Mackenzie King convened his ministers for one of the gravest cabinet meetings in many months. At it the European crisis and its potential effect upon Canada came under discussion.

The prime minister entered the privy council chamber at 10.50 a.m. and was the first to arrive. He said he anticipated an all-day session.

Cabled dispatches covering the latest developments in Europe were rushed into the council chamber as fast as received by the external affairs department.

The meeting follows telephone consultations held yesterday by the prime minister with the leaders of the three opposition parties in the House of Commons.

Parliament will be called together at once if it becomes apparent efforts to settle the European problem

(Continued on Page 3, Col. 3)

NICE WEATHER FOR OPENING

There will be nice weather for the opening of the "Ex", the weatherman says. "Mostly fair and warm today and Friday," he said. Yesterday's high was 80, at 2.10 p.m. The low for last night was 62 at 6.45 a.m.

BRITAIN READY AS IN 1914 TO SAVE WEAK FROM BRUTAL

People Still Hope War Can Be Averted—Jubilation in Berlin

POLES STAND FIRM

By WILLIAM H. STONEMAN
Special Cable to The Chicago Daily News and The Toronto Star

London, Aug. 24.—If Great Britain goes to war this week-end she will be fighting to save a smaller nation from the brutal, lawless attack of another great power. To this extent she will be fighting for a principle, just as she did 25 years ago when she went to the aid of Belgium.

Thus the British feel as they stand on the threshold of the inferno that the battle will be both honorable and necessary. Because of this conviction the British people, who are fundamentally both decent and brave, are fully prepared for whatever awaits them, even though it may be death and destruction. There is no grumbling in England today; everyone is ready to take his medicine.

Strive to Save Peace

London, Aug. 24.—Grave-visaged, the King returned to London today and heard his people cry "Bring us peace, your majesty!" Meanwhile Britain strove with all her power and ingenuity for a last-minute settlement, and yet made sweeping preparations for war.

Parliament came back for an emergency session, in which Bri-

(Continued on Page 3, Col. 4)

HITLER FLIES BACK TO BERLIN SUDDENLY

Causes Rumors of Action at Once

Berlin, Aug. 24—Fuehrer Adolf Hitler returned unexpectedly to Berlin from Berchtesgaden today, leading to reports of some early new move in Europe's crisis.

The Fuehrer flew to the capital from his Bavarian retreat, reaching the chancellory shortly before 8 p.m. (1 p.m., E.D.T.). He was greeted by Field Marshal Goering.

Immediate conferences were scheduled with Foreign Minister Joachim von Ribbentrop, now on his way from Moscow, and other key men. Hitler was due to meet Von Ribbentrop at 8 p.m. (3 p.m., E.D.T.), and the others shortly afterward.

Nazi officials tonight described Prime Minister Neville Chamberlain's speech as "unquestionably of tremendous importance".

LAKE TEMPERATURES

Sunnyside	66
Simcoe Park	66
Kew Beach	68
Centre Island	65

CELEBRATES 90TH BIRTHDAY BY WINNING GAME OF BOWLS

S. B. Brush "Very Abstemious"—Only Smokes From Dawn to Bed-Time

By R. E. KNOWLES

Still another festive Torontonian has reached the "90's" of his years with undiminished joy of life and marvellous liberty of both work and play.

This latest is Seely B Brush—who, let me seriously appraise, would pass anywhere, for a denizen of mid-seventies (at least). On Lowther Ave., (garden attached) is the home where he spends, and enjoys, his vesper years.

Seely B. Brush

To establish his "enjoyment" claim, it is only necessary to state that on his 90th birthday, which came along on Saturday last, Mr. Brush (who has been the head of the "greens" committee there for all its later history) repaired to the

(Continued on Page 9, Col. 1)

LION RUNS LOOSE IN SHIP OFF N.Y.

Terrorizes Crew — Rush Tamers to Vessel

New York, Aug. 24.—A lion that broke loose from a cargo of wild animals today was terrorizing the crew of the Royal Netherlands steamer Amazon, which left New York yesterday for Venezuela.

No guns were aboard the Amazon, and in response to frantic calls for help by the master, a coast guard boat from Cape May, N.J., was preparing to put out with doctors and two lion tamers who will attempt to capture or shoot the beast.

The master of the Amazon radioed that one crew member already had been mauled by the lion.

The ship's cargo includes several lions, tigers and snakes being shipped from Trinidad to a Zoo at Laguayras, Venezuela.

RUSHES WITH WOOD IN HOPE YOU'LL SEND HIM TO CAMP

Jimmy, 10, Head of Household, Busy on Winter's Fuel

FUND NEEDS HELP

By JESSIE MacTAGGART

Maybe you've seen him, this 10-year-old head of a household.

He usually can be found pushing a big wooden dump cart down behind the warehouses by the railroad yard.

That's where he was the day we called, so we sat on the top step, which wasn't broken, and waited.

We saw the cart first. It was piled high with discarded wooden boxes, and, when it arrived in front, we saw him, a thin little boy whose head did not nearly reach the height of the cargo he pushed.

"Hey, Jimmy," we called. "We've been waiting to see you."

He gave us a brief glance, dumped the cargo of old boxes into the open, sashless, cellar window and without a backward glance

(Continued on Page 2, Col. 8)

$1,047 EVERY DAY FUND'S BIG NEED

Time does not wait for you to send your donation to The Star Fresh Air Fund, so please send your contribution immediately, before it is too late. There are only seven more August days and on each day the fund must receive $1,047 if it is to reach its objective of $28,400.

Today the grand total acknowledged is $21,075.77, of which $364.81 has been donated in the last 24 hours.

You can dry the tears of disappointment of many of Toronto's needy children by sending your donation immediately to The Star Fresh Air Fund, 80 King St. W., or by bringing it in personally to the front counter of The Star.

LIST OF DONATIONS TO FRESH AIR FUND

Amount previously acknowledged ... $20,710.96
Sunday offerings at Severn Falls Sunday School, Severn Falls ... 10.00
A.J. ... 5.00
B.S.C. ... 10.00
In memory of Norman ... 5.00
In memory of Hilda G.H. ... 5.00
Liverpool ... 5.00
Proceeds of baseball game between East End Firemen and McGowan Manufacturers, Main St. ... 4.00
Members of the Lazy Nine Club: Shirley Hutchison, Ruth Harris, Beverley Barbour, Frances Maunsell, Jean Smallman, Marjery Dixon, Janet Harbron, Margaret Ferguson, Virginia Burkholder ...
J. A. Young, Hamilton ...

THE WEATHER

THURSDAY-FRIDAY, AUG. 24-25

The local and lower lake region forecast: Mostly fair and warm today and Friday with scattered thundershowers tonight; moderate southwest to west winds.

'England Expects' Again And Everyone Answers

Cozy Suburbs See Strange Sights as Bomb Shelters Appear in Gardens, Children Don Gas-Masks and Families Prepare for Air Raids

London, Aug. 24—(CP)—Today walk into "The Limes," heretofore calm, prosaic home on Brent Rd. in our middle class suburb, and don't be surprised to see sharp reflections of a disturbed world.

For in these hectic days with peace precariously tilting with war the family routine, which used to start with bringing in the milk and end with putting out the cat—and had nothing more exciting in between than a call from the vicar, now embraces the deadly earnest business of ARP—air raid precautions.

The "Knockout Blow"

The radio and press has broad-

that if the knockout blow had been delivered last September casualties might have mounted to 500,000 the first two weeks.

Meantime night aerial "warfare" complete with bombers, barrage balloons, blackouts and batteries of guns and searchlights has been realistically illustrating the message of civilian population organization.

And that's where our suburb comes in. Our next door neighbor was one of the first to sign up as an air raid warden. The need for speedy organization was brought home to him when his wife, a confinement case, was sent home because her maternity hospital was cleared to make ready for the ex-

5,000 CHEER PARADE OF VISITING BANDS

Five thousand people cheered lustily in city hall square today when the band of the Royal Marines, the Royal Canadian Mounted Police musical riders and the Dagenham Girls' band from England marched up Bay St. and were received by Mayor Day and the board of control.

Major F. J. Ricketts, director of the Marines band, was presented by Elwood Hughes, C.N.E. manager, to the mayor and controllers. Then he laid a wreath on the cenotaph. Rev. Capt. Sydney Lambert dedicated it in a brief memorial service.

BRITONS TO QUIT TIENTSIN

Shanghai, Aug. 24—(UP)—A

Toronto Motor Toll Lowest Among North American Cities

Toronto has become the safest city on the continent, figures of the National Safety Council showed. These were made public by Chief Constable Draper, who noted an increase in motor fatalities here in the last month.

Last year Toronto ranked sixth among the large cities in North America. Its motor traffic death rate per hundred thousand population now stands at 6.5 for the first six months of this year. St. Louis is next with 8.2, Los Angeles had

duction in traffic fatalities," Chief Draper said. "But can we hold this favorable record? Fatalities have increased from 21 at the end of June to a total of 28 today.

"Be safety-conscious," the chief urged. "Think of your own safety and the safety of others. Don't be afraid to let your neighbors and the children on your street know that you are a believer in safety. Practise it. Set a proper example for your children to follow. Toronto police are conscientiously endeavoring to save human lives and to pre-

DEATH NOTICES
In Today's Star

As war became imminent in 1939, Mr. Atkinson refused to contribute to any mass hysteria.

ABOVE: J. E. Atkinson surrounded by his great-grandchildren in 1947

BELOW: Mr. Atkinson, right, delighted in honouring old employees. William Stewart, left, retired after fifty years with *Star*

describing the hardships of the families of underpaid workers, of children left fatherless, of families in which there was sickness. Subtly the message was conveyed that mothers' allowances, family allowances, unemployment insurance, and sick benefits were needed. At the same time the public was conditioned to the necessity of larger relief grants, slum clearance, and public housing.

Despite the battery of high-powered writers who worked on these charities, the amount collected never reached the all-time peak of 1921 when *The Star* Fresh Air Fund raised $40,835. Since 1926 the amount raised has averaged around $30,000 a year in good times and bad. By the end of the 1962 season it had raised around $1,310,000 in total. *The Star* Santa Claus Fund, with its more sentimental appeal, usually raised more than the Fresh Air Fund, its total to the end of 1962 exceeding $1,753,000.

In its earlier years *The Star* Fresh Air Fund had been used to take children on day outings. During the depression it began paying the expenses of 35,000 to 50,000 children and their mothers for a two weeks' holiday in the country each summer. These were usually at fresh air camps operated by churches or welfare agencies. *The Star* did not run any camps. When the board of education opened an open air school in Victoria Park for children of poor health the Fresh Air Fund provided a noon lunch for fifty.

During the depression *The Star* promoted a number of projects to ease the burden of the unemployed. In 1931 representatives of four welfare agencies came to Mr. Atkinson with a request *The Star* help them recruit women who would work part-time on a volunteer basis. He acceded and the result was the Friendly League which, in the first year recruited 135 volunteers. The program was so successful that in succeeding years it was extended to include men. *The Star* also promoted a "Get a Man a Job" campaign in which advertisements were run free of charge for men looking for work. Many hundreds of unemployed men found jobs through this campaign.

In 1935 Mr. Atkinson helped organize the Society for Crippled Civilians, and provided it with its first small office rent free. For several years it was given more publicity in *The Star* than any other charities except the newspaper's own two funds, and its present commodious workshops and store on Jarvis Street were made possible by a fund-raising campaign conducted in *The Star*.

Chapter 17

DEPRESSION LABOUR POLICY

When *The Star* moved into its beautiful new building on February 3, 1929, the nation was enjoying a prosperity most Canadians confidently believed would last forever. Nine months later, on October 24, occurred the first of the series of stock market crashes that preceded the greatest depression of all time. At first Mr. Atkinson seems to have believed the decline presaged only a healthy return to normal conditions. He had always been opposed to stock market speculation, as he was to all forms of gambling, and while other businessmen were hazarding tens of thousands on the rise or fall of stock prices, he would take only an occasional nervous little flutter for a few thousand dollars, usually in shares of a paper manufacturing company.

He had invested *The Star*'s reserves in securities like Latin American bonds, than which there were none better according to President Hoover. When one after another Latin American republics repudiated their indebtedness *The Star*'s reserve fund was virtually wiped out. To this misfortune is attributed the provision in the charter of the Atkinson Charitable Foundation limiting its investments to securities of the Canadian and Ontario governments and the city of Toronto. To this is also attributed a lasting prejudice against Latin America, with the result that *The Star* virtually ignored that part of the world as long as he lived.

By mid-December the effects of the stock market crash were being felt throughout the national economy and *The Star* did not escape. Pre-Christmas advertising was below expectations, the average for December being only slightly higher than for October. Characteristically Mr. Atkinson's thoughts turned towards economizing; he may have become even a little panicky.

A few days before Christmas he summoned Hindmarsh to his office. Bone had died in 1928 and Hindmarsh had been responsible for spending the editorial budget for only a year. An executive in whom Mr. Atkinson reposed considerable confidence was present during the interview. Atkinson told his managing editor he must reduce expenditures by a certain amount before the end of the year. Hindmarsh replied it could not be done in such a short space of time. Atkinson retorted that it must be done. Economy waves were not unusual at the *Star*, but one in December was unheard of. The fiscal year began October 1, and Hindmarsh still had nine months in which to cut back expenses.

The following morning Hindmarsh had a second interview with Mr. Atkinson at which he repeated his statement of the previous day that expenditures could not be so drastically reduced in such a short time. Present throughout this interview was an employee who held a responsible position in the business office.

"The only way I can reduce expenditures by such a large amount is by cutting every reporter's salary or by laying off fourteen or fifteen men," he quotes Hindmarsh as saying.

"You are the head of your department, and it is not for me to tell you how you should run it," Mr. Atkinson replied. "I simply tell you that by the end of the year you must have reduced expenditures by . . .," naming a figure. Hindmarsh departed without further word.

On Friday, December 20, Hindmarsh called city editor E. B. (Tim) Reid to his office and handed him a list of fourteen reporters who were to be given a week's notice that day. As Reid, now a government public relations man, relates it, he protested against the timing of the dismissals. Hindmarsh, he says, replied that he did not like it either but it had to be done. However, Reid says, after further discussions Hindmarsh told him to take no action until after the New Year "and in the meantime we will take another look at things." Reid states categorically that nobody was given his notice until after the New Year, but that in the first six weeks of 1930 ten reporters left *The Star*.

Payroll records in the main confirm Reid's recollection. It shows ten men left between January 1 and February 19, but some of these are known to have departed voluntarily. Charles C. George, a former city editor of the *World*, went off the payroll January 1 to join the public relations staff of the Canadian National Exhibition. Stephen M. Jones departed January 2 to become a photographer. Of the other eight, one left January 9, one January 21, one January 22, one January 29, two January 30, one February 14, and one February 19. Two of these eight, both now working on other Toronto newspapers, say they left voluntarily. One of these left after being given an assignment by Hindmarsh to which he objected. This may have been Hindmarsh's way of "taking another look at things." Five of the eight soon returned to *The Star*, one within ten days of leaving.

In addition to these, and in no way connected with the economy dismissals, one man had been removed from the payroll on December 2 for chronic alcoholism, but was soon rehired and remained with *The Star*, on and off, for another twenty-five years. One went off the payroll on December 6 after several warnings that his conduct was unsatisfactory. He never returned. Norman MacLeod quit on December 13 to become head of the Ottawa bureau of the *Montreal Star*, and a young man named Smythe, who had not been particularly successful during a trial period as a reporter, left on December 24 to become a teacher. None of the fourteen had been employed by *The Star* for more than six months, though two were old-time newspapermen who had been on and off various Toronto newspapers for several years.

Yet this was the seed from which grew that hardy myth once referred to by the *Guild Reporter*, organ of the newspaper editorial workers' union, as "the annual pre-Christmas firing bee, long a *Star* institution." Most persistent and most distasteful of all the legends that cluster about Canada's most colourful newspaper, it has been mentioned in every write-up about *The Star* in the past twenty years.

Yet it is only a myth, invented by a scurrilous scandal magazine. It was circulated with avidity by those opposed to *The Star*'s program of social reform, for they welcomed eagerly any evidence, however circumstantial, that Holy Joe was indeed the sanctimonious skinflint they claimed he was. Everybody knew what Hindmarsh intended, for city editor Reid was a convivial soul who warned his friends of impending doom at a Christmas party. In time it was forgotten Hindmarsh had not carried out his intentions.

Nevertheless, *The Star*'s practice of hiring reporters for a short trial period "on voucher" lent an appearance of plausibility to the story. There were usually two or three reporters "on trial" at any one time. They were not on staff but they came to work each day. If the city editor gave them an assignment, or if they wrote anything "on their own" which was published, they were given a petty cash voucher for a day's pay. A man who demonstrated ability might be taken on staff after two weeks. Some who did not make the grade and had no other job might continue coming in every day for weeks in the hope of being given an occasional assignment. Their fellow workers did not always know they were not on staff.

Since petty cash vouchers are destroyed by the accounting department after five years there is nothing to show whether anybody was working on voucher in December, 1929. Anybody who was would most certainly have been told he could expect no more assignments. But this can be said positively—nobody on *The Star*'s payroll was ever dismissed for reasons of economy during the Christmas season, either in 1929 or any other year.

After these unprecedented economy dismissals at the start of 1930 the year passed without incident until mid-August when, with the editorial budget nearly exhausted, twelve reporters were laid off staff over a period of six weeks. Several office boys nearing the age-limit of eighteen were also let go. At the time *The Star* was attacking the provincial government for doing nothing about unemployment, and in a counterattack Premier Ferguson accused it of "itself adding to the number of unemployed."

After the start of the new fiscal year on October 1, 1930, *The Star* began rehiring. By this time nearly every newspaper in the country, including the other Toronto newspapers, were reducing staff and the city was swarming with unemployed newsmen. With fresh money in his poke and a year in which to spend it, Hindmarsh would give a job to almost anybody who applied. He was particularly partial to old newspapermen who had seen better days and hired several who had been laid off by the *Mail and Empire* and *Globe*.

It was about this time that he began to realize the full possibilities of the voucher system. Heretofore it had been used sparingly, and only to pay applicants for employment during their period of probation. But beginning fairly early in 1930 some capable newsmen were kept on voucher for months at a time. Like photographers, they were regarded by Hindmarsh as free lances, readily expendable. One of the charms of the system was that they did not show up on the payroll changes reported regularly to Mr. Atkinson.

Occasionally a problem drinker was kept on voucher for months, paid only when he showed up for work. Thus alcoholics who could not hold a job on any other paper drew fairly regular pay from *The Star*, and the newsroom displayed as fine a collection of old crocks and alcoholic drifters as ever graced the craft. There was more than a grain of truth in the jest that all one had to do to get work at *The Star* was to prove he was a confirmed drunk—that is, if he was a good newspaperman when sober.

The payroll records show that only one editorial worker went off staff after September, 1930, receiving his notice on December 5, yet in an article on Hindmarsh in a national magazine in 1955 a writer said he "fired 13 reporters at Christmas 1930." As 1931 rolled along and the number of unemployed newspapermen increased, the voucher system got quite out of hand. Some were remaining on voucher for months. Hindmarsh was even putting unemployed Buffalo newspapermen on voucher, then forgetting about them. The city room became as crowded as a New York subway train which was wonderful, for instead of sending reporters out in gangs of eight or ten they could be sent out in armies of twenty. There is no way of checking how many reporters were on voucher, but some who worked on *The Star* at that time maintain the number of reporters on staff and on voucher had reached sixty-six by September, 1931, compared with a normal complement of thirty-four. Reid, who had to approve all vouchers, says this is an exaggeration, and the number on voucher at no time was more than half a dozen.

Be that as it may, orders were given in September, 1931, that the editorial staff must be reduced, and in the last week of that month six on payroll were given their notice. On Friday, October 9, the Friday before Thanksgiving Day, another eight were given their notices. At the same time orders were given that none on voucher were to receive assignments, and a couple of men who had been working on the desk on a day-to-day basis were told they were no longer needed. Thus the number thrown out of work by this economy wave was higher than the payroll records show. Men still working for *The Star* recall the panic that swept the city room, with every reporter expecting to get his notice any day.

It must have been apparent to all that the over-staffing could not continue indefinitely, but that was slight consolation to those laid off. And unfortunately, a man discharged after six months seldom remembered *The Star* had given him an opportunity to earn some money in a period of depression when no other newspaper would give him a job. Since the dismissal notices were usually signed by Hindmarsh, resentment was centred on him—which was not wholly unjust, for he was to blame for allowing the situation to develop as it had.

The economy wave that accompanied these dismissals was the most drastic *The Star* had known. Reporters had to turn in the stubs of pencils before being given a new one; no one was given a streetcar ticket or allowed to take a taxi at *Star* expense, no matter how important the assignment, and office boys sometimes had to walk the length of the city to pick up a parcel, or pay their own way. Supper money was reduced from 50 cents to 35 cents, and hours of work, always long, were extended. Ceiling lights were fitted with individual pull-cords so they could be turned off if no one was working directly beneath one, and Mr. Atkinson used to make periodic tours of inspection to make sure they were.

Economy waves, sometimes one or two a year during the 1930's, usually extended throughout the organization, but were never as drastically enforced in the other departments, or accompanied by such large-scale staff reductions, as in the editorial. This was mainly because the others were not subject to the large, unexpected expenditures inherent in Hindmarsh's method of covering the news, but also in part due to the literal and impetuous manner in which Hindmarsh carried out what was sometimes no more than a casual suggestion from Mr. Atkinson. "If you have something unpleasant to do, do it at once," he used to say, and the manner of his doing it at once sometimes increased the unpleasantness.

But even in the business office, the 1931 economy wave was unusually harsh, aggravated as it was by Mr. Atkinson's concern over Britain's financial position. There was some reduction in staff, with subsequent hirings at a lower salary scale, and some pay cuts. The *Telegram* published affidavits from two adult men that they had been hired by the circulation department for $6 a week for work in connection with a puzzle contest, and demanded an investigation by the provincial government into *The Star*'s alleged "low wage practices."

The Star's economy waves have often been the subject of ribald jokes, but the drastic economies effected in 1931 may have saved the paper from disaster. Profits had begun to decline in the latter half of 1931, and Mr. Atkinson had foreseen conditions were likely to get worse before they got better. Despite the stringent economies, profits continued to decline alarmingly and by mid-1932 were only a quarter what they had been. After that they increased slowly to a reasonably safe level, then slumped in the first three months of 1933 to half their former level. Each decline in profits was accompanied by an economy wave throughout the organization.

Hindmarsh's literal enforcement of specific measures of economy was not without a touch of sardonic humour. On one occasion, for example, Mr. Atkinson put a limit on the size of the colour illustration on the cover of the *Star Weekly* full-length novel, ostensibly to save zinc. Several cover illustrations were already in metal. Hindmarsh and his picture editor solemnly measured these. All were over the limit, so all were destroyed—about $250 worth of cuts.

So far as the editorial department is concerned, the 1931 economy wave ended with the beginning of the new fiscal year. By Christmas Hindmarsh had hired thirteen new reporters. But whereas most of those laid off had been in the $45 to $50 salary range, most of the new ones were hired at $18 or $20 a week. These newcomers were all paid the Christmas bonus of one full week's pay, though some had worked less than two weeks. *The Star* was the only Toronto newspaper to continue paying a Christmas bonus throughout the depression.

Then one bright day in 1932 the scandal magazine *Hush* appeared on the streets of Toronto with a horrendous exposé of the way wicked old Holy Joe was treating his employees. For the first time there appeared in print the story that *The Star* had fired employees on Christmas Eve. Since the *Hush* story was characteristically vague as to the year in which this had taken place, or who was involved, and nobody could remember very definitely, it was agreed it must be happening every year.

The *Telegram* was engaged in a circulation drive at the time, and its canvassers went from door to door with a copy of *Hush* in one hand and an order form in the other, thus assuring widest dissemination of the story. But significantly, the records department of the *Telegram*, which has been most helpful in searching old clippings, has not produced evidence that the *Telegram* published the story at that time, though it was usually alert for anything it could print derogatory to *The Star*.

In the years that followed new stories of this alleged Christmas Eve firing burgeoned wherever reporters met to bend an elbow, and with each telling the story became more fanciful until fiction became inextricably interwoven with fact. Any number of newspapermen can be found to claim they were among the victims, or had friends who were. They remember the panic that reigned during the economy firings of 1930 and 1931, and long familiarity with the myth has caused them to associate it with Christmas. Nearly all those laid off on October 9, 1931, the Friday before Thanksgiving, will solemnly vow it happened the day before Christmas.

In gathering information for this history the writer talked with fully two dozen people who claimed to remember the alleged Christmas firings well.

Some put them as late as 1935, only one as early as 1929. Pressed for names, they usually mention one or more of those laid off in September and October, 1931. Only one person was mentioned in connection with the 1929 episode, and he was the one dismissed on December 2 for chronic alcoholism. None recalled two office boys who departed December 24, 1930, but there is nothing on record to show whether they left voluntarily or were dismissed.

One man who tells a circumstantial story of bearding Mr. Atkinson in his office to demand his Christmas bonus after being fired "the day before Christmas, 1931," is shown by the records of an advertising agency to have been working for them at the time he says *The Star* fired him. *The Star*'s records show his name was removed from payroll at Thanksgiving. Another related in an interview with a magazine how he returned to the office the day before Christmas from an out-of-town assignment, staggering with weariness after giving his heart and soul to the cause, only to be handed a notice of dismissal. Actually it was much earlier in December than Christmas, it was not weariness that caused him to stagger, and he had given his heart and soul so ineffectively that he had been badly scooped.

As late as December, 1937, when economy lay-offs had been definitely ended on *The Star*, the *Guild Reporter* claimed there had been "a recurrence of the annual pre-Christmas firing bee." Yet careful reading of the *Guild Reporter*'s story shows that the twelve persons it lists as having been "fired before Christmas" in 1937 left *The Star*'s employ at various times in October and November, and had worked in several departments. Two were office boys, two were girls who had been employed in the syndicate as temporary help, one had been employed temporarily in the library. None departed within the month before or after Christmas.

The Star's payroll records show that in the ten years following 1929 only the two office boys in 1930, and a telegraph editor went off the payroll during the Christmas season, or at a time indicating he was given his notice at Christmas. In those ten years only four reporters were dismissed from *The Star* in December, none within two weeks of Christmas. One was an alcoholic who was rehired after an appropriate period of drying out; one was a communist organizer whose newspaper career ended, sometime after he left *The Star*, with a jail sentence for publishing obscene literature; one had fallen down badly on an assignment; and one is but a misty memory on the newspaper scene.

Older employees of the payroll department recall that when the story was first told they surmised it referred to photographers who were paid by the picture, since they knew no names had been removed from the payroll near Christmas except in 1929. Photographers who worked for *The Star* in those years say this surmise is incorrect, though they were usually the first to be affected by an economy wave. A possibility, which can neither be proven nor disproven at this date, is that some reporters on voucher were told at Christmas they would be given no more assignments. At least one man on voucher is known to have been personally dismissed by Hindmarsh the day before Christmas when Hindmarsh learned he had been trying to get an office girl drunk in the photographic dark-room.

Though the *Telegram* never printed the story as fact, for several years when its editor, C. O. Knowles, felt particularly rancorous towards *The Star*, it would call on either Atkinson or Hindmarsh to deny the story if it was not true. Atkinson, only once, and that in 1941, denied anything said about himself or *The Star*, in keeping with Timothy Eaton's advice to "keep store." Hindmarsh at the same time was busy creating his own legend of tough, hard-boiled Harry Hindmarsh, in which he took some pride. By the time they realized how persistent the fable was, and the harm it was doing *The Star*'s reputation, it was too late to deny it. They would not have been believed.

A curious feature about the editorial firings over a span of eight years is the small number of persons actually affected. The same people were hired and fired several times. The main body of editorial employees went about its work with few changes. Of thirty-seven reporters and deskmen on the payroll at the beginning of the depression, twenty-five were still there eight years later though several had been promoted to more important positions. Eleven editorial workers whose names appear in a 1927 directory of employees are still working on *The Star* as this is written in 1962, while twenty-four others listed in 1927 as writers, editors, deskmen or reporters remained with *The Star* until death or retirement.

It would seem *The Star* kept a basic staff of about twenty-four reporters, as indomitable and ingenious a crew as any newspaper ever employed, and their exploits are legendary. They roamed the world and the less pleasant parts of their own country when occasion demanded, and counted the day lost when they did not scoop a rival. They worked incredibly long hours and with amazing competence, and they cursed Hindmarsh from Halifax to Vancouver.

But Hindmarsh was extraordinarily proud of them and they were just as proud of him even when they cursed him the most. And his loyalty to them, which was immense, begat a similar loyalty. With one or two exceptions this valiant crew suffered no pay cuts even when the depression was at its most dismal worst, and their salaries ranged from $45 to

$180 a week. These are the men who will relate, as Gordon Sinclair does, that "Hindmarsh fired me eight times," but they knew he did not mean it and he knew they knew he did not mean it.

Outside this inner group was a rolling mass forever trying to get "in." Some, like Matthew Halton, James V. Kingsbury, and Ken Edey, did get "in," usually to replace one of the select group who left or was promoted. Until they got "in" their jobs were never secure and their pay might be as low as $12 a week, though university graduates usually started at $20. Scholarship winner Matthew Halton started at $24 after studying a year in Europe. Most of them were young men, but there were a few old-timers who had trouble holding a job even at the best of times. Some were able young men who were to distinguish themselves later in journalism or other occupations, but in Hindmarsh's opinion were prima donnas. It is not clear whether Allister Grosart, the man popularly credited with building up much of Mr. Diefenbaker's appeal in 1957, was a prima donna or not. He worked for *The Star* from 1928 to 1933. But he was clearly a stubborn character or he would have been more receptive to *The Star*'s brand of liberalism. Hugh Garner never reached the prima donna class, for he was dismissed as an office boy without being given an opportunity to demonstrate his talent as a writer.

For a while there was a regular circuit between the *Toronto Star* and the *Windsor Star*, which operated along similar lines, with an occasional asteroid straying briefly into the firmament of the *Sudbury Star*. But one and all, they would come streaking back to the *Toronto Star* on word Hindmarsh was hiring, for to get "in" was to win the highest accolade of newspaperdom. Why they would put up with the intolerably long hours, and the insecurity, is one of the mysteries that made newspapermen what they were. The morale on *The Star* was a marvel and a thing of joy that seemed able to withstand any shock.

Despite these recurrent economy waves, on average *The Star* was one of the few newspapers anywhere that operated on an increased editorial budget throughout most of the depression. With other newspapers tightening their belts, Mr. Atkinson looked upon the depression as an opportunity for expansion. How right he was the record shows.

Sometimes an economy wave followed the expenditure of an unusually large sum in covering a story, and this gave rise to other myths. An example is the Moose River mine disaster of April, 1936, in which a rescue crew worked ten days to free three trapped men. *The Star* hired planes, leased telegraph lines, and sent a large crew of reporters and photographers to Nova Scotia to cover the story. This was followed by an economy wave in which two or three men were laid off and a limit was placed on pictures bought on assignment.

A Toronto left-wing publication, the *New Commonwealth*, carried an article reporting *The Star*'s so-called "injustice" to its reporters on this story. Its article was wrong on nearly every count. It said *The Star* spent $25,000 covering this story but actually realized "a handsome profit" because *The Star Newspaper Service* syndicated the reports to other newspapers for more than they cost. Nevertheless, it affirmed, "because each department had to stand on its own feet," syndicate profits could not be used to offset editorial losses, and as a consequence it said, "15 men were fired." This piece of fiction is still being repeated.

The facts were that *The Star* did not make a cent out of the story, syndicate profits could be and usually were used to offset editorial expenses, the story cost considerably less than $25,000 to cover, and the number of reporters laid off was far short of fifteen. Mr. Atkinson had a rooted aversion to making money out of other peoples' misfortunes, and profits from syndicating disaster stories invariably were applied to the relief of disaster victims. If there was a fund for a specific case, they were donated to that fund. If there was no fund, they were given the Red Cross. These were among Atkinson's many secret acts of charity. Syndication of the personal story of Alfred Scadding, one of the rescued men, produced $10,600 gross. Of this Scadding was paid $10,000. All revenue from syndication of other stories of this disaster was given the Red Cross.

When stories of a general nature or reports from foreign correspondents were syndicated, *The Star Newspaper Service* paid the editorial department 40 per cent of the revenue they produced. This helped cover the cost of maintaining *The Star*'s large staff of roving reporters, but the syndicate was never the big money-maker it was popularly supposed to be. Its most profitable period was in the 1920's when it ran a telegraph news service similar to Canadian Press. But by 1930 Canadian Press was firmly established and *The Star* dropped its rival service.

The syndication of their stories without them being given any share in the profits was long a grievance of *Star* writers, who felt they should be paid some extra compensation. Their sense of grievance mounted when, after the death of Bone, the rule was firmly enforced that an employee of *The Star* could not write for any other publication. Mr. Atkinson justified this on the grounds that if a reporter was good enough to have his articles regularly syndicated, he was paid a salary in keeping. Moreover, the policy of *The Star* as of most daily newspapers in America at that time, was that a reporter was on call twenty-four hours a day, seven days a week, and that anything he might produce was the exclusive property of his employer. Hindmarsh did not agree with his father-in-law on this point, and one of the first things he did on becoming president was to relax this rule.

Another cause of resentment for several years was the capricious dismissal of reporters for inconsequential misdeeds. Some editors, notably news editor John Drylie, were temperamentally unsuited for directing a large staff harmoniously, and it was not unusual for him to fire a reporter for "insolence" or "insubordination" where none was intended. Hindmarsh, too, earned a reputation for firing in anger and with slight provocation, though his ire was usually directed against relative newcomers for whom he had not yet acquired a sense of paternal responsibility.

Thus, though the alleged "annual pre-Christmas firing bee" was mostly myth, and some of the other stories must be discarded as malicious fancy based on very slight fact, the truth must still be admitted that during eight depression years *The Star* at times showed a cold ruthlessness towards its employees out of keeping with its previous record, and one would think, out of keeping with Mr. Atkinson's character as he had previously shown it.

W. A. Hewitt referred to Atkinson as running "a happy paper" in earlier years. *Star* reporters had always been the highest paid in Canada, and on his twenty-fifth anniversary as publisher of *The Star*, on December 13, 1924, they presented Mr. Atkinson with a grandfather's clock and a testimonial letter praising him as a generous and understanding employer. This clock now has an honoured position in the hall of his son's home. At the same time editorial employees of the *Star Weekly* presented Mr. Atkinson with a similar testimonial letter, and a silver tea service, which are now the treasured possessions of Mrs. Hindmarsh.

Why this seemingly inexplicable change? Cranston blamed it on the death of Mrs. Atkinson after a long and painful illness in 1931 which deprived the publisher of his "good Angel," and employees of an advocate. Yet the change had set in nearly two years before her death. Gregory Clark says Mr. Atkinson was moved by the misfortunes of humanity in the mass, but not by those of individual humans. This fails to explain his many, many, acts of kindness to persons he scarcely knew. B. K. Sandwell said he was proving what his enemies had said all along, that he was only a humanitarian, a liberal, and socialist because it was good for circulation. Against this we have his youthful attraction to liberalism, his rejection of the flattering offer from the *Montreal Star* in 1899, and his coolness towards the Liberal party when it dragged its feet in implementing his welfare program. M. E. Nichols said he saw in the depression an opportunity to expand while his less confident competitors were retrenching, and he exploited it ruthlessly. But he had already knocked out two of his competitors and a third was tottering. Pascoe said he had made so much money he was greedy for more. Yet he lived plainly and without ostentation, and his generosity to innumerable charities was inconsistent with one who loved money. The *Telegram*, always given to seeing things in unrelieved black and white, expressed it more starkly. He was "a wicked old man."

The editorial workers who bore the brunt of the recurrent economy firings, and were the most articulate in their protests, blamed the man nearest at hand, tough, hard-boiled Harry Hindmarsh who, said they, had to have his story at whatever cost of human suffering. A former news editor called him a "sadist," and Hemingway said working under Hindmarsh was "like serving in the Prussian army under a bad general." But a former newspaper Guild organizer termed him "a big softie inside a hard shell," and a psychiatrist who analysed him by remote control said he was the typical "adamant father personality."

A former news executive relates a revealing interview he had just after being given a promotion. Hindmarsh asked him what his ambition was. The young man replied it was to be successful enough as an editor that he could retire while still reasonably young and travel, or perhaps write. "That is a poor ambition," he quotes Hindmarsh as saying, "You should strive for power. Power is the most important thing in the world." Did Hindmarsh feel the glow of an absolute monarch as he surveyed the city room, and enjoy his power over men's destinies?

There is no doubt the pressure on the reporting staff began to increase as Hindmarsh assumed more authority after the end of the First World War and had become intense by 1923. It mounted as Hindmarsh usurped more authority from Bone, but there were no staff troubles until December, 1929. After that there were economy firings and low pay in departments not under Hindmarsh, though working conditions were always better than in the editorial department and there was never the same ruthlessness.

The amazing thing is that, for whatever reason, *The Star* should have for eight years pursued a policy towards employees that could only result in casting suspicion on the sincerity with which it held the liberal and pro-labour principles it supported.

Chapter 18

ENTER THE GUILD

A notable improvement in pay and working conditions for editorial employees on *The Star* coincided with a drive for membership in Toronto by the American Newspaper Guild. The Guild had been organized in Cleveland in 1933 as an independent craft union for reporters and other editorial workers, but soon became an industrial union open to all employees of newspapers not organized in other unions. It demonstrated a remarkable strength from the beginning and by 1937, when it joined the CIO, it had conducted nineteen successful strikes and won eighty-four contracts. It had lost only one strike, on a small town newspaper.

On August 31, 1936, nine young newspapermen met in a room at Toronto Union Station to organize the first Guild local in Canada. Harry R. Farmer, an editorial writer on the *Globe*, was elected president. Ralph Foster, of *The Star*, was secretary-treasurer. Their initial efforts to recruit members met with faint success and on February 28, 1937, they invited all newspaper workers to an open meeting at the King Edward Hotel.

About a hundred attended, including Mayor W. D. Robbins, a labour man, who brought fraternal greetings.

On April 30, 1937, Farmer wrote Mr. Atkinson, officially informing him of the establishment of a Toronto local, and taking "the opportunity of acknowledging the absolute fairness of your attitude on labor questions." He disclaimed any intention on the part of the Guild to use *The Star* "as a means to press organization on the staffs of the other dailies," but, he added, "at the same time, naturally, it has learned to look upon *The Star* as a friend, and for that reason has taken advantage of a favourable atmosphere in the matter of organizing."

Then he concluded his letter with a paragraph that was to cause a great deal of trouble and misunderstanding in the next four years. "Will you please accept the assurance of the Guild," he wrote, "that no underhand action with respect to *The Star* is contemplated, and that when the organization attempts to open negotiations for the betterment of working conditions the request to be allowed to do so will be made to all three papers without discrimination."

This assurance was given as a result of fears expressed by Mr. Atkinson that the Guild would take advantage of *The Star*'s well-known support of organized labour to force upon it a contract which would place it as a disadvantage in competition with other Toronto newspapers. Later the Guild was to repudiate Farmer's letter on the grounds that unions have never accepted the principle that all firms within an industry must be organized before a union seeks a contract with any one of them.

The Guild's efforts to organize employees of the *Telegram* and the *Globe and Mail* encountered immediate and determined opposition. On July 2, 1937, the *Globe and Mail*, which had come into existence a few months earlier with the merger by George McCullagh of the *Globe* and the *Mail and Empire*, ran an editorial declaring the Guild was "a threat to freedom of the press." A few days later it discharged Farmer as he was about to leave for the Guild's international convention. At the same time the news editor posted a "declaration of loyalty" on the bulletin board with a suggestion all reporters sign it. Farmer's dismissal was protested by the Allied Printing Trades Council, but McCullagh told a delegation from that organization that he had been discharged for incompetence and his case could not be reconsidered. McCullagh at the time was waging a campaign in his newspaper to "keep the CIO out of Canada," and the Guild was a CIO affiliate.

In November, 1937, Ralph Foster, one of the more radically inclined of the younger Guild leaders, was dismissed with two weeks' pay by news editor John Heron, who had recently succeeded John Drylie. Foster was told it was for reasons of economy but when he learned the following Monday that *The Star* had hired the son of a friend of Hindmarsh he was convinced it was because of his activities in the Guild. He wrote to Mr. Atkinson protesting his treatment and received an immediate invitation to discuss the matter with him. "Somebody thought he was pleasing me," Atkinson told Foster sourly, and ordered his immediate reinstatement. He assured Foster no employee of *The Star* would be penalized for Guild activity.

Shortly thereafter the Guild asked Mr. Atkinson to open negotiations for a contract. Atkinson replied by quoting Farmer's letter. The Guild responded that because of intimidation at the *Telegram* and the *Globe and Mail* it had been unable as yet to organize those newspapers. Mr. Atkinson retorted that the Toronto newspapers had negotiated jointly with the mechanical trades since 1917, and the Guild committee got the impression from his conversation that there was an undertaking among them that none would make a separate agreement with any union. The *Guild Reporter* said Atkinson promised that as soon as the Guild had a sufficient number of members on each newspaper to warrant joint negotiations he would see it was undertaken. He repeated his promise that no obstacle would be placed in the way of the Guild organizing *Star* employees.

About this time *The Star* and the *Globe and Mail* began giving reporters "dismissal pay" amounting to one week's salary for each year of unbroken employment, and this was welcomed by the *Guild Reporter* as an indication the newspapers had abandoned the practice of periodic economy firings. This practice had not by any means been resticted to *The Star*, and McCullagh had added materially to the number of unemployed newspapermen when he merged his two papers. The *Guild Reporter* also noted that both papers had raised the minimum starting pay for inexperienced reporters to $20 a week, the minimum for office boys to $10 a week, and had given a general pay increase to advertising solicitors. The Guild's goal was $25 a week starting pay for reporters, rising to $45 a week after four years' experience.

In the next two years only three reporters were dismissed from *The Star* for any cause. The period of insecurity in so far as employment was concerned may therefore be considered as having ended in 1937.

"*The Star* . . . seems to be the only newspaper as far as can be judged that has openly, though not officially, allowed its workers all the freedom they want to organize," wrote Edward Dix, a member of the Guild executive, in the June 11, 1938, issue of *Satuday Night.* He said management of the *Globe and Mail* was hostile to the Guild, while management of the *Telegram* ignored it.

The Guild held its international convention in Toronto in 1938. The more aggressive Fred Payne, of *The Star,* had meantime succeeded Farmer as president of the Toronto local, and when the convention elected Roger Irwin of *The Star* as international vice-president Farmer disappeared from the Guild scene leaving only his troublesome letter behind. In connection with the convention a mass meeting of Toronto newspapermen and white-collar workers was held, sponsored by the Guild and the Inter-Professional Association, at which Guild founder and president, Heywood Broun, was the speaker. Morley Callaghan was chairman.

The *Telegram* completely ignored the convention, printing not a line about it. The *Globe and Mail* made passing reference to it, but did not cover the sessions. *The Star* sent five reporters to cover it, but they got surprisingly little in the paper.

The convention gave a boost to organizational activity in Toronto, and it was soon proceeding openly on the *Globe and Mail* as well as *The Star.* A notice was posted on the bulletin board of the *Telegram,* however, warning that any reporter who joined the Guild would be immediately dismissed. In midsummer 1939 a bulletin issued by the Toronto local contains this statement: "The Toronto local's existing relations with the publishers of *The Star* and the *Globe and Mail* leave very little to be desired at this stage. Publishers will do what they can, on economic grounds, to hold off negotiations for a contract, but there is no trace of hostility in their attitude. It's simply business, on both sides." It was also reported in this bulletin that a *Star* unit had been organized under the chairmanship of reporter Alf Tate and a *Globe and Mail* unit under columnist Judith Robinson, but "the *Telegram* chairman is still, by force of circumstances, underground."

That same summer *Star* reporters were informed none would be expected to cover more than two night assignments a week, and that those who had a night assignment need not report for work until noon the next day. This was a notable improvement over the working conditions that had prevailed previously.

In the fall of 1939 the Guild again approached the publishers of *The Star* and the *Globe and Mail.* They were met with a flat refusal to negotiate from McCullagh and Atkinson waved the Farmer letter before the eyes of the delegation. Organize the *Telegram* before requesting negotiations, he told them. An effort along that line was made but it met with total failure, while the *Globe and Mail* unit collapsed after Miss Robinson was discharged in 1940 with the excuse that criticism in her column of the King government was hampering the war effort.

However, organizational work on *The Star* continued openly and without interference. In July, 1940, six *Star* employees and Miss Robinson founded the *New Lead,* still the official organ of Toronto guildsmen, and their names appeared on the masthead as an "editorial committee." At the same time the Guild rented the third floor of 101 King Street West, across from *The Star*, as a press club. Here *Star* employees met after work and Guild business was discussed at meetings open to any who chose to attend. It was known that a full report of what was done and said, and by whom, was given Hindmarsh the following day, and the identity of the reporter was known, but no effort was made to interfere with him.

One day when Foster, who was picture editor of the *Star Weekly*, entered Hindmarsh's office for his daily conference he found the latter poring over the September issue of the *New Lead*, which had developed into a breezy eight-page newspaper. "Why don't some of those boys write like that for us?" Hindmarsh demanded. "They will, when the editors of *The Star* give them as good assignments as the editors of the *New Lead* do," Foster retorted.

"Who on the *New Lead* gives them these assignments?" Hindmarsh asked, then noticing Foster hesitate he quickly continued, "Don't misunderstand, I think he is doing a splendid job. We should have a good position for a man like that." He was told the editor was George Fairhead Rogers, a relatively inexperienced young man then working on the copy desk. Four months later Rogers was appointed executive editor of the *Star Weekly*.

By November, 1940, *The Star* unit claimed a membership of 107 out of the 147 editorial workers on the two *Star* publications, and it was decided to approach Mr. Atkinson again. The principal topic discussed at a membership meeting was how to persuade him to evade his agreement with other publishers not to negotiate separately with the Guild.

Mr. Atkinson himself supplied the answer a day or so later when he encountered Jessie MacTaggart in the corridor. Miss MacTaggart had been president of *The Star* unit since February, Tate having joined the navy as a public relations officer.

"Did I ever tell you how I settled the Oshawa strike?" Mr. Atkinson asked.

When Miss MacTaggart said that he hadn't, he related how leaders of the United Automobile Workers had come to his home for advice in the early morning hours, and he had suggested that as a face-saving compromise General Motors sign a contract "with its employees who are members of the United Automobile Workers," but not with the union. Then looking knowingly at Miss MacTaggart, Atkinson hurried away, audibly chuckling. When Miss MacTaggart reported this conversation at the next Guild meeting a committee was appointed consisting of Roger Irwin, Gordon Sinclair, Edward Dix, Jessie MacTaggart, and Ross Harkness, to inquire if *The Star* would negotiate an agreement along the lines of "the Oshawa formula," as it was known.

The committee was referred to Hindmarsh, who assured it *The Star* would negotiate, and that he had been appointed by Mr. Atkinson to treat with a committee of employees. He said he personally felt that a paper which supported organized labour as strongly as *The Star* did should be fully organized. When it was remarked that the overtime provisions sought by employees would necessitate a radical change in *The Star*'s method of covering big stories he said the day was gone when *The Star* could cover stories in the massive way it had in the past.

After this committee reported back to the membership, a negotiating committee was appointed consisting of Foster, Payne, Sinclair, Irwin, and MacTaggart. The *New Lead* reported that "collective bargaining between publisher and editorial staff . . . began at 9:45 a.m. on Dec. 19." It said that though *Star* employees are members of the Guild "their representatives are negotiating in behalf of organized *Star* employees rather than in behalf of the union itself." Simultaneously with the opening of negotiations, *The Star* raised the pay of forty-two editorial employees, by amounts ranging from $4 to $9 a week.

Writing later in the *Canadian Forum* under the pseudonym Rex Morgan, a man who has been identified as a member of the Guild executive and associate editor of the *New Lead* said "management intimated it was prepared to consider favorably as a basis of negotiation such measures as a five-day, forty-hour week, overtime allowance, and a $45-per-week minimum wage for experienced reporters." This was the minimum goal aimed at by the Guild in negotiations with all newspapers. Actually in 1939 *The Star* had unofficially adopted a minimum of $45 in hiring experienced reporters, and had stopped hiring for a trial period on voucher. Not all experienced reporters on staff, however, had their pay increased to $45.

Only one negotiation meeting, December 19, was held before Christmas. At a meeting scheduled for the day after Christmas Hindmarsh told the Guild committee a crisis demanding his immediate attention had arisen in the *Star Weekly* as a result of the resignation of the *Weekly* managing editor, T. J. Wheeler, and he asked that the meeting be postponed a day or two. When they met for the postponed meeting he said the *Star Weekly* business still was not straightened out. Since he had made reservations for his annual January vacation in Nassau, he asked the Guild to agree to suspend negotiations until the first Thursday of February.

The Guild committee filed from his office, but instead of asking a membership meeting for instructions it decided on its own to submit an ultimatum. Half an hour later it re-entered Hindmarsh's office and handed him a letter accusing *The Star* of bad faith and stating that unless *The Star* resumed negotiations within two days the Guild would consider negotiations broken off. This ultimatum was reported in the *New Lead*.

"Wait here a minute," Hindmarsh told the committee, and hurried with the letter to Mr. Atkinson's office on the floor below. A few minutes later he returned and handed the letter to Irwin.

"All right," he said, "negotiations are broken off."

"You mean, *The Star* is breaking off negotiations?" Irwin asked.

"No, I mean you have broken them off," Hindmarsh replied.

The meeting at which the negotiating committee reported to the membership what had transpired was one of the stormiest ever held, with much of the anger directed at the Guild's own committee rather than at *The Star*. Irwin said he wrote the ultimatum, though against his better judgment, because all the other members of the committee were in favour of it.

The collapse of the Guild began with this meeting. It can be attributed to a loss of confidence by the membership in their leaders, though the knockout blow was delivered by news editor, Ken Edey, who had succeeded John Heron in 1938. Many felt Hindmarsh's request for a postponement of one month in negotiations was not unreasonable under the circumstances. They also felt that anyone familiar with Atkinson's and Hindmarsh's temperaments should have known better than to deliver an ultimatum charging bad faith after only one meeting had been held, and on such slight evidence.

The Toronto local appealed to New York headquarters for advice, and John Dunn, one of the Guild's most successful negotiators, was sent to Toronto. He criticized the negotiating committee for its ill advised action and advised appointment of an entirely new committee which would seek to reopen negotiations. This was done, but Hindmarsh had left on his vacation and Mr. Atkinson refused to meet the committee or Dunn. Some individual labour leaders agreed to intercede on behalf of the Guild with Mr. Atkinson, but neither CIO nor AFL unions would promise to support the Guild. The Allied Printing Trades Council declined its support, and unofficially the mechanical trades at *The Star* indicated they would not back the Guild in the event of a showdown. The mechanical trades had always enjoyed excellent relations with Mr. Atkinson, and blamed the Guild for what had occurred.

Over a period of a month members had been resigning, and a meeting called February 4 to take a strike vote was attended by only 41 per cent of the editorial employees. The *New Lead* reported the vote of those attending was 42 to 19 in favour of a strike. When apprised of the vote by an intermediary, since he would not see any of the Guild executive, Mr. Atkinson stated that in about a year's time, "when harmony has been restored," he would consider negotiating with an organization of employees, but would not negotiate with the Guild or members of the existing executive of the Toronto local or *Star* unit. Some of them had attacked Mr. Atkinson in speeches that can best be described as hysterical, and had printed circulars for distribution among downtown shoppers asking them not to patronize stores advertising in *The Star*.

At this point, according to the *New Lead*, C. H. Millard, director for Canada of the Steelworkers' Organizing committee, advised against a strike and suggested the Guild apply for conciliation. It must have been clear to all that with only 42 of 147 editorial employees voting for a strike it could not possibly succeed. Nevertheless the Guild executive decided on an immediate strike and called a meeting for February 8 to confirm its decision.

The morning of that day Edey began calling Guild members two by two into his office, he says so he would have a witness that he did not threaten anybody. Now head of public relations for the University of Toronto, he states he acted entirely on his own initiative and that neither Hindmarsh nor Atkinson indicated what he should do. He says it was quite evident not enough employees would strike to make it effective, but they would interfere with getting out a paper. He says he believed in a union of editorial employees, but felt the only way he could save it from catastrophe was by persuading the rank and file to break with the executive. He says the argument of the Guild executive that a pro-labour paper like *The Star* "couldn't afford to have a strike" was fallacious because organized labour had already condemned the Guild and had indicated it would not support it in a strike.

The article in the *Canadian Forum* said the news workers were told by Edey "their jobs were in no danger and they were not being intimidated, but that they would be better off outside the Guild, and asked for carbon copies of their resignations." Edey states this is correct. Some reporters indicated a reluctance to resign under such pressure, and it was suggested to these that they might simply abstain from attending the meeting as a demonstration of non-confidence in the executive.

Only nineteen attended, and they included twelve who were not interviewed because they were considered to be hard-core troublemakers. One of these twelve was Borden Spears, who later helped reorganize the Guild, was on the committee that won the first contract, and eventually became managing editor of *The Star*. In a parting statement in the *New Lead* Dunn said they voted to rescind the strike motion. Spears states this is incorrect. In a last gesture of defiance, he said, they voted 17 to 2 to strike anyway, but since a strike obviously was impossible that was the end of it.

The next day a funeral wreath was hung on the bulletin board, centred by a Guild button, and with the motto "Requiescat in Pace." It was placed there by Claude Pascoe at the suggestion of Hindmarsh, who personally paid for it. Pascoe had opposed the Guild from the beginning and had tried unsuccessfully to organize a committee of employees against it. He said this was done entirely on his own initiative because he believed the Guild members were "disloyal."

The Guild was no more, but in a story headed "$20,000 in Raises Won by Starmen, Strike Called Off" the *New Lead* of March, 1941, reported that almost everything asked except a contract had been granted. *The Star* introduced the five-day week for editorial employees—the first Canadian newspaper to do so—with a minimum of $40 a week for experienced reporters. The Guild in the US was demanding $45 a week but settling for $40. In some individual cases, the *New Lead* stated, "the raises amount to $15 a week." Commenting on developments, the *Guild Reporter* observed: "As is customary when increases are handed down by any management, a number did not get an increase," but these were all men receiving more than the minimum. No cash payment for overtime was provided, but without any promise the practice developed of giving reporters equivalent time off for overtime worked.

The *Canadian Forum* observed that during the period of Guild activity only an inexperienced reporter and an editorial secretary had been dismissed, neither for Guild activity, though "a number of news workers who had been prominent in Guild activities were given new positions which, it is alleged, lowered their status." Roger Irwin, a former financial editor, was assigned on Hindmarsh's instructions to writing obituaries. After February 8 their "status" was restored and "most of those who led the Guild activity" were among those given the larger pay increases. Two were promoted.

Ralph Foster, who now heads one of Canada's biggest producers of television films and commercials, said recently: "We would have got our contract if we hadn't been so impatient. Hindmarsh wouldn't have spent the time he did with us if he hadn't been honest in his intention to negotiate, but we rubbed him the wrong way." On the other hand, though insisting he was given no lead whatever by Hindmarsh, Edey suggests he may have been glad of an excuse to break with the Guild. While Hindmarsh resented the fact that printers were being paid more than reporters, and had welcomed the organization of the Guild in the first place because it strengthened his hand when he sought equal treatment for editorial workers, he may not have wanted it to become too strong. By merely being in existence it accomplished his purpose.

Be that as it may, *The Star*'s failure to sign an agreement in 1941 with editorial workers has been cited for twenty years as an example of the "contradictions" between Atkinson's professions and his practices.

In contrast with the troubled relations with white collar employees, *The Star* and Mr. Atkinson personally always enjoyed a cordial relationship with the printing trades. Beginning in 1917 all Toronto daily newspapers negotiated jointly with the mechanical trades. Atkinson was a sort of unofficial chairman of the publishers' committee, not by any formal election but because he enjoyed labour negotiations and was the most able of the group at that sort of thing. Only once while he was chief negotiator for the publishers was a strike seriously threatened, and that resulted from the opposition of the other newspapers to introduction of a five-day week. The Typographical Union had made the five-day week its main objective in 1934 and in the next two years nearly every contract signed in the United States provided for it. Canadian locals, however, had not pressed for it.

In 1937 international headquarters warned the Toronto locals that unless the contract then being negotiated contained provision for a five-day week it would not be approved, and they would be expelled from the international organization. Around the bargaining table the publishers appeared united against this concession, but the union suspected Mr. Atkinson was in favour of it. A delegation from *The Star* chapel (as a Typographical Union unit is called) accordingly met with him in his office. "If you can show me how a paper publishing six days a week can operate on a five-day week, I'll see that you get it," Mr. Atkinson told them.

The employees followed the example of big business and hired a firm of management consultants to study how it could be worked out. They were able to demonstrate that by hiring thirty more men *The Star* could put its composing room on a five-day week without loss of efficiency.

"You've convinced me," Mr. Atkinson told his own employees, but speaking for all the publishers, he objected to the extra cost entailed. The union offered to "split the cost" with management by accepting a reduction in pay of $5 a week each. When this concession was rejected they notified the publishers they would "not be at work" the following day.

Mr. Atkinson went to see C. O. Knowles of the *Telegram*, who had been the principal hold-out, in a last-minute effort to persuade him to agree to a five-day week. Knowles insisted he would never agree. "Then I am notifying you formally that *The Star* is no longer negotiating jointly with the other newspapers," Atkinson told him. "I will not have a strike on my newspaper. I am agreeing to a five-day week in the mechanical trades on *The Star*. You may do as you please."

After his conversation with Knowles, Atkinson returned to *The Star* and told his composing room employees he was meeting their conditions. Later that day Knowles also agreed, and a contract was signed. "You will have your five dollars back within three years," Mr. Atkinson told the union negotiators after the signing. He was right. By 1941 all departments of *The Star* were working only five days a week. For several years it was the only newspaper in Canada with a five-day week throughout.

The knowledge of what had happened in 1937 led some members of the executive of the editorial workers' Guild to argue in 1941 that *The Star* "could not afford a strike," but the situation was entirely different. The Typographical Union had shown a friendly and conciliatory attitude throughout its negotiations and had made the unusual concession of accepting a cut in pay in order that the five-day week would not be too burdensome all at once, whereas the attitude of the negotiating committee for the editorial workers was hostile from the beginning.

Mr. Atkinson's refusal to introduce a pension plan for his employees puzzled many people. He usually paid a generous retirement allowance to old employees, but sometimes the amount of the allowance depended upon the extent of Mr. Atkinson's personal acquaintanceship with the employee. He was always reluctant to see an employee retire, believing that "the longer a man remains in harness, the longer he lives," and very often a man was kept working at full pay long after his days of real usefulness had passed.

Soon after coming to *The Star*, J. S. Atkinson began urging his father to introduce a pension plan that would give employees an adequate retirement pay as a matter of right. Hindmarsh, also, would have liked to see a pension plan, and at least six different schemes were laid before Mr. Atkinson. On one occasion the firm's accountants were able to demonstrate that *The Star* would actually save money, having in mind the tax structure and the fact retirement allowances were already being paid a considerable number of employees. But to their undying mystification, Mr. Atkinson rejected it without explanation.

Atkinson seldom felt called upon to justify his actions, but he told his editorial writers, who sometimes had to justify them for him, that he could not introduce a company pension plan while *The Star* was advocating a uniform, non-contributory federal old age pension of an amount adequate to maintain an elderly couple in comfort. He objected, he told them, to company pension plans on the grounds that only a portion of the public would be covered, and that they would have the effect of freezing workers in their jobs, thus reducing the mobility of labour. As between the seeming inconsistency of refusing to set up a pension plan for his old employees while professing concern for the welfare of aged workers in general, and the real inconsistency of setting up a company pension plan while opposing such in principle, he chose the former.

This almost awesome adherence to consistence as he saw it is to be found throughout Mr. Atkinson's career. Viewed in the light of his reasoning, many actions that seemed inconsistent to others, and were inconsistent in the short term, are found to be in complete harmony with the principles he preached. His approach to liberalism and humanitarianism was intellectual. It could never be understood by those whose approach was emotional—still less by those whose opposition was emotional.

Chapter 19

THE KING STREET PRAVDA

On May 12, 1938, *The Star* was awarded a gold medal for distinguished service in journalism by the School of Journalism of the University of Missouri. Accompanying the medal was the following citation:

> For outstanding enterprise in covering world news—witness the Greenely Island 'scoop,' world rights on the Dionne quintuplets, staff correspondence from Russia and Spain—yet devoting tremendous energy to the bringing of local aid to the needy—witness its Santa Claus fund at Christmas time, its Fresh Air Fund at the peak of summer heat; for publishing an intelligently and independently liberal newspaper in a conservative stronghold of the Dominion; for scrupulously respecting the interests of minority groups in selecting its news; yet for maintaining editorial independence always, and for fighting the battle of free speech not only against alien dangers, but against local and powerful threats as well—for publishing a great North American newspaper.

The Star "voices the feelings of the man in the street," said the *Halifax Herald*, praising the award.

It is doubtful if any newspaper was ever under more outrageous attack for maintaining its principles than *The Star* was at the time this award was made. Some of the very things for which the University of Missouri commended it were those for which it was most violently assailed. "The King Street Pravda," it was dubbed by a journalistic contemporary; the "Red Star of Toronto," the Tories called it; "a Moscow-tainted publication," condemned a radio priest.

The years of the 1930's were an unending struggle in Canada, and more particularly in Toronto, to maintain free speech, freedom of assembly, freedom of workers to organize in a union of their choice, a free press, and civil liberties for all. Communists, fascists, and even the Ku Klux Klan had organized to overthrow democracy, and many who professed democracy were declaiming that it could be saved only by using the methods of totalitarianism. Because communists were the most numerous and the best organized they were the most feared by people with little faith in free institutions. Canada passed through its period of McCarthyism twenty-five years before the United States, and as *The Star* was to comment later in comparing the two, "it posed a greater threat to freedom because it was so secretive."

Throughout these years *The Star* defiantly maintained that no country ever lost its liberty by granting more liberty. It maintained that workers should have the same freedom to organize as employers; that it was not communists who encouraged communism but employers who would not bargain in good faith with their workers; and that the good sense of the people would lead them to detect the errors of communism. Above all, it maintained the right of the people to be informed, even though they might learn some of the bad things about Italian fascism, which many people secretly admired, and some of the good things about Russian communism, which most people openly detested. Bolshevism had to be beaten, but it could never be beaten if those opposed to it buried their heads in the sand.

And the public responded, as it usually responds to a newspaper that trusts it and in which it has trust. Year after year the circulation of *The Star* increased while that of its evening opposition remained static and that of its morning contemporaries declined. The very years in which reactionaries screamed most stridently at *The Star*'s liberalism were those in which the circulation of *The Star* gained the most. *The Star*'s detractors said Joe Atkinson played up to the "commies" and "the labour agitators" to get circulation. It played up to neither, but it defended the democratic rights of both. A newspaper that was truly liberal and concerned with the preservation of democracy and civil liberties could have taken no other position.

Canada's peculiar brand of McCarthyism made its first appearance in the years of labour unrest that followed the First World War, though it did not become a serious threat to civil liberties until after the election of R. B. Bennett as Prime Minister in 1930. In the anti-communist frenzy that had gripped the Conservative party in the last days of the Borden government, Parliament passed a law which, for sheer outrageousness, had never been equalled in a democratic country. It was the notorious "Section 98," an amendment to the Criminal Code.

This section did not mention the Communist party by name, but it made it a criminal offence punishable by twenty years imprisonment to belong to an "unlawful assembly." An "unlawful assembly" was so loosely defined that it made almost anybody who was against the government a criminal. But the most abhorrent feature was that proof of membership or even a trial according to the rules of justice were not necessary. Its provisions were so sweeping it was a criminal offence to pick up a communist handbill from the street and hand it to a friend.

Police were authorized to "arrest on suspicion" that an unlawful assembly was about to be held, and persons were sent to jail on mere suspicion of being communists. The property of suspected communists could be declared forfeit to the Crown by the RCMP without due process of law. Finnish and Ukrainian halls all over the country were seized between 1930 and 1935 because some of their members were known to be communists. Provincial governments cancelled the licences of theatres for permitting plays "likely to cause unrest." Four times before 1930 a Liberal House of Commons voted to repeal this section and four times the Conservative majority in the Senate vetoed the bill.

Toronto, which refused to be reconciled to King and his "pampering of subversives," hired tough-fisted Brigadier-General Dennis C. Draper as chief of police in 1928 to keep the communists in their place. Since he included among communists almost anybody who struck for higher wages or who suggested in public that the Canadian social order had not attained the apex of Christian civilization, his police provoked more disturbances than they prevented. Consequently, *The Star* waged unending campaign against his rough-shod methods. And since it was at the same time declaring that even a communist is entitled to the protection of the law, and urging that Russia be admitted to the League of Nations (for the same reasons it today is urging that China be admitted to the United Nations) it was accused by panicky people of being an admirer of communism and of Russia.

But an editorial of May 16, 1929, clearly shows it was not influenced by admiration for the Soviet system. At the same time it just as clearly indicates that, as one who believed that a radical reform of the social system was necessary, Mr. Atkinson was inclined to welcome agitators, even though they be communists. Said *The Star*:

> There is no free speech, no liberty of the press, in Soviet Russia. There is no free speech, no liberty of the press, in Fascist Italy. Nowhere under these dictatorships are liberties allowed . . .
>
> Always we have had discontented men, agitators, disturbers, railing at existing conditions. Always, too, we have had conditions that deserved to be railed at. The social history of Ontario has been a continuous example of mending and improving. There is scarcely a complaint that was made . . . by William Lyon Mackenzie in 1837 . . . that has not long since been remedied. Those who agitate are not always right. Very often they are absolutely right in the protest they make, but absolutely wrong in the remedy they propose. But if they set everybody thinking, a solution in due course evolves.
>
> [The communists] may be absolutely wrong in the program they advocate. They may even want to agitate for agitation's sake. They may, as some say, be filled with a chronic and profitless discontent. Yet they should not be permitted to provoke democracy into adopting the errors of dictatorship by forbidding the right of free speech and the right of public assembly.

At the time this editorial was written *The Star* had just succeeded in obtaining permission for its resident London correspondent, Henry Somerville, to visit Russia. Until then Russia had been closed to foreigners, and, though *The Star* had published a good deal on that country, most of it was second-hand material. Mr. Atkinson, therefore, looked forward with rejoicing to having his own reporter get first-hand information. But Somerville lost no time in demonstrating he was determined to see no good, hear no good, and above all, write no good. He began his first article by expressing surprise Russians "look more normal than a visitor would expect." Then he launched into a narration of how surprised the Russians were at finding him normal, because their press is so controlled they live in a state of primitive ignorance. His second article a week later was an interview with Madame Kamenoff, sister of Trotsky. He began it by saying he was impressed by "the social and economic progress of the country" after which he devoted nearly a column to debating with Madame Kamenoff about Russia's easy divorce, free love, anti-religious laws, and disfranchisement of the upper classes, with all of which Canadians were quite familiar. Not another word about "the social and economic progress of the country," which he had been sent to investigate.

Except for a few short items, those were all of Somerville's highly publicized "series on Russia" that ever saw the light of print in *The Star*. By June 1 he was back in London. It had been a mistake to send him. No doubt Somerville wrote other articles about Russia but they were not used. Unknown to *The Star*, he had become so active in the Catholic Social Movement in England that he had already come to regard the fight against communism as a religious crusade, and one never admits that the Devil may have his good points. A year later *The Star* tried to send him on a second trip to Russia, but the Reds refused him a visa.

In 1931 Prime Minister Bennett ordered a nation-wide crackdown on communists and W. H. Price, Attorney General of Ontario, had nine party leaders in the province rounded up and brought to Toronto on charges of being members of an illegal association. *The Star* was on the horns of a dilemma. It hated Section 98 under which they were charged, and had repeatedly urged its repeal. But at the same time, it had been pointing out to Chief Draper and the Toronto police commission that communism had never formally been declared an illegal association under Section 98. Instead of forcibly dispersing communist meetings, it admonished, the proper course would be to arrest the leaders, bring them to court, determine by trial whether communism was illegal and whether they were communists, and if they were guilty to impose the penalty prescribed by law.

It solved the dilemma by commending the court for the fairness with which the trials were conducted, Price for his wisdom in taking its advice to use lawful means against the communists instead of encouraging police to beat them over the heads, but adding that the law under which the communist leaders had been convicted and sent to prison for five years was vicious and should be repealed.

To tell the truth, *The Star* was more than a little shocked at the result of its appeal to the rule of law, while in certain left-wing though not necessarily communist quarters it was blamed for the plight of the persons whose rights it had professed to defend. Had it left well enough alone they would have suffered an occasional beating at the hands of Draper's police but been free to walk the streets. As it was they were locked in the penitentiary for five years.

Like many liberals of his day, Mr. Atkinson had never been overly fond of the concept of the rule of law, believing that an unjust law was just as oppressive as an unjust decree by an arbitrary ruler. Hereafter *The Star* was to appeal to justice more often than to law.

As unrest increased with the worsening of the depression the Tories' fear of communism became a frenzy. Armed with Section 98 they were jailing men for attending a communist meeting or for showing a friend a communist handbill, without any inquiry as to whether they were communists themselves. At a hearing in Toronto on February 22, 1932, before Wesley Gordon, Minister of Immigration and Defence, it was disclosed that witnesses who testified that persons on trial were not members of the Communist party had been arrested, convicted, and in some cases deported on the sole grounds that they could not have so testified unless they were themselves members of the party.

Arvo Vaara, editor of the Finnish language daily newspaper *Vapaus* of Sudbury and his translator, Martin Parker, were arrested in a midnight raid on *Vapaus* by the RCMP in 1932 and quite literally were never heard from again. The Minister of Justice, the Minister of Immigration, the Attorney General of Ontario, and the Crown Attorney at Sudbury all protested that they knew nothing whatever of what might have happened to these two men. Communist party officials said they had been rushed to Halifax and deported without a hearing. Parker had lived in Canada since he was a year old.

After some judges balked at convicting under Section 98 on the flimsy evidence so often produced, the burden of protecting Canadians from communism was transferred to the immigration department. Most of the communists were of foreign birth, but many who had been brought to Canada in childhood did not realize they were not Canadian citizens. These with later arrivals were hunted down and deported. J. S. Woodsworth told Parliament that of three men seized by immigration officers in Winnipeg one night and deported without a hearing, one had been in Canada thirty-four years and another twenty-four years. The Minister of Immigration replied that even if they had spent a lifetime in Canada, "if they are found to be undesirables they have no right to be in Canada." It was because of such secret deportations that organized labour adopted as part of its program the right to an open hearing.

The case that forced the government to begin holding open hearings on deportations was that of Steve Worebek and Nick Machuk, officers of a Ukrainian-Polish club in Montreal. They were charged with being members of an illegal assembly after transmitting to Premier Bennett a resolution from their club asking for repeal of Section 98. But instead of being tried they were rushed to Halifax and deported. On the insistence of opposition members, a transcript of the hearing before an immigration officer was made public. It showed the immigration officer had ruled the men were "subversives" because a pamphlet called "The ABC of Communism" and a book of Plato's writings had been found in a trunk in Worebek's attic.

"It is reassuring to believers in lawful methods of law enforcement to be told that the men will be given a fair hearing," *The Star* commented when Bennett announced that thereafter hearings would be public. "They will, presumably, be given this fair hearing just before they are pushed on to the boat in Halifax and banished for life. The Canadian Cheka will, it is hoped, not grab off any citizen whose looks it does not like and whisk him away two thousand miles, there to be given a 'fair hearing.' "

Yet very much like that happened. For example, nine men who had been working on a relief works project at Cranbrook, British Columbia, were dismissed as "troublemakers." When they then applied for direct relief they were picked up on orders of the immigration department, taken across the continent to Halifax, given a hearing, and deported as "indigents."

In late 1932 it was disclosed that nine men brought from central and western Canada were being held in cells in Halifax without trial while deportation proceedings dragged on. None had been convicted of breaking a Canadian law. In 1933 *The Star*'s London correspondent reported that the Soviet embassy in London had received applications from the Canadian government for visas for forty men Canada wished to deport. There was no Soviet representative in Canada and visas had to be secured from the embassy in London.

At the same time Manitoba was waging a senseless persecution of Mennonites. In the panic over communism every foreigner was suspect, and the Mennonites were the most obstinate of foreigners for they insisted on educating their children in church-run schools in which German was the language of instruction. Moreover, most of them had been born in Russia.

When the anti-communist frenzy first threatened the Mennonites in 1929 *The Star* sent D. B. Rogers, now news editor of the Regina *Leader Post*, to the frontier between Russia and Germany to report on the exodus of Mennonite refugees from Russia. He showed they had been driven from Russia by religious persecution and had no affection for communism. But the prosecution of Mennonites in Manitoba continued, and since Russia refused to accept them back, many were clapped in jail. Testimony that a German-language Bible was the only book in the house was used against some of them at hearings. After the US ambassador to Argentina reported that Mennonite refugees from Canada had established a "socialist colony" at New Australia in Paraguay, Premier Taschereau of Quebec issued an order forbidding even Mennonites of Canadian birth to buy land in Quebec.

The Star was unceasing in its condemnation of this betrayal of democracy. The way to defeat communism, it insisted, was to free the workers from the fears on which communism thrives. This could be done, it said not once but many times, "by unemployment insurance, health insurance, minimum wages and maximum hours of work for men, old age pensions at sixty-five, a national works program, and a federally administered relief system"—in short, by the program proposed by Mr. Atkinson for the Liberal party in 1916 and endorsed by King.

But the Canadian Manufacturers' Association solemnly predicted a flight of capital from Canada unless the radical elements were curbed, by which it meant unless industrial labour unions were banned. The Ontario government was trying to keep "labour peace" by denying the right of workers to organize, though it did not go as far as the government of Saskatchewan which authorized police to fire upon strikers at Estevan, with the result that three were killed. The rise of the CCF in that province may in part be attributed to the excessive zeal of the Conservative provincial government in suppressing "subversion," a fact that was noted by *The Star* when the CCF adopted its "Regina manifesto."

On the other side of the coin Stewart Smith, a Communist party official who became a member of Toronto's board of control, was reported in *The Star* to have told a meeting in 1935 that the *Labour Gazette* had correctly reported that the Communist party had organized 536 strikes in five years; ninety per cent of all strikes in Canada in that time.

The repressive measures of the Bennett government were in large part responsible for its defeat in October, 1935, for they were an issue in the campaign. The Conservatives elected only forty-two members in a house of 245, and twelve of these came from the Toronto area. But even in Toronto and the Yorks the Conservative candidates drew only 38 per cent of the popular vote. Most of them owed their election to the fact the anti-Bennett vote was divided between the Liberals and the new CCF party. With unusual restraint *The Star* refrained from deploring this division of liberals. Instead it declared, "the CCF has set men thinking as seldom before . . . It has been a beacon lighting the way toward reform. Its work is not done." Apparently it anticipated the role the CCF was to play as a goad to keep

Mackenzie King unswervingly on the road to reform, and approved of it.

The Star had been friendly to the CCF since its inception in 1932. When the CCF adopted the famous Regina Manifesto, which was to be the platform of the party for many years, it observed on July 26, 1933: "The spirit is the spirit of a broader humanity which looks to a new dawn in which ordinary human beings will be happier and more blest . . . Reformers within the Liberal party, while they may not accept the letter of the Regina manifesto, will feel they can share its crusading spirit and aspire to the goal which it has visualized—the greatest happiness of the greatest number."

While these disturbances were going on in Canada, *The Star* had been reporting as best it could on developments in Russia. After Somerville's trip in 1929 it had been unable to get a reporter into the Soviet Union until June, 1932, when permission was received for Frederick Griffin to visit the country. At the same time the *Globe* was allowed to send Pierre van Paassen, former Paris bureau chief for the New York *World*. Van Paassen had begun as a reporter on the *Globe* after his return from the war in 1918.

Griffin had no experience whatever in foreign affairs, and slight interest in politics or ideologies. He had established a reputation as a writer of descriptive prose, more concerned with actualities than with motives. But that was exactly the kind of reporter Mr. Atkinson wanted for the Russian assignment. Because he was an honest reporter he would report honestly what he saw. Because he was a good reporter he would see more than most. Because he had so little interest in ideologies he would have an open mind.

Fifteen years had passed since the revolution began, and for most of that time Russia had been a closed country. There was intense interest in it, mostly because local communists were forever harping on its "wonderful achievements" though few were allowed to go and see for themselves. Mr. Atkinson believed the public was eager to know what Russia was like from a source that could be relied upon, and he was as curious as anybody to learn whether communism was accomplishing what its partisans in Canada claimed for it. Thus Griffin's instructions were simple—"Write what you see, not what you are told, coloring nothing to suit either Canadian prejudices or Russian propaganda."

He followed his instructions to the letter. The articles he sent back over a period of two months were described at the time as being "quietly impressionistic." Like a latter-day Marco Polo he did not dig beneath the surface. He expressed neither approval nor condemnation. He told what kind of homes the Russians lived in, how they dressed, how they worked, and what their farms were like, leaving the reader to render his own verdict on the facts presented. He described the mass discipline "from which nobody escapes," the intense activity in the cities of Leningrad and Moscow, with new buildings and new factories rising everywhere, and he described the poverty and backwardness of the rural districts of the Ukraine, where the workers on the land lived in sod shacks as primitive as those of our own prairie pioneers in 1900. His articles were, in fact, an unemotional and objective travelogue by an unusually observant writer.

Van Paassen, like Griffin, began his tour at Leningrad and his first stories also were of booming cities, crowded schools, and cheerful people. And almost every day the *Globe* had an editorial saying, in effect, "do not believe what our correspondent writes for he has obviously fallen victim to Communist propaganda." Commented *The Star*: "No doubt the *Globe* sent van Paassen to Russia expecting to get a very different line of stuff from what he is sending."

A couple of weeks later articles by van Paassen began appearing in *The Star*. The *Globe* observed that he was "temporarily separated" from its staff without giving a reason, but van Paassen said he objected to an editor three thousand miles away deciding whether what he reported came from the Soviet propaganda mill or was the result of personal observation. The *Globe* printed a sarcastic editorial about *The Star* using articles which it, in its wisdom, had decided should not be published. *The Star*, it hinted, was not concerned with the truth but only with printing anything it could find favourable to communism, for the once-liberal *Globe* had become even more frenetically anti-communist than the Conservative *Telegram*. Its surrender to hysteria contributed as much as anything else to its rapid decline in popularity, and by 1932 what had once been the most powerful champion of reform in Canada was trailing the other three Toronto newspapers in circulation, its influence negligible.

A few brave souls declared *The Star* was serving the world by reporting the achievements of the Russians as well as their failures. One of these was Professor King Gordon of McGill University, son of the author Ralph Connor. Talking with Griffin after his return from Russia he said: "Communism is not a system outside our world, but inside our world. The time will come when the implications of this experiment will be brought home to us, whether we like it or not. The Capitalist world can no more disregard the existence of Sovietism than could the Roman Empire disregard the rise of Christianity."

Griffin's standing as a reporter was too high for anybody to accuse him of misrepresenting what he saw, but *The Star* was attacked for sending anybody "to write up the Russians" no matter how truthful his report. There were also accusations Griffin had been shown only what the Russians wanted him to see. This he denied, declaring "newspapermen are humiliated by the childish notion they are led around Russia by a ring in the nose."

Van Paassen's articles were more opinionated than Griffin's and he was soon to be expelled from Russia because of opinions he expressed in *The Star* on what he observed in the Ukraine, whereas Griffin, who described the Ukraine with even more brutal realism, was allowed to stay because he confined his articles to observable facts. Van Paassen returned to the *Globe* after his Russian tour, but resigned on September 27. "The divergence of the *Globe*'s views and mine are really too wide," he explained in a cablegram to the editor. Correspondence published at the time indicated that before setting out on the Russian tour he had been instructed by the editors of the *Globe* how to slant his reports to conform with *Globe* policy.

The Star promptly announced it was engaging him as its roving European correspondent, a position he occupied for the next four years though he was never on staff. He devoted most of his attention to events in Germany and Italy, for he correctly judged that the rise of fascism posed a more immediate threat to peace than the rise of communism.

The Star held the same opinion. On February 2, 1933, it declared that "the difference between the Nazis and Reds is more apparent than real." Any difference there might be, it explained, lay mainly in the fact the Nazis were nationalists whose objective was a world ruled by Germans, whereas the Reds were internationalists, whose objective was a world ruled by their Marxist doctrine. Both were prepared to use force to achieve their objectives. Because the Nazis were quite evidently preparing to be the first to strike and had the greater industrial machine, they were, for the time being, the more dangerous. History demonstrated the correctness of this view.

About the time it engaged van Paassen in 1932 *The Star* sent Matthew Halton to London to replace Somerville. He became without question Canada's greatest foreign correspondent, both as a writer for *The Star* and after 1943 as a reporter for the Canadian Broadcasting Corporation. Somerville returned to Canada and became editor of the *Catholic Register* of Toronto and one of the most severe critics of *The Star*'s policy with respect to Russia and communism.

Halton spent most of his time in England, but he looked in occasionally at the League of Nations. He made a trip to Germany in 1934 to see what Hitler was up to and with remarkable foresight predicted almost exactly the course the Nazi leader would follow in his attempt to conquer Europe. He covered the Munich conference in 1938 and by this time his prestige was so high the NBC chose him to broadcast the commentary on the conference over its national network. " 'Give me what I want or I'll run amok,' said Hitler. We gave it and got peace. If later, strengthened and enriched, he threatens war again, do we give him what he asks?" Halton wondered. For the first few years, however, Halton confined himself to the British scene and British politics, leaving the continent of Europe for the most part to van Paassen. In the four years that van Paassen was *The Star*'s European correspondent he showed a remarkable insight into Nazi objectives and methods, and the accuracy of his predictions brought considerable fame to *The Star*.

As early as March 15, 1932, a year before Hitler came to power, he said in a dispatch to *The Star*: "Hitler holds the fate of Europe in his hands." In late 1932 he predicted Hitler would seize power in Germany "and crush the workers' movements." In 1933 he covered the German elections and correctly predicted both the excesses of the Nazis during the campaign and the outcome. He was one of the first foreign correspondents to report the persecution of Jews in Germany, for which *The Star* and three British publications had the distinction of being the first banned from Germany by Hitler. The official announcement said *The Star* was banned "because of its articles by a Dutch Jew." Van Paassen, in fact, had no Jewish blood. He was a member of the Anglican Church, though his parents were Dutch Reformed.

"You should be proud your newspaper is the first in America to be banned by Hitler," wrote James W. Gerrard, former US ambassador to Germany, in a letter to Mr. Atkinson, while W. Arnold-Foster, a British diplomat, praised *The Star* as "one of the leaders in the war on war." Arnold-Foster disclosed that what he described as "a well-reasoned editorial" from *The Star* had been a deciding factor in persuading the British government to co-operate with the World Court in 1927–28.

But the *Globe*, which was carrying on an atrocious campaign against Canadians it believed were communists, even demanding that they be denied their democratic rights as citizens, condemned *The Star* for its "sensational reports from Germany which have brought official denial." Concluded the *Globe*'s editorial of April 18, 1933: "It will be a sorry day if this sort of thing becomes mistaken for Canadian newspaper accuracy."

Six million Jews soon had tragic reason to know the accuracy of *The Star*'s reports, but in Canada thousands of otherwise sensible people were blindly hailing Hitler and Mussolini, and later Franco, as the saviours of Christian civilization.

In March, 1934, van Paassen predicted in *The Star* that "every German Jew is doomed to death, slavery or exile." The same month he wrote that sooner or later Hitler would attack Russia. He predicted an alliance between Germany, Italy, and Japan to make war on the rest of the world. He foresaw Mussolini's war of conquest on Ethiopia, and covered it for *The Star*. Because of the excellence of his reports his name was inscribed in the Honour Book of the Hungarian Nation, and he was made an honorary citizen of Tel Aviv. His assessment of the situation in Europe was reinforced by the sound judgment of Matthew Halton, writing from London.

Largely influenced by the despatches of these two able reporters, *The Star* was one of the few newspapers in Canada persistently to hammer at the theme that unless Hitler and Mussolini were curbed the world was in for dire trouble, but many thought Holy Joe was only trying to divert attention from the communists.

After the Soviet Union was admitted to the League of Nations in 1935, Alexandrine Gibb was sent on a tour of Russia and the Near East. Without any background or experience in the kind of stories she was supposed to do, her tour was a failure. A tour the following year by Margaret Gould was more successful. Miss Gould had been executive secretary of the Child Welfare Council of Toronto since 1929, and made the trip with a party of social workers studying welfare agencies in Britain, the Scandinavian countries, and Russia. She had been born in Russia of Jewish parents and spoke the language.

Over a period of two months she wrote almost an article a day dealing entirely with welfare matters, mingling commendation with criticism. These articles were widely praised by welfare workers in the United States and Canada, but almost from the appearance of the first one on June 24, 1936, they were attacked in the *Catholic Register* by Henry Somerville, who accused Miss Gould of being a communist.

In August of that year the Spanish Civil War broke out, and van Paassen was assigned to cover it for *The Star*. His dispatches were to cause it more embarrassment than anything it has ever published. The war had to be covered from the Loyalist or Republican side, for the rebel leader, the present dictator Franco, invading Spain from North Africa with a legion of Mohammedan mercenaries, had prudently banned correspondents from his army. Moreover, the Republicans were soon joined by a detachment of Canadian volunteers, including Hugh Garner and Dr. Norman Bethune, and Canadians were naturally interested in their exploits. Most of these were fervent democrats though there was a sprinkling of communists among them. Like liberals all around the world, *The Star* supported the Republican government, even though it contained some communists. "The Loyalist forces are supporters of a regularly constituted government which was returned to office by an overwhelming majority of the electors," commented *The Star*. "This is a Liberal government, not a Socialist or Communist government . . . The rebels are those who challenge the right of the people to rule."

This it should be noted, was the official position of the governments of Britain, France, the United States, Canada, and other democratic countries. Moreover, with things as they were in Germany and Italy, *The Star* and other democrats felt fascism had to be scotched wherever it reared its ugly head.

At the time Roman Catholics in general regarded communism as a greater threat than fascism and many supported Franco. Somerville was one of these. He saw the Civil War as a religious crusade against communist atheism. His view was shared by Reverend Charles B. Lanphier, director of the Radio League of the Little Flower, also a former reporter on *The Star*, who broadcast every week from St. Michael's Cathedral. They began at once to attack *The Star* and van Paassen. At first they accused van Paassen merely of sending biased dispatches, and Fr. Lanphier visited Mr. Atkinson with a request he dismiss the reporter. Later they accused him of deliberately "faking" his stories from Spain, particularly those relating the atrocities committed by Franco's Moorish mercenaries. Hindmarsh was unconcerned, but J. S. Atkinson wrote his father, then holidaying in the north, enclosing a copy of the *Catholic Register*.

"The matter can rest until I get to the city," Mr. Atkinson replied. "It is unlikely we will be drawn into a controversy about the latest attack any more than by the previous one. Their writer, as you know, is Henry Somerville, whom we dismissed as unsatisfactory when he was our London correspondent. He is trying to get some of his own back. I don't think he gets as much effect as might be the case if we began defending van Paassen or Margaret Gould's Russian articles."

Heretofore van Paassen's reporting had proven to be wholly trustworthy, and Mr. Atkinson was reluctant to believe his hatred of Naziism and fascism had led him into the sort of fanatical misrepresentation some anti-communist writers were showing. But by September the *Catholic Register* was declaring van Paassen was not in Spain at all, but was living in Paris and either drawing upon his imagination or rewriting the dispatches of other reporters. When it was able to demonstrate that certain events van Paassen said he had recently witnessed had been reported days earlier by correspondents for French newspapers Mr. Atkinson sent Hindmarsh at once to Paris. The question so far as *The Star* was concerned was not whether the events van Paassen reported had actually occurred, for they were amply corroborated by impartial observers, but whether he had seen them occur, as he said he did.

Leaving word that he and Mrs. Hindmarsh were leaving on a cruise of the Caribbean, Hindmarsh took ship instead for Europe. Accompanied by his wife he went to the address of van Paassen's home in Paris. The writer was not in but Hindmarsh had a chat with the servants, who told him where he could be reached. He also had a chat with the neighbours on both sides, and with the milkman. He did not see or speak with van Paassen. As a result of the report he made to Mr. Atkinson on his return home, van Paassen was informed by letter enclosing a cheque for $1,000 that his services were no longer needed.

Van Paassen was a man who found endless fascination in international intrigue and revolutionary plotting, and saw them wherever he looked. The humdrum people who stay at home in Canada found some of his stories hard to believe, and he was accused of having a too vivid imagination. Van Paassen said this worried *The Star*, and that *Star* agents kept popping up in the most unlikely places, introducing themselves as readers of *The Star* or friends of Mr. Atkinson, and asking "Were you really there?" or "Did you really see this?"

The present writer, visiting Yugoslavia in 1953, was surprised when a man high in the government of that country suddenly asked during an interview: "Do you know Mr. van Paassen?" Then he related an incident in which he and van Paassen had participated. King Alexander, he said, had closed Parliament and was ruling by decree. Van Paassen arrived in Belgrade to see what was going on and immediately began sniffing out plotters against the king. His investigations led him to one of those murky cellar cabarets familiar to everybody who has watched a spy movie. He arranged to make contact there with some of the plotters, but before he could do so three Serbian army officers, completely accoutred with sword at side, invaded the cafe and demanded that van Paassen surrender. The reporter leaped on a table and began fending off the officers with a chair.

These drew their swords and there ensued a merry mêlée reminiscent of Dumas. Since most of the habitués of the den were revolutionaries and therefore on van Paassen's side, the officers were soon tripped and *The Star*'s writer made his escape. Such, at least, is the story told by the highly placed Yugoslavian.

Van Paassen said in a letter to a friend after this Yugoslavian episode that on his arrival safely in Austria he was accosted by a missionary newly come from Toronto with the guileful question: "Were you really in Yugoslavia?" As the missionary conveyed the story back to Toronto van Paassen had been engaged in some sort of a bar-room brawl. The fact is, this world is teeming with spies and plotters of revolutions, and never more so than in the years between the wars.

After van Paassen's dismissal *The Star* sent Halton to the Franco-Spanish border to cover the war as best he could from communiqués and interviews with refugees. He remained there until the abdication crisis recalled him to London in December. By November 28 Griffin was with the Republican army in Barcelona. *The Star*'s support of the Republicans was unshaken, for it was convinced this was a dress rehearsal for an impending war between Hitlerism and democracy. This conviction was strengthened when Hitler and Mussolini sent troops to Spain to aid the fascist General Franco, while Russia sent planes to the Republicans.

The dismissal of van Paassen did not appease Somerville or Fr. Lanphier. They demanded nothing less than that *The Star* stop publishing reports and articles favourable to the Republican cause. In particular they took exception to the articles of Dr. Salem Bland, a United Church minister whose radical social views have already been mentioned. Dr. Bland's sympathy for the cause of the Spanish Republic led to the establishment of the Salem Bland Home for refugee children outside Barcelona. He had been instrumental in having the Toronto conference of the United Church pass a resolution in 1935 condemning the capitalist system for its emphasis on profit-making.

When *The Star* printed on its editorial page a long article sympathetic to the Republicans by George N. Shuster, managing editor of *Commonweal*, a liberal Roman Catholic review, the *Catholic Register* said Shuster did not know what he was talking about. It charged "even some Catholics" with "presenting a largely false picture" of events in Spain. "If anything the *Catholic Register* has been more emphatically anti-Red than other Catholic weeklies," it declared proudly in an editorial.

In a radio address Fr. Lanphier accused *The Star* of printing faked pictures showing atrocities committed by Franco's Moors. Two months later he wrote Mr. Atkinson a lengthy letter of apology, saying he had learned the pictures were genuine. Fr. Lanphier continued his vendetta against *The Star* until ruled off the air by the Canadian Broadcasting Corporation in January, 1939, for unlawfully delivering an election address the day before the municipal election.

However, the most sensational feature of this address was not its unlawfulness, but a threat to call for a boycott of *The Star* by all Roman Catholics. *The Star* was supporting the re-election of two communists to city council, J. B. Salsberg and Stewart Smith. In its reports of city council meetings the preceding year it had given equal space with other aldermen to the remarks of the communists. In the opinion of *The Star* they had shown themselves to be hard-working and intelligent aldermen, and had not used their position on council as a sounding board for communist propaganda. In deciding to support them Mr. Atkinson remarked that they were feared most because they were demonstrating that a communist might be a more able alderman than many an anti-communist. That same year *The Star* also supported Donald Fleming, later Conservative Minister of Finance, for council.

Father Lanphier, in words addressed to Mr. Atkinson, said that since his fruitless efforts of two years before to have *The Star* alter the nature of its coverage of the Spanish Civil War "your paper has . . . continued to show a more definite and decided Red trend until today it is now publicly considered to be but a Bolshevistic organ of propaganda . . . How long, Mr. Atkinson, do you think the Christian people of this community are going to suffer and permit your Moscow-tainted publication to be disseminated in our homes among impressionable young minds?"

After admitting that *The Star* had helped Roman Catholics on the separate school question and had been generally friendly towards them, he said all other questions were "infinitesimally insignificant" compared with the necessity of defeating communism, "the deadliest enemy of Christianity in the history of Christian civilization." "Should your paper obviously persist in the glorification of Russia and Red doctrine, then I state to you plainly that I personally will lead a delegation to the leading ecclesiastical authorities of this province and request them to bar your paper from our homes," he declared. Then he followed with a call to the working men of Toronto to turn out in force on election day and defeat the communist candidates. It was this open intervention in politics the day before balloting that was unlawful.

An immediate protest against this broadcast was sent W. Gladstone Murray, president of the CBC, by the Toronto Fellowship for a Christian Social Order. The Toronto Fellowship was one of a number of similar groups that had been organized across Canada to combat both communism and fascism as a result of a resolution of the General Assembly of the United Church of Canada in 1932. One of its distinguished members was Sir Robert Falconer, principal of the University of Toronto.

"You will note a direct incitement to murder however unwittingly this was made," the Fellowship wrote, commenting on the impassioned language Fr. Lanphier had used. It linked an election-day assault on a man who admitted he had voted for a communist candidate on the incitement of Fr. Lanphier's address. It declared Fr. Lanphier's "poisoning" statement "is not in keeping with Christian honor and truth nor with social good."

> *The Toronto Daily Star* has not to our knowledge glorified the Communist doctrine as alleged. It has indeed recently published in good faith a series of articles written by a reputable and competent engineer who has been working for the Soviet for several years and who now reports the conditions which he found to prevail. This in no way is a glorification of Communist doctrine. Nor in its statement of fact did it go beyond the succinct declaration of Sir Edward Beatty that the Russian experiment is succeeding though at the price of some confusion and suffering.
>
> To threaten a ban upon *The Star* for such bonafide reporting indicates a desire to suppress any information which may lead to a Christian criticism and reorganization of our own social order. Moreover, it is only fair to point out that *The Star* has in an outstanding manner sought to present a Christian view of life devoting several columns of its editorial page every week to comment on matters of current interest by mature Christian clergymen of national reputation, not one of whom is Communist.

The *Globe and Mail* said on January 6, 1939, that the Canadian Broadcasting Corporation was right in taking the action it did against Fr. Lanphier for his Sunday broadcast. "While we disagree with the Communistic principle sympathetically treated in *The Star*, and while we regard it as the more dangerous when they are subtly infiltrated into the public mind under the dignity of a metropolitan publication, we have nothing against Mr. Atkinson personally," it continued. "We shall continue to use the influence of the *Globe and Mail* in full view of the public to combat these insidious doctrines, but we can't sympathize with Fr. Lanphier's threat against the paper—that if it does not do this or that in accordance with his views he will lead a movement to boycott it."

"There is no doubt whatever that *The Star* has printed a great many articles and news stories that have presented various aspects of the Communist regime in Russia in a favorable light," commented the *Kingston Whig-Standard*. "But there are aspects of the Communist regime in Russia which probably have to be presented in a favorable light if a description of them is to be true . . . *The Star* gives fair reports of the activities of the Communist aldermen in Toronto's city council. Such practices do not justify anyone in labelling *The Star* 'Red.' " It added that both *The Star* and Fr. Lanphier "ordinarily do very useful work, *The Star* in attacking and unmasking Fascism and Fr. Lanphier in attacking and unmasking Communism." That probably expressed the opinion of a majority of the citizens of Ontario.

In an editorial published only a week before Fr. Lanphier's address, *The Star* had stated its own position. Society, it said, is not perfect, but there is no better way of improving it "than in the democratic way." Democracy, like the human body, "needs nourishment and exercise, and not to be 'saved' from inactivity." A healthy democracy and "the greatest good to the greatest number" cannot be achieved "by restricting groups of law-abiding people from participating in the responsibilities and functions of government." Even earlier *The Star* had castigated a group of demonstrators who had tried to break up a fascist meeting in Massey Hall. "*The Star* has no use for Fascism . . . but this is not an issue of political doctrines," it said editorially. "It is an issue as to free speech."

To Fr. Lanphier's charges that it was "the Bolshevistic organ," *The Star* pointed out that its reporters were barred from entering Russia. Both Halton in London and Gregory Clark in Toronto had been trying since June to get visas, and had been given a final refusal on December 2.

Soon after this incident the Archbishop of Toronto called upon Mr. Atkinson, and apparently everything was smoothed over. A prominent Toronto Roman Catholic later said he had suggested the visit to the Archbishop, pointing out that *The Star* "is the greatest friend of minorities in Toronto and has always been a friend of Catholics." He said he told the Archbishop, "Mr. Atkinson will never come to you, you had better go to him."

In March, 1939, Gregory Clark was sent to Rome to cover the coronation of the new Pope and thus show there were no hard feelings. This was Hindmarsh's idea. Mr. Atkinson had been piqued by the attacks of Roman Catholics and was toying with the idea of sending somebody to Italy "to find out why the country that is the seat of Roman Catholicism has more Communists than any other country in Western Europe." Hindmarsh persuaded him of the unwisdom of this course. This was not the only occasion on which Hindmarsh exercised a moderating influence on his father-in-law.

Clark's reports from Rome were so fulsome that to pacify Protestants *The Star* felt it necessary to deny he was a Catholic. However, it ignored whispers the paper had been secretly bought by Catholics, just as it had ignored rumours it was secretly owned by Catholics when it was advocating an equitable share of taxes for separate schools in 1935. The extravagant coverage from Rome was a typical Hindmarsh job. Lacking the subtle touch of Mr. Atkinson, when he set out to prove *The Star* was a friend of some person or cause he was likely to go so completely overboard as to defeat the purpose he intended.

The Star could usually be counted upon to support revolutionary movements in backward countries. It had been friendly towards the Mexican revolution from the beginning, and had approved the expropriation of foreign-owned properties. When Canadian and American businessmen in 1938 tried to persuade their governments to sever relations with the government of President Cardenas on the grounds he was a communist *The Star* argued Cardenas was right in trying to break the grip of "mercenary foreign investors" on the economy of his country. That did not make him a communist, it said. Events proved *The Star* was right, for Cardenas set Mexico firmly on the road to stable, democratic government.

To accuse *The Star* of communism was to misunderstand completely its position. So far as Canada was concerned, it argued only that every Canadian, regardless of religion, race, or ideological beliefs, should have the right to contend lawfully for principles in which they believed. So far as foreign countries were concerned, it argued that such people as the Spanish Loyalists and the Mexican revolutionists were in the main simple folk, fighting with the only means at hand for a better life.

Nevertheless, it can be truly said that Atkinson believed the Russian people were better off under the communist dictatorship than they had been under the autocracy of the Tsars. He also believed the Russian people would eventually turn to liberalism, as nearly all revolutionists have done, perhaps by a gradual evolution within the communist party.

His faith in Russia was first shaken when Stalin signed a mutual non-aggression treaty with Hitler on August 23, 1939. But resolutely *The Star* looked on the bright side. This treaty, it thought, immobilized Japan as a possible enemy. As a matter of fact, at the time *The Star* was doing exactly what it had done before the outbreak of the First World War—it was playing down the possibility of war. Other newspapers were full of reports of ultimatums and mobilizations and the marchings of troops, and frightening reports from special correspondents in Berlin and Warsaw, but *The Star* restrained its news stories to a bald recital of facts.

The day Russia and Germany announced their mutual non-aggression treaty, thus making war almost a certainty, it calmly put its eight-column banner on: "Toronto Man New Salvation Army Head." Editorially it judiciously conceded the possibility of war, but thought it might be averted if nobody panicked, and everybody kept his head. "Steady, Aye, Steady" it rallied the nation in an editorial.

Chapter 20

PACIFISM RENOUNCED

Mr. Atkinson had been a lifelong pacifist, but shortly after the outbreak of war on September 3, 1939, he protested to Reverend Charles H. Huestis against a "Witness Against War" based on the pacifist declarations of the United Church, which Dr. Huestis and several other United Church clergymen had signed. "I think you are courageous, and I admire your courage, but I think you are wrong," he wrote.

On disclosing this correspondence several years later, Dr. Huestis said Mr. Atkinson was "a deeply religious man . . . but he did not think that a nation that called itself Christian could be bound by the imperatives of Jesus in the Sermon on the Mount when its existence as a nation was threatened." Dr. Huestis added that even before the war Mr. Atkinson had "accepted with diffidence" one or two articles of a pacifist nature from him "saying he could not agree with me."

The activities of Hitler and Mussolini had completely effaced Mr. Atkinson's native pacifism. As early as 1934 he had reluctantly admitted the probability of war between the democracies and the dictatorships of Germany and Italy. By 1938 he regarded it as inevitable—a just war the democracies could evade only at peril of their very existence. Thus when *The Star* played down events preceding the war it was due to Mr. Atkinson's conscientious aversion to glorifying war or to doing anything that might inflame war passions, and not with any hope of averting the impending holocaust.

With the outbreak of war *The Star* went immediately on a war footing. Cable editor William Walling was made war news editor, the position he had occupied in the First World War, with telegraph editor James Kingsbury taking over the afternoon war desk. Editorial writer W. R. Plewman began writing his "The War Reviewed" column, as he had done in the previous war. Arrangements were made with the Chicago *Daily News* to have its staff of foreign correspondents cover enemy countries for *The Star*, and the staff of the copy desk was doubled to handle the increased flow of news.

Gregory Clark was accredited as a war correspondent and told to stand by to proceed overseas with the first Canadian contingent, but until things "hotted up" Matthew Halton covered events from London. After Poland was smashed in a matter of days there was little activity until November 30 when the Soviet Union launched an entirely unprovoked war upon Finland. This was a greater blow to Mr. Atkinson's faith in Russia than even the Stalin-Hitler pact. "They have betrayed me," he exclaimed to Maitland, with tears in his eyes. "They have betrayed me, and I cannot trust them again. They have betrayed the hopes of humanity. Why have they done such a terrible thing?"

"For sheer inhumanity and barbarity Russia's attack upon Finland can hardly be exceeded in the whole record of supposedly 'civilized' warfare," *The Star* said editorially the next day, while a cartoon showed a huge Stalin crashing through a paper billboard reading "Down with Imperialist Wars" to attack a tiny Finland with a bayonet.

Halton was sent immediately to the Finnish front. When a Canadian Aid to Finland committee was established under the chairmanship of Senator Arthur Meighen, Mr. Atkinson was one of the first to pledge his support and two members of the staff were assigned to full-time duties with the committee. The surrender of Finland in March ended its work.

Halton was still in Finland when Clark went overseas with the first Canadian troops in December. On a tour of British and French forces in France he was horrified to find them preparing to fight the heavily-armed Germans with obsolete First World War equipment. He was even more shocked at the complacency of the British high command, and the insane feuding within the French army. He was prevented by censorship from reporting any of this, but in February he sent an urgent message to Mr. Atkinson telling him he had private information he should know. Atkinson cabled him to return at once.

Largely on the basis of Clark's information, Mr. Atkinson concluded Canada's most important contribution for the time being would be military equipment and supplies, and he decided *The Star* should oppose conscription or the building up of a large Canadian armed force until the men could be spared from munitions factories. This was soon declared to be the policy of the Canadian government. It was supported by General A. G. L. McNaughton, commander of the Canadian army, and Winston Churchill, but was bitterly opposed by an element within Canada headed by George Drew; the "sabre rattlers," Atkinson called them.

After Germany overran Denmark and Norway in April, Clark, Frederick Griffin, and Claude Pascoe were sent overseas. Griffin was assigned to British headquarters, which was presumed to be planning a counter-invasion of Norway. Pascoe was to live with the Canadian troops in England and write on life in the army. Clark went to the "front" in France, arriving by coincidence on May 10, the day Germany launched its attack upon France through Holland and Belgium. He was in the thick of the fighting, witnessed the evacuation of Dunkirk, and reported on the fall of France.

The three war correspondents and Halton were recalled to Canada shortly after the evacuation of Dunkirk. After a speaking tour of Canada and several broadcasts over the CBC and US networks, Halton was sent to Washington as *The Star*'s resident correspondent, the first it ever had in the US capital. His series of "Let's Face the Facts" broadcasts from Washington established his reputation as a radio reporter of the first rank. "This is the stuff of authentic eloquence, but even more important, it is a picturesque and accurate survey of the things at stake in this war," said the *Ottawa Journal* of these broadcasts.

One of the reasons *The Star* withdrew its correspondents from England in the summer of 1940 was Hindmarsh's aversion to having them risk their lives merely to duplicate stories the news services were sending. The German bombing of Britain began on July 10 and was at its peak after September 7. Canadian Press and other wire services were covering it as thoroughly as staff correspondents could hope to do in view of the strict censorship, and some correspondents were killed.

The Star was more solicitous than most newspapers of the safety of its war correspondents. Usually they were told to let the wire services cover the front-line fighting, and to concentrate on writing background, interpretive articles, or colour. None of them followed these instructions to the letter, for it is against a reporter's instinct to keep away from where the action is; and perhaps they were not really expected to. In addition *The Star* insured its war correspondents and their dependents for a pension equal to that of a brigadier in the Canadian army in the event of disablement or death.

Halton returned to Europe in April, 1941, to cover the war in Greece but arrived just too late. He went to Syria, then to Egypt, and then accompanied the British army across North Africa. There he performed the spectacular feat of making his way through enemy lines into besieged Tobruk, whose British defenders had been under attack by the Germans, for eight months. Halton did his finest writing of the war in this campaign. On the invitation of the British government he toured England lecturing on the gallant defence of Tobruk.

While Halton was in Canada on furlough in April, 1943, Hindmarsh told him he was sending Griffin and Clark to cover the impending allied invasion of Italy, an assignment he had expected to get. When Halton's protests proved unavailing, he had himself appointed war correspondent for the CBC, then told Hindmarsh he was leaving *The Star*. Hindmarsh retorted by offering to take an article a week from him for the *Star Weekly* as in the past, the payment per article to be the same as he had been receiving per week as salary. It was a good arrangement for *The Star*, for the CBC would now be paying Halton's expenses. Halton remained a regular contributor to the *Star Weekly* until his death in 1956.

Griffin went overseas for the second time in the midsummer of 1942 and except for a brief trip home for Christmas, 1944, he was there until after the war ended. He covered the ill-fated Canadian landing at Dieppe, then went to North Africa and on up through Sicily and Italy with the Canadians accompanying the joint British-American army under General Eisenhower. Clark reached Italy in September, 1943. Griffin returned to England that winter and was accredited to SHAEF, headquarters of the joint command preparing for the invasion of France. Just before the invasion Clark went to England and had himself accredited to the RCAF, with which he remained until the war ended.

Griffin covered the D-day landings from a naval craft. One of his descriptive articles was hailed as the finest piece of writing the war had produced, and was widely reprinted. Clark covered the landing from the air.

After the invasion was accomplished, Griffin accompanied the Canadian army through Holland and Belgium. Bill Kinmond, a former *Star* reporter, who had been a year with the RCAF, was sent to help him shortly after D-day, but had the misfortune to be taken prisoner a few days after arriving at the front. Kinmond was succeeded by John Clare, another former *Star* reporter who had served most of the war with RCAF public relations.

Wessely Hicks, also a former *Star* reporter, was released from navy public relations at the same time and given a roving assignment. Paul Morton was sent to be dropped by parachute among the Yugoslav guerillas, but never succeeded in making contact with them. Ross Harkness was accredited to General Eisenhower's headquarters, SHAEF, which permitted him more freedom of movement throughout the war theatre than the others. He accompanied General Patton in the last days of his spectacular drive to meet the Russians, and was the last to be recalled. Thus in the final months of the war *The Star* had seven correspondents in the field, a number said to be unexceeded by any other paper.

The Star remained cool to Russia after the war with Finland, and even after Germany invaded the Soviet Union in June, 1941, it was slow in warming up. This did not affect its attitude towards Canadian communists. It objected to their internment in the first days of the war on the grounds that they were Canadian citizens, not enemy aliens, and while they might be unenthusiastic about the war they had done nothing overt to impede the war effort. It severely criticized the government for confiscating Ukrainian halls and suppressing Ukrainian cultural activities, as it was later to condemn it for its "unnecessarily cruel" treatment of Japanese-Canadians.

When Canadian communists were free again to participate in local politics, after the German invasion of Russia in June, 1941, *The Star* renewed its support of Joseph Salsberg for the legislature and Stewart Smith for Toronto board of control on the grounds they were able men and should not be held responsible for the sins of Stalin.

In October, 1942, the Canadian Aid to Russia Fund was organized and after that the National Council for Canadian-Soviet Friendship. *The Star* immediately took them under its wing. This was to be cited later, even in US publications, as an example of Mr. Atkinson "cuddling up" to Communism, but if so he was in good company. Sir Ellsworth Flavelle headed the council, while on the directorate were such doughty champions of capitalism as Clifford Sifton, J. S. McLean, John David Eaton, Walter Gordon, Norman Wilks, and General Lafleche.

The truth is, by this time there was great goodwill throughout Canada towards Russia as an ally, without in any way condoning the communist system. Most Canadians understood that giving aid to Russia was one way of helping win the war. At Mr. Atkinson's request, Prime Minister King used his influence to persuade Wendell Willkie, later Republican candidate for president of the United States, and Hon. Joseph E. Davies, former US ambassador to Moscow, to speak at the first two mass meetings in Maple Leaf Gardens. The Prime Minister was chairman of the meeting at which Davies spoke in June 22, 1943. "The Canadian Aid to Russia society is in good hands and the result of its activity promises to be creditable to all associated with it," Atkinson wrote King.

It is understandable that Mr. Atkinson should grasp at Hitler's invasion of Russia as at least partial justification for Russia's earlier "defensive measures" against Finland. But his son and son-in-law, both of whom were by now vice-presidents, did not. They disapproved of *The Star*'s renewed friendship towards Russia and its support of communist candidates, and they blamed Margaret Gould for what they considered to be a too-trusting attitude towards the communists. Her partiality towards Russia, country of her birth, had long been known.

Miss Gould had joined the reporting staff of *The Star* on September 1, 1937, several months after returning from her tour of Russia. On February 24, 1938, she was appointed an editorial writer. The next day Mr. Atkinson sent her to Mackenzie King with a letter of introduction. "I think you will consider you have made the acquaintance of an exceptionally brilliant young woman," he wrote.

There is no doubt this remarkably able woman exercised a considerable influence over Mr. Atkinson for several years. Maitland attributes this mainly to the fact she was the only person Mr. Atkinson could hear without a hearing aid, for she had a clear, piercing voice, the trained voice of a public speaker. Mr. Atkinson used to enjoy talking with her because he could hear her without effort. Besides, Miss Gould flattered him, and he was not immune to flattery. A common interest in social problems and an almost identical approach towards them was another link.

On September 22, 1942, Mackenzie King wrote Mr. Atkinson that he would like to appoint Gerald Brown, city editor of *The Star*, as chief information officer for the RCAF, and asked that he be granted leave of absence. "It is felt that he has outstanding qualifications for the work which is proposed for him," King wrote. Brown, he said, had been recommended by Charles Vining, the recently appointed head of the Wartime Information Board.

Mr. Atkinson replied that the editorial department had already given forty-five of its members to various war services, and was carrying on with difficulty. He would not like to release a key executive without Hindmarsh's agreement, and Hindmarsh was in the North where he could not immediately be reached. A week later he informed King that Brown would be given the leave of absence as requested. Brown was succeeded as city editor by James Kingsbury.

By this time *The Star* was having considerable trouble getting editorial workers, but the five-day week and salary increases which had been introduced April 1, 1941, after the Guild collapsed, plus its reputation for liberal expense allowances and its practice of sending reporters on extensive trips all over the continent, lured many reporters from other papers.

Following a precedent that had been established when the cost of living rose in the First World War, *The Star* gave all employees a cost of living bonus dating from July 4, 1941, amounting to 10 per cent of their salaries for all earning $25 a week or less and a flat $2.50 a week for those earning salaries between $25.01 and $50 a week. Retroactive pay to July 4 was included in the September 12 pay envelope.

Even in wartime *The Star* retained some of its dizzy flamboyance. One day when there was little exciting news from Europe, managing editor Ken Edey showed Ross Harkness a picture of an unusually beautiful woman dressed in some sort of Spanish costume. The caption identified her as a female bull-fighter who had been injured in the Mexico City bullring the preceding Sunday. "Go to Mexico and ask her why such a beautiful girl is fighting bulls," Edey directed.

The lady had left Mexico on Monday and the pursuit led through six countries until she was finally caught up in Bogota, Colombia. She said she liked to fight bulls. Harkness was ordered home by way of Los Angeles to interview a lady wrestler. Nobody seemed to know or care that Los Angeles was four thousand miles out of his way.

One day Hindmarsh called Gregory Clark and photographer Norman James to his office. "Go out to British Columbia and look around," he directed. "There must be something doing there." There was, and they got several good stories. Once cub reporter Paul Morton was sent to Detroit on some insignificant assignment. The day he arrived the worst race riot in Detroit's history erupted. Morton was sent to Kingston. A student pilot fell out of a bomb bay and was miraculously snatched from death in midair by an accompanying plane. Morton went to Montreal. There was a riot in St. Vincent de Paul prison.

Hindmarsh was delighted. Here was an authentic Jonah. Calamity (and news) followed wherever he went. Hindmarsh gave him a raise and decided to train him as a parachutist to be dropped in occupied Europe thus bringing calamity upon the enemy. The inevitable calamity resulted. Morton broke a leg in a practice jump.

It has been said that nothing increases a newspaper's circulation like a war or a sensational murder, and the war gave Toronto newspapers a boost at a time when they needed it. They had been selling for two cents a copy since August 1, 1917, but increasing costs had forced them to raise the price per copy to 3 cents on January 3, 1938. Between that date and the outbreak of war *The Star*'s circulation dropped from 249,661 to 218,391 and that of the other Toronto papers proportionately. Circulations jumped the first year of the war, but *The Star* did not fully recover until 1942. The other papers were even slower in regaining lost readership.

Undoubtedly, the most important factor in *The Star*'s more rapid gain over its rivals was the superiority of its war coverage both at home and abroad by writers of familiar and established reputations. However, the fact that the *Globe and Mail*, which was bitterly opposing the King government and its war policies, gained circulation more slowly than the other Toronto papers and was nine years in recovering its losses, suggests that another factor in *The Star*'s popularity may have been its support of a federal government that had been returned with the largest majority until then on record.

The effect of the war on the *Star Weekly*'s circulation was even more remarkable than its effect on the *Daily*. Its 1939 average circulation was 362,396, an increase of 38,000 over the preceding year due mainly to its coverage of the Royal tour. Instead of losing much of this, as would normally be expected, it gained an additional 36,000 in the first year of the war, almost without promotional effort. This was attributed by Hindmarsh to the spectacular war pictures it carried and the excellent articles by Halton, Griffin, and Clark. The *Star Weekly* was giving its readers a good overall picture of the war and world events through the eyes of Canadian writers, whereas some US publications were antagonizing Canadian readers by an attitude which seemed to many to be anti-British and isolationist.

As early as July, 1940, the government was being urged by some people to ban certain US publications because of the possible adverse effect they might have on the Canadian war effort. Strangely enough, one of those who objected most vociferously to criticism of the Canadian government in US publications was Hon. R. B. Hanson, temporary leader of the opposition.

By the end of 1940 the *Star Weekly* was selling close to 60,000 copies on news-stands in the United States, mainly in Detroit, Buffalo, Cleveland, Niagara Falls, and Boston. No particular effort was made to sell in the United States. These cities have a large Canadian population, but most of the readers were Americans who wanted a broader picture of the war than US newspapers were giving them.

By this time the adverse balance of trade with the United States was so heavy that Canada was running out of US money. In order to conserve US currency for essential war purchases, Parliament passed the War Exchange Conservation Act, effective December 16, 1940, which, among other provisions, barred from entry into Canada publications "consisting largely of fiction or printed matter of a similar character" including comics which were not "bona fide supplements used with newspapers."

A measure of that nature had been proposed first by Hanson and Meighen, leader of the Conservatives in the Senate, after Mackenzie King had declined to forbid entry of isolationist or anti-British periodicals. They appear to have conceived this as a means of keeping out publications they disliked without laying themselves open to a charge of advocating interference with the free flow of information. It may be that King also was glad of an excuse to keep out publications that were critical of his government. At any rate, he acted with good precedent, for both Britain and Australia were banning US publications to conserve exchange and the Canadian act was modelled upon that of Britain.

In a report to Parliament in March, J. L. Ilsley, Minister of Finance, said 140 American periodicals were affected. Most of them were of that large and popular class of fiction magazines known as "the pulps," but also affected were Sunday newspapers which had been the principal competitors of the *Star Weekly*. Better class "slick paper" publications like *Saturday Evening Post* were excluded from the ban. Later some US "pulps" and comic books were printed in Canada but never very many.

For the next six years the *Star Weekly* had the weekend newspaper field in Canada pretty much to itself, and had only slight competition from fiction magazines. Its principal competitor was the Montreal *Standard*, which circulated mainly in English-speaking sections of Quebec and the Maritime provinces. The effect could be anticipated. By the end of the war the *Star Weekly*'s circulation had reached 782,157 or more than double the highest pre-war figure. The increase had been so rapid and so large that when the Canadian government rationed paper it had to drop its US circulation and about 12,000 copies it had been selling in England, in order to get enough paper for its Canadian circulation. Before long it had to drop its news section also to keep within its ration, and this has never been resumed. The *Star Weekly*'s remarkable growth continued for four years after the war, until by 1949 it had a circulation of 905,142 comprised almost entirely of news-stand sales.

In addition to a wartime shortage of newsprint, by 1941 newspapers were being handicapped by a shortage of gasoline and tires for their delivery fleets. At one point J. S. Atkinson bought an old Brooks steamer with the intention of studying the practicability of converting some of *The Star*'s truck fleet to steam power. Later, several staff cars were converted to use propane gas and tests of a long-lasting storage battery were carried out to discover the mileage limitations under normal truck loads. The electric truck did not complete the round trip to Hamilton and was towed to *The Star* Garage. However, the gasoline crisis was eased when the federal government ordered *The Star* and *Telegram* to pool their delivery operations for the duration. It was estimated that this pooling arrangement, which became operative April 20, 1942, saved about four thousand truck miles a day.

The Star never became so obsessed with the war that it neglected what was, above all, Mr. Atkinson's lifelong passion, social betterment. And just as they had done twenty-five years before, Atkinson's thoughts turned towards plans for the brave new world to which he hoped our soldiers would return. And just as he had done twenty-five years before, he scrutinized the Liberal party and was displeased with what he saw. As early as 1941 he detected those trends within the party that led eventually to its downfall.

King had called the Liberals slightly left of centre, and this was true at one time. But in an editorial on November 13, 1941, *The Star* referred to "the already somewhat rightist Liberal party leaving in fact, if not by profession, the advanced reform position to the CCF." Mr. Atkinson was anxious to see some sort of understanding between the Liberal and CCF parties, either a coalition or absorption of the CCF by the Liberals, which would end this drift to the right. He also detected within the Liberal party an increasing intolerance of civil rights, and the inclination toward authoritarianism which was so flagrantly displayed in the last months of the St. Laurent regime. Repeatedly *The Star* protested against the denial of right of trial to persons interned during the war, and the treatment of Japanese Canadians. These were the points, it said once, on which Mackenzie King was most vulnerable.

King's diary shows that by 1943 he also was disturbed by the drift of his party away from liberalism. But whereas King, as a party leader was alarmed at the increasing strength of the CCF, and hoped to contain it, Mr. Atkinson welcomed it in the hope the Liberals would be frightened back to liberalism. It was not until January 14, 1944, however, that he wrote King asking him to come to Toronto for a chat, "just the two of us." "We have seldom talked politics, have we, but now I would like to," he said in his letter.

King came to Toronto on January 19 for Sir William Mulock's one hundredth birthday, and dined with Atkinson. In his diary King wrote that they had discussed the future of Liberalism and Mr. Atkinson assured him *The Star* would like to make a real fight.

"He would undertake a campaign along the lines that *The Star* had fought for the Aid-to-Russia fund were he to get the things to fight for," King recorded in his diary.

> He thought family allowances was a very absolutely necessary and right measure. He would like to see the age for old age pensions reduced at once. Felt the health policy was also good and should be followed up . . . He doubted we could hold labour as we had in the previous campaigns . . . The words he seemed to wish to impress upon me were: Not too little or too long, meaning not to do too little in the way of social reform or to wait too long in what we had to do. He thought if we had a strong program announced in the speech from the throne, we would gain right along from now on.

As their private chat ended and the two men entered a room in which others were awaiting them, Atkinson was overheard to remark to King: "Family allowances would be a wonderful thing for the children and for the family —and for the King government, too, because, Mr. King, people are not going to vote against a government that gives them money like this."

On January 26 King wrote Atkinson: "I hope, though some things may still have to come, you will not be disappointed in tomorrow's speech from the throne." The speech contained almost everything Mr. Atkinson had suggested, with family allowances heading the list. Full health insurance and a national contributory old age pension scheme, both promised in the speech, have yet to become a reality.

While Mr. Atkinson was presenting King with a post-war social program, *The Star* was prodding the Liberals by encouraging the CCF. "We support the CCF except at elections," Atkinson once remarked. *The Star* hailed the victory of the CCF in the Saskatchewan elections of June, 1944, as a victory for the common man. "The overwhelming CCF landslide in Saskatchewan serves notice on the older parties that an increasing number of electors believe in the possibility of a more abundant life than they have hitherto enjoyed—or than the other parties will give them," it declared. It said a CCF government is much to be preferred in any province than a Liberal-Conservative coalition such as there was then formally in British Columbia, informally in Ontario.

A year later it sent feature writer B. H. Honderich to Saskatchewan to report on the results of a year of CCF government. His series of articles were so favourable the Saskatchewan government had them reprinted and circulated in pamphlet form. In April, 1946, Honderich was appointed financial editor at the age of twenty-seven.

The end of the war presented *The Star* with a new problem. Under the Re-Instatement in Civil Employment Act of 1942, employers had to give workers who served in the armed forces their old jobs back when they returned. Many chose not to return, because they had to start where they left off, while men who had been exempt from military service had been promoted into jobs they felt they would have been filling had they not entered the armed services. Nevertheless, a sufficient number returned that *The Star* was considerably overstaffed.

A drastic economy wave was introduced, and subtly the impression was conveyed that there was not much future for anybody at *The Star*. The feeling of uncertainty was increased by Mr. Atkinson's advancing age, and uneasiness as to what might happen when he passed on. Gradually departures whittled down the staff to more manageable proportions.

This process was hastened by Hindmarsh's decision that a lot of prima donnas had to be cut down to size. The prima donnas included most feature writers and all war correspondents, for it was regarded as axiomatic that any reporter who had his by-line attached to a big story on page one every day for months would get a swollen head. It is true Halton had quit in a temperamental huff, but most war correspondents understood quite well that their dispatches received the display they did because of the exciting news they conveyed and not because there was anything exceptional in their reporting or writing.

One of the first to feel the rod was Frederick Griffin. He had returned from overseas a man of 57, physically and nervously exhausted after two years of covering front-line fighting, and was plunged immediately into general reporting. He died of a heart attack on January 15, 1946.

The wave of departures which began in late 1945 took from *The Star* some of its finest writers and most promising young editors, including managing editor Kenneth Edey, who was succeeded by Kingsbury. Employee morale was at the lowest it has ever been in *Star* history, and it never quite got back to what it had been. The names of several of those who left at this time became well known in the newspaper and writing professions, and some were rehired by *The Star* several years later.

Among the first to quit was Gregory Clark, and it is doubtful whether Hindmarsh ever knew why. The indirect cause was the death of Greg's son, Lieutenant Murray Clark, who had been killed in action in Normandy one year earlier, on September 17, 1944. Mrs. Clark suffered a nervous breakdown and was under the doctor's care, and it was natural Greg should want to be with his wife in their mutual bereavement.

After visiting his son's grave Greg cabled *The Star* asking that passage be arranged with the RCAF, which controlled all flights, for his return home. He was puzzled that authorization was not received for ten days, for he knew all *The Star* had to do was ask and passage would be arranged immediately. On his return home he asked that the "Greg and Jim" series be dropped for two weeks. While he was overseas the *Star Weekly* had been reprinting old articles he had written with new illustrations by Frise. Since the *Star Weekly* circulation had increased two-and-a-half times since they were first used, they were not recognized as reprints. Greg did not want the public to think he was writing such humorous nonsense just after his son was killed. Hindmarsh refused to drop them. This rankled.

A year later Clark learned *The Star* had merely requested his passage home without indicating there was any urgency or compassionate grounds. At the same time he learned his passage had actually been arranged by Norman Robertson, Under-Secretary of State for External Affairs, within twelve hours of being informed that Hindmarsh had brusquely refused to discuss accelerating it with friends of the family.

The day after learning this Clark stomped into Hindmarsh's office and declared he was quitting. Hindmarsh did not ask him why, but with Olympian impassivity removed his cigar and announced that the *Star Weekly* would continue to accept a weekly "Greg and Jim" feature, for which it would pay a sum exactly equalling Clark's salary, though he would not be on the payroll. This was a good arrangement for Greg, for it freed him from other work he had been doing for *The Star* and allowed him to write for other publications. Though taken aback at the calmness with which his "bombshell" had been received, he accepted at once. His resignation was announced September 8, 1945, with the explanation he was going into radio work but would continue his popular series with Frise.

From Hindmarsh's office Clark went directly to Frise and informed him he intended to continue writing for *The Star* only until he could find another market. This need not affect Frise, whose "Birdseye Centre" was still the *Star Weekly*'s most popular comic, but Frise was already upset at the pressures being put on old employees to force them out, he believed, without pension. The new market turned up a year later, in December 1946, when the proprietors of the Montreal *Standard* were preparing to transform it into *Weekend Magazine*. Offered a job, Clark and Frise agreed at once to move to the *Standard* for only slightly more than they were getting from *The Star*, but they would share in income from syndication, something *The Star* never allowed its staff.

On the train back from Montreal after signing with their new employers they discussed how they should notify Hindmarsh. "Tell him on Christmas eve, Greg," Frise suggested. It was close to Christmas, but they told him at once. "Aren't you giving us a chance to bid against their offer?" Hindmarsh exclaimed in surprise. "I have never put myself on the auction block," Frise retorted, "and I don't intend to now."

On learning that the *Star Weekly* was to lose its two oldest and most popular features, "Birdseye Centre" and "Greg and Jim," Mr. Atkinson declared that *The Star* must never again be put in the position where a feature or a writer was so popular as to be nearly indispensable. Characteristically, Hindmarsh interpreted this ruling as meaning, "A writer must never again be allowed to consider himself indispensable." Hereafter, prima donnas would be nipped in the bud before they flowered.

The sensational Evelyn Dick murder trial was under way in Hamilton at the time and *The Star* had four of its top writers covering it. Abruptly by-lines were removed from their stories. Police reporter Gwyn Thomas, who later won an award, did a remarkably fine job on a local crime wave; no by-line. Reporters at Queen's Park and the city hall lost their by-lines, and for several weeks H. R. Armstrong at Ottawa was the only staff writer, with the exception of sports writers, whose name was attached regularly to his stories. Reporters who had gradually been working themselves up to getting good assignments again found themselves unaccountably in the doghouse. For nearly a year Marjorie Earl, now a successful magazine writer in England, did not receive more than one or two assignments in a month. Staff-written articles vanished from the pages of the *Star Weekly,* to be replaced by mediocre syndicate articles on Russia, the Suez, Denmark, anywhere but Canada. There was another wave of departures, and when it was over only one of the seven war correspondents was still with *The Star*, and only one feature writer remained. The *Star Weekly* became a very dull paper.

It would be unfair to blame Hindmarsh entirely for this. He was, it is true, the man who gave the orders, who selected the pictures and the articles, and his obsession against prima donnas undoubtedly resulted in the *Star Weekly* failing to take advantage of the feature writing potential on the staff of the *Daily Star*. But Hindmarsh was never allowed to carry out for very long a policy that did not have the approval of his father-in-law. The fact is Mr. Atkinson was anxious to save all the money he could in as short a time as possible, and both papers were running short-staffed and using syndicate material. He was planning to erect a great building for the *Star Weekly* that would be his lasting monument, and he wanted to pay cash for it.

Had this pinching on features and writers affected the circulations or the revenues of either paper the purse strings would undoubtedly have been relaxed, but newsprint rationing was still in effect, American periodicals were still banned, and people were starving for something to read.

The effect was not felt, therefore, until after newsprint rationing ended on June 30, 1947, and competing Canadian publications were able to step up production. Restrictions on the entry of American publications were not lifted until January 15, 1951.

Even after newsprint rationing ended, *The Star* voluntarily rationed itself, purely for reasons of economy. At one time the number of columns of news and features in the *Daily Star* was reduced to 104. By comparison, it averaged about 158 columns a day in 1962. At the same time the size of advertisements was limited. While these measures reduced revenue from advertising, they reduced production costs even more. Restrictions on classified advertising were not removed until August 24, 1948, while even later some display advertising was being taken on a "we will get it in if we have room" basis.

Except for those who were personally affected by the staff shortage and stringent economies, the *Daily Star* seemed to be carrying on in its razzle-dazzle traditional way. W. G. Wittels began an article in the *Saturday Evening Post* of March 16, 1946, as follows:

> In Toronto, Canada, there is a newspaper which makes a liar out of all those veteran newspapermen who have spent years vainly trying to convince laymen that the newspaper business is not as depicted in *The Front Page* and sundry other books, plays and moving pictures. All sound newspapermen in the United States know that reporters no longer kidnap newsworthy characters to keep them away from the opposition. They know that managing editors don't say, "Jones, go out somewhere and get me a scoop." They know that even Hearstlings have quit chartering planes as if they were taxicabs. But on *The Toronto Star* they do all those things apparently under the impression that the newspaper business is still the newspaper game.

Nevertheless the razzle-dazzle period was drawing to a close and despite sporadic outbursts it never flamed again as brightly as in pre-war days. It would almost seem that when *The Star* occasionally engaged in its old-time shenanigans it was regretfully and only because a new publisher of the *Telegram*, who wanted to be known as a razzle-dazzler himself, forced it to.

Mr. Atkinson had never quite recovered his confidence in Russia's good intentions after the invasion of Finland. Nevertheless, in an editorial on May 10, 1945, three days after the war ended in Europe, *The Star* said Russia's splendid record in the war called for a re-examination of communism, not only as a social but as an economic system. It repeated the warning of the Presbyterian Synod of Toronto and Kingston that "soon, very soon, a flood of emotion will be released against Communism, that is, just as soon as some of the dictators have been destroyed." Canadians, it warned, should guard against being caught in this flood of emotion. Before condemning communism out of hand, it suggested we should examine the deficiencies of our own social system. The social emphasis of the Christian gospel has not been given the emphasis it deserves. Christianity, it continued, has been so intent on saving the individual from the consequences of his own sins "it has done all too little to save the masses from the sins of others."

Before long Russia's intransigence and the discovery of an extensive spy network in Canada cost the Russians any goodwill Mr. Atkinson or *The Star* may have had for them. Nevertheless, *The Star* expressed a reluctance to pass judgment until all the evidence was in.

The spy suspects were arrested in mid-February, 1946, and held incommunicado until their trials. While conceding that those charged with spying for Russia deserved punishment if proven guilty, *The Star* was deeply troubled about the way the suspects were treated. "Those who value civil liberties cannot but be concerned about the detention of thirteen persons for interrogation; persons who are not permitted to consult their legal advisors and are thus arbitrarily deprived of a fundamental right," it said editorially. It was not until a month later that Prime Minister King summarized the results of the RCMP investigation for Parliament.

"I liked your address," Mr. Atkinson wrote him on March 20. "It was so completely objective that it didn't surprise me. If it can be said of anyone, then it can almost be said of you, that you are always right. I don't know if anyone ever tells you what is being printed in *The Star*, but if they do you will know that we don't like the way the spy suspects are being treated, but you have also been told that you are entirely right in your housecleaning." In the same letter Atkinson informed King that the

$2,200,000 which the Canadian Allied Relief Fund had allotted to Russia had been reduced to $500,000. "The significance of this change will hardly be lost upon the Russian embassy," he commented. "As you know, I almost never trouble you with my opinion of government policy, but I have not been able to get out of my mind that I ought to at least let you know about this Russian matter, about which you might otherwise not have any knowledge, and might wish to do something if it is brought to your attention."

Chapter 21

THE TORONTO CLIQUE

One of the more famous feuds of recent Canadian journalism was the bitter one between J. E. Atkinson on the one hand and Mitchell Hepburn, George Drew, and George McCullagh on the other. Hepburn and Drew were successively Liberal and Conservative premiers of Ontario; McCullagh was publisher of the Toronto *Globe and Mail.*

The feud began when Hepburn declared war in April, 1936, on the CIO, "foreign labor agitators" and the welfare state. It was carried even into the grave, for Drew and McCullagh were architects of the bill which upset Mr. Atkinson's will.

"The Toronto clique" these three and those who subscribed to their social and political doctrines were called, even in the columns of the *Telegram.* Mr. Atkinson believed that the policies they advocated could lead only to the establishment in Canada of a one-party state based on fascist principles. Mackenzie King shared his fears, but in a letter to Atkinson referred to McCullagh as "an amateur" who, in ignorance, had been sucked into something he did not understand. On their part the three professed to believe, and probably did at first, that Mr. Atkinson was the chief spokesman for international communism in Canada, though later they referred to him simply as "an evil old man."

Correspondence published in 1938 indicates that Hepburn and Drew began flirting with the idea of a one-party government for Ontario early in 1937. Earl Rowe was the provincial Conservative leader and Drew was not yet a member of the legislature, but as chairman of the Conservative campaign committee he was an influential member of the party.

The Star broke the story of the Drew-Hepburn dickering on May 6, 1937, after Drew announced he had resigned as chairman of the campaign committee because, he said, he could not agree with the tolerant attitude of his party towards the CIO. Both men denied the truth of *The Star*'s report.

However, on December 3, 1938, Rowe made public a letter dated April 30, 1937, to him from Drew in which Drew said: "It did not seem to me in our conversation this afternoon that you clearly understood the reasons why I had urged you to accept Mr. Hepburn's proposal for a coalition before you saw him this morning. . . . Even assuming that the threat of the CIO were greatly exaggerated, I still believe that this is an opportunity to do things for the future welfare of the province that it seems to me not likely could ever be done by one party alone." In making public the letter, Rowe said the conversation Drew referred to took place in the Albany Club, Toronto. "Col. Drew finally stated to me that the time had come to end the two-party system in Ontario," Rowe related. "He said that he strongly favored coalition, and said that unless I agreed to coalition he would resign."

The Star published Drew's letter and Rowe's accompanying statement in full, but made no editorial comment until Drew was chosen provincial Conservative leader a few days later. Then it somewhat plaintively remarked that the Liberal leader was causing it too many worries for it to spare time to worry about the Conservative leader.

Meantime a convert had been made of George McCullagh, who had bought the *Globe* and the *Mail and Empire* in 1936 and merged them into the *Globe and Mail*. As a broker, McCullagh had made the acquaintance of Drew while the latter was chairman of the Ontario Securities Commission from 1931 to 1934. As an active member of the Young Liberals his acquaintance with Hepburn was of even longer standing. He had supported Hepburn at the Liberal leadership convention in 1930, and his newspaper supported the Hepburn government.

McCullagh also declared war on Communism, the CIO, and Mackenzie

King, and on February 12, 1939, he launched his Leadership League. In a series of radio addresses to the nation he proposed the abolition of all political parties, the elimination of provincial boundaries and provincial legislatures, and the establishment of one National government of the best brains headed by a strong man fit to rule instead of "poor, bumbling Mackenzie King." He attacked Canadian Press as "a creature news service" that printed only good about Mackenzie King, indicating his proposed National government would compel it to print the "truth"—as, of course, the National government would see it.

"Authoritarian and bureaucratic," was the way *The Star* described his proposals. What he advocated, it said, was nothing less than the abolition of democracy and the setting up of a fascist state along the lines of Italy and Germany.

In November, 1939, McCullagh took to the air again to advocate replacement of Mackenzie King by a strong-man government which would wage total war. His proposals were endorsed by Hepburn and Drew, who had called a wartime truce to party politics and were waging a similar campaign. On January 18, 1940, without the notice of motion required by the rules of the House, Hepburn introduced in the legislature a motion censuring King for alleged weakness in prosecuting the war. It was passed 44 to 10 after he threatened to resign if it was not adopted. Some thirty-six members, most of them Liberals, succeeded in absenting themselves when the vote was taken.

The Star promptly called for Hepburn's resignation as Liberal leader on the grounds that only a minority of the Liberal members had voted for the motion. Hepburn retaliated by repeating the story, with variations, that Mr. Atkinson had threatened to hound him from office because of his anti-labour policies. In a short editorial *The Star* denied there was any truth in this story, adding that it was the second time it had been formally contradicted.

Thereafter *The Star* carried almost daily rumours and reports of a grass-roots movement among Liberals to get rid of Hepburn. "There is a lot of wishful writing in *The Toronto Star* about the demand for Hepburn's retirement," B. K. Sandwell commented in *Saturday Night* on February 3. "But Mr. Hepburn's members like their seats. They know that without Mr. Hepburn they would not have been elected, nor would they stay in office."

Nevertheless, events were soon to justify *The Star*'s reports. King used the Ontario motion of censure as an excuse for dissolving Parliament the day the session opened and calling a snap election for March 26. "Mr.

King took the democratic course" in the face of censure by a provincial legislature that was ostensibly Liberal, *The Star* approved, but Hepburn and Drew teamed up to stump the province against him. Harry Nixon, provincial secretary, declared he was shocked by Hepburn's activities, and resigned. The alliance between Hepburn and Drew "is particularly repugnant to me" because "it seems to exist for the sole purpose of concentrating every possible attack and embarrassment upon the federal government," he said in his letter of resignation to Hepburn on March 11. It was released to the press the same day.

On March 13 *The Star* reported that the provincial cabinet had met and served Hepburn with an ultimatum. He must make no more speeches against the King government, he must remove the ban he had imposed on cabinet ministers participating in the campaign on behalf of Liberal candidates, he must end his alliance with Drew, he must consult his cabinet in the future on matters of importance, and he must restore Nixon to his cabinet position. *The Star* attributed its information to two unnamed members of the cabinet.

Next day Hepburn denounced the report as wholly untrue, and issued an order forbidding *The Star*'s legislative correspondents access to his office. Mindful of the hot water Ferguson had got into when he barred *The Star* from all government offices, he emphasized that this was a personal breaking off of relations, but he invited all cabinet ministers to follow his example. Later the same day he called a press conference with all twelve ministers present.

"Show me which of these men gave you such a totally untrue story?" Hepburn demanded of Jack Hambleton, who had recently replaced H. R. Armstrong as *The Star*'s legislative correspondent.

"I do not believe it is untrue, and obviously, for ethical reasons, I cannot give you the source of my information," Hambleton replied, as quoted by the *Telegram*.

Hepburn then ordered Hambleton from the room. The *Telegram* reported that after *The Star* man left the Premier polled each minister individually, and each denied giving out the story. Commenting on this, *The Star* said in an editorial that the interviews were "given out in part over the telephone and in the case of one minister was followed by personal contact . . . *The Star* published what both ministers said."

The next day Attorney General Gordon Conant wrote Hepburn that he had closed his office to *The Star* because its report, which did not name any minister, "places me under suspicion of having violated my oath of cabinet secrecy." His example was followed by Hon. T. B. McQuesten, minister of highways, and Hon. Eric Cross, minister of municipal affairs. "It's a silly ban," commented the *Ottawa Journal*. "*The Star* . . . is giving a public service in its way vastly more important than the service rendered by those who accept the vagaries of Mr. Hepburn and who shrink with horror from carrying their convictions to the final test of resignation."

The accuracy of *The Star*'s report was soon confirmed. Hepburn personally called upon Nixon and asked him to reconsider his resignation, he took no more part in the election campaign against King, and his open partnership with Drew was ended for the time being.

Hambleton's mistake was in acknowledging that he got his information from a cabinet minister. The ministers had got into the habit of talking somewhat frankly with members of the press gallery and Hambleton, a newcomer, did not realize the importance of protecting them. When he was replaced by Greenaway, who had known Hepburn for years, the ban was quietly forgotten.

This was the second time Hepburn had penalized *The Star*'s legislative reporter. Several months earlier Armstrong's desk in the press gallery had been rifled, and in some manner memos he had exchanged with the office found their way into Hepburn's possession. Some of them were couched in terms decidedly uncomplimentary to the Premier, and he made his displeasure known by refusing to give Armstrong any news, a situation that lasted until the reporter was transferred to *The Star*'s bureau at Ottawa.

Drew, Hepburn, and McCullagh had manoeuvred Dr. R. J. Manion, the Conservative leader, into endorsing a National government, and the federal election was fought mainly on that issue. It resulted in a return of the Liberal party on March 26, 1940, with the largest majority ever given any government until that time. Manion lost in his own riding.

"The traducers of Mr. King and his government have had their answer," *The Star* began its lead editorial the next day. "Dr. Manion," it said, "fought a gallant fight . . . The dissolution of Parliament found him fighting his campaign under great difficulties." It said he did not realize the implication of "a government of the best brains." The tenor of the editorial was that the Conservatives had a better leader than they deserved.

In the two years Dr. Manion was leader of the opposition *The Star* gave him every encouragement in his efforts to reform the Conservative party, without in any way slackening its support of Mackenzie King and the Liberal party. After his defeat the Conservatives discarded him as their leader, naming R. B. Hanson as temporary leader until a convention could be held. Manion wrote Atkinson asking for a job on *The Star* as a columnist. "Though you and I have been on the opposite side of politics, our ideas apparently travel along the same grooves of progressive thought," he wrote, "for on more than one occasion you have been good enough to compliment me on some attitude of mine toward social questions."

Mr. Atkinson replied briefly that there was no place on *The Star* for Dr. Manion, but he telephoned Mackenzie King about the former Conservative leader's situation. King wrote in his diary that Dr. Manion was very hard up, for "the Tories" had made no provision for him, and he promised Hanson to find some "government post in connection with the war" for him. The post eventually found was that of director of civil air raid precautions, which he occupied until his death.

Early in the legislative session *The Star* pulled one of those frightful boners the thought of which causes the hair of editors to turn white. The legislature had appointed a special committee to investigate charges of corruption in the Department of Lands and Forests. *The Star* had been pressing for an investigation. Mayor Charles W. Cox of Port Arthur, who was also a Liberal MPP, delivered to the press early on February 22 typewritten copies of a statement he said he intended to make before the committee that afternoon. It accused certain unnamed departmental employees of accepting bribes. *The Star* printed the statement in full in its Home and Sport edition, which went on the street at the same time the committee began its afternoon session. But Cox got cold feet and never made the statement. In the mistaken belief he would make it later in the day, *The Star* allowed the false report to run in all subsequent editions.

Next day Drew rose in the legislature to express his indignation at "this venomous publication" and to demand that a charge of criminal libel be laid against "Joseph E. Atkinson and *The Toronto Daily Star* for its dastardly and criminal attack on the integrity of the civil service." Advance copies of Cox's threatened "revelations" had been widely circulated and Hepburn must have known what had happened, but for a month he pretended to be considering laying criminal charges before admitting, regretfully he said, that *The Star* had broken no law.

That summer the Drews moved into a house on Dunvegan Road which stood back-to-back with Atkinson's home on Warren Road. A few days after they moved in Mr. Atkinson spied Mrs. Drew in her back yard. They had never met but he waved to her, she waved back, and soon they were chatting amicably over the back fence. Atkinson invited Mrs. Drew to call on him with her husband some evening for a get-together. "She suddenly stiffened as though alarmed and broke off the conversation," he related later. "She said she would have to speak to her husband first." At a social event that evening Mr. Atkinson spied the Drews half-way across the room, and started towards them. Mrs. Drew smiled as he approached, but Drew, after staring stonily at Mr. Atkinson for a moment, turned his back. Atkinson turned aside without speaking to them.

Despite her husband's attitude, Mrs. Drew was always friendly to Mr. Atkinson, while he considered her one of the most charming women he had known. They often chatted over the back fence when Drew was not around. But Drew's posture towards Atkinson was one of studied contempt which turned as the years passed into raging hostility.

The Star had given him no personal cause to behave in this manner. Indeed it had been careful to explain on occasion that it was not criticizing him for acting as it believed the leader of an opposition party should be expected to act, and most of its barbs were aimed at Hepburn. Newspapermen who covered Queen's Park in that period believe it was simply that the ultra-Conservative, extremely imperialistic Drew considered Atkinson's radical liberalism and nationalism to be "evil," a word he used himself later. He could not believe that a man intelligent enough to make a lot of money could be a sincere Liberal.

The resounding victory of the King government at the polls in 1940 did not end the campaign for a National government and an "all-out" war effort. Those who recalled *The Star*'s vigorous campaign for a "National government of the best brains" in the First World War, and its eventual support of a Union government, professed puzzlement at its opposition to National government now. The only explanation, they suggested, was "flagrant partisanship."

But an entry by Mackenzie King in his diary on March 9, 1941, hints that though *The Star* was opposing National government, Mr. Atkinson was favourably inclined towards it provided King was its leader. King had come to Toronto to see his dentist and spent the evening of March 8 with Mr. Atkinson at his home. Atkinson told him that Clifford Sifton had been to see him recently to get the support of *The Star* for National government. "Atkinson," King wrote in his diary, "said he believed national sentiment would be better satisfied with National government or at least with a few outstanding Conservatives, though he could see practical difficulties in effecting anything of the kind." He felt that "there is no feeling anywhere for anyone supplanting myself."

No doubt one of the "practical difficulties" Mr. Atkinson saw to

National government was King's unconquerable opposition to it. King had fought Union government in 1917 and was never convinced it was necessary. But aside from the practical difficulties, Mr. Atkinson was terribly afraid of the men who had lined up behind the National government movement: prominent businessmen for the most part, industrialists, financiers, and the like, some of them had fought the Liberal social welfare program and labour unions before the war, and were now fighting to prevent the government from imposing excess profits taxes to pay for the war.

He was prepared to see them given administrative positions, but not taken into the cabinet, for he was afraid they might get control of the government and turn the clock back on social welfare and liberalism. However, he did not fear the influence of a few Conservative politicians in a Union government headed by King.

In the entry in his diary previously referred to King said Atkinson told him "that he knew from his association with businessmen in the city that, once the war was over, they would fight as strenuously as ever for retaining their possessions, and he felt sure if I took in the Cabinet any of those who wanted to come in for Union government reasons, they would be a thorn in my flesh in trying to control financial policies, etc. That he thought all the wealth that was coming from the war should be taxed and returned to the state."

If Mr. Atkinson was fearful of the influence of "big business" men, they detested him with an equal fervour. Here was a multi-millionaire untrue to his class, one who urged conscription of wealth and abolition of the profit motive in time of war. When Meighen protested that munitions-makers would not produce without their profits, *The Star* mildly remarked that they should not object then if their workers also put the profit motive first and demanded higher wages.

Maitland tells an anecdote that illustrates Mr. Atkinson's attitude. After the Minister of Finance had proposed increases in the rates of personal and corporation income taxes, Maitland wrote an editorial approving of these changes. Mr. Atkinson laid the proof on Maitland's desk, unchanged. "Splendid," he said; "this will cost me $65,000 a year."

By coincidence, the day King visited Atkinson there was printed on the editorial page of the *Globe and Mail* the most violent diatribe ever published against *The Star*. The previous day *The Star* had printed, under the heading "Mr. King and the Rumor Factory," an editorial in which it demonstrated from speeches of Opposition Leader Hanson as quoted in

Hansard that a number of accusations levelled against the King government by the *Globe and Mail* and the Montreal *Gazette* were false. Without denying the accuracy of *The Star*'s editorial the *Globe and Mail* retorted with an editorial headed, "From the Journalistic Gutter."

> *The Toronto Daily Star*, of all papers in Canada, has undertaken to lecture the *Globe & Mail* and the Montreal *Gazette* on newspaper morals. This slavish party organ, with a reputation for violating every known code of newspaper ethics and all other ethics to gain its ends, which colors its news to suit its aims, is a strange creature to pretend to principles of honest journalism. For months it has been trying to "get" a provincial premier by methods no self-respecting journal would countenance. It puts on a face of sanctity, filling its columns with benevolent platitudes, and observes the opposite in practice. Fooling the public is its chief vocation, because it finds this pays in mass circulation, and full coffers are all it cares about.
>
> Does *The Star* think its racket pulls the wool over the eyes of thinking people? Honest journalism! It doesn't know the meaning of the words.

Against the advice of all his associates, including his son, and contrary to his long practice of simply "keeping store," Mr. Atkinson issued a writ charging libel on March 10, and claimed $100,000 damages. The *Globe and Mail* retorted that you cannot libel "a product," and that the editorial referred to "a product," *The Star*, nowhere mentioning Mr. Atkinson. The court ruled that the nature of a newspaper is such that the "publishers and proprietors" cannot be distinguished from the newspaper, and the case went to trial before Mr. Justice Keiller MacKay on April 8, 1942. His Lordship ruled that the *Globe and Mail* editorial had been published "on a privileged occasion" and the question at issue was whether the protection of privilege had been exceeded.

Mr. Atkinson was the only witness called and his examination was brief. Counsel for *The Star* went through the offending editorial clause by clause asking Mr. Atkinson "Is this true?"—did it "lecture" the *Globe and Mail*, is it "a slavish party organ," and so on. And clause by clause Mr. Atkinson answered, "It is untrue," until counsel came to the question: "It puts on a face of sanctity, filling its columns with benevolent platitudes, and observes the opposite in practice. Is that true?" Mr. Atkinson looked at the jury, smiled benignly, and replied, "The last part of that is untrue." He said also it was untrue that *The Star* was trying to "get" a provincial premier, a denial defence counsel apparently thought too sweeping under the known circumstances, for he assured the court no objection was being taken to the statement *The Star* was trying to "get" the Premier, only to the accusation that it was trying to "get" him "by methods no self-respecting journal would countenance."

Other newspapers, including the *Telegram,* commented on the fact the *Globe and Mail* made no attempt to prove the truth of its editorial. Its defence was almost entirely that *The Star* had started the name-calling by referring to the *Globe and Mail* as "a rumor factory," and that this was a case of "tit for tat." The jury found there was no libel.

Personal responsibility for this editorial cannot be attached to McCullagh, for he was in the hospital when it was written. After the libel action had been disposed of he called on Atkinson to express his regret that such unbridled language had been used. "Mr. McCullagh, a public affront requires more than a private apology," Mr. Atkinson replied sternly. But McCullagh would not say publicly in his newspaper what he had said privately.

The *Telegram* had mellowed towards *The Star*, possibly because it too distrusted Drew, McCullagh, and Hepburn, but the *Globe and Mail* was carrying on the vendetta against *The Star* with a vigour that outdid the *Telegram*'s past efforts.

In the meantime Senator Arthur Meighen, the architect of Union government in the First World War, had emerged as a leading spokesman for National government while Hepburn and McCullagh were temporarily out of the fight, the former because his followers in the Legislature had clipped his wings, the latter because he was a sick man. Moreover, these two had fallen out. Early in November, 1941, Hanson resigned as leader, and the Conservative caucus in Parliament offered the national leadership to Meighen. He accepted. Drew had sought the leadership and McCullagh had gone to Ottawa to support him.

"History will probably regard him as the most unfortunate of Canada's Premiers; Premier twice, but less than a year and a half in all, and never the winner of an election," *The Star* commented of Meighen. On the whole its editorial and news coverage was friendly, though Atkinson believed Meighen represented dangerous interests.

Writs were issued for four by-elections to be held on February 9, 1942, and Meighen chose to run in the presumably safe Conservative seat of York South, the sitting member resigning to make way for him. The Liberals did not enter a candidate, but the CCF entered Joseph Noseworthy, a high school teacher. When Farquhar J. MacRae, who had been Liberal candidate in the previous election, indicated an intention of running in defiance of his party's decision not to enter a candidate, Mr. Atkinson sent a personal emissary to him with a warning that if he took any action that would divide the anti-Meighen vote he would be jeopardizing his own future ambitions.

Mr. Atkinson was anxious to see Meighen out of public life entirely, the more so after he was informed that McCullagh had stated he was "almost ashamed" to support Meighen because the men who had engineered his choice as leader were more concerned with opposing price controls than with winning the war. He was shocked, therefore, to find there was no law requiring Meighen to resign from the Senate before contesting a seat in the Commons. He set out to shame him into doing so.

Armstrong was instructed to call every morning on Meighen and ask him, "Have you resigned from the Senate yet?" Each day *The Star* ran on page one a short item to the effect that Meighen had not yet resigned from the Senate but was considering doing so. A week of this and Meighen's nerves were thoroughly on edge. He would shout "No" as soon as Armstrong opened the door. Then came the day, January 19, when he shouted: "Yes I have, now get out." Meighen had wanted to keep his seat in the Senate in case he did not win the by-election, but he knew that if he did so it would be used against him as an admission he did not expect to win.

Because of the Liberal promise not to oppose Meighen, *The Star* did not take an active part in the campaign until January 30, when the Conservative leader was reported to have told a tea of women electors that: "If we have to conscript wealth to win the war we will, but people of common sense do not advocate that until the last gasp." Six days later Meighen denied he had expressed himself in quite that fashion, but in the meantime *The Star* had leaped to the defence of a measure it had been advocating since the start of the war.

Meighen is prepared "to take the widow's last son before touching the millionaire's first dollar," it scornfully commented, and thereafter threw its support strongly behind Noseworthy. Meighen was supported by the other Toronto papers, by the Hepburn government, and by an organization called "The Committee for Total War" which had been formed on January 12. *Saturday Night* said the committee was George McCullagh. The *Globe and Mail* said it consisted of businessmen whose sole object was "to make articulate the British element in Canada." One of the businessmen was a large advertiser in *The Star*. For some years he refused to speak to Atkinson, but never withdrew, or even reduced his advertising.

Meighen was defeated, a result he blamed on "an unholy alliance between *The Star*, Communism, and un-British forces." Drew fumed that "*The Toronto Star* [is] the worst influence in Canada." Mr. Atkinson offered a different explanation. York South embraces the wealthiest suburban residential areas of Metropolitan Toronto. "The master and his wife voted for Meighen," he chuckled, "but the cook, the chauffeur and the upstairs maid voted for Noseworthy."

A few minutes after Meighen conceded defeat the telephone rang on the desk of night editor Jimmy Nicol. His answer was greeted by the excited voice of Mackenzie King: "Isn't this wonderful news, Mr. Atkinson!" Then the connection was cut as the operator realized she had put the Prime Minister's call on the wrong line.

By this time the Japanese had attacked Pearl Harbour, bringing the United States into the war, and the campaign for conscription had been stepped up. Though Mr. Atkinson had two grandsons, John and Harry Hindmarsh, Jr., in the air force, both having enlisted on the outbreak of war, *The Star* contended that conscription should be introduced only after it had been conclusively demonstrated that more men were needed than could be raised by voluntary enlistment.

Editorially it recalled the riots that had occurred in 1918 as a protest against conscription and the division in the nation that was still unhealed. In July, 1941, it had conceded "that conscription is the fairest way to raise military forces," but it did not believe that, with Quebec strongly opposed, it was the wisest way. When riots occurred in Quebec in 1944 it recalled its forebodings.

When King first proposed a plebiscite on conscription, the same solution he had asked Mr. Atkinson to support in 1917, *The Star* was not enthusiastic, for it foresaw a bitter campaign. But when, in January, 1942, the Prime Minister disclosed that the question would only ask the voters to relieve him from a pledge he had made in the 1940 election not to introduce conscription *The Star* approved of it. "Unparalleled cowardice," on King's part, Drew called the plebiscite, which was set for April 27.

"The cynical view that governments should be free to pursue a course diametrically opposed to their definitely stated election pledges . . . is not to be encouraged in a Democracy," *The Star* retorted, and it campaigned vigorously for a full turnout of electors and a "yes" vote. The vote was overwhelmingly affirmative in every province but Quebec.

Two weeks later King introduced a bill providing for conscription for home defence, with voluntary enlistment for overseas service. But it also provided authority for conscription for overseas service if more men were needed than volunteered. Throughout the summer the opposition campaigned for conscription at once for duty anywhere, and coupled with this was a demand for an inquiry into the catastrophe at Hong Kong, whose British and Canadian defenders had been overwhelmed by the Japanese. "I have been completely with you in everything that developed about Hong Kong and the conscription issue," Mr. Atkinson wrote King on August 11, 1942.

Nevertheless, when Drew was charged under Defence of Canada regulations with delivering addresses in connection with the Hong Kong inquiry which were likely to discourage enlistments, *The Star* rushed to the defence of free speech. Drew, it said, had a right to criticize the report of the Hong Kong inquiry if he believed information had been suppressed.

While King was in Toronto on October 9, 1942, to address the convention of the American Federation of Labor he conferred with Atkinson and Hindmarsh. Both assured him *The Star* was solidly behind him. Mr. Atkinson told him "he thought the Tories, who had been pressing for total war . . . were beginning to feel that they had had quite enough of total war, and were beginning to wish they had not said so much about it." This was evidently a reference to complaints about high taxation. At this meeting King first disclosed to Atkinson that Louis St. Laurent was his choice as a successor.

On December 9 the Conservatives met in Winnipeg to choose a new leader to succeed the defeated Meighen. Before it began *The Star* devoted a slightly ironical editorial to candidate John Bracken who was, it commented, "a pleasant man" who in a variegated career "has always managed to please everybody," first the Farmers, then the Progressives, then the Liberals, and next it would appear the Conservatives. Bracken was chosen on December 11, and the following day, still in slightly ironical vein, *The Star* remarked that "the Tories did well to choose him."

The new leader decided to lead his party from outside Parliament and was, in fact, not elected to Parliament until June, 1945. He stumped the country delivering speeches on free enterprise, which *The Star* called "free to get and keep enterprise," and after a couple of years of listening to him *The Star* remarked regretfully that "the man who promised to be a crusader has become simply an opposition leader of ordinary type."

Hepburn resigned as Premier of Ontario in October, 1942, appointing Gordon Conant as his successor without consulting caucus. "To what a shameful pass at this time of war affairs of government have come in

Queen's Park," King wrote Mr. Atkinson. "I am pretty sure there is more behind it all than meets the eye. It causes one to reflect on what happened in France, and served to bring that country into its present appalling plight." Atkinson agreed with King. He regarded Conant as a reactionary, and deplored the way Hepburn, and Ferguson before him, had bequeathed the premiership as though it were their personal possession. But this opinion was not reflected in *The Star*'s editorials. Conant resigned May 18, 1943, being succeeded by Harry Nixon, whom *The Star* had called "the only strong man in the Hepburn government," and one of the few liberals.

Nixon called an election for October 4, 1943, campaigning on the record of the Hepburn government. This put *The Star* in an uncomfortable position, which it got out of nicely by distinguishing between the government's record in administering the province, which on the whole it considered good, and Hepburn's personal record with respect to the Liberal government at Ottawa. Nixon, it said, was "a King Liberal," and should be supported.

The Star covered the election in a manner without precedent. Early in the campaign Drew, leading the Conservatives, had complained that *The Star*'s reports of election meetings were slanted against him. Instructions were then given reporters that meetings, regardless of party, should be covered "dead pan." The attendance at every meeting should be counted and given exactly in the first paragraph of the report. Reporters were not to inject any colour into their reports, which except for noting the size of the audiences were to deal exclusively with the speeches. Editors were to put "label" headings on election stories.

The Liberals suffered a crushing defeat, electing only fifteen in a legislature of ninety. Conservatives led with thirty-eight. The CCF was second with thirty-four. Toronto and the Yorks elected eight CCF, seven Conservatives, and two Communists.

The Star reporter who had accompanied Drew on his tour of the province went to congratulate him at his committee room that night. The Premier-elect glared at him for a moment before taking his outstretched hand. "I'll shake hands with you," he said grudgingly, "but I want it understood that no reporter from *The Star* will ever have access to my office, or ever be welcome at the Parliament buildings." Then he turned away.

Next morning Mr. Atkinson came bustling into the city room for late election results. The news editor made some comment about the extent of the Liberal defeat. "We had two horses in the race, you know," Atkinson smiled, "and one of them did pretty well."

Hindmarsh asked for a measurement of the space that had been given each party during the campaign. It showed the CCF led by a large margin. This was unintentional on the part of *The Star*, and can be attributed to the intelligent public relations work of Mrs. E. B. Jolliffe, wife of the CCF leader, who personally saw to it that speeches of CCF candidates were condensed to two or three pungent paragraphs before being sent to the newspapers.

"While [the Liberal] party was defeated, the result of the election was the emergence of an advanced form of liberalism as a new and powerful factor in provincial affairs—and one may be sure in federal affairs as well," *The Star* commented. "It may be the beginning of the end of the power of the Liberal party federally," King agreed. In a later editorial *The Star* said the result was "largely due to the determination of the great masses of the people that a better day will dawn for the common man." It was "a declaration of faith lost in the old way of doing things."

Drew carried out his warning that *Star* reporters would not be welcomed at the Parliament buildings while he was there. He did not ban them, as Ferguson had done, and *Star* reporters always had access to any office except Drew's own. But ministers, though greeting them politely, never had any information for them. Even provincial police officials would express blank ignorance of events in their jurisdiction. Press releases were always issued after 4 p.m., too late for evening papers but just right for McCullagh's morning *Globe and Mail*. This discriminated against the *Telegram* too, but since ministers and other officials miraculously recovered speech and memory in the presence of its reporters, that newspaper fared quite well.

Greenaway, who had been working for two or three years on other assignments, was sent to Queen's Park again. He discovered that T. L. Kennedy, Minister of Agriculture, was no admirer of Drew, and was the one minister who had never discriminated against *The Star*. Before long Kennedy was providing Greenaway with reports for every department. This could not have been done without the knowledge and tacit consent of the other ministers, who deplored Drew's pettiness but lacked Tom Kennedy's courage to defy him.

In spite of Drew's attitude, *The Star* was not noticeably more critical of him than it would have been of any leader of a political party with whose views it disagreed until in 1944 he set himself up as the chief opponent of family allowances, and tried to rally the other provincial premiers behind him. This was a project dear to Mr. Atkinson's heart. He was then seventy-eight and desperately eager to see the social welfare program he had enunciated in 1916 completed before his death.

It was in January, 1944, that Atkinson had his chat with King in which he advised the Prime Minister to introduce family allowances. In a radio address on August 9 Drew declared his intention of blocking them. "I assure you, the government of Ontario intends to do everything within its power to make sure that this iniquitous bill does not go into effect," he stated. He said Quebec would benefit from family allowances at the expense of the rest of Canada.

Under the heading "To Balkanize Canada," *The Star*'s editorial the next day blasted Drew's "offensive and ill-timed speech directed against Quebec." The *Montreal Star* agreed with its Toronto namesake that Drew "hopes to make Quebec the political scapegoat." After this Drew could do no good in *The Star*'s eyes. It attacked him not only for his "Toryism" in opposing social welfare measures, but also for his failure to implement the 22-point program on which he had been elected. "They have proven to be nothing but hollow promises," it declared. Day after day it told off Drew's string of broken promises like a rosary, repeatedly accusing him of insincerity. "He is not only a Conservative, he is a Tory of the Tories, out of tune with the trend of the times and unsympathetic with the trend of humanitarian reforms which is to bring a measure of justice to the masses of the people," it declared. Reports from Queen's Park were flagrantly slanted. And once in a while the *Telegram* chimed in to condemn the Drew-McCullagh alliance, which it said was trying to get rid of Bracken because he was too progressive.

The Drew government was beaten on March 23, 1945, in the vote on the speech from the throne, and an election was called for June 4. "The people of the province will have the opportunity of declaring whether they want Ontario to be brought into line in a modern, humanitarian outlook on legislation and its objectives, or whether they are content to have their province saddled with a Premier and government oblivious to all this and incurably reactionary," *The Star* commented.

Since a federal election was being held a week later, Drew escaped comparatively lightly until, in a radio address on May 24, the CCF leader E. B. Jolliffe accused the government of having a secret police force in the nature of a "Gestapo" to spy on labour unionists and others it considered its foes. After delivering his address, Jolliffe telephoned

Greenaway, and accompanied him to *The Star* offices where he left in Greenaway's possession photostatic copies of reports on a number of citizens, mostly prominent members of the CCF, which had been abstracted from the "special force" files by an employee. Next day Greenaway delivered them to Hindmarsh. Jolliffe placed responsibility for this "Gestapo" on Drew personally.

The following day Maitland wrote an editorial in which he suggested that because of the sensational nature of the charges the Legislature should appoint a committee to investigate them. On seeing the editorial in proof, Mr. Atkinson hastened to Maitland's office. "Oh no, no, no, Mr. Maitland," he protested, "this won't do. I've talked to Jolliffe, got all the information from him, and we're going to back him up." Then Atkinson sat down and told Maitland exactly what he should write. Thereafter *The Star* had an editorial every day until the election on Drew's "Gestapo," which was likened to that of the German Nazi leader Himmler, and most of them were dictated in large part by Mr. Atkinson. Every day it had new "revelations" from Jolliffe on page one.

In a statement to Canadian Press, Drew denied any knowledge of such a "special force" and said he had never authorized secret inquiries. *The Star* printed his statement in full, but retorted that his denial was worthless. When Drew announced he was appointing a royal commission to investigate the charges, *The Star* said that would do no good, since it could not report until after the election. Hepburn had emerged from retirement on his onion farm to lead the Liberals, but *The Star* scarcely mentioned either him or his party.

Drew won with sixty-six supporters. The CCF was in third place with only eight. *The Star* filled nearly two pages with tables and graphs to demonstrate that actually both Toronto and the province had voted against Drew, the city by 20,000 votes. A front page story was headed: "Popular Vote Strong against Drew's Party." Mr. Atkinson was displeased at this churlish attempt to minimize Drew's victory, but Hindmarsh had ordered it and liked it, and he was allowed to have his way.

Editorially *The Star* blamed the result on "fear that a Socialist government might be established in Ontario," and predicted that fear of socialism would also result in a Liberal victory in the federal election of June 11. The prediction was accurate. "People who normally are Conservative voted Liberal as the surest way of keeping the CCF out," it explained after King's victory.

The day after the provincial election Drew sued *The Star* for $100,000 claiming the entire series of "Gestapo" editorials were libellous. The case did not come to trial until March, 1947, when a jury under Mr. Justice D. P. J. Kelly found there was no libel and assessed costs against Drew, His Lordship having told them "qualified privilege" existed during an election campaign.

Drew appealed, and five justices of the Court of Appeal ordered a new trial. Chief Justice Robertson commented that the jury should have considered whether *The Star* went beyond "fair comment" when it likened the Premier to Himmler. In a written decision he observed: "If the defendant pleads fair comment he must establish that the facts are true. No attempt was made in evidence to establish their truth." *The Star* appealed this order to the Supreme Court of Canada. Its appeal was dismissed on October 5, 1948, three days after Drew had been chosen federal leader of the Progressive-Conservative party at a convention in Ottawa. On April 1, 1949, Drew announced he would not seek a new trial, and the case was dropped.

The royal commission headed by Mr. Justice LeBel began hearings July 6, 1945, only two weeks after Jolliffe made his charges, and on October 11 His Lordship reported that he found the "special branch" had been set up by the Commissioner of the Provincial Police to inquire into communist activities without Premier Drew's authorization or knowledge, and that except for its "unwarranted intrusion in CCF affairs" its activities were non-political. The evidence showed that most of the reports on CCF members were made by two amateur "counter-spies" on their own initiative, and had not been asked for. They had turned to the provincial police after the RCMP refused to take their reports of communist-CCF plots seriously.

The feud between *The Star* and Drew raged unabated for the next three years, and nothing Drew did found favour in *The Star*'s pages. His prewar writings in which he had accused prominent Canadians of being communists, had said the Russian people would never fight for their country, and urged a one-party government for Canada, were paraded again and again, as were also the promises he was said to have broken. On his part Drew used the floor of the legislature as a privileged forum from which to attack *The Star* and all it stood for.

His most famous speech against Mr. Atkinson was delivered in the legislature on March 22, 1947, just one week after the libel action against *The Star* was dismissed. *The Star* had accused him in an editorial the day before of turning down a federal offer to help 15,000 crippled children in the province. He denied this was a fact. Canadian Press reported his reference to Atkinson as follows:

"Freedom of the press is part of the freedom of speech which must not be prostituted to the evil ends of any man prepared to use his place as owner of a great newspaper to his own evil purpose," he said. The Premier said he was proud of Ontario's press with the exception of *The Toronto Star* and "its associate, the Canadian *Tribune*." [The *Tribune* was the Communist organ]. Nothing appeared in *The Star* editorial without the permission of that "very evil old man Joseph E. Atkinson," said Col. Drew. "It was a most vicious and malicious appeal to sentiment" in the editorial page, said Mr. Drew, by the "incorrigible liar who directs the editorial page."

A few days later Atkinson encountered Attorney General Price in a hotel lobby. "I do not like that leader of yours," he said, pressing a bony finger against Price's chest. "He called me an evil old man. I resent being called old." Then unsmilingly he went on about his business.

"I don't hate George Drew," he told a reporter to whom he was giving instructions. "But he is an exceedingly dangerous man because of the things he stands for, and he must be eliminated."

By early 1948 Bracken was on the way out, and Drew was in the running for leadership of the federal Conservative party, to be decided at a convention in October. Mr. Atkinson thoroughly approved of his ambition. He thought there was no better way of rendering Drew harmless than to make him leader of the federal Conservatives.

When Drew announced plans on February 26, 1948, to convert Ontario's hydro-electric power from 25-cycle to 60-cycle, thus bringing it into uniformity with the rest of the continent, the city editor expected *The Star* would, as usual, oppose him. He summoned his corps of political writers at Toronto and Ottawa to pontificate against the change, and assigned reporters to spend the evening interviewing by telephone anybody who might conceivably be opposed, including housewives who knew nothing about it.

Next morning Mr. Atkinson came to the office unusually early, and asked the city editor for proofs of what had been written. After glancing quickly through them he laid them gently on the desk. "Don't use this," he said. "Use Drew's own statement in full and verbatim, with a lead provided by Canadian Press. It is a courageous thing he is doing."

Mr. Atkinson was in ill health all that winter. On April 20 he was at his office on the third floor of the *Star* building for the last time. The family were told he was nearing the end of his long and useful life.

On May 7 Mackenzie King wrote Mr. Atkinson the long, rambling letter of an old friend. He recalled their youthful friendship, their experience as reporters together more than fifty years before, the many years in which they had fought side by side for the social betterment of Canada. "Throughout the whole of that period I have had in you the truest of friends, both political and personal," the Prime Minister wrote. His letter was delivered with the mail the next morning.

There was something infinitely fitting, infinitely touching, in the fact that the last letter Mr. Atkinson received should have been from his oldest living friend, the man on whom he had pinned the hopes of the people of Canada, and who had not failed him; the man he had done so much to raise to the highest office in the land, and who himself, before the year was out, was to pass on the torch he held to others.

That evening, May 8, 1948, Mr. Atkinson died quietly at home. He was in his eighty-third year and had been publisher of *The Star* for forty-eight years, four months, and twenty-five days.

Above All . . . Humanity

In memory of the late J. E. Atkinson, whose life of philanthropic endeavor is crowned in his death with the bequeathing of his two great newspapers to the Atkinson Charitable Foundation.

He that has fought the good fight and has finished the course with rejoicing
  Now has passed on to his rest. In the aeons of light he is sleeping
Deaf to the praise of his name that the least and the greatest are voicing.
  All that he patiently wrought he has left in humanity's keeping.

He was a message of hope for the weary of heart, the forsaken;
  This, of his struggles the fruit, of his humble upbringing the token.
Eagerly, always, he sought in the minds of mankind to awaken
  Pity and brotherly love for humanity toil-worn and broken.

Aging or needy or sick—'twas for these that his bright sword he wielded,
  Making their battle his own, that their lot might be shorn of its sadness.
Victims of life and of fate—it was these that his kindliness shielded,
  Turning despair into hope, and their sorrow at last into gladness.

Out of the depths of his heart, from the well-spring of deepest emotion,
  Clear flowed the waters of love for the suffering children of sorrow.
These were his care to the end, at the shrine of his earnest devotion,
  These—that their ills of today might be lost in their brighter tomorrow.

All that his talents had won with the God-given skill of a master,
  All that his genius had fashioned, and all that his zeal had promoted
Now to the people returns, for the healing of grief and disaster,
  All the news empire he built to humanity's cause is devoted.

He that has fought the good fight and has finished the course with rejoicing
  Now has passed on to his rest. In the aeons of light he is sleeping
Deaf to the praise of his name that the least and the greatest are voicing.
  All that he patiently wrought he has left in humanity's keeping.

Toronto, May 11, 1948 G.H.M.

G.H.M. is George H. Maitland, editor of *The Star,* 1937-55.

Chapter 22

A WILL FRUSTRATED

Joseph E. Atkinson died on a Saturday night. The following Monday *The Star* carried the sensational announcement that "*The Star* and *The Star Weekly* are willed in perpetuity to a Foundation—The Atkinson Charitable Foundation—which will devote their profits as periodically distributed to religious, charitable and educational objects in Ontario."

This was, as many news story leads are, an over-simplification of the facts, and this over-simplification was to lead to some misunderstanding in the future. While Mr. Atkinson controlled The Toronto Star Limited and Toronto Star Realty Limited, which owned the papers and publishing plant, and their direction was subject to no will but his own, he was not the only shareholder. He could bequeath only the 16,570 shares he owned himself of the 20,000 issued.

The remaining 17.5 per cent of the shares were owned by his son, Joseph S. Atkinson, his daughter, Mrs. Ruth Hindmarsh, and William Pate Mulock, grandson of Sir William Mulock. Before his death his son and daughter indicated their approval of the way he left his estate by agreeing that the shares they owned should go on their deaths to the Foundation, and in return Mr. Atkinson directed that certain annual payments be made to them and their survivors for life as a first claim upon the estate. There was no such undertaking in the case of the Mulock shares.

Mr. Atkinson's intention was made clear in three paragraphs of his will, which were quoted as follows in the announcement:

> It is my desire that the ownership and operation of the newspapers known as *The Toronto Daily Star* and *The Star Weekly* shall not fall into private hands, and that the shares in the capital stock of The Toronto Star Limited and Toronto Star Realty Limited held by me shall be held in trust for and ultimately belong to The Atkinson Charitable Foundation or [under certain conditions] shall be held in trust for or transferred to charitable organizations which carry on their work solely in Ontario, selected by my Trustees.
>
> This should accomplish two things: (1) The publication of the papers will be conducted for the benefit of the public in the continued frank and full dissemination of news and opinions, with the profit motive, while still important, subsidiary to what I consider to be the chief functions of a metropolitan newspaper; (2) The profits from the newspapers will be used for the promotion and maintenance of social, scientific and economic reforms which are charitable in nature, for the benefit of the people of the province of Ontario.
>
> It is my hope the newspapers and the Foundation will be operated for these purposes by the Trustees whom I have chosen and by their successors, all of whom will be closely related to the newspaper business and familiar with the doctrines and beliefs which I have promoted in the past. It is my desire that the Trustees shall have the widest freedom possible in the decisions which they make in the operation of the newspapers and the charitable causes which they promote and maintain.

The "certain conditions" mentioned elsewhere in the will, were the possibility the provincial or federal governments might decide the Atkinson Charitable Foundation was not a true charity and therefore bequests to it would be subject to succession duties. He suspected that should he die while George Drew was Premier of Ontario an attempt would be made to frustrate his last wishes. He was also alive to the possibility he might even be prevented from leaving control to established charities. Thus he gave his trustees authority, as a last resort, to sell the shares he left or any portion of them to such persons, or in any manner, they thought most likely to further the objects he had in mind.

The *Globe and Mail* and the *Telegram* were quick to point out that *The Star* had always advocated substantial death duties on big estates, and they professed to see an inconsistency in the steps Mr. Atkinson took to free his estate of these duties. But they missed the point that *The Star* advocated taxing big estates because, as it said on several occasions, "their heirs have not earned this money," and in most cases the imposition of death duties was the only way of returning the profits to the people from whom they were derived. This did not apply if the estate was left to the people by way of a charity.

Mr. Atkinson knew the policies he had advocated were unpopular with people who had money, and he was described by Alexander Stark, *The Star*'s solicitor, who helped establish the foundation, as being "desperately afraid" his newspapers or a controlling interest in them would have to be sold to some of these people to raise money for succession duties. The only way he saw of making certain his papers would be preserved as spokesmen for "the little guy" was to leave them to a tax-free foundation.

To the end of his days Mr. Atkinson retained the missionary zeal of the boy who wanted to be a Methodist minister. *The Star* was the sword of his crusade, and it had to be kept strong. If sometimes he used Machiavellian methods to further ends he believed to be desirable, so have churchmen of repute and honoured memory. In 1942 a reporter who had been assigned to write his obituary, to be held until needed as is newspaper practice, expressed concern over what might happen when Mr. Atkinson passed on. "There need be no worry on that point," the Chief told him. "I am fixing things so nobody can destroy my paper." Yet in the end it was the determination of his son that saved it from being destroyed, or at least blunted.

J. E. Atkinson had been accused so often of inconsistency and insincerity by foes of his social program that many refused to believe his will expressed his true intentions. Yet his career reveals an awesome consistency and a sincerity that was close to fanaticism. His will fitted exactly into the pattern of his creed.

The Atkinson Charitable Foundation was incorporated in 1942. It was not Mr. Atkinson's wish that the Foundation should restrict its good works to Ontario, but in order to qualify for tax exemption under Ontario law it had to be so limited. For six years it carried on in a small way with donations from *The Star* or Mr. Atkinson. Its first grant, in 1946, was to the Toronto Hospital for Sick Children for research on hearing defects and diseases of the ear. Mr. Atkinson was hard of hearing, as was his father before him. But the Drew government steadfastly refused to give the slightest indication whether or not it would accept the Foundation as a charity.

At the same time Mr. Atkinson was trying to have the federal government change its law with respect to bequests to charity. At the time the Foundation was established federal tax exemption was allowed on only half of large charitable bequests. J. S. Atkinson and Stark went to Ottawa to ask Mackenzie King to amend the law to allow total exemption on charitable bequests. King promised to make the change, but he kept procrastinating. During Mr. Atkinson's last illness Stark made a rush trip to see King, but before the change could be enacted into law Mr. Atkinson had died. However the amendment, when passed in 1950, was so worded as to be retroactive to a time before his death.

It should be kept in mind that the only portion of his estate that would be free of succession duties was the shares he left to the Foundation. In addition to these shares the estate included sundry stocks and bonds, personal property, his home, and $1,999,260 in life insurance.

There were also other beneficiaries than the Foundation, the two largest being bequests of $35,000 a year for life each to his son and daughter. There were bequests of $5,000 a year for life each to Mrs. Hindmarsh's four children, payment to start upon her death, and a bequest of $25,000 cash to grand-daughter Catherine Atkinson. Other relatives and servants were also remembered. Succession duties were paid on these amounting to $333,299.36 to the Dominion and $208,400 to Ontario. The total amount paid individual beneficiaries, including capitalized value of life bequests, was $1,079,349.

At the time of Mr. Atkinson's death the directors of *The Star* were also trustees of the Foundation, though this was not an essential condition. In fact, for two years Mr. Atkinson himself had not been a trustee. In his will he directed that the trustees of the Foundation should also be trustees of his estate. But he provided that his son should be a trustee of the estate for life, regardless of whether he was a trustee of the Foundation.

The number of trustees had stood at seven, but only five survived Mr. Atkinson. They were J. S. Atkinson and H. C. Hindmarsh, both vice-presidents of *The Star*; George Maitland, editor-in-chief; F. L. Tate, business manager; and Alexander Stark, the *Star*'s solicitor. William Wallace, advertising manager since 1936 and a director, had died the previous December.

On May 15 it was announced that J. S. Atkinson had been elected chairman of the board and president of the Atkinson Charitable Foundation, and H. C. Hindmarsh president of *The Star*. Atkinson exercised general supervision over the business and production departments, while Hindmarsh headed the editorial departments. These two men had never worked well together, but this was of no great importance as long as J. E. Atkinson was present as a dominant unifying factor. But the division of management after his death into two watertight and mutually suspicious compartments was to prove a weakness. Evidently J. E. Atkinson had hoped the board of trustees would be a unifying element, but the other trustees were never assertive enough to be effective.

Even so, the conflict of personalities might not have been of major importance had the two men not differed on a matter that was fundamental—the interpretation of Joseph E. Atkinson's real intention as expressed in his will. Was it to further his doctrines or was it to aid charity?

All the trustees believed Mr. Atkinson had hoped that both the objectives set out in his will would be achieved. But J. S. Atkinson believed that should it ever be necessary to choose between the two, his father would have preferred to keep the papers strong and in the hands of men sympathetic to his views, that they might carry on the fight for social justice and the liberal principles he cherished. Hindmarsh held that the charitable objective should be put first, and he was not averse to having the papers retreat from long-held policies with which he may not have been in full accord or perhaps had not understood.

Doubt as to how the will might be construed by the courts if a conflict arose had been expressed even before Mr. Atkinson's death by Kaspar Fraser, the distinguished lawyer who had drawn up the will, though he had no doubt the terms of the will complied with the law with respect to charitable bequests. This uncertainty worried the trustees from the beginning, for the other Toronto newspapers were clamouring for the provincial and federal governments to collect the full amount of the succession duties on the estate.

"The question in the minds of the trustees was whether a reading of the whole will by either the courts or the taxing authorities would so construe its intentions as one designed, not to further charitable work, but to carry on or perpetuate a newspaper business," explained J. M. Armstrong, manager of the trusts department of the National Trust Company, which was the executor of the estate. Armstrong was testifying at a Supreme Court hearing to determine what compensation should be paid the executor.

The trustees knew that sooner or later they would have to come to grips with the problem, for fundamentally there was a conflict of interest between the two positions they held. As directors of *The Star* it was their duty to keep the papers strong in the face of increasingly severe competition. As trustees of the Foundation it was their duty to get as much money as possible from *The Star* for charity. That was at the base of the discord that arose between J. S. Atkinson and Hindmarsh.

But for the time being they agreed that their first responsibility was to have the provincial and federal governments formally recognize the Atkinson Charitable Foundation as a legitimate charity, and this the Ontario government resisted doing. If it was not so recognized Ontario could collect an estimated $3,328,358 and the Federal government another $2,300,000 in succession duties. The only way the trustees in that event could avoid paying these duties would be to exercise the second option under Mr. Atkinson's will and distribute the profits, and ultimately the shares, among other charities that had already been recognized, and this they were reluctant to do except as a last resort. The fact that he had made established charities the alternative beneficiary refutes charges made at the time that Mr. Atkinson had established the Foundation as a "wily scheme" to assure his heirs good-paying jobs. He had, as we have noted, made other provision for his children and grandchildren.

For a while officers of the trust company were in almost daily contact with *Star* management, but did not interfere in editorial policy or try to influence it. They gave some consideration to having a representative on the board of directors, but decided against it. "It was our view these directors had been brought up in the business by the deceased . . . and were conversant with the policies he had expounded," Armstrong explained. "So long as the financial operations were successful, and so long as we were in the picture we had no intention of interfering in editorial policy."

There were two vacancies on the board of directors due to the deaths of Atkinson and Wallace. When the five remaining directors could not agree whom to appoint to succeed them, Hindmarsh and Stark suggested the five remaining carry on. The trust company reluctantly agreed to this compromise.

It gave orders at once to stop work on the projected plant for the *Star Weekly* on 7.66 acres The Toronto Star Limited had purchased on the waterfront. Mr. Atkinson, it will be recalled, had begun saving money as the war ended in order to build this enduring monument. He wanted to pay cash for it, and his goal was to have $7,500,000 in a surplus account which could be readily converted to cash. An architect had been engaged and $60,000 had already been spent on plans, and there was a liability of between $1,500,000 and $2,000,000 for presses and other equipment ordered several years before but not yet delivered.

The executor ruled that the trustees could not proceed with this plant until the Ontario government decided whether the bequest was to charity or not. If not, some of the funds in the surplus account, which stood at well over $6 million, might be needed to pay succession duties. Eventually a much less elaborate plant than Mr. Atkinson had planned was built.

Armstrong said the trust company had some difficulty in evaluating the estate because J. E. Atkinson had kept financial statements secret, not even showing them to other shareholders. Eventually they arrived at a figure of $8,760,496. They allowed nothing for goodwill on the grounds Mr. Atkinson had exercised such firm personal control over the enterprises that all goodwill died with him. They estimated the loss of Mr. Atkinson reduced the value of the properties by 10 per cent.

The other Toronto newspapers loudly protested the valuation, the *Telegram* declaring the estate was worth "at least $25 million" and that the people of Ontario were being robbed of $10 million in succession duties. Actually, if the residue of the estate was going tax-free to charity, the valuation placed on it was of no practical importance. The federal government accepted the appraisal and ruled the Foundation was a charity, but the Ontario succession duties department sent in its own valuation of $16,162,000 "just so the people of Ontario will know how much taxes they are being deprived of," a government spokesman said. Eventually the executor and the succession duties department reached a compromise agreement of $12,200,624 of which $10,550,000 was represented by Mr. Atkinson's shares in *The Star* companies.

This valuation was reached by comparing *The Star*'s worth with that of the *Telegram*, which had been sold on November 25, 1948, to George McCullagh for $3,610,000 by the trustees of the John Ross Robertson estate. Directors of *The Star* had considered buying the *Telegram*, for J. E. Atkinson had emphasized during his lifetime that *The Star* should buy the *Telegram* when it was offered for sale, as it had to be when the period of trusteeship set by John Ross Robertson ended. When it came on the market in 1948 two of the directors and most of the senior executives of *The Star* were eager to make the purchase. They set up an amount to offer which would have been sufficient to buy the paper because it was higher than the reported purchase price. The papers would not necessarily have been merged, though that was considered. Some of the senior executives believed the papers could be profitably operated independently, and tried to persuade the directors to set up a separate company to buy and operate the *Telegram*. Hindmarsh opposed the purchase, mainly because he was afraid it would weaken the Atkinson Charitable Foundation, and the directors decided not to enter a bid.

After he bought it, McCullagh lost no time in hurling the *Telegram* into his personal vendetta against *The Star*, for he regarded the men then running it as no better than Mr. Atkinson had been. "The outstanding thought that brought me into the evening newspaper field was to knock off *The Star*," he told a mass meeting of *Telegram* employees the day after he bought it. "*The Star* has done enough to the profession of journalism that we ought to go in and teach it a lesson . . . I'm going to knock that - - - - rag right off its pedestal."

When an interviewer for *Time* reminded McCullagh that he had succeeded in adding only 21,697 circulation to the *Globe and Mail* in the twelve years he had owned it, while in the same period the "slow-poking *Telegram*" had added 42,290 and *The Star* 121,059, McCullagh cracked: "The smart talk will soon be about the waning *Star*."

"That fellow Hindmarsh is so ugly that if he ever bit himself he'd get hydrophobia," *Time* said he retorted to an editorial in *The Star* which stated the *Telegram* had "lost its independence" as a result of its purchase by McCullagh. *The Star* nicknamed the two McCullagh-owned papers "the gold-dust twins," a reference to McCullagh's well-known link with gold-mining interests.

The municipal election campaign, just getting under way, provided the first opportunity for a test of strength, and McCullagh dashed recklessly into the fray. The issue was whether the elections should be held annually, as in the past, or every two years, with *The Star* supporting the one-year term. In a series of front page editorials the McCullagh papers accused *The Star* of "lying, dishonesty and trickery." A typical blast under the heading "Don't be a Dope" accused *The Star* of "joining hands with the Communists" and asked "are you going to be a dupe of this dishonest journal?" The one-year term supported by *The Star* carried with a majority of more than twenty thousand.

"Those who watched from a distance the campaign of vituperation McCullagh's newspapers unleashed upon *The Toronto Star* . . . will feel some satisfaction at the outcome," commented the Ottawa *Citizen*. "Not content with debating the merits of the case, they turned the contest into an effort to carry out McCullagh's threat to 'cut *The Star* down to size.' "

A few weeks later alarming rumours reached *The Star* that the Ontario government intended to introduce legislation with respect to Mr. Atkinson's will, but its nature was still a secret. The Brockville *Recorder and*

Times stated editorially, "This newspaper . . . actually heard in Tory circles boasts to the effect that the Conservative government of Ontario is 'going to fix *The Toronto Star*.' " McCullagh was reported to the trustees to have made a similar statement. Drew was no longer Premier of Ontario, having been chosen leader of the federal Progressive-Conservative party in October, but with aging Tom Kennedy only a caretaker Premier until a convention chose a new provincial leader, he was still a power in provincial politics.

John G. Hungerford, then general manager of the National Trust Company, told the Supreme Court hearing that from the beginning he had been "very much alive" to the problem that might be created by the fact *The Star* was "not in popular favor with the government." Because of this he had taken a more personal interest in this estate than would normally have been the case, he said.

The Charitable Gifts Act, introduced in the legislature on March 25, 1949, by Hon. Leslie Frost, provincial treasurer, was more drastic than even the worst anticipations, for to quote Mr. Hungerford's testimony, "it completely nullified Mr. Atkinson's wishes as expressed in his will." The Atkinson Charitable Foundation was not to be allowed to own more than a 10 per cent interest in *The Star* newspapers.

Section (1) provided that "wherever any interest in any business that is carried on for gain or profit is given to or vested in any person in any capacity for any religious, charitable, educational or public purpose, such person shall dispose of such portion thereof that represents more than 10 per cent. interest in such business." Existing charitable foundations had to comply with this provision before April 1, 1952.

In introducing the bill, Mr. Frost said that when a charitable foundation is set up to run a business "the charitable object may become secondary to the interests of the directors, managers and officers who would be by themselves and their successors trustees in perpetuity. . . . It is necessary and desirable that there should be some safeguards to assure that the charitable intent is carried out." He said that without regulation a business run by a charitable foundation would "no doubt become a menace to competitive business and provide extremely unfair competition to businesses which are endeavouring to pay taxes and provide dividends for shareholders."

However, the Liberal and CCF members of the Legislature argued that the measure was inspired by political motives and a desire to harass a newspaper unfriendly to the government. This was the opinion of the trustees and executors of the Atkinson estate and it found wide acceptance.

Armstrong told the Master of the Supreme Court at the hearing previously mentioned that in the opinion of the National Trust Company officials one of the main purposes of the bill was to put the trustees of the Atkinson estate "in a position of having a forced sale."

Replying in the Legislature to these and like charges, Frost said the fact that *The Star* was the first business affected "is merely incidental to a measure of broad principle and general application." There is no evidence that Frost did not genuinely believe that an important principle was at stake. With this in mind, the passage of the Charitable Gifts Act by a Conservative government may properly be regarded as the final episode in the long dispute between Mr. Atkinson, who believed that a little socialism now and then is a good thing, and those who presume that private enterprise, spurred by the profit motive, will always run things better.

Frost told the legislature that Mr. Atkinson's will "was drawn up to continue promotion of the doctrines and beliefs of the owner [of *The Star*]. Charity was secondary." He held that "concentration of control of business in perpetuity in charitable trusts or foundations" is "undesirable."

"If we had to choose between *The Toronto Star* belonging to The Atkinson Charitable Foundation and *The Toronto Star* in the hands of some wealthy corporation, our choice would be the Foundation," replied the *Ottawa Journal*, a Conservative newspaper, in an editorial more than a column long. "The more we examine this law the less we like it." "*The Toronto Star* always has upheld the interests of the minorities, of the poor, the unfortunate and the downtrodden," observed the *Windsor Star*. "Never has it presumed to speak for special interests. If it has to be sold, it will be sold to somebody with a lot of money . . . The lower income people in the Toronto area might end up without any newspaper to speak on their behalf."

The Ottawa *Citizen* linked the Charitable Gifts Act with *The Star*'s "longstanding feud with Mr. George Drew," and observed that "the fact Mr. George McCullagh . . . a close personal and political friend of Mr. Drew, is *The Star*'s sole daily newspaper competitor gives a sinister aspect to the proposed measure . . . If *The Star* is forced to sell it may, of course, be picked up by moneyed interests in sympathy with the Tories." The glee with which McCullagh's two newspapers greeted the Charitable Gifts Act strengthened the suspicion that political and personal motives were involved as well as the principles enunciated by Mr. Frost. "Bill May Force Sale of Toronto Star," the *Globe and Mail* headlined its story, while editorially it asked: "If all the declared profits are to be given away, what is to prevent the trustees from running their concern in so unprofitable a way as to put their competitors out of business?" Rightly or wrongly, the trustees of the Atkinson estate were convinced Drew and McCullagh were behind the Charitable Gifts Act. An editorial in *The Star* referred to it as: "This adopted law child of his [Mr. Frost's] whose parentage is undisclosed."

"Personally, I relish the blame," retorted McCullagh, as quoted by *Time,* while the *Globe and Mail* said "Mr. McCullagh can have no interest in seeing *The Star* pass from the control of the incompetents now guiding it to a new and more able management."

The day the bill was introduced the trustees met and decided to fight it with all the powers of publicity at their disposal. They succeeded in stirring up such a storm of protest against the bill from labour organizations, churchmen, opposition parties, and newspapers of all political persuasions that it must have been abundantly clear to the Ontario government that they would be endangering their own future if they passed it without amendment. At the same time, the National Trust Company was greatly disturbed, as executor of the estate, at what it called "this frustration of the testator's intentions." Officers of the company met with Frost and urged him either to remove the retroactive feature or to extend the time in which the papers would have to be sold.

When the bill was introduced for its second reading on April 6 it had been amended by extending the time limit from three to seven years. After seven years the trustees might apply to the Supreme Court for an extension of time. There was also a clause providing for determination of profits and filing of information with the public trustee.

The most important amendment, however, was a provision permitting sale of the properties to trustees, officers, or directors with the approval of the Supreme Court of Ontario. Without this provision it might not have been possible for the present six directors to buy *The Star* in 1958. The Act went into effect April 8, 1949, the forty-fifth birthday of the chairman of the board and present publisher.

The trustees were left with four choices. They could distribute the shares Mr. Atkinson left in the *Star* companies among ten or more charities, "like 10 pieces of pie," in which case *The Star* would almost certainly flounder from lack of unified control. They could sell the shares and give the proceeds to the Atkinson Charitable Foundation, in which case there was a strong possibility the papers would fall to interests of which Mr. Atkinson had disapproved. They could buy the papers themselves provided they

J. E. Atkinson at wedding of a relative

TORONTO DAILY STAR

56TH YEAR | Authorized as second class mail, Post-Office Department, Ottawa | TORONTO, MONDAY, MAY 10, 1948—48 PAGES | 3 PER COPY, 18c PER WEEK

THE WEATHER
Toronto and vicinity — Tuesday: Cloudy and cool. Low tonight, 40; high Tuesday, 55.

JOSEPH E. ATKINSON DIES AT 82

Final Gift Climax to Philanthropies

STAR IS LEFT TO CHARITABLE FOUNDATION

HOME AND SPORT EDITION

CONTROL FROM WITHIN FOR ATKINSON PAPERS PROFITS TO FOUNDATION

The death of Joseph E. Atkinson will naturally arouse speculation as to the future of The Toronto Daily Star and Star Weekly. Such speculation can be at once set at rest. Since taking charge of The Star at the close of 1899, he had built up these properties out of their own earnings. No outside influence controls them. No outside influence will control them in the future. The news of their proprietor's decease is accompanied by one of the most unusual announcements in newspaper history. This:

The Star and The Star Weekly are willed in perpetuity to a Foundation—The Atkinson Charitable Foundation—which will devote their profits (as periodically distributed) to religious, charitable and educational objects in Ontario.

The seven trustees of the Foundation, or a majority of them, will be employees of The Toronto Star Limited. The Star and Star Weekly will also be controlled and operated by these; operated by working newspapermen with no interest but to give the public the best newspapers possible. That was the purpose which, over a period of years, took form in the late Joseph E. Atkinson's mind, and to which his family readily agreed.

NO OUTSIDE CONTROL

It may be stated in his own words:

"It is my desire that the ownership and operation of the newspapers known as The Toronto Daily Star and The Star Weekly shall not fall into private hands, and that the shares in the capital stock of The Toronto Star Limited and Toronto Star Realty Limited held by me shall be held in trust for and ultimately belong to The Atkinson Charitable Foundation or (under certain conditions) shall be held in trust for or transferred to charitable organizations which carry on their work solely in Ontario, selected by my trustees.

"This should accomplish two things: (1) The publication of the papers will be conducted for the benefit of the public in the continued frank and full dissemination of news and opinions, with the profit motive, while still important, subsidiary to what I consider to be the chief functions of a metropolitan newspaper; (2) The profits from the newspapers will be used for the promotion and maintenance of social, scientific and economic reforms which are charitable in nature, for the benefit of the people of the Province of Ontario."

"It is my hope that the newspapers and the Foundation will be operated for these purposes by the Trustees whom I have chosen, and by their successors, all of whom will be closely related to the newspaper business and familiar with the doctrines and beliefs which I have promoted in the past. It is my desire that the Trustees shall have the widest freedom possible in the decisions which they make in the operations of the newspapers and in the charitable causes which they promote and maintain."

FOUNDATION CARRIES ON

So while Joseph E. Atkinson is dead, the Atkinson Charitable Foundation carries on. What the people of Ontario and of Canada gave to its Founder in their support of his newspaper enterprises, he returns to them, conserved, multiplied and established in the form of newspapers to be operated for the public benefit. The Atkinson Charitable Foundation passes on forever the spirit of public service which animated its founder throughout a remarkable life whose many philanthropies now reach a climax in this greatest gift of all.

The Atkinson Charitable Foundation will take possession of the great resources of The Toronto Star and Star Weekly. Its purposes and objects, as set out in its charter granted May 1, 1942, are "to receive and maintain a fund or funds and apply the income thereof, in perpetuity, for religious, charitable or educational purposes within the province of Ontario." The income of this fund will consist largely of profits of The Star and Star Weekly. These, as periodically distributed, will be available to the trustees either for disbursement for religious, charitable or educational purposes, or as capital additions to the fund itself.

By his will Mr. Atkinson turns over to the Foundation which bears his name the vast enterprises which he built and which will thus be operated wholly for the public good.

STAR GREW FROM WITHIN

In this dramatic announcement, the life of one of Canada's greatest sons finds fulfilment in a perpetual contribution to the public weal. Joseph E. Atkinson started life with far less than most men. He reached the end as one of Canada's richest citizens. He built The Star and Star Weekly entirely out of their own earnings. He did not speculate. His financial interests were confined to the newspapers which he created out of their own profits. Gifted with talents of the most extraordinary character and quality, he placed these at the disposal of the public not only through his newspapers, but in the promotion of many philanthropies. The sincerity of his public service, never doubted by an ever-growing majority of newspaper readers in Ontario, is made manifest in this: that the splendid financial reward which he reaped he has permanently consolidated and returned as a public service to those who entrusted him with it. He has crowned a lifetime of service to the public by an act which passes on his spirit of service for all time.

Those who knew J. E. Atkinson best were not surprised to learn that the public would profit to a substantial degree by his bequests, although the extent of this final and perpetual service to humanity exceeds what anyone could have anticipated. From the very beginning of his career as a publisher, service to the public, especially to the workers, to minorities, and to victims of social injustice, has been his passion.

CHAMPION OF SOCIAL JUSTICE

But it was a controlled passion under the direction of a shrewd and brilliant mind. He had the utter and passionate conviction as to social justice that the sincerest of penniless zealots possesses. Yet his mind was that of a business genius. Beneath his gentle manner there was an iron will, which, with his genius, accounted in part for his financial success. But his success did not lead him to forget his early life in a very humble home, and the need of such homes for a better livelihood. He often said that he did not think much of people who "forget their beginnings."

The disposal which he has made of his newspaper properties is not a philanthropy only. It is a guarantee against outside non-newspaper interests controlling The Star and Star Weekly—and this not only during the life of some individual or individuals, but in perpetuity. It is as near as a newspaper could come to being an unbiased public property; its control being vested entirely in its own employees.

JOSEPH E. ATKINSON

—Photo by Violet Keene

Champion of the Less Fortunate

Great Journalist, Zealous Reformer, True Canadian

Prime Minister King's Tribute

Special to The Star

Ottawa, May 10—"The passing of Mr. J. E. Atkinson, president of The Toronto Star, is to me a great personal loss," Prime Minister King said today. "Mr. Atkinson and I were life-long friends. Our friendship began when he was a young reporter and came to Berlin (now Kitchener), to report the criminal assizes, and I was a student at the Berlin high school. At the time, he was a visitor at our home, 'Woodside,' and the friendship he then formed with members of our family, and which, after their marriage, was enlarged by that of his wife, Elmina Elliott, well-known by her writings as 'Madge Merton,' continued throughout the years.

"When for a short time during the general election campaign of 1896, I was a reporter on the evening edition of the Toronto Globe, I shared Mr. Atkinson's desk. He was then on the staff of the morning paper. When he subsequently became editor of The Toronto Star, and I was pursuing studies abroad, he accepted articles from me from time to time, the payment for which was a welcome supplement to my slender income.

UNFAILING SUPPORT AS LEADER

"Throughout the years of my public life, Mr. Atkinson, as is well known, was as unfailing in his support of myself as leader of the Liberal party as he was constant in his personal friendship. The life-long bond between us was our mutual interest in social problems.

"Mr. Atkinson's business and journalistic success was achieved all but wholly through his own energy and initiative, his foresight and keen business acumen, inspired by broad human sympathies. Always modest about his own amazing achievements, he kept himself much in the background. Through the powerful medium of the press, he centred his attention on the promotion of liberal ideas and ideals. His was a crusading spirit. He was a pioneer in the cause of present day social reform. His life was devoted to the cause of human betterment.

CHAMPION OF LESS FORTUNATE

"Phenomenal success in business and the possession of great wealth in no way altered Mr. Atkinson's political philosophy or social outlook. A champion of the less fortunate, from his early years, he became, with the passage of time, more ardent than ever in his support of every cause which he believed would enlarge the opportunities or further the well-being of those in humble circumstances. In season and out, the editorial page of The Star has advocated measures of economic security and social justice.

"Mr. Atkinson was a great believer in Canada, and in Canada standing in her own right as a nation among the nations of the world. In his splendid half-century of public service, he did much to create throughout our country, the growth of a truly Canadian spirit, as well as a liberal spirit in the broadest and finest sense of the word. He leaves behind him the memory of a great journalist, a zealous reformer and a true Canadian."

JOURNALIST 64 YEARS PUBLISHED STAR FOR 48 GREAT CAREER IS ENDED

Joseph E. Atkinson, president of The Toronto Star Limited, owner and publisher of the Toronto Daily Star and Star Weekly, died late Saturday night at his home on Warren Road, Forest Hill Village, in the 83rd year of his age. He had been in his office in The Star building, taking his usual active part in the production of his newspapers, until within a week or two of his death. It was found that his heart was affected, and from the first it was apparent that a fatal termination might be possible.

Beloved by his staff, and widely known for his philanthropies and for his phenomenal success in the newspaper world, he was one of the deans of daily newspaper publishing in Canada. Born near Newcastle, Ontario, on December 23, 1865, and brought up by a widowed mother, he began his newspaper career as a collector of accounts on the Port Hope Times at the age of 18. His whole subsequent life was devoted to journalism. From Port Hope, where he practically "ran" the Times, he moved to Toronto to take a position as reporter on the late W. F. Maclean's World, where he graduated to the editorial columns. He moved over to the Toronto Globe and became its Ottawa correspondent; went to Montreal as managing editor of the Herald; returned to Toronto to manage The Star at the close of the last century.

The late Mr. Atkinson's wife was Elmina Elliott, well known to journalism as Madge Merton. She predeceased him in 1931. Surviving him are a daughter, Ruth, Mrs. H. C. Hindmarsh, of Oakville, whose husband is vice-president of The Toronto Star Limited, and a son, Mr. Joseph S. Atkinson, of Forest Hill, vice-president and secretary-treasurer of The Toronto Star Limited. There are five grandchildren and eleven great-grandchildren.

TOOK OVER IN 1899

It was at the end of 1899 that a group of Toronto Liberals acquired (as told on another page of this issue) a newspaper which was at the time dying on its feet—The Toronto Star. They paid for it the sum of $32,000 and they brought Joseph E. Atkinson back from Montreal to run it. He made two stipulations: There must be a provision whereby he could buy stock, and the paper must be operated as a business enterprise as he thought best, and without interference from any of the interests represented by its owners.

Thus, from the very inception of Mr. Atkinson's connection with The Star, no outside interest has been able to dictate its policies. And now that "the Chief" has passed on, it is to be operated by a directorate of its own employees in the public interest as they see it, without any outside control whatever, while its profits, as distributed, will go to a Foundation which will use them for religious, charitable or educational purposes.

The story of Joseph E. Atkinson's early days and of his experiences prior to undertaking the management of The Star is told elsewhere in this issue. Because of the unique and public-spirited disposal which he has made of the great newspaper properties he owned, the history of his connection with these is of supreme interest. It is the history of an achievement made possible by financial genius, unusual journalistic capacity and wide experience utilized for a high purpose. Without that purpose—the purpose of public and humanitarian service—it would be only a "success" story, one of absorbing interest indeed, but falling far short of the actual accomplishment.

MUST BE HONEST WITH THE PUBLIC

One of his strongly held beliefs was that a newspaper should be honest with the public. He gave practical evidence of that conviction when he took charge of The Star on Dec. 13, 1899, and promptly reduced its circulation from a fictitious "over 14,000" to about 7,000, the actual figure.

It was characteristic of the man that his mind was always open to new ideas. He let them into it, but he had an uncanny way of using only those which were worth while, and these he generally improved upon.

He believed in tolerance. Asked once by a magazine writer what it was he most disliked, "intolerance" was the answer. Thus his newspapers presented the views of unpopular minorities as well as those more generally held. All down the years, minorities have felt that they could secure fair treatment from The Star.

How he entered upon the management of it, and the characteristics which he developed as a great newspaperman and fine citizen will be found on Page 4 of this issue. On Pages 2 and 3 are articles which follow his career from childhood up to the time of taking over The Star. On the Section Front page are further accounts of the life of this outstanding figure of Canadian journalism.

MAYOR LEADS CIVIC HEADS IN HONORING MR. ATKINSON

"It was with a great sense of loss that I learned of the passing of Mr. J. E. Atkinson," Mayor H. E. McCallum said today.

"The city of Toronto has lost an outstanding citizen and a great publisher and newspaperman. Mr. Atkinson was a man of wide interests and broad sympathies and played an important part in the development and progress of his city and country.

"His beneficent interest," the mayor continued, "was not confined to the direction of The Toronto Daily Star, which grew in size and importance under his guidance, but extended to many fields of philanthropic and cultural activity. He took an intense interest in plans for the development of the city and of its people and his counsel and advice will be surely missed.

"Personally, and in the name of the council of the city of Toronto and on behalf of the citizens, I extend our heartfelt sympathy to his family and associates in the great loss they have sustained."

Members of city council and aldermen joined the mayor in expressions of regret at the passing of Mr. Atkinson.

"Toronto has lost a great leader and a Christian gentleman," said Controller David A. Balfour. "And it has lost a man who had the wel-

(Continued on Page 11)

FUNERAL SERVICE FOR J. E. ATKINSON AT 3 P.M. TUESDAY

Funeral services for the late Joseph E. Atkinson will be held tomorrow afternoon. A private service will be held at his Warren Rd. home at 2.15, followed by a public service at 3 o'clock in Timothy Eaton Memorial church. The services will be conducted by Rev. David A. MacLennan, pastor of Timothy Eaton Memorial church, and Very Rev. Peter Bryce, pastor of Metropolitan United church. Mr. Atkinson will be buried in the Atkinson plot, beside his wife, who predeceased him in 1931, in the Oakville cemetery on the Queen Elizabeth Way.

ABOVE: H. C. Hindmarsh, president, 1948–1956

LEFT: the first intimation to the public that Mr. Atkinson was leaving his fortune to charity was in *The Star* when it announced his death in 1948

ABOVE: George Maitland, editor-in-chief, 1937–1954; director, 1944–1951

UPPER RIGHT: Alexander Stark, director, 1944–1956

LOWER RIGHT: Frederick L. Tate, business manager, 1934–1956; director, 1944–1956
Ashley & Crippen

could secure the financial backing. Or they could carry on, trusting the Charitable Gifts Act could not, or would not, be enforced.

They chose the last. This decision was not unanimous. Collectively and individually the trustees had consulted legal authorities. These agreed that since Mr. Atkinson had made payment of the annuities a first claim on his estate the courts might very well rule that the shares need not be transferred to the Foundation and thus the papers need not be sold until the last remaining life interest under the will had expired, that is, until the last grandchild was dead, which might be forty or fifty years. At the same time they warned that a government that had not hesitated to pass a law to alter provisions of Mr. Atkinson's will might also be expected to pass legislation to set aside the decision of the court.

With this latter consideration in mind, J. S. Atkinson felt that rather than fight the government they should try, within the framework of the Act, to devise some means of carrying out his father's wishes, particularly his desire that the paper be perpetuated as the voice of liberalism. But for several years he stood alone. The method of countering the Charitable Gifts Act was, therefore, another cause for disunity among the trustees.

While the trustees, or a majority of them, had decided to ignore the Charitable Gifts Act, the National Trust Company felt it should try to work out some plan of complying with the law in a manner that would conform most closely with Mr. Atkinson's will. Officials of the company testified they dismissed any thought of offering the shares or the papers for sale to the highest bidder, since Mr. Atkinson had made it plain he did not wish that, but they worked on several other plans. They testified their first plan, prepared in April, 1949, contemplated sale to a syndicate in which the directors of *The Star* would have a majority interest.

"We find that as a rule the best market for shares is to try to get the management of any company interested in acquiring shares and ownership," explained Thomas A. Morrow, trust accounting officer, to the Supreme Court. But the huge sum in the surplus account was a stumbling block. This was not J. E. Atkinson's personal savings. It was company savings from undistributed profits and was thus partly the property of the three minority shareholders. The only way of getting it out was to declare a dividend, and the tax on a dividend of such proportions would be almost confiscatory. The minority shareholders alone would have had to pay more than $650,000. Therefore this plan had to be dropped. For the same reason a plan to sell the papers, or perhaps a half-interest in them, to the employees had to be abandoned.

Morrow said other schemes were considered but every one "had the fundamental objection that it was contrary to the testator's intentions" though a sale to either the directors or the employees would have most nearly conformed to his wishes. Despite differences of opinion on other points the trustees were agreed that in order to establish the Atkinson Charitable Foundation as a legitimate charity, and lay the groundwork for a public demand for relaxation of the strict provisions of the Charitable Gifts Act, it was important to get a substantial sum of money into the Foundation as quickly as possible.

They were influenced in this decision by the advice of Prime Minister St. Laurent. Hindmarsh and Stark had gone to Ottawa to discuss with the Prime Minister the possibility of having the Act disallowed by the Dominion government. St. Laurent's advice was to leave the Charitable Gifts Act alone, but to start the Foundation operating in a big way and with as much publicity as possible, thus building up such strong public feeling in favour of the Foundation that Frost would not venture to take action against it.

There were two ways of getting money into the Foundation: sell shares in *The Star* companies or dip into the surplus account of $6,000,000. The trustees rejected any thought of selling shares as contrary to Mr. Atkinson's wishes. That left only the surplus account, but a gift from it could not be made without injustice to the minority shareholders, since it was partly theirs.

J. S. Atkinson and Mrs. Hindmarsh raised no objection at the time to a gift, but the 750 shares in each company owned by Mulock presented an obstacle. It was decided the estate should buy these. The Ontario government recognized the Foundation as a charity in March, 1950, but funds had to be transferred from the estate to the Foundation before June 1, 1950, to conform with the legal requirements of a charitable bequest. The Mulock shares, therefore, had to be bought before that date. They were purchased a few days before the deadline for $500,000, about 10 per cent more than the valuation that had been placed on them by the trust company.

Immediately after this purchase $3,000,000 was transferred to the Atkinson Charitable Foundation as a "gift" from The Toronto Star Limited. It was announced in a press release on July 24. Other gifts, though smaller, were made from surplus directly to the Foundation until 1952, when the shareholders were advised that such gifts were contrary to the will of J. E. Atkinson. Under the will, dividends had to be declared to the estate, and from the estate would pass to the Foundation. As a result, subsequent transfers of funds from *The Star* to the Foundation were in the form of dividends.

The Foundation had been dormant since the passing of the Charitable Gifts Act, but after this transfer of $3,000,000 to its capital account J. S. Atkinson threw himself with zeal into its work. The first large grant of $100,000 payable over a five-year period was made to Toronto Western Hospital School of Nursing on July 27, 1950. It was to help finance the setting up and operation of a new two-year demonstration course in the training of nurses, in which students would be relieved of much of the drudgery long associated with nursing schools. In recognition of Mr. Atkinson's long association with Toronto Western hospital, the school was renamed the Joseph E. Atkinson School of Nursing. Seventy-seven girls registered for the first class. By the end of 1950 the Foundation had made twenty grants, paid out $296,210 and pledged twice as much for "continuing grants" in future years. It had paid $15,000 in bursaries to help worthy students continue their education.

Earnings of *The Star* in 1950 provided $809,000 for charity which were duly transferred to the Foundation. *The Star* itself, as a separate organization, donated $99,170 to charity.

Early in 1951 the trustees decided that small grants for services that would not normally be subsidized or sponsored would be the most useful form of assistance. One of the principal tasks they undertook was to provide Ontario's small hospitals with modern equipment. In the next five years more than 75 per cent of the hospitals in the province benefited from the more than $1,600,000 spent on hospital equipment and another million was granted for medical education or research.

By 1953 the Atkinson Charitable Foundation was being praised in Parliament and the legislature, even by Conservative members, for its splendid work. Introducing his estimates in March, 1953, Hon. W. A. Goodfellow, Ontario Minister of Welfare, declared the Atkinson Charitable Foundation was setting a fine new trend in charity. "They have engaged in pathfinding endeavours for the government and our people as a whole," he declared. The next year even Premier Frost praised it, though he hastened to assure the legislature he had never objected to charity, only to a charitable organization owning a business, which he still believed was wrong in principle.

On May 18, 1954, the Foundation was presented with the fourth annual award of the brotherhood of Beth Sholom synagogue, Toronto, "for splendid achievements in the field of humanitarian services in the province of Ontario." J. S. Atkinson accepted the award on behalf of the trustees.

By the end of 1962 the Foundation had distributed $3,648,403 in the field of health and $1,526,321 on social welfare projects. The building fund of nearly every hospital in Metropolitan Toronto was given some assistance, in some cases up to $150,000. To the same period the Foundation had distributed $2,552,312 in the field of education, one of the larger grants up to that time being $200,000 to Carleton University to establish a graduate school in public administration. Some 4,185 students have been given financial assistance with bursaries in their first year, and 2,500 students in later years.

The National Trust Company completed its duties as executor on April 8, 1951, and prepared to turn the estate over to the trustees. On April 12 Maitland resigned as a trustee and was succeeded by Mrs. H. C. Hindmarsh. The announcement of the change said she would serve without pay. The National Trust Company submitted a bill of $375,000 for its services as executor of the estate. Stark submitted a bill of $60,000 for his duties as solicitor of the estate over a three-year period. Both accounts were challenged by Armand Racine, the public trustee.

Judge T. H. Barton approved the accounts. His decision was appealed by the public trustee. The Court of Appeals referred the matter to the Senior Master of the Supreme Court of Ontario, A. S. Marriott, and it was before this hearing that most of the testimony quoted earlier in this chapter was given. As a result of the hearing, the Court of Appeals reduced the compensation to the trust company to $149,124. The company appealed to the Supreme Court of Canada, which, on June 8, 1953, upheld the decision of the Ontario Court of Appeals.

Though the trustees of the Atkinson estate and of the Atkinson Charitable Foundation were now free from supervision of the National Trust Company, they were still a long way from being out of the legal woods. They were still under supervision of the public trustee, one of whose duties was to see that they complied with the terms of the Charitable Gifts Act.

Chapter 23

THE STAR UNDER TRUSTEES

Occasionally it has been advanced that the ideal newspaper would be an endowed journal, endowed like a university, hospital or other public institution. The danger to a publication working under such auspices would be the development of self-righteousness and Phariseeism. If the canker of these things began to work usefulness would cease. Moreover, the assertion is at least open to argument that a staff who feel their work is good enough to reap a profit to the man, or men, who supplies the capital, and that he is getting that profit, adds an additional self-respect.

This is a quotation from an article by Joseph E. Atkinson in 1905. It is true *The Star* was not an "endowed journal," but the arguments he used are equally applicable to a journal owned by a foundation which only theoretically is required to make a profit. A man of eighty-two should not be bound by opinions he expressed at thirty-nine, but even some of the trustees of his estate came to wonder if Atkinson's earlier judgment in this respect was not more sound than that of later years.

A year after his death *Saturday Night* commented in a dispassionate discussion of the Charitable Gifts Act that *The Star* was already demonstrating that a trust is "an unsatisfactory owner for a popular and sensational paper." It observed that whatever the reason might be the paper is "already less effective than it was a year ago." If *The Star* had become less effective so soon the fact was apparent to few but the perceptive editor of *Saturday Night*. Its editorials, it is true, had lost some of the incisiveness they had when Mr. Atkinson scrutinized them all, and the executive editor, Alex Givens, was quoted as saying, "We're trying to be respectable now," but it was still very much on top of the news. Moreover, it had just beaten back a *Telegram* attack in a six-weeks circulation war in April and May.

Nevertheless, some very significant changes, as yet unrecognized by most readers, had taken place in *Star* policy. It had become more partisan and in an editorial was soon to label itself for the first time in its history as a frankly Liberal party paper. In the past it had supported the Liberal party only when the party supported liberal principles. It was drawing away from the CCF and left-wing influences, despite the fact the CCF had fought more vigorously on its behalf than the Liberals when the Charitable Gifts Act was introduced. It joined the hue and cry against communists, and by 1951 was calling on the electors to end an "intolerable" situation by ejecting the last of them from city council.

Its first noticeable departure from established practice was in October, 1948, when it sent the largest number of writers it had sent to any political convention to cover the one at which George Drew was chosen leader of the federal Progressive-Conservative party. Their reports, prominently displayed on page one, were markedly unfriendly. On the day of the balloting it had three editorials on various aspects of the convention or platform. The day after the convention it had a long and snarly editorial about Drew. "The Conservatives have the first Conservative leader since R. B. Bennett," it commented. Past practice had been to withhold comment on new party leaders when it did not wish to commend.

The federal election was held June 27, 1949, with Drew leading the Conservatives and Louis St. Laurent, who had succeeded King the previous August, leading the Liberals. As the campaign advanced *The Star* became progressively more hysterical in its demands that Drew be beaten. It fought all over again the issue of the Charitable Gifts Act and the nefarious scheme of the Tories to silence a Liberal paper. It almost ignored the CCF.

In the last week of the campaign it had as many as eight election stories a day on page one, of which one or two would be about the Charitable

Gifts Act. In the last days of the campaign it made the issue an alleged secret deal between Drew and Premier Maurice Duplessis of Quebec to get the former mayor of Montreal, Camillien Houde, into the cabinet as leader of the Quebec Conservatives. Givens was sent to Quebec to mastermind an anti-Houde campaign, while photographers were sent to dog Houde's steps wherever he went and photograph him in the most unflattering of poses. A gross man with an enormous paunch, Houde made a perfect target and some dandy pictures were taken, particularly at banquets.

The crowning achievement was the front page of the first edition on the Saturday before election day, which was on a Monday. If not a classic, it at least has the doubtful distinction of being the most ridiculed front page in *The Star*'s history. Across the top of the page were three lines in 110-point condensed Gothic type:

KEEP CANADA BRITISH
DESTROY DREW'S HOUDE
GOD SAVE THE KING

Beneath this was the most revolting picture of Houde in shirt sleeves that an imaginative cameraman had been able to capture. "This man will be one of the rulers of Canada if voters Monday elect George Drew as head of a Conservative government," said the caption beneath it. "He is Camillien Houde, isolationist, ex-internee, foe of Britain." Every story on page one was anti-Drew.

This was probably the first time in its history *The Star* called upon Canada to remain British in the name of the King. Stark was so shocked he came plummetting down sixteen floors from his office to urge Hindmarsh to amend it, but Hindmarsh had left for home and could not be reached. Stark then called it to the attention of J. S. Atkinson, chairman of the board, and they decided it had to be altered. The third line accordingly was changed to "Vote St. Laurent." The banner lines as originally written appeared, therefore, in only one of the day's six editions. Hindmarsh was not pleased when he learned what had been done, for he had written the lines himself.

All this frenzy was quite unnecessary. The Liberals won by one of the largest majorities ever polled, leading all across Canada. There is no evidence *The Star*'s hysteria gained them any votes in its circulation area.

The McCullagh papers had waged almost as fantastic an election campaign, ignoring the Liberals and St. Laurent and directing their attacks at *The Star* and the memory of J. E. Atkinson. In the last week of the campaign McCullagh took to the air in a coast-to-coast national broadcast which he entitled "Shocking Political Pay-Off." With complete misunderstanding of the true relationship between King and Atkinson, he said *The Star* had "sold its support to the so-called Liberal party" in return for a "pay-off." This pay-off, he said, included $528,000 worth of free radio time on the CBC for twelve years and an alleged $108,000 subsidy to the *Star Weekly*.

The "free radio time" was, of course, *The Star* newscast from CBL which had been authorized while the Conservative Bennett government was in office, and by an appointee of that government. It had been cancelled by the CBC in 1946, under a Liberal government. McCullagh did not make it clear how *The Star*, under new direction, was still being influenced by an alleged pay-off that had ended three years before. The subsidy to the *Star Weekly*, he alleged, had been accomplished by the "cute trick" of having it classified as a magazine instead of a newspaper, thus exempting it from an eight per cent tax on newsprint. The fact was, the *Star Weekly* had not printed a news section since early in the war, and had been removed properly from the newspaper classification when it ceased to print news.

The Star's next venture into politics had important repercussions, for it gave the Ontario government some warrant for claiming public support of the Charitable Gifts Act. A by-election was called for October 31, 1949, to fill the seat in the legislature vacated by the death of the member for Leeds. The Conservative candidate was W. B. Reynolds, the Liberal candidate, Ernest Miller. Leslie Frost, the provincial treasurer who had sponsored the Charitable Gifts Act, was now Premier of Ontario. *The Star* decided to make this the testing ground for public opinion. It could have chosen no worse field for battle than this normally Conservative, largely rural riding on the fringe of its own circulation area, and whatever the result it would prove nothing anyway. But *The Star* gave this minor by-election the full treatment it had given the federal election four months earlier.

For two weeks there were seldom less than three election stories a day on page one, all set double column. One story invariably dealt with the iniquities of the Charitable Gifts Act. Photographers roamed the countryside taking pictures of farmers who deplored what was called this affront to democracy. Leaders of the provincial Liberal party were goaded into the fray with *The Star* picking up the tab. Pictures eight columns wide designed to illustrate the issue and show what a fine man Ernie Miller was compared with the Tories, or any Tory, usually occupied a third of page one. One layout even showed what a fine man J. E. Atkinson had been, playing with his great-grandchildren, compared with a picture of a flint-faced Leslie Frost. Conservative candidate Reynolds won, as almost everybody knew he would, by 10,800 to 8,000.

The Star, commented Premier Frost, had taken its case to the jury of public opinion, and had picked the jury itself. Now it had to abide by the verdict. Thereafter his attitude hardened against amending the Charitable Gifts Act.

In the provincial election of November 22, 1951, *The Star* suffered an even more disastrous political defeat after a campaign that brought upon it the wrath of Liberals and labour organizations alike. The notoriety that attended this campaign has been more persistent than even that of the 1949 federal election.

A year earlier the Liberals had chosen Walter Thomson, member of Parliament for Ontario riding, as leader. Just after this, Hindmarsh sent two men to attend several Thomson meetings and report privately to him their opinion of the new leader. It was not very high. Nevertheless Hindmarsh decided to make him the man of the hour, and in April assigned Dick Ryder, one of *The Star*'s more able reporters, to "build him up." Ryder completely sold himself on Thomson, but as events were to demonstrate, made few other converts.

It was decided in *The Star* office that the Liberals should stake all on a promise to introduce a prepaid hospital care plan, and attack Frost for allegedly refusing an offer from the federal government to aid hospitals. Thomson agreed to go along with this, and on October 6 his plan was unveiled.

The Star's campaign was about as fantastic as one can imagine. Speeches of Conservatives were unreported, *The Star* acknowledging they were delivered only to refute them. Only speeches by the leader of the CCF were reported except when the speaker said something good about Thomson. Horrendous "case histories" were printed, without names, of infants and old folk who had died from lack of hospital care. The *Globe and Mail* complained that Premier Frost was being pictured as a murderer. Even the *Star Weekly*, which J. E. Atkinson had kept strictly neutral in politics, carried Liberal election stories. It has never been neutral since.

On October 23, the Toronto and Lakeshore Labour Council passed a resolution condemning *The Star* "for its policy of unbalanced coverage, suppression of news and headline distortion" of provincial election news, the first time an important labour organization had ever turned against *The Star.* The resolution and the discussion of it were published fully by *The Star.*

As the campaign progressed *The Star* began to use stock pictures by professional models from New York and Hollywood agencies, showing crippled children, mothers and old folk in pathetic poses. Only by a careful reading of the cutlines would one know that these were not real people who had actually suffered from Frost's "hard-hearted policy."

Page one of the issue of November 10 has been framed and hangs in the office of the *London Free Press* with the notation above it: "It can happen . . . sentimentality and headline editorializing defeat their purpose and destroy confidence in a newspaper." The eight-column line in 110-point reads: MAY BE YOUR MOTHER—THOMSON. Beneath it, running across the entire width of the page in 14-point, are quotations from a speech by Thomson in which he said "the minds of 10,000 elderly folk" could have been saved had Frost accepted a hospital plan proposed by the federal government. Beneath this is a model agency picture of an old couple, five columns wide, across it the caption: "Should dear old people such as these go to mental institutions?"

R. A. Farquharson, editor of *Saturday Night*, analysing *The Star*'s coverage in the last thirteen days of the campaign, said a year's growth from 600 acres of pulp forest were required for the paper to print its pro-Thomson stories alone. In that period it devoted 157 columns of type and almost as many columns of pictures to boosting Thomson, but only 44 columns to international news and 83.5 columns to local news. In the last edition before election day it had not a line of international news.

The Liberals suffered their worst defeat of all time in Ontario, polling only a third of the popular vote and electing only eight members. Conservatives elected seventy-nine, CCF two, and Communists one. The CCF, which had always counted on *The Star* to give it a break, never forgave it for what they regarded as a betrayal. In 1953 CCF delegates to a convention were urged to boycott *The Star* because of its Liberal partisanship.

Thomson called a caucus on December 10, attended by seventy Liberal candidates. They decided *The Star*'s campaign was largely responsible for the magnitude of their defeat. The Hamilton East Liberal Association discussed a motion "that we divorce ourselves from *The Toronto Daily Star* until it presents its news in a more sensible manner." However, after a rancorous discussion the Ontario Liberal Association passed a motion by a small margin thanking *The Star* for its support.

Yet strangely enough, while this weird campaign was under way *The Star* experienced a steady and substantial increase in circulation, followed by a sharp drop after polling day in November. The normal pattern is for a moderate increase in the fall, accelerating in December and the winter months.

The question has often been asked why *The Star* conducted the kind of campaign it did. At the time Hindmarsh was solely responsible for the editorial conduct of the paper. To him the most intolerable feature of the Charitable Gifts Act was the power it gave Frost, a political foe, over the destiny of *The Star*. He saw a threat, never expressed though none the less real to him, that some day the politicians might tell him, "You be a good little boy or we'll put your paper out of business." At that very time Peron was closing down the opposition newspaper *La Prensa* in Argentina, and Hindmarsh thought it could happen in Ontario.

He had to remove that sword of Damocles from over the head of *The Star* and he struck at it furiously. He felt he had to prove to Frost and to the people of Ontario that he could not be intimidated, and he did it in the only way he thought was open to him. He supported the Liberals because after their big victory in the federal election he thought they had a better chance of winning than the CCF. He threw the CCF to the sharks because he did not want the anti-Frost forces divided. He proved his point that he could not be intimidated, but at the same time he made it impossible for Frost to amend the Charitable Gifts Act without appearing to back down and lose face.

During the campaign, on November 16, *The Star* published a statement on page one, signed by all the trustees. It said the trustees were only asking that the Charitable Gifts Act be amended to remove the forced sale clause, not that it be repealed. It said they agreed that foundations should at all times be accountable to the public and "to the extent that the purpose of the Charitable Gifts act is to provide this protection we welcome it. But to the extent the act is designed to force the sale of *The Toronto Star* within seven years, and thus silence a Liberal newspaper that at times is critical of the government of the day, we fight against it . . . That is the only part of the Charitable Gifts act with which we quarrel."

The Star's experience in municipal elections was not much more successful than in provincial affairs. In late 1950 Allan A. Lamport announced he would oppose Hiram E. McCallum, who was seeking a fifth term as mayor. *The Star* did not like Lamport. Still less did it like his platform, which was a promise to have removed restrictions on the playing of commercial sports on Sunday. It did not think McCallum could beat Lamport so it persuaded

Nathan Phillips, veteran member of council, to run and lavishly supported him. McCallum won; Phillips was a poor third.

The next year it supported Phillips again, against Lamport. Lamport won with a two-to-one majority. In his election there was the unique situation that all three daily newspapers opposed Lamport, thus his large majority was interpreted by some as a vote of want of confidence in all Toronto dailies. On the other hand it may have been due mainly to the popularity of Lamport's platform of commercial sports on Sunday.

If it was a vote of non-confidence it may be attributed to the extravagant competition of *The Star* and *Telegram* for sensational news. McCullagh had set out to scoop *The Star* as often as he could, and an article in *Maclean's* commented on the "wholesale kidnapping" of news-worthy persons by both newspapers to keep them from talking with the opposition.

The kidnappings began when *The Star* snatched a woman the *Telegram* intended to fly to the Arctic to visit her sick husband, a radio operator. It thus got the story, and the credit for a humanitarian act exclusively for itself. Thereafter gangs of "kidnappers" roamed the city sweeping up sweepstakes winners, murder witnesses, or others of news-worthy interest for their respective newspapers. At the same time local stories became ever more sensational and it was not unusual to find the front pages of both papers monopolized by stories and pictures of crimes, train wrecks, and sex fiends.

As they tried to outdo each other in sensationalism on page one, so they strove to outstrip each other in piety inside. Each had three religious columns running simultaneously, playing no favourites between Protestants, Catholics, and Jews. When the *Telegram* announced it was running a "Life of Christ" *The Star* sent a reporter calling on publishing houses for a "life" it could hurl into print at the same time. It sent another reporter to scour the art galleries of Europe for religious paintings. He came back with a lovely lot, some as gruesome as the war pictures had been.

Even in charity they tried to outdo each other, and a professional fund raiser who came to manage a campaign on behalf of the building fund of Toronto General Hospital was astounded when told the amount of free publicity the papers would give him. It was almost worth it for the newspapers, for they were able to pry out some medical stories that must have made the flesh of their readers crawl. "I don't think our newspapers are very ethical, but they sure are a lot of fun," a woman told an interviewer from *Maclean's*.

Nevertheless, to picture a blind, frenzied sort of competition would be completely incorrect, at least so far as *The Star* was concerned. It is true *The Star* went further than it needed to in matching the sensationalism of its rival, but at the same time it did a great deal of workmanlike and constructive news-gathering. The post-war economy wave, which had lasted an unprecedented five years, was ended as soon as the executors released enough money to permit some freedom of action. By 1950 *Star* reporters were again roaming the world for news. William Stevenson was sent to Yugoslavia, J. E. Belliveau to the West Indies, and Ross Harkness made the first of several trips to South America. After that there was usually at least one *Star* reporter prowling the world.

In 1951 Beland Honderich was sent to Argentina to report on Peron's muzzling of *La Prensa* and later was sent around the world. Stevenson was the first Canadian reporter to enter Communist Poland, the first representative of a Western newspaper in China, and the first Canadian reporter to reach the Korean war zone. Douglas Blanchard was sent to Cairo, Algeria, and South America. He was the only Canadian reporter in Argentina when Peron was overthrown, and was jailed in the round-up of rioters. He was the only Canadian newspaperman to reach Budapest in the Hungarian uprising. Monroe Johnston visited Europe, accompanied royal tours of Africa, and was the only Canadian reporter to cover the British-French attack on the Suez canal.

Despite the fact he married a newspaperwoman, J. E. Atkinson had never thought much of girl reporters except for such feminine jobs as writing weddings and social notes, and even the social editor was as often as not a man. There was usually a female sob-sister available for general assignments, but her desk was in the *zenana* of the social department, safe from the contaminating influence of male speech and manners. After his death the number of women reporters was increased and they were given better assignments.

The second great royal tour was in August and September, 1951, when the then Princess Elizabeth and her consort visited Canada. Norman James and Jack Karr, who had covered their wedding in 1947, flew to England for advance stories and pictures. Eight reporters were divided into two shifts to give round-the-clock coverage, or to write on specific angles. Photographers were legion, and Prince Philip used to quip "Are you from *The Toronto Star*?" when he glimpsed an unfamiliar face in the press party.

To put the public in the proper mood, just before the tour *The Star* ran a series called "Our Heritage of Freedom" depicting in pictures great moments in the history of the English-speaking world. As in 1939 circulation figures reflected the public interest in the tour. The *Star Weekly*'s circulation jumped from 812,000 in August to 881,000 in September when the pre-tour articles and pictures started running. In October it reached 905,000, attributed largely to splendid pictures. Much of this new circulation was retained. The effect on the *Daily* was not so noticeable, though circulation began to rise in September and reached the monthly peak for the year in November.

The new circulation almost compensated for that lost by the *Star Weekly* when the price outside Ontario and Quebec was raised to fifteen cents on January 28, 1950. The shortage of newsprint was still a problem at the beginning of 1950, but public demand for both papers was increasing and the directors had to choose between holding the line on circulation or reducing the size of the papers. On the advice of the executors of the Atkinson estate they raised the price of the *Star Weekly* in eight provinces with the deliberate intention of limiting its circulation. Sales dropped enough to free sufficient newsprint to allow an increase of 20,000 in the *Daily Star*.

King George VI died on February 6, 1952, and the new Queen was crowned June 2, 1953, *The Star* sending four reporters to cover the coronation. The RAF rushed pictures by Canberra jet planes to Montreal, where they were met by planes engaged by *The Star*. In April, when the *Star Weekly* was running pre-coronation pictures and features, average circulation for the month reached an all-time high of 1,002,986, an increase of almost 110,000 over the previous month. By this time the *Star Weekly* was going regularly into almost half the English-language homes in Canada. Circulation held to over a million until after the coronation, then dropped, though about half the increase brought by the coronation remained. By this time newsprint was available for all needs.

The experience of the newspapers should settle the question of whether Canadians are interested in royalty. They are, intensely. It is noteworthy, however, that almost the entire increase in the *Star Weekly* sales attributable to the coronation came from outside the Metropolitan Toronto area. Moreover, it had a comparatively slight influence on the circulation of *The Daily Star*. It would seem, therefore, that the citizens of Toronto do not share to the same extent the interest of the rest of Canada in royalty.

It may be of interest that the feature which sold more *Daily Stars* than any other, at any time, was not a news story at all, but an advertisement. On November 15, 1949, *The Star* inserted one page printed on Miracloth, a new fabric being introduced. It was the most expensive single advertisement ever published in Canada, the retail value of the fabric alone being

$73,900 and the printing had to be done by a special, costly process. The press run was 511,734 copies, still the biggest of any daily newspaper in Canada.

Shortly after the death of Mr. Atkinson employees in the editorial department began to consider reviving the Toronto local of the Guild, which had been dormant since 1941. After consultation with several other employees, Norman Phillips, then cable editor, wrote Sam Eubanks, executive vice-president of the Guild in New York, asking for any assistance international headquarters might be able to give. Eubanks came to Toronto and met Phillips, Alf Tate, who had been the first president of *The Star* unit in 1938, and Dennis Braithwaite.

This was followed by another meeting with Eubanks, attended by twelve members of the editorial office who had agreed to be charter members of the revived local. Phillips was the temporary chairman and he accepted the charter which was given the number 87, the same number as the charter granted in 1937. International headquarters assigned Charles Crissey to help with the organization.

One of the first things the committee of twelve did was to notify Mr. Hindmarsh that Local 87 had been revived, and intended to begin recruiting members. All twelve signed the letter. Hindmarsh did not reply, but it was soon known he was not unfriendly. Before long 185 members had been signed up. While recruiting was still actively under way the committee of twelve called a meeting of members, and the local was properly organized with financial editor Beland Honderich, who had been one of the twelve, as president.

Local 87 was certified by the Ontario Labour Relations Board in November, 1948, and negotiations for a contract were begun immediately. The Guild was represented by Charles Crissey, Ben Rose, Dennis Braithwaite, Joe Beauclerc, Marjorie Earl, Borden Spears, and Beland Honderich. *The Star* was represented by Alexander Stark, George Maitland, and Mr. Hindmarsh. Spears was appointed city editor while negotiations were in progress and had to retire.

"Hindmarsh scared the life out of the rest of us; he wanted to give the Guild everything it asked for," Maitland said later. Hindmarsh had long chafed at what he considered to be the preferential treatment given the strongly organized mechanical trades, and was determined an experienced reporter should be guaranteed pay equal that of a craftsman. A union contract would strengthen his hand against the executors and the other trustees who wanted to keep costs down by holding the line on salaries.

Sometime before J. E. Atkinson's death Hindmarsh had tried to have a general increase for all reporters approved. He sent one of his senior editors on a tour of Canadian and US newspapers, and as a result of his report on the pay scale on other newspapers, Hindmarsh sent a memo to Mr. Atkinson recommending that experienced reporters be paid a minimum of $60 a week. Mr. Atkinson ran his pen through the "$60" and wrote "$55" and that was, at the time the Guild reorganized, the unofficial minimum.

One day while negotiations were in progress Hindmarsh outlined to Alex Givens the kind of working conditions he hoped to see introduced for editorial employees.

"Nobody will ever believe this of tough, hard-boiled Harry Hindmarsh," Givens commented. "Mr. Givens, tough, hard-boiled Harry Hindmarsh was buried with J. E. Atkinson," Hindmarsh replied. This was probably the first formal intimation of what came to be known in newspaper circles as "the mellowing of H. C. Hindmarsh." Before another year had passed it was being widely talked about, and even found mention in the column of a popular writer for a rival newspaper.

A contract with the Guild was signed April 12, 1949, the first between any Canadian newspaper and the Guild, though three other newspapers had contracts with editorial workers who were members of other unions. "It's the kind of a contract union men dream about but seldom get," remarked the *Financial Post*. "The contract is reported to be a combination of the best features of the scores of Guild contracts in the United States." In some cases individual pay increases amounted to $25 a week.

Somewhat to Hindmarsh's dismay the Guild did not stop at organizing editorial workers, for he had regarded it only as a union to protect his "boys." But as a CIO union it had been chartered to embrace all newspaper employees, and it took advantage of the favourable climate on *The Star* to organize non-union workers in other departments. Though Hindmarsh grumbled that editorial workers were limiting their own pay by trying to raise the salaries of stenographers and clerks, on April 6, 1950, the Guild was certified to bargain for circulation and business departments. After eight months of negotiation a contract was signed giving pay increases averaging 14 per cent to 350 employees.

On July 18, 1951, the Guild was certified as bargaining agent for the truck drivers. In January, 1952, it signed a contract on behalf of eighty employees of the Star Realty Company, which included elevator operators, maintenance workers, and the like. On June 10, 1953, it signed a contract on behalf of ninety garage and delivery employees. When the advertising department staff voted for the Guild in 1957 *The Star* became the most thoroughly unionized newspaper in America.

McCullagh would never sign with the Guild, but after his death on August 5, 1952, the new owner of the *Telegram*, John Bassett, readily agreed to open negotiations, and the first contract with the *Telegram* was signed in the latter part of June, 1953. The *Globe and Mail* held out until 1955, but when it was put up for sale in February employees hastened to join the Guild. The new owner signed a contract on December 10.

Purchase of the *Telegram* by John Bassett was a significant event in the history of *The Star*. For one thing it put an end to the stream of abuse and personal vituperation that had been poured upon *The Star* and its publishers by the *Telegram* almost continuously since the death of John Ross Robertson. Relations between the management of *The Star* and the *Telegram* have not always been cordial since 1952, but they have always been correct. More important was the fact that for the first time in many years *The Star* was faced with competition that was as intelligently directed as it was aggressive.

McCullagh had spent a million dollars in promotion and greatly increased his editorial payroll, but in the four years he owned the *Telegram* it gained only 19,240 in circulation. In the same period *The Star* gained 62,328. Admittedly part of the disparity is due to the fact the *Telegram* raised its price from three cents to five cents on December 2, 1949, while *The Star* remained at the old price, but even before the *Telegram*'s price increase *The Star* had been gaining two-to-one on it.

In 1950 *The Star* forged ahead in one of the most profitable fields, classified advertising. Heretofore the *Telegram* had advertised that it was "the paper with the want ads" but in 1950 *The Star* published more than the other two papers combined.

On March 31, 1962, four months before McCullagh died, the price of *The Star* was raised to five cents a single copy, the first increase in fourteen years. Almost overnight circulation dropped by 32,000. There is no reason to suppose these former *Star* readers began taking the *Telegram*, but the new owner exploited with audacity and judgment the improved competitive position resulting from reduction of the *Star*'s long circulation lead. Before long the *Telegram* was gaining circulation faster than *The Star*.

This may have been in part due to the change in public support of Canada's two major political parties. With the exception of the election of 1911 there has always been a noticeable correlation between the fortunes of *The Star* and those of the Liberal party. In Ontario the Liberal party was at its lowest ebb, and *The Star*'s campaign on behalf of Thomson had done nothing to enhance the prestige of either the paper or the party. At the same time the Liberal party at Ottawa had ceased to be truly liberal and was coasting along on the memory of Mackenzie King and the personal popularity of "Uncle Louie." Though it was to win one more election, it had already lost public confidence.

It would be strange if this did not redound against *The Star* which had deliberately pinned upon itself the label of a Liberal party paper. By doing so it had lost not only the support of many independent voters, but had also antagonized some people of liberal temperament who were not within the Liberal party. It had alienated the reform and radical elements, mostly those within the CCF, which ideologically were neither liberal nor conservative but which had depended upon *The Star* to put their case before the public.

It had weathered other periods of Liberal party decline by supporting liberal and reform elements whenever they appeared, whether they were within the Liberal party or not, or even if they were antagonistic to it. By so doing it had been a potent force in compelling the Liberal party to return to liberalism, to the mutual advantage of *The Star* and the party it favoured. Now it failed to show any understanding that the Liberal party, as in 1916, was again flailing issues "as dead as Caesar." It was not until the famous "pipeline debate" and the federal election of 1957 that it showed alarm at the departure of the Liberal party from liberal principles.

After the plans for an elaborate *Star Weekly* building on the waterfront had to be discarded following Mr. Atkinson's death it was necessary to find some alternative. The presses at 80 King Street West were being pushed to the utmost and the circulation of the *Star Weekly* was limited by their capacity. Moreover, they were nearly obsolete and were no longer capable of the kind of fine printing that was wanted.

When McCullagh died his executors found it necessary to get some money quickly into his estate, and they offered *The Star* a modern, high-speed, four-colour press which had recently been installed in a rented building at Pearl Street and University Avenue. It had been bought to print a coloured comic section for the *Telegram*, and had been used for a while to print coloured comic books from plates imported from the United States. *The Star* bought it and thus was able to improve considerably the colour reproductions in the magazine section of the *Weekly*.

But this was only a stop-gap, and it was decided to build a rotogravure printing plant and an ink factory on the waterfront property. On June 10, 1953 the first pile was driven. With the memorable address, Number One Yonge Street, it went into operation in May, 1954. Covering a site seven acres in area, it has its own dock, is on the rail lines serving the harbour area, and on the route of the Gardiner expressway, Toronto's main highway leading to the east and west.

On November 3, 1956, the *Star Weekly* went to tabloid size with all except the comics and the full-length novel printed by rotogravure at the new plant. The rotogravure process gave a much better reproduction of colours and pictures. Type is still set at 80 King Street West, where the editorial offices remained.

Meantime an important change was made in the printing of the *Daily Star*. Reversing the trend of the preceding thirty years towards smaller papers, it expanded the size of its pages from eight columns to nine columns on January 16, 1953. This permitted it to print more news and advertising without substantially increasing its consumption of newsprint. Its example has been followed by other newspapers, including the Toronto dailies.

Even before Atkinson's death it had become apparent that the fight for a national retirement pension sufficient to live on without hardship had been lost. But at the same time, changed circumstances had greatly increased the cost of setting up a company pension plan for *Star* employees. It is probable that in his later years this, rather than considerations of consistency, led him to oppose a pension scheme for his own workers.

In 1954 a company-wide pension plan was introduced with *The Star* undertaking to pay the full cost under the plan arising out of the employees' pensionable service prior to September 30, 1953. Employees are free to contribute or not with respect to service subsequent to that date. For employees who choose not to join the plan on a contributory basis, a smaller non-contributory pension is made available, except in cases where a negotiated pension is provided under the terms of a collective bargaining agreement between *The Star* and one of the unions. Originally, four of the major craft unions forbade their members to become contributory members of the Star pension plan, but in 1959 two of these four unions removed the restriction.

On April 23, 1955, H. C. Hindmarsh was paid a remarkable tribute of affection and esteem when some two hundred former members of *The Star*'s editorial staff, along with some of the older employees, gave a dinner in his honour at the Royal York hotel. It was not the "mellowed" Hindmarsh they were toasting, but the hard-driving newsman they had loved while they cursed, praised while they reviled, and been most loyal to when they railed at him the most.

The guest list read like an honour roll of Canada's great names in publishing, radio, television, public relations, politics, and business. Hindmarsh was presented with a silver cigar-box inscribed with the five letters so familiar to all *Star* employees, "OK—HCH," and with a scroll prepared by, of all persons, the master mind of Conservative election strategy, Allister Grosart.

The trustees had never been completely unanimous in their judgment as to the course they should pursue with respect to the Charitable Gifts Act. Sometime in 1954 a three-way split began to develop among them regarding the eventual disposition of the newspapers, in view of the provisions of the Act. J. S. Atkinson believed the trustees or members of the family should buy them as the means best fitted to assure the attainment to the greatest degree possible under the circumstances of both objectives of his father. Hindmarsh did not look with favour upon the directors buying *The Star* though the failure of his initial campaign against the Charitable Gifts Act had caused him to lose hope the government could be forced to amend it. He was therefore predisposed towards acceptance of an offer from outside interests. Stark stood by the letter of Mr. Atkinson's will. He favoured fighting the Charitable Gifts Act politically and through every court in the land if necessary. He believed that when it came to a showdown the government would not dare force the sale of *The Star*. He believed that if it should attempt to do so the courts would rule that the papers need not be sold until the death of the last annuitant.

In the late fall of 1954 John Angus McDougald, an associate of E. P. Taylor, who had visited Hindmarsh at his home during the Community Chest campaign a few weeks earlier, asked him if the trustees would consider selling *The Star* to outside interests. Hindmarsh replied that so far as he was concerned he had changed his mind about the public ownership of newspapers. It gave politicians, he said, an excuse for interfering. He had concluded, he said, that of the two evils, a publicly owned newspaper under the thumb of politicians or a privately owned newspaper representing private interests, the latter was the lesser of the two.

The Taylor group contacted Hindmarsh again in June, and on October 18, 1955, met the board of directors of *The Star* for what were referred to as "informal discussions." The following day the board met again and adopted a motion that the "informal discussions" with the Taylor group proceed no further since sale to it would be contrary to the wishes expressed by J. E. Atkinson in his will.

Some months later Taylor told J. E. Belliveau, a staff writer for the *Star Weekly*, that he had not been particularly keen himself on buying the paper but his associates "thought we should have it." "My friends tell me that for an afternoon paper to be successful in Toronto it must be sensational, and I am not anxious to own that sort of paper," he said.

The seven-year deadline set by the Charitable Gifts Act expired April 8, 1956. *The Star* had not been sold, but the government took no overt action. Opposition members in the legislature asked Frost what he intended to do. He replied with an eulogy of the work done by the Atkinson Charitable Foundation, which up to that time had given $3,247,642 to charity, and concluded with the statement that he did not intend to repeal the Act.

"If the Prime Minister is not going to repeal the Act, he is going to force the sale of *The Star*," commented CCF leader Donald MacDonald.

"That's what you think," Mr. Frost replied.

The Premier was in a pickle. If he forced the sale of *The Star* there would be criticism that he was trying to silence an opposition newspaper. If he did not the other Toronto papers might stir up a rumpus. All concerned must have been agreeably surprised when the deadline passed without the other papers calling for enforcement of the Charitable Gifts Act. However, though Frost took no action, the public trustee exerted what Hindmarsh called "gentle pressure" to bring about a sale.

It was in the atmosphere of a directorate sharply divided on the question of whether or not *The Star* should be sold that Hindmarsh approached his seventieth birthday, which would have been on January 13. This is retirement age under *The Star*'s pension plan, but an employee may be granted a "postponed retirement" with the approval of his department head. Observing the formalities, Hindmarsh wrote the board of directors asking that he be allowed to postpone his retirement.

This request came before the directors December 12. Stark had been waiting for an opportunity to break the deadlock among the three factions and this seemed to provide it. Hindmarsh had not been well for several months and had two or three falls. In one he injured an arm, in another he suffered a fractured hip. These appeared to have been the result of slight strokes. Stark reminded the directors that they had never been apprised of the cause of these falls or of the nature of the illness that had confined

Hindmarsh to his home for several weeks. He proposed Hindmarsh be required to produce a medical certificate to the effect he was capable of carrying on as president, and that in the meantime action on his request be deferred a week. Hindmarsh agreed to this.

The next day J. S. Atkinson visited his sister and brother-in-law at their home in Oakville and there was a family reconciliation. It was perhaps a good omen that this reconciliation took place on the fifty-seventh anniversary of their father joining *The Star*. Following this meeting Stark and Tate resigned. W. J. Campbell, advertising manager and Burnett M. Thall, production manager, were appointed to succeed them at a meeting on December 19. At the same meeting Hindmarsh presented a medical certificate from his family physician that he was in good health, and his request for deferred retirement was granted.

At 3 o'clock on the afternoon of the next day he suffered a heart attack in his office. He died at 6.10 that evening in Toronto Western Hospital. Counting his summer work while at university he had been a newspaperman for fifty years. He had been an employee or executive of *The Star* for forty-five years. He was its president for almost nine years.

Chapter 24

NEW OWNERS, NEW WAYS

An exciting period in the history of *The Star* came to an end with the death of H. C. Hindmarsh. Only one of the trustees appointed by J. E. Atkinson before his death was left—his son, Joseph S. Atkinson. With him as trustees and directors were his sister, Mrs. Ruth Atkinson Hindmarsh, and two men of his choice, W. J. Campbell and Dr. B. M. Thall. On January 26, 1957, Beland Honderich was appointed to fill the vacancy left by Hindmarsh's death, and the board was at full strength again.

All of them are people of liberal temperament and a consciousness of their social responsibilities as publishers of a great newspaper. All but one had served under or been trained by J. E. Atkinson. They could be expected to support the principles and doctrines he had furthered in his lifetime. But none of them is an admirer of the razzle-dazzle school of journalism.

Campbell had come to *The Star* on his return from overseas in 1919. He was head of the collections department until 1926, when he transferred to advertising. Eighteen months later he was assistant to national advertising manager William Wallace. In 1929 he became advertising manager of the *Star Weekly* and in 1948 was advertising manager of both the daily and weekly newspapers. In 1956 he was awarded the gold medal of the Association of Canadian Advertisers, "An advocate of absolute truthfulness in advertising, he has played an active and significant role in molding the profession's high ethical standards," read the citation accompanying the medal.

Dr. Thall joined *The Star* in 1950. A research engineer, he holds a Ph.D. from the University of Toronto. He worked for a time with the National Research Council on atomic reactors and as a research physicist at the Chalk River atomic energy plant. As production engineer for *The Star* he has worked closely with J. S. Atkinson.

Honderich began as a reporter on the Kitchener *Record*. He came to to *The Star* in 1943, became a relief editorial writer in 1945, and financial editor in 1946, in both positions working under the supervision of J. E. Atkinson. He was appointed editor-in-chief January 1, 1955. In announcing his appointment, an editorial in *The Star* described him as "a selective reformer rather than a doctrinaire progressive."

Mr. Atkinson became president of *The Star* on February 2, 1957. At the same time Mrs. Hindmarsh was appointed secretary-treasurer of the Atkinson Charitable Foundation. "For as long as I can remember *The Star* has been part of my life," Mr. Atkinson said in a statement to employees.

> It is my aim as President to publish a newspaper that will command the public's confidence and at the same time be worthy of our great *Star* traditions.
>
> From its inception in 1892 *The Star* has been a champion of social and economic reform, a defender of minority rights, a foe of discrimination, a friend of organized labor and a staunch advocate of Canadian nationhood. We shall continue to support these principles with all the vigor at our command.
>
> Our principle object as a newspaper is to print the news as fully and objectively as possible, remembering at all times that the dissemination of news and opinions in a free society carries with it a high responsibility. A free society cannot function effectively without informed public opinion; and public opinion cannot be formed unless the public are given the facts upon which they can form intelligent conclusions . . .

The new management's aversion to sensational handling of news was made immediately plain in orders to the news department to tone down stories and headlines.

"*The Toronto Star* turned grey one day last week," mourned *Time* in its issue dated February 25. "Banished overnight were the sensation and

ABOVE: Joseph Story Atkinson, president, 1957–19—

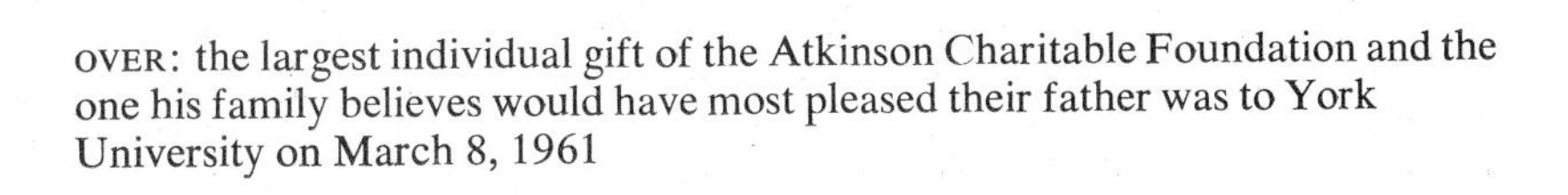

OVER: the largest individual gift of the Atkinson Charitable Foundation and the one his family believes would have most pleased their father was to York University on March 8, 1961

York University To Open Night College

TORONTO DAILY STAR

METRO WEATHER Overcast, colder, freezing rain, snowflurries tonight. Low 28, high 35. Details P. 2.

Authorized as second-class mail Post-Office Department, Ottawa. WEDNESDAY, MARCH 8, 1961—56 PAGES 10¢ PER COPY 55¢ PER WEEK HOME DELIVERY

CONGO ARMY DEFIES U.N. WON'T GIVE UP 2 PORTS

Atkinson Foundation Grant of $782,000

The establishment of The Joseph E. Atkinson College of York university with a grant of $782,000 from The Atkinson Charitable Foundation, largest in the Foundation's history, was announced today by Dr. Murray Ross, president of York university.

The main object of the new college is to enable adult students to obtain university degrees by attending evening classes and thus it fills a serious gap in the educational facilities of Metropolitan Toronto. It is hoped to admit the first 100 to 200 students in the fall of 1962.

College For Night Students

The new college is named for the late Joseph E. Atkinson, founder of The Toronto Daily Star and Star Weekly, who himself had to leave high school in Newcastle at the age of 14 for economic reasons, and who set up The Atkinson Charitable Foundation in 1942.

It will be Canada's first institution of higher learning established for night time students primarily. Plans call for the college to be a distinct unit of York university in its own right, with its own building, campus, library, common rooms, seminar rooms and dining hall by 1965. A gradual build-up of the student enrolment to 3,000 by 1970 is forecast. At the beginning, the students of Joseph E. Atkinson College will attend classrooms and use other facilities such as science laboratories at York university at Glendon hall on Bayview Ave.

The college is expected to attract office and industrial workers, housewives, new Canadians, school teachers and former university students who had to interrupt their studies in earlier years.

The York university board of governors hailed the $782,000 grant from The Atkinson Charitable Foundation as a generous gift. The board said the purpose of the college, to provide opportunities for formal education for those who were denied such opportunities but are now willing to work for them, "is consistent with the ideals and philosophy of Joseph E. Atkinson."

JOSEPH E. ATKINSON

Own Schooling Interrupted

Though his own schooling was interrupted, the late publisher of The Star continued his self-education through intensive reading of Tolstoy, Henry George, John Stuart Mill, John Ruskin and other writers of the humanist school.

The grant is to be spread over a five-year period and is to include acquisition of a site and erection of a building. The first step made possible by the Foundation grant will be appointment of a director within the next few months to plan organization of the new college.

The college will offer courses aimed at the interests and mature capacities of adults. The curriculum is to be adapted from the program of general and liberal education of York university. At first it will emphasize broad survey courses such as the history and philosophy of science, great literature of Western civilization, cultural conflicts in the modern world, the origin and development of life in the universe, and will be followed by highly specialized courses in the field of the student's choice.

(Continued on Page 8, Col. 3)

Aim To Boss U.N. Troops

LEOPOLDVILLE — (UPI-AP) — The Congo central government refused today to return the strategic supply ports of Matadi and Banana to U.N. control.

An announcement said the Leopoldville regime had decided to assume control of U.N. troops and supplies moving in and out of the Congo.

Five-Point Demand

It also presented a five-point ultimatum to Rajeshwar Dayal, Indian head of the U.N. Congo operation, and said it must be fulfilled before U.N. troops can return to Matadi.

The U.N. was considered certain to reject the demands which included:

Dayal must be recalled and replaced by an "impartial" U.N. official.

The Congolese must control the flights of all U.N. aircraft in the Congo and all river traffic.

The United Nations must hand over all strategic bases to the Congolese.

Solve Own Problems

Meanwhile, in Tananarive, Malagasy republic, Congolese leaders ended a five-hour round-table session with a plea to the U.N. to hold off from further action on the Congo and let the Congolese solve their own problems.

The conference was called by Katanga president Moise Tshombe.

Tshombe earlier urged the rival Congolese leaders to join forces for unified action against the U.N.

He gave up a fruitless wait for the possible arrival of Antoine Gizenga, Communist-supported boss of Oriental province, and called the first session of the conference to order without him.

In Cairo, a spokesman for Gizenga said he had no intention of attending the conference.

In the official communique, the delegates outlined their varying points of view and agreed unanimously to send identical telegrams to the U.N. General Assembly and Secretary-General Dag Hammarskjold.

The telegram said the conference answered the wish of the Congolese, the Security Council and the General Assembly "to see the Congo crisis solved by the Congolese themselves."

"In view of the tension in the Congo as a result of the Security Council resolution of last month, the delegates draw the particular attention of the General Assembly to the fact that any new action or execution of that resolution would aggravate the situation very seriously in the Congo," it said.

It was understood that all the Congolese delegates agreed with Tshombe the system left to the Congo by the Belgians was unworkable and that the provincial boundaries would have to be redrawn.

Asks for Mother

Liz Back From Brink Of Death

LONDON — (AP-UPI) — Elizabeth Taylor appeared to be winning her desperate fight for life today with a steady rally against double pneumonia. There was an indication that she might soon be out of danger.

Doctors said that for the first time since the 29-year-old movie star was stricken four days ago she was "sufficiently conscious to be able to assist in her own treatment."

The actress made an amazing comeback during the night from the brink of death.

Then an hour later they reported her condition "greatly improved."

Just before darkness fell last night the film star roused from a coma and whispered "I want my mother."

She apparently did not recognize that her mother, the former American actress Sara Sothern, was in the room.

Miss Taylor whispered another message for nurses to carry to her husband—singer Eddie Fisher—"I love you."

A report tonight said Miss Taylor's condition is "vastly improved."

Fisher left the hospital smiling and cheerful. He told reporters:

"She is doing very well. I have spoken to her just now."

Asked whether Miss Taylor knew how ill she had been, Fisher replied that "she has a pretty good idea."

—AP Wirephoto via Radio from Leopoldville

GUNS SILENCE OUR RADIO

Congolese soldiers poke over Canadian radio equipment they captured in port city of Matadi after driving out Canadian and Sudanese U.N. troops. Canadian signalmen kept working their equipment through height of battle, but finally had to surrender to superior numbers of Congolese.

Private TV Backs CBC in CFTO Row

Top executives of five Ontario private television stations affiliated with the CBC yesterday offered strong support to CBC President Alphonse Ouimet in his football duel with Toronto's CFTO-TV.

Mr. Ouimet failed Monday in a last-minute attempt to regain Big Four football telecast rights and he forecast destruction of the publicly owned network if CFTO were allowed network rights with CBC private affiliates.

Six stations were polled for their opinions on Mr. Ouimet's strong stand against splitting the network so that private stations outside CFTO's proposed Toronto-Ottawa-Montreal hook-up could carry game telecasts.

Ralph Snelgrove, president of Barrie's CKVR-TV, said: "Preservation of the CBC network transcends Big Four football. We think the national network is far more important than a quick buck.

"Of course we have little problems with CBC, but it wouldn't be worth the price of losing the national network for us, or anyone, to sabotage the CBC by leaving it. The net result of the CBC network is good for TV, and most important, good for Canada."

Mr. Snelgrove said the move by John Bassett, CFTO board chairman, to get the Big Four telecasts was part of a far larger plan. "They don't really want football, they want the second network."

Mr. Snelgrove said the popular football telecasts last year reached 45,000 homes in his station's area, and, although the station lost money by carrying the games, he would like to have them again handled by the CBC.

Roy Hofstetter, manager of CKWS in Kingston, said: "We're not prepared to break away from the network. We are very happy with the CBC affiliation. We'd love to carry the game, but it's up to the CBC."

He said CKWS reached some 25,000 homes with football telecasts last year.

W. T. Cruickshank, president of Wingham's CKNX-TV, said: "We would hate to see anything done to disturb

(Continued on Page 2, Col. 1)

SIR THOMAS BEECHAM one of the world's most noted orchestra conductors, died early today in London of cerebral thrombosis at the age of 81. See page 41.

EXILED BY WIFE, LIVES IN CUPBOARD

SAINT-BRIEUC, FRANCE —(AP)—Jean-Baptiste Bellec, a 46-year-old bricklayer, has been living in an oversized wardrobe in a Brittany field for three years, ever since his wife turned him out of the house.

Bellec makes his bed in the drawer of the wardrobe, stores his food under the bedding and hangs his clothes in the upper part.

What about winter?

"Then I close the doors of my house," he said, smiling. "To be free and happy one must be ready to suffer a little."

Icy Rain, High Winds Forecast for Metro

Slippery streets and sidewalks are forecast for Metro this afternoon as freezing rain and high winds move into Southern Ontario carried by a storm from Missouri.

Freezing rain, slated to hit Metro at noon will change to rain during the afternoon as temperatures rise, the forecaster said.

He said spring weather again would be delayed as dropping temperatures tonight and tomorrow bring snowflurries.

Today's dull skies will be accompanied by milder temperatures than in recent days—with a high of 45—before the thermometer drops again tomorrow, the forecaster said.

But 30 to 40-mile-an-hour winds are expected late today.

PRIME MINISTERS' CONFERENCE

Hint S. Africa To Stay In

By JEANNINE LOCKE
Star Staff Writer

LONDON—The 10th Commonwealth prime ministers' conference opened today at Lancaster house with all signs pointing to a victory for Britain's aim of keeping South Africa inside the club.

None of the 12 prime ministers, it now seems certain, will stand up and be counted against South Africa when its application for renewed membership as a republic reaches the conference agenda, probably this weekend.

Prime Minister Diefenbaker, who was regarded here as the mystery man, the prime minister most likely to lead an attack on Dr. Hendrik Verwoerd's apartheid policies, has so far failed to live up to his advance billing.

Won't Cast First Stone

On his arrival yesterday he restated the British argument which is that none of us is so righteous that he can cast the first stone at Dr. Verwoerd.

Last night at a meeting of the Canadian club, Mr. Diefenbaker declared that the Commonwealth should not set itself up as a court "to sit in judgment on fellow members." Instead, he suggested a declaration of Commonwealth principles that would recognize the equality of all men "whatever their race and color."

He deplored apartheid "with the utmost compassion and the recognition that our own record is not perfect."

He added it had taken many years to achieve a similar declaration in Canada.

A Commonwealth bill of rights, he acknowledged, would not be achieved "now or next year."

Disarmament, in his opinion, would be a "paramount issue" at the current conference.

Canada, although its "economic difficulties have been exaggerated," according to the prime minister, is concerned about keeping its agricultural markets should Britain move toward the European common market.

Nehru Speaks

Prime Minister Nehru of India today opened the conference with a wide-ranging discussion of East-West relations.

Prime Minister Macmillan, who normally speaks first on international affairs, asked Nehru, who has attended all nine past Commonwealth "summit" sessions, to start the discussions at Lancaster house.

Nehru was followed by Prime Minister Diefenbaker and the leaders of Pakistan, Nigeria, New Zealand and the Rhodesia-Nyasaland federation.

They reviewed such issues as the future of Western relations with Russia and Communist China, disarmament and the Congo.

This afternoon Mr. Diefenbaker was to have an audience with the Queen at Buckingham Palace.

Today, as the prime ministers survey the world generally at morning and afternoon sessions, the organization of exiled South Africans, the South African United Front, is desperately trying to make contact with Mr. Diefenbaker and his Afro-Asian colleagues, President Ayub Khan of Pakistan, Sir Abubakar Tafawa Balewa of Nigeria, Nehru of India, Tunku Abdul Rahman of Malaya, Mrs. Bandaranaike of Ceylon, Robert Menzies, Australia, and Keith Holyoake of New Zealand.

May 31 Is Day

They want to present their arguments against South Africa's staying inside the Commonwealth when it becomes a republic May 31.

They regard its exclusion as a necessary first step in bringing down the government of Dr. Verwoerd.

But the five leaders of the outlawed African congresses—Oliver Tambo, Nana Mahomo, J. Kozonguizi, Dr. Yusuf Dadoo and Tennyson Makiwane — are pessimistic about the likelihood of a receptive hearing.

STOP THE PRESS NEWS

Board of Control approves Easter Sunday plans for painting Yonge St. pink.

Sydney, N.S. — Several passengers shaken up in head-on train collision.

Shrewsbury, Eng. — Bus taking 10 passengers to hospital bursts into flames, five burned to death.

Birmingham, Ala. — Tornado in Northern Alabama injures 15 persons, destroys 53 homes.

Jakarta — 64 insurgents killed by government troops in Central Sumatra.

OTHER LATE NEWS ON PAGES 2, 3, 8, 9 AND 29

Lesage Wants Lottery

QUEBEC —(CP)— Premier Jean Lesage said today he has had conversations with federal Justice Minister Fulton on the possibility of establishing a provincial lottery.

Mr. Lesage, told a delegation of the International Railway Brotherhoods, he and Mr. Fulton held "unofficial" exchanges on the possibility of changes on the criminal code so provinces could organize lotteries.

Inside

U.S. Twists Our Economy With Its Tariffs--Coyne

Special to The Star

NEW YORK—James Coyne, governor of the Bank of Canada, told a U.S. audience last night that U.S. tariff policy has been misshaping Canada's economy.

Low U.S. tariffs on raw materials, Mr. Coyne told the Economic Club of New York, have led to the extreme development of resource industries useful to the U.S.

At the same time, high tariffs on Canadian-manufactured goods have prevented development of industry in Canada.

Nothing Canada can do in protecting the domestic market for manufactured goods has been adequate in overcoming the two-sided U.S. tariff, he said.

It was the first speech Mr. Coyne has made since the debate over monetary policy boiled up in the House of Commons.

Last night's address on balance-of-payments problems in North America touched on the issue of laws to deal with unemployment.

[The] country's balance of payments is the plus or minus figure reached by subtracting the value of all pay-

(Continued on Page 2, Col. 1)

THE TWO FACES OF LESLIE FROST

For six years Star columnist Ron Haggart has kept a searching eye on the municipal affairs of Metropolitan Toronto.

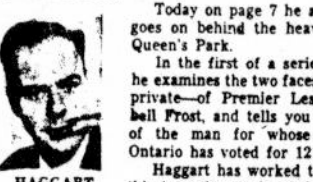

HAGGART

Today on page 7 he analyzes what goes on behind the heavy portals of Queen's Park.

In the first of a series of articles, he examines the two faces—public and private—of Premier Leslie Miscampbell Frost, and tells you the make-up of the man for whose government Ontario has voted for 12 years.

Haggart has worked two weeks on this intensive study of Canada's most successful Tory. He has talked to those who have known Mr. Frost longest, to those who know him best.

sudden death once trumpeted in blazing, two-inch headlines. Staffers were forbidden to mention the nude bodies and sanguinary scenes that once covered Page One; crime reporters could no longer identify criminal suspects until they had been formally charged . . . Young Joe ordered drastic cutbacks, told editors to drop far-flung junkets."

Time concluded its article by reprinting page one banners from the two afternoon newspapers of the same day. The *Telegram*: "Mother, 4 Tots in Terror as Men Chop in Three Doors." *The Star*: "5-Inch Snow, Hundreds Crash."

The new policy was strictly observed in the federal election of March, 1958. Pierre Berton, then the managing editor of *Maclean's*, reported that a two-week study of Canadian newspapers showed *The Star* to be the most objective in its election coverage. *The Star* and the *Ottawa Journal* were the only newspapers that gave the CCF adequate coverage, he said.

Throughout 1957 the public trustee continued to exert his "gentle pressure" to get the trustees to sell. The pressure usually consisted in demanding more revenue for charity, leaving less for normal business expenses. It was becoming apparent that without any overt action to force a sale *The Star* could be bled into subjection or even into collapse. An increase in price to ten cents a copy on December 9, necessitated by increased costs, did not solve this problem but lost it readers, even though the *Telegram* followed its example a week later.

On January 24, 1958, the five trustees announced they would seek the approval of the Supreme Court to buy *The Star* newspapers, as provided under the Charitable Gifts Act. Associated with them in the application was Harry A. Hindmarsh, a grandson of J. E. Atkinson, who was at the time associate city editor and picture editor. Except for service with the RCAF as a fighter pilot for four-and-a-half years he had spent his adult life with *The Star*.

"The trustees have been endeavoring for several months to find a formula for the purchase of the paper that would carry out the expressed wishes of Mr. Atkinson and also enable employees to participate in the future ownership of *The Star* and *The Star Weekly*," an announcement said.

They engaged the American Appraisal Company of Milwaukee and A. E. Ames and Company, of Toronto, to assess independently of each other the saleable worth of the properties. W. H. Bosley Co., realtors, were asked for an independent valuation of the real estate.

On March 24, 1958, their application was heard by Mr. Justice J. L. McLennan. The public trustee approved of the application, and after hearing evidence that the bid of the trustees was at least equal to a fair valuation of the properties, the court authorized the purchase of the properties by the trustees for considerations totalling $25,555,021. The only other bid was from an employee, B. A. Griffis.

The Star fetched the highest price ever paid up to that time for a single newspaper property anywhere. The next highest was $18,600,000 paid for the Birmingham, Alabama, *News* in 1955, but included in that deal were three radio stations, a television station, and a small town newspaper in Alabama.

An offering to the public of bonds, debentures, and preference shares totalling $16,500,000 was over-subscribed in twenty-four hours. An offering of $500,000 to employees was over-subscribed by $200,000.

On May 27, 1958, Joseph S. Atkinson, president of Toronto Star Limited, was appointed publisher also of the *Toronto Daily Star* and the *Star Weekly*. At the same time, Harry A. Hindmarsh was added to the board of directors. Two weeks earlier he had been appointed a trustee of the Foundation.

The taxpayers gave up $5,600,000 in succession duties on J. E. Atkinson's estate in 1948. In the next 14 years they got back $7,210,377 in grants for educational, medical, and charitable purposes. The sale of the newspapers resulted in an immediate increase in the capital of the Atkinson Charitable Foundation to more than $14,000,000. In addition something in excess of $5,000,000 remains in the Joseph E. Atkinson estate most of which will eventually be transferred to the Foundation. The exact sum will not be known for several years, since it is out of this that the annuities provided for in Mr. Atkinson's will are being paid. Meanwhile the Foundation receives about $150,000 a year income from the estate.

Early in 1961 the Foundation made its 605th grant, the biggest of all. It was for $782,000 to establish the Joseph E. Atkinson College of York University, Toronto. The main object of the new college is to enable adult students to obtain university degrees by attending evening classes. Plans call for the college to be a distinct unit of York University, with its own buildings and campus sufficient to handle an enrolment of 3,000 students.

The late Joseph E. Atkinson had to leave school at the age of fifteen. He educated himself by reading, but he always felt the task of self-education without formal direction was such an immensely difficult one that few could accomplish it. Yet thousands of able men and women are so situated economically that they cannot attend day classes or full-time university.

It is probable that few grants the Foundation has made would have given more satisfaction to the man whose wealth makes them possible.

Index